Advance Praise for

This book is a radical break from past traditions in lesbian and gay studies, which have stressed the importance of covert places in creating a penumbra that protected marginalized populations. Instead *Queers in Space* is an imaginative cartography of the enormous diversity of public and private spaces and places that play an integral part in the daily lives of contemporary queer communities. The book is both a revelation and testimony to a new maturity in research and writing on queer experiences.

—***Michael Dear***, Professor, Department of Geography, and Director, Southern California Studies Center, The University of Southern California

It is so refreshing to see the discourse about space opening itself to questions it has repressed for so long. This book constitutes yet another important step in the ongoing confrontation with the politics of space.

—***Beatriz Colomina***, Professor, School of Architecture, Princeton University

Exploring the interactions between queer identity, experience, and activism and a range of communal and public spaces, *Queers in Space: Communities, Public Places, Sites of Resistance* opens up a new direction in gay and lesbian studies.

From gay space in Mexico City to the now legendary baths of New York and San Francisco, *Queers in Space* travels to bars, parks, beaches, neighborhoods, and cities to follow the expansion and transformation of queer communities beyond the gay ghetto. In the process *Queers in Space* grounds queer theory in the sites and locations of everyday life to confront homophobia and inequities in access to housing, security, and safety. Using memoir, historical anecdote, field studies, and images, the contributors construct maps to represent queer experience and devise strategies for queer activism.

By focusing on the geography of queer social relationships *Queers in Space* raises critical and timely questions about the role of social space in shaping identities, the meaning of communal space for marginalized peoples, and the significance of public spaces for social visibility.

Photographs not bearing a photographer credit are by Gordon Brent Ingram.

"The Bathroom Line" and "Riis Park" in "Restriction and Reclamation: Lesbian Bars and Beaches of the 1950s" ©1987 by Joan Nestle. Reprinted from *A Restricted Country* (Ithaca, NY: Firebrand Books). Used with permission of the publisher.

"The City of Desire" in "Revisiting the City of Desire" ©1994 by Pat Califia. Reprinted from *Public Sex: The Culture of Radical Sex* (Pittsburgh, PA: Cleis Press). Used with permission of the publisher.

"The Queer Nation Acts Up: Health Care, Politics, and Sexual Diversity in the County of Angels," by Ty Geltmaker, was originally published in *Environment and Planning D—Society and Space* 10 (1992): 609-650.

"Constructing Manchester's 'New Urban Village': Gay Space in the Entrepreneurial City," by Stephen Quilley, was originally published in *Transgressions, A Journal of Urban Exploration.*

"Invisible Women in Invisible Places: The Production of Social Space in Lesbian Bars," by Maxine Wolfe ©1992 Swiss Federal Institute of Technology, Lausanne Switzerland. Originally published as "Invisible Women in Invisible Places: Lesbians, Lesbian bars, and the social production of people/environment relationships" in *Architecture et Comportement/Architecture and Behavior* 8(2): 137-158.

"Leather Nights in the Woods: Locating Male Homosexuality and Sadomasochism in a Dutch Highway Rest Area" by Maurice van Lieshout ©1995 The Haworth Press, Binghampton, NY. Originally published as "Leather Nights in the Woods: Homosexual Encounters in a Dutch Highway Rest Area" in *Journal of Homosexuality* 29(1): 19-29. Used with permission of the publisher.

Printed in the United States of America

1 2 3 4 5 6 7 8 9 10

Bay Press
115 West Denny Way
Seattle, Washington 98119-4205

Library of Congress Cataloging-in-Publication Data
Queers in space : communities, public places, sites of resistance /
edited by Gordon Brent Ingram, Anne-Marie Bouthillette, and Yolanda Retter
p. cm.
Includes bibliographical references.
ISBN 0-941920-44-5 (paper)
1. Gays—Identity. 2. Lesbians—Identity. 3. Gay men—Political activity. 4. Lesbians—Political activity. 5. Gay communities. 6. Lesbian communities. I. Ingram, Gordon Brent. II. Bouthillette, Anne-Marie. III. Retter, Yolanda, 1947-
HQ76.25.Q395 1997
306.76'6—dc21 97-11611
CIP

Cover and interior book design by Philip Kovacevich

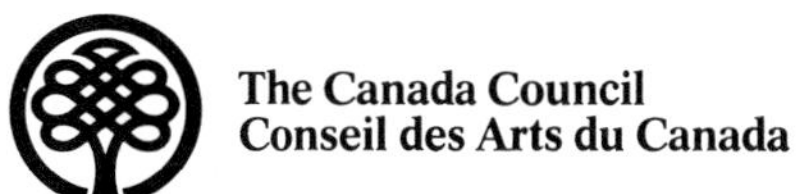

Queers in space:

Communities | Public Places | Sites of Resistance

Edited by Gordon Brent Ingram, Ph.D., Anne-Marie Bouthillette, M.A.,
and Yolanda Retter, Ph.D.

Contents

vii Acknowledgments

3 **Lost In Space: Queer Theory and Community Activism at the Fin-de-Millénaire**
Gordon Brent Ingram, Anne-Marie Bouthillette, and Yolanda Retter

17 **Queer Space**
Jean-Ulrick Désert

27 **Marginality and the Landscapes of Erotic Alien(n)ations**
Gordon Brent Ingram

Part 1 — Experience / Place / Maps

55 **Narratives of Place: Subjective and Collective**
Gordon Brent Ingram, Anne-Marie Bouthillette, and Yolanda Retter

61 **Restriction and Reclamation: Lesbian Bars and Beaches of the 1950s**
Joan Nestle

69 **The Interim Photographs**
Bill Jacobson

77 **People and Their Streets, Places**
Sarah Schulman

81 **One-Handed Geographies: An Archaeology of Public Sex**
David Bell

Part 2 — Queerscapes

91 **Surveying Territories and Landscapes**
Gordon Brent Ingram, Anne-Marie Bouthillette, and Yolanda Retter

95 **"Open" Space as Strategic Queer Sites**
Gordon Brent Ingram

127 **"No More Shit": The Struggle for Democratic Gay Space in Toronto**
John Grube

147 **From Landmarks to Spaces: Mapping the Territory of a Bisexual Genealogy**
Clare Hemmings

163 **Domestic Dykes: The Politics of "In-difference"**
Elsie Jay

Part 3 — Regional Dynamics and Community Formation

171 **Queer Zones and Enclaves: Political Economies of Community Formation**
Gordon Brent Ingram, Anne-Marie Bouthillette, and Yolanda Retter

177 **San Francisco: Revisiting "The City of Desire"**
Pat Califia

197 **Gay Male Places of Mexico City**
Alvaro Sanchez-Crispin and Alvaro Lopez-Lopez

213 **Queer and Gendered Housing: A Tale of Two Neighbourhoods in Vancouver**
Anne-Marie Bouthillette

233 **The Queer Nation Acts Up:**
Health Care, Politics, and Sexual Diversity in the County of Angels, 1990–92
Ty Geltmaker

275 **Constructing Manchester's "New Urban Village":**
Gay Space in the Entrepreneurial City
Stephen Quilley

Part 4 — Queer Sites

295 **Placemaking and the Dialectics of Public and Private**
Gordon Brent Ingram, Anne-Marie Bouthillette, and Yolanda Retter

301 **Invisible Women in Invisible Places:**
The Production of Social Space in Lesbian Bars
Maxine Wolfe

325 **Lesbian Spaces in Los Angeles, 1970–90**
Yolanda Retter

339 **Leather Nights in the Woods: Locating**
Male Homosexuality and Sadomasochism in a Dutch Highway Rest Area
Maurice van Lieshout

357 **Queer Spaces in New York City: Places of Struggle/Places of Strength**
Betti-Sue Hertz, Ed Eisenberg, and Lisa Maya Knauer of the REPOhistory Collective

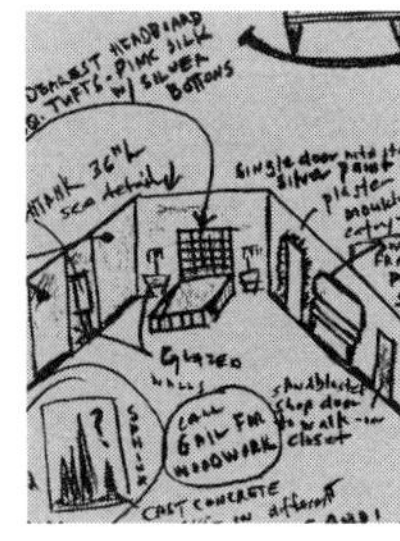

Part 5 — Queerscape Architectures

373 **Making Room: Queerscape Architectures and the Spaces of Activism**
Gordon Brent Ingram, Anne-Marie Bouthillette, and Yolanda Retter

381 **Having Something to Wear: The Landscape of Identity on Christopher Street**
James Polchin

391 **The Meaning at the Wall: Tracing the Gay Bathhouse**
Ira Tattelman

407 **This Is about People Dying:**
The Tactics of Early ACT UP and Lesbian Avengers in New York City
An interview with Maxine Wolfe by Laraine Sommella

439 **Do You Love the Dyke in Your Face?**
Carrie Moyer and Dyke Action Machine!

447 **Strategies for (Re)constructing Queer Communities**
Gordon Brent Ingram, Anne-Marie Bouthillette, and Yolanda Retter

459 **Notes**

497 **Bibliography**

523 **Contributors**

Acknowledgments

The major parts of compiling, editing, and curating the graphics for this book were funded through The Canada Council Explorations Programme grant #2550-95-0008 "Queersville." I am grateful to the courageous jurors—Phillip Todd, Margaret Dragu, Christine Welsh, Catherine Lewis, and Pierre Coupey—who recommended support for this avowedly queer project, and for the careful grant administration by Richard Holden and Margaret Dryden of The Canada Council.

Earlier phases of the research benefitted from the extensive resources of the University of British Columbia (UBC), including the Landscape Architecture Program, particularly through the studio course "Open Space Planning" in buildings adjacent to Wreck Beach. I am grateful for the fine secretarial assistance provided by the Department of Forest Resources Management and for the support of colleagues on the Ad Hoc Committee on Lesbian and Gay Issues of the Faculty Association. This book was begun at a time of exceptional hostility to notions of activist queer theory and public open space, especially as related to human rights law and stewardship of public lands. I am deeply grateful to the British Columbia Public Interest Advocacy Centre and the BC Human Rights Coalition for their counsel, especially Chuck Reasons, David Fathi, Susan O'Donnell, and Peter Beaudin.

In contrast to the chilly climate at UBC, I remain indebted to numerous staff and faculty at Berkeley, particularly in the Department of Landscape Architecture, who, while fighting backlash and cutbacks in the University of California system, found time to support my research. Kris Albert gave a tremendous amount of support and encouragement, as did numerous people at University of California libraries, particularly Elizabeth Byrne and Kathryn Wayne of the Berkeley College of Environmental Design library.

Good friends Kathleen Morrissey and Melinda Wong redrew, scanned, and enhanced many maps and other types of graphics, and Colin James, of Smith Photo in Vancouver, printed many of the photographs. Their patience and interest were crucial.

Lynne Fernie, the director of the film *Forbidden Love*, generously shared her research on pre-decriminalized queer spaces in Canada. Willie Walker and Gerard Koskovich of the Gay and Lesbian Historical Society of Northern California kindly gave assistance on San Francisco. I am grateful to the following individuals for their support, ideas, and or information: Kwame Anthony Appiah, Kass Banning, Allan Bérubé, Thomas Boellstorff, Judith Butler, Bill Coleman, Beatrix Colomina, Samuel (Chip) Delany, Jeffrey Escofier, Linda Farthing-Kohl, Andrea Fatona, Vera Frankel, Ken Gardels, Amber Hollibaugh, Michael Immel, Victor Janoff, Isaac Julien, Moira Kenney,

Larry Knopp, Ruth Maheney of Modern Times Books-San Francisco, the unforgettable Tedde Matthews (1952–1993) of Modern Times Books, John Bentley Mays, Haris Metaxa, Henry Myers, Shirin Neshat, Stephen O'Murray, Cindy Patton, Jean Pauline of Modern Times Books, Daniela Porta, Tom Radulovic, Robert Reid-Pharr, Eric Reyes, Robert Rothon, Stephen Shapiro, Stephen Shotland, Henry Urbach, Gill Valentine, Jacqueline Woodson, Cory (Cornelia) Wyngaaden, and Eric Zinner. Important ideas and information came from Queers in Space Vancouver, particularly from Anne-Marie, Kathleen, Michael Howell, Michael Hoeschen, Michael Carroll, and Bart Reid.

Special thanks go to my family, particularly my mother Wilma (Pire-Brochu) Ingram, my sister Fay Hennekes, my unstoppable daughter Reed Marie Stannard (who was born and learned to talk as this book was being developed). Benita Dibdin, Anne Davis, Todd Pittson, Lady Lurex aka Rita Morris, Sarah England, Sally Ogis, Catherine Laurente, and Franco Studiale gave crucial support.

Thanks to Kim Barnett and Sally Brunsman of Bay Press for their early belief in the project and their support for its publication, as well as Wallis Bolz, Julie Sullivan, Lauren Byrne, and Lee Damsky who were crucial in production.

Finally, our greatest thanks go to the many article authors and artists who all worked to make *Queers in Space* a reality.

gbi
Vancouver and San Francisco, 1997

Introduction

Preceeding page: Pride March, New York, 1993. Photograph © Morgan Gwenwald

Lost in Space: Queer Theory and Community Activism at the Fin-de-Millénaire

Gordon Brent Ingram, Anne-Marie Bouthillette, and Yolanda Retter

In this time of increasing displacement stemming from the globalization of capital and destruction of the biosphere, "queer space," used for refuge, habitation, and play, has expanded and diversified. Global ghettos, villages, nations, alienations, and, most important, global communalities and communities have become possible as never before. In the 1990s the ghettobusting of queer nationalism and the rapid globalization of real estate markets have transformed queer space, pushing it beyond the bounds of the ghetto and inspiring new linkages within and among communities. Yet the unique cultures, aesthetic sensibilities, and politics of a particular place must inform and shape its alliances with other groups if "concrete" improvements in queer communities are to be made effectively. Queer space enables people with marginalized (homo)sexualities and identities to survive and to gradually expand their influence and opportunities to live fully. In the fragments of queer-friendly public[1] spaces available today, a basis for survival, contact, communality, and sometimes even community has begun. But the term *community* is problematic[2] in light of the "politics of difference."[3] To talk of the gay or lesbian "community" in 1997 is to beg the question "Which one?" Only analytical frameworks that take into account the full range of spaces and marginalities across cities and landscapes can provide tools for confronting homophobia and chronic inequities in access to housing, security, and comfort, resources whose availability still is closely tied to gender, race, ethnicity, language, age, and narrow notions of physical ability.

Queers in Space provides a basis for "constructing interests"[4] of specific sexual minorities with more care—and more results. Individuals, networks, or whole communities can make use of the theories, pragmatic strategies, shared experiences, and inspiration presented here, as they seek to gain more public and semipublic space, access to homes and privacy, and greater security and freedom to make contact. We explore queer civic activism related to urban, suburban, and rural public spaces, considering issues of access, safety, comfort, design, representation, and artistic expression. With a nod to what Adrienne Rich called the "politics of location,"[5] we recognize that an underlying homophobia by design constrains and even maims queer people, resulting in a complex limitation of movement and self-expression that has been simplistically lumped into the single term *ghettoization*. This anthology takes

Dyke March, Seattle, 1994: Angel, Gwench, Amii, and Lori. Photograph by Dana Schuerholz, Impact Visuals.

part in a broader effort to define a new "spatial politics" rooted in specific locales, desires, and communities, and the aesthetics that emerge from their confluences.[6]

The central argument of *Queers in Space* maintains that studying and understanding the perceptions, ideas, and priorities that characterize each community and its relationship to its environment are necessary prerequisites to building "effective affinities,"[7] which in turn can lead to new alliances between lesbians, gay men, bisexuals, transsexuals, and other groups of "sexual minorities" perceived by some to threaten the heteronormative status quo. Such diversity requires very supple "theory"[8] to guide discussion and resolve the myriad questions that will certainly arise as a variety of groups join forces to "privatize public space and publicize private space."[9] Though it may seem that cyberspace[10] is outpacing physical space as a locus for social and cultural interaction, the role of real, physical public space is actually increasing for some kinds of contact. Both "queerness"[11] and "space," in all their different forms, stand at crucial historical junctures on the map of political and cultural thought at this *fin-de-millénaire*. Given the contradictions of the current period—juxtaposing new gains with new assaults on networks and enclaves of sexual minorities—the theory of queer activism has never been more unresolved and "up for grabs." The development that began with the emergence of the Mattachine Society, the Daughters of Bilitis, the Stonewall riots, the scattered gay liberation fronts, lesbian feminism, and the more recent emergence of ACT UP, Queer Nation, and Lesbian Avengers is leading us into new territory and "uncharted space." It is time to take stock.

Science Fictions

Back in the 1960s, there was a television series *Lost in Space,*[12] in which a barely functional heterosexual family was stranded on a distant planet and was desperate to find home. In the same period, and at a time of an explosion of lesbian and gay activism,[13] references to "queers"[14] in public "space"[15] were limited to pejoratives. Imaginings of new communalities, of queers with more and more varied space, were often found only in the works of Samuel R. Delany.[16]

Early activism in Los Angeles, San Francisco, and New York City, culminating in the Stonewall riots, was among the first conscious modern attempts to claim and reconstruct queer public space.[17] But gay liberation and lesbian feminism did not provide all of the theory[18] needed to interpret a diversity of relationships, networks, and contexts. The emphasis on generalized ideologies and a unitary vision of sexual minorities was, by the sex wars[19] of the 1980s, reduced to "broken totalities."[20] In addition, the gay liberation and lesbian feminism of those times were often framed in Eurocentric, particularly white North American terms that excluded people of colour and much Third World activism.[21] In the years that followed, the ravages of AIDS, increasing globalization of both capital and "gay culture," the declining importance of national identities,[22] and further confrontation of racism and cultural chauvinism (processes of a broader "decolonization") shook the expanding gay and lesbian networks, enclaves, and ghettos. In the past decade, improvements in life in communalities of sexual minorities have progressed unevenly. The media-oriented actions of ACT UP and Queer Nation, especially between 1987 and 1991, targeted privatized "public space," including the growing electronic realm that we now call cyberspace. Due to the impact of globalized capital on real estate markets, access to housing and social services, and the flow of ideas across public

Mark Robbins, *Borrowed Landscape: 36 Views,* Museum of Modern Art, Saitama, Japan, 1994.

media, queer space has been dissected, stretched, pummeled, fragmented, cordoned off, and spread in ways that decades before would have been possible to imagine only in science fiction. Although some new and exciting public spaces have been created, most of the "gay ghettos" of today have become remarkably similar and exclusive, like Christine Boyer's chronicle of New Orleans, *Vieux Carré*: "What once was a bizarre landscape and set of mythological hieroglyphs beckoning the wanderer to stray had become a fixed and purchasable commodity."[23]

We titled this anthology *Queers in Space* because the phrase connotes being "out there floating," disconnected and separated from the planet. Although people who experience marginalization might like to be more "grounded," inequity in access to public space continues. For minorities, including people marginalized through (homo)sexuality, these forms of "uneven development"[24] have often compounded their sense of isolation and rootlessness. Although in the late twentieth century space[25] has become recognized as a signifier of a group's status in a society, this realization has not yet transformed society or yielded real inclusion. At least in terms of visibility, most of us remain "out there," constrained by marginalization. This problem complicates current activism and development in most queer communities. "Coming out" on an individual basis and increasing visibility, the tactics that emerged from lesbian feminism and gay liberation of decades back, have little diminished the disparities in access to public resources for queer people and networks. In many homophobic contexts—and

Demonstration with the Lesbian & Gay Immigration Rights Task Force, Inc., Seattle, 1995. Photograph by Dana Schuerholz, Impact Visuals.

many still exist in North America, Europe, and other parts of the world—the more we try to connect in new ways, the greater the obstacles and the prices become. This discouraging dynamic influences the size of our enclaves and our attempts to build more functional networks and communities. Most of us are still struggling to stake out psychic or cognitive space, as well as physical space, in the world. In this context *space,* an inherently vague word, lessens in importance as a trendy postmodern codeword and becomes the defining element in tracking chronic inequities.

Gender(ed) and Queer(ed) Theory

Lesbian, bisexual, and transsexual history, placemaking, and territorialization are currently undertheorized and underdocumented. The recent work focusing on gay males is still tentative, both in its theoretical frameworks and stated uses. Much queer theory is based on white male experience and privilege, severely limiting its relevance in informing activism. Numerous lesbian scholars, notably Hoff,[26] Jeffreys,[27] and Zita,[28] have noted how particular tenets of queer theory have affected particular communities and places. A major criticism is that queer theory presents a canon written largely by white and decidedly Eurocentric males and therefore excessively reflects their ideas. The majority of lesbians and gays whose quotidian lives are overshadowed by homophobia do not necessarily want to or cannot make sense of the language and concepts used in this growth area of philosophy and social theory.

Women, people of colour, and transgendered people are wrestling with the complex array of differences and similarities that complicate the building of alliances, and few canons exist to help define the specific subjectivities of women, people of colour, and transgendered people. The majority of people who "run" visibly queer ghettos and municipalities are white, middle-class gay men. Although doubly marginalized groups, including lesbians of colour such as Gloria Anzaldua[29] and Barbara Smith,[30] have been thinking and writing about what it means to "live within and manage life at the intersections," the way their experience has been framed in current theories remains uncomfortably simplistic.

Much queer theory continues to be, at best, "thin" on gender and race. In recent years, some chronicles of lesbian and gay communities have appeared deceptively inclusive of people of colour; but the richness and the contradictions that characterize these communities have often been stifled through the overuse of generalizations in describing and interpreting them.[31] *Queers in Space* revisits "difference" and relates it to political economy, aesthetics, and the designed environment, allowing paradoxes and unresolved difficulties to surface—instead of presenting a false front of unity when diversity is the dominant flavor.

A Queer and Not-So-Manifest Destiny

Space[32] has increasingly become a concern in our lives and the politics of our communities. In a time of great mobility, "the triad of local, locale, and location"[33] and the politics to celebrate and deepen community and sense of neighbourhood become increasingly central to queer life. In "place," we can confront the "injustices [that] are justified in the name of the immediate."[34] As our erotic, communal, and political identities have become more visible, they seem to grow more complex, tangled in a host of unresolved social questions; similarly, as more actual and potential queer space has become more visible, it seems more contradictory and baffling in nature. *Queers in Space* helps identify what Frantz Fanon calls "homosexual territory,"[35] explores and encourages the conscious "making of space" (called, in postmodern jargon, "territorialization"), and points out external and internal obstacles to this venture. We look at places of every size: closets, buildings, cities, and regions. At any scale, place invariably encompasses theoretical and spiritual dimensions. This book's essays evoke the social and biophysical textures of regional queerscapes, the shifting and often hidden locations of erotic and increasingly politicized alien(n)ations in the form of new queer networks, institutions, and locations, and what they mean for us and the communities in which we live.

Queers in Space unties some of the conceptual knots involving visibility, communality, community, and a host of possible physical interventions in the environment. These unresolved questions have kept many of us from utilizing the powerful insights of postmodern and queer theory, which, unfortunately, can be dry and obscure. Space, both as habitation and as arena for power, can be described through words but also by way of maps, sketches, photographs, and plans; it can be considered on physical, metaphorical, and theoretical levels. Representing queer experience in space through these means can lead to guidelines for constructing communities with fuller diversity of sexual expression and equity in terms of gender, race, language, culture, class, age, generational differences, and mobility—resulting in more authentic means of "recognizing differences while forging (provisional) unity."[36] Gross inequities must be squarely faced and addressed.

In charting the gendering of space, we highlight divergent analyses based on queer theory, various frameworks of feminism,[37] and postcolonialism. We depart from Lisa Duggan's optimistic view that "it is precisely from within feminist theory . . . that a 'queer' critique of the dominant categories of sexuality and gender is emerging most imaginatively and persuasively."[38] *Queers in Space* examines the didactic but often partially accurate notion that queer theory is weak in identifying gender-related disparities and that some aspects of feminism are "sex-negative" and complacent about obstructing free consensual sexual expression. We explore the arguments of Elizabeth

Still from *The Attendant,* directed by Isaac Julien and produced by Mark Nash, 1993. Photograph by Liam Longman. Courtesy of Normal Films, London.

Grosz, stipulating that "feminist"[39] theories are in crisis and that their proponents are often unable to discern the subtle differences between patriarchal and phallocentric domination.[40] In this book our arena, our means of tracking and auditing homophobia compounded with patriarchy, (neo)colonialism, and globalizing capital,[41] is space and the landscape.

Spaces Communal and Erotic

A tension exists between the roles of eroticism and communality in the formation of queer space. Twenty years ago it would have been easy to accept the false notion that a permanent dichotomy characterized queer space: for men, it was defined by erotically charged, phallocentric experience; for women, by a communal, cooperative, often "sex-negative" experience. This false duality has trammeled the study of queers and space. And the sex-negative versus sex-positive reductions that emerged in the lesbian feminist sex wars pertaining to pornography have done nothing to explain the richness and complexity of places of queer presence. As Australian geographer "Elsie Jay" states in this volume, "Our difference is not proclaimed solely in terms of sexuality." But this statement is not meant to undermine the importance of sexuality. Desire and sex are as much an aspect of human experience and use of the landscape as any "more legitimate" activities "programmed" into public space and landscapes. Still, this gender-based divide colours much discussion of queers and space.

The idea for this book gestated in 1993 to counteract the trend in which sites and landscapes of queer contact and communalities were being conceived in narrow reductionist terms (although such landscapes often were used by different groups and for many purposes other than finding sexual satisfaction). The importance of queer environments and the impacts of different groups and acts on them was being discounted; lessons in community formation and the making of new places and relationships were being overlooked. One of the most insidious facets of homophobia has been equating queer communality with sex alone. To avoid stereotyping and "essentializing" queer identities, we must recognize the importance and the positive nature of erotic expression without restricting the concept to a reductionist phallocentrism. Sexual expression is more varied and protean.

Two decades ago the notion of "claiming territory" was often considered a "boy thing." But today, as lesbian and transgender presence emerges to claim and reorganize public space in most large cities, these old simplistic notions of queer(ed) territory and territorialization must be transformed. This is important in order to "appropriate"[42] and degender public and private queer spaces and to identify new possibilities for the public realm. This book explores how queers can more purposefully make (activist) space, in essays that recount resistance to isolation, invisibility, and violence; its survey of "sites" includes parks used for public sex, lesbian and gay male bars, and recent lesbian land trusts, demonstrations, and street fairs. Several writers envision new representations and designs.

Although we searched diligently to find a broad range of contributors, *Queers in Space* still reflects the dichotomy of women forging communality in space and men having sex in it. Is this because lesbians are more sexually repressed or have less interest in sex, or because men are apathetic about communality? Hardly. In our time desire, sex acts, and pleasure are still framed in largely phallocentric and androcentric terms, and the nurture of children and the preserves of home and neighbourhood are considered women's realms. Divisions based on gender, race, nationality, and language continue to dominate public and private space, including that which we had hoped, by this late date, would be fully "queered." In this anthology writers from a wide range of locations, backgrounds, and theoretical positions paint a sober picture of queer space that, as architect Jean-Ulrick Désert stresses, remains as tenuous and vulnerable as the lives of many queers.

In *Queers in Space* we hope to fully explode the old dichotomies. Spaces of lesbian communality are often highly eroticized, even if the women do not have sex on site; and even the densest localities of male public sex involve considerable cooperation and communal culture. Also, severe, historically rooted misogyny has blocked the development of female eroticized space. Much lesbian literature on sexuality

Del LaGrace Volcano, *Monica and Elena,* Bologna, Italy, 1994.

polemically defends or responds to women's experience, rather than stating the author's own ontology and experience. Gay men have been writing about outdoor spaces of cruising and contact for half a century, suggesting activist agendas to enhance security, contact, and pleasure; now it is time for women to more fully deconstruct the phallocentric and gendered generalizations about public sex. New visions, strategies, and tactics are sorely needed in order to liberate spaces for women's erotic satisfaction.

In the 1970s lesbian feminists sanitized sexuality in order to make themselves more palatable to heterosexual feminists and the public, leading to a "civil war" of S/M women and other sexual liberationists versus lesbian feminists. Though often effectively "sex-negative" toward many forms of queer expression,[43] lesbian feminists focused their efforts on questions of domination in intimate relations (an issue of immediate concern) rather than on options and spaces for pleasure. Over the past two decades, writers on the subject have typically aligned themselves with either the sadomasochist and anticensorship activist Pat Califia or the antiphallosex feminist Andrea Dworkin. But this polarized discourse has severely constrained discussions of community, communality, place, space, and the roles of the public and the private. The debate must be expanded in order to create a truly diverse set of queer possibilities and, occasionally, even communities.

Truth in Advertising

> "What kind of girl *are* you?"
>
> —The concierge (Duran Duran) to Barbarella in the 1968 film *Barbarella*

We want *Queers in Space* to inspire a new generation of theoretically grounded activists to consider queerer geographies and designs. Thus these pages contain not a single manifesto but the rough beginnings of many. This book asks more questions than it can answer in a new field of study that is beginning to forge better alliances, more sustainable habitation of the planet, and, yes, more love, in the sense that a better environment can encourage love. People usually learn theory to help them make sense of complex experiences and problems; the frameworks that we propose are only as strong as their grounding in and knowledge of real places, conditions, and the divergent viewpoints that arise from particular situations.[44] This collection is oriented to the relatively affluent cities of the industrialized world. Discussion of the spaces and experiences of people of marginalized sexualities in other cultures and economies is sorely needed.

Rather than construct dogma, we seek new ways to link many different stories, valuing the contrasts and contradictions that may surface. In order to build successful political alliances and to solve complex environmental and design problems, the diverse experiences that characterize a given landscape and queerscape must be acknowledged and respected. For these queer geographies to have an impact on planning and public policy, collective activism is needed. We hope this book will give you new ideas for strategies to confront disparities in access to places and resources where you live (compared not only to heterosexuals, but also to other groups such as lesbians, gay men, bisexuals, and transgendered people). Addressing specific inequities can bring together authentic alliances and have a real effect on particular public places and neighbourhoods. We explore the implications of more gendered, erotic, and radical conceptions of "site-specificity."[45]

The postmodern city and rural landscapes are difficult environments in which to survive and to take part in a community. There is, as Christine Boyer has observed, "a veil over the spatial politics restructuring the heart and fallow fringes of the contemporary city . . . [that] . . . declines to challenge the process of colonization that has appropriated the image and representation of the city for private concerns."[46] In cities, towns, and less controlled landscapes, older social groups are fragmenting and most groups, except a few élites, are being marginalized. At the same time, new aggregations of communities are forming the new queer "city of inner discordances and retinal distortions."[47] The underlying agenda of *Queers in Space* is both activist and tenaciously spatial, valuing physical sites and the communality of neighbourhoods and public events. We want to confirm and describe new forms of queer "localization," which Michel Foucault has tied to a "space" and a trajectory "opened" by Galileo.[48] Foucault foresees a "desanctification of space," in which the old boundaries of sacred and profane become scrambled. Sites once shunned as ugly may one day be considered sacred due to the communalities that they have harboured. To be queer and to be involved in lesbian, gay, bisexual, transgendered, or queer politics at this end of the millennium is to walk cautiously across both the hyperspace of theory and the often brutal environmental and social realities of sites, neighbourhoods, and regions. In these dizzying Dantesque journeys, nothing is "pure;"[49] not the planet at this period in time and not theoretical determinations—they will continue to shift and proliferate, as they should.

Tony at the March on Washington, April 25, 1993. Photograph by Dana Schuerholz, Impact Visuals.

Queers have "reterritorialized the city"[50] for several centuries, though they lacked a comprehensive theoretical framework to use in interpreting these activities. Similarly, words such as *commodification* and *reappropriation* of space, along with more familiar terms, such as *community, marginalization,* and *ghetto,* need to be reviewed and more carefully defined for our times and specific contexts. (See this book's conclusion beginning on page 447 for definitions of important terms.)

This book is for people who can see the relevance and importance of new concepts of constructed sexualities, socially based notions of "landscape ecology," and "postmodernism" to our political efforts, to our respective communities, and to our most intimate relationships.

Questions in Theory and Activism for Queer Space

Queer environmental activism has been constrained by a host of unresolved issues concerning the entitlement of sexual minorities to public space in patriarchal and heteronormative contexts. The following questions are starting points for an activist and experiential theory of queers in space:

- What constitutes queer space, and how is the concept useful or obstructive for different groups—particularly lesbians and queer people of colour?
- Are queer neighbourhoods effective refuges from homophobia, or are they just places where there are a lot of lesbians and gay men?
- What are the points of similarity and divergence between lesbian and gay male experience, use of public space, and the formation of concentrated and scattered nodes of communalities? How central is gender in community formation? How stable can the space of bisexuality ever be?
- What are the potential uses of a theory of queers in outdoor space in terms of forging new identities and communities, for organizing activity to address local issues, and for increasing security, communication, and the diversity of means of contact, expression, and pleasure?
- How have the uses of historically queer sites changed over time? What are the trends and emerging opportunities for claiming and remaking these places?

From Outer Space to Home

The sections that follow present opportunities for the construction of a new cultural and political "localism" on various scales: the region, the neighbourhood, the building, and the room. Recognizing these different spatial scales enables the shaping of precise strategies to address a host of specific problems, thus transforming our communities. The essays explore a wide range of ties to where we live, work, play, and venture on the earth: places that are outdoor and indoor, public and private, highly eroticized and more communal.

In order to create a blueprint for making community, the heteronormative realities of particular places and environments must be contested and reconstructed. We begin to sketch the broad outlines of this project in two general discussions: one viewing queer space in the mood of the new "queer camp"[51] and one presenting a theoretical review of erotic alienations played out in the landscape. Part 1 explores the uses of queer "maps"—verbal, written, sketched, collaged, or Cartesian—for representing experiences and forging communal bonds. These maps, which integrate the subjective experiences of their creators, help identify collective experience and inequities within a given landscape. This queering of "local knowledge" can bring queer people together to claim status as stakeholders in civic activism.

Part 2 explores the gestation and formation of the presence of sexual minorities in territories that include only a small amount of queer space. We examine forms of queering public space and gradients of communality, isolation, repression, and resistance. We pay close attention to factors including housing and employment, repression and tolerance, the presence of particular services and institutions, and demonstrations and other forms of activism.

Part 3 looks more closely at regional dynamics and community formation, examining how queer enclaves emerge as refuges in relatively inhospitable territory. In Part 4 we explore the relationships between neighbourhoods and queer sites and, in particular, the social, cultural, and economic dynamics of placemaking. The dialectics of public and private space, the site-specific tactics that can be used to create zones of security and opportunities for contact, are presented as well.

In closing this anthology, we move from the subjective to the collective, from the genesis of site-based alliances to the aboveground enclave, and from the region to the room. While linking arenas for discussion and intervention (which might be conceived of as the queerscape), we explore avowedly activist forms of expanding and reconstructing queer communality. Maxine Wolfe describes the designs and choreographies of influential queer public demonstrations, and others in the anthology acknowledge the power of public art to reorder landscapes and communities; together, these essayists catalogue recent tactics that have been used to claim and transform public space.

The emerging architecture of queerscapes has resulted in broad environmental impacts, and the fruits of "queerings" remain vulnerable to regional political economies. We end *Queers in Space* with an optimistic vision of purposefully entering the stream of civic politics in order to (re)construct queer spaces, choosing strategies that will connect private sites with public landscapes. Within any territory, urban or rural, it is time to make room for deeper forms of queer communality and, where viable, community. We hope this book will help spark new initiatives and interventions in all environments—the home, the neighbourhood, the landscape, the region—so that we can all live, prosper, and love well on earth.

Becoming Visible: The Legacy of Stonewall exhibition, The New York Public Library, June 1994. Photograph by Kathryn Kirk.

Queer Space

Jean-Ulrick Désert

My earliest recollections of self-identification stem not from gayness but rather from a sense of place(ment)—a centered place, bridging my maternal family with my more obscure paternal family. I served as the locus of adoration for my grandmother, a *grande dame* of her Port-au-Prince suburb. My sense of "blackness" was mute. We were all beautiful in the Caribbean sun; variations of blackness were as natural as variations of orchids.

I inherited a legacy of classism, and I was privileged—but in Haiti there was and is always someone more (or less) privileged than yourself. America ripped me from my center, into an exile I had yet to understand, beyond the obviousness of politics. My personal growth toward self-inscription would be arrested by the imposition of an identity. Ulrick—no, *Eric*—yes, that's more normal. Teachers, other children, and their parents were unwittingly complicit in isolating me from one's most basic sense of self—one's name.

I became *negro* and *colored,* an undesirable trait, redeemed only by my "frenchyness," which rendered me an exotic, like a caged bird. I did not feel oppressed but rather . . . bewildered. What was the fuss? Where were the eloquence of language and gestures and familial breadth I had once known so warmly? Why couldn't I understand Bill Cosby, though I was supposed to? Why was Diahann Carroll so beautiful and yet so solitary and isolated? Why, in fact, were they both alone—no partner, male or female? "Negroland in America" was fraught with land mines I could not perceive. Even "hipness" did not register with me.

My "queerness," with no regard to the erotic, was well inscribed for me. My queerness became heartfelt, my isolation a convenient vantage point to witness normality. Sexually, I perceived boys and girls as the same, interesting and curious. The sexual presence of grown-ups was more compelling. The looming ubiquity of female sexual exploitation numbed me early on. What I saw least compelled me most. But alas, new labels were to be inscribed in a fascist manner once again: "*pédérast,*" "sissy," "faggot," and so on. But this time, I had the choice of disclosure or deception, whereas no choice was offered before. I unwittingly walked into a large dark closet, unaware of its true size. Its architecture was not unlike what I already knew, its boundaries were fluid, sometimes only for a moment. It shared the same streets, the same people. Its only difference was silence—a silence that fostered and still fosters overwhelming complicity.

"Queer"

My general definitions would begin as follows: queer space is virtual space. I embrace this tenet though I continue to struggle with the plausibility of the very question that such *identified space* explicitly exists. Is such space preconceived and designed? Is it an intrinsically spatial condition? The general trend in defining "difference" and the implicit politics of that gesture strike me as suspect. Queer culture, or gay culture, is the operative term bantered about today. For this reason I approach the subject with caution and trepidation. But is it really a culture? Is it really a cultural space? Is it really a physical space? Is it a cultivated history, a lineage transferred albeit not by, some may argue, genetic inheritance? Is it really a "shared" culture that knows no national boundaries? "Culture" as it is reinvented today may indeed be a garden path to a virtual utopia, an escape from the dominant culture that benefits from a minority's self-imposed exile. Diederich Diederichsen, an art and social critic, warns of the disturbing trend in establishing difference and cultures of the "other."

> [Turkish] "culture," it's different from us . . . "violence" and "foreigners" often would be combined, a peculiarity of the German language, to terms like "foreigner violence" or "foreigner criminality" as if there was something violent intrinsic to "foreigners" . . . these strategies create a world outside of ours, a zone, to use this word, where all these nasty things such as racism, separatism, homophobia and homosexuality, violence and culture take place and we have nothing to go with it: it's a conflict that they have with each other: the Turks and the Kurds, the gays and the Turks, the homophobes and the homosexual, the racist victims of racism and the other racist victim of racism. We are somewhere else and observe . . . The major difference between the right and the mainstream (in Germany) is this: the right wants a homogenous society, the established left accepts difference, if the difference is content with the name culture: since then we have youth culture, foreign culture and so on.[1]

Queer culture has in the past decade been promoted in the universities under the auspices of Women's and Gender Studies, and has fostered full-fledged Gay Studies programs at such places as Columbia University and UCLA. "Queer," an antiquated pejorative for homosexual, has in recent times been appropriated by lesbian and gay activists to subvert its negative denotation by an act of positive redefinition. The implied rudeness of "queer" snaps back at those who would actively use it as an injurious slur. Matthew Ehrlich of MIT, in his introduction to *Civil Wars: Queer Theory and the Arenas of Activism*,[2] notes that "The notion of civility is used to counter certain kinds of activism: whenever we [queers] are being impolite, indiscreet—we are told to be more civil. Civility itself, the relation of politeness to politics, is [currently] under examination . . ."

This turnabout of language and labeling as self-inscription is seen not only with the rehabilitation of the word queer[3] but also with such symbolic emblems as the inverted pink or lavender triangles (though, oddly, not the black triangles used to denote homosexuals during the holocaust years of World War II).

"Queer" is therefore consciously active and aggressive toward its detractors. Queer culture would not be queer if there were no other culture from which to establish its difference. I argue that to reinforce an isolationist stance rather than engage in an evolution of perpetual differences would be detrimental to any notion of a living queer culture. Queer culture exists because of the dominant normative culture. And in many instances the fluidity and blur between the cultures are the very richnesses and contradictions that should be embraced. Isolationism would be the death of such fertile ground. Repatriation to the dominant culture and an acknowledgment of de facto inclusion by all parties lies at the heart of understanding our place, our spaces.

Our private lives require no veil of secrecy in the socially inclusive context of a shared cultural production. The current adage, "the private is public," is a manifesto for this end. Queer activists, Richard Mohr points out, stress opposition to the dominant culture's mandatory privacy, or maybe here the word "secrecy" is more apropos: "Privacy, especially enforced privacy, is the closet . . . what is needed is not gay privacy but gay publicity—to break through the silence and taboos surrounding gay issues and to confront people's unsubstantiated fears of gays." Mohr goes on to argue that "a rough distinction drawn between privacy and secrecy will allow for publicity, since not all that needs to be private needs to be secret . . ."

In the realm of the sexual, privacy extends to specific acts and not to other types of behavior or even telltale signs of specific acts. For example, some might argue that a conspicuously pregnant woman out in public has violated to some extent the requirement of sexual privacy that society places over (hetero)sexual performances, because anyone can make the inference that she has had sex, been raped, or practiced alternative or artificial insemination. And heterosexual couples who wear wedding bands are, to some extent, publicly committing to having had sex and perhaps children. In sharp and painful contrast, there remains a general requirement for secrecy covering homosexual desires and behaviors. Thus the obligation for secrecy is often brutally unequal for sexual minorities. Sometimes the inequity is blatant, such as public kissing, which is socially or legally tolerated between heterosexual couples but violently suppressed between same-sex couples.[4]

"Queer" can be defined elastically to include sensibilities other than the normative with a propensity toward, but not exclusive of, the homoerotic. "Queer" is therefore a liberating rubric encompassing multiple sensibilities exclusively or in tandem. We might also clarify "homosexual"[5] to the degree that this inadequate label currently establishes sexual preference as the primary and only defining mode of a person's being. This is incorrect and must be redefined. In the United States over the last century, the homosexual/heterosexual duality has become a major ontological dichotomy. Foucault expressed unease at the reification of a gay identity or of homosexuality, declaring that "even on the level of nature, the term 'homosexual' doesn't have much meaning." Foucault also called for the abolition of "homosexuality" and "heterosexuality" in favor of "an infinity of sexualities."[6]

Sexual orientation or drive plays a natural role in our personalities, but does physical erotic engagement need to occur in order to establish an identity politic? Not really. Must a "homosexual" engage in homosexual acts to be homosexual, or a "heterosexual" take part in heterosexual acts in order to be heterosexual? One's "visceral" identity remains independent of these actions, allowing for a "visceral perception" rooted in self-identity.[7] Therefore, "visceral identity" establishes predisposed sensibilities beyond the erotic and into all facets of human engagement. Celibate queers, by choice or otherwise, are no less queer nor are they any less involved in occupying and creating queer spaces within and without a heterocentric context of the dominant culture. Alexander Doty, in his introduction to "Making Things Perfectly Queer," cites Judith Butler and Sue-Ellen Case and argues that queerness is something that is ultimately beyond gender—it is an attitude, a way of responding, that begins in a place not concerned with or limited by notions of binary opposition: the male and female or homo versus hetero paradigm usually articulated as an extension of this gender binarism.

> The notion of queer and queerness . . . borrows Queer Nation's goal of inclusivity . . . a quality related to any expression that can be marked as contra-, non-, or anti-straight . . . by pointing out the queerness of and in straights and straight cultures, as well as that of individuals and groups who have been told they inhabit the boundaries between binaries of gender and sexuality: transsexuals, bisexuals, transvestites, and other binary outlaws.[8]

"We are everywhere" (a Stonewall-era rally cry) defines the parameters of these [queer] spaces.

"Space" is commonly defined as a delineated or loosely bounded area occupied cognitively or physically. The potential for exploration under this rubric may provide greater substance to the typical vagueness of queer theory. This terrain of physical and often, designed, space, increasingly includes literary, media, and electronic space. Queer space crosses, engages, and transgresses social, spiritual, and aesthetic locations, all of which is articulated in the realm of the public/private, the built/unbuilt environments, including decoration. Though the erotic nature of space is, by itself, difficult to categorize, the act of sex—witnessed or instigated by the inhabitant and the designer—need not be what defines queer space. The definition of queer space by erotic program would be as limiting as the word *homosexual.*

The City and the Realms of Public and Private

The possibility of any space is latent until the moment it doubles and is devoured by the contradictions of its program and the actual events of its construction, use, and eventual destruction. A queer space is an activated zone made proprietary by the occupant or *flâneur*, the wanderer. It is at once private and public. Our cities, our neighborhoods, our homes are loosely defined territories inscribed not merely by the laws of proprietary ownership but by implicit and shifting inflections of presence, conspicuous or otherwise. Queer presences lend an inflected turn of meaning to such places as Greenwich Village in New York City or the intersection of Castro and Market Streets in San Francisco. The general perception and belief, in part from the mistaken notion that most other places are really straight, is that these are gay/queer zones. This implication, seductive as it is, invites the occupant or observer into a complicit act of faith. Queer space is in large part the function of wishful thinking or desires that become solidified: a seduction of the reading of space where queerness, at a few brief points and for some fleeting moments, dominates the (heterocentric) norm, the dominant social narrative of the landscape. The observer's complicity is key in allowing a public site to be co-opted in part or completely. So compelling is this seduction that a general consensus or collective belief emerges among queers and nonqueers alike.

The emergence of queer zones evolves in varying circumstances. Their presence elicits just as many responses. A *New York Times* article reflects on the acknowledged presence of queers and the landscapes they/we affect. "They've stabilized a lot of neighborhoods where they've stayed," said a real estate agent of twenty-five years from Chicago. Seattle's Capitol Hill, for instance, has in the last twenty-five years seen an influx of gay men and women who have rehabilitated houses in the formerly working-class area. The Montrose neighborhood in Houston, once a declining working-class section, is now the geographic center of a lively gay community. In Miami, there is South Beach; in Denver, the Cheeseman area; in Cincinnati, Liberty Hill and North side; and in St. Louis, the South Grand Street area. There are also concentrations in smaller cities throughout the United States heartland.

Perhaps nowhere is the phenomenon of "gay neighborhood as urban pillar" truer than in the Dupont Circle section of central Washington, a half-mile north of the White House. In the past twenty years, it has been transformed from a run-down area of stores and apartments badly in need of renovation to one of the most vibrant and desirable places to live in the district and the source of a recent war cry of gay rights advocates: "We're here. We need a realtor."

Our cities and landscapes double as queer spaces, just as Washington, D.C. doubles as the seat of United States governmental mayhem. The most active doubling of space is in the public space. The squares, the streets, the civic centers, the malls, the highways are the place of fortuitous encounters and juxtapositions. It is the place in which our sensibilities are tested, it is the place of "show." The public space is the place of romance, seen as landscape, alleys, and cafés. The public space is the space of power in the form of corporations or factories. It is the (blue, white, or pink collar) ghetto of the everyday. This fluid and wholly unstructured space allows, in its publicity, a variety of readings, re-readings, and misreadings, given the observer's individual propensities toward power, mystery, and how these desires fold into the passive space of Eros.

By passive, I mean to suggest a space where desire intertwines with visceral sensibility, in the space of the everyday. The doubling of public space requires that a catalyst such as the observer's perception or a collective consensus of readings bring forth that queer latency from being merely implicit to explicit. The more localized space of home(s) may require not merely a collective perception but objects and images that, when strung together, cognitively serve as a suite of (queer) evidence. The catalyst of disclosure may be a matter of capital, mathematics, program, or design. The images/objects may present evidence in their conspicuous absence. Where is . . . the bed? the photos? the linen?

In America the heterocentric domestic house is defined ironically by the suburban home. Programming intrinsic to the home's configuration presupposes and encourages heterocentric activity. Its interior ideal is reinforced by domestic examples such as Donna Reed and the Brady Bunch. Gender roles (within the space) are prescribed by proximities programmed into the house itself, as well as by media simulations surrounding the user. The Master Bedroom, set in isolation over a litter of smaller bedrooms, orchestrates a social order of age, sexuality, and ownership. The prescribed domestic work of wives as nannies, cooks, and "homemakers" provides a blueprint of sequential spaces such as kitchen, rec room, and sewing room in proximities marketed as convenience.

Queer homes do not necessarily negate these characteristics, but rather they reinterpret and often (re)appropriate them, constructing new spaces as the occupants redefine the parameters for domesticity. Queers, queer couples, triads, and more than a few tribes have always existed—though with varying degrees of isolation, marginality, and self-consciousness. The act of redefinition, so central to today's notion of queer, is always present in such spaces, as the normative condition always looms near the edge of (ill)-defined boundaries. The housing market, cognizant of the onslaught of nontraditional families, is slowly capitalizing on and reconstructing a notion of home by establishing spaces of great permeability and flexibility. The loft building is only one example.

Implicit rather than explicit programming in buildings and landscapes may be evolving as the new norm in an industry currently more occupied with the bottom line of marketing rather than the dictates of "family values."[9] Queer lives are in many ways similar to their heterosexual counterparts. Love, family, dysfunction, and pathos exist in varying degrees. The occupant is the catalyst that facilitates this shift from implicit programming to the explicit space of queer living. The interior scape may be as commonplace as a sitcom set or as theatrical as Liberace's mansion. Both, in part by the details, will engage the structure of the space to double into that elusive and boundless queer space of the everyday.

The Public Gaze

I mention the public (queer) gaze only because of its ubiquity. The expanding pantheon of sexual imagery in the service of commerce is astounding, but when sexual titillations are aimed at consumers of the same gender, I must question the overt queerness of the action. The Calvin Klein underwear ads, initially exclusively male, are one such example. Popular media is the most powerful venue for this queer space. When RuPaul is attractive to self-identified heterosexual men, who are fully aware through publicity of "her" two balls and dick, I question the queer space the nonqueer male observer must confront, having created it himself with his knowledge and undeniable attraction. And there is also the question of the female attraction to such a clearly only partially transgendered figure. RuPaul's success has been twofold—creating a queer space for nonqueers and queers. This phenomenon, though accelerated with the variety of media available, is not new.

The public (queer) gaze has been present in such spaces as the viewing rooms of Michelangelo's *David* or *Dying Slave*. Here a piece of art, produced for contemplation, invites the observer to seduce, if only with one's eyes, and is questionably covert. Similarly, the thinly veiled "Last Supper" by the painter Jean Delville is misleadingly entitled *The School of Plato, L'école de Platon* (1898). The viewer is asked to enjoy this display of nudity—a nudity that shifts, between its context, between nakedness and the nude. Another Frenchman, in the tradition of Michelangelo, surrounds the observer with his tattoos—the same tattoos of his infamous *cahiers blanches,* a diary of his queer lust. The displacement or oscillation between the spiritual and the erotic space cannot be lost in these examples because, remember, we are still talking about the public space doubling into the queer and blurring the communal and the private.

"High" Art (A Public Discourse among Aesthetes)

"Outhouse," a site-specific installation piece by Leone/MacDonald, renders a rather open interpretation of queer space. Fabricated in steel, it simulates an actual door and door frame situated on a path. Reminiscent of Marcel Duchamp's 1927 *Porte, 11 Rue Larrey,* a threshold is established in nature where the visitor is confounded by two bronze door knobs—one engraved "Us" and the other "Them." As well as subverting any fixed notion of its parameters, I argue that this is queer space at its most radical state, due to its ability to remain relatively open and to absorb a multiplicity of oppositions. The genius of "Outhouse" in establishing and yet confounding oppositions by labeling is the very moral I find most suspect and dangerous. Labels are utilized in everyday life and we collectively participate in reinforcing them, as the artist Simon Leung points out so eloquently in his discussions of the "architectural apparatus" of gender-defined door signs such as Ladies or Gentlemen. Here the occupant is forced into complicity with a labeling system that goes far beyond defining biological anatomy to establishing clear lines of civil behavior.

If it were generally known (and accepted) that a significant number of cultural contributors to this society have been and are queer, then queers and others alike might clearly see through the current blur of complicit secrecy—this vain closeting of space and the landscape. This knowledge might assist in a history of sensibilities, vocabularies, and mappings from Sappho to Roland Barthes. How oddly universal and yet inclusively queer are such literary and philosophical observations, which are integrated into heteronormative narratives of place.

Language is a skin; I rub my language against the Same and the Other. It is as if my body has language without words. My language trembles with desire. The emotion derives from a double contact: On the one hand, a whole activity of discourse discreetly and indirectly focuses upon a single signified, which is "I desire you," and releases, nourishes, and ramifies it to the point of explosion; language experiences orgasm upon touching itself. On the other hand, I enwrap the other in my words; I caress, brush against, and talk up this contact; I extend myself to make the commentary to which I submit the relation endure.

> To speak amorously is to expend without an end in sight, without a crisis it is to practice a relation without orgasm.[10]

The artist Lyle Ashton Harris has taken, as his charge, to investigate an even more complicated terrain of metaphorical space buttressed against the pervading structures of power, cobbled with divisions defined by race and lust.

> Interior space of Black sexuality . . . [we] need to question the lack of discourse on sexuality in the Black community—homo and hetero.

His goal is

> to reconstruct the Black body as a site of value and pleasure.

Harris confesses,

> I am hurt by the indifference of white gays and lesbians, mainstream avant garde, by their resistance to actually participate in a discourse where race and sexuality intersect. . . . It's important that we begin to

> question the positioning of sexuality as the transcendental signifier. We must begin to engage in a self reflexive sexual space. I am very interested in that space—that contradictory *liberatory space*.[11]

Media Space and Popular Culture

"Cybermind" is an electronic forum for the discussion of the philosophical and psychological implications of subjectivity in cyberspace. In its increasingly queer spaces, many new framings of issues emerged, including the psychology of intimacy, the role of gender in the experience of even electronic space, the phenomenology of the terminal screen, neurosis and paranoia on the Net, the relationship of lag to community and communication, sex/gender/sexual orientation theory and electronic subjectivity, the role of the symbolic or imaginary in computer communication, the implications of symbolic extensions of the human external memory, and "the psychoanalysis of lurking."[12] "Queers in History aka Lesbians and Gays in Herstory/Fags and Dykes in History/Queers through the years" is a CD-ROM currently available for the edification of "digital inverts" with proclivities toward compiling a knowledge of "homo-notables from across the nations and professions, dating back to 612 B.C. Clerics and soldiers, directors and designers—each historic figure is listed with a pithy description and one reference work."[13]

Camp and Kitsch

I argue, as Susan Sontag did so long ago, that "camp," the mainstay of "gay" stereotyping and the domain of the "homosexual," serves as one of a myriad of implicit gestures to redefine place and even history. Queers have often produced camp or kitsch rather than articulate subjective sensibilities born of their sense of difference. Camp subverted the brutal heteronormative universalism of modernism—under every patriarchal edifice was a shifting and queer geomorphology. This parallel landscape has served as the lens and catalyst for defining both physical and phenomenological space.

Closing: Homosex, Lust, and Yearnings of Penetration

> Querelle has forgotten his jersey in my cabin. It's lying on the floor, just as he left it. I don't dare touch it. The striped sailor's jersey has the power of a leopard skin. More than that, even. It is the animal itself, hiding there, wrapped up in itself, showing only its outward form. "Someone must have thrown it there." But if I should stretch out my hand to touch it, it would instantly swell up with all the muscles in Querelle's body.

The . . . drawing . . . shows a woman.[14]

Querelle's relationship with (homo)sex is as tenuous as our abilities to conceive of a "place" for it. It is tenuously serious, tenuously sexy, tenuously camp and—most importantly—tenuously there.

From a performance of *Undressing Icons: Looking for Langston,* directed by Isaac Julien, Minneapolis, 1991. Photograph by W. H. Schelling. Courtesy of Normal Films, London.

Marginality and the Landscapes of Erotic Alien(n)ations

Gordon Brent Ingram

> Despite its bludgeoning absolutions, its vicious wars, the Twentieth Century may yet be known as the age of sexual efflorescence . . . The home, the garden, the park, must be planned for lovers and love-making: this is an essential aspect of an environment designed for human growth.
>
> —Lewis Mumford, 1938[1]

> A landscape tradition a thousand years old in our western world is yielding to a fluid organization of space that we as yet do not entirely understand. . . . Out of a ruin a new symbol emerges, and a landscape finds form and comes alive.
>
> —John Brinckerhoff Jackson, 1994[2]

Coming from Great Distances

For most people whose sexualities have been "marginalised"[3] through some experience of same-sex desire,[4] who therefore feel or are made to feel "queer," we travel great distances in order to live in the ways that enhance fuller contact with one another.[5] The spaces that we cross and in which we live—to which we adapt, create, and sometimes reconstruct—have great bearing on how we come to express ourselves. Surviving queer, no matter how invisible, often requires knowing how to travel across hostile territory—whether it be physical, emotional, cultural, or theoretical. Most likely it is space with a combination of all of those dimensions. And central to the recent emergence of queer politics, since roughly the advent of the first ACT UP chapter in New York City in 1987, has been the ideal of purposeful (re)construction of relationships, alliances, and (where they exist) communities.

The notion of reconstructing what often is still referred to as "the ghetto" is usually based on experienced or perceived threat to our bodies in public or commercial gay spaces, as well as in our homes. These heightened perceptions of risk and emergent opportunities involve physical "landscapes"[6] and other kinds of "designed" or managed environments and geographies. Space has become a way to track transactions and to envision a host of new relations. In this essay I outline some of the social forces and associated environmental factors that currently support and constrain the development and enrichment of queer relations, whether they be two people, or networks and communities.

Del LaGrace Volcano, *Hampstead Heath,* summer 1995.

In this exploration of the differences and synergies of marginality and alienation as related to "minority" sexualities, I outline the relationship of "sites"[7] and space inhabited by sexual minorities to the broader landscape. Cities and more natural terrains have supported layered and often contradictory social transactions related to queer communality, love, and sex that involve and are between sites. These cumulative interactions and the associated environmental constraints and opportunities can be called the "queerscape."[8] The central argument of this essay is that there emerged before the Stonewall riots[9] a well-defined trajectory to "queer" [the verb] "public space"[10] as a key element of cultural expression and community activism, and—as some forms of homophobia and violent repression decline and others become more subtle—the importance of and opportunities for such "placemaking" are now increasing. I am not suggesting that much of this reconstruction of public place will lead to domination and segregation by particular communities of sexual minorities—far from it. Instead, exploring the queerscapes of a community can lead to the recognition of the presence (and the inherent rights for expression in public arenas) of a range of minorities' sexualities and experiences. This is not necessarily to suggest that such sexual expression should ever emerge in ways that are truly oppressive—as the homophobic right has argued in recent decades. In the queering of public space, some forms of sexual expression, both queerer or more heterosexual, may occasionally get out of hand in public space; it always does and always will. More importantly, the thorough queering of the landscape will mean that the existing poorly recognized barriers to equitable use of public space will be removed.

In beginning to chart queerscapes and in tracing some of the forces that create and transform them, I argue that "marginality"[11] and erotic alienation are always present. These sometimes related but different conditions are never static, and they can contribute to the temporary formation of various queer networks, identifications, movements, communities, and—in contrast to heteronormative mythologies—even erotic "alien nations." This includes all "sexual minorities" such as gay men, lesbians, bisexuals, "transvestites"[12] and other participants in drag, and transsexuals, as well as people who engage in consensual "adult" practices that are not tolerated by the state. Within this dynamic of marginality and alienation, the former condition is due to the domination of heterosexuality and produces the latter in people who do not experience sufficient benefits from it. Marginality of queer desires, acts, and communalities produces alienation, and responses such as the formation of alternative social networks can produce more marginalization—especially in times of more organized homophobic repression. I argue that one process feeds off the other: an erotic marginality leads to an internalized and environmental alienation, and this constitutes the core, the queerness, the queasy antipodean, of "queer space." Such synergies provide key clues to the nature of the extremes of the queer space gradients—exceptional starkness

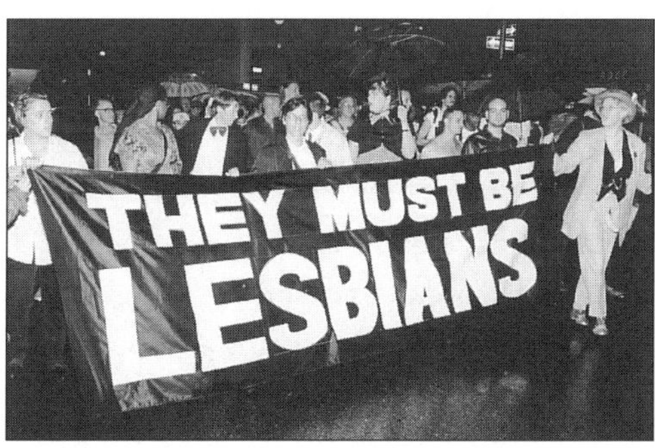

Drag March, New York City, June 1995. Photograph by Saskia Scheffer.

Drag March, New York City, June 1995. Photograph by Saskia Scheffer.

replicated in warehouse aesthetics, contrasted with exceptional richness and complexity rivalling the decorum of royal courts.

I also argue that the notion of extremes and the instability of queer space have overshadowed much of the inventories and descriptions of the public and private spaces of sexual minorities. Clichéd notions of victim and hero, poor and rich, accommodation and revolution, kitsch and conformity, have overshadowed understandings of more complex and supple relationships. One discredited strategy for better coping with the queer intensification and the compounding of marginality and alienation was invisibility and "the closet." Invisibility allowed the feedback loops between marginality and alienation to be lengthened and internalized, giving some breathing space in the attempts at obtaining social recognition and resources provided in "normal lives." Another strategy, only sometimes chic since Stonewall, has been detonation to form raucous spaces of rebellion. But neither of these kinds of "spaces" nor the survival strategies that they represent have allowed for very satisfying lives. The short-lived chapters of the Gay Liberation Front of 1969–1971[13] and Queer Nation of 1991 confronted the marginality and alienation dynamic in the overly optimistic hope that by collectively intensifying the unlivability, new forms of community would automatically and swiftly take root. This strategy works in relatively liberal ghettos and perhaps even a few suburbs. But the shopping malls that were queered long ago are still fairly inhospitable to and unrepresentative of queer relations. Strategies of confrontation, without a strong emphasis on focused education, are often exhausted before alternative social relationships can take form. The marginality/alienation dynamic always has uneven impacts across space and time. Desires, collectivities, and repression all fluctuate across uneven landscapes with unique sites and opportunities.

Virtually every "community" where sexual minorities are present is a system of public or private spaces and the social relationships that maintain them, and, as such, the community embodies contradictory impulses, opportunities, and communal dynamics. Virtually every wave of homosexual, lesbian, gay, and queer activism in the twentieth century has questioned or actually confronted the "heterosexist" dichotomies of public and private space.[14] This stratum of marginalized and alienated eroticism in the landscape can be described in specific and cumulative terms as various "scenes." A queerscape is, first of all, a plane, a "scape"[15] of points of homoerotic desires, some more actualized than others, and many heavily constrained and limited to the realms of imagination, talk, and "culture."[16] My concept of the queerscape is directly linked to an expanding framework for understanding marginality, with homophobia being only one part of the political-economic processes that contribute to uneven social access to resources. I argue that, as a result of demographic marginality, aspects associated with lower numbers and isolation will always be present but that the largest obstacle to creating new and richer space—homophobia—can be fully confronted by activists in the coming centuries. I envision queerscape as a landscape of erotic alien(n)ations, ones that shift with demographics, social development, political economies, interventions of "the state,"[17] aesthetics, and—yes—desire. The conditions of these erotic "alienations"[18] and erotic "alien nations" and respective networks vary greatly across neighbourhoods, cities, metropolitan areas, regions, countries, and even broader geopolitical blocks. But the power behind these queerscapes remains the minority status of same-sex and related desires and the broader forces such as misogyny, homophobia, and patterns of capital that enjoy the benefits of enforcing the inequities resulting from initial marginalization—only some of which are directly related to homophobia. In a theory of queers in space, this is where race, culture, language, age, and disability come into play. A queerscape is just as much the product of marginalizations derived from inequities based on gender,[19] race,[20] culture, language, class,[21] age, and disability[22] as queer desire and acts.

In beginning to explore how to describe and find locations in landscapes of erotic alien(n)ations, I construct a framework that begins with (queer) marginality, which has tangible impacts in space, territory, and communities. I outline three other arenas of that over-used term "difference,"[23] as related to gender, race and culture, and class. I then review notions of "queer space" and the subjective and collective natures of its experience and use. Out of these explorations of the landscape and public places, I explore activism as part of the response to increased globalization of capital[24] and the loss of other forms of neighbourhood cohesion, as well as de facto access to public resources. Finally, I relate queer activism of the last decade to new efforts to confront homophobia as well as inequities in the distribution of environmental benefits and costs, and in the design and management of public areas that better recognize the "natural" rights of individuals to consensual contact.

The queerscape is a way to look at social transactions, landscape flows, and environmental impacts related to minority sexual identities and the marginalization of erotic expression. A queerscape is larger than a closet and usually involves outdoor and unbuilt landscapes, but it is smaller and more locality-specific than broader zones of queer "geopolitics"—ones that are becoming increasingly merged and defined more in terms of language and access to technology since the invention and marketing of cyberspace. A queerscape is a locality of contests between the domination of heteronormative constructions of identities, which Judith Butler has called "the heterosexual matrix,"[25] along with the acts that are considered acceptable and less "socially acceptable" forms of consensual contact. Lauren Berlant and Elizabeth Freeman allude to physical space and configurations of power in recognizing, "The multiplicity of social spaces, places where power and desire are enacted and transferred, needs to be disaggregated, specified . . ."[26]

Marginality and the Social Ecology of Queerscapes

Sometimes being queer feels like being an alien. Too many of the streets have no names, and there are not many friendly places to go. When you are living on the edges of things, the margins, "home" can be hard to find. Making new "home territory"[27] can be more difficult. Lesbians, gay men, bisexuals,[28] and other groups that are perceived as threatening to heteronormative "hegemony" are marginalized as "sexual minorities." In this sense "queer" extends to transsexuals[29] and transvestites,[30] as well as to networks of people with erotic desires that are also deemed "perversions"—especially those increasingly public practitioners of sadomasochism, "S/M."[31] This "otherness" of queer sexualities is played out at different scales—across neighbourhoods,[32] regions, and landscapes. The new emphases on uniqueness of place, on more democratic forms of "site-specificity"—sometimes as parts of new "identificatory practices"[33] and the confluences of people who inhabit them—emerged in part from site-based art[34] and political ecology, but is being increasingly applied to other questions of community and activism. Where we live and our passages across space are central to our identities, outlooks, priorities, strategies for survival, "community," and for finding various forms of communality and "communion."

The early days of gay liberation, feminism, and environmentalism in the 1960s and 1970s saw the emergence of these new ways of looking at the world. They were oriented to finding simple unified theories that were still basically "normative." There was one way to be—the nonnormal was queer. Blame it on Hegel, though it has been the core of the modernist "project" for some time. There was still a search for absolute truth—essentially one way of looking at the world, usually some kind of science-based objectivity. Experiences of marginalized sexualities flew in the face of a total theory of psyche-sex-family-political-economy, and they were too often considered unimportant, impotent, or wrong. Over the last two decades, some feminist theorists and some lesbian, gay, and environmental activists have worked to construct a "space" sufficiently expansive to allow for multiple voices. These new "locales" have nurtured a more diverse set of queer experiences and "uses" of the landscape. In recent years this

Del LaGrace Volcano, *On Top of Soho,* London, 1989.

emergent theoretical framework began to be articulated through various interpretations of postmodernism:[35] an increasingly overused and poorly defined term. For example, Elizabeth Wilson has talked of the city as comprising contradictory sites—new freedoms for women, along with renewed constraints and increasing dangers.[36] Douglas Crimp noted that much "postmodernism" has been in opposition to modernism, with its emphasis on singular objectivity that subordinates and negates subjectivities. Such unified theory too often obscures local relationships and reenforces centralized power relationships.[37] In contrast, the central concept in postmodernism, or "pomo," is the emphasis on historic and site-specific interpretations that extend to culture and include the marginal and anomalous erotic and other social relationships.[38]

A queer(ed) "postmodernism," especially for environmental design, would not be a kind of "cultural relativism," where certain well-defined and privileged groups of gay men and lesbians are considered fixed subcultures that simply had been overlooked. Rather, queer "pomo" nurtures a kind of "pluri-normativeness,"[39] where human relationships and cultural expression are considered in terms of their possibilities for diminishing inequitable access to resources and distributing certain environmental benefits and "costs." Out of these possibilities could emerge more authentic alliances and identities, most of which would have erotic dimensions, as played out in specific communities and "places."[40] Such a shift would cause big changes in how people, including sexual minorities, view themselves and their place in the world.

There are three forces that currently highlight the need to understand better our communities as queers in space. The increased globalization of capital, often today referred to as "the postmodern condition," has destabilized the fabric of many non-sexual identities and communities, including those constructed around "race,"[41] submerged nationality,[42] and class. Because of the requirements to survive hostility and subsequent marginalization, queer enclaves—when they actually become established—have tended to be relatively resilient. The pedestrian-oriented, public-space-intensive gay ghetto is now being reappropriated by the middle class in the name of Hillary Rodham Clinton's "village." As "the family" becomes less rooted and more anonymous, the cohesion and sense of place found in (queer) neighbourhoods—which is in large part derived from the recognition of local histories[43]—begin to appear as viable alternatives. Sometimes this alternative coherence and cohesion abet gentrification by middle-class white men, but there are few analytical frameworks and "tests" for looking at more egalitarian and sustainable forms of communality that can occur while real estate values climb. In this sense, there are key relationships between locality and identity, with the queer(ed) municipality, such as Benjamin Forest's West Hollywood,[44] following the creation of new "moral narratives" across the landscape that counter homophobia and renew the importance of community and neighbours. But "narratives,"[45] especially those played out in inevitably cultural

Gay male gentrification in Chelsea, New York City, 1995.

biophysical landscapes, are often more ambiguous and contradictory. Only sometimes can they be read, almost literally, as "texts which are transformations of ideologies into a concrete form."[46]

Problematically, both homophobia such as "queerbashing" and the efforts to counter it often involve new forms of identifying public outdoor space as contradictory sites—both strategic and dangerous. The new homophobia will continue to make queer space the higher risk areas—foreshadowed by broad societal indifference to the ravages of the gay ghettoes in the first decades of the AIDS pandemic. There are also intensifying contests over public outdoor sites, including the remaining "open" space in many cities where sexual minorities are involved only "peripherally." Patterns of access to a range of landscape amenities are often good indicators of persistent broader disparities in distribution of environmental costs and benefits, freedom of expression, and security. These inequities are increasingly obvious among sexual minorities along lines of gender, race, nationality, ethnicity, language, age, and mobility disability, and they are being increasingly questioned and confronted.

In order to construct an analytical framework for identifying important public outdoor sites for sexual minorities, this essay outlines solutions to three theoretical problems. First, the vocabulary for social relationships that involve sexual minorities in the landscape needs to be expanded. In particular, the notion of "community," with all of its divergent meanings and uses, must be clarified—along with ancillary terms such as communality, alliance, and movement. Second, an expanded analysis of the rather fluid and overlapping hierarchies of oppression involving homophobia, patriarchy, and colonialism/neocolonialism is needed in order to track disparities in access to public spaces. Third, it is necessary to construct matrices to identify more clearly the social uses and functions of particular sites for networks of sexual minorities.

Queer Communities versus Strategic Sites

The roles and nature of "community" for sexual minorities have been radically transformed over the last three decades. At various points, public places in or near certain gay enclaves[47] have had crucial roles in making social contact and in the formation of broader milieux. The notion of the homosexual community[48] goes back to the early homophile movements and to "liberal" (though often somewhat hostile) sociological studies.[49] Since the 1969 Stonewall riots in New York, there has been a plethora of visions of lesbian, gay, or queer community, most notably that of Wolf in 1979,[50] D'Emilio in 1983,[51] Lauria and Knopp in 1985,[52] Di Augelli and Hart in 1987,[53] Murray in 1992,[54] and Almgren in 1994.[55] In recent years there has been some discussion of communities based on electronic networks[56] without common territory. And there have been some well-founded challenges to the entire notion of communities. In support of the deconstruction of the mass of associations under the label of community, Michael Warner argued in his *Fear of a Queer Planet* that, "Queer people are a kind of social group fundamentally unlike others, a status group only insofar as they are not a class."[57] Warner goes on to identify correctly the notion of a gay and lesbian community as generated by "Anglo-American identity politics."[58] My response is not to completely abandon the use of the multiple and often contradictory visions of community, but, when using them, to highlight the inherent ethnic and cultural specificities of each construction. I argue that given the extent and chronic nature of overt and more submerged homophobic repression and hostility, few such queer(ed) zones have so far been able to be constructed as interdependent communities—territorialized or just imagined. But it is just a matter of time and countering homophobic constraints. Such an optimism avoids the difficult question of what constitutes "communities" of individuals who possess only vaguely similar desires, practices, and sensibilities, and who demonstrate a great disparity in their vulnerability to economic and cultural inequities. Community, therefore, is always in large part a reflection of the level of repression and unequal distribution in resources and access to them. It may, in fact, be possible to make new kinds of communities, and I want to believe that it is largely a matter of social education, theoretical clarity, and the time necessary to form alliances.

On the Margins of Marginalized Desire: The "Differences" of Race, Culture, Language, Class, Disability, and Age

> It is currently quite fashionable to speak about race, class and gender. I think we have to address empire first. You cannot situate race, you cannot situate class, you cannot situate gender, unless you begin with empire.
>
> —Cornel West, 1994[59]

Most people who experience marginalization because of same-sex desire also contend with unequal access to social and environmental resources because of at least one

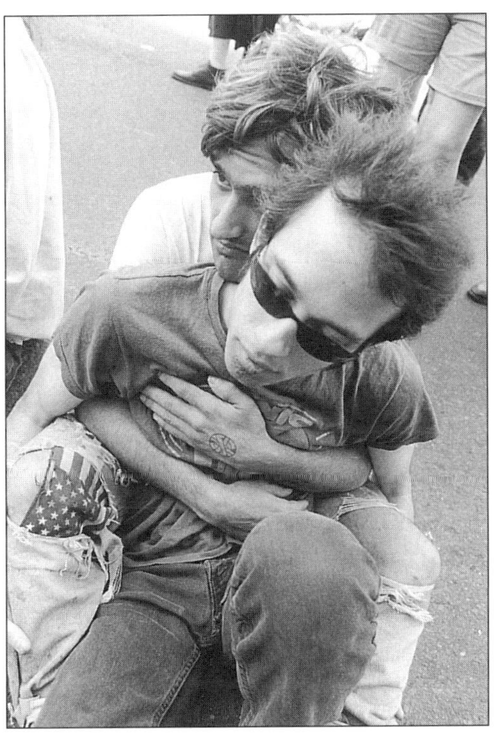

Lover boys and the United States flag. Photograph by Dana Schuerholz, Impact Visuals.

other condition such as their race, culture, language, class, disability, and age—not to mention their gender. Most of these conditions are regulated in terms of the overlapping vestiges (the societal artifacts) of colonialism and empire, as well as today's flows of globalizing capital. Confronting such combined and cumulative inequities has been the greatest weakness of gay liberation, lesbian feminism, and queer "nationalism."[60] Lack of recognition and the subsequent inability to negotiate authentic alliances has remained the Achilles heel of activism to confront homophobia and to build queer communities. To distill and reduce such a multitude of inequities to generic difference or even to problems of "decolonisation" tends to obscure the full extent of what might have been conceived, jumbled together, as overlapping oppressions two decades ago. Today, "postcolonial boundary crossings"[61] remain problematic because, in large part, many of the boundaries remain "underacknowledged" by privileged groups and "underdocumented" by the less privileged combined majority. The most common element of queer experience is marginalization by same-sex desire, and this is compounded or overshadowed by other social obstacles to resources. Having a framework for these, especially marginal alterities, is crucial to understanding the historical development and current options for the queerscape.

Certainly some queerscapes are more colonial or liberatory than others. Some queerscapes are little more than plantations or company towns, and some are closer to country clubs. Some queer networks are heavily constrained by state interventions, even totalitarianism or a heavy emphasis on consumption. In every queerscape, no matter how egalitarian, there are environmental and political economic forces that enforce some inequities. The formation of networks and even more territorialized communities often parallels these hierarchies of oppression. In racist landscapes there are ghettoization and partial containment[62] of racial identities that largely define those in the marginalized sexuality. For example, in the confluence of African-American and homosexual space in the Harlem Renaissance,[63] racial and erotic identifications were key to self-protection and access to cultural activities in the early pre-white-tourism period. Being in a cultural or language minority often constrains an individual's options for public space where he or she can make contact and find peer support. These differences often overwhelm and further distort the de facto spatial apportionment that a queer individual experiences. These forces of inequity work to limit the amount of space, both private and public, that is effectively available to minorities.

The places where sexual-minority identities can express themselves sexually, as well as the spaces where acts can be transformed into identities, are some of the more strategic and transformative queer spaces. Such zones of exploration date well before the emergence of modern notions of gay men and lesbians as part of an "alternative modernist enterprise"[64] that were associated with homosexual subcultures of the 1920s, particularly in Paris and New York City. Today, such places exist as much in fantasy as in reality. In every queerscape there is a current of imagination, of only partially recognized and territorialized desire, that is as much about an open space as its vegetation and designed fixtures. For example, Nicole Brossard recently described a fantasy for a cruising park "for women only" in Barcelona.[65] Similarly, Annemarie Jagose[66] has argued that the word "lesbian" always has embodied a vision of utopian space and a displacement of patriarchical sites.

Recognition of the queerscape provides a basis to better inventory and monitor transactions and inequities in enjoyment of landscape amenities as well as the distribution of costs across public and private environments. Other forms of containment and isolation, derived from social hierarchies other than homophobia, can be more precisely mapped. But it is easy to reduce the analyses to what was once referred to as "primary contradictions," especially those persisting in postcolonial times, related to race, culture, and class. It is more difficult, but as important, to consider the inequities that are related to language, disability, and age—conditions that in the global labour market could become greater generators of inequities than race, class, and gender are today. "Class" position in the postmodern condition is more the cumulative result of older exclusions, including those rooted in homophobia. Today, nationalities function less around shared territories and more around the lines that link local experience to global exchange.[67] For sexual minorities these forces are increasingly filtered through the experience of the neighbourhood, whether as the gay ghetto as regional centre for goods and suburbs or the suburb where childcare is convenient and affordable. In this time when state-sanctioned and science-based reality is breaking down and any pretense of objectivity is disappearing, confrontation of racism and gender inequities along with their host of synergies in disparity of access to information and public space become central to queer activism. The strategies to confront homophobia and the calculated indifference of power to sexual minorities[68] often require more of the educational actions and confrontations that emerged with ACT UP and the organizations that followed than the more established realms of electoral politics. In other words, queer civic politics will increasingly be based on strategies for queer (re)appropriation of public space, whether it be safety from violence in a park or ten seconds on national television.

The Boundaries of the Public and the Private

The lines between domestic and state issues have always been constructed, have always been fluid, and have always been site-specific. Sexual politics have always had a direct relationship within these dynamics, and this relationship dates back before the *publicus* and *privatus* of Roman law.[69] Significantly, according to Habermas, "a public sphere in the sense of a separate realm distinguished from the private sphere cannot be shown to have existed in the feudal society of the High Middle Ages."[70] In other words, public space, like both conventional and marginal sexual identities, has been and will continue to be constructed and reconstructed. Paradoxically, many of the attempts to create universally accessible public space have been part of the totalizing narratives of modernism, especially as related to natural rights and in contrast to what have often been conceived of as unnatural acts. The emerging publicness of outdoor sites made them centres for traffic in commodities, ideas, sexual identities, and sex.

The notion of public space, where citizens had rights and were somewhat equal, emerged more fully during the French Revolution.[71] But almost simultaneous with the

Muff divers in front of the Treasury Department, Dyke March, March on Washington, Washington State contingent, 1993. Photograph by Dana Schuerholz, Impact Visuals.

movement to transform "natural law" into rights, state surveillance apparatus began to expand—with one of the major groups targeted for repression being sexual minorities. In fact the need to police public spaces was often justified by invoking the largely overblown spectre of the (public) threat of the (homosexual) "molester." More destructive than policing per se were the more comprehensive efforts by heteronormative patriarchy, which became known as "the family," to dominate public spaces in the latter half of the nineteenth century and the first half of the twentieth. In effect, public places and networks of open space were programmed and constructed to exclude queers, and to reenforce an exclusive *ordre naturel* that reflected the desires for maximized profit by capitalism and the state in the Industrial Revolution and in periods of colonial expansion.

Provisional Sexualities/Marginal Spaces

Space may not be the final frontier of queer theory[72] but it is taking on an increasingly pivotal role in identifying inequities within and *between* networks and communities of lesbians, gay men, and bisexuals and in developing new strategies for making alliances to counter homophobia. This decade, the last of the first century of prolonged urban activism by sexual minorities, is seeing an explosion of theories about queers in urban and rural space[73] that involve a range of scales from the closet to the transnational region. And like most other environmental amenities in late capitalism, queer space[74] is increasingly commodified. Indeed the notion of queer space has emerged nearly a decade later into a wave of renewed activism that has redefined communities of sexual minorities and more seriously confronted a wider range of inequities as related to gender, race, class, and culture.

Queer space has an inherent oppositional relationship to homophobic space. "Homophobia"[75] is a remarkably recent concept, one that emerged in the post-Stonewall period and has central implications for the management of public space. The notion of homophobia, constructed to counter a range of inequities, suggests an illness or at the very least an overprivileging by certain heterosexuals (or closeted homosexuals) that, in turn, functions to justify denying rights and respect to people who are engaged in or forming identities around homoeroticism. The most extreme tactics by homophobes involve assaults on sexual minorities, and these attacks often function to destroy spaces where autonomy and free expression were formerly controlled, however temporarily, by the (queer) targets. In recent years in North America, one of the most common themes in the rhetoric of homophobic violence is to reverse "queering"[76] processes in order to "cleanse" neighbourhoods.[77] As ethnic cleansing has reemerged as a tactic for domination, the constant attempts to clean up state-neglected queer space continue unless economic forces are particularly strong.

A queerscape is not only a landscape (as based on the Flemish root *schap*) with sexual minorities. A queerscape is also an aspect of the landscape, a social overlay, where the interplays between assertion and marginalization of sexualities are in constant flux and the space for sexual minorities is "decentered,"[78] in terms of increasingly supporting stigmatized activities and identities. Queerscapes embody processes that counter those that directly harm, discount, isolate, ghettoize, and assimilate. A queerscape is, therefore, a cumulative kind of spatial unit, a set of places, a plane of subjectivities constituting a collectivity, which involve multiple alliances of lesbians, gay men, bisexuals, and transsexuals and which support a variety of activities, transactions, and functions. At least for some time to come, a queerscape nearly always overlaps with and is surrounded by social groups where heterosexuality is the "norm." Like the landscape, the queerscape is a cultural construct that provides a territorial basis for considering opportunities for and persistent disparities in access to public space and various respective services and amenities, as well as options for personal and collective expression. Activism for the management and (re)construction of spatial[79] aspects of various queer enclaves for more purposeful formation of sites for various functions, particularly where there are pressures for increased equity in access[80] and enjoyment, can become the initial core of a kind of queerscape architecture. But a kind of environmental design that clearly confronts the impacts of erotic desire and power has barely been imagined.

A queerscape embodies constellations of sites of various habitudes and utilities. There are invariably key relationships among commerce, power, and sex.[81] Cindy Patton outlined three basic types of uses of queer space, which could include strategies that she conceived as "complex sets of practices that lead to alliances across space."[82]

1. With greater visibility, bodies marked as queer create specific forms of space around them. Personal erotic expression and individual resistance to homophobia at the level of "body space"[83] provide the most basic elements of queer space. Here, there is only queer space because there are queer bodies. Today, body space is a central discourse in culture, monitored and designed, but remains rooted in the German concept of private space, the *intimsphäre* and the earlier Greek notion of personal realm, the *idia*.[84]

2. With large numbers of people identified as queer, there is a "queering" of adjacent environments in terms of a limited safety in numbers as a means of countering repression and developing more diverse and dependable relationships. This kind of queer space emerged in the nineteenth century as a blurring of public and private into small scattered "intermediate zones"[85] often occupied by disproportionately higher numbers of women and female and male homosexuals. Here badly needed information can be exchanged and various forms of socialization can take place. This is the queer space of the ghetto where, because of homophobic targetting, the vulnerability of sexual minorities may actually increase. Perhaps this is the diametric opposite of the heteronormative "exclusionary space"[86] erected in the nineteenth century that functioned to reenforce, more comprehensively, power relationships of gender and sexuality.

Tomb of Oscar Wilde, Père Lachaise, Paris, 1995. The genitals on the figure are often vandalized.

3. There is the creation of usually designed places of aesthetic conflicts and ruptures, such as Tschumi's "disjunctions" of use, form, and social values,[87] that force social, cultural, and personal reassessments and reconstructions. Such jarring landscapes and sites can contribute to the reconstruction of sexualities or at least challenges to patriarchy and heteronormative controls and have some links to Foucault's notion of the *heterotopia*[88] of the rich courts and theatres that emerged in Europe in the Middle Ages, where designed spaces are "endowed with the curious property of being in relation with all the others but in such a way as to suspend, neutralize, or invert the set of relationships designed, reflected, or mirrored by themselves."[89]

Such oppositional use of public space, indeed a construction of *des espaces autres*[90] as part of strategies of *détournement,*[91] has provided key arenas for collective visibility and expression by sexual outlaws. This, the most revolutionary and utopian use of queer space,[92] has rarely been applied to architecture and planning though there are increasing attempts to disorient[93] or to reconstruct memory through theatre, opera, performance, interior design, monuments and markers, and public art.[94] Related to such spaces of deconstruction, Manfredo Tafuri described a neo-Marxist process of "self-disalienation" launched by "negative design."[95]

Some of the first queer spaces were formed through communal responses to sites of resistance to homophobic repression. In one sense, queer space is always a response to homophobia. A queer site is a singular point of expression, exchange, sexuality, or resistance in the landscape that counters loss of use and habitation because of social changes and events rooted in homophobia. The binary notion of ghetto/nonghetto gives way to subtle maps of pleasure, threat, isolation, opportunity, and communality.

Queer Space as Collective Subjectivities

> The city is a map of violences anticipated.
>
> —Samuel R. Delany[96]

Queerscapes are derived from highly individualized experiences. What we know and how we feel about where we are has tremendous implications for how we interact with other people and what is perceived as community.[97] While ideologies have impact on cultural imagery in ways that influence individual development and perspectives, the experience of place is largely individual and subjective. A queerscape is essentially a sum total of subjectivities, some more closely linked, for a time, than others. There are the biophysical environment, social relations, culture, and desire that create their own geographies and actual places. The textures of these sum totals, how they shift over time, and where they stabilize—the communalities and communities—have direct implications for the spaces, networks, and coalitions that are possible at any given time. Homophobic intimidation, policing, and other forms of repression can regulate desire but can rarely destroy erotic motivations to gaze and make contact.

"Mapping" becomes important to make sense of the tremendous changes going on in both cultural and physical environments.[98] For sexual minorities, more careful recognition and use of such maps, as well as the range of respective subjectivities, may be key to survival. For example, Eric Estuar Reyes explored the implications of cognitive maps for "queers of color" as part of a program to distribute safe-sex information to different Pacific Rim ethnicities and different same-language groups defined in terms of age, culture, and citizenship/immigration histories. He asks,

> Just as there is a physical structure of the spaces we inhabit, there is a cognitive structure that we use to locate ourselves in the landscape. For queers and for queers of color, what is this cognitive structure? Is it spatial? How is this important to being, becoming, or negating a queer individual and/or communal identity?[99]

Comparisons of such cognitive maps emerge as opportunities for charting commonality and divergence in activist efforts "to construct a more concrete collective space."[100] These notions were preceded by Debord's 1955 "Introduction to a critique of urban geography,"[101] where he coined the term "psychogeography." Much of Debord's conception of personal spatial relationships is underlaid with a critique of Haussmann's bourgeois reconstruction of Paris and is inherently activist. His "Psychogeographical Game of the Week"[102] linked subjectivity to activism. The 1957–92 Situationist Movement,[103] of which Debord was one of the founders, informed what Maxine Wolfe termed the "collective direct action" tactics of ACT UP[104] and Queer Nation[105]—particularly the "zaps,"[106] "kiss-ins"[107] in suburban shopping malls, and funerals in highly public areas. Such events can be used to illustrate and confront intimidation, terror, and alienation along with disparities in enjoyment and access to urban areas while holding some promise of security and even pleasure through new forms of communality.

ACT UP and the Wealth Care Bus, San Francisco, June 1980. Photograph by Dana Schuerholz, Impact Visuals.

Homophobic Repression and Sites of Resistance

> There is a residuum that hooks "queer," this violent rejection and despoliation of the norm by the exiled, to the newly disposable populations produced by a state characterized by casual despotism.
>
> —Philip Derbyshire[108]

If the denial of access to certain forms of standing in public space and typical levels of freedom of expression, comfort, and security have been central to the experience of sexual minorities in the twentieth century, what are the cumulative social impacts of these losses, and how are they enforced? How much of these losses has been internalized and will persist indefinitely in queer subcultures and social relations? The following is a list of some of the most important processes working against queer “open” space.

- homophobic and misogynist violence
- police repression
- de facto privatization of public open space
- site design and landscape management to discourage contact and queer placemaking
- censorships of relevant cultural representations

The dynamic geography of dyke and gay bashing and murders has had a huge impact on the mental maps of most people who are sexual minorities. Sometimes it takes a great deal of extra thought and energy to minimize the possibilities of being targeted. These internalized defensive maps have an influence on where we choose to go and to live and on the subsequent physical forms of our neighbourhoods and communities. Police surveillance and repression,[109] which go back to the early use of urban homosexual sites, have reenforced strategies of avoidance. At various points in the last century, and in large parts of the world, the state has attempted to suppress queer challenges to “normative gender and sexual arrangements”[110] by containing the visible presence of “perverts” in the public sphere. In times of repression, public open space has had particularly crucial roles in making contact and subsequent socialization, education, nurturing, and protection. This was often the case in the 1950s in the United States, as suggested by Jim Kepner[111] and Joan Nestle.[112] In much of the developing world, a shortage of queer indoor space is still acute, and reliance on furtive night landscapes continues, especially for groups of men who normally pass as heterosexuals and where certain sites, at night, become the major identifiers of queerness. As well as claiming public space, the birth of the modern Women’s Liberation and Gay Liberation movements coincided with redefinitions of the lines between public and private space. In the industrialized West, housing options became increasingly more available for people outside

Antientrapment activism, Buena Vista Park, San Francisco, 1980.

of the traditional nuclear family units,[113] as did, more problematically, greater travel between city centres and suburban housing. For example, early Canadian gay activist John Grube[114] explored the effects of Toronto's 1950s and early 1960s zoning laws, by which it was difficult for single men to find accommodation where "friends" could stay over. Outdoor sites were, therefore, central to the social lives of many of these gay men; they were one of the few alternatives to bars and washrooms, though such environments posed other risks and exclusions. Lesbians, as well as less "masculine" men and transsexuals, had even fewer options for and access to indoor and outdoor space.

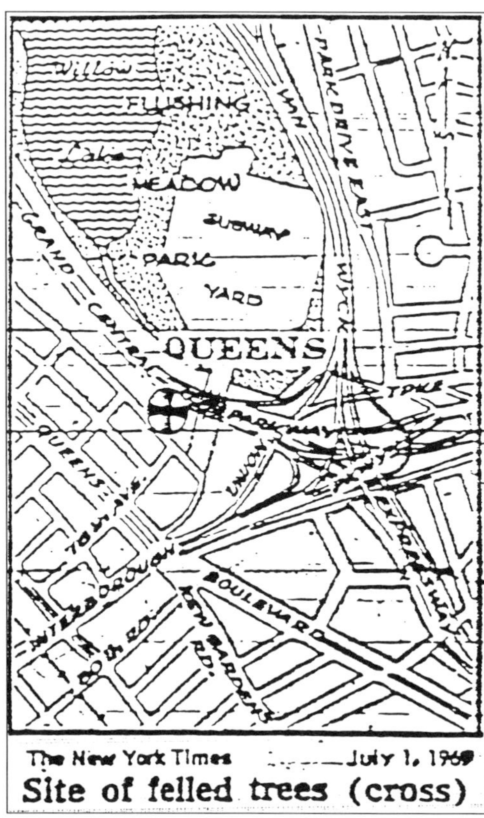

Kew Gardens, Queens, site of the June 1969 conflicts over cruising that preceded the Stonewall riots in lower Manhattan. *The New York Times*, July 1, 1969. Courtesy of *The New York Times*.

The Stonewall riots were the first communal "reterritorialization"[115] that was recognized by mainstream media,[116] as they involved a contest over a bar and the street adjacent to it between the police, the Mafia, and nascent activists. But the notion of Stonewall as a singular event obscures the full extent of the activism of those times.[117] Similar, though slightly less militant confrontations with the police had been going on for several years, especially in Los Angeles and San Francisco. Stonewall embodied stiff resistance because there was a perception that the raids were part of a renewed attempt to "drive the fags out of the Village."[118] The Stonewall riots raged for well over two nights and did not end abruptly.[119] In the same month Kew Gardens, a cruising area in Queens, was badly destroyed by extensive tree cutting and violent vigilante attacks intended to discourage the presence of gay men. Within a week after Stonewall, there were public actions showing conscious visibility, and the first gay liberationist environmental group, Trees for Queens,[120] was formed to restore the park. In Manhattan's gay ghettos,[121] confrontations with the police continued for over a year in response to what a coalition of gay and lesbian feminist groups termed "stepped-up police intimidation and harassment" and "on-street assaults by heterosexual bigots."

In the decades since Stonewall, there have been waves when privately owned semi-public queer spaces were acquired, often at considerable cost[122] and at the expense of more collective projects. Gay businesses have sometimes conflicted with activists over organizing parades and outdoor demonstrations and, indeed, over the underlying purposes of social events. Inherent in the post-Stonewall era ghettoes were relatively stable disparities in terms of access to jobs, income, and consumerism, including housing stock, and divergent patterns for use of open space. Yet in North America, for example, the inequities within gay ghettoes—which followed lines of gender, race, and language—have barely been assessed.

The first ACT UP demonstrations in 1987 in New York City—which came in response to calculated government indifference to the AIDS pandemic—confirmed a shift in the politics of North American sexual minorities back to more collectivist uses of public space, even if only to make a point. People were dying quickly, and some kind of "(re)appropriation"[123] of the public realm from and through the corporate media was desperately needed, if only as pressure for more resources for treatment and to better educate the population about unprotected sex. Just as significant was the fact that those years of the Reagan presidency saw some of the first significant "rollbacks" in the gains of women, while their invisibility in the equations of the early gay male AIDS activists was untenable. And the increasing globalization of the real estate markets of North American cities was driving up prices and making the already cramped ghettos more difficult for already marginal living. The early ravages of AIDS share a disturbing trajectory with increased homelessness. Some tactical uses of choreography and architecture[124] were developed by Queer Nation and Lesbian Avengers for the symbolic[125] and temporary appropriation of public attention, as a kind of subversion of "spectacle." These strategies have been part of a project of deghettoization, which Lisa Duggan[126] argues is central to queer politics, as opposed to those of earlier lesbian and gay activism—to consciously move presence, placemaking, and representation[127] into more public and homophobic zones.

The 1969 Stonewall riots and the ACT UP and Queer Nation actions marked three exceptional points in an ongoing trajectory of increased purposefulness in queer community building and placemaking. There has even been a kind of militaristic "delocalization" and a renewed "localization,"[128] with outdoor sites being aggressively contested and reappropriated, sometimes only for short periods. It is important not to underestimate historical context in the impact of various celebrations, remembrances, and other activities with ritual quality, as well as the power of these episodes for queer groups so culturally and emotionally marginalized. Today, there often is more than just the temporary assertion of what Foucault suggested was power over points and territories. The experience of collective resistance, with new relationships and vocabularies, transformed the ways in which we as sexual minorities have viewed ourselves, our networks, and our sense of inherent rights, transforming the nature of respective identities. Outdoor sites of sexuality, communality, and remembrance have been particularly contentious between communities of sexual minorities and within broader society. In virtually every North American and European neighbourhood with sizable lesbian and gay male populations, there have been controversies about safety and public sex,[129] as well as the conception, symbolism, interpretation, and delivery of sculptural and pictorial information for public places. Art that explicitly explores queer sensibilities and relationships to public space has only begun to be designed and installed[130] out there, although it is already supporting a wide range of cultural and political functions.

Activist Responses to Globalizing Market Forces

The emergence of Queer Nation and ACT UP in New York City[131] date not only from the early ravages of the AIDS pandemic but also from the years of intensified globalization in the real estate markets of large North American and western European cities. This disruption of place has become synonymous with experience of community since the decline of modernism.[132] Except for Berlin under the Nazis, the scale of death and displacement was unprecedented in the history of any of the historic gay and lesbian enclaves. In the same period, emergent lesbian enclaves were stymied by some of the same forces. Perhaps the recent invention of the notion of queer space reflects new uses of coding,[133] which resists avowedly capitalistic parameters of identity and resource apportionment in favour of more communal needs and desires.

As the de facto privatization of public space has intensified[134] over the last decade, and as capital has flowed more freely, urban environments have deteriorated. The dissociated shifts in capital and land values have pushed a wide range of social groups out of valuable and strategic urban areas. Paradoxically, enclaves of sexual minorities have been particularly vulnerable to privatization of public space and yet highly adaptable to it. In queer activism two very different constellations of tactics have emerged, roughly paralleling "right" and "left" political ideologies, and which might be conceived as private-oriented and public-oriented, respectively. There has been the creation of semipublic commercial space, coupled with commodification of such amenities as safety in the prolifer-

Poster for the exhibition *Queer Space*, Storefront Art and Architecture, New York, June 18–July 31, 1994.

Martha Judge, *Poster #1* (top) and *Poster #4* (bottom), *Localmotive Project,* 1992.

ation of bars, resorts, cafés, and gatherings that are run for a profit. In contrast, there has been the defense and expansion of queer commons and the claiming of turf. This public/private dialectic in political strategies forms an initial dynamic of queerscape architecture that will probably persist indefinitely in various forms.

Queer activism around space and place has emerged in part because of its intensifying commodification by business groups, many of whom have resisted the label "queer." The increasing commercialization of communal sites is causing many to be expensive and increasingly unavailable to less privileged queer groups. The greater the commodification of space and loss of secure access to formerly public sites (a central characteristic of globalized capital), the more the preclusion of collectivity with its subsequent retardation in forming local queer commons. Today, instead of authentic access to space and community, sexual minorities active in civic politics have been granted a poor substitute of the globalizing-capital standard fare, the "spectacle"[135] where capital is accumulated to such a degree that it actually becomes an image,[136] rather than authentic access to resources.

Historically, queer space has been largely hidden. But today it is increasingly interesting to a wider audience. Globalizing media is enabling an increased heterosexual voyeurism, something of a new and slightly more liberal "panopticon." Yet in this context, queer space continues to be largely unstable, vulnerable, "nomadic,"[137] and "deterritorialized"[138]—to the detriment of many important kinds of communality, exchange, and enculturation. Paradoxically, where queer space is better established, it is often what Virilio called "delocalized,"[139] not to be confused with deterritorialized. Thus San Francisco's Castro Street looks and functions much like New York's Christopher Street and other areas, such as the "touristic" Rue du Temple in Paris, oddly similar and reworked to conform and reiterate an easily marketable subset of desires, images, and transactions.

Conclusions: Identifying Queerscapes as a Prerequisite for Their Reconstruction

Despite the gains made since partial decriminalization of homosexuality and the modern North American gay liberation and lesbian feminist movements, urban landscapes are still high in diverse forms of homophobia and low and scattered in tangible levels of communality. In this provisional context, new queer sites and their respective territorialization represent crucial confluences of desire, values, imagination, cooperation, and place. The increase in both public and more private sites indicates a host of nascent relationships, and it should no longer be trivialized—particularly by planners, designers, civic governments, and activists.

Any new architectures of queerscapes must function to counter homophobia, both to organize against violence[140] and to confront the inequities and added risks resulting from design decisions, whether they be in "programming"[141] or ongoing management of the landscape. A huge amount of public funds still goes into design and management decisions that make some sites effectively inaccessible or uncomfortable for certain groups with marginalized sexualities. This inaccessibility or discomfort extends well beyond furtive sexual contact. In 1997 queer outdoor space offers points of conflict over safety, comfort, communication, sexual expression, and "collective memory."[142] Landscape architecture, including what is innocuously termed "landscaping" and "urban design," is too often used to exacerbate inequities under the guise of balanced management and fiscal restraint. Until recently, issues of sexual minorities, including security for women, have been tacitly neglected in most landscape design programming. Negative reactions to sex in the landscape function as smoke screens for broader hostility and indifference towards individuals who act independently of heteronormative families and for the continued interest in regulation of public behaviour. Even the few activist administrations that have attempted to concretize gains in increased protection and services for lesbian and gay presence have often been largely ineffective due to internal bureaucratic "containment"[143] that reasserts inequities.

Development of vocabularies for recognizing the breadth of different alliances and community-formation processes across landscapes becomes a prerequisite for strategizing queer architectures of (re)appropriation and community. Queerscape architecture tactics can extend from creating ephemeral presence, as in lesbian and gay parades, to concretizing interpretations of events such as AIDS memorial sites. In turn, more spontaneous site-specific interventions of various durations require new levels of coordination and planning. There are a number of overlapping theatres and scales for queerscape architecture. There are more systematic reforms related to policies and laws that, in turn, influence the impact of police, homophobes, and economic constraints—which, in turn, regulate the use of designed and more natural public space. Social pressures can be analyzed in relation to the needs and interests of specific groups as part of efforts for greater inclusion. Measures for intervention in these spheres can be grouped under such categories as legislation, the courts, administration and planning, finance, information access, civic participation, and culture.

Are queerscapes simply another layer of erotic and social reality neatly sheared off social space with only a small gap and minor footprint? Hardly. As long as there are some forms of marginalization and alienation, there will be queerscapes that function as closets, undergrounds, and hyperpublic arenas. Queerscapes are just one of the many layers of social-environmental relationships in the landscape, but they remain highly contentious—generating numerous opportunities to expose the horizons of power, communality, and lusting and loving creative expression. Does any form of homoerotic contact transform its environment and become part of a queerscape? Yes. Do queerscapes always embody conscious and contradictory purposes to both assert and to suppress homoerotic expression? Yes. Given the diversity of networks that have been emerging, with a wide range of motives for assertion and suppression of presence, queerscapes will remain unique cumulative reconnings of specific histories, locations, and experiences. The queerscape will remain both vulnerable and volatile, and its texture and trajectories are worthy of careful examination before we can hope to survive as viable networks and communities or to begin to effectively protect and enrich the relations for which many of us have crossed such great distances.

Part 1—Experience / Place / Maps

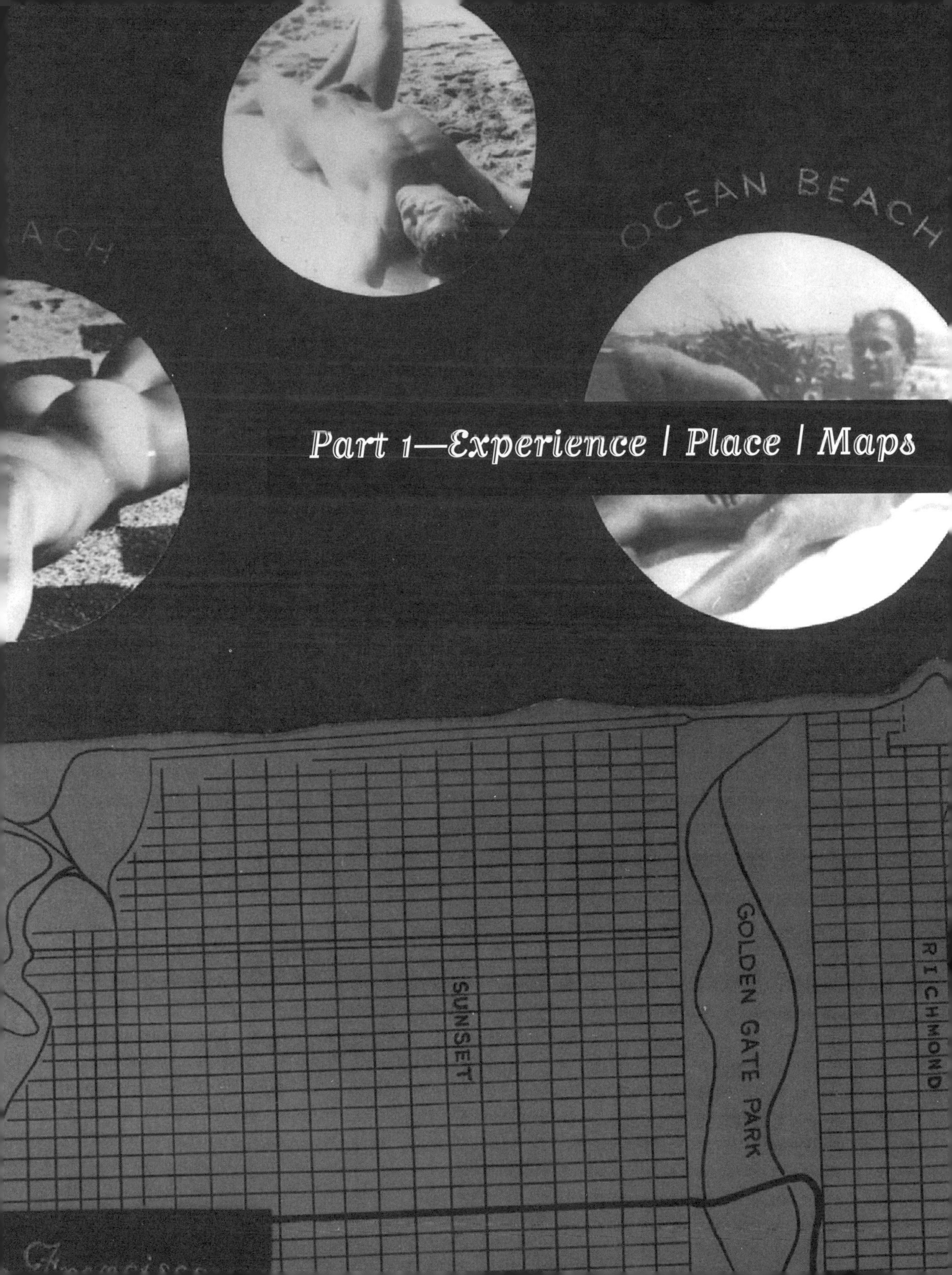

Preceding page: Photograph from the Tim Wood collection, with map of San Francisco open space in the 1950s. Courtesy of the Gay and Lesbian Historical Society of Northern California.

Narratives of Place: Subjective and Collective

Gordon Brent Ingram, Anne-Marie Bouthillette, and Yolanda Retter

How do literature, photography, video, and other forms of creative expression fit into a book on marginalized sexualities and environmental design? They help to expand the discussion of queer civic politics by expressing "reality"—that web of daily life that includes both external places and events, and internal states such as fear or desire—as experienced by sexual minorities. Instead of using charts and graphs, or maps marked with labels and elevations, they use metaphor, image, wit, and reminiscence to make that reality real to the reader or viewer. These selections show how the lives of queer individuals and groups both reflect and shape the landscape; such accounts have often been ignored or only partially asserted. Such imaginatively reconstructed experiences reveal the epistemological connections between mental theoretical spaces and tangible biophysical and designed spaces.[1] They lend immediacy to the more theoretical discussions of place and space by showing unique instances of courage, vulnerability, empowerment, and insight, which can motivate meaningful political action more than sterile plans or studies can.

Just as there are (queer) sexual acts and related personal identities, there are maps that report the physical geography of a landscape and more subjective maps that exist "in our heads." In queer experience, this "sense of place" map plays a key role, affecting how people go about their individual lives and how they interact in social networks. It defines the points where a person's friends, lovers, potential sex partners, and allies can be found, and where danger may exist. Experience of place involves coping with social conflicts (homophobia is only one example) and building strategies for self-expression and fulfillment, including sexual exploration. Although we all experience our lives and our locales in unique ways, asserting these individual experiences—each person's unique "take" and "cognition"[2]—can help identify civic and environmental conflicts, the problems faced by queer "stakeholders" in the community and other vulnerable groups, and the affinities that need to be developed among groups in a given landscape if they are to find solutions to these problems.

In Part 1 of *Queers in Space,* we present four subjective descriptions of place, isolation and communality, and social conflict. Each work includes descriptions of people and places over time, constituting a fragmentary narrative. Each cluster of stories and impressions forms an organic and supple "map" that may be as important as "objective" cartographies of elevations or vegetation in building an understanding of a community and its biophysical environment. Generating these maps based on the experiences of different individuals leads to pooled knowledge, experiences, and

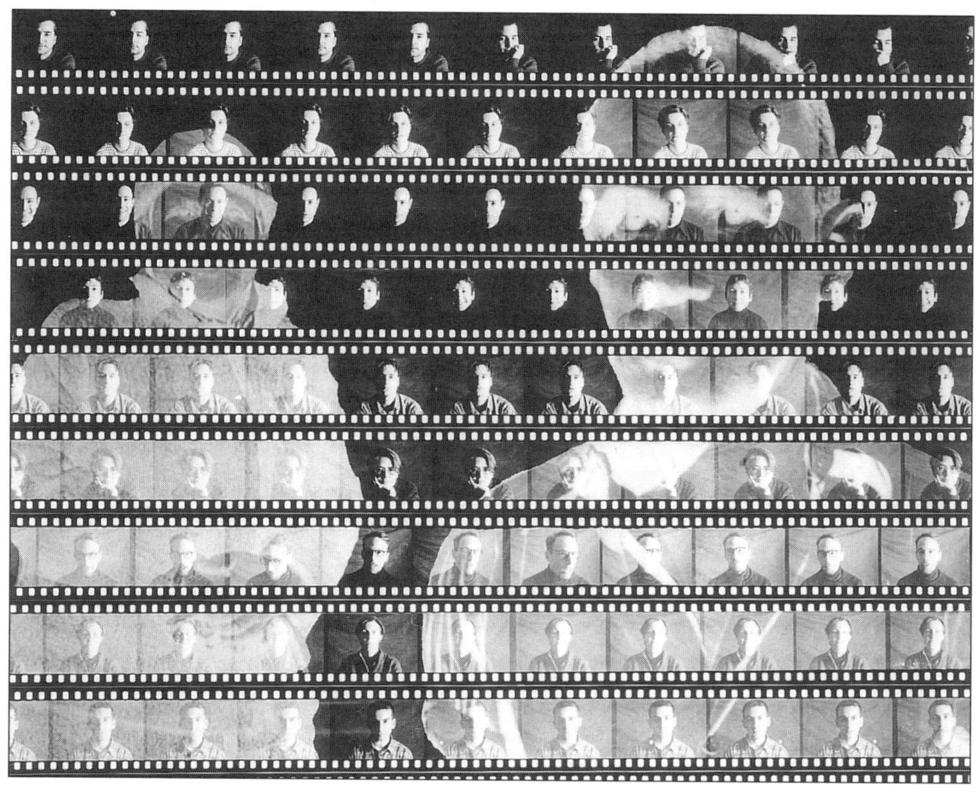

Blake Goble and Robert Ransick. Gertrude Stein and Jean Genet from *The Walls Speak: Passages from Queer Places, Queer Space* exhibition, Storefront Art and Architecture, New York, 1994.

concerns that could ultimately result in new forms of local civic polity. Whether written, spoken, or expressed in various media, maps of experience radicalize shared subjective experience and build alliances leading to effective activism, ranging in scale from a street or neighbourhood park to the entire globe. Each person's "map" is usually part autobiography, part mythology, and part the embodiment of tensions concerning forms of marginality, such as sexual politics, gender, race, ethnicity, or culture. But rather than representing a fairly complete *gestalt*, each map constitutes a page in the ongoing atlas of individual life and communal history. It contains emotional, political, and economic dimensions and involves both individuals and groups. Although erotic dynamics always figure in these pictures, the roles of sexuality and how they are played out in place and over time vary greatly.

If we were to ask a few hundred residents of a neighbourhood to draw their public open space and to talk frankly about it, different experiences (reflecting various levels of privilege, access to resources, and risks) would emerge, in many ways defined by gender, race, culture, age, mobility, and sexuality. The mental maps of most gay men and some lesbians show secret hidden spaces. These less public queer spaces formed a major part of the lives of gay men before gay liberation—indeed, they were central to our communities, especially when gay bars and other gay-owned businesses were repressed. As well as identifying these furtive islands of meeting and pleasure, mental maps point out the terror of violence, which is especially acute for women. Mental maps show that lack of queer space, including lack of basic physical safety, is all too evident in too many communities.

Considering its evident usefulness to local activism, why has cognitive mapping, or a queer version of what environmental educator Mitchell Thomashow has termed "sense-of-place mapping,"[3] not been used more often to inform queer activism? And where mapping techniques have been used, emphasis on "environmental autobiography"[4] and on the links between people's experience of and activities in a particular place and their respective life histories has been limited. Although broad self-knowledge is a prerequisite to effective work with neighbours, activists, and decision-makers, very focused techniques are often needed to flush out common issues of concern among groups and neighbourhoods. A more serious obstacle has been the almost chronic inability, in much of queer culture, to acknowledge the full range of open divergent experiences and environments and to build authentic solidarity and effective alliances.

For recent investigations of different experience of, and access to, outdoor space for communities of sexual minorities, the implications of cognitive maps are myriad. For example, cognitive mapping processes inform decisions on choice of routes and their associated distances and risks.[5] These affect the formation of queer spaces in many ways—deciding where to live, where to cruise, where to demonstrate, and where to shop. However, after a decade of growing recognition of the central role of spatial issues in postmodern theory and more than two decades discussing cognitive maps in a wide range of fields, from environmental psychology to planning to design, the implications of these maps for the (re)construction of queer communities have barely been explored. Each urban and rural queerscape embodies numerous subjective maps of spatialized social relations, including erotic desire and expression, both current and remembered, as part of what Christine Boyer has called "topographical travelogues and city views."[6]

Since at least as far back as the Renaissance, the notion of the "landscape" has been linked to the "search for certainty rather than a vehicle for individual subjectivity" and tied to an often gendered and masculinist "exercise of power over place."[7] The idea of landscape offering opportunities for collective subjectivities has generated radical critiques of scientific and heteronormative "objectivity,"[8] especially where communalities have been ignored and discounted. Comparison of the cognitive maps of different individuals and groups highlights disparities in access to resources, security, freedom of expression, and pleasure. Recognition of these inequities as well as the underlying factors that reenforce them could serve as a powerful organizing force for political action and community formation. Use of cognitive mapping in queer

The graves of Gertrude Stein (top) and Alice B. Toklas (bottom), Père Lachaise, Paris, 1995.

strategizing could begin with recognizing shared experiences and desires, then lead to pinpointing of inequities, and finally result in the formation of alliances across and between sites and entire communities and regions. Differences and inequities can be best described in the voices of ignored or censored "subjects," and their dialogue can shape particular objectives to correct these problems.

Many places inhabited by lesbians and gay men are "contested" sites, where the forces of homophobia challenge the survival and formation of communities of sexual minorities. Also, conflicts exist regarding collective expression in public space; capitalistic interests often focus on creating relatively privatized, elite, and expensive queer space. Such disparities generate new needs and uses for queer maps. Correlating "mental maps"[9] with the social and developmental differences between individuals[10] reveals "differential cognition"[11] of the same places and different "affinities." Exploring such affinities can reveal the broad outlines of minority experiences[12] and can point up specific needs, such as improved access for people with disabilities. Understanding how a sexual minority experiences marginalization can run counter to the "generalizable system of environmental categories"[13] that has dominated much of environmental design and civic politics—regardless of the impact of "identity politics," which has occasionally been able to create alternative "queerer" places.

The relationships between power and the assertion and flow of "information"[14] are crucial to heightened queer presence in civic politics. As long as "subjective" information is devalued, sexual minorities will be at a distinct disadvantage, whether or not queer persons ascend to positions of power. In the phraseology of postmodernism, there is talk of "breakup of any master subject location."[15] Architect Bernard Tschumi has a vision of an activist "environmental knowledge"[16] related directly to a radical, though perhaps what can now be seen as a somewhat naïve, notion of "counterdesign" grounded in the upheavals of Paris in 1968. More recently, feminist theoretician Donna Haraway has proposed "situated knowledges"[17] as alternatives to both the arrogance of scientific objectivity and the limitations of earlier gender-based analyses. Central to these attempts at more localized and site-specific relationships between knowledge and power, as information becomes increasingly globalized and readily available, are ideals of "radical subjectivity"[18] as "webbed accounts"[19] that engender renewed activism.

The narratives of place chosen for *Queers in Space* represent a range of experience, means of expression, and disciplines. We begin with a profoundly personal and yet historical set of recollections: Joan Nestle, one of the founders of the Lesbian Herstory Archives, conveys powerful recollections of lesbian bars and beaches of New York City in the 1950s, providing a contemporary basis for confronting homophobic repression and the day-to-day struggles to maintain dignity and build community. The historicizing of some of her early experiences as a lesbian leads to some questions.

How is the concept of queer space defined and envisioned by younger activists? How does it differ from that of older activists who carry memories, what Nestle has called "the final site of reclamation," of how lesbians "transformed themselves, right under the fist of the state"?

The small portfolio of the work of Bill Jacobson, "The Interim Photographs," constructs a vision of childhood yearning, a sort of nascent cruising that begins to map the intersection of exploration, desire, and identity. Jacobson's blurred portrayal of the landscapes of childhood and memory often infer loss. But the vulnerability and hope (so central to the experience of sexual minorities of any age who are trying to survive and make contact), the broad communal landscape that encompasses these few fleeting moments and places, is hinted at.

Sarah Schulman's short story "People and Their Streets, Places" focuses on a small portion of Manhattan's Lower East Side near the northwest corner of Tompkins Square Park. Here, "community" is perceived through experiences of hazards, such as garbage, pests, racism, homophobia, and gentrification. Schulman's story maps environmental and social problems in far more compelling ways than dry "planning studies" can.

David Bell's "One-Handed Geographies: An Archaeology of Public Sex" forms a postmodern scholar's collage in which personal narratives and theoretical expression run together. Weaving British sexual humour and sarcasm into his narrative, Bell envisions an activism that confronts persistent homophobia and hostility to consensual sexual expression, which exists in much of the landscape of Britain and in many other parts of the world.

These narratives foreshadow the queer politics of the coming decades—the identity politics, affinity politics, and new intersections that have yet to be categorized. They express the many different attachments to and interests in home, place, community, and region. In these fast-moving times, the heart of environmental design concerns the common ground on which people live, work, and play—sites that are only superficially defined by the lines and symbols on maps and plans.

Restriction and Reclamation: Lesbian Bars and Beaches of the 1950s

Joan Nestle

When I published *A Restricted Country* in 1987,[1] I did not think in terms of queer spaces, but a basic tension in the narratives is the existence of restricted territories and my need to deconstruct them into sites of lesbian freedom. Images of geography and metaphors of place came naturally to me as I tried to re-create the pre-Stonewall struggle for lesbian survival, whether concretely as a neighborhood—the Lower East Side in the 1960s—or abstractly as historical disenfranchisement—"When the Lions Write History."

Silenced and policed,[2] we congregated in allotted spaces. Borders were marked and real; vice laws, police, and organized crime representatives controlled our movements into and out of our "countries." But what could not be controlled was what forced the creation of these spaces in the first place—our need to confront a personal destiny, to see our reflections in each other's faces and to break societal ostracism with our bodies. What could not be controlled was our desire.

A 1950s lesbian bar in the South. Courtesy of the Lesbian Herstory Education Foundation, Inc./Lesbian Herstory Archives, Brooklyn, New York.

The Bathroom Line[3]

We had rituals, too, back in the old days—rituals born out of our lesbian time and place, the geography of the fifties. The Sea Colony[4] was a world of ritual displays—deep dances of lesbian want, lesbian adventuring, lesbian bonding. We who lived there knew the steps. It was over twenty-five years ago [now over thirty], but I can still peer into the smoke-filled room, feel the pressure of bodies, look for the wanted face to float up out of the haze into the circle of light, a tumult of recognition. "I wondered how long it would take for you to come here," the teacher welcomes her adoring student and then retreats into the woman-made mist.

Because we lived in the underworld of the Sea Colony, we were surrounded by the nets of the society that hated us yet wanted our money. Mafia nets, clean-up-New York nets, vice-squad nets. We needed the lesbian air of the Sea Colony to breathe the life we could not anywhere else, those of us who wanted to see women dance, make love, wear shirts and pants. Here and in other bars like this, we found each other and the space to be a sexually powerful butch-fem community. We entered their nets with rage, with need, and with strength. The physical nets were visible, and we knew how to sidestep them, just as we knew, holding hands in the street—clear butch-fem couples—which groups of straights to stay away from or which cars flashed danger as they slowed down at the corner of the curb. We knew how to move quickly. We had the images of smashed faces clear in our memories: our lovers, our friends who had not moved quickly enough. It was the other nets, the nets of the righteous people, the ones that reached into our minds, that most threatened our breathing. These nets carried twisted in their invisible windings the words *hate yourself because you are a freak, hate yourself . . . you use your tongue, hate yourself you look butch and femme, hate yourself because you are sexual.*

The powers of the mainland controlled our world in some obvious ways. The cops would come in to check their nets, get their payoffs, joke with the men who stood by the door. They would poke their heads into the back room to make sure we were not dancing together, a crime for which we could be arrested. Of course, the manager had flashed the red light ten minutes before the cops arrived to warn us to play our parts. We did, sitting quietly at the square tables as the cops looked us over. But if they had looked closer, they would have seen hands clenched under the tables, femmes holding on to the belts of their butches, saying through the touch of their fingers: "Don't let their power, their swagger, their leer, goad you into battle. We will lose, and they will take pleasure in our pain, in our blood."

But the most searing reminder of our colonized world was the bathroom line. Now I know it stands for all the pain and glory of my time, and I carry that line and the women who endured it deep within me. Because we were labeled deviants, our bathroom habits had to be watched. Only one woman at a time was allowed into the toilet because we could not be trusted. Thus the toilet line was born, a twisting horizon of lesbian women waiting for permission to urinate, to shit.

The line flowed past the far wall, past the bar and the front room tables, and into the back room. Guarding the entrance to the toilet was a short, square, handsome butch woman, the same woman every night, whose job it was to twist around her hand our allotted amount of toilet paper. She was us, an obscenity, doing all the man's tricks so we could breathe. The line awaited all of us every night, and we developed a "line act." We joked, we cruised, we commented on the length of time one of us took, we made special pleas to allow hot-and-heavy lovers in together, knowing full well that our lady would not permit it. I stood, a fem, loving the women on either side of me, loving my comrades for their style, the owner of their stance, the hair hitting the collar, the thrown-out hip, the hand encircling the beer can. Our eyes played along the line, subtle touches, gentle shynesses weaved under the blaring jokes, the music, the surveillance. We lived on that line; restricted and judged, we took deep breaths and played.

But buried deep in our endurance was our fury. That line was practice and theory seared into one. We wove our freedoms, our culture, around their obstacles of hatred, but we also paid the price. Every time I took the fistful of toilet paper, I swore eventual liberation. It would be, however, a liberation filled with a memory.

Public space for the pre-Stonewall working-class lesbian bore all the tensions of a stigmatized private self. The public bar was a privately coded place. Its awning and darkened street window never revealed its secret, yet going to the bar meant going out. Our exposure was enclosed, but the secrecy was also disclosure. The space was both a gift and a torment. It replicated the wonder of desire and the burden of its condemnation. But almost every night, there would be times when the spirit of the enclosed community threatened its enforced containment. These were the early signs of deconstruction, the first cracks in the wall.

Riis Park, 1960[5]

I may never change my name to nouns for sea or land or air, but I have loved this earth in all the ways she let me get close to her. Even the earth beneath the city streets sang to my legs as I strode around this city, watching the sun glint off windows, looking up at the West Side sky immense as it reached from the river to the hills of Central Park. Not a Kansas sky paralleled by a flat earth, but a sky forcing its blue between the water towers and the ornate peaks that try to catch it.

And then my deepest joy, when the hot weekends came, sometimes as early as May but surely by June, when I would leave East Ninth Street early on Saturday morning, wearing my bathing suit under my shorts, and head for the BMT, the start of a two-hour subway and bus trip that would take me to Riis Park—my Riviera, my Fire Island, my gay beach—where I could spread my blanket and watch strong butches challenge each other by weight lifting garbage cans, where I could see tattoos bulge with womanly effort and hear shouts of the softball game come floating over the fence.

The subway wound its way through lower Manhattan, out to Brooklyn, and finally reached its last stop: Flatbush Avenue. I always had a book to read but would periodically cruise the car, becoming adept at picking out the gay passengers, the ones with longing faces turned toward the sun waiting for them at the end of the line. Sometimes I would find my lesbian couple, older women, wide-hipped, shoulders touching, sitting with their cooler filled with beer and cold chicken.

The last stop was a one-way, long, narrow station, but I could already smell the sea air. We crushed through the turnstiles, up onto Flatbush Avenue, which stretched like a royal highway to the temple of the sea. We would wait on line for the bus to pull in, a very gay line, and then as we moved down Flatbush, teenagers loud with their own lust poured into the bus. There were hostile encounters, the usual stares at the freaks, whispered taunts of *faggot, lezzie, is that a man or a woman,* but we did not care. We were heading to the sun, to our piece of the beach where we could kiss and hug and enjoy looking at each other.

The bus rolled down Flatbush, past low two-story family houses, neighborhoods with their beauty parlors and pizza joints. This was the only time that I—born in the Bronx—loved Brooklyn. I knew that at the end of that residential hegemony was the

Femme women at the beach, c. 1950s. Courtesy of the Lesbian Herstory Education Foundation, Inc./Lesbian Herstory Archives, Brooklyn, New York.

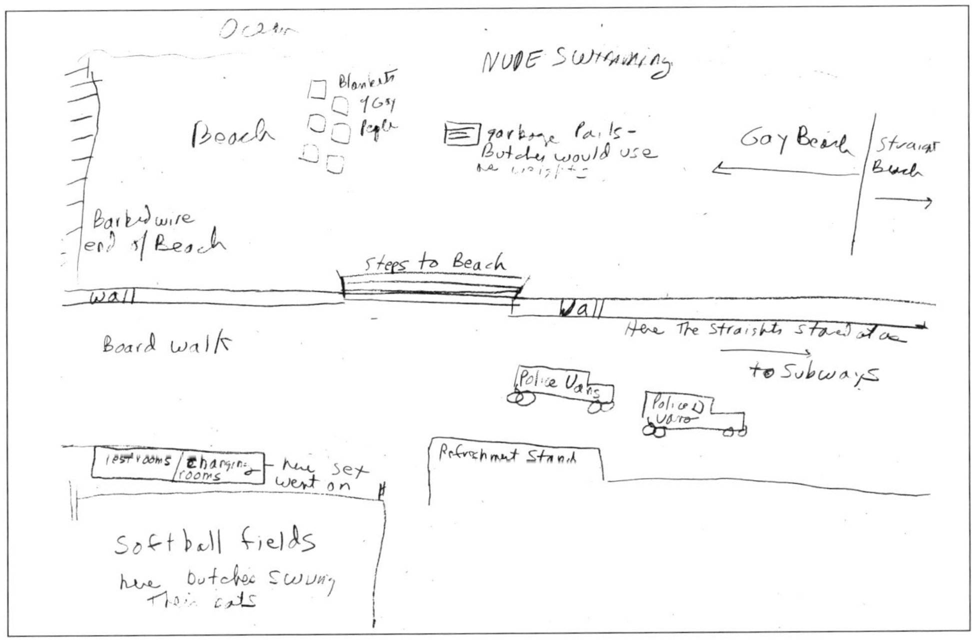

Riis Park c. 1958. Map by Joan Nestle.

ocean that I loved to dive into, that I watched turn purple in the late afternoon sun, that made me feel clean and young and strong, and ready for a night of loving, my skin living with salt, clean enough for my lover's tongue, my body reaching to give my lover's hands the fullness I had been given by the sea.

I would sit on the edge of my blanket, watching every touch, every flirtatious move around me, noting every curve of flesh, erection, nipple hard with irritation or desire. I drank in the spectacle of lesbian and gay men's sensuality, always looking for the tall, dark butch who would walk over and stand above me, her shadow breaking the sun, asking my name.

And the times I came with my lover, the wonder of kissing on the hot blanket in the sunlight, the joy of laying my head in her lap as we sat and watched the waves grow small in the dusk. The wonderful joy of my lover's body stretched over me, rolling me into the sand, our wrestling, our laughter, chases leading into the cooling water. I would wrap my legs around her, and she would bounce me on the sea, or I would duck below the surface and suck her nipples, pulling them into the ocean.

Whenever I turned away from the ocean to face the low cement wall that ran along the back of our beach, I was forced to remember that we were always watched—by teenagers on bikes, pointing and laughing, and by more serious starers who used telescopes to focus in on us. But we were undaunted. Even the cops deciding to clean up the beach by arresting men whose suits were judged too minimal, hauling them

Home of the Lesbian Herstory Archives in Park Slope, Brooklyn. Courtesy of the Lesbian Herstory Education Foundation, Inc./ Lesbian Herstory Archives, Brooklyn, New York.

over the sand into police wagons, did not destroy our sun.

Only once do I remember the potential power of our people becoming a visible thing, like a mighty arm threatening revenge if respect was not paid. A young man was brought ashore by the exhausted lifeguards and his lover fell to his knees, keening for his loss. A terrible quiet fell on our beach, and like the moon drawing the tides, we formed an ever-growing circle around the lovers, opening a path only wide enough for the police carrying the stretcher, our silence threatening our anger if this grief was not respected. The police, sinking into the sand under the weight of their uniforms, looked around and stopped joking. Silently they placed the dead youth on the stretcher and started the long walk away from the ocean. His lover, supported by friends, followed behind, and then like a thick human rope, we all marched after them, our near-naked bodies shining with palm oil and sweat, men and women walking in a bursting silence behind the body, escorting it to the ambulance, past the staring interlopers. The freaks had turned into a people to whom respect must be paid.

Later in my life I learned the glories of Fire Island, the luxury of Cherry Grove. But this tired beach, filled with the children of the boroughs, was my first free place where I could face the ocean that claimed me as its daughter and kiss in blazing sunlight the salt-tinged lips of the woman I loved.

When I look over my narratives that grew out of this time period, I am struck by the competing language of control and liberation, of colonization and autonomy. These forces always exist together just as they did in the physical public spaces we occupied. As I grow older, I still return to these memories as the most compelling, as the truest metaphors for how it was to love. Since the seventies, I have been to fully liberated spaces like the Michigan Women's Music Festival, Sister Space, and other all-women gatherings, but while I have enjoyed the openness, homogeneity, and safety of them all, they do not call to my imagination in the same way. Perhaps it will always be the site of the first kiss, of the first entry, of the first battle for erotic life that will call for commemoration. Surely the struggle between our public expression and societal control has not gone away, yet I think there is something deeper calling out from these places, the dark and red-lit bars, the liberated zones of sea and sand. It was here that women transformed themselves, right under the fist of the state. It was here, on continuously shifting ground, that we created the semblance of communal permanence. It was here that we found a way to be real in places that were never our own, by deed or laws of property. Whether it was the bar or the beach, we claimed these places by the courage of our often-wounded bodies and the persistence of our need. We created moments, afternoons, nights of liberation out of the mortar of surveillance.

Now they live in my memory, the final site of reclamation.

The Interim Photographs

Bill Jacobson

Childhood Cruising

I was born in a small Connecticut town in 1955, fourteen years before the Stonewall riots. Eventually I realized that people my age who grew up in cities, even in those years, at least knew of the existence of homosexuals. Growing up in a small town with conservative parents, I did not.

It wasn't until high school that I caught my first oblique glimpses of what I sensed inside and found manifestations of it in the world at large. I have vivid memories of first hearing Lou Reed's "Walk on the Wild Side" while getting dressed in the morning to go to high school. The refrain "shaved his legs and then he was a she" has never left me. About the same time, someone gave my father a copy of the first Diane Arbus book,[1] which he immediately sequestered to the highest bookshelf in the den. I immediately scrambled up there to retrieve it, almost smelling something I needed to discover. Indeed, opening this book opened my eyes simultaneously to the possibilities of photography and different gender experiences. And while the pictures were far from pretty, they brought me to a deeper place in myself than I had ever gone before.

The years prior to realizing that I was gay were avidly spent searching for something unknown, unnamed, and mostly unfathomable. As a child, I was constantly cruising, yet for what I did not know. Trying to understand my own early desires and what they implied about my future in the world was a blur in many ways, and I can recall countless hours staring at life in an often futile attempt to find clarity. The bodies of men and the gestures of women, the relationships between family members, the bonding of boys in school from which I was or was not included; all were open to scrutiny and to question.

I started taking photographs as a teenager, nearly twenty-five years ago—soon after Stonewall. Since then, my work has been an ongoing meditation around desire, loss, and the role of photography as a vehicle for remembrance. My pictures often function as metaphors for the way the mind works: simultaneously collecting images and letting others go, fading in the way that memories fade, and alluding to the fact that, historically, photographs have always faded as well.

Decades later as I lose more and more friends to AIDS, the world is still a blur. I am still struggling, though in different ways, to make sense of it all. While my photography is not specifically about AIDS, it refers to what I have learned from being part of a community ravaged by the epidemic. By losing a steady stream of friends and acquaintances these past fourteen years, I have come to understand the transient nature of existence.[2] Most photographs are meant as documents of moments we wish to hold onto forever. My work suggests that these moments, like life itself, are constantly fading into the past. For me, the Interim Photographs[3] have been a way of recording these feelings in an ongoing attempt to define myself in this impermanent world.

Bill Jacobson, *Interim Figure* (2121), 1989. Photograph courtesy of the Julie Saul Gallery, New York.

Bill Jacobson, *Interim Landscape* (186-8), 1989. Photograph courtesy of the Julie Saul Gallery, New York.

Bill Jacobson, *Interim Landscape* (185-6), 1989. Photograph courtesy of the Julie Saul Gallery, New York.

Bill Jacobson, *Interim Landscape* (134-14), 1989. Photograph courtesy of the Julie Saul Gallery, New York.

Bill Jacobson, *Interim Landscape* (219-8), 1990. Photograph courtesy of the Julie Saul Gallery, New York.

Bill Jacobson, *Interim Landscape* (180-18), 1989. Photograph courtesy of the Julie Saul Gallery, New York.

People and Their Streets, Places[1]

Sarah Schulman

Last summer the mayor of New York decided to cut back on rat extermination. He also cut back on streetlights. As a result, night increasingly meant the dark outlines of buildings surrounded by the scampering of 18-inch varmints. Ten million of them at least. My best friend Killer and I spent a lot of nights that summer just walking around because we didn't have any money. I was saving up to move out of New York, and Killer hadn't had a job in two years. She came over every night to eat, and then we'd take a walk. She'd forgotten even how to look for a job. She'd forgotten how to sound employable on the telephone. One day I glanced over her shoulder at the Help Wanted pages of the *New York Times,* only it wasn't what you'd call *pages.* It was more like half a column. One Saturday we saw a kid get shot in front of The Unique Clothing Store Going Out Of Business Sale, and the next day we watched a guy go crazy and throw glass bottles at people for twenty minutes. I've always wanted to shoot rats.

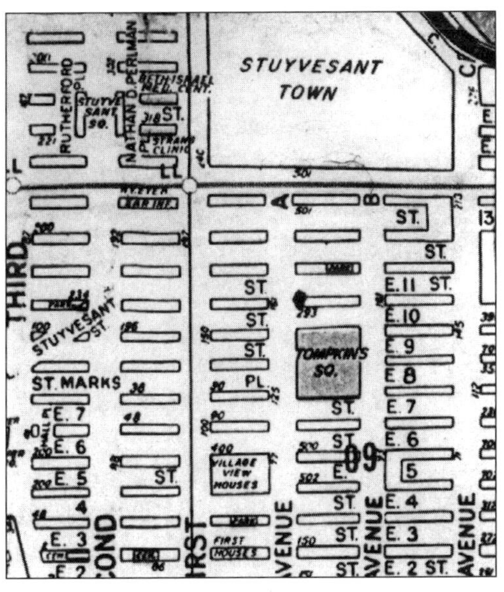

The Lower East Side of Manhattan, west of Tompkins Square Park, where much of the story takes place.

Killer and I are hard-core New Yorkers. But when we were kids, the only homeless person you'd ever see would be a wino on The Bowery or an occasional bag lady. You never saw anyone sleeping on a subway car unless they were coming home from the night shift. The streets were not covered with urine then; that was considered impolite. There have always been rats, though. As a teenager waiting for the Seven train to get me out of Jackson Heights, I remember watching them run around on the subway tracks. But mostly, when I was a kid, rats were something that bit babies in an unreal and faraway ghetto. You never saw them hanging out in the middle-class sections of Queens.

An average rat litter is twenty-two little ones, and rats can reproduce at the rate of six litters a year. Some time in the 1980s I started to see them scampering regularly

Poor garbage storage at East 9th Street and Avenue A, 1995.

in the playgrounds of Central Park. Reagan had just become president, and I held him directly responsible. Rat infestation felt like something the U.S. government should have been able to handle. That's when I started thinking about getting a gun and shooting every rat on sight. Picking them off the way hillbillies shoot squirrels.

That guy, last Sunday, who was throwing glass bottles? All he cared about was himself. His personal expression was more important to him than other people's eyes. That's the kind of attitude that makes this town a dangerous place to live. You never know when danger can hit. The shooting in front of The Unique was more reasonable. It was just a bunch of friends killing each other. Don't have friends like that, and it will never happen to you.

Every morning I go over to the old Veteran's Administration building on West 25th Street and wait on line to go through the metal detectors. The lobby walls are covered with these old World War II murals of soldiers getting fitted for artificial legs by nurses in starched caps. The women lift up the veterans' new legs and demonstrate how to use them. Once I make it through, I have to ride up in the elevators with all the whacked-out veterans scratching and getting into fights. I get off at the seventeenth floor, where there is The Food and Hunger Hotline office, and I walk past them to my office. Then I sign in at Pest Control, and I waste about half the day unless I get sent out on a job.

When I'm sitting in Pest Control hanging out waiting, I pay close attention to the goings-on at Food and Hunger. I want to see everything I can. Everything. I want to be a witness to my own time because I have a sneaking suspicion that I'm gonna live a lot longer than most of the people I meet. If I'm gonna be the only one still around to say what happened, I'd better pay close attention now.

Killer usually stops by the office at ten for coffee and peanut-butter sandwiches. Then she checks in at a couple of restaurants to see if they need any prep cooks. I know for a fact that they're only hiring Mexicans and Israelis. Everybody knows Americans aren't good for restaurant work. They want to talk on the phone in between

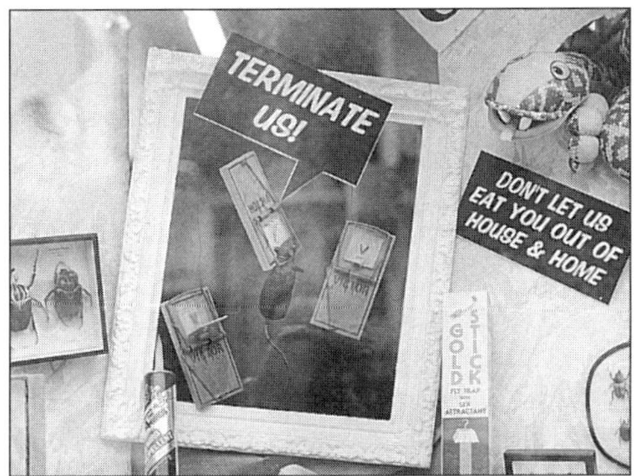

Pest control, the Lower East Side, 1995.

getting high salaries and free meals. In the meantime Killer is living on forty dollars a week from watering plants for a couple of offices and boutiques. The rest gets paid by The Bed and Breakfast guests she hustles at those four-dollar cappuccino places. Mostly Swiss people or Germans. They think it's quaint. She gives them a bed and then tells them to make their own breakfast. Then she comes to the office to eat some of mine. We've been living this schedule for a long time already. It is one big fat habit. You know one thing I don't like about homeless people? They ask you for a light and then hold on to your lighter for forty-five minutes, blabbing on and on about some misfortune. The whole act is designed to make it seem that they don't realize they've got your lighter. But the fact is, they know they've got it.

Killer was brought up to be a racist. One night I went over to her place to watch TV, and her parents brought over some food. Next thing you know the news came on and it was all "Nigger" this and "Nigger" that. Her parents had these sharp teeth whenever they said that word. It wasn't said calmly. They scrunched up the skin around their eyes. Killer knows better, but when she gets emotional, that's what she falls back on. Like one time some Puerto Rican guy was beating up his kid in the hallway and Killer said, "Look at that low-rent over there."

"Shut up," I said. "You haven't had a job in two years. If you had enough patience to stand in line you'd be on Welfare yourself."

"I'd be on Welfare if it wasn't for the strength of the Eurodollar," she said as some blonde couple rolled over in the bed. That was the way she looked at things.

God that summer was hot. There's that way the Puerto Rican girls sit close together on the stoops. They have skinny arms and those ten-dollar pink dresses. They smile and wear their hair long with a headband.

Everyday homeless people come into Food and Hunger looking for food, but they only get Contact Cards. I gave Killer one of those cards but she said the food they advertised wasn't nutritious.

One time, before breakfast, Killer walked me to work but she wanted to stop off on Tenth Street at the copy store that was run by some Moonies. They were clean-cut, peculiar, and wore polyester pants up to their necks.

"They give away free bread and free Chinese buns," Killer said.

Pest control, the Lower East Side, 1995.

When we walked in the store, it was kind of slow and real hot. It stank of copier fluid. The polyesters had a few day-olds sitting on the counter and a bag of day-old buns.

"Don't eat it," I said. "It's old pork."

"Hi, Killer," they said handing her two loaves. Then they turned to me. "What about you?"

"I don't need free food," I said.

"Look," Killer whispered. "Take it. I need it. I'll give you a fresh one later for your birthday."

"OK. No, wait. I don't want bread for my birthday. I want a colander."

"Do you think I need a professional portfolio?" she asked. Killer was still thinking about jobs.

"How is everything going?" Killer asked the Moonies, remembering to be gracious.

"We're having problems with rats," they said.

That woke me up. "Do you have big ones?" I asked. "One pounders?"

"Yep," they said.

"Did you put out poison?" Killer asked.

"Poison doesn't work," they said. "They're too strong. Besides, if you kill one that way it's just gonna stink up your place and bring maggots."

"Did you try traps?" Killer asked, trying to cut me off because she knew what I was about to recommend.

"Traps don't work," I said ignoring her. "The rats are too smart. They spring the traps and get the bait."

"What about walk-in traps?" one of the Moonies asked.

"Too expensive," I said. "Doesn't work on a massive scale."

"Well, what do you suggest?" he asked.

"You gotta shoot 'em," I said. "You gotta get 'em one by one."

One-Handed Geographies: An Archaeology of Public Sex

David Bell

> On the Heath someone choking in the dark giving a blow job, said loudly: "The ghost of Christmas Past."
>
> Picked up a tough looking skinhead who said: "Fuck me."
>
> "OK," I said.
>
> "That's a bit risky," he said, and had a good laugh.
>
> "I was only thinking it," I said.
>
> "Fuck everything," he said.
>
> —"Derek"[1]

I

In thinking about the shifting meaning of the "public" when twinned with that old devil called "sex," we can begin to envision how erotic and eroticised topographies can be created, reworked, and reclaimed. Outdoor scenes, nudism, exhibitionism, voyeurism, cruising—made by marking the erogenous zones of the city and the country, the bodies at play publicly map out new landscapes of desire.[2] The spaces of sex in this context are an endless psychogeography of perverse possibilities:[3] a sensuous geography of sadomasochism in deserted warehouses, circle-jerking in woodlands, the sewage worker's birthday party, cruising the perfume counter, watching your suburban neighbours getting carpet burns, fucking in the school toilets, talking dirty on the phone, ladies' nights at the health club—a sexscape of alleys, cars and carparks, the beach, the town hall steps, the mall. These are all locations

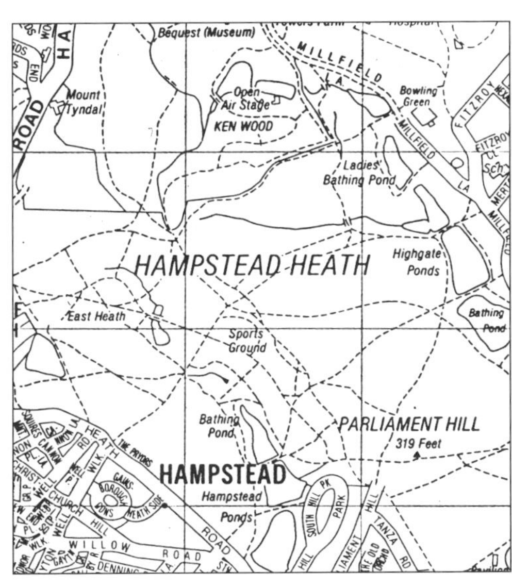

Hampstead Heath, London.

for polymorphous decentered exchanges in polymorphous decentered landscapes.[4] By telling the stories of these encounters, we participate in the project of a "queer archaeology," marking the traces of our erotic selves passing through the public spaces that surround us.[5]

II

> The true picture of erotic spaces barred from what is structurally possible flits by. Such spaces are recognizable only as images which flash in an instant; fleeting gaps that defy words, left-overs from some unacknowledged sacrificial meal. These uncanny spaces involve the ghostly reappearance of what's been made to disappear; hearing what's been silenced; tasting what's forbidden; touched by the smell of rotting fruit.
>
> —"Stephen"[6]

> I do like sex in the open. When I lived in Hammersmith there was a part of the river bank that was great. A lot of the student nurses from Charing Cross Hospital went there, among others. Also, the bushes in Brighton were a good place to meet. A lot of the time the guys wouldn't bother going into the bushes, but would have sex on the path; the more daring under the lighting. I learned a lot from watching them.
>
> —"Grant"[7]

III

The strategic (re)claiming of privacy remains part of the project of queer citizenship. In tension with calls "never to go underground," the right to be private clashes with campaigns of outing, with the perverse parade of pride marches, and with the celebrations of public sex.[8] Discussions about the propriety of place for sex acts and performances always tread a fine line between desiring a selective privacy and needing to confront a heterosexist public by "flaunting it." "When once the gay good citizen comported him/herself with dignity and avoided public flamboyance,"[9] a queer citizen must be aware of the strategic positioning of the sexed body in space as a site of resistance against the dead weight of heteronormativity.[10]

IV

> After midnight and tyres burn at one hundred miles an hour down wet-dream streets as a Mazda Xedos 6SE screams past lighted shop-window

displays and performs a sudden turn (aided by power steering) into a dark, unlit back-street leading to a car-park, empty except for a handful of vehicles abandoned for the night. Very quietly, it proceeds to the roofless and carless top floor of the building and eases into position close to the small wall dividing car and eternity. A joyrider gets out and stares out at the twinkling city prostrate before the twelve-story car-park. After several transfixed seconds, the joyrider climbs up onto the windscreen of the Mazda and, after a rearrangement of clothing, begins a ritual of isolated relief for all the heavens to see, starting in a slow and delicate manner, rapidly rising to a faster, sharper handling. During the working day a car-park has only one possible function, and people have no desire to stay longer than is necessary, just park the car and get out of there. At night this rigid structure can yield itself to the sexual fantasy, but which, somehow, remains as limited as the car-park's day-job. But for the moment the joyrider is gripped by the insistency of sexual urges, the contrasting nature of the car-park's space through the twenty-four-hour cycle rather adding to the enjoyment.

—"Prof"[11]

V

Within a portfolio of queer performativity,[12] transgressing public heteronormativity remains one of the most forceful and challenging tactics.[13] Queer nights out to straight nightspots, kiss-ins in shopping malls, safer sex workshops, and forms of public sex all

Camley Street, London, an area of black/white cruising, in a performance of *Undressing Icons: Looking for Langston,* directed by Isaac Julien, 1990. Photograph by Isaac Julien. Courtesy of Normal Films, London.

perform a resonantly troubling political pleasure-praxis, which might articulate the disruptive potential which queer is said to embody.[14] Casting aside the arguments about empty transgression,[15] we can envision an erotically charged *detournement* of the heterosexist city into a flickering spectacle of sites for queer play.[16] What might this city be like? We can only imagine the pleasure zones it might contain and then contrast that image with the reality of the cities we live in. The maps have yet to be drawn.[17]

VI

> Arriving home with excellent fuel consumption in a Peugeot 309, seven joyriders charge into the three bedroomed, suburban semi and start fucking, rampaging through the house in every possible combination of twosomes, threesomes, foursomes, same and mixed gender sex, etc.; kitchen sex, lounge sex, bathroom sex, toilet sex, stairs sex, garden sex, etc. The geography of the family home echoes the developments in the control and surveillance of the city, in the way that space has been divided into specified areas of activity to control the activites that take place there. In the home, sex is invisible, masturbation is never mentioned, in keeping with the heterosexual agenda of normalisation, and not even seven joyriders engaging in loud sex can tear down the walls.
>
> —"Prof"[18]

> Lesbian identity is constructed in the temporal and linguistic mobilization of space, as we move through space we imprint utopian and dystopian moments upon urban life . . . In an instant, a freeze-frame, a lesbian is occupying space as it occupies her. Space teems with possibilities, positions, intersections, passages, detours, u-turns, dead-ends, and one-way streets; it is never still.
>
> —"Sally"[19]

VII

If we are going to embark on revisioning the public as a future site of queer performativity freed from the pressures of heteronormativity, what will become of the private? While we might try to assert that a private sphere would be unnecessary in the kinky city of queer play, we must at the same time realise that the need for privacy remains a fundamental requirement for those whose erotic configurations and tastes pass into forbidden zones.[20] There must be a private realm into which the state and law cannot pry, a realm where—beyond the basic human rules of mutual consent, respect, and

Performance of *Undressing Icons: Looking for Langston,* directed by Isaac Julien, Kings Cross, London, 1990. Photograph by Peter Barker. Courtesy of Normal Films, London.

Performance of *Undressing Icons: Looking for Langston,* directed by Isaac Julien, Newcastle, 1992. Photograph by Peter Barker. Courtesy of Normal Films, London.

tolerance—anything can happen.[21] For every loud 'n' proud queer guerilla there is someone for whom the closet is, at least in part, the chosen home. Demolishing all closets might be a politically desirable aim, but there must also be sensitivity shown towards those who freely choose a *private* life.[22] Of course, we must constantly question freedom of choice in societies that routinely deny this basic freedom to sexual dissidents.[23]

VIII

> [L]et me just says that these words—dom, Master, bottom, whore-fem, butch, Daddy-boy, cruising, play, play-mate, and so on, have their place, or rather they take a place and make a place. They make an impossible place take place. They describe, circumscribe, inscribe a spectacular space, a spectacle of space: an invented, made-up, unreal, larger-than-life-and-certainly-more-interesting space that people like myself sniff out and crave and live in and want to call "Home;" a home I want to suggest that is entirely Urban; an urbanness I want to say that is entirely City and not at all—or not exactly—Community; a queer (kind of) city (or better yet, cities), that finally, not only privileges the Joke but has something to do with the cry: "Freedom."
>
> —"Sue"[24]

> For those in the know, the alfresco fuck is the original fuck.
>
> —"Derek"[25]

IX

The quest for sexual adventures in heteronormative environments is part of the mission to rearticulate both public and private spheres.[26] But equally important is the campaign for a queer private sphere that is out of sight and reach. By resisting the pressures that would place certain acts and actors firmly within a nonpublic space away from public gaze, while trying at the same time to deny the right to privacy by intruding and starting all that sex talk, the creative and wild possibilities for a new urban sex-political and sex-pleasure praxis are made manifest.[27] The closing come-shot is always already loaded with this contradiction: what we wish to remain private will be rendered public, what we would take into the public will be projected back into the private. Continuing to challenge such hegemonic narratives of the propriety of place for queer acts must be central to any activist queer project.[28]

x

I cut my hair short, took off my earrings, put on a leather jacket and,
armed with KY and poppers, took off into the night . . .
I was happy.

—"Derek"[29]

Part 2—Queerscapes

Preceding page: Fertility ceremony with dildo performed by the newly formed Sisters of Perpetual Indulgence, San Francisco, 1980.

Surveying Territories and Landscapes

Gordon Brent Ingram, Anne-Marie Bouthillette, and Yolanda Retter

In Part 2 of *Queers in Space,* we move from expressions of divergent realities experienced by sexual minorities to discussions of new means of surveying queer presence and marginalized eroticism across territories and landscapes: conditions of ambiguity, isolation, repression, strategic invisibility, and carefully constructed visibility. In surveying nascent communality and community, we first examine notions of queer "commons"[1] involving "sharing" and uneven distribution of spatial, ecological, social, cultural, and aesthetic resources. Many landscapes are still contested, and even mild assertion of queer identities and sexualities can ignite powder kegs of social conflict. Overt, ongoing queer presence in such public space has been a major target of homophobic attacks for more than a century. How common areas are queered by some sexual minorities and avoided by others textures these regions and neighbourhoods.

Hostile versus Queered Territory

Lesbian, gay, and bisexual habitation of outdoor and indoor environments has become a major topic in queer theory, and such spatial issues represent new frontiers in the politics of our various communities. Both queer communities and homophobia are key social "layers" of urban and rural environments. Homophobia can sometimes function in ways that are similar to environmental racism—no matter how pretty ghettos are made to look. And ghettos are increasingly unstable communities where early gentrifiers are often later forced out. The metaphor of homosexuality rather than homophobia as a kind of pollution still dominates a majority of the world's cities and towns.

To determine what sort of space sexual minorities have lost or have never possessed, it is necessary to situate erotic expression both spatially and historically. The following essays on landscapes and territories explore spatial apportionment and the notion of "lost landscapes"—the experience of denial of access, assault, intimidation, or perceived risk in relation to particular sites because of sexual identity and behaviour. For the majority of communities of sexual minorities, these losses of access, safety, comfort, and freedom of expression are compounded by their experiences as women, people of colour, or poor people. In developing cities around the world, these groups endure hypermarginalization and invisibility because of poverty and lack of basic environmental resources—including raw space.

Homophobia, Violence, and Lack of Access to Landscapes

How are denied access and limited freedom of expression enforced? How many of these losses have been internalized and will persist indefinitely in the lives of queer people? One of the most effective means of control is the threat of violence. For example, the threat of dyke and gay bashing has had a tremendous impact on where we choose to live and to socialize, and the subsequent formation of our communities and neighbourhoods. Police repression has had a similar effect.

The de facto privatization of public open space, which increased in the 1980s in much of the world, has pushed many local populations off sites strategic to them. For some sites and some groups, a form of homophobia by design has functioned to discourage contact through certain landscape design and park management decisions.

Most public open space offers little representation of queer experience and imagery. Billboards, statues, memorials, and outdoor art depicting aspects of our lives are scant—even in neighbourhoods with large gay communities. Most queer sites, especially those inhabited by racial and cultural minorities, are virtually invisible, and only informed members of those communities know how to find them. This can lead to a sense of cumulative discouragement about claiming outdoor space as queer territory. The essays in this section describe experiences of marginality that feel distinctly "pre-Stonewall," but these conditions continue in many areas of North America and Europe, as well as in the rest of the world, to this day.

The Genesis of Queerscapes

The following essays explore the almost universally experienced polarities of isolation and communality, and the tension between repression (both internalized and state-sanctioned) and resistance. They describe moments in the genesis and development of queer enclaves and identify nascent social and environmental relationships. Before enclaves and ghettos form, scattered sites across regions, landscapes, and neighbourhoods provide opportunities for contact and support. Over time, these points of contact have a subtle impact on broader areas. Thus queerscapes evolve from conditions of isolation and invisibility to increasingly rich and complex sets of social relationships across space.

In " 'Open' Space as Strategic Queer Sites," Gordon Brent Ingram reviews the significance of outdoor public areas in community formation and seeks more precise concepts of communality. He looks at the changing roles of the open spaces of Vancouver, a quintessential peripheral city, in its development from logging town and small port to an international destination. In a related vein, John Grube, in " 'No More Shit': The Struggle for Democratic Gay Space in Toronto," uses historical analysis to expand on the notion of "democratic streets"[2] and other public spaces

The Ladder 1, no. 1 (October 1956). An early lesbian monthly published by the Daughters of Bilitis. Courtesy of the Lesbian Herstory Educational Foundation, Inc./Lesbian Herstory Archives, Brooklyn, New York.

"with a healthy balance of freedom and control." In both articles public space becomes the matrix for a contemporary "archaeology" of sexual minorities and public confrontations concerning sexual politics. Grube, a long-term activist and political historian, outlines the formation of local cultures of resistance and the explosive creative episodes in which they confronted repression. In Toronto, the defining event for the expanding gay and lesbian enclave was not the Stonewall riots of 1969 but rather the 1981–82 demonstrations against massive bathhouse raids and the police violence that accompanied them.

In her essay "From Landmarks to Spaces: Mapping the Territory of a Bisexual Genealogy," Clare Hemmings explores contemporary tactics of invisibility, naming, visibility, and placemaking among bisexuals. Many specifically bisexual sites are forming in ambiguous territories that already have been strongly queered. Some forms of territorialization are similar to and others profoundly different from those that emerged in gay male enclaves and lesbian spaces. Hemmings's search for a genealogy of "spaces," both physical and cultural, takes her across two continents. Her efforts to piece together a history of bisexual sites and placemaking bring her to many ironic conclusions and profoundly queer sites.

In the only extended discussion of children in this book, "Elsie Jay," an Australian lesbian who does not want to use her real name for fear that her children will be ostracized, explores "Domestic Dykes: The Politics of In-difference." She describes the fact that, for lesbians with children, invisibility can still be a necessary tactic. Because assertion of presence in public space involves such high risk of inviting hostility and reprisals, the issue is still largely irrelevant to this group. But life within the home and the backyard, with a few friends and key, mainly indoor, institutions, still has an effect on the broader social and biophysical landscape. These domestic spaces socialize an increasing number of children, and such sites form strategic pockets of resistance and influence when efforts to establish more secure and public queer space are scuttled by state-sanctioned homophobia. Yet even these hidden sites are connected with and vulnerable to "the outside world."

In these four discussions, the authors reveal how various and competing social groups as well as political and economic forces vie for the same queerscapes. By beginning to survey the full range of realities, experiences, and sites in landscape not yet marked as queer, their explorations and insights challenge the isolationism and complacency that effectively deny many queer people access to large portions of public space.

"Open" Space as Strategic Queer Sites[1]

Gordon Brent Ingram

> . . . the demand for the "right to privacy" can transcend its liberal antecedents and become a radical demand for change in the relationship between private and public life. This is the real threat posed by so-called "public sex."
>
> —Jeffrey Weeks, 1985[2]

For sexual minorities "open"[3] space is often not so open, and communality does not always make for community. The unraveling of these riddles is becoming increasingly central to queer theory, activism, and civic politics. This essay expands the debates concerning use and requirements for outdoor space by various sexual minorities. My focus in this discussion is parks and "open space"[4] in urban and suburban areas and, in particular, networks of public places that Christine Boyer has called "topoi."[5] I am particularly interested in the role of public outdoor open spaces as nuclei for queer "enclaves" and "pockets,"[6] sites that serve as "rupture points"[7] in power structures. I explore the implications of the presence of queers in outdoor space, both in community formation and in the landscape planning and design decisions of communities and territorial units. My intent is to construct an analytical framework for expanding the queer use of open space; I pursue a queer environmental design instead of using highly fragmentary and site-specific information to support sociological or even historical hypotheses.

In many parts of the world, particularly where repression and violence persist, the prerequisites for communities of lesbians, gay men, bisexuals, and transsexuals are not present, and only more modest kinds of social intercourse can take place. I construct a framework for identifying the various strategic relationships among outdoor sites, public space,[8] and the broader cultural and political economic processes that may lead to relatively free use of open space by particular groups of sexual minorities.

I outline four kinds of overlapping relationships, referred to here as "alliances," around outdoor sites—relationships that are central to the formation of queer space, no matter how temporary. These social processes can lead to various forms of "queering" across landscapes—at least in terms of greater visibility, some increase in freedom of behaviour, and the lowering of perceived risk of assault or other forms of repression. Even these fragmentary types of social intercourse can lead to more cumulative processes of community formation. With the recognition of alliances within the context of various fluid cultural and political movements, there is the beginning of an analytical framework for defending, assembling, constructing, and reconstructing strategic[9] and public queer space. While not wanting to "essentialize"[10] use of open space in terms of either gender or sexual acts and identities, I look for underlying relationships that have similar relevance for lesbians, gay men, bisexuals,[11] and transsexuals.[12]

The central argument in this essay is the potential in the notion of alliances, whether they are between sexual partners or between very different groups, in understanding how networks and more visible communities are formed. I connect these social processes to aspects of design and management. In response to closeting sexual minorities in the typical programming of landscape design and planning, I outline a matrix for identifying strategic sites and for uncovering homophobia—a sort of queerscape architecture. I use "architecture"[13] in this term because social policy decisions can yield concrete changes to particular places and their associated social relationships.

In the following sections, I describe some competing notions of "public space"[14] use by sexual minorities that are related to divergent interpretations of acts and identities.[15] I sketch the central, but sometimes contradictory, role of gender in these landscape dynamics. I then examine the emerging notion of queer (public) space as a partial solution to several problems in identifying strategic sites, and I propose four basic kinds of potentially overlapping alliances that could provide more precise alternatives to the various notions of queer communities. Finally, I explore ways to consider more honestly the many activities, needs, and preferences of (queer) users of this often not-so-open space and to interrogate respective landscapes for homophobic and anti-erotic biases, involving decision-makers and their planners, designers, and managers.

Open and Obstructed Space

In virtually every urban area on the earth, there are public outdoor areas regularly frequented by members of sexual minorities. Many of these sites can be considered, as Barbara Weightman suggests, "zones of discard."[16] Regardless, most are becoming desirable to a range of social groups and are often contested by the state and heterosexuals. Today, the forces that are working to destroy these public queer spaces are growing in number as urban populations increase, natural areas dwindle, and social groups diversify. A disturbing consequence of this competition for space is the increase in violence against women and gay men in public areas. Less noticeable is the "homophobia by design" of many park agencies, municipalities, and governments, which effectively discourages visible queer presence. This effective loss of queer access is often maintained and initiated by local residents and bureaucrats at the expense of authentic programmes for public safety.[17] For example, in western North America, there have been numerous conflicts over public beaches.

Jodie, a young lesbian activist, Lions Bay (north of Vancouver), 1994. In the late 1980s, this beach had a well-established lesbian scene, much of it topless or nude. In recent years, the presence of women who might possibly be lesbians has brought harassment from residents in the expensive beach homes and the Royal Canadian Mounted Police.

The notion of open space, particularly its preservation, has been one of the cornerstones of North American urbanism and environmental advocacy in this century. Kevin Lynch's 1965 essay, "The openness of open space," exemplifies the links between the modernist ideals of universal access to outdoor areas and the contradictions in early- to mid-twentieth-century liberalism in stating,

> We proceed directly from the meaning of "open": free to be entered or used, unobstructed, unrestricted, accessible, available, exposed, extended, candid, undetermined, loose, disengaged, responsive, ready to hear or see as in open heart, open eyes, open hand, open mind, open house, open city. Open spaces in this sense are open to freely chosen and spontaneous actions of people . . .[18]

It is difficult not to suspect allusions to erotic expression in this passage, even to marginalized or minority sexual identities. But Lynch wrote this passage in the midst of one of the most repressive and homophobic periods in the twentieth century in North America.[19] "Progressive" urbanists, such as Jane Jacobs, were still talking publicly about "pervert parks"[20] only a few short years before the Stonewall riots.[21] Jacobs, a great urban reformer of the 1960s who has gone on to write books on liberal ethics, also promulgated notions of "wholesome" public space and "wholesome surveillance,"[22] which were used to justify homophobic repression under the guise of reform and equity. Her influence is still very much evident in environmental design. Such an

Homophobia by design, Lions Bay, 1994. The dividers were recently installed by the British Columbia Ministry of Highways, in response to lobbying by local homeowners to curtail parking in an effort to stop the influx of lesbians onto a public beach.

inherently hostile view of sexual minorities and the nonrecognition of access rights to public meeting places has left legacies of confusion in feminist and queer theory.[23] These homophobic and antisexual contradictions in urban activist movements persist to this day and are very much embedded in both academic and professional spheres of landscape architecture and urban design. It did not take poststructuralism or deconstructionist techniques to perceive, as Lynch did in 1979, that, "Freedom of action in public spaces is defined and redefined in each shift of power and custom."[24]

In these times of nascent human-rights protection under the category of sexual orientation, homophobia often has gone underground in a growing number of jurisdictions. It is necessary to reexamine notions of "open" space, "pervert parks," and the nature of the politics and programming that actively support not-so-subtle homophobia in landscape designs and subsequent management[25] decisions, which include police harassment. The central question of this essay, albeit a somewhat rhetorical one, is: Are public outdoor spaces strategically important to certain groups of sexual minorities? A second rhetorical question is: Do some planning and design decisions made by professionals and governments consciously limit or destroy queer access to and enjoyment of outdoor sites? I believe that both questions can be answered with a resounding "yes," but that the extent of the importance of such outdoor sites and homophobic design and management responses vary greatly between specific networks of sexual minorities and across landscapes and jurisdictions.

The roles and nature of "community" for sexual minorities have been radically transformed over the last three decades. At various points, outdoor sites in or near certain gay enclaves[26] have had crucial roles in making social contact and in forming milieux into broader assemblages.[27] Since the 1969 Stonewall riots in New York, there has been a plethora of visions of lesbian, gay, and queer community and communities. One of the earliest descriptions of a homosexual community was written by Donald Webster Cory in 1951,[28] at the onslaught of McCarthy repressionism in the United States. Cory described a "submerged world,"[29] layering the analogy of an ethnic community with his use of "gay society," and mentioning strategic public sites, as in the following case of sites for male "cruising,"[30] as a basic sort of unit of community.

Not long after Cory there was recognition of multiple communities. The first exhaustive study was of gay men in the mid-1950s in Montréal, funded by the Canadian Social Science Research Council in a period of increasing state repression and a full decade and a half before partial decriminalization in Canada.[31] This study found cliques and emerging tensions between secret and overt groups.[32] The male homosexual community was framed in terms of "his dependence upon other deviants for the satisfaction of sexual needs . . . ,"[33] and acknowledged that contentious and stygmatized forms of sexual contact, with all their inherent challenges to the lines between public and private, could provide a gradually expanded basis of community regardless of how limited. Edward Delph, in his 1978 *The Silent Community,* wrote "'Public sex,' when perceived as a threat to society, refers to sexual acts so situated as to result in the involuntary accessibility of others as sex objects or witnesses."[34]

But in the same post-Stonewall period there was an equally simplistic argument that anonymous and promiscuous contact was inherently the result of alienation and internalized oppression.[35] In his infamous study of toilet sex in a Chicago suburb, Laud Humphreys[36] was a nonparticipating "watch queen" who noted that "these men seem to acquire stronger sentimental attachments to the buildings in which they meet for sex than to the persons with whom they engage."[37]

Sense of (public) place and casual and playful sexual contact began to be linked with a kind of alienation that was supposedly absent in the formal introductions, parlours, and bedrooms of the sexual revolution. Moreover, the de facto designs of certain spaces, such as the dependence on automobiles in suburban areas,[38] have been a major factor in the queering of certain sites and adjacent neighbourhoods, especially as cultural scenes have diverged between urban cores and the expanding suburbs and edge cities.

Perhaps more significant to the analysis of the "strategicness" of open space than the symbolic claiming of public space in the Stonewall riots was the emergence of feminist interest in tracking disparities in gender, some involving space and resources. This perception that sexism is as relevant as sexual transactions has provided a clearer basis for recognizing community formation processes and obstacles to these processes. But recently there have been some well-founded challenges to the entire notion of communities and related concepts (such as the singular lesbian community) for a particular piece of territory, given inevitable contests over ideology and between what noted theorist Gill Valentine recently referred to as "cliques."[39] My response to this crucial juncture in theory of queer relations, environments, and activism(s) is to not entirely abandon the notion of queer communities but to conclude that, given the extent of repression and hostility, few such areas have been very successful. But even without community, there is still a lot of scattered communality, no matter how unsustainable and vulnerable. To look more closely at communality without community, one needs a more precise geographical unit, larger than an individual, that can be tracked both in time and space. One solution is the notion of "constellations of strategic sites" for sexual minorities, with various associated behaviours, forms of contacts, and alliances across the landscape. While it is difficult to chart the full extent of queer communality in various public spaces, the idea of strategic sites provides opportunities for identifying fluid groups through contemporary and "site-specific"[40] queer archaeologies. As Cindy Patton said, "We have deployed our secret 'queer knowledges,' in essence, have been the archaeologists (and architects) of our own marked desires."[41]

In the term "archaeology," I include the impacts that specific relationships between individuals and within groups of sexual minorities have on biophysical and cultural contexts. Such influences, no matter how subtle, can cumulatively affect the fabric of broader interactions—some of which make or break communities. Sites and associated queer space provide fragmentary evidence of and opportunities for drawing on local institutions for mutual support and satisfaction, no matter how secretive and elusive the broader communalities prove to be.

Mapping Communalities through Identification of Alliances Around Public Sites

Preceding the recognition of places, neighbourhoods, and regions, there are individual (queer) acts and personal relationships. Often rules and hierachies are established, though—as in any society—there is much change over time. When transactions become relatively dense, rapid, and regular for particular sites, there is the basis for claiming and transforming territory. At the end of the twentieth century, in the west, these early communal processes are often reductively labelled "pre-Stonewall." In fact, most of these relatively isolated acts occur today and, if examined carefully, can tell us much about how our more "sophisticated" networks and communities function or do not function.

To begin to explore any queerscape ecology,[42] and any open space system for that matter, is to establish a range of subjectivities and then group experiences in terms of commonalities such as desire, activities, and constraints (such as from policing) against particular geographic locations, no matter how fine the scale. Thus we can look at regions, at small parks, even at the microgeographies of cafés and bars. It is in inventorying the particular nature of the connective power of subjectivity[43] in a landscape, as well as the social relationships that come to be associated with particular sites, that there is the basis for determining the more crucial and vulnerable queer space. The social transactions that take place on particular sites comprise the "matrices"[44] of a queerscape. There are various means to track types of relationships and exchanges, no matter how unique each transaction is, but it is usually necessary to start with a small number of functions of mutual benefit.

From my own limited experiences of queer open space, formed along with my own post-Stonewall identity, I know of at least four types of social-environmental alliances. Such ongoing interactions result in some greater communal awareness—in an increased "situating" of collective queer space. Underlying these types of alliances are a host of transactions that, for the purpose of this introductory discussion of outdoor space, can be grouped under solidarity, entertainment, sex acts, and information. While these processes can be remarkably rudimentary and incomplete in terms of their potential for richer forms of social and cultural expression, they constitute the basic relationships, the building blocks, underlying much of today's queerscapes. I begin this discussion with four archetypical and mythologized examples taken from culture, though the descriptions are largely autobiographical.

Samuel R. Delany's Landscapes of Abjection

There are kinds of cooperation in the landscape formed between people who have nowhere else to go—or who engage in certain contact or activities that are not tolerated elsewhere. Homelessness is the most extreme form of this abjection, in that it forces people into public space. Delany's 1994 novel *The Mad Man*[45] is about a graduate student who has sex with homeless men. There are aspects of the book that echo some of Delany's rich personal history, including sex and relationships with indigent men and his formerly marginalized position in academia.[46] The novel's character bases his doctoral research around a long-dead gay male graduate student who was murdered in a bar frequented by hustlers. There are a number of long passages portraying sex in derelict public spaces[47] such as on the margins of city parks.

The landscapes of sexual abjection in *The Mad Man* illustrate one of the most basic of the community formation processes, that of forced proximity. The outdoor site becomes a strategic place, almost a home, because there are few other places to go. The bonds that form between these homeless people, including the "gay" men portrayed by Delany, may be partially from necessity but are remarkably viable. There is a comraderie that overcomes some of the hostility and threats from the urban core. One of the most poignant passages describes sex between a homeless man and the graduate student. It takes place in a cardboard box in a park because they have nowhere else to go and because it is a place where the homeless man feels relatively at home.

> "Do it right here." He sat back, looking around the church-porch steps. "It'll be okay. . . ."
>
> "It's all right" he repeated. "I got my cardboard. We get under that, nobody'll see."[48]

It would be a great mistake to suggest that these urban spaces of gay male sexual abjection, with their slightly cooperative and interracial dimensions, constitute sites of resistance for building and remaking a wide range of social relationships. The opposite is more often true. But these are definitely crucial alliances formed across space: They have environmental impacts, and they extend well beyond survival.

Della Grace's Site-Based Transgressions as Fetish

People sometimes *choose* to make contact in outdoor sites as part of a complex response to and appropriation of the patriarchal dynamics of the gaze and spectacle. Many of the city centre parks in North America and Europe were first established or were redesigned in the late nineteenth century with an emphasis on the public promenade, the male gaze, suppression of public sexual contact, and team sports as a means to lift up working-class morality. Such public parks have usually been programmed for what are sometimes conscious displays of androcentric heterosexual desire, courtship, and conquest. There is some caché in playing in these artifact landscapes. Recently, some of the trappings for making scenes in public spaces have been appropriated by women and artists. But for much of the last century, such pleasures in public areas have been pointedly denied or heavily constrained to sexual minorities. The acts of cultural resistance that turn private acts semipublic can be a kind of fetish, which recently has had increasing use by some lesbians.[49]

Much has been said about *Love Bites,*[50] the controversial and sometimes-censored[51] photographic collection of lesbian erotica accompanied by vague political implications,[52] the work of London-based, California-born photographer Della Grace.[53] This celebration of relatively mild scenes of sadomasochism engendered a tremendous reaction from more conservative elements of British feminism, even though Grace only wanted to use her images "to create a space for the exploration and celebration of diversity and desire."[54] While there was a great deal of hostility to the images of dog collars and chains as unabashed "fetishes,"[55] the greatest transgression was not the art marketing of overpriced fashion accessories for recession-bound British consumers. Rather, the transgression was taking consensual acts between women into what is normally male-dominated public space.[56] Cathy Griggers noted, "We see a lesbian body appropriating the codes of straight porn while assimilating S/M sexual practices arising specifically out of the situationality of gay male bar culture."[57]

Grace appropriated masculinized public spaces and turned aspects of the landscape into props for female pleasures, forming vague resistance to the controls of the state and associated ideologies. She creates, at least within the imagination, "hysterical zones."[58] But to reduce Grace's imagery to simply a "fetishization" of landscape as sex prop would be to ignore some important possibilities for new forms of relationships and alliances. These women are engaged in consensual sexual acts in places where they are vulnerable but relatively well-prepared to defend their turf. These spaces and sites are, for a time, theirs and theirs alone. Problematically, these atomized sexual couples define a relatively clean line around reduced body space. And time will tell whether these "bad girls" become good consumers, even if their buying power continues to be limited due to their gender and marginalized erotic cultures.

Del LaGrace Volcano, from the *Nympho Cabbie* series, London, 1993.

Tom of Finland's Pleasure Park

There are alliances formed for heightened communal pleasure that may lead to sexual satisfaction through complex transactions involving various partners. Such use of public space is not limited to sex acts but is more often about space for complex group interactions, which can include women's softball and political demonstrations as well as anonymous orgies in a park. Public outdoor space becomes strategic because it is difficult to engage in such activities indoors and to find room for larger groups of people. These public spaces for groups, whether officially sanctioned or outlawed, are key sites for learning social skills, for exchange of information, for peer support, and for identity formation. The role of sites of public sex in inverting the standard homophobic proscriptions for social contact were described by Michael Immel for some parks in San Francisco: "It is a pathway, or a series of pathways, that narrow from the open area and allow for closer inspections of others. . . . Silence is maintained as cues and visual presentation excite interest."[59]

Furtive sexual contact in public places is often limited and fetishized, but the opportunities for new social interaction allow for new kinds of alliances. The related notion of self-conscious promiscuity as a response to repression of homoeroticism, a driving force in the formation of geographies of communality, was illustrated somewhat uncritically in John Rechy's *The Sexual Outlaw.*[60] Rechy's Los Angeles queerscape was clearly automobile-oriented and was bounded by the beach farthest west[61] and the public sex of Griffith Park to the east.[62] The landscapes in between were structured around a highly eroticized and commodified landscape of constant sex and individual gratification. Today, even after a decade and a half of the ravages of AIDS, these types of queerscapes exist in every major city in the world, and the structures of these transactions have continued impacts on the textures of neighbourhoods.

The cartoon fantasies of the late Tom of Finland celebrate a wide diversity of hypermasculine[63] "(homo)sex."[64] Much has been said about Tom's exaggeration of masculinity,[65] with its supposed links to misogyny, though most of it has only been speculative.[66] He freely confirmed having had sex with Nazi soldiers in occupied Finland,[67] flirting with fascist aesthetics,[68] and to progressively exaggerating male bodies—particularly proportions, musculature, and genitalia to satisfy consumers and gain wider acceptance. But from the vantage point of the alienations in this *fin-de-siécle* work, the images of fetishized masculinity are less significant for their uniforms and props (which by now have already been heavily marketed) than for their rich nuances, intimations of comraderie, and the cooperation implied by the sexual acrobatics. Most importantly, Tom of Finland created space to conceive of an "erotics of lubricious power"[69] informed by and having relatively positive impacts on the outdoor environment and public space. In these cartoons of recollections and fantasies,

Gender-based entry to the Pleasure Park: part sexual fantasy and part chronic inequity. Tom of Finland, *Kake Pleasure Park,* c. 1969-1970. Drawing courtesy of the Tom of Finland Foundation, Los Angeles.

desire and its relatively equitable satisfaction—particularly that which is communal—makes and re-creates place.

In the 1984 *Kake Pleasure Park,*[70] we are presented with a vision of an all-male public space based on mutual and somewhat expanding erotic satisfaction. Perhaps this vision is closest to Jacob's viciously constructed spectre of the "pervert park." Two forces create this gay male site. Exclusion is indicated by a "Men Only" sign at the entrance to the pleasure park.[71] The second factor is the world of uniforms and the organizations and sectors that they represent, particularly for marginalized groups in need of employment and points of entry into hierarchies of social standing. It remains to be seen whether public sites of highly charged homoeroticism can generate the resources for their own protection and management, as relatively sustainable plateaus[72] in communal life. Many such marginal places are only intermittently or diurnally queer, and the outskirts of such "pleasure parks" are often sites of homophobic assaults.

From Community to Communality in Andrea Fatona and Cornelia Wyngaaden's *Hogan's Alley*

If we use the metaphor of the nineteenth-century train station, there are places for changing tracks and making connections that are particularly strategic for sexual minorities. Outdoor public spaces often support shifting alliances and communal identifications. *Hogan's Alley*[73] is a half-hour video about the first black neighbourhood in Vancouver. Hogan's Alley was a neighbourhood of flimsy wood-frame shacks, barely large enough for extended families, built on a filled salt marsh, at that time a block from the port. A neighbourhood identity emerged in the 1920s, and a strong black presence was established by the outbreak of World War II. By the time of the United States and Canadian civil rights movement, a new generation of Hogan's Alley residents was involved in the arts and the production of imagery—much of which exoticized African Americans for largely white audiences. The function of community for these Vancouverites of African heritage had changed, and given the lack of state-initiated ghettoization, people scattered. This community had been first defined by race, and it shifted from one that was tight-knit and functioned for survival, centred around church, businesses, and unions, to something that was more provisional and related to specific experiences and sensibilities with their underlying economic and cultural relationships. As the heart of the community was destroyed, new waves of black immigrants from the West Indies and farther afield settled in other parts of the city.

The narrative in *Hogan's Alley* is based on the reminiscences of three women who grew up in the neighbourhood. A major part of the second half of this video involves the contentious relationships between one of the three, Leah Curtis, and both the black community in which she grew up and Vancouver's lesbian community of the 1960s. Early on she confronted racism in the Vancouver lesbian community.

Main Street, Vancouver, 1922. Tracks near the West Coast terminus of the Canadian railways, the principal infastructure behind the formation of the state and national culture. Courtesy of the City of Vancouver Archives.

Typical alley open space in the vicinity of Hogan's Alley and the Canadian Pacific Railway terminal, early 1960's. Photograph by Eric Lindsay. Courtesy of the City of Vancouver Archives.

Leah Curtis, from *Hogan's Alley*. Video by Andrea Fatona and Cornelia Wyngaarden. Courtesy of Video In, Vancouver.

> So I used to go back and forth from the New Fountain to the Vanport [lesbian bars] but I really didn't like the Vanport too much because it was mostly just white uppity people there. And I wasn't really accepted there because there was a lot of prejudiced women . . . There was an older dyke there that was callin' me names. I said, well, "You call me that name again and I'm going to fix you." . . . And then it was just like a western bar scene where two people start fighting then the whole club starts fighting. . . .

Curtis then described how difficult her life was as a teen taking care of children in her extended family. She chose to trade that traditional role of unmarried woman as caregiver for the surveillance (the "panoptic gaze of heterosexism"[74]) of her racially and ethnically defined community and then to break with it for an only slightly multicultural lesbian network.

Hogan's Alley, Vancouver, 1954. Hogan's Alley was the first African or "coloured" enclave of the city, adjacent to the early lesbian enclave in the tough bars along Main Street (visible in the centre of the photograph). This marginal space was crammed between the railroad station to the south, Chinatown to the north, and the port to the west. Courtesy of Maps of British Columbia.

> I wanted some freedom. . . . So how they dealt with my lesbianism was they just totally disowned, ostracized me, which suited me fine because the black community, was really tight. . . . After when I decided that I was not going to go home again, ever, that was my home, the gay community, and at that time, it was The New Fountain. . . .

What Curtis describes is a central experience for a majority of North American lesbians and other sexual minorities for whom redefinition of identity and "coming out" is linked to going from one minority community that is based around networks of heteronormative families defined by race, culture, language, and class, to another that is often more narrowly conceived in terms of some increase in individual expression, erotic satisfaction, tolerance, and mutual support. The multiple dilemmas she confronted in that walk from Hogan's Alley to The New Fountain resonate in the not-so-open spaces along the way. Her dilemma was peculiar to small and chronically Eurocentric and neocolonial cities in the north of North America, where membership in the so-called "gay community" required a kind of faux assimilation in terms of race, because demographics and politics constrained the formation of networks, for example, of black lesbians.

Vancouver Open Space as Queerscape[75]

Open space and other strategic queer sites do not exist as isolated points in the landscape. There always is a context with a horizontal plane, across which are points of key transactions—connecting lines such as paths, roads, and conduits—and territorialized polygons. Such open and queer space involves constellations of "traversable sites."[76] Within each of these environments are a series of dialectics, including those between expanding sexual expression and repression, between zones of public and private, and between sexual acts and various communal identities. Each queerscape is a matrix of desire and power with, as Deleuze and Guattari envisioned, the smooth spaces of the game Go and the striated niches of chess.[77] A queerscape also includes indoor and outdoor sites (some privately owned), but the open space, that which is outdoors and publicly owned, often forms the most strategic nodes. These sites of recreation, along with options for housing and work, determine the texture of a queerscape.

The following is an example of how to begin to describe the queerscape through linking cognitive maps: recognition of the full range of differences, inequities in access to landscape resources, repression, and various forms of alliances that can influence the formation of more extensive enclaves of sexual minorities. In this example, as in many around the world, colonialism, neocolonialism, and only partially successful efforts at decolonization have created broad templates that continue to dominate social, political, and economic relations.

Vancouver is a relatively new city,[78] built on the sites of Salish-speaking villages that date back over five thousand years. Vancouver was established as a city in 1886 as the Trans-Canada Railway was completed. Soon after its founding, Vancouver also became the northern terminus of the United States's Great Northern Railway. At the city's founding, the Crown Colony of British Columbia had already been in the Canadian confederation for fifteen years, but Vancouver remained, for much of its first century, a colonial landscape and way station in the British Empire—not particularly strategic in the economic hegemony of the United States.

Like nineteenth-century San Francisco, with its similar pattern of frontier town labour and immigration, Vancouver became a major site for "sexual, racial and gender crossings"[79] and the institutionalization of racist policies. This contradiction was to dominate its social relations for a century. For example, as the Trans-Canada railroad was being completed by Chinese workers in 1885, an anti-Chinese "head tax" was enacted for the next thirty-eight years, followed by active exclusion until 1949. Vancouver was incorporated in the months following the criminalization of sodomy in Britain. This chill was soon felt in the margins of the Empire, particularly in emergent centres of sodomy such as Vancouver. In the first half of the twentieth century, Vancouver was a hard port and terminal city where vice, including male and female homosexuality, was often partially tolerated even when it was not flourishing.

Similar to more segregated cities in the British Empire, Vancouver has since its inception supported at least four very different homosexual subcultures and cultural discourses around marginalized sexualities: white gay male, primarily white lesbian, gay or lesbian Chinese, and Native/aboriginal. Other cultural groups have tended to be attached to the first three of these, inevitably overlapping social strata of the queerscape. In such a small city, there has been a remarkable amount of spatial segregation, especially in the lives of sexual minorities. Public parks were often sites where racial and cultural boundaries were blurred and where conflicts were played out. Soon after the city was established, the streets that were west of crowded, expanding, and repeatedly cordoned Chinatown and Main Street became the boundary between "whites" to the west and non-European communities to the east. The West End, often considered a gay ghetto, was remarkably white, Eurocentric, androcentric, and middle class well into the 1960s. The West End functioned far less like a ghetto than Chinatown. In contrast, lesbian bars, as part of a working-class port subculture, first emerged along and to the east of Main Street. As the lesbian feminist networks went aboveground and started involving more childrearing in non-male-centred households in the 1970s,[80] a scattered "enclave," if the word is applicable here, expanded eastward toward Commercial Drive.

Within every homosexual underground are discordant and invisible networks that threaten to explode and become visible when broader political economic factors eventually permit it. In contrast to the primarily white gay male enclaves, a nineteenth-century homosexual Chinese subculture was established after the Trans-Canada railroad was completed, when more than ten thousand male workers were crowded into the Chinatowns of Vancouver and neighbouring Victoria. There were ongoing cultural links to the large homosexual enclaves in Chinese cities of the time. After World War I, south Asian enclaves began to take root, especially in the suburbs farther east in the slowly expanding metropolitan area. Even in a city with a history of state-sanctioned segregation less overt than many others in North America, the fractured and invisible nature of large networks, indeed of much of the queerscape, is remarkable. It is probably no coincidence that, as the de facto divisions described previously

The West End from the edge of Stanley Park, Vancouver, 1994.

finally began to break down over the past decade, there emerged finally a "queer" politics for sexual minorities that was somewhat less Eurocentric and antiracist and more sex-positive. Integration processes have barely begun and will remain appropriate only for particular forms of communality, exchange, and erotic contact where modicums of equitable power relationships can be assured.

In less than half a century, Vancouver has evolved from a violent frontier town to a cosy outpost for the élite among the rapidly integrating economies of the Pacific Rim. But the ghosts of the initial struggles for gender equity and sexual expression linger. In recent decades Vancouver has spawned numerous global corporate institutions. In the past decade it also has emerged as a centre for film and television production, exporting queasy and often pretentiously "postmodern" mythologies with series such as *The X-Files*, *Outer Limits,* and *Millenium.*

The landscapes of North America often embody competing and overlapping neocolonial reiterations from its three major European sources: Spain, Great Britain, and France. Within this uneasy detente, the position of Vancouver in maintaining its part of this triad is increasingly insecure. The patina of Britishness is long gone. Like

Los Angeles, any pretense of solidly Anglo roots was largely a racist fabrication. Heritages primarily British were rarely a majority in the city, and this portion of the total population has been declining throughout much of this century. But within this contradiction of the growing "unBritishness" of British Columbia, constructions of sexual identities largely have remained rooted in anglophile frameworks. In this quiet cultural crisis, the land and the public spaces that have formed on it have remained under the control of the more neocolonial government agencies, notably the British Columbia Ministry of Forests, which still controls the majority of the province.

The development of this terminal city has paralleled the formation of modern notions of the homosexual and queer. In Vancouver, built through curious contradictions of colonial and corporate monopolies and the subsidies and interventions of a distant federal government, heterosexuality was solidly associated with the state.[81] The construction of this colonial landscape was also simultaneous with systematic forms of homophobic repression and isolation of sexual minorities. The ambiguous potential of open space as an arena to control, hide, and tolerate minority sexualities became intrinsic to those Victorian and Edwardian landscapes. Perhaps more than most large North American cities, prostitution and reactions to it have been major factors in the formation of Vancouver's neighbourhoods. Partially because of a chronic shortage of skilled labour, known homosexuals, especially those from more privileged European groups with command of English, tended to be better tolerated than in less-urbanized areas of the British North American frontier. In addition Pacific Canada has a heritage of sex radicalism associated with radical trade unionism and utopianism going back to the early socialist movements of the Victorian period.[82] Though somewhat homophobic, the contradiction opened some more space for homosexuals.

The public spaces of this mercantile town were built on contradictory pressures for commodification of sex and creation of commons resilient to the vagaries of short-term market forces. But the government reserves and parks have also tended to obliterate prior ownerships and claims by "First Nations." Multiple use, often the rhetoric for wholesale liquidation of ancient forests and open space, has been rooted in colonial strategies for control of land, resources, and labour. Notions of "nature" in these false commons are highly contentious.[83] Today in this port city, beaches such as Vancouver's English Bay have become surrogates for more purposeful forms of public space[84] and the fulcra for social discourse ranging from cruising to political demonstrations that typically go on

Clearcut, Clayoquot Sound, Vancouver Island, 1995.

Tom of Finland, *Finlandia,* 1974, from *The Men of Finland* (1984). Drawing courtesy of the Tom of Finland Foundation, Los Angeles.

Gay men's softball team, San Francisco, 1975. Photograph by Emery Reiff. Courtesy of the Gay and Lesbian Historical Society of Northern California.

in urban centres. Many of the urban parks in central cores of North American cities, including Vancouver's Stanley Park, are nineteenth-century artifacts with multiple layering of changing morals, ideologies, and activist movements. Urban parks in North America are derived from the nineteenth-century articulations of landscape architect Frederick Law Olmsted of a vague commitment to "parks for people." The contradictions within these notions can be read in today's networks of city parks and open space. In the late nineteenth century, there was a movement for greater presence of women in city parks, often involving team sports, leaving a legacy in lesbian and other queer sports groups. Just as Eve Kosofsky Sedgwick argued that nineteenth- and early twentieth-century cultures functioned as something of a big closet for avoiding homoeroticism, there are parallels in Vancouver's open space. In this context lesbians and gay men of colour had few options, often with a "hypermarginalization" rather than "ghettoization," which limited contact to a few hazardous indoor establishments or a small number of risky outdoor sites. But the needs for outdoor space and the pressures to claim them if only for brief periods were constantly reiterated in contests between heterosexual user groups over space and buildings. The level of competition for the public spaces of Vancouver, between heterosexuals and sexual minorities, has varied over the decades. There were periods after World War II when there were contests for space between courting heterosexuals and cruising gay men—contests similar to those that led to, for example, the severe anti-homosexual repression in Atlanta[85] in the same period.

Vancouver has had substantial numbers of gay men and lesbians since a decade after its founding. There has been tolerance of the sexual activities of single men, in light of their status as badly needed workers, with disposable income and in need of entertainment. Historically male prostitution has been partially tolerated in the city, with corners on the margins of the city's core relegated to hustling. Vancouver's city police have been less violent and intolerant of sexual minorities than in other major Canadian cities, and though extensive harassment has continued well into the late 1980s, it has occurred without much of the violent and organized harassment of

Transexual Menace basketball team, New York City, 1995. Photograph © Morgan Gwenwald.

queer groups in Toronto and Montréal. At times, there has been considerable surveillance[86] of known homosexuals,[87] and this continued well after the partial decriminalization of homosexuality. After 1968 the emphasis on repression shifted to bars and clubs, political organizing, public sex, and child pornography. In Vancouver, police entrapment and harassment in response to cruising[88] and public sex intensified in the 1970s and did not decline until considerable monitoring and organized resistance by the gay community into the 1980s.[89] As late as 1976 there were regular incidences of city police viciously attacking openly gay men, to the point of their requiring hospitalization.[90] Compounding this checkered history of municipal repression, the Royal Canadian Mounted Police (RCMP, the Mounties) were carefully inventorying, monitoring, and mapping sites of queer desire in public space into the late 1960s,[91] and some of this surveillance extended to Vancouver. Until the 1960s federal government officials would denounce people as homosexuals and cause them to lose their jobs. Thus the dynamic of repression and resistance was a primary force, comprising another matrix in the ecology of this queerscape.

Rather than just a response to repression, gay male and lesbian presence in public space was driven by numbers, concentrations, and desire. By the end of the Depression, a period of major social displacement that brought many single men and women to the Pacific coast, there were well-known rooming houses and apartments inhabited by gay men. By the 1960s Vancouver, like most large ports in North America, had developed a host of illicit commercial establishments and underground networks. For example, by 1967 there were roughly eight lesbian-only or lesbian-gay male commercial establishments in the city and a comparable number of relatively exclusive gay male spaces.[92] For a metropolitan area of not much more than one million people, this was extraordinary. And these gay populations were highly mobile in terms of employment and residence, with particularly strong links to Seattle, San Francisco, and Toronto.

The first homophile organization in Canada, the Association for Social Knowledge (ASK), was formed in Vancouver in 1964,[93] a year of continual police presence and repression of activity in the city's gay bars.[94] Vancouver's first lesbian and gay centre opened in 1967.[95] The following year saw the partial decriminalization of homosexual acts by the Canadian Parliament, but the law had only limited day-to-day impact on these networks and respective neighborhoods,[96] particularly since police repression continued. For gay men—particularly white anglophiles—there were quasi-underground pre-gay liberation "courts," such as the Dogwood Monarchist Society, which continued to play substantial social roles until well into the 1980s. In Canada lesbian feminism emerged as a movement and a community in 1968,[97] and political lesbian feminists tended to gravitate to Vancouver, particularly in the 1970–72 period.[98] In the same period, downtown Vancouver's representative in Canadian Parliament was a closeted gay man who rose, in the early Trudeau cabinets, to be Minister of Urban Affairs—a particularly short-lived portfolio[99] but one crucial to creation of the extensive public areas such as Granville Island, now central to the network of open space.

In 1970 the Vancouver Gay Liberation Front (GLF) was formed, but because it did not find a support base in the gay male ghetto in the city's West End, it was defunct a year later[100]—soon succeeded by the more conservative Gay Activist Alliance and the slightly radical Gay Alliance Toward Equality (GATE). Vancouver's first resource centre exclusively for lesbians opened in 1972.[101] Gay people first began organizing for a gay studies curriculum at The University of British Columbia in 1972, though so far they have been unsuccessful in developing comprehensive programmes.[102] It was also in this period that gay liberation, in contrast to only decriminalization, was first championed by an elected Canadian official: black, human rights activist Rosemary Brown represented part of Vancouver in the Provincial Legislature.[103]

In this same period of explosive growth of lesbian and gay movements and institutions, there was increased resistance to police entrapment and harassment as well as to other forms of discrimination. There was a wave of police harassment of gay clubs in 1973,[104] the same year that Gay Pride Week brought out a demonstration of about one hundred people.[105] Gay and lesbian service organizations had formed by 1974.[106] The first organization against gay harassment was the moderate Society for Education, Action, Research, and Counselling on Homosexuality (SEARCH). The group was formed in 1974 with considerable antipathy to members of GATE. SEARCH initially limited its concerns to police harassment in and around private establishments and other gay institutions, not including open space such as Stanley Park. By the late 1970s a women's and lesbian enclave had formed in the eastern part of Vancouver, along Commercial Drive, an area that provided lower rents and more services to women and children.

As with many parts of the world where gay ghettos became more visible, homophobic violence intensified in the 1980s. The city's lesbian and gay bookstore, Little Sisters, was firebombed in 1988, with a second attempt months after the first. Over the last decade, there has been some gaybashing attributed to neo-Nazi groups,[107] some involving trainees from the Aryan Nation-associated camps in northern Idaho, in a remote rural area that borders on the British Columbia interior. As is the case with many other cities with gay ghettos, much of the violence, abuse, and lesser discrimination continues to occur in neighbourhoods with large numbers of lesbians and gay men, in places where people feel most secure.[108] Street crime in Vancouver is low in comparison to similarly sized North American cities, although violence against women, visible lesbians, and gay men remains a constant threat. This relative freedom from violent crime has allowed a greater presence of women in public spaces, sometimes alone and at night, though outdoor sites that are well-used at night—such as some parts of the West End's Seawall—remain exceptions. Repeated assaults in public areas, particularly parks, were a major concern for the short-lived cell, Queer Planet, in 1991.

In recent years the city has been particularly vulnerable to international capital, with linkages to Hong Kong, Japan, and China. This monetary flow has contributed to transforming Vancouver into what some, including Paul Delany, have argued is a quintessentially postmodern city.[109] Delany argues that formerly marginal cities that have been outside of colonial and modernist centres of power and generation of cultural icons, such as Vancouver has, hold more space for hybridity and new perspectives. Less optimistic Vancouverites are convinced that the power brokers are hell-bent on concocting "fictional histories" of the city.[110] Today, Vancouver is relatively affluent and multicultural, with high levels of social services. The heritages of the metropolitan-area residents are between 30 and 40 percent non-European. But in this increasingly Disneyesque and hyped centre for the production of imagery, which once brought the world Greenpeace and the United Nations Habitat Conference and today specializes in macabre (and mediocre) television fantasies, a comfortable sort of alienation is the standard fare. And the rare engagement from spontaneous meetings in public outdoor spaces may be one of the most dependable forms of social intercourse.

Various forms of outdoor-space contact leading to acts of homosexuality, especially involving gay and bisexual men, have been occurring since the city's inception. Such communality has been regulated by the particular nature of the persistent "closet colonialism," the patterns of immigration,[111] and the distribution of housing, public transportation, and services across the city. The result is a highly fragmented and impermanent set of queer enclaves and personal networks of varying levels of invisibilities structured, in no small part, along lines of race, language, ethnicity, class, and sexual desire. In this context that is more neocolonial than postcolonial, most non-European groups have been either ignored or exoticized. There are few spaces to speak languages other than English, making silent-contact sites particularly strategic for some groups.

In the mild and rainy weather of Vancouver, with the same latitude as Paris, southwest-facing shores are the most comfortable year-round. In the central part of the city, the two largest beaches with this condition have relatively high presences of gay and bisexual men and, to a growing extent, lesbians and bisexual women. Nature aside, in comparison to other liberal North American cities, such as neighbouring Seattle (which is roughly the same population size), Vancouver has relatively underdeveloped organizations and institutions for lesbian, gay, and transsexual populations. With Vancouver's queer communities somewhat scattered at the margins[112] of North American urban activism, certain outdoor sites remain strategic for exchange of information, socialization, and mutual support, if not for sex. Perhaps because of lower rates of violent crime, outdoor areas of gay male sex are large for a North American city and have grown rapidly in the last three decades.[113] However Vancouver has seen continuing anti-gay violence, and there have been organized responses to this for nearly two decades[114] including, in recent years, a queer street patrol.

The City of Vancouver banned discrimination on the basis of gender and sexual orientation in 1982.[115] In the same decade, the Canadian Constitution finally enshrined protection against gender discrimination, and the Province of British Columbia amended its Human Rights Code to outlaw more blatant forms of homophobic discrimination in 1992. There were extended debates on whether the Canadian Constitution inferred protection on the basis of sexual orientation, and federal legislation to clarify limited protection was finally enacted in 1996. All of these changes have had tangible impacts on the queerscape. One of the most dominant regulating factors in this erotic landscape has been shifting legal notions of privacy,[116] both through interpretations by the state in tolerating homoeroticism[117] and in the fluid lines between public and private zones as related to the permissibility of sexual acts.[118] Notions of privacy around sexual contact and information on sexuality, particularly for but not limited to gay men, was transformed greatly in the 1980s with the ravages of the AIDS epidemic. Pacific Canada has had particularly high rates of HIV infection.[119] Over the last decade, various organizations have come and largely gone, including ACT UP, Queer Planet, and Lesbian Avengers.

The open spaces of Vancouver were formed as part of an infrastructure to expand dominion by anglophile culture, the Canadian and British Columbian states, and capitalism and modernist technological "development." Yet today all three of these historical projects are in crisis, and only the third, in this city of railway terminals, is still on track. The queerscape as a regional tension between homoerotic desire and communality on one hand and the forces of heteronormative conformity on the other is rapidly giving way to a tension that is more directly structured for the benefits of discriminating "blind" capital that only faintly echoes the racism and cultural chauvinism of the past century. Increasingly the city is less a centre for dissemination of the English language and more for the multitude of languages from south China and Asia, as well as French, Italian, and other western European cultures. In these times of globalization of capital and neoconservativism, the Canadian state is in retreat, especially in providing both social repression and social entitlements. In the face of aboriginal sovereignist movements and declarations, the validity of the Province of British Columbia, as the heir to the Crown Colony of British Columbia and as a means to concentrate resources and pay for the state is increasingly in doubt. And while indulging in the paranoias of impending United States domination is a major Canadian pastime, the influences of this particular city state, Vancouver, now extend south to below the border. Vancouver is slated to become the largest metropolitan area in the Pacific Northwest in the coming years. All of these dynamics are reflected in the textures of the public spaces of Vancouver—in expanding options, at least for now, for contact and communality, a major aspect of which is erotic.

If we look at the network of open space in Vancouver as the matrix of a queerscape, with shifting nodes and connections and with each supporting some or all of the following alliances, there is the beginning of a comprehensive analytical framework for inventorying the most important communal relationships and points of transaction. Some sites support a wide range of activities for gay men, lesbians, bisexuals, and transsexuals and include a wide range of cultural, age, and mobility groups. Most areas harbour a small number of uses and user groups, and for only brief periods. While this is still an elite and neocolonial queerscape that allows considerably more options for white gay men, the gendered and eurocentric aspects of these templates of relationships and transactions are being transformed.

Abjection

People are often forced out into outdoor areas because there are problems with their homes, such as crowding and lack of privacy and light, or because of homelessness. Outdoor nights become refuges for contact, privacy, and sex. Parks and parking lots have been crucial sites for erotic contact between individuals who cannot have guests at home and for people in heteronormative households who have needed somewhere "to get some space." Solidarity in such disparaging settings as stifling morality, crowding, poverty, and homelessness can involve tracking police and spouses or looking after someone else's children. Street prostitution, male and female, can be a form of

Photograph from the Tim Wood collection, San Francisco, 1950's. Courtesy of the Gay and Lesbian Historical Society of Northern California.

abjection: Brothels are illegal and more lucrative forms of "sex work" involving arrangements by cellular telephone are unavailable. But in times of state repression and serial murders, the high degree of solidarity and mutual protection on the streets may be preferable.[120]

The entertainment afforded by open space often involves more complex stimuli such as light, panoramas, and nature than is available from indoor queer sites. In contrast, sexual activity in parks, when there is nowhere else to go, is often limited and of a short duration. Exchange of information can be quite miscellaneous, but for the homeless or transient, for example, it can often be key for survival, shelter, and access to social services and economic opportunities. In recent years there have been programmes to provide information on safer sex practices to hustlers and people engaged in public sex.[121]

Transgression as Fetish

One of the greatest transgressions by sexual minorities in recent decades has been to conduct sex in public as some sort of performance or, in the case of the exhibitionistic hustlers of Yaletown, cheeky advertisements. The transgression is in moving sex from the private to the public realms and in "doing it under their noses." This is a crude and very temporary form of appropriation of space. In the case of forested park lands, fetishizing nature in a political economy engaged in its increasing commodification and destruction has a particular appeal. Solidarity, in this case, involves watching and assisting actors in not getting caught. The transgression is half of the entertainment. Recently, women and transsexuals are moving into typically all-male and masculine areas as increasingly conscious forms of reappropriation. The education provided in such episodes is often fairly limited unless there is a specific message, as in the case of art performances or political demonstrations.

Communal Pleasures

In the case of the overworked, a park is a place to finally find some relaxation. Sexual expression in this context, no matter how anonymous, is less reduced and compartmentalized from the rest of a person's tastes, desires, and aspirations. Outdoor areas provide opportunities for high levels of social contact and, when desired, numerous partners. But to reduce communal pleasures to Tom of Finland's recollections and fantasies of group sex forgets the hundreds of lesbian softball and grass hockey teams that regularly "queer" the playing fields of North America as well as the many cultural events and festivals. Communal solidarity in the mild, cool seasonal shifts of Vancouver is punctuated by a Lesbian Visibility March in the chill of February, a Stonewall Festival in June, a Gay Pride March in early August, a charity AIDS Walk in late September, and long lines snaking outside queer films at the Vancouver International Film Festival soon after. Vancouver, as a link in the expanding circuit parties, has been weak. At dusk on warm nights when it is not raining, there are sometimes orgies on Wreck Beach and lines for sex in the Enchanted Forest of Stanley Park.[122] But these remain furtive, ephemeral, and spontaneous, whereas less overtly erotic events are often more dependable. And along with films, pamphlets, posters, performances, and word of mouth, these pleasurable communalities often provide key information on health care, fighting bigotry and organizing, upcoming parties, and new consumer services.

Network Entry

"Coming out" for most people has a key function of "coming in" to new social networks with changes in habits and routes across landscapes. Use of public space can be part of the expansion of personal networks to include people who share perspectives, sensibilities, and pleasures. In the rough and tumble frontier of Pacific Canada, before decriminalization of homosexuality, bars with furtive gay spaces and parks were the few places where a stranger had any hope of finding peers, allies, and friends. But in the past two decades, both institutions have become decidedly ancillary as sources of networks after support groups, clubs, political caucuses and other organizations, and increasingly spectacular "benefit" parties. Today, instead of the pub in the Vanport Hotel[123] of Leah Curtis's youth being a destination and a refuge from the homophobic surveillance of heteronormative public space, similar bars are only minor stops with the less furtive public space along the way now holding more promise for a range of social contact and solidarity.

Queries and Hypotheses: The Not-So-Open Spaces of Queerscapes as Analytical Frameworks

The previous outline of Vancouver as queerscape is far from a conclusive inventory, description, or analysis. Certainly the notion of the queerscape is as constructed and shifting as is that of the landscape. But the framework of networks of outdoor public space as nodes of contact and activities for sexual minorities poses some increased opportunities for confirming the existence of and obstacles to various forms of queer communality. Given that invisibility and nonrecognition remain chronic obstacles to developing viable strategies for queer politics, the concept of the queerscape reappropriates some of the surveillance techniques of the malevolent and indifferent state. Whereas ACT UP queered militarily through actions that verged on guerilla tactics, and Queer Nation laid the basis for a cultural activism whose promise is largely unfulfilled, the vision of the queerscape could contribute to the reinvigoration of queer civic politics and a more prolonged focus on particular neighbourhood conditions, at a time when self-styled gay and lesbian leaders are increasingly careerist and technocratic.

The analytical framework that I have outlined begins with recognizing spatial subjectivities, moves to identification of functions and alliances, and focuses on strategic points—with transactions involving sex acts only a small portion. Space becomes a means for tracking such transactions rather than generating them. The relationships and connections between these points can then be assessed in biophysical and social contexts as part of broader scaled conditions, such as freedom and repression, across queerscapes. But perhaps all that can be achieved in the coming years for most cities is an expanded vocabulary and appreciation for diverse communalities across networks of open space. This alone could have a tremendous impact on civic policies. In a world of declining green space,[124] design questions for parks become political issues. In Vancouver, election to the City of Vancouver Parks Board is one of the least difficult entry points for ambitious lesbian and gay and environmentalist politicians. More than just a fetishization of the landscape, a political culture of the "opening" of public space has taken root, one that will require expanded analytical frameworks employing sophisticated environmental conceptualizations.

Conclusions

The history of the city park in the twentieth century has been dominated by state-sanctioned neglect of the safety of women, partial exclusions and marginalizations of racial and cultural minorities, and often vicious attacks on the presence of sexual minorities. Paradoxically, the park has been one of the most strategic and poorly explored battlegrounds in the recent sexual, cultural, and political wars. Public space in the twentieth century, more than in any other time in history, has been dominated by the state's attempts to suppress, constrain, and otherwise regulate sexual desire and consensual activity—particularly for women and sexual minorities. The notion of the queerscape is one more analytical framework to track desires, marginalities, transactions, and communalities across landscapes and communities. Within such contradictory environments of hatred, risk, anxiety, empathy, and pleasure, queers have often subverted the state-constructed divisions between public and private, and for short periods they have appropriated intermediate zones as spaces for mutual support and satisfaction. The tactics[125] used to queer these not-so-open spaces have varied greatly over the years as state policies and social and economic options have fluctuated.

Community always has both site and territorial aspects, ones which function very differently as a result of the nature of the transactions and respective networks. For sexual minorities, there has often been exclusion and invisibility with only exceptional nodes and modest levels of regular presence. Transactions that are part of alliances associated with strategic sites may provide a more accurate basis for understanding territorialization for sexual minorities—at least in the context of repression, limited liberalization, and closeted patriarchy, and neocolonialism. The importance of such sites and their respective activities are radically different during periods of criminalization, partial decriminalization and rights advocacy, more comprehensive forms of women's/gay/lesbian/bisexual liberation, and today's more indefinite and provisional intersections of queer theory and activism. How outdoor sites are transformed by the configurations of queer alliances associated with them will be central determiners as sexual minorities set civic agendas for decades to come. I have initiated an argument that the importance of outdoor space and landscapes to sexual minorities is never totally by default nor is it from systematic marginalization. The landscape is never just a backdrop; it transforms and is in turn transformed through pleasure, danger, sacredness, and contentiousness in the process of its use as queer site. And such cultural processes are extending well beyond bedrooms, closets, and dark outdoor sites of anonymous sex.

As for simple definitions, there is a basis for more precise usage of the following terms. A (queer) "node" is a place that involves more than one strategic site, with respective transactions and alliances. A (queer) "enclave" constitutes a relatively dense set of nodes that includes homes and relatively permanent habitation. A (queer) "network" involves shared interests and desires, along with regular communication, but is not necessarily spatially specific. A (queer) "community" involves multiple and possibly divergent networks for a particular area that include various degrees of interdependence and mutual support along with respective organizations and institutions.

A queerscape intrinsically embodies contradictions involving various pressures for and constraints on erotic, familial, and communal desire—ones that have biophysical environmental impacts and others that are developmental, social, and cultural. The monitoring framework that can be created to understand the shifting nature of queerscapes and the extent of the refuge that is afforded to particular groups requires frank recognition of specific acts, identities, and alliances as well as their biophysical and political economic contexts and impacts. This environmental information can be integrated into decision-making frameworks for landscapes as part of the strategies for including more queer networks, for confronting homophobia and violence, for popular education, and for better stewardship of natural areas.

Even in the most severe forms of exclusion from space, such as homelessness, there are alliances between individuals that create the basic forms of queer space. There is protective interdependence between individuals as well as shared pleasures. There are opportunities for constructing more complex and representative identities that lead to life choices somewhere between heteronormative families and various queer possibilities. All of these dynamics are played out simultaneously across the landscape. Uncovering and reconstructing the social architecture of queerscapes, in terms of implications for physical design, public policy, and redefinition of cultural perspectives and functions, is a central political task for new queer activism, as well as environmental planning, urban design, and that massive closet called "landscape architecture." If networks of open space are to be made increasingly safe, enjoyable, and inclusive, the homophobia that is consciously or inadvertently "programmed" into the landscape will have to be confronted in the academy, in the design and planning professions, and in civic politics.

In looking at Vancouver as a queerscape, remarkable amounts of residual colonialism and misogyny become apparent. For most minorities in this city, such a statement comes as no surprise. Queer sites nearly always have specific ethnic and cultural associations. Identifying strategic sites and recognizing the relationships that they support, and which in turn transform them, as part of more spontaneous forms of queerscape architecture becomes part of more advanced phases of decolonization. And establishing new and more accessible queer outdoor space can be linked to a host of other prerequisites that contribute to deconstructing and eventually confronting and destroying gender and cultural hierarchies—at least for the inherently multicultural but increasingly problematic cultural landscapes of countries such as Canada.

Just as we experience sensoral aspects of the landscape that indicate a diversity of natural and social processes across space and time, so too are there indications of the social interactions that comprise queerscapes. Underlying these queerscapes are contradictions between desire and repression, heterosexuality and homosexuality, homosexuality and bisexuality, gender stability and transgendered fluxes, equality and elitism, communality and more individualized alliances, and separatism and assimilation. It is these unresolved social relationships that can determine the patterns of competition for resources, which are often made artificially scarce across the not-so-open spaces of cities, suburbs, towns, farmlands, and wildlands, and that often centre on social groups defined in terms of gender, race, class, language, culture, and age.

Like other forms of territory, queerscapes have shifting and unresolved relationships with various forms of state apparatus. Queerscapes are as natural and intrinsic to human environments as any other aspect of the cultural landscape. Learning better to read the queerscapes around us is the basis for discussing more precisely how to inhabit, use, and modify them. In pre-postmodern times, it would be easy to suggest, however naïvely, simply to liberate these spaces and to conceive of them as being truly opened. But by delving into and more consciously engaging the queerscape, a richer and more contradictory set of social processes become apparent—a set that creates more space for expression of desire, a set that is far more indefinite than the initial promises of gay liberation and queer nationalism.

"No More Shit": The Struggle for Democratic Gay Space in Toronto

John Grube

If you asked the average citizen of Toronto to take pencil and paper and draw a sort of freehand mental map of the city, the first item to appear would likely be Yonge Street. It is our Main Street. It starts at Lake Ontario and runs north fifty miles through the downtown business district, a tacky patch of discount stores, the smart midtown, and the suburbs. When a rebellion broke out in 1837 against the autocratic Family Compact, the farmers and workingmen marched up Yonge Street. In 1981 when the government of the day decided to raid every gay bathhouse in the city on the same night, the protest demonstration had to march up Yonge Street—even though none of the raided bathhouses were located there. No other street would do. Yonge Street has always been and is still felt to be the psychological "spinal cord" of Toronto. For the last 150 years gay men have sought, in the streets that branch out from lower Yonge Street, the anonymity of the downtown core—before World War II in rooming houses, from the 1950s onward in the high-rise apartments that have taken their place.

In urban environments, many groups have to share the public space. In this essay I show how gay men[1] have partially transformed public space for their own use. The parks, ravines, and streets laid out by others become, in part, appropriated as our own "sacred ground." My central argument is that a dichotomy of pre- and post-Stonewall space is too simplistic. Gay space has expanded or contracted as a result of complex interplays between the state's attempts to restrict it and the resilience of networks that continue to deepen links under repression. Instead of simply before and after, I have seen a number of interwoven shifts: from largely invisible to more visible; from one set of rules and regulations defined by small élites, to multiple memberships in more fluid and democratic "communities";[2] from social interaction defined by persecution to that defined by other social categories—notably gender, ethnicity,

John Grube, Yonge Street, Toronto, 1995.

and sexual desires. I believe that the real progress in building queer public space has been slow and incremental, rather than sudden.

In this essay I outline a notion of "democratic" gay public space that has often been suggested in terms such as "after Stonewall." I argue that this type of queer space is not exactly the same as spaces of the "gay ghetto," and certainly it did not automatically emerge after the New York City riots of June 1969. Instead public spaces where there are sexual minorities—which comprise a key strand of postmodern "democracies"—are fought for, appropriated, and constructed. In North America the militant presence of gay and lesbian groups in strategic urban open space has tended to be an essential prerequisite to forms of "placemaking" that nurture a wide array of activities for specific sexual minorities and respective networks. Street activism to fight homophobic attacks, as part of broader processes of community formation, goes far back in Western social traditions—at least to the urban centres of the Renaissance.[3]

What is "democratic" gay space in a time of suspect democracies that often involve substantial coercion by state apparatus and manipulation by the media? It is the freedom to engage in social intercourse that is taken for granted by the heterosexual citizen.

Hierarchical Homosexual Space	Democratic Gay Male Space
Identity hidden	Identity visible
Evidence of sexually related contact hidden	Evidence of sexual contact obvious
Rules within gay male networks made by a singular élite	Rules and organizational structure set by multiple groups through open discussion

Change did not happen overnight, nor were gains won without prolonged struggles that still continue. A key turning point in the Toronto gay community's taking of public space occurred in the two or three years following a massive raid on all the city's gay steam baths on February 5, 1981. Hundreds of gay men were arrested and charged. Contrary to the expectations of the authorities, the decision was taken to fight back by all means necessary, and the attack helped the Toronto gay and lesbian communities coalesce as we now know them. In Toronto the defining moment of gay male public space, as well as the lesbian sites which increasingly overlap with it, was not the Stonewall riots in New York City in 1969, but the cohesion that emerged in response to the 1981 bathhouse raids.[4] The enclaves that formed during and since the 1981–83 demonstrations bear the signature of both the specific resistance of those years and traces of the earlier and only-partially-outmoded strategies of communality, mutual protection, and identity construction.

The common chant of those 1981 demonstrations was "no more shit." The associated rage contributed to a sort of gay cultural and political "template" for a range of more purposeful acts that expanded public, communal, and residential gay presence in Toronto. In this essay I unravel the key social and cultural currents that led to the placemaking that created the fabric of downtown Toronto. Gay male communities emerged in public spaces from secretive and highly structured networks, which were often relegated to less contested sites. Several types of movements and alliances were necessary before more purposeful placemaking was possible. In chronicling the progression of these, I question the mystique around Stonewall as has George Chauncey.[5] Riots and the once fashionable rhetoric of Gay Liberation alone did not create public areas where sexual minorities could be safer and relatively more open about themselves and their desires. Instead, more complex demographic, cultural, institutional, economic, and political factors gelled to allow the formation of neighbourhoods that embody archaeologies of past social relations. Every public place is part artifact and part a "cleaned slate" for new social relations. This contradiction and the ambiguity that it produces have become synonymous with (postmodern) public places. And this

Lobby of the Kind Edward Hotel, Toronto, 1952. The lobby and the adjoining bar were important pre-decriminalization cruising spots, with cruising at its peak from 1948 to 1958. Courtesy of the City of Toronto Archives, Gilbert Milne Collection.

element of conflict, discontent, and assertion around and experienced by sexual minorities has become an almost essential ingredient of life in urban cores of large North American and European cities, as well as in the less repressive and impoverished zones of Third World cities.

The structure of this essay embodies both a chronicle of social changes in the gay male community of Toronto[6] since World War II and a progression across various strategic types of gay male outdoor space. My research was a series of interviews[7] with a group of gay men, primarily white, Canada-born, native English-speakers.[8] I describe cruising before 1969, when homosexual acts were highly illegal[9] and access to indoor spaces for contact was very limited. The essay's discussion moves to the initial decriminalization period,[10] which has often been deceptively referred to as "after Stonewall," and then moves to the 1981 raids and the subsequent formation in Toronto of the more stable and less contested gay male outdoor space that we know today—such as that along Church Street and not far from Yonge Street.

Mental Maps as Gay Archaeology

Before World War II a gay man's freehand mental map of Toronto places for recognition and contact would begin on Yonge Street. Then it would move on to the extensive ravines that have retained a fairly wild state, to the downtown parks, to the beaches on Toronto Island[11] and the eastern end of the city on Lake Ontario, and to several well-defined outdoor hustling locations. By the 1950s discreet gay bars near Yonge Street would start to appear on this mental map, as would the slender beginnings of the gay ghetto—in the form of indoor businesses such as gay steam baths, for example. There was also the once-a-year street spectacle of the Hallowe'en drag.[12] In the post-Stonewall 1970s, aboveground gay businesses and service organizations became visible and part of the off-Yonge Street streetscape.[13] My associates and I interviewed over forty older gay men from Toronto, allowing maximum latitude in recording their recollections. In the following sections, I excerpt these recollections for interviews about "gay space." I use "gay space" rather than "queer space," because no lesbians or bisexuals were interviewed. It is important to note that many changes have taken place in gay men's use of public space since Stonewall, but also important to state that many other elements have remained constant.

Cruising as Placemaking

Casual street cruising has been with us since ancient times. The extent, functions, and outcomes have changed with particular sites, communities, and social climates. Gay cruising has its own logic that new members have had to learn. Cruising in Canadian cities such as Toronto when homosexuality was illegal played many crucial roles in the lives of gay men—much more than just for casual pleasure. Cruising was a way to gain

The Pearson Hotel, Toronto Island. For decades, large numbers of gay couples (mostly closeted) stayed in this hotel. Courtesy of the City of Toronto Archives, Toronto Island Collection.

entrance into networks that could provide the socialization—through a system of younger protégés and older mentors, often referred to as "queens"—necessary for a sexually active person to survive in a hostile world. This was the initial "transaction" that created the basis for gay space in Toronto, and it is significant to note that the system functioned as much for socialization as for leading to sex. The secrecy of the closet was necessary for network-building until the late 1960s, when the objective conditions allowed the emergence of an aboveground community.

If a person was lucky, his furtive homosexuality could be given access to indoor social contact. One of my informants, speaking of the period at the close of World War II, reported that "young people didn't have apartments, everybody lived at home," whereas "older gay people had soirées, Sunday tea sort of thing, that you went to, and you made contact." Another informant reported that in the 1950s—in addition to large parties at private houses—there were dinners, card parties, and weekends at cottages. It would be difficult to exaggerate the importance of these social occasions for a community under siege. These were, for example, the only venues where gay men could safely appear in drag. But for most gay men who were young or new in town or not desirable for such gatherings, homosexuality—the acts, identities, and culture—was placed in one zone of social discourse: the public anonymity of the street and the park.

The Street

Cruising is a deceptively simple social transaction. For Fred, who came out into the Toronto gay scene in 1917, cruising did not involve a high level of communication and exchange.[14]

> John Grube: How did you guys meet? I mean it must have been awfully hard to meet other gay people, wasn't it?
>
> Fred: Well, you usually met them, there were no bars, anything like that, you usually passed them on Yonge Street, and you stop and look in a window there, and he'd stop and look in a window farther up the street, and the first thing you know, you're both looking in the same window!

As the two men walked off together, straight passersby would be totally unaware that a connection had been made. Gay men and their activities were invisible. In fact that was a condition of survival—space was straight. Gay men could use it only if they and their behaviour appeared normal.

The Ravines with Green Space

In Toronto the nocturnal use of ravines and parks was a crucial element in pre-Stonewall gay communities. Such "open space" was not only a place for sex but also for touching base with other members of the community. Ravines are slightly different from parks as sites. They have steep slopes on either side and dense underbrush, ideal for completing sexual intercourse and difficult for straights to penetrate at night. City parks, which tend to be flat and have more of a plan—with flowerbeds, ornamental trees, and the like—are great for initial contacts but less likely to accommodate completed sex acts. Clarence Barnes, a great frequenter of ravines long before Stonewall, explained why he chose to make out late at night in Toronto's David Balfour ravine:[16]

David Balfour Park, one of the most heavily cruised ravines in Toronto.[15]

> The hundreds of gay men who visit it each seasonable night of the year do so because it is heaven, a lovely and democratic place to be. You go there, not because you are trying to find Mr. Right, but to get as much sex as you can handle. Orgies easily start and continue with changing personnel. . . . It is really quite civilized.

> Nearly complete silence is observed—except for "thank you" at the end . . . The exchange medium is touching and sex. You don't become raucous, wild, and woolly. The rule is to be well-behaved, the code is silence. . . .
>
> I would arrive on my bicycle, then take off all my underwear . . . depending on the weather, I would put on very cut-off shorts or tight-fitting overalls, then begin cruising around slowly—strolling, promenading. You tend to stray off, and not to move fast.

Barnes had a pleasant home where he took sex partners he met on the street or in the park, but he *chose* sometimes to have sex in the ravine.

> It is a holy spot for gay men, where you can always find someone—a beautiful spot from early spring, on a summer's night, and well into the autumn, the sort of place cruising has been going on since time began.

There were of course dangers—the police and gay-bashers. Corpses of gay men stabbed to death turn up there from time to time—crimes the authorities are not likely to investigate too thoroughly. Gay men, like many other groups, have not yet entirely succeeded in making their community and its folkways legitimate.

City Parks

City parks were not only a well-used place to connect with potential sex partners; they could lead to a sponsored entry into the gay social life of the time. Bernie, now a highly successful, retired businessman, started life in a poor Jewish immigrant family. At fourteen he was cruising parks and ravines for sex, but as he grew older he wanted more. He wanted an entry into the gay social life he observed from a distance. A downtown park, Allan Gardens, provided the space for this connection.

> Bernie: Paul Almond had a lover called Bruce Williams who was sort of a Greek god type, beautiful features . . .
>
> John Grube: This would be about 1938?
>
> B: Yes, 1938 or 1939, and I happened to see him out in one of the parks sunning himself. . . . I walked over to him and said "You must be Bruce Williams," and he said, "How would you know about me?" So I says "Well, you're so beautiful and everybody knows about you," which touched his ego of course, and he sat down and we became very good friends. We talked that time and I said "I'm on the outside of all this and I see what's happening because sometimes I stand in front. . . . I see all

Allan Gardens, a major Toronto cruising area since at least 1840. Today the drug trade drives out much of the cruising.

> these people going in, and here, I'm on the outside." So Bruce says, "Well, why don't you come to a party that we're having?" and I did.

At this point Bernie's social life took off, and he never looked back, but acknowledges that it all started in the democratic environment of the gay cruising area of a public park, in broad daylight, where casual social interaction was possible. This was not the behaviour code of the wooded ravine at midnight, with its silent orgies.

Not that completed sex couldn't take place in parks after sundown. Historically some gay men have always challenged the tight control of the straight majority with outrageous behaviour. Phil's account of a completed sexual encounter in a public park after nightfall clearly contains something of this anarchic gay challenge to the established order. The following encounter took place on the grounds of the Ontario Provincial Legislature, the province's "Parliament Buildings," which at the time was a major site of conservative Canadian politics.

> The bandshell was still there in the park, and it was a late summer night, August probably, and I was in the park, and the park was fairly active and then this thunderstorm broke out and it was a lulu, thunder, lightening, deluge, and everybody ran right out of the park for shelter, cars, whatever, and I ran up into the bandshell, which was an empty bandshell, right? And I stayed there because I loved storms, love to see nature in its

> violence, always wanted to see a volcano erupt, but the thing continued and people were actually gone, they weren't just hiding out, they'd moved, gone away, called the park quits . . . and while this was going on, some car pulled up on Queen's Park Crescent there, and a guy came out with a raincoat thrown over his shoulders, right into the park and up into the bandshell, he was a little older than I was, maybe five years, and we got talking about it, and he loved storms and I loved storms, and he got closer and closer and closer, and we began to feel each other up, eventually we ended up taking all our clothes off, and rolling around and having wild sex, in the bandshell while the elements—it was like something out of *King Lear*—I expected any minute the lightening to go ZAP! And we enjoyed ourselves so much, and of course the rain had swept in and we were all wet, and all those soggy clothes to put on! But it was joyous. It's one of the joyous things that I remember, I love wild, spontaneous moments like that where, you know, two people or more just really, something just happens, and it just goes crazy, and it's wild and everybody enjoys themselves, and there's just a little bit of a laugh about it.

Barry started life years ago in a prosperous Jewish family in Forest Hill. From age eleven his urge to have sex with other males motivated him to slip out of the house in the middle of the night, have sex in the David Balfour ravine, and sneak back into his

The Queen's Park bandstand, north of the Ontario legislature building, Toronto, 1952. Courtesy of the Metropolitan Toronto Research Library, J. V. Salmon Collection.

bedroom before his parents got up. A significant percentage of the men we interviewed had started having sex in their early teens with much older strangers encountered in public space. Because of the inherent danger to the older party, it is sometimes hard for a boy in his early teens to make out. This is Barry's account:

> Yeah, I met a man in a bush and before we had sex we chatted, and he wanted to know who, why I was in the park at such an hour, it was about two o'clock in the morning, where my parents were, and what was going on, and I basically said to him, well, look, I'm here to have sex, I'm not here to discuss my parents or why I'm here, I'd rather do something. . . . He took me home, we fucked. . . . He thoroughly enjoyed the sex, *I* thoroughly enjoyed the sex.

Hustler Streets

Although it is contrary to all the received wisdom, none of the men who had started off their gay sexual careers really young, as Barry did, seem to have suffered in later life from doing so. They faced the usual problems of growing up, earning a living, and being gay in a straight universe. Many men also seem to have turned casually to prostitution from time to time when younger, again without any specific ill effects that we could detect. Barry did so at fourteen, when he began to have difficulties with his Orthodox Jewish family. There were clear and defined uses of space. The most desirable location for hustling was Grosvenor Street just off Yonge, but you had to earn your right to work there:

> John Grube: How did you actually at fourteen establish your *droit de cité*?
>
> Barry: By being aggressive.
>
> JG: Give me an illustration.
>
> B: My first couple of nights on Grosvenor Street I was told, like, to get lost. And my reply was "You get lost! I'm here to make money, I know exactly what I'm doing," so the introduction was immediate, I had to fight my way in, OK? The problem with the street-organized trade at that point was to chase off the "carp," which was someone who was giving sex for free. . . . I knew all the guys that worked there, and I just announced, "There's a carp back there in the street! We got to get rid of him," and six guys were marching down there and approaching him and saying, "This is where we work."

As in any other trade or profession, there was an initiation, a set of tests to pass before you were admitted to the professional group.

> B: If you want to hustle, then you, like, get out on to Yonge Street where the work is really bad and getting busted is real easy. You work your way *onto* Grosvenor Street, you know, by showing up really early, in the evening, by working really shitty nights when there was nobody around, I mean that's how you *earned* your right to be on Grosvenor Street, at that point. I mean it was a transient business for sure but it had, for the year that I spent there, it had a very strong sense of community.
>
> JG: Can you think of an incident where they tapped you on the shoulder and said something like, "You're now a member of Skull & Bones," like they would at Yale or something?
>
> B: The first time I actually felt I was *not* going to get the shit kicked out of me was showing up early in the afternoon, and staking out a piece of Grosvenor Street . . . making a clear decision that tonight I'm spending the evening right here. And I'm going to work. And at that point most of the regular guys knew who I was, they had seen me, and they had chased me away, and that evening I didn't get chased away. The guys watched me work, knew that I was actually cash trade, you know, that I was not giving it away, that I was not going to jeopardize prices or anything like that. . . . It's not that consistent a community, it's possible to get in.

While cruising was one of the few outlets for homoerotic contact well into the 1960s, the state—primarily through the city police—was relentless in its attacks on "queers." This destabilization of gay male activity generally took place, almost as a lesson from the state, in well-known cruising areas. George Hislop, a well-known Toronto activist, recalls a typical incident from 1954.

> I was out walking in the park, I wasn't working and there's a pavilion in the middle of the park. . . . This was just an empty pavilion but the washrooms were open and they were typically smelly washrooms of the day, and they had been entrapping people there, and a friend of mine had been entrapped there, so I had cruised the place and . . . I went into the washroom and came out. Later I came back and a man came out as I was going in. He was quite attractive, so I walked in, then he came back in, and this other plainclothes officer, huge man, no shoes on, came out of this doorway which led to a kitchen and just picked me up and smashed me in the face, called me "queer" and everything. The other man, they played the good guy, bad guy, and the other guy was writing notes, and all this stuff, but I was hurt badly. They almost broke my nose, it was very badly bruised, and they had nothing on me. . . . They told me to stay out

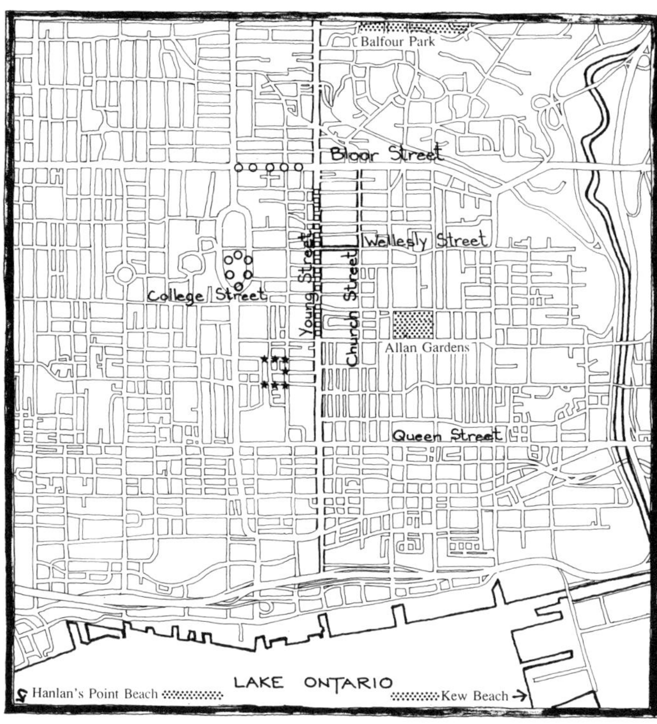

Gay male use of public space: 1960.

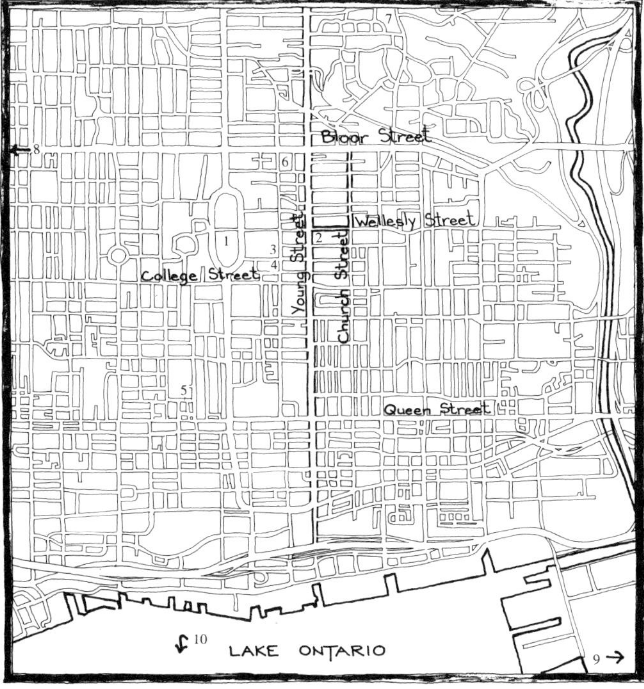

Gay male use of public space: 1974.

> of the park and all that stuff. The one man, the one I followed in, now holds high office in the Ontario Provincial Police. . . .

In Toronto homosexual morals charges were usually dealt with by either knuckling under to humiliating plea-bargaining, a cash bribe—sometimes on the spot—or intervention through straight networks. As far back as 1840, political figures accused of sodomy were disgraced for life and removed from politics, but there were no humiliating public trials.

Repression Through Design

When Queen's Park and Hanlan's Point became well-known gay spaces, the bushes were cut down. When St. Joseph Street and Philosopher's Walk became popular cruising spots, social "morality lights" were installed. The whole Central Island community in Lake Ontario, in earlier decades one of the first identifiable gay neighbourhoods in the city, was bulldozed into sterile parkland. The "development" forces around Lake Ontario beaches have been carefully manipulated to discourage nudity and the presence of gay men.[17]

Wherever the authorities suspect nocturnal gay activity, whether in parks or ravines, they chop down the underbrush and install "morality lights," as happened in a ravine whose steep banks were originally created by the Don River. Just when the authorities had succeeded in stamping out gay activity in the Don Valley, 1990s ecologists started a move to "green" the Don, to restore the original course and vegetation of the riverbed. When the trees and bushes started to spring up, earlier flora and fauna returned, including gay men cruising!

Public space in Toronto has been, in effect, a battleground between the forces of homophobia and the state's apparatus for regulating sexual behaviour and the forces for gay communality and coalition building.

The Environmental Impacts of Gay Liberation

Gay Liberation provided a vague ideological framework for appreciating the importance of groups and crowds in public space—a recognition that there is an inevitable impact and concretization of gay sex. In this period people who were once terrified of sharing personal details with anonymous sex partners for fear of being exposed began talking more openly[18]—allowing for more peer learning and support—and in this way social options were expanded.

What seems to have happened regarding gay space in Toronto is that, prior to 1969 or so, the use of public space by gay men was always surreptitious; but after 1969, an aboveground straight-modelled gay community began to emerge alongside the traditional one. The two communities are symbolized by the two polar coordinates of the gay year: Hallowe'en and Pride Day. Hallowe'en has always been the one

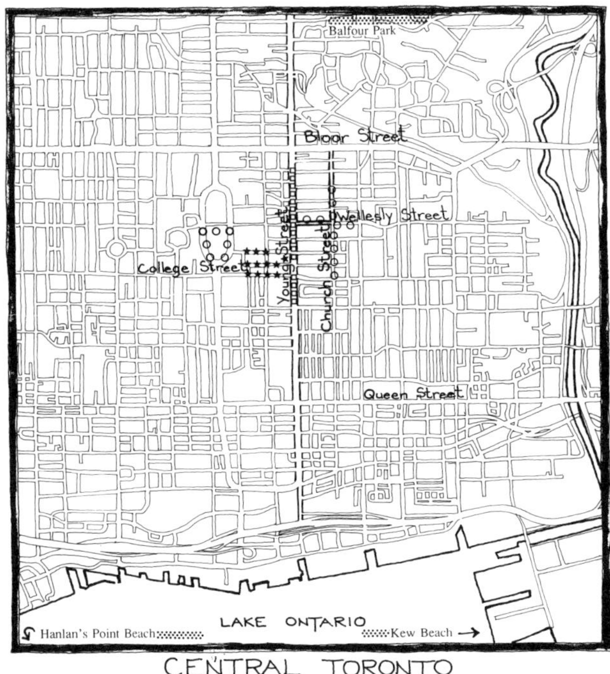

Gay male use of public space: 1980.

straight festival where drag queens can camp it up under the guise of "costume parties." It's the Protestant equivalent of the Latin carnival. In earlier times—the 1950s, for example—drag queens would line up on Yonge Street to enter the Parkside Tavern. There might be jeers and missiles from the hostile straight crowd, and a newspaper photographer or two might record it all, but the drag queens insisted on their right to use Yonge Street on that particular night and the police generally complied.

While Hallowe'en high jinks look back to our underground past, Pride Day celebrates our aboveground progress since Stonewall, as well as our hopes for the future. Hence Pride Day has been open, public, and political. On that day we own the streets, the parks, the public transit system. We wear Gay Pride buttons. We salute each other in our tens of thousands. Straight sympathizers take part. Once again the police generally recognize our right to these spaces for that day; whole sections of the "gay ghetto," on Church Street one block over from Yonge Street are blocked off from traffic. For that day, the gay use of public space is legitimate.

The Street Demonstrations of 1981[19]

> It was the night the mainstreet of Canada's largest city belonged to us.
>
> —Gerald Hannon[20]

> It looks like we finally may be getting something we've been saying we've had for the last ten years.
>
> —Hannon et al.[21]

In the 1970s aboveground organizing activities by both radicals and moderates led to increased police repression in spite of the partial decriminalization of 1969. Sexual activities in public places, including bathhouses, remained vulnerable to various archaic laws; and there were several raids in the 1970s, most notably on December 9, 1979.[22] In the same year there was intensified resistance by men who were attacked or actually charged in "indecency busts" in parks.[23] The culmination of the gay activist-police conflict came on the evening of February 4, 1981, when police raided every gay bathhouse in Toronto, and every individual present was charged as being either a "bawdyhouse keeper" or a "found-in." The next day, leaders of the organized gay community met and decided, as one said, that "this is our Stonewall," that a strong and immediate response was imperative. A demonstration was scheduled for the night of February 6, at 11 P.M. Organizers hoped to attract two hundred demonstrators. To their amazement, five thousand people, mostly gay men and lesbians, showed up. The speeches thrilled the crowd, which marched as directed, and against police wishes, up Yonge Street.

By 1980 or so, the structure of Toronto's gay community had changed from a large underground group of intersecting networks, where the mentor/protégé couple was the basic structural unit, to an aboveground straight-modelled society with its own newspaper, charitable organizations, recreation clubs, and most other characteristics of an ethnic group. The forces of order felt they had to act, to break up and destabilize the growing legitimacy of this society. The historical significance of the police action is that instead of harassing individual gay men, here and there, mostly in well-known gay space, for the first time the police abused gay men collectively; just as at Sheridan Square in New York City in June of 1969, the result was a collective response.

The viciousness of these highly coordinated police attacks on the bathhouses was exceptional. When the police attacked, it took a while for Bob Chambers to figure out what was happening. He was smoking peacefully with a sex partner in his cubicle at the Barrack steambath.

> All of a sudden we heard a lot of noise, and voices in the distance. We both stopped talking and, you know, like, what's wrong? What's going on out there? And then we heard this big scuffle, right outside our door, and I figured it was a fight, I thought hoods had broken in, or a fight between you know, people coming to the Barracks . . . and then I heard the pounding on the door with basically just voices, "Hey, open up," this kind of thing, no admission of "This is the police, open up," you know . . .

I heard no broken glass, it sounded more like wood, and then the door just flew right open and then these two men just came right in, and I was pushed immediately up to the left corner without any admission and then they just said, "It's a raid," and they also didn't identify themselves then . . . and they were in civilian clothes wearing blue windbreakers, with Sears labels on them . . . and I was pushed so close my nose hit the wall, because as you know it's rather uneven brickwork, and my knees had abrasions on them, my nose bled from a cut, of which there is still a scar today . . . and then I heard a lot of scuffling in the halls, and it looked as though the people who were under so-called arrest, were being led to the steam area, so gradually they emptied the room . . . we heard the so-called police calling to one another, and a few of them would taunt the inmates, they would say "Get your hands up against the wall," they would call such comments as "Well, it's too bad these steam or shower vents aren't hooked up to gas," and then another comment was "Well, if these guys run, we can certainly get them for evading police."

A police assault of this scale was a relatively new and untested tactic in Toronto, where two centuries of a "hear no evil, see no evil" policy had prevented the massive police bar raids common in some U.S. cities. By the time of the 1981 raids, a key development was that most Toronto gay men, including most arrested that night, had come to see themselves as full citizens entitled to protection by the police. Coming at a time when the general population had declining patience with police behaviour, the raids came off as fascist, opportunist, and inept. To the emergent citizen-consumer of Toronto—only some of whom were gay men—the obvious bad management in the attack fueled a rage that was linked to a general frustration with the declining competence of police and provincial officials.[24]

The gay bathhouse has been an authentic institution of the gay community for over a century, so the police attack brought out thousands, not hundreds, of demonstrators. The injustice of the police intrusion on bathhouses—in terms of transactions of space, money, and power—suggests why so many people were finally galvanized into action. The police raids were on territory that normally required fairly expensive admission costs and into space that was essentially "private,"[25] as in commercial, and certainly in terms of actions by two or more consenting adults. The gay male community was paying high prices while often feeling ripped-off; the assumption was that the higher prices bought a sort of privatization in the communal but certainly not "public" space in the interiors of these bathhouses. In the post–World War II period, these higher prices went, in part, to pay off police. But the emerging consumer consciousness of the time, as well as Gay Liberation theory with its ambivalent perspectives on "gay ghettos," destabilized the earlier détente during yet another period of social reaction and police repression. For more conservative gay men, the canon—the unspoken deal of paying more for temporary private space in gay public space—was shattered, and more radical elements channeled the subsequent energy into appropriating public space. In the minds of many, the result was the basis for consciously constructing the gay commercial neighbourhood on Church. As territory, rather than zone of discard, the Yonge Street commercial area represents significant parallel symbols of power, public life, and consumerism.

Ordinary gay men with no previous political consciousness were prepared to defend their community, while members of the organized gay community began to realize that there was a gay world out there, honeycombed with networks they could now contact. The temporary fusion of these two social forces released a tremendous surge of energy in the years after 1981. The Right to Privacy Committee, set up to defend found-ins in a previous bath raid, was reorganized, and it raised large sums of money for those prepared to plead non-guilty. In the end almost 90 percent were acquitted. In the gay male community the tradition to plead guilty was so strong that the Committee had to retrain lawyers to fight this type of case to the end.

In the first demonstration in 1981, thousands of gay men and their allies turned up on Yonge Street to demonstrate and march on the Parliament Buildings a few blocks away. Strong powerful street demonstrations followed in the next two years. Sometimes they were marked by anger, sometimes by disco dancing to a sound truck—February can be extremely cold in these parts of Canada. The police tried to reroute the march, to get it onto some side street, which is a standard police tactic. But the gay community insisted on Yonge Street, on the most public and visible presence possible. Those who took part in the demonstrations experienced a surge of solidarity they will never entirely forget. They are what I think of as the Class of '81. One of the older men I interviewed—a cautious lifelong member of the Progressive Conservative Party, which had fought decriminalization in 1969—felt impelled to take part in the first Yonge Street demonstration he heard about on the radio. He felt he had waited his entire life for that moment, a moment when gay men could repossess the public space denied them for so long.

Bob Gallagher acted as the chief marshall for many demonstrations. He described his earlier experiences in the United States, which

> were mostly involved with anti-war movements and a few ecology and antinuclear movements, and it seems to me that the period between, say, 1970 and 1973, was important for me in terms of the skills I learned which I later used for the gay activities in Toronto. And this was around demonstrations, around marshalling, around sit-ins, and that, because I was involved with, as I mentioned, the moratorium, which I believe was 1970 in Washington, D.C. . . . I don't know how many workshops I sat through, and some of which I led during that time period, in how to publicize a demonstration, how to run one, what kind of behaviour will

> cause retribution from the police. It was straightforward learning, technical training for me at that point, and I think that, as a matter of fact there's no doubt, it's very explicit, my activities in the bathhouse raids and the post bathhouse raids, here in Toronto. I mean I was conscious of having had a certain amount of technical training that I thought I could put to use.

Like so many other individuals caught up in the that struggle, Bob felt as the first demonstration started that "[I] hadn't really ever until that moment—I think—ever been so strikingly aware that it was my community, that it was a personal commitment as well as a political commitment, and that community was very important in my life."

The demonstrations went on from 1981 until 1983, each time involving thousands of gay men, lesbians, and their allies from various community and Left groups. Each demonstration required careful and intricate negotiations with the police. Nowhere was the influence of such movements on recent gay organizing more vividly illustrated; on the other hand, the gay community itself contributed numbers and a clandestine jungle telegraph. Some older and traditional gays gave grudging admiration to the radicals—even in the form of financial support. The numbers of people involved forced both the police and politicians to pay attention.

The Toronto gay community was changed permanently by this fusion. A climate was created for prolonged resistance,[26] and the police stepped up park surveillance and arrests.[27] Significantly, the first Lesbian Pride March was on May 18, 1981,[28] and this claiming of public place was also met with police resistance.[29] There was now an expanded base for organizing social events and, indirectly, funding gay-friendly businesses. For several years after the 1981 raids, the Gay Community Dance Committee was able to hold fund-raising dances attended by over two thousand lesbians and gay men. Well over thirty organizations were involved in the operation of the Dance Committee, collaboratively preparing refreshments, putting up decorations, serving drinks, selling tickets, providing security, and cleaning up.

The protests of the early 1980s were so strong that the police never again attempted to destabilize gay institutions such as bathhouses by mass arrests. In a low-key way, however, the police have continued to harass and arrest gay men in well-known cruising areas. They have again and again harassed Toronto's only gay bookstore, Glad Day. Fifteen years later, the anger and energy generated by the bathhouse raids have died down, and many of the institutions to which this crisis gave birth have simply passed away—particularly with the focus on AIDS treatment and prevention.

Conclusions

Nearly five hundred years ago, a group of young men stood outside a prison in Florence protesting the incarceration of friends whose only crime was enjoying sex with other men. We must learn to understand the implications of such historic gestures of solidarity for activism, placemaking, and neighbourhood formation today. What has changed in the realm of gay male public space in Toronto? Stonewall had no direct effect. Prime Minister Pierre Trudeau's 1969 change in the criminal code had no direct effect. But the police attacks in 1981 and the ensuing concerted community response to them did. From then on Yonge Street[30] and the streets around it belonged to everyone, including openly gay men. And it was only after that time that the gay ghetto, with its bars, terraces, and street cruising, became visible, even flamboyant.

In conclusion,[31] the evidence suggests that the gay community changes, but slowly, and different strata at different speeds. Older forms persist and function (for example, the mentor/protégé couple or entourage) at the same time as different structures are introduced (such as straight-modelled services, sports, and political organizations). Initiation procedures and external relations are still crucial, although the forms have changed. Outdoor and public space remain important for many forms of contact, but the uses of specific sites have diversified and been enriched; through cumulative victories against repression, they no longer provide the only option for contact.

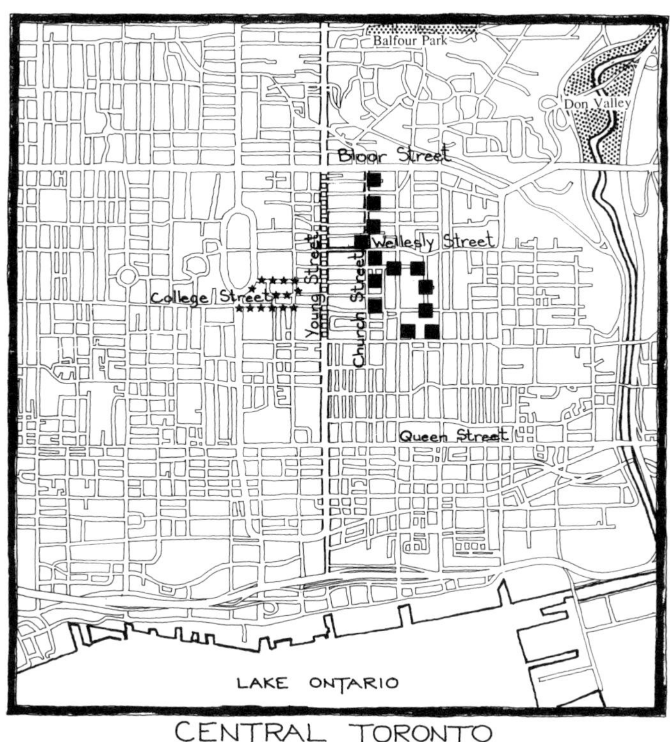

Gay male use of public space: 1995.[32]

From Landmarks to Spaces: Mapping the Territory of a Bisexual Genealogy

Clare Hemmings

I

I have been thinking through the possibilities of theorising bisexuality in and through spaces in the last two years[1] and writing about it in the last year, after I went to the Organizing Sexualities Conference in Amsterdam in June 1994.[2] The conference was organised to coincide with EuroPride 1994. For once, academic and activist worlds did not seem completely at variance. Amsterdam was buzzing; the streets were decked with pink triangles and banners; it was warm. Performances, workshops, dance clubs, academic presentations, all jostled for my attention, were all part of the conference experience. The subtitle of the conference was "Gay and Lesbian Movements since the 1960s." I was the only person giving a paper on bisexuality and—as far as I was aware—the only out bisexual delegate at the conference. Although none of the organisers was actively biphobic, bisexual space—both concrete and theoretical—was not part of the conference format. Unsurprisingly, the only space given to bisexuality as a relevant area of concern was created by my presentation or by specific interventions.

One paper at the conference was on the different kinds of spaces in Amsterdam that mark out a young gay male's identity.[3] In the discussion after the paper, the importance of public spaces—streets, parks, backrooms, and baths—in the formation of a contemporary gay and lesbian[4] identity was tentatively explored. At a certain point one participant turned to me—as the holder of all bisexual wisdom—to ask what and where are bisexual spaces? While I was thinking about it, another delegate answered that perhaps both gay and straight spaces are bisexual spaces. This is true in certain respects. Bisexuals certainly occupy both lesbian or gay and straight spaces and may call one or the other or both "home." One might also highlight the fact that both gay and straight spaces—including bars, clubs, restaurants, and "political" spaces—have been partly formed through the intervention and work of bisexual people as well as gay or straight people. But in this conference discussion about gay male spaces, and in many other more general discussions about "queer" spaces, spaces were being viewed as linked to identity. In that sense, neither gay nor straight spaces could be said to be bisexual spaces per se. A bisexual's identity is never the dominant identity being produced, delineated, or contested in either gay or straight spaces. "Bisexual" may be added on, may be seen as included, but it is never seen as inclusive.

This exchange raised a number of issues for me, issues that I thought about after the conference and am still pondering now. If the conclusion is that bisexual space is not both gay and straight but rather neither gay nor straight, what are the implications for a positive bisexual identity or for bisexual theorising? If bisexual identity is not inclusive but rather always partial, if there are no "bisexual spaces" per se, then how do we represent bisexuality, and what is the relationship between bisexuality and space? This is the quandary that faced me a year ago: a sense of my own identity as bisexual, some temporary bisexual spaces such as conferences and support groups,[5] but few examples of a bisexual culture that could be read through analysis of particular public spaces at particular times. Add to that the lack of much that could be termed "bisexual theory" to provide alternative models or alternative ways of reading predominantly lesbian and gay or straight spaces, and you begin to get a sense of my frustration. The problem of spaces and bisexuality has kept returning to me, has kept presenting itself as a series of questions to ask about bisexual theorising: What is a bisexual space? How do bisexuals negotiate sexual spaces that do not take their name or confirm their identity?

The Amsterdam conference took place more than a year ago. In part, my concern with bisexual spaces arose at that point because of the growth of bisexual writing and bisexual movements in the United Kingdom and the United States. Ten years previously it might not have been possible even to articulate the lack of bisexual spaces to analyse and from which to theorise. Let me backtrack a little. When three influential works on bisexuality were published in the space of the three years between 1975 and 1978—Margaret Mead's often referenced Bisexuality: What's It All About? (1975), Charlotte Wolff's *Bisexuality—a Study* (1977), and Fritz Klein's controversial *The Bisexual Option* (1978)[6]—they broke a virtual silence about bisexuality that had stretched since Kinsey's 1948 findings that two-thirds of American males behaved bisexually.[7]

Before Kinsey, bisexuality was represented in fictional works such as Djuna Barnes's *Nightwood* (1937) or in sexological works such as Wilhelm Stekel's *Bisexual Love* (1934).[8] After the late 1970s bisexuality again almost disappeared as a public subject of discussion.[9] Apart from the occasional article, writing on bisexuality as a viable personal and political concern or choice did not come into the public eye again until the early 1990s. In the last few years in the United States and the United Kingdom, there has been what might be termed an explosion of bisexual writing and more particularly of bisexual anthologies.[10]

The lack of publications in the 1980s does not mean, of course, that no activism around issues of bisexuality was taking place. In fact the steady growth of bisexual groups and local conferences in both the United States and the United Kingdom throughout the 1980s could be said to have been the driving force behind much of the writing in recent anthologies on bisexuality.[11] This increase in writing on bisexuality is heartening, but when I was at the Organizing Sexualities Conference in Amsterdam there was still next to no bisexual theory. When I began working on bisexual theory in 1991 in the United Kingdom, the subject of my master's thesis—bisexuality and feminist theory—would provoke at best blank stares and at worst scarcely veiled hostility. Since then some inroads into mainstream academia have been made. Robyn Ochs's course, "Contexts and Constructs of Identity: Bisexuality," at Tufts Univerity in 1992[12] was the first and only course to date to take bisexuality as its core topic. The year 1992 also saw the publication of Elizabeth Däumer's article in *Hypatia* on bisexuality and lesbian ethics.[13] In the United Kingdom in 1992, a few bisexual writers, researchers, and academics met up at the 11th National Bisexual Conference in Nottingham and formed the national network for research on bisexuality, Bi-Academic Intervention.[14] But it is really only since 1994 that bisexual theorising has emerged as a serious academic field of enquiry in its own right. Two volumes of bisexual theory have been published, one, *Representing Bisexualities*,[15] in the United States and the second, *The Bisexual Imaginary*,[16] in the United Kingdom. In cyberspace, too, bisexual theory has finally come into its own. For example, the use-net group Bisexual Theory (Bithry-L) has been supplemented by other more specific groups such as Bigrrls, which was set up by a group of bisexual feminist activists and researchers.[17] Bisexual writers are also being asked increasingly to submit their work to anthologies that are not specifically bi-focussed, but which consider a bisexual perspective to be a useful and necessary one.[18]

The highpoint of all this new interest in bisexual theorising came in 1995 with the publication of Marjorie Garber's *Vice Versa: Bisexuality and the Eroticism of Everyday Life*.[19] Garber looks at bisexuality as it has been understood mythologically and historically; its role within sexology, psychoanalysis, and psychology; its function in relation to literature, art, and culture; and the farthest reaches of its possible meanings (for example, Is sexual attraction to a grapefruit bisexual attraction?). Garber's reputation was established after the 1992 publication of *Vested Interests*,[20] and the large number of early reviews[21] indicate that *Vice Versa* may create a lasting place for bisexuality on contemporary scholarly agendas.

The question is no longer whether we should be theorizing bisexuality but rather, how. Eve Sedgwick comments:

> Could we ask, about a concept like bisexuality that is gaining new currency, not so much "What does it 'really' mean?" or "Who owns it and are they good or bad?" but "What does it 'do?'—What does it make happen? —What (in the ways that it is being or 'could be' used) does it make easier or harder for people of various kinds to accomplish and think?"[22]

How is bisexuality being used at present? Might it be used differently? Can bisexuality be theorised in ways that do not set it up in opposition to other sexual identities but that move theories about sexual identity forward more generally?

In this discussion I want to experiment with an imaginative and theoretical move from seeing bisexuality as a sexual identity with a conventional linear narrative and history, to looking at bisexuality as it is produced and negotiated in relation to particular queer sexual spaces. Accompanying this move is another one that focuses on bisexual desire, on bisexual bodies and acts, rather than on bisexual identities. Bisexual desire does not always correlate to a self-identified bisexual subject. To limit my analysis to people who identify as bisexual would be to ignore the complex history of many individuals' desire for more than one sex, for more than one gender, or for a changing gender position.[23] By moving away from a focus on identities, I am not advocating an oppositional emphasis on "performance," on a postmodern disembodied "play."[24] Neither am I advocating a move to distance theory from the experience or politics of individuals or communities.[25] Differences can only be acknowledged by attending to specific bodies, to the shared and different histories of particular queer bodies and their relationships with one another, politically, theoretically, and personally. By focusing on bisexual desire rather than identities, I hope to reemphasise that queer desire takes place in particular spaces at particular times and that desire is enacted through our bodies. It is our bodies that pay the price, our bodies that experience the pleasure.

Primarily, my decision to write about bisexuality in terms of spaces, in terms of desire and bodies, is a response (and I hope not merely a reactive one) to prevalent ways of reading, writing, and articulating sexual identities as boundaried, as separable from one another, as separate. Conventionally bisexuality has not been seen as an identity at all, because it is not structurally consistent in terms of gender of object-choice,[26] a gendered subject position,[27] or chronology.[28] Politically bisexuality has also been "denied" legitimacy in terms of sexual identity. Commonly a bisexual woman is understood as "a good example of inauthenticity in a lesbian."[29] Only existing models of sexual identity will do, it seems. As a response to exclusion, most bisexual writers have argued that bisexuality is a valid sexual identity, that it has its own form of consistency, its own coming-out narratives,[30] its own unique culture.

The problem is that, in the courageous effort to grant bisexuality some sense of authenticity, the same identity frameworks are often adopted. Bisexuality becomes separated off as if it were discrete and separate from lesbian and gay or straight identity, from lesbian and gay or straight history. The identity narrative plots the progression of sexuality through identity above all.[31] A bisexual history along these lines sees the emergence of a bisexual identity as more critical than, say, histories of bisexual behaviour and desire that surface unexpectedly without the consciousness of contemporary bisexual meanings. Only a few souls that amount to bisexual tokens and icons can be rescued, those who are created in "our" own image, to show how we progressed to the contemporary moment of awareness or self-identification. Sappho, Oscar Wilde, Virginia Woolf are all being reclaimed as bisexual because of their relationships with more than one biological sex.[32]

Another, relatively recent, way of trying to separate bisexual identity out from other forms of sexual identity is through the use of the term "monosexuality." Bisexuals, both activists and researchers, use the term to distinguish between bisexuals, who desire more than one sex, and "monosexuals," who don't; monosexuals are lesbians, gay men, and heterosexuals. The term has begun to appear, often unquestioned and unclarified, in most recent bisexual publications in the United States, including *Vice Versa, Bi Any Other Name, Closer to Home,* and *Bisexual Politics.*[33] Rather than challenging identity categories, the invention and use of the term monosexual re-emphasises the primary significance of sex and gender in the formulation of a sexual identity, while simultaneously attempting to mark out bisexuals as somehow "beyond" sex and gender. In this rubric bisexuals are uniquely oppressed by monosexism and are therefore politically entitled to their own oppressed minority status and identity. By setting up this division, the differences between lesbians and gay men and heterosexuals in terms of power are elided. The politics of identity fade away.[34] It is precisely the fact that bisexual desire blurs the boundaries between heterosexual, gay, and lesbian desire and blurs the separation of heterosexual, gay, and lesbian communities that marks it out as politically and theoretically important at this time.

To return once again to the experience at the Organizing Sexualities Conference in Amsterdam, to the realisation of the lack of what might be called bisexual spaces, the relationship between bisexuals and other sexual identities and communities is key to beginning to theorise bisexuality. Bisexuals never find themselves represented or reflected wholly in gay, lesbian, or straight spaces or communities.[35] We may be part of heterosexual culture in terms of access through a partner and of privilege, however temporary or illusory. We may also be part of lesbian and gay culture, again in terms of relationships and politics. Our histories may be within both heterosexual and gay and lesbian cultures, sometimes sequentially, and sometimes simultaneously. Often it is not our own sexuality that grants us access to a particular community but that of our partner(s) and friends.[36]

Because of bisexual presence—sometimes overt and sometimes not—in what are assumed to be gay, lesbian, or straight spaces, bisexual history is partly lesbian and gay history, and vice versa. Bisexuals are not outside lesbian and gay movements and spaces, banging on the door trying to get in. Bisexuals are already there, are already part of what shapes the particular spaces where sexual identity is grounded, determined, and enacted.[37] For all of us whose sexual behaviour and acts mark us out as "other" to mainstream heterosexual culture, we are closer to one another than we might like to think—even though that closeness is not always comfortable. We share spaces and lives, dance, tred on one another's toes, lose ourselves in each other, find ourselves, cruise, talk, move, eat, mourn. But some of those bodies that I dance, cruise, and fight with write bodies of theory that ask if I should be allowed to share, "that space where I sweated with you, showed fear with you." They are theories that reinscribe sex-gender-sexuality connections and ideas of identity in ways that do not allow me to recognise myself, not even in part.

Let me be clear that I do not think that identity narratives are a "bad" thing, as such. Narratives are what enable us sexual "perverts" to make sense of ourselves in a hostile world. In fact my need for this "re-imagining" is precisely because there is a lack of a clear bisexual narrative, a lack of spaces where my sexuality is "read as" bisexual. We need stories—desperately. My purpose here is to consider ways that bisexual stories and histories can be written that emphasise that familiar sense of partiality that bisexuals commonly experience, rather than looking for narratives that emphasise only individual and community consistency and identity. Bisexual identity narratives and the reclaiming of a unique history serve an important purpose, but they do not make sense of the discontinuities and misrepresentations that also make up my life and are part of bisexual history. If I tell my own past as internally consistent (I always knew I was bisexual; I always found both men and women attractive; once I came out as bisexual I found my identity and community that had always been there) that tells part of the story. But the time I have spent in the lesbian community, my three years as a lesbian separatist, the moments where I am "read as" something else in the present, the always partial sense of "homecoming"—these things also make up my sense of self as bisexual—determine what it means to me to be bisexual, not just whether or not I am bisexual. These experiences are as much a part of my experience of self-identifying as bisexual as is my desiring men and women.

The overlaps between different sexual communities are always going to be an important part of the history of bisexuality. I want to do justice to our histories of being closeted, of exclusion, of misrecognition, or of desire accepted and rejected, as much as I want to be proud of out, visible bisexual identities and communities now. Only a genealogy that focuses on those contradictions can explain where we are now. A chronological history of bisexual identity ends up reading like the coming-out narrative of self that seeks to release or reveal the "true" bisexual story at the expense of our desires, our commitments, both political and personal, and our very bodies. To focus on bisexual desire, on spaces where that desire plays out, is one way to begin documenting that complexity. My desire is to "re-member" a genealogy of bisexuality, not through the lens of a distant past but through the perception of a complex present. I seek to pinpoint the formation of sexual spaces by making the margins of bisexuality the main focus, which does not require other discourses being phased out or being made out of focus. I want to re-member the margins and their relation to the centre and to one another. In that sense I am re-membering a genealogy that already exists in the present, in my body, and in my body's relationship to other bodies.

II

> [A]n individual's perception of a landscape changes with the experience of moving through it. It is less obvious but equally true that an apparently

> unified landscape may actually be composed of several fragmentary ones, some sharing common elements of the larger assemblage. Indeed this may be the only way to make sense of certain landscapes.
>
> —D. Upton[38]

For the purposes of this essay I use the notion of space in a number of different ways. Firstly, I am referring to geographically concrete spaces, such as bars, clubs, restaurants, urban/rural areas, individual living spaces, and so on. Secondly, I am referring to what might be called "spaces of articulation." By this I mean the scope and range of meanings that concrete spaces have outside their specific geographical confines, as well as the effect that those meanings have on other spaces. For example, a lesbian and gay culture or subculture may be built up around specific bars and clubs primarily in cities or towns, but the meaning of those spaces within discourses of sexuality will often extend beyond those walls to create a larger sense of "lesbian and gay culture." Lesbian and gay spaces of articulation can also be produced, changed, and discussed in other concrete spaces that may have no direct relation to concrete lesbian and gay spaces per se. Feminists, who may or may not be lesbian, who may or may not occupy lesbian S/M cultural spaces, have discussed, negotiated, and affected the issue of lesbian S/M, but not exclusively in lesbian spaces. Thirdly, I am interested in "performative space," by which I mean temporary spaces where relationships occur between members of the same and different communities, often spontaneously, as well as the new spaces that are created within and outside those relationships. These spaces are, if you like, experiential ones that are formed and negotiated by lovers and friends, which may have an influence on the formation and meanings of larger sexual spaces.

Of course those three senses of space are not discrete. In most cases elements of all three uses are combined. In the rest of this paper I look at some examples of how bisexuality plays out in particular spaces—mixed gay and straight spaces, women-only space, bisexual conference space, lesbian and gay space. My aim is to see whether and how bisexuality might be theorised through those spaces, not as separate and not as a discrete identity, but as one part, a very important part, of queer space and queer meaning.

A Bi Place to Be? A Place to be Bi?
The North Star, Northampton, Massachusetts

The North Star bar and dance club formerly of Northampton, Massachusetts (it is now The Grotto), is one of the main focal points for queer social interaction in a town known in the popular press as "lesbianville."[39] This lesbian-owned bar is located on the corner of Green Street, at the top of Main Street and close to Smith College. Inside, the bar is on the right and a dance space and a pool area slightly raised and next to the dance floor, are on the left. The North Star Seafood Restaurant and Bar (the restaurant closed in early 1995) has provided a venue for lesbian performance, music, and workshops on anything from teaching to sales management since 1989. The North Star is open more or less daily in the afternoons and evenings, offering weekly special events such as Latin music evenings, with Latin music dance class in the early evening. Friday and Saturday nights are club nights, Friday for eighteen and over. The music is eighties and nineties bop, with the usual smattering of seventies favourites. Although the North Star is lesbian-owned and known as a lesbian bar, it has a wide clientele of nonlesbians including the growing gay male population of Northampton, trendy straight people who like the music and the ambience, bisexuals, and older straight men who appear to turn up by accident or for whom the North Star is the nearest local bar.

Arriving at the North Star on a Saturday night around 11:30 P.M. (it's open until 1 A.M.) a straight doorman takes your $4. The bar is jam-packed, two people deep. The barwomen are curt and overworked. The place is busy, but not so busy that you can't look or move around. The club is on the small side, low lighting but not gloomy. The majority of the men, who are mostly gay in style, stand around in the space between the bar and the dance floor; some are dancing, and these men are mostly in their early twenties or so. The women are spread out over the whole club. The pool area is dominated by butches who are mostly young. But some are older women, probably in their forties, who shoot pool or lean nonchalantly against the walls, drinking bottled beer and smoking, looking at the women dancing, but not really cruising, certainly not hard cruising. Mostly, men talk and dance with other men; women talk and dance with other women. Some men and women talk and dance together—friends, lovers, gay, lesbian, straight, or bi? Butch and femme is common, particularly among the older women, though not exclusively. The predominant style is casual—there are no leather men or dykes—though some femmes are high femme, and some of the butches (if they are butches) are cross-dressed.[40] A lot of people know one another—the atmosphere is intimate and friendly.

It seems that at the North Star people from different communities with different identities coexist fairly easily. Because the club is so small and because Northampton does not have much to offer in the way of places to socialise past midnight, people make room for one another. It appears that everyone has their own piece of territory. But with such mixing, misrecognition and blurring of the boundaries also occurs. Does this mixing of straight and queer make this a bisexual space? Some of the dynamics at the North Star relating to this question can be partially illustrated through the following:

> A friend of mine, Jane, goes to the North Star fairly regularly. She is a lesbian: she identifies as femme, and presents as high femme. She is white

North Star Bar, Northampton, Massachusetts.

and middle class, in her late twenties. Most of her friends are gay men, and she sometimes goes to the North Star with them at the weekend. Jane is not a "scene dyke"; and so is not well-known within the lesbian community. Unless people know otherwise she is assumed to be straight more often than not. At the North Star, dancing with her gay male friends, Jane is assumed to be a straight "fag hag," comfortable in queer space, but not queer. Were Jane to be dancing or talking with a butch, however, she would be more likely read as femme.[41] Interestingly, when Jane and I go to the North Star together, Jane gets read more easily as femme, by association with me, because I am more easily read as lesbian (my femme style is not as "high"). Jane says that she likes going with me because she is more likely to be cruised by the butches she desires, in other words she is more likely to be read as the femme that she is. Of course, this recognition of Jane relies on a misrecognition of me as lesbian. When with gay men, Jane is misread as straight; when with me, she is read as lesbian. Someone is always misread in order for the straight or lesbian reading. No one is being read as bisexual.

Another friend, Alex, is a Mexican-American gay man in his twenties. He sees a man standing in the corner opposite the pool table area whom he thinks is attractive, and he goes over and asks him to dance. In answer, the man, Chicano and probably in his early twenties, says, "I'm straight."

This was obviously by way of a "No." This incident could be read in a number of ways. The man in the corner might be gay or bisexual, but might not have wanted to dance with Alex. Rather than offend him, it may have seemed easier to be seen to be refusing all men as potential sexual partners ("I'm straight") rather than Alex in particular. He might be straight and assumed that an acceptance of Alex's offer to dance would mean he would be read as gay. He might be a closeted gay or bisexual man, and Alex's approach was too upfront for him. He might have wanted to be the sexual aggressor, equating active roles with heterosexuality, passive roles with (effeminate) homosexuality. Whichever it was, he realised that he was being read as gay or bisexual, and because of the mix of people at the North Star, was able to proclaim his sexual identity as straight.

Myself and my then-lover, Mark, are at the North Star on the same evening. I identify as a bisexual femme; Mark identifies as FTM. Mark is pre-upper or lower body surgery and has only recently begun hormones. He is read as male in heterosexual spaces almost all the time; queer, and particularly lesbian, spaces produce more ambivalence. We are both in our late twenties. We are dancing and are obviously lovers. How are we being read? As a heterosexual couple? As a butch/femme couple? As both? At a certain point, an older butch (we both assumed she was butch, rather than FTM) comes and stands close to us, her pool queue planted firmly on the ground, blocking our way to the pool table. She doesn't say anything, but her attitude is telling us, "This is my territory." Are we threatening to her territory because she sees us as a heterosexual couple who "shouldn't be there," or as an unknown butch/femme couple who might be "on the up"! These different readings are complicated by the fact that we have our own debates about what the nature of our relationship is. I insist that I am not in a heterosexual relationship because I am not heterosexual. But just because I identify as bisexual does this mean that all my relationships are bisexual? If we are in a heterosexual relationship, what does it mean that we may be read as butch/femme, as a lesbian couple?

It would seem that the North Star is a mixed space, one that can accommodate a range of sexual orientations and gender positions. But this does not make it a "bisexual space." One is read as gay, lesbian, or straight, even though those identities can mix. What the North Star does provide, though, amongst other things, is a place to be bisexual, a place where bisexual people can dance and cruise with people of either sex and still feel part of queer culture. The North Star is also a place where desire can find expression, even if that desire is misread as signaling an identity that is other than the identity claimed. In relation to the third scenario, for example, the North Star is a space where my lover's and my desire could be expressed safely even though it may be misread, even though we may misread one another in terms of identity. My point is not that people should not be misreading identity but rather that identity is impossible not to misread. Identity always allows itself to be misread. The three examples of reading and/or presenting identities that I have given highlight the ways in which identity is used to maintain a clear sense of boundaries among recognizable sexual identities. "Straight" is used to create distance from lesbian and gay, either in terms of desire, as in the case of the man my friend Alex asked to dance, or in terms of style and association, as in the case of Jane's high femme style and gay male friends. And the choices in terms of reading my and my lover's desire is as straight or lesbian. It is unlikely that we were being read as bisexual femme and FTM, and it is unlikely that we ever would be.

An analysis of places such as the North Star could be used to highlight the complexity of queer social spaces in a number of ways. Although there may not be any bisexual clubs and bars, it is clear that (1) bisexuals currently occupy space within queer and straight spaces, and (2) that an individual's desire for people of more than one sex (as well as gender) may be expressed in those spaces, even if their identity is "misread." It is not only bisexual desire that gets "misread" as signaling a particular identity. Femme desire, style, and identity, for example, are often also read as "straight," even though femme desire has been a founding part of lesbian culture. Gaps among identity, desire, and style always emerge in sexual spaces and not just when bisexuality is the issue. Those gaps form part of the sexual tension that ebbs and flows in queer sexual spaces—Is she or isn't she? Will she or won't she? It will be interesting to see whether spaces such as the North Star become more "bi-conscious" in the next few years. As bisexuality becomes more visible, as bisexual identity becomes more solidified (if it does), will there be a way of being "read as" bisexual?

Creating New Spaces of Experience

Sexual desire and sexual identity are, as we have seen, not the same thing. But I do not want to suggest that they are totally separate either. One's desire for people of the same sex, in particular, is usually the motivating force behind challenging the notion that one is heterosexual and claiming a different identity—lesbian, gay, or bi, usually—or rejecting identity labels at all. Desire can consolidate a particular sexual identity; it can also disrupt it, or force a reevaluation of that identity. If a lesbian desires men, she may respond in a number of ways. She may decide that her desire is important enough to reevaluate her sexual identity, or she may not. She may act on her desire, or she may not. She may subsequently identify as bisexual or as straight. She may identify as a lesbian who sleeps with men, or she may not consider her desire to be significant enough to change or modify her lesbian identity in any way.

It is not just desire for a different sex than the one your sexual identity would ordinarily suggest that can cause reevaluation of that identity. Desire for someone whose sexual identity is different from yours may also provoke a reexamination of the meaning of sexual identity, even when the sexed object of desire is consistent with that identity. For example, relationships between lesbians and bisexual women commonly cause some identity confusion in both parties, even when the sexual object of desire is consistent with both identities. In bisexual support groups that I have been a part of, in both the United Kingdom and the United States, bisexual women often talk about how long-term relationships with women, in particular, shake their sense of bisexual identity.[42] A typical question would be, "If I am able to have a relationship with a lesbian, why do I not call myself a lesbian?" This is less likely to be an issue for bisexual women who are in relationships with other bisexual women, bisexual or gay men, or heterosexual men.

Typically, bisexual women feel that their identity as bisexual is of great importance in their relationships with men. Part of this is political. A lot of bisexual women feel more uncomfortable being seen as straight and may feel some internalised guilt about having relationships with men at all. Bisexual women who are in relationships with lesbians also speak, though less frequently, about how their lesbian partners may question their own identities as lesbians because of being involved with a bisexual. A reported question might be, "If you identify as bisexual even though you are in a relationship with a woman, what's to say that I'm not bisexual too?" This question is particularly apt if the lesbian partner also acknowledges desire for men (to whatever degree).[43] Even in what could be termed a "bisexual space," such as a bisexual support group, expressions of how desire, commitment, and identity interrelate is far from uniform. The relationship between sex of object-choice and identity can be called into question when both parties do not conclude that their identities are the same, even when the desire would seem to fit both identities.

This reevaluation of the relationship between desire and identity is not restricted to long-term relationships either. A bisexual feminist who organises sex parties for queer people was talking to me about how, to her mind, new territory is carved out during and after some of the interactions that occur in the "play spaces" that she creates. She gave the example of a lesbian and a bisexual woman having sex, without prior knowledge of each other's sexual orientation. While previously both parties were hostile to each other's identity, in the afterglow this knowledge was shared, and a connection was acknowledged and discussed. Each woman shifted her perceptions, not only of the other woman's perceived identity but of her own as well. Our very sense of ourselves is produced in those connections; it is not separate from them and does not wholly precede them. You do not go to a particular space already fully formed to play out your sexual identity; that identity is partly formed in and through the spaces where your desire is expressed. Further, the relationships between people create new spaces, new ways of looking at and seeing others and self, which in turn influences larger, more permanent sexual spaces. It is possible that the more spaces of "bisexual recognition" that are created on interpersonal levels in spaces such as play parties, the more likely it is that bisexual desire will be recognised in spaces such as the North Star.

Tracing Bisexual Histories

In August 1994 I met Lani Ka'ahumanu[44] for coffee in Josie's Cabaret and Juice Joint in San Francisco, where we spent a couple of hours comparing experiences of bisexual communities in the United States and the United Kingdom. Lani told me a story about the interrelationship of the bisexual and lesbian and gay communities in San Francisco through retelling the history of one particular queer cafe and performance spot—the Valencia Rose, which eventually became Josie's Cabaret and Juice Joint. This place where some of the most famous queer artists were introduced to their adoring public was managed by a bisexual, and bisexuals have always been involved in the management and general operation of this cafe/cabaret venue. The story of a particular place, in a particular town, at a particular moment, is rich to overflowing with bisexual specificities.

The Valencia Rose is marked as having been a lesbian and gay space. Yet a history of this space would also be a history of bisexuality, a history of the ways in which lesbian and gay space does and does not include bisexuals, a history of the negotiations between the different identities. Telling the stories of spaces or moments that are assumed to be straight, lesbian, or gay provides much-needed empirical data about the histories of bisexual people and their lives, and the ways in which we have negotiated spaces that have not been seen to "belong" to us. To my mind these "negotiations" are as much a part of a bisexual genealogy as documenting the First National Bisexual Conference. In many cases, bisexual history is a history of misrecognition, of expression and repression in spaces that do not signal a bisexual identity. It is also a history of coexistence with lesbians, gay men, and heterosexuals, of shared political and managerial effort. This is particularly important given that a large number of self-identified bisexuals "come out" after having identified as lesbian or gay, after having spent a long time as active members of lesbian and gay communities.[45] Their narratives are part of the history of lesbians and gays and of bisexuals—even if those narratives deny the "truth" of having been lesbian or gay.

The final space that I want to look at briefly in this paper is what might be understood as a "concrete" bisexual space, the First National Bisexual Conference, held in San Francisco June 20–24, 1990.[46] What interests me here is how a "bisexual conference space" evolved, what and whom it included, and which debates were formative in this respect. The organisers of the conference were bisexual activists in the San Francisco Bay area, and they received help from activists in Seattle and Boston. Interestingly, most of the organisers lived in the area between San Francisco's Castro and Mission districts. The Castro is the gay male area of town, the Mission is the Hispanic and dyke area of town. The bisexual conference meetings ostensibly took place in the uncharted territory that cannot be defined as either gay or lesbian.

The Bisexual Conference steering committee was concerned with issues of space from the very beginning. Twelve subcommittees were set up to negotiate areas such as logistics, media, housing, site,[47] access, parade,[48] entertainment, and the people of color caucus. The aim was to be as inclusive as possible. The statement of purpose presented the conference as "a celebration of the bisexual community and the diversity that is our strength as well as the challenge."

Every effort was made to include people with disabilities: there was a cable car for people with AIDS and anyone unable to walk during the Pride Parade; tapes of materials were made for blind delegates; ASL people were at every plenary and where requested; the conference was one of the first to take account of environmental illness.

A People of Color Caucus was organised and mobilised well in advance,[49] and workshop leaders and presenters were asked to make their sessions cross-culturally relevant.[50] During the conference a Jewish bisexual caucus was formed, which is still

Josie's Cabaret and Juice Joint, 16th and Market Streets, San Francisco.

running in San Francisco in 1995. Training was also provided for volunteer workers to deal with "conflict-resolution" and "unlearning 'isms.'"[51] Issues around politics, feminism in particular, became hotly debated in the run-up to the conference. The statement of purpose highlighted that the conference aimed to be "progressive" and "feminist."[52] In the feedback sheets following the conference, most people responded that the conference was not political enough for their liking. Other comments noted that although it was clear that a huge effort had been made for the conference to be inclusive, it was overwhelmingly white, middle-class, and able-bodied.

Many of the problems seem to centre around the issue of who should be included in a bisexual conference, a bisexual identity, and a bisexual space. Should partners of bisexuals be included in bisexual space, for example? Time was scheduled to include lesbians and gay men.[53] Can a bisexual space be all-inclusive? And if the answer would evidently appear to be "no," what are the priorities for diversity? As a final comment, the majority of the people at the conference mentioned in feedback that the conference was a place where they could feel at ease being bisexual, where they did not feel it necessary to explain their desire, and where they felt part of a larger bisexual community and movement for the first time.

Conclusions

The above are just some of the kinds of spaces where bisexuality and bisexual desire are expressed, played out, negotiated, and formed. This approach to theorising bisexuality is obviously still in its early stages. All I am trying to do at this point is highlight some of the ways bisexuality could be understood in terms of desire, and in terms of connection rather than separation from other sexual identities. It is clear from the preceding examples that queer sexual spaces are places where the boundaries between desire and identity are blurred, and that those blurrings are as much a part of the history of bisexual desire as moments where the boundaries are more sharply defined.

One of the central questions that emerges from this brief look at space and bisexual desire is, do we actually want separate bisexual spaces? Do we want a bisexual bar? A bisexual dress code? If there were "permanent bisexual spaces," as well as conferences and support groups, who would they include? Would everyone be "read as" bisexual, all desire be "read as" bisexual? As I have tried to suggest, a significant part of the history of bisexuality is the ways that bisexual desire unsettles, or the ways that bisexuals have negotiated "other" spaces. My fear is that, with the growth of a bisexual movement and the creation of more specifically bisexual spaces, history risks getting lost and bisexual desire becomes separated, and separable, from the very contexts in which it has flourished. A place for everything and everything in its place. The ways that desire and sexual identity—whether bisexual, lesbian, gay, or straight—do not always map onto one another; the complex, subtle, intricate ways may become subsumed under a generalised attempt at bisexual inclusion that loses, not only its edge, but the tension that gives it life. Bisexuality, as we see in Garber's book, seems to mean almost anything that you want it to. Any desire that is not wholly gender-determined —that is, any desire—can count as bisexual desire.[54] Would bisexual space end up eliding specificities, meaning that everyone is still "read as" something, only this time it's bisexual?

This does not have to be a question of choosing either separate bisexual spaces, which of course will never be "separate," or negotiation in and with queer and straight spaces, which are never only queer or straight. Different issues arise in each case, and different histories are told. What is important to me is that the connections between different spaces are also made, that we don't just end up with a series of arbitrary spaces. Specific spaces, the forms of expression that bisexual desire finds in those spaces, have a relationship. A line could be drawn between them to highlight similarities, but that line does not form a cosy linear narrative.

Taking snapshots, if you like—freezing a moment to delineate a space. You rarely get out your holiday snapshots and show your (grudging) audience just one picture. You present them with a whole series of images—some repetitious, some amusing, and some "you had to be there's." The "order" of the pictures is mixed up, rarely following a chronological order. To continue the metaphor, you share these snapshots with other people who've been to those places, who might even have been there with you. The pictures don't pretend to tell the whole story, but they serve to jog the memory, to prompt further recollections, to precede the stories we tell each other. Just take away the nostalgia that the snapshots usually induce, along with the simplistic narrative they precede, "Those were the days. The sky was always blue, friends were more loyal, politics more active. . . ."—take away the boredom of being forced to witness other people's irrelevant reminiscences. In other words, how many straight people seriously read queer theory? Probably not many. This essay provides an idea of the kind of bisexual genealogies I am interested in theorising. Sometimes the most interesting pictures are the ones that didn't come out the way we wanted them to, the out-of-focus ones, and the ones with the inevitable stranger who just happened in front of the lens. Instead of the linear coming-out story, we could begin to document a highly ironic, always eclectic, never-ending "family album."

Domestic Dykes: The Politics of "In-difference"

Elsie Jay

The wooden floors echo to the soft shuffle of tiny feet. As thoughts and eyes are wrenched from sleep, the bedclothes disappear, a blast of cold air swirls, and a flying lamb's wool heralds his arrival. I gaze at the green fluorescence on the bedside table—3:27A.M.—about the usual time. The "busy-ness" of arranging Lamby, Humphry B. Bear, Big Monkey, and Little Monk is followed by a kiss, a snuggle, some more wriggling, and then absolute stillness. He is asleep. And here I am. Wide awake. Left wondering why on earth four-year-olds cannot sleep in one place!

Wondering if all mothers have this nightly visitation.

Wondering if there is any difference between this night and those my mother had with me, and the thousands of other parents have in this city with their nomadic four-year-olds.

Committing myself to some serious thinking on the subject, I suddenly heard the radio click on and another school day begins.

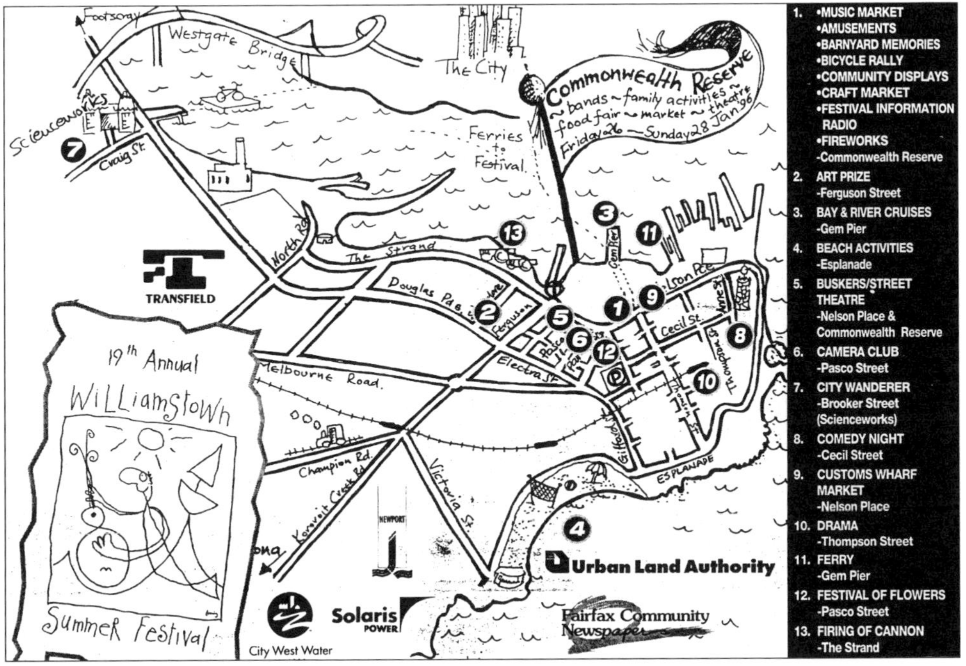

The place and life of Williamstown.

Up for a shower, heater on, kettle on. Hurried breakfast. Eight o'clock. Time to rouse the boys.

Julien is there, high up on his bunk sound asleep. At first a gentle call: "Julien." "Jules." A gentle stroke over his blonde hair. A brushing over the smooth rested skin. But then the calls get louder as the body remains unmoving. "JULIEN"! More shouts now. A tickle. And then a growl.

"Go 'way . . . I hate you . . . I don't wanna go to school . . . You choose my clothes. No, don't. You never get it right. No, not those ones. I don't like them. Where's my purple stuff? Why isn't it washed?"

"Cereal? You want cereal? Porridge? Toast?" Silence. "Will you answer me? Try getting up . . . You'll be late and I don't care. So what do you want to eat? No, I don't know where your boots are. Where did you throw them last night? So what did you say you wanted to eat?"

"I wanna bubble!" A call from my room. Tynan is up. Dragging his lambs wool down the hallway, he drops it at the toilet door. Retrieved, it is carried and thrown onto the lounge for early morning cartoons and a warm milk bottle. He sits there, eyes glazing before the coloured movement, hand working hard twisting his hair. The tangle grows as the bottle empties.

The pace quickens.

Sharon is up, dressing wriggling bodies. Tempers flare. A football hurtles through the kitchen. Fights erupt over . . . over . . . what? God! I don't know. It's never clear. But the screaming. The tears. And then it's all over. Replaced by the sound of quiet talk and laughs.

Finally with bags slung over both shoulders, toast stuck midway between mouth and stomach, a quick kiss, and then with heart racing and keys in hand, the car door fumbles open. Seat belts. Forgotten toys. Lunch orders. Ignition.

Silence breaks out behind the windows as the engine coughs into life. A wide sweep across the road sends them off.

I wave to Nina across the road as she pulls in the emptied garbage bin, up the ramp and into the darkened house. She looks as she always does at this hour, all decked out in her pink gown and fluffy slippers. Teeth not in, but happy to see us.

Next door, a similar scene of harried departure is unfolding. In front of the neat verandah with its colonial stripes and Georgian symmetry, Ellie is looking dazed. She too is not quite dressed. Her fine blonde hair is uncombed, her socks are crooked. She is crying out for her . . . her . . . something. I can't hear, but it's obviously important in that life-threatening, desperate way that everything is important to four-year-olds. Carol sinks behind the wheel, looking exhausted, as Mike peddles off to work. Older children are walking down the street. They watch the chaos with indifference—talking football and video games.

And then all goes quiet. I turn to go in. Now is the time for a desperate tidying binge before the solitude of books and writing. It is not an unusual start to a usual day. Located in an older Australian suburban street, the scene is being replicated a million times over across the city as each parent negotiates the morning ritual with their young children. Except that this couple is female. Gay. Lesbian.

Queer. Different.

Or so much of the literature, political agitation, and community identification have decreed. It is to these proclamations of difference that this essay is addressed.

* * * * *

"Difference" is a term that has gained a great deal of currency in academic and feminist circles. Initially used by those grappling with the differentiation of women from men, it has now come to be associated with differences *between* women, especially those generated around ethnicity, race, and sexuality.

My argument is that such an emphasis on difference heightens some elements of identity and oppression at the expense of others—gay at the expense of gender, class, and ethnicity in my own case. It is a politics which is only exercised in the public arena, so that the politics of the private, the suburban, the network, the invisible, and the nonaligned are not admitted. It is also a categorisation which can silence differences within. As a result, the micropolitics which exist outside identifiable public gay spaces are rendered insignificant, ignored, or even condemned, while those of the rally, the ghetto, the parade, the beat, and the commercial strip are elevated. The outcome is that the politics—and often pleasant realities—of sameness and acceptance are denied. This argument will be developed in two parts.

Firstly, I will engage critically with some of the queer and gay literature, especially that coming from my home discipline of geography, to suggest that while "difference" has indeed been made into an issue, and great political and social victories have been won in its name, there has also been a cost. This cost is the heightening of one dimension of identity and oppression above all others, with the result that other aspects are ignored or downplayed to the point of invisibility. Secondly, as a consequence of the politics of visibility, a whole array of invisible activities and the politics of commonality are thereby lost, along with an appreciation of the possibilities and complexities of change at micro scales.

Queers in Geographical Space

Geographers have long been interested in a fundamental element of difference, that which occurs between places.[1] Over the last ten years, they have also begun to study the identity and sexual experience of gay communities in order to recognise that sexuality has an impact on the constitution and character of places. In these enquiries there has been as emphasis on gay men and on their visible and public spaces in the city. Thus, for example, in his study of San Francisco, Manuel Castells delimited an identifiable gay urban territory by using "key informants" from that community: multiple male households on voter registration files; the presence of gay bars and other social gathering places; gay businesses, stores, and professional offices; and votes for a gay political candidate.[2] From his investigation Castells concluded that the predominance of gay men in creating a distinctly homosexual neighbourhood reflected a profound gender difference, whereby men seek to dominate space while women emphasise nonlocalised relationships and networks.[3] Similarly, in their studies of gays and gentrification, Micky Lauria and Larry Knopp use housing occupancy and the presence of gay businesses and entrepreneurs as key indicators of class. They also studied the gendered power of gay men to constitute urban territories as their own—powers which women cannot wield, because of their generally poorer socio-economic position.[4] While these studies are commendable in making visible the role of gay men in certain cities, they tend to be white, affluent, and middle-class men who are active in the constitution of a particular form of urban neighbourhood. The studies are also self-fulfilling investigations, for the quest is to find concentrations of gays in cities and to detail the ways in which gay male power is used to define particular public and private spaces. What is omitted from such studies, therefore, is a strong sense of difference *within* the gay male community. There is no focus on the gender differences between gay men and lesbians nor any admission of private spaces onto the research agenda.

The bias in favour of gay men in these investigations has been altered somewhat by a few studies on lesbian spaces. Building on a solid tradition in psychology, anthropology, literary studies, women's studies and sociology,[5] as well as more recent work within poststructuralist theorising,[6] geographers such as David Bell, Gill Valentine, Sy Adler, and Johanna Brenner have begun to research lesbians in North American and British cities.[7] The importance of their work lies in correcting a gender imbalance in gay geographies, in recognising the specificities of women's experiences, and bringing to valuable scholarly notice a neglected group. Despite this, I would argue that they accept a key assumption of earlier studies, namely, that public visibility and collective presence is vital to recognition and political legitimacy. Sy Adler and Johanna Brenner, for example, use Castell's techniques to map lesbian spaces in a North American city as they search for equivalent territorial claims made by lesbian women. Gill Valentine draws on friendship networks to construct skeins of lesbian presence and social activity across an unnamed British city.[8] In Valentine's work, along with examining the importance of housing for lesbian women,[9] there is some movement away from public visibility as the definer of community, though spatial concentration remains central to the research approach and conclusions drawn.

In contrast, I see my own life and that of some other lesbians around me as very different. Instead of prioritising a physical or social community defined by sexuality and adopting agreed markers of difference, there is geographical fragmentation. There is a libertarianism which consciously resists politically correct sexuality and a community defined more by class, ethnicity, life cycle, propinquity, social needs, work practices, and political interests than by sexuality.

The resulting micropolitics of (in)difference traverse a number of terrains. There is a work life which gives a certain privileged class position. This position is shaped by feminism, a feminism which is informed by but not determined or insistent upon a personal lesbian identity. Rather, my academic work draws on a feminism which is alert to the critiques offered by women of colour and, in the Australian context, by those of Aboriginal and non-English speaking backgrounds. This work is also shaped by a particular class politics and understanding of Marxism, which regards sexuality as but one of a number of social dimensions of difference and inequity.

Another life, identity, and politics revolve around home and neighbourhood. Here there is a politics that builds a community *within* a preexisting locality. This is not an exercise of territorial colonisation in the name of sexual difference. The quest is not to create a ghetto, to build a spatial concentration of women defined primarily by their sexuality, but to choose housing on the basis of a host of other considerations. In our own case, this is a stunning coastal and historical environment close to my employment but which is also perfect for young children. In choosing such a location, there was a commitment made to "fit" and also to challenge, to assert difference in being two women living together and raising children. This household sought neighbourhood support, company, and acceptance as parents, feminists, and writers. It was not a suburban occupation which proclaimed and demanded acceptance as lesbians, though this has been achieved. On these terms, it does not matter to those around us unless we insist on the difference and demand some recognition of it. The reaction to such a loud declaration could well be negative enough to destroy the quality of life we have engendered. Alternatively, it could be indifference or celebration. My point here is that such a challenge can lead to either a positive or negative response; the outcome is unpredictable but critical to the quality of domestic life that we can enjoy.

It is not that we are "passing." Clearly the household is different. It is just that our difference is not proclaimed solely in terms of sexuality. The change process of acceptance is worth far more to the quality of our life than demanding "equality" as gay women. The reality is that we already have it. As a result, there is the construction of a community of sameness and difference. The community is one of propinquity, life stage, and tolerance of (often unarticulated but nevertheless evident) difference.

Friendships radiate out from such a domestic base. A few are defined by common sexuality, but most are defined by politics, parental status, and a mutual acceptance of divergent sexualities. Social life may sometimes connect into the lesbian life of the city, but mostly it doesn't—in part because being a parent of young children makes it so difficult to do so, but also because such a life is multifaceted. It is not only based around the spatial ghetto, or those organisations and businesses which declare their sexual identity as gay but, as has been documented by Valentine, lesbian households interact mostly with each other within these spaces. I would draw again on my own experiences to suggest that social interaction occurs across a range of other centres of identity, such as paid work, sporting or cultural interests, parental status, age, ethnic group, political causes, and so on. Many of these connections include no involvement at all with lesbian women, even though sexual identity inevitably remains a crucial dimension in the negotiation of these relationships. Identity, social life, and mobility are not shaped by one dimension. Indeed the politics of difference insists that many other dimensions are important and contribute to power, to oppression, and to the social life of the city.

The politics of domesticity is therefore only superficially one of indifference. Rather what appears to be domestic sameness—for example, getting young children off to school—also has within it many dimensions of difference. For each of these dimensions there is a politics and set of personal identities. Both of these flow as much from class as from ethnic, ideological, or sexual difference, and they traverse the private sphere as much as the public. Indeed, it is in the intersection of these spaces—especially in the negotiation of neighbourhood occupancy by those who do not proclaim their sexual identity through their urban location—that a neglected queer space is constructed.

Part 3—Regional Dynamics and Community Formation

Preceding page: Gay father and his sons at the March on Washington, 1993. Photograph by Dana Schuerholz, Impact Visuals.

Queer Zones and Enclaves: Political Economies of Community Formation

Gordon Brent Ingram, Anne-Marie Bouthillette, and Yolanda Retter

In Part 3 of *Queers in Space,* we move from discussing the hidden relationships and partially identified enclaves that exist within landscapes and instead explore the formation of communities that have arisen within and among both rural and metropolitan areas. We examine the political, cultural, and sexual economies that enhance and constrain these zones of communality. In these regions, global and local forces combine to shape the cultures, sexualities, and communities that make up particular queer "scenes." At the end of the 1960s, gay liberation largely emerged from the politics of inner-city enclaves of gay men, areas that began to be labelled "gay ghettos." Less focused on these relatively enriched urban neighbourhoods, lesbian feminism has tended to be based in suburbs and on rural land. Although a rural gay men's movement developed in North America in the mid-1970s,[1] the ghetto continued to dominate notions of queer communality until the advent of queer nationalism. Today, the word *ghetto,* when used to describe lesbian and gay communities, draws contention. Most lesbians, gay men, and bisexuals do not live in classic ghettos—visible enclaves of

Some of the only open space in the original exceptionally crowded "ghetto" of late fifteenth-century Venice.

Del LaGrace Volcano, *Italian Dykes Come Out to Play,* Florence, Italy, 1994.

a particular minority, such as the Jewish neighbourhoods in Italy from which the term is derived. The term has a different meaning for invisible minorities.

In the past two decades, the little study of emergent lesbian and gay neighbourhood presences has often emphasized gentrification,[2] particularly by gay men. We have neglected to examine the fundamental obstacles to community formation[3] and how capital hinders the territorialization of "communities of desire." As capital and culture are globalized, territories that support large clusters of queer space are increasingly governed by forms of municipal government that echo the less stable, more complex medieval[4] alliances that preceded the rise of nation-states. Linkages across regions are leading to new forms of queer "sovereignty," determined as much by shared ideologies, desires, and resulting networks as by spatial proximity. Yet though these physically scattered neighbourhoods are connecting and communicating on a variety of issues, each specific locale primarily defines its own problems and reaches its own policy solutions. And consistent with the contradictions of the postmodern condition, queer ghettos are dissolving at the same time that the ghettoization of pleasure and communality is increasing for many sexual minorities.

Queer politics is evolving to include new forms of neighbourhood and spatial politics.[5] Related to older environmental politics, this perspective views the landscape, the ecosystem, and the site as an embodiment of cultural and historical forces. This view of queer human ecologies provides basis for both heightened contention and strengthened alliances with other social groups defined by proximity, identity, environmental linkages, and affinities. As different sexual minorities have moved outside the old inner-city ghettos, this political perspective has spread to the older suburbs and sometimes affects the development of "edge cities."[6]

Where are the expanding zones of queer presence in the world's cities? What are they like? How are they different and similar? Some of the better documented, established, and most rapidly expanding of the "cities within cities" often link urban cores, suburbs, and rural resorts. Although discussions in the following essays emphasize the more visible urban cores, these queer metropolises increasingly integrate urban and rural areas and are linked with other cities. We chose to focus on somewhat "peripheral" cities (reflecting the status of queer enclaves in the political economies of cities).[7] We start with the West Coast of the United States, move to the marginal Third World "development" in Mexico, proceed to the interface of Canada and the Pacific Rim in Vancouver, shift to the increasing fragmentation of Los Angeles, and end this part by exploring the emergence of gay urban space in economically depressed Manchester, England.

In "San Francisco: Revisiting the 'City of Desire,'" we reprint Pat Califia's essay, augmented with recent interviews concerning the current direction of this city, one of the first of today's "gay meccas." More than most other cities, San Francisco has grown up around its gay and lesbian networks and subsequent enclaves. The focus of Califia's notion of "the city of desire" is the South of Market Area (SOMA), which has a long history as a site for single men, homosexuality, street life,[8] and the sex trade. For a time in the 1970s and 1980s, it was a major centre for "underground" sexualities, particularly those associated with leather. Yet despite its history as a "liberated zone," the vulnerability of the city's strategic sites and networks of the sexually marginalized finds voice in this essay.

In sharp contrast to the review of well-established, partially institutionalized queer enclaves in San Francisco, Alvaro Sanchez-Crispin and Alvaro Lopez-Lopez's "Gay Male Places of Mexico City" looks at the still tentative distribution of queer sites across one of the largest metropolitan areas on earth. Despite the gay liberation and lesbian activism that began around the time of the Stonewall riots,[9] the emergence of gay male places as visible centres in Mexico City is far more recent, associated with a period of liberalization in the early 1990s. Underdevelopment, government corruption, and the AIDS pandemic have all constrained queer presence and visibility in the metropolitan region. Given the huge population of Mexico City and the sudden shift from total repression to limited levels of social and political tolerance, the pace and processes of "becoming visible" in the coming years could be some of the most spectacular ever. So far, a flowering of Mexican queer territorialization appears a long way off, especially given the country's economic crisis. Tactics of invisibility have a long history in Mexico City's gay population, and this fact continues to dominate current queer sites. More than simply cataloging the most important gay male places, Sanchez-Crispin and Lopez-Lopez describe the whole process of using, marking, coding, and claiming sites, and how this affects a chronically hostile culture governed by a corrupt state that is much compromised by North American economic interests. Despite the obstacles, the new visibility holds out many opportunities to develop communality and to diversify social relationships.

In "Queer and Gendered Housing: A Tale of Two Neighbourhoods in Vancouver," Anne-Marie Bouthillette explores the relationships between erotic and consumer desire, options for housing, and social and cultural currents that form and change identifications with particular neighbourhoods and local "scenes." The west side of Vancouver harbors an old, somewhat classical gay male ghetto, and the east side of the city, an old working-class ethnic neighbourhood that offers institutions and public spaces focused on women. But this dichotomy is barely two decades old. Within a city vulnerable to, and the product of, international flows of capital, the greatest social divisions within the combined queer communities of Vancouver are, not surprisingly, gender and class. Although Bouthillette sees signs of reversals and integrations—for example, single lesbians are increasingly attracted to the areas formed around gay male consumerism, and gay men with children are heading east to streets formed by women's institutions—the high cost of housing and its limited availability are fueling diffusion and "suburbanization," which may redistribute many of the queer amenities and nodes across the city.

In "The Queer Nation Acts Up: Health Care, Politics, and Sexual Diversity in the County of Angels 1990–1992," Ty Geltmaker recounts years of conflict in the fight against AIDS and in the assertion of gay, lesbian, bisexual, and queer communality in metropolitan Los Angeles. The years 1990–92 were both an intensive period of activism for ACT UP Los Angeles and the formative years of Queer Nation LA. These organizations took part in a territorialization that was less about establishing physical localities and more about creating a queer "infrastructure," a safety net that would develop resources for health care, shelter for homeless AIDS sufferers,[10] and other needs. Geltmaker chronicles his involvement in ACT UP at the International Conference on AIDS in 1990 in San Francisco,[11] the violent responses of the state and the police in the early 1990s, and the movement to provide clean hypodermic needles.[12]

His story ends before the 1992 riots[13] that have had such an impact on Los Angeles. Geltmaker's recollections describe a relatively new form of community formation, linking small and diffuse enclaves with suburbs in response to the emergence of the "HIV landscape."[14] Gay organizations' educational and disruptive strategies, including opportunities and obstacles presented by public space, present strategies for confronting the homophobic narratives that produce new variants on "a technology of social repression"[15] in cities such as "Citadel-LA."[16]

Where do we find the best glimpse of the near future of gay, lesbian, and other forms of queer formation of communities? Surprisingly, we look at Manchester, England, that industrial giant of the nineteenth century, which in recent decades has lost much of its traditional economic base. In "Constructing Manchester's 'New Urban Village': Gay Space in the Entrepreneurial City," Stephen Quilley explores the way that queering of neighbourhoods has been used politically to develop a new local economy based on the "service" sector. As this "Gay Village" was forming, the left of the Labour Party took over city government. The party's historical power base, the industrial working class, had declined as an electoral base, and in their search for a new core of constituents, leftist politicians formed an alliance with small businesses, the forces of gentrification, and the service economy. One result has been the development and publicized promotion of the city's gay and lesbian enclaves and their commercial and cultural establishments. But the fit of these alliances has been awkward and only partly successful. Reliance on this recent, consciously constructed gay enclave as a political linchpin in the power struggles of municipal politicians is paradoxical, especially in the context of an explicitly homophobic nation-state. This somewhat desperate project, in a declining city, owes its success to a level of cooperation, collaboration, and compromise seen in few other municipalities, even those with large queer populations. These new strategies for queering neighbourhoods reveal emerging power structures that may come to define the urban cores of the future.[17]

San Francisco: Revisiting "The City of Desire"

Pat Califia

"The City of Desire" was written in 1985, languished for years on the desks of editors, and was first published in 1991.[1] The original essay from the 1994 *Public Sex: The Culture of Radical Sex*[2] is reprinted here. Published with this essay are two 1996 interviews at the Café Flore in San Francisco. The interviews explore the subsequent changes in San Francisco, particularly for the South of Market Area (SOMA) and the Castro and Valencia Steet neighborhoods to the west.

"The City of Desire": Its Anatomy and Destiny

The city is a map of the hierarchy of desire, from the valorized to the stigmatized. It is divided into zones dictated by the way its citizens value or denigrate their needs. Separating the city into areas of specialization makes it possible to meet some needs more efficiently; it also attempts to reduce conflict between opposing sets of desires and the roles people adopt to try to fulfill those desires.

In the city there are zones of commerce, of transit, of residence. But it is not possible to be so matter-of-fact about the purposes some zones of the city serve. These are the sex zones—called red-light districts, combat zones, and gay ghettos. Although a city's legal code may specify where these areas will be, community leaders will rarely admit that there is anything deliberate about the construction of these areas. They will say they would rather such places didn't exist at all. Yet there is no city in the world which does not have them. In part because of these zones, the city has become a sign of desire: promiscuity, perversity, prostitution, and sex across the lines of age, gender, class, and race.

The sex zone does not exist independently; no area of the city is dedicated solely to this use. It is usually superimposed upon another area: a deteriorating neighborhood where poor people, especially those who have recently arrived in the city, must live; an area that has very few residents because it is designed for the manufacture or transport of goods; or one of those offerings to eco-guilt, a city park. The warning, "Don't go into the park after dark," has achieved folklore status and is more than just a simple notice of potential physical danger. It is also an acknowledgment of the shift in the park's function that takes place when the sun goes down—from a place where nature lovers eat lunch and children feed squirrels, to a place where one can buy drugs or get one's cock sucked.

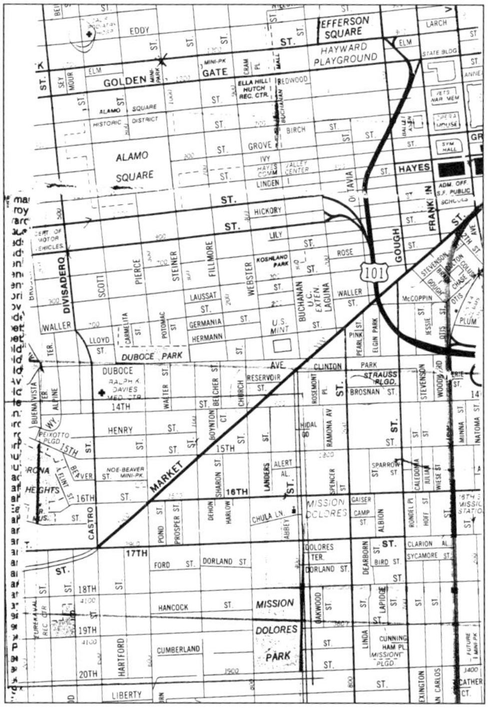

Street map of Castro and Market Streets and Mission neighborhoods.

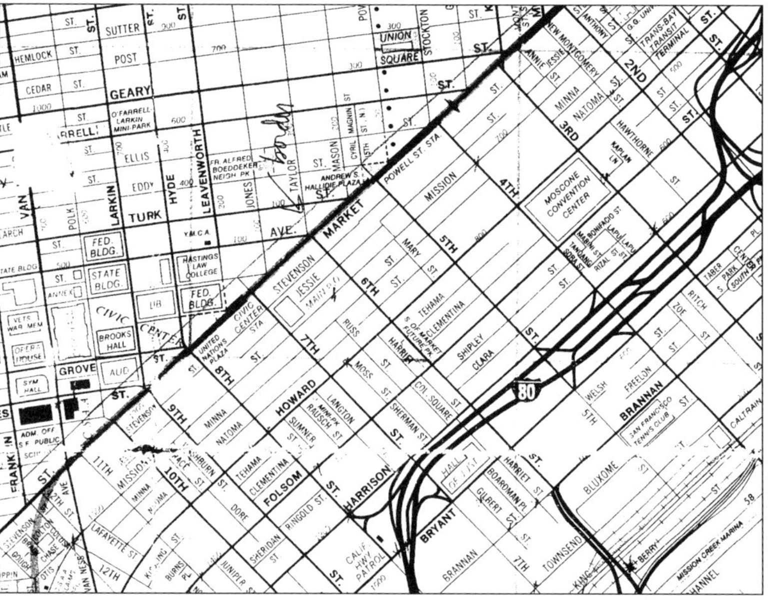

Street map of the South of Market Area (SOMA), San Francisco.

The sex zone is just one example of the many types of urban marketplaces that sell goods and services to urban residents. But the sex zone is a black market, and its wares are not limited to sexual pleasures. Most types of contraband appealing to the low end of the market (drugs, stolen goods, counterfeit and gray-market merchandise) are available in the sex zone. In some ways, this black-market status is an advantage for those who operate and profit from it. Many of the commodities offered here would not be sought in an aboveground pleasure economy because of their adulterated contents or the dangers of enjoying them. For example, once a piece of pornography is produced, it never completely loses its value as merchandise in the black market. During crackdowns on obscenity, pornography sellers can warehouse their stock until strictures are eased and then sell it at a high profit, even if the clothing worn by the models is no longer fashionable or the magazines have suffered mildew or water damage. Fortunes are made in the sex zone by peddling ersatz or adulterated drugs that could be produced very cheaply in purer and more potent form in pharmaceutical company laboratories.

Most people won't admit that the legitimized pleasures available outside the sex zone "for free" (a concept that warrants critical examination) may be less prized or enjoyable than the illicit delights consumers hope to obtain when they enter this black market. Perhaps this is because all members of society are supposed to possess automatically the legitimate pleasures, which are in turn supposed to be sufficient to keep any "decent, sane" person happy. It is embarrassing to admit that this supposed birthright has proven elusive and unsatisfying. It is like admitting you are not a human being or, at least, not a good one. In other words, despite the fact that people are willing to pay inflated prices for sex-zone products, even its most compulsive customers pretend that everything for sale there is trivial, worthless, and unnecessary. They pretend, in fact, that this marketplace does not exist at all. So a sex zone must acquire at least a token invisibility to avoid threatening its customers, as well as the authorities. This means that if one visits a sex zone at the wrong time of day, it may be unrecognizable. This type of marketplace is usually tolerated only between sunset and dawn.

A hidden market permits its customers to remain hidden. This gives all other neighborhoods in the city a double meaning, a hidden semiotic, since their relationship to the sex zone remains uncharted. The most obvious illustration of this unacknowledged relationship is the fact that the ostensibly safe residential enclaves designated for child rearing and monogamous marriage are also full of johns avid for forbidden pleasure. The sex zone is never allowed to flourish within or even in close proximity to the place where most of its customers live. An inappropriately located adult-movie theater or bookstore will find its presence—even if it is completely legal—hotly contested, and often by the same people who patronize similar businesses in the heart of the sex zone. So, johns must make an effort to travel to the black market for sex, and the risk of theft or assault they usually face along the way is a threat that most of them accept without protest. The punitive aspects of the sex zone are some of its most irrational—and most fiercely defended—characteristics.

The map of the city pits responsibility against shiftlessness. Within the sex zone, the privileged are innocent; the poor are culpable. From those who have much, less is expected. Only those who have very little are expected to pay their dues.

The sex zone is an area of resistance and acquiescence to gender polarization and male domination. Often johns and hustlers view their exchanges in very different ways. For example, a john may assume that a prostitute is fulfilling a passive, traditionally feminine role. The transvestite hooker may feel that he has suborned another man's privileged heterosexual identity and suckered him into paying to be humiliated or at least deceived. He may feel this way even if his true gender is not discerned. The deception simply reinforces the hooker's belief that the john is stupid, a born mark.

The costumes women wear to make themselves identifiable as streetwalkers—and to increase the amount of money they can demand from their tricks—are often exaggerated versions of mainstream feminine apparel and lingerie. However, this exaggeration does not simply create a form of ultrafemininity; it creates something that is both related and in opposition to it. Hookers and office workers do not wear the same kind of high heels, stockings, skirts, foundation garments, wigs, or makeup, and these items do not have the same meanings, either. The two systems of similar signs do not

Consolidation of Castro and Market Streets as gay public space in the 1970s. Photograph by Crawford Burton. Courtesy of the Gay and Lesbian Historical Society of Northern California.

Consolidation of Castro and Market Streets as gay public space in the 1970s. Photograph by Crawford Burton. Courtesy of the Gay and Lesbian Historical Society of Northern California.

indicate that one can expect equivalent behavior from each class of women. Indeed, their whole purpose is to indicate just the opposite. Any confusion stems in part from the fact that both the performance of menial tasks and the performance of sex for money are gender-linked in our culture. An office worker can be paid to do anything except perform sex. A proposition toward her is "sexual harassment." By her manner of dress, the hooker marks herself as an outlaw. She can be paid *only* for sex and has little communication about anything else with her clients. It is interesting to note that when an appeal is made for stepped-up enforcement of laws against solicitation the complaint most frequently heard is that hookers are bold, aggressive, and persistent. The same "gender-inappropriate" behavior that is a necessary part of their trade is used in argument for the suppression of that trade.

Gay ghettos operate differently from other types of sex zones. There are likely to be residential districts for gay men, as well as places where they can find entertainment. Although johns still enter gay ghettos in quest of pleasurable activities unavailable within their nuclear families, they have better luck scoring if they camouflage themselves as residents of the area.

Gay men comprise the only sexual minority that has established its own enclave in the modern city. The lesbian community is still at an earlier point in its development, although it could be argued that neighborhoods like Park Slope in Brooklyn

Women's Building, Valencia Street, San Francisco, 1996.

and Valencia Street in San Francisco are nascent "lesbian ghettos." The fact that male sexuality is recognized to be a valid strong organizing principle in men's lives contributes to the greater ability of gay men to structure their own ghettos. So do their greater amount of money, freedom to travel, and ability to live away from their parents—conditions more enjoyed by all men than by women.

Other sexual minorities—lesbians, transvestites and transsexuals, sadomasochists, etc.—tend to make parallel use of any gay male social space when their presence is tolerated. Historically, these sexual minorities have "followed" gay men out of the red-light districts and into the gay ghettos. Before there were gay bars, there were hooker bars and burlesque clubs where the presence of homosexuals was tolerated. Some social spaces that can be used by gay men (for example, drag clubs that cater primarily to straight tourists) continue to exist in red-light districts, and other sexual minorities maintain even closer ties to them. In the black market for sex, enclaves of sexual minorities are like Third World countries: dumping grounds for poorly produced goods that have little or no relationship to the needs of the people who buy them; pools of cheap labor; and sites for the elites who want to go slumming or take exotic vacations.

It is difficult to envision a heterosexual porn consumer paying for a video showing two unattractive people who are not heterosexual doing something that only vaguely resembles heterosexual intercourse. Nor would that consumer pay for the services of a prostitute who was willing to do everything *except* make them come. Yet this is nearly the only sort of pornography or prostitution available to sadomasochists. Another minority, pedophiles, must settle for material that depicts youths but has almost no sexual content, or else material that depicts adult models wearing youthful attire but rarely appear younger than they are. Pornography that more accurately depicts pedophiles' interests—even if it is homemade only for individual use, and not for commercial distribution—subjects them to the threat of horrific legal penalties.

If toys for infants were made as shoddily as most sex toys, they would be recalled by the various United States government regulatory agencies. Lingerie sold in sex shops for the stated purpose of wearing during sex—a vigorous and athletic activity—seems constructed to fall apart within the first half hour, yet it costs many times the price of lingerie sold in department stores. It is ironic that a pair of crotchless panties winds up being so much more expensive than cotton briefs. It is difficult to interpret the existence of sex toys that can injure their users and costuming that deteriorates upon use as anything other than punishment for expressing an intention to have sex.

It is also difficult to envision conformist heterosexuals accepting the low-paying jobs that the staff members of sex clubs, adult bookstores, and gay bars accept with gratitude because such employment allows them to keep their sexual identities full time (i.e., become lifestyle deviates). Heterosexuals would not tolerate the presence of, for example, a well-dressed group of drag queens who invaded a singles bar, took pictures, interrupted couples to interview them about what happened in their childhoods to cause them to become patrons of this bar, pressured them to accept drinks in exchange for this information, and then attempted to pick them up and take them home for a spot of crossdressing. Yet something very like this scenario happens nearly every weekend at many lesbian bars in many cities and large towns.

It is understandable that sexual minorities would like to sever their ties to the red-light district and model their aspirations upon the primarily white male gay ghetto. Since they are unable to control large amounts of their own social space, the more marginalized sexual minorities attempt to "share" the protected space gay men have designed for their own use. The assumption about such space is that the customers' money is going to "one of their own." This obviates the need to examine what one is paying for and whether or not it ought to be a saleable commodity. Currently, a bar or other business that caters to gay men must maintain the appearance of being gay-owned. In fact, most are not. This gives rise to the myth of the "gay mafiosos" who supposedly own gay bars. It also prompts straight owners to employ gay managers and maintain near-complete invisibility. One of the punishments for a gay-oriented business not showing a profit is the sudden visibility of its real owners, who use the humiliation of reasserting their control, as well as threatened or actual violence, to improve the gay male manager's performance.

Bo from the series *City of Wounded Boys & Sexual Warriors,* 1982. Photograph © 1997 Mark I. Chester.

There is considerable tension between the gay male majority and its "camp followers." Some gay men simply enjoy the opportunity to reverse their usual positions in society, and they attempt to become supercilious elites who have the right to condemn and limit the parameters of other minorities' pleasures. Some male homosexuals are made uncomfortable by the differences between their own sexuality and the practices or appearances of other groups. For example, to the extent that a gay man has eroticized his sexual identity in an all-male, masculine environment, he may be hostile to the presence of women or crossdressed males. To the extent that a gay man (or a lesbian) has eroticized a sexual identity based on differentiating between two genders and preferring one exclusively over the other, he or she will be hostile to bisexuals, to preoperative or nonpassing transsexuals, and to people whose sexuality is based on factors other than gender distinctions—these factors including age differences, use of fetish substances like latex or leather, desires for specific sensations and experiences such as humiliation or pain, erotic play with body fluids, and the sexual use of nonhuman animals. This tension is sometimes eased by the overlapping specialized aspects of gay male sexuality and other deviant sexualities. There are gay male transvestites and sadomasochists, and the establishments that cater to these subpopulations often have less ambivalent attitudes toward heterosexuals or lesbians who share their erotic predilections. These establishments are more likely to be located in the red-light district than in the gay ghetto proper.

There will probably always be cyclically recurring periods of stress when the gay ghetto will not be a safe haven for other sexual minorities. Paradoxically, these periods can occur either in response to mainstream society's increased hostility toward the gay ghetto—hostility in the form of police harassment, overt denial of equal civil rights, escalating and unchecked street violence, or forced closure of gay male social spaces, or to token gestures by mainstream society indicating increasing acceptance of the gay male community. Both kinds of gestures often encourage some gay-community leaders and members to attempt to purge fringe elements or at least to disassociate their own groups from those who are more stigmatized—all in an attempt to keep and increase their improved, and often precarious, status in the city.

To the extent that lesbians and other sexual minorities can organize independent social forces and claim and defend their separate social space instead of being restricted to the margins of the gay male ghetto, they will be able to more reliably meet the needs of their own communities and attract and acclimatize new members. But at least three factors mitigate against these new levels of community formation.

First, these groups possess very little capital. In a country where the state will not subsidize the formation and self-promotion of sexual minorities, without substantial private financial resources, little or nothing can be done to change the amount or kind of territory these groups occupy. As long as the activity itself is illegal or at least stigmatized, it is impossible to obtain capital by marketing the activity in the mainstream

South of the Slot Hotel, SOMA, 1982. Photograph © 1997 Mark I. Chester.

economy. Much of the black market for sex is controlled by "businessmen" such as the Mafia. These people often are *not* self-acknowledged members of sexual minorities, so no capital can be funneled from the sex zones into the creation of new types of sex ghettos. The very structure of at least one sexual minority, lesbians, makes it impossible to package that group as a commodity for sale to johns—at least in a way that benefits lifestyle lesbians as opposed to female sex workers, who are willing to pose for photos or perform in sex shows that depict male heterosexual fantasies about what lesbians do. The fact that some of these models are in fact lesbians does not usually alter either the kind of images they are used to produce or the poverty of their community. A sexual minority, as a whole, may also cut itself off from any resources generated in the sex zone by ostracizing members who work there. For example, few lesbians know any sex workers because prejudice against prostitutes keeps dyke hookers in a very small closet. Many leather organizations are hostile to professional dominants and will not allow them to advertise in their publications.

A second mitigating factor derives from the reality that without the support of a well-organized, powerful, and visible subculture, most sexual deviants are unwilling to identify openly with their sexual preference and organize for the interests of those who share it. Isolation begets invisibility, which perpetuates isolation—giving these variations a furtive and unattractive appearance to prospective members. It becomes all the more difficult for newcomers to identify as members of these minorities or even attempt to gain admission into their social spaces. One strategy for dealing with oppression is to eroticize certain signs which symbolize the oppression and transform them into signs imbued with meaning supplied by the minority. For example, the dangerous neighborhoods and filthy conditions in which leather bars are located—once symbolizing the insignificant social status of their patrons—have come to symbolize their daring and adventurous nature. Refusing to acknowledge desperation is one way to preserve one's dignity. To an uninformed outsider or prospective member, it may seem that this attempt to boost morale means that lifestyle deviants choose or prefer a marginal existence. In fact, a shift in membership would probably occur if, say, S/M were an aboveground activity;[3] that is, if no penalties followed disclosure of membership in this sexual minority. The members for whom genuine danger and filth are an important prerequisite to arousal would switch to a more persecuted activity or move their current practices to a less protected milieu. However, the number of people who would drop their membership in a sexual minority under such circumstances is probably much smaller than the number of people who would join it if they did not have to worry about stigmatization, discrimination, or violence.

A third factor is derived from the reality that the number of people who acknowledge their own membership in these groups is relatively small, even in comparison to the gay male minority. Members of these groups often feel as much hostility toward their counterparts in other sexual minority groups as gay men or even agents of the state feel toward *them*. The needs and goals of one minority are perceived as being incompatible, even inimical, to another's. This explains the acrimonious exchanges between lesbians and transsexuals, sadomasochists and pedophiles, and so on, as well as even the willingness of some deviant individuals to cooperate with the state's efforts to suppress other sexual minorities. There are also lines of stress and fragmentation within sexual minorities. The lines of sexual orientation become barriers, even within variations not based on gender. Lesbian, gay male, and heterosexual sadomasochists may identify less with each other than they do with the members of their sexual orientations who have no interest in S/M. Boy-lovers may be contemptuous of girl-lovers. Postoperative transsexuals may want to sever all ties with any deviant identity and attempt to form heterosexual partnerships, while others seek to become members of the lesbian or gay male community. Still other transsexuals refuse to "complete" the process of surgical sex reassignment and thus, in some sense, remain alienated from any identity or readily labeled group. Horizontal hostility precludes a joining of forces or sharing of what capital is available.

Conclusions

The term "sexual minority" is probably a misnomer, since the range of valorized sexual activity is extremely narrow. If these standards were taken seriously and applied without hypocrisy, very few people would escape being labeled a deviant of one sort or another. The existence of the sex zone serves to perpetuate a mythology of sexual normalcy that has little or no relationship to the actual frequency of perverse sexual fantasies and practice.

This is not a static immutable situation. For example, the economic status of women is improving, albeit gradually. Even if women did not want to experience the range of sexual pleasure available to men, the fact that they have more money means that there will be continual efforts—largely by men—to design and market erotic opportunities that will persuade women to part with their cash. Because many of the male attempts are inept, and because women do in fact want to make their lives as enjoyable as possible, there will be more rewards for female sex-industry entrepreneurs. And if women obtain access to more resources, there will be more material and labor available to create lesbian enclaves.

Some socialist countries have provided models for state-mandated repression and persecution of sexual variation. Others provide models for the state-subsidized outreach, education, and organization of sexual minorities and the decriminalization (or at least the benign neglect) of practices such as sodomy, prostitution, narcotics use, and public sex. Even in America, there seems to be some tendency toward the consensus that a state collecting a high percentage of taxes ought to insure a certain minimum standard of living for its citizens. If the American economy were not in recession, more liberal countries might be employed as models for change in the city's social policy toward the sex zone. And we cannot overlook the past and future impact of deviant individuals with unusual amounts of insight or resources, who attempt to alter the boundaries of the city—an anatomy that most people accept as if it were the map of their own bodies.

1. Traffic Flows

GORDON BRENT INGRAM: How has the map of San Francisco as a "hierarchy of desire" shifted since you originally wrote "The City of Desire"?

PAT CALIFIA: There have been a bunch of changes. One is that gay sex territory in SOMA [the South of Market area of San Francisco] has radically shrunk. Instead of bathhouses, sex clubs, and leather bars with back rooms in San Francisco, we have a handful of small, underground private sex clubs and more or less three leather bars. In SOMA, the Eagle is just about the only leather bar left. There are now two leather bars on Castro Street, which would have been unheard of in the late 1970s and early 1980s. There is only one "bathhouse" in the same sense as the early 1980s and that is the EROS Center on Market and Church. There are some other changes. The Tenderloin is still a major center of street prostitution. And Polk Street is still a hub of teenaged male hustlers. But there is a new center for straight prostitution on Valencia Street between 15th to 18th Streets. That has spilled over on to Mission Street while Valencia Street, just a block away, has finally been established as a lesbian neighborhood.

GBI: Can you still apply Gayle Rubin's three zones of "good," "contested," and "bad sex,"[4] or is an increasing amount of sex just "contested" with the label of "bad" a fairly ineffective form of control?

PC: That question is complicated because in the gay community there is a large conservative segment that wants to rehabilitate gay sexuality as a normal variation on monogamous reproductive heterosexuality such as with Bruce Bawer's *A Place At The Table.*[5] One of the consequences of the polarization that the New Right brings to the public discourse about morality is that acts that used to be contested have moved into the "bad" category and the "good" category is even more restricted than twenty years ago.

GBI: In San Francisco, has the "conflict between opposing sets of desires" been increasing or diminishing over the last decade?

PC: I do not see a big change in that. I think the major change is that many gay people are trying to separate gay oppression from sexual desire and claim that queer identity has little if anything to do with desire. One area where we can see more conflict between opposing desires is on the internet. A huge number of people are communicating with each other in a very explicit way about sexual topics, and this has collided with the dictum that sexuality should not cross the boundaries of the family and into childhood.

GBI: What have been the functions of city parks, green space, and "eco-guilt" in mediating between gay ghettos and sex zones?

PC: Gay men still fuck in parks and alleys, and whenever bathhouses are closed, traffic in those areas increases. Those spaces also serve the needs of men who are not able to participate in gay culture as consumers either because of economic reasons or because they do not want to take the risk that participation in that commerce would result in their being labeled homosexual. The link between parks and poverty has also entered the public's consciousness in connection with debates about how to regulate the homeless. Ambivalence about queer "public sex" space in the city has increased since these places are widely perceived as gathering places for "undesirables."

GBI: Does the sex zone always have to be a black market? How do you think that the economy of San Francisco's sex zones differs from those in more state-interventionist European cities such as Amsterdam, or Third World cities like Bangkok?

PC: Obviously, in countries like Holland and Germany where some forms of prostitution have been legalized or there are some policies to tolerate them, it would no longer be accurate to label sex work there as totally black market. Decriminalization moves most prostitution off the street. But then sex workers who are also addicts often do not want the expense of rent. Male hustlers and transvestites are often not included in social policy and so remain in the black market.

GBI: Today, what are San Francisco's most important "sex-zone products," and how do the economies of metropolitan areas such as Los Angeles and San Francisco, which generate a huge amount of increasingly electronic global imagery such as "pornography," differ from areas that are clearly more "colonized"? What are the trends for San Francisco?

PC: AIDS has transformed the sex industry. Today, the industry's most popular product is fantasy and sexual release without physical contact. This means that phone sex, on-line chat rooms, and electronically transferred photographic and video imagery and other ephemeral pleasures that are increasingly difficult to detect and regulate are acquiring increasing market value. But you can always guarantee that sex workers are not the ones who will get rich. The porn industry has become more secretive and more transient in an attempt to avoid prosecution—which has been relentless.

GBI: You said "a sex zone must acquire at least a token invisibility" but as the traffic in erotic imagery accelerates, does not invisibility become problematic? Is not some visibility necessary from the standpoint of successful marketing, especially with increasing competition?

PC: The point of that statement is that it is a token invisibility because real total invisibility would make it impossible to find the zone. So we make irrational bargains that allow supposedly bad things to happen but only in very limited ways. So "invisibility" may mean sex activity that can be visible only after dark. Alternatively, the boundary markers may have to be in code that can only be broken by people who already possess "spoiled" identities. For example, any time you see a bar called the Eagle, you know it is a queer leather bar.

GBI: One of the most central points in the essay is your argument that "A hidden market permits its customers to remain hidden. This gives all other neighborhoods in the city a double meaning, a hidden semiotic, since their relationship to the sex zone remains uncharted." Can you describe some of these relationships between neighborhoods in San Francisco?

PC: For example, the Avenues, which is a suburban family area on the west side of the city, is every bit as much of a prostitution zone as the red light district because that is where the customers live.

GBI: "The sex zone is an area of resistance and acquiescence to gender polarization and male domination." How is this the current case in San Francisco?

PC: I was responding to a certain kind of simplistic feminism that figures prostitution as a metaphor for the subordination of women. I was saying that the sex industry has another layer of meaning. While prostitution in its present form would not exist in a society that was not male-dominated, the sex industry is also a magnet for women who are rebelling against the strictures of traditional femininity. Sex work funds female rebellion. Without the money that comes from that economy, the lesbian community, for example, would be even more impoverished, as would various kinds of women's cultural and political activism.

GBI: How do gay ghettos operate differently from other types of sex zones in San Francisco?

PC: One big difference is that ghettos are residential zones. People do not just go there for pleasure; they live there. And gay ghettos eschew the protection of invisibility that red-light districts still need.

GBI: What are the prospects for lesbian and gay male "territorialization" that involves more explicitly nonwhite identities? In San Francisco since gay liberation, there are neither ghettos nor many "nodes" that are not defined in terms of anglo gay men. But even white men are now decidedly a demographic minority in the sum total of queer communities. But have other groups, networks, even communities formed their priorities for use of resources and public space?

PC: The biggest obstacles to the formation of nonwhite gay territories are economic forces. As long as economic privilege is linked to race, gay men and lesbians of color will not be able to afford to sever their ties to their heterosexual families and define their own neighborhoods.

GBI: How is queer space a "saleable commodity" in San Francisco? What are the trends? How do you see supply, demand, costs, and patterns of access—particularly as San Francisco's economy is further integrated into those of the Pacific Rim and remains increasingly vulnerable to what Gayle Rubin called "the high-stakes politics of urban real estate."[6]

PC: Gay space is still a commodity in short supply in San Francisco. It has become more expensive like every other space here. Access and visibility have improved dramatically. I think the trend is toward small, more mobile social gatherings and networks that meet the needs of smaller, more specific groups in the gay community. This is partly in response to increased competition between queer groups. Generic gay space is no longer sufficiently rare to be profitable.

GBI: Much of your essay employed a lesbian/gay-male duality. Has there been a diversification of spaces in the ghettos and sex zones to include bisexuals, transsexuals, transvestites, and sadomasochists, or are these other groups just paying higher prices in what still amounts to "ghettos" controlled by white gay men? How do different communities of lesbians come to play in this?

PC: Those groups of people still have fairly marginal positions in gay space in San Francisco. In this city, we are in an era of the Lavender Mainstream. The position of sexual minorities, other than white gay men, has not really improved in the last two decades.

GBI: What has happened to leather/sadomasochist spaces as SOMA has been gentrified?

PC: Some of SOMA is still a sex zone, but it is now more a zone for young heterosexual club hoppers with a combined consumer power decidedly greater than the people they have replaced. One of the most interesting things lately is that a woman has acquired a warehouse that used to be a straight house of professional domination. It is now a party site for the women's S/M community and the closest thing we have ever had to a bathhouse.

GBI: Can you still say that "leather bars are located" in "dangerous and filthy conditions?"

PC: In most cities, yes.

GBI: If "the existence of the sex zone serves to perpetuate a mythology of sexual normalcy," will they not be spaces that dissolve as more sites and neighborhoods are "queered"?

PC: Yes, to some extent. But this is not happening as quickly as I would like. In San Francisco, you can see so many visibly queer people and there are so many artifacts of queer communities, that no one could pretend we do not exist. However, this heightened visibility still often triggers even more extreme statements about morality and certainly can be used to justify crackdowns to reestablish the old boundaries and sexual hierarchies. Changing people's ideas of right and wrong is very difficult.

GBI: In terms of "making space" for the widest possible range of "erotic minorities"[7] in San Francisco, from the broadest set of backgrounds, that myth of "diversity" so central to the city as a (queer) tourist mecca, what are your priorities for advocacy, planning, design, and "construction"?

PC: The first one, which is not explicitly gay, is to decriminalize prostitution and provide off-street locations where people could work safely. Brothel licenses would be granted on the condition that workers be treated as employees, with health insurance and other benefits. The second thing is that I would make it legal to open sex clubs. Right now, they are in a grey area. Making the clubs legal would encourage investors to make more spacious establishments in safer neighborhoods. I have yet to hear of a good system for encouraging safer guidelines and instead must design these commercial spaces for more effective forms of education, practice, and motivation. The third thing, which at first sounds like it's not related to sex, is to finally have universal health care.

2. *Sites & Artifacts*

GORDON BRENT INGRAM: In the first interview, we concentrated on broader urban dynamics and some relationships between neighborhoods in San Francisco. Now, I would like to ask you about the evolution of the constructed and interior queer spaces in which you have personally lived, had sex, and done political work such as around women and sadomasochism and anticensorship.[8] I want to start with the original Catacombs of 1979–82 just before AIDS began to ravage gay communities.[9] Why was the Catacombs a landmark space in the formation of both sexual minority and queer space?

PAT CALIFIA: The Catacombs offered gay men the opportunity to further diversify and specify their sexuality. Instead of generic homosexuality, it delineated a community of men who were drawn to masculinity, fisting, and S/M. Because it was owned by an iconoclastic and brilliant man, Steve McEachern, who delighted in upsetting paradigms, the Catacombs also played a role in the development of a leather dyke identity.
GBI: What exactly happened at the Catacombs on a busy night?
PC: Anywhere from twenty to a hundred and fifty men would show up, get naked, get stoned out of their minds, and plunder one another's orifices. There was not much hard-dick sex until about 4 A.M. when the drugs wore off. Ninety percent of the sex was fisting. There was some S/M but some of the fisters did not like it—found it noisy and counter to relaxation and deep massage. Rather than top/bottom sex, the roles were fluid. Switching was the norm. There was a strong feeling that a "top-only" fister was probably not safe to play with.
GBI: Were there separate "communities," such as those people primarily interested in fisting, or were the identities somewhat more overlapping and vague?
PC: That varied a lot. Some old-fashioned leathermen thought fisting was dreadful and had nothing to do with S/M. They were not about to get Crisco on their leather. Some fisters thought S/M was violent and extreme. Old-guard leather was a beer and bourbon scene; fisting was MDA and poppers. But there was also a small outspoken group of men who considered themselves to be both fisters and either S/M or leathermen.
GBI: Back then, with rising levels of violence against women and gay men, where were the most secure spaces and neighborhoods to express what the French call *le hard* sex?
PC: There have been no "safe zones" because bashers came into gay neighborhoods like the Castro and South of Market to confront us. In neighborhoods with a high concentration of gay residents, we could organize patrols and respond to calls for help. So there was this weird dynamic of queer areas of San Francisco being simultaneously under attack and yet often well-defended.
GBI: What were the obstacles to the presence of "leather communities" in public space, particularly in demonstrations, parades, and street fairs?
PC: The greatest obstacles to increased visibility for the leather community were hostility from mainstream gays and lesbians, who wanted us gone, and our own fragmented condition. Lots of people who did S/M or had leather fetishes did not think of themselves as members of a sexual minority community and actively resisted seeing any political implications in the way they experienced pleasure.
GBI: How long had there been strategic outdoor sites for public sex and other contact? And especially for women?
PC: As far as I know, I threw the first leatherwomen's sex parties in the late 1970s. But there has always been public space for man-to-man sex in San Francisco. Always. This city was founded by cornholing gold miners.

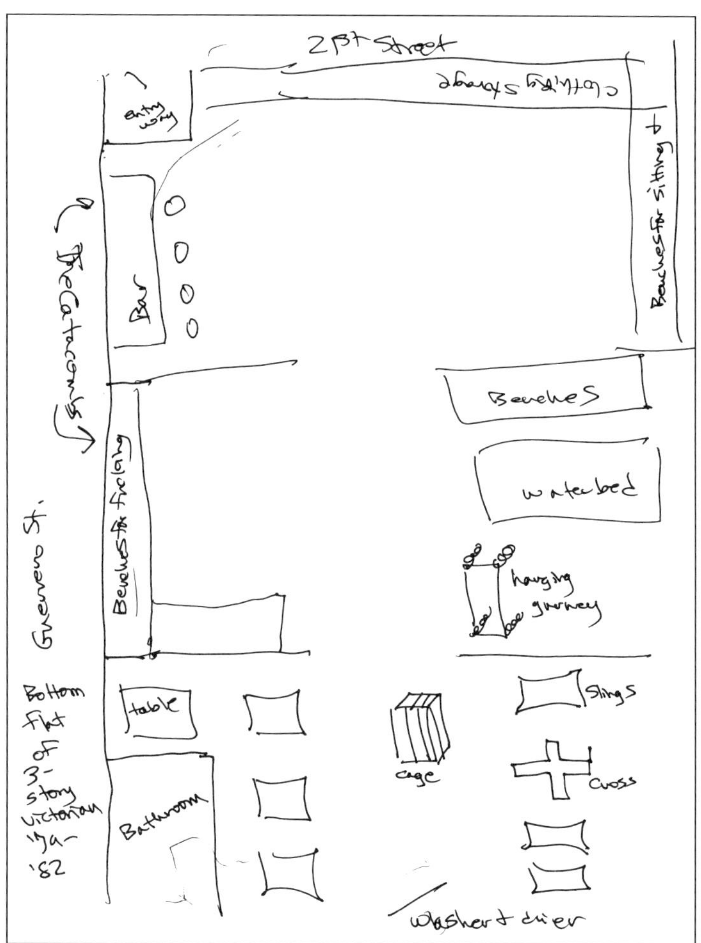

The Catacombs (1979–1982).

1. First Zone: The Entryway
   The entryway was designed so you could not see the rest of the club past the body of the person who answered the door. There was also a sign on the front that said, "If you did not call first, do not ring or knock now." You had to have a reservation to come to the parties.
2. Second Zone: The Bar and Social Area
   This was where people took off their clothes and stashed them under the benches. Things got ripped off all the time. The deal was you were not allowed to have clothes on or the owner, Steve, would harass you. People would sometimes bring bottles of liquor that they would stash at the bar. However, the drug of choice was MDA, not alcohol. There were only a few stools at the bar for people to sit down on and drink before they would go in the back and play. The club was full of erotic art but not porn magazines or videos because Steve wanted people to touch each other and not just jack off. He kept the thermostats way up so if you did not take off your clothes you were very uncomfortable. Even though this area was primarily for socializing and cruising, everything was coated with a thin layer of Crisco.
3. Third Zone: The Play Area
   More private scenes went on here, and there was less voyeurism. The benches were padded for fucking, and Steve and his favorites tended to reserve the waterbed and the gurney for themselves. There was a pecking order, and if you were lower down on that hierarchy, you moved aside for the "Alpha males" or did not get asked back. Except for all-women parties, there were never more than three women there. Friends of Steve's tended to be higher in the hierarchy. Most of his friends were experienced and heavy bottoms. Exclusive tops were derided at the Catacombs, but men who usually topped and occasionally bottomed were highly valued.
4. Fourth Zone: Crisco Alley/Sling Row
   This was where the heaviest S/M and longer fisting scenes went on. It was the most popular room for play. The cage locked, and sometimes a person who had pissed off someone important enough to have the key found himself stuck there for much longer than he would have liked. Towels were provided. Everybody brought poppers. It was kind of like being in a womb that was slippery and warm, and there was constant music.
5. Fifth Zone: The Bathroom
   The bathroom was really small. It was always crowded. For girls, it was considered a rite of passage to walk into a room full of guys, some douching, and piss in the sink. The place was not about how sex looked, it was about how sex felt. The Catacombs had more diversity in terms of age and race than vanilla bathhouses of the time.

Pat Califia and recent tattoos, Café Flore, 1996.

GBI: In the late 1970s, women with a whole range of sexual desires and established practices, from S/M to bisexuality, started to be denied access to women's spaces such as festivals, or at least marginalized in ephemeral outdoor events. How much of a problem was this for these ultra-marginalized communities?

PC: Being denied entry to women-only or lesbian-only or feminist events had both positive and negative results. It scared some women who were interested in S/M away from experimentation. But it also made us more visible. We had not had so much publicity before. It made it clear that varieties of lesbian sex did exist and had to be debated.

GBI: When were issues of physical access and disability first articulated in women's leather and S/M circles in San Francisco?

PC: This is still an issue that hardly anybody talks about, though there's an attempt to make events wheelchair accessible and signing for deaf leather people.

GBI: Looking back over the last fifteen years of debates on both public sex and safer sex, there seem to be some emerging links between space and risk. Is it too simplistic to identify a correlation between access to greater quantities of queer space for public sex, with rich environments for contact, play, and opportunities for learning, and effectiveness at negotiating safer sex?

PC: In a conversation with Michael Callen about closing the Mine Shaft, he told me that "they" (meaning safer-sex activists who had pressured the city to do this) would have let the Mine Shaft stay open if they took down the slings and removed the piss tubs. I said, “Are you really trying to tell me people get AIDS from slings and bathtubs?” This attitude, in my opinion, is a great obstacle to AIDS prevention efforts. We are fighting a virus, not decadence, perversion, or promiscuity. Big clean spaces that allow us to use our sexual imaginations make it easier to negotiate, eroticize, and have safer sex. And using or getting condoms in a tea-room environment is next to impossible.

GBI: Over the last twenty years, you have seen considerable growth in spaces of public sex for women and men, as well as various waves of repression and censorship. How would you link your anticensorship work and your own writing[10] to longer-term strategies for building various sex-positive queer communities?

PC: First of all, we cannot fight state repression without knowing its extent. And we need to have a dialogue about what repression is, how it operates, how we are often co-opted and become complicit with it. The state will always try to interfere with our attempts to create our own culture, and without it, we have no community. It is the visible artifacts of our existence—our poetry, fiction, photography, graffiti, street demonstrations, bumper stickers, newspapers, and pornography—that alert potential new members of our community to our existence and help them to locate us. Resistance to censorship, and the broader political and legal battles around it, are vital!

Gay Male Places of Mexico City

Alvaro Sanchez-Crispin and Alvaro Lopez-Lopez

This article describes the more public gay places of Mexico City, a mega-city with more than twenty million people. Because of the number of people in Mexico City, it contains one of the largest gay populations anywhere in the world. In spite of the size and economic importance of the Mexican gay community, the local gay scene has been examined infrequently in terms of either its social connotations or its territorial dimensions. For a variety of reasons, geographers, Mexican and otherwise, have not contributed significantly to the understanding of the spatial issues of the gay community in Mexico City. In this discussion we begin to explore the emergence of public gay places across the metropolitan area. This survey is particularly timely given the relatively recent emergence, over the last decade, of visible gay space in Mexico.

At the beginning of the 1990s, in a slightly more liberalized political and urban context, the local gay scene became a visible part of the social structure of the Mexican capital. As part of a short-lived expansion of consumerism in the late 1980s and early 1990s, more places effectively became available to the gay population, particularly to gay men. Most often these places were visited by local clientele from their respective

Denny's—Juarez, a cafe patronized by gay men, Mexico City, 1995. Photograph by Alvaro Sanchez-Crispin and Alvaro Lopez-Lopez.

neighborhoods. However, for the size of the city and the number of people living in it, there is still a gap—effectively a sort of shortage—in terms of the availability of local gay businesses and services.

The aim of this discussion is to analyze the pattern of spatial interaction of gay men in the largest city of the world, based on more empirical information than has been available before. To do this, a research strategy was followed with a questionnaire designed to gather relevant information, which was later transferred onto maps. The maps revealed striking patterns in the socio-spatial interaction of gay men in Mexico City. A number of relationships are worth mentioning at the beginning of this discussion. First, there remains a relatively small number of visible and public gay male places for the size of the city. Second, the majority of these strategic sites remain concentrated in the central areas of Mexico City. Third, the decisions of gay men about where to socialize remain strongly tied to membership in specific classes and networks, as well as identification with the specific styles and sensibilities often associated with, for example, one café, one cantina (bar, tavern), or one disco.

A Historical Overview of Gay Spaces in Mexico City

Only a few studies deal with the issue of how gay men in Mexico City have built their own spaces for socializing. Sociologists and anthropologists have examined some of the cultural and social issues of the local gay scene (Lamundsen 1991 and Taylor 1985). But in this context, gay or lesbian geographies are practically nonexistent in the current literature. As stated by Bell (1991), the "insignificant others," meaning gay men and lesbians, have largely remained outside the interest of geographical research anywhere in the world. The intention of this paper is to start filling that gap by undertaking an empirically-based study aimed at unveiling social gay interaction in specific places in Mexico City.

After having done a literature review on the subject, it became apparent that much of the theoretical debate regarding the analysis of gay places and territories in the United States and Western Europe has not so far contributed significantly to the understanding of the Mexican gay scene or, for that matter, Latin American gay spaces. Unlike the urban gay housing and commercial neighborhoods of New York, Los Angeles, or San Francisco, spatially differentiated gay ghettos are not present in Mexico City. As a group gay men and lesbians have been less visible in Mexican society in terms of their use of space and their social and political participation at both local and national levels. Thus, until recently, most inhabitants of Mexico City assumed that there were no gay people present, nor gay places.

In this study the lack of a solid theoretical framework is counterbalanced by the empirical knowledge of both the spatial structure of the city and the expanding and shifting nature of the local gay scene in the last decade. Traditionally, as in many other

A pedestrian street in the Zona Rosa frequented by hustlers, gay men, and tourists alike, Mexico City, 1995. Photograph by Alvaro Sanchez-Crispin and Alvaro Lopez-Lopez.

countries, gay places have been linked to areas where both female and male prostitution is practiced (Curtis & Arreola 1991; Lerma 1993; Zendejas 1993).[1] Streets, cinemas, and bars located in the historical city centers of Mexico City, Guadalajara, and Monterrey are frequently associated with both prostitution and gay male cruising. As late as the early 1980s, these places were hidden from the general public and only aficionados knew about their existence. At the end of the 1980s, as a result of a general trend in Mexican society toward modernizing many aspects of the economy, as well as society and politics, the gay population witnessed the implementation of more open-minded policies. This resulted from local government initiative and from a more tolerant view of homosexuality by large sectors of the population.

The increasing visibility of gay spaces is thus a new phenomenon in the urban arena of Mexico City. As early as the first half of the 1970s, some central areas of the city housed a handful of businesses catering to gay men. Engulfed by a larger number of establishments catering to heterosexuals, these gay spots remained open mainly because their location in a tourist area of Mexico City made it easier to explain that these gay places were for "outsiders" rather than for locals. In reality, the opposite was true. There were some places in the downtown area, particularly in the so-called Zona Rosa, where gay men used to socialize: a disco-bar, some theaters, and certain restaurants. The latter—although not specifically gay—had a large gay clientele and included some of the Sanborns and VIPS chain restaurants.

The number of gay places grew slowly during the 1980s, featuring an important change in their spatial distribution; the periphery of the city started to be the recipient of some of these establishments and public sites. Some bars were open in areas as far as twenty kilometers from the city center, such as in Satélite in the northwest and Nezahualcóyotl in the far east, and in slum areas as well as some of the most affluent districts of the towns. Another characteristic of the 1980s was that businesses were opened, run for two or three years, and then closed down. This dynamic depended a great deal on the individuals in powerful political and administrative positions in the *delegaciones,* the municipalities within Mexico City. This is particularly true of the *delegación* of Cuauhtémoc, in the heart of Mexico City, where authorities apparently have always been sympathetic to the opening of gay places. However, such tolerance is more accurately an interest in the money generated by the businesses rather than a mature political and social attitude toward minorities in the city. Patronage and corruption were and still are at the basis of establishing new businesses, at the end of which everybody seemed to be satisfied: money ended up in the *políticos*' pockets, businessmen made good profits, and gay men gained new places to have fun on the weekends. The major problem with these kinds of urban alliances is their volatility, which was reflected in a very movable spatial context for the gay people of Mexico City in that period.

In the 1990s Mexico City's gay population benefited from the spatial consequences of a new stage in the relationship among gay people, the local authorities, and Mexican society as a whole. One of the most important benefits was the publication of new Mexican gay magazines including *Hermes,* which was formerly called *Macho Tips; Del Otro Lado* (*The Other Side*)*;* and, more recently, *Apolo* and *Diferente.* Of these, only *Hermes* has so far received an official permit for printing and distribution.[2] One of the major contributions of these magazines to the gay community was that they listed, for the first time in the history of the Mexican capital, the location of gay places in the city and even in other cities of the country. This information is no longer given in the magazines, apparently due to the possibility of raids by the police and attacks by homophobic groups. However, the gay community of Mexico City considers the publication of the magazines a step forward in their social recognition. As a minority group, gay men increasingly perceive their right to use part of the city space, including the urban land base, for specific social and economic purposes.

Another set of indicators of the new openness toward gay establishments is the willingness of local authorities to license new gay places, especially discotheques and bars, in central Mexico City. The process of opening new social gay places is a continuation of actions linked to patronizing relationships between owners and representatives of the local government. In this context, a handful of new gay places were opened in the 1990s, particularly in the downtown area where licenses are granted by authorities of the *delegación* Cuauhtémoc. A third aspect of the current stage of increased claim and visibility of gay male space is the laissez-faire policy of the capital authorities with respect to straight pornography in theaters. As a result of this attitude, many heterosexual porno movie theaters have sprung up all over the city, occupying old cinemas—some of which were frequented by gay men prior to this liberal attitude. Ironically, with the spread of heterosexual porno movies, gay men gained more spaces for meeting and socializing in Mexico City.

The impact of the illegal sales of gay porn videos, as part of the rampant informal economic growth in the city, remains to be determined. This may be significant given the current spatial mobility of many gay men today, with many travelling great distances across the city to meet. With increasing access to video, many may prefer to stay at home watching videos instead of socializing in public. Another force that might affect the move toward increased public visibility is fear brought about by the AIDS pandemic; however, so far this fear does not seem to have resulted in any sort of paralysis around public homosexual contact in Mexico City.[3]

It would be easy to assume that, given the more liberal conditions for establishing gay places in the city, gay men can now choose from a wider variety of places for socializing. However, the actual number of gay businesses providing services and space in Mexico City is not large—especially in comparison to other cities. Based on the information provided in one of the world gay guides, it is clear that Mexico City lags behind many medium-sized American cities in the number of gay establishments per total population numbers. The 1993 *Ferrari*'s guide lists the following entries for Mexico City: five bars, four discos, two bathhouses and two "bookstores."[4] Per this guide, thirteen places exist altogether, many fewer than the gay businesses found in Phoenix or even El Paso, cities twenty times smaller in population than Mexico City. We generally concur with the information contained in these gay guides, which varies from year to year, and it is safe to say that the basic information for Mexico City is usually correct. The number of businesses catering to gay men, or lesbians for that matter, is rather limited for the massive size of the city. In this context, the value to some groups of gay men of additional public outdoor sites, particularly for cruising, remains high but difficult to gauge.

No gay establishment in Mexico City has been in continuous operation on the same site for more than fifteen years. Therefore, the majority of gay businesses in the city are quite new, and their locations and signs of historic recentness within the urban fabric can be traced easily. Most of these commercial establishments do not offer physical safety, especially due to overcrowding, particularly during the weekends. Overcrowding at bars and discos could be seen as one of the consequences of lacking sufficent numbers and total areas for gay socializing space in other parts of the city. In this respect, indoor capacity is not always a constraint, and the frequent conversions of spaces from one use to another, plus overcrowding, make them potential traps in the event of fire or earthquakes. For instance, the most popular gay bar-disco in downtown Mexico City, Butterflies, has an official capacity of three hundred persons, but on Fridays and Saturdays it is packed with over five hundred people. Another feature of many of these gay indoor establishments is their gloomy location near shantytowns, next to empty mall parking lots, and in the darkest streets of the center of Mexico City. Only in the Zona Rosa do gay places enjoy more comfortable and accessible locations.

From 1990 onward, various gay places have been open in the downtown area under "neutral" names, in order to hide their raison d'être from the heterosexual public. However, Mexican gay men find it easy to guess the meaning of these names and of numbers such as thirty-three, forty-one, and forty-two. Other establishments are less concerned with the suggestiveness of their names: Men, Spartacus, Le Baron, and Crazy Boys are publicly saying that they cater to a gay clientele. None of these businesses are or have become specialized in terms of S/M, leather, or denim. In contrast to these rather defined locations, almost as bastions of safety surrounded by hostility, the latest fashion in the gay scene of Mexico City involves a kind of nonspatialized interaction between gay men and masseurs, waiters, strippers, and escorts—often arranged through telephone calls.[5] The advertisements for such specialized companies are published in nearly all the local gay magazines; services are offered at the company's premises or through home visits. This new social phenomenon may diminish the possibilities for gay people to go out and make more public spaces. Nevertheless one has to bear in mind that, in spite of the comparative affluence of some gay male groups in the city and in relationship to Mexican society in general, the economic options of many gay men in Mexico City are more limited. Most cannot afford a one-night stand with a male stripper or masseur in their own home. In this context, for the vast majority of the gay men of Mexico City, the pressures for more spaces to socialize will continue to increase. After briefly examining the spatial and social connotations of the gay places in Mexico City, our key research question emerged:

> How do gay men living in Mexico City perceive and socialize in their own social space?

The remainder of this discussion begins to answer this question.

The Questionnaire Survey: A Profile of Gay Men in Mexico City

In order to construct a clear picture of how gay men interact in Mexico City, we chose a questionnaire survey as the most workable instrument to gather data on the specific activities, places, and territories within the urban sprawl that were often visited by gay men. Two methods for selecting interviewees were employed. First, interviewees were chosen through a gay friend or through friends of friends. Second, gay men were interviewed at random, in known gay places of Mexico City such as parks, cafés, outside underground stations, and streets located in the downtown area.[6]

The questionnaire contained four main sections. The first dealt with general data about the interviewee. Another section functioned to gather information on places within the city that were visited most often by gay men when they wanted or needed to socialize. A third section was geared to obtaining information about the perceptions of gay spaces by gay men from Mexico City, as well as from other parts of the country. Data from the fourth section were used to sketch a socio-economic profile of the interviewees. Altogether the questionnaire consisted of thirty-two items, most of which were relevant to the spatial and territorial aspects of the gay scene in Mexico City.[7]

During six weeks between June and July 1992, a total of 131 questionnaires were filled out. Once this stage was completed, the information was codified and processed to make computer analyses. In accordance with the results, some tentative statistics were produced, revealing the best known and most visited gay places in the city. This information was, in turn, condensed and mapped on specific sheets of central Mexico City. As far as our literature review is concerned, this type of information is not contained in any other paper or book published on the city, nor is there any map at the scale presented in this study showing the places and areas of Mexico City where gay men actually meet and socialize.

The basic profile of the gay men surveyed is as follows: Most of the interviewees are originally from Mexico, particularly from Mexico City.[8] A substantial portion of the interviewees living in the city were originally from other states, and even from abroad. Ages of the gay men interviewed ranged from sixteen to fifty-two, but the sample was slightly biased, with young people more numerous and a median age of twenty-four. This fact is significant to the survey since young people are assumed to be the most intense and frequent users of the urban space for socializing. The responses that they gave to the questionnaire were, therefore, fundamental to understanding the more vital dynamics of socio-spatial relationships of gay men in Mexico City.

With regard to formal education, these urban gay men had a mean of two years of high school, and most of the interviewees earned a monthly salary of above $500 (U.S.). Both of these are well above the average for Mexico as a whole and for the inhabitants of Mexico City in particular. The gay men surveyed were employed in a variety of places, from universities to private travel agencies, as civil servants, skilled workers, and businessmen, as well as informal workers, including hustlers .

All interviewees went out to gay places at least once a month. When the men went out, they spent up to $33 in each outing, which is rather expensive by Mexican standards. This is mainly because entrance fees to gay places are high. For example, to get into some bars and discotheques, a minimum of $8 is charged, which often includes

Figure 1: Place of Origin of Interviewees by State

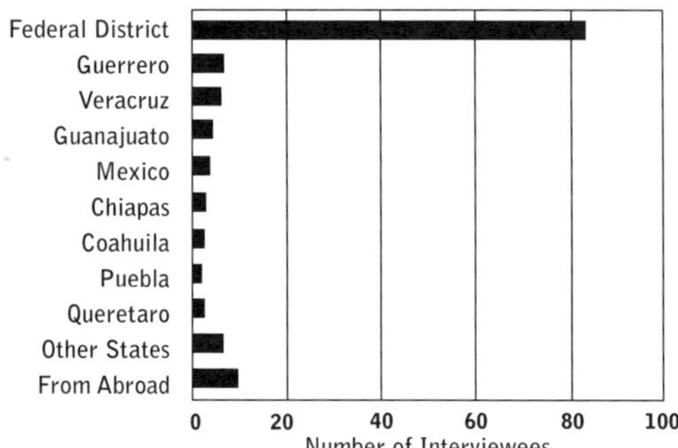

Figure 2: Formal Education of Interviewees

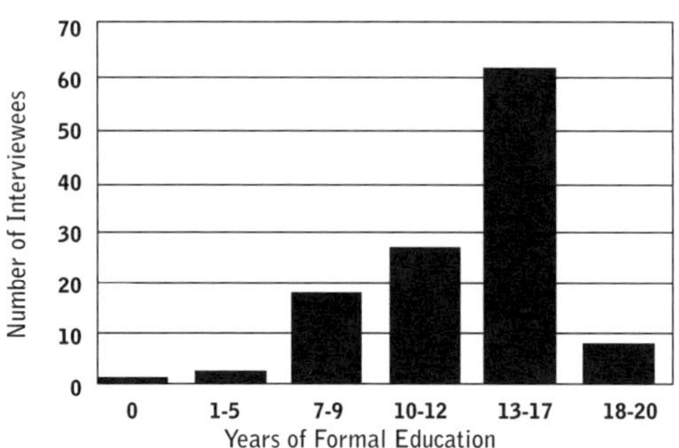

Figure 3: Monthly Income of Interviewees

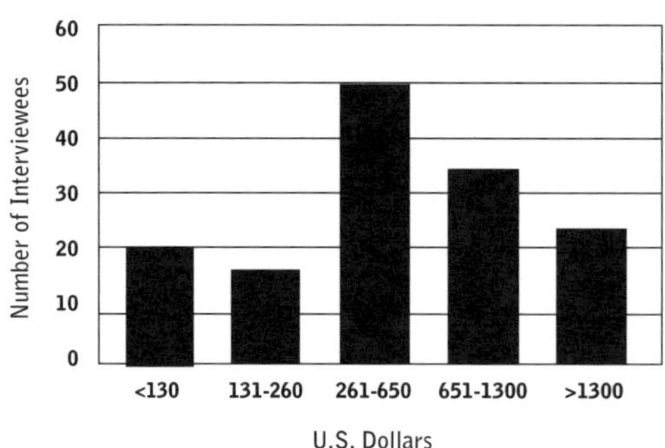

Figure 4: Occupation of Interviewees

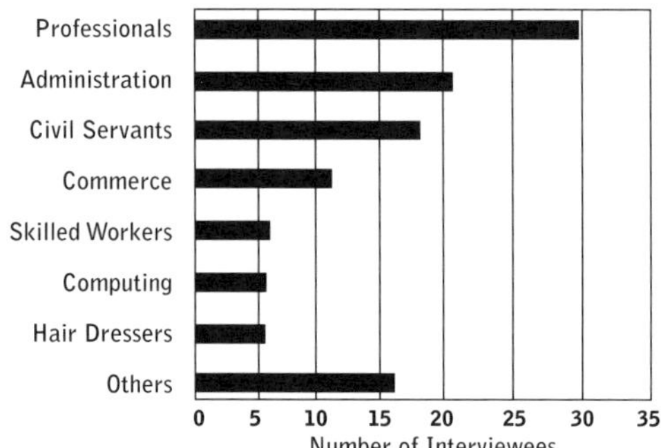

Figure 5: Time Needed by Interviewees to Get to Gay Places

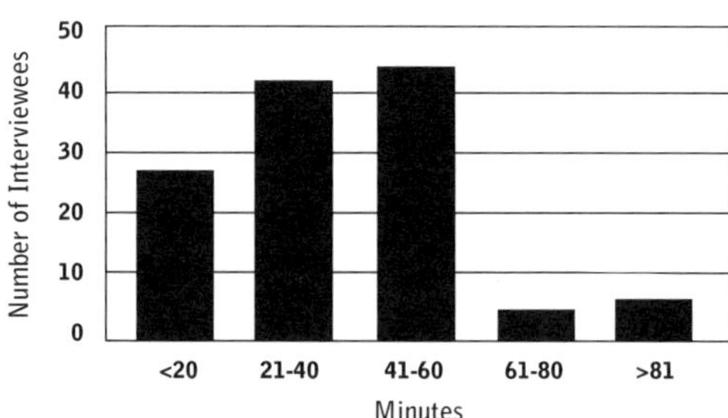

Figure 6: Place of Residence of Interviewees (areas of Mexico City)

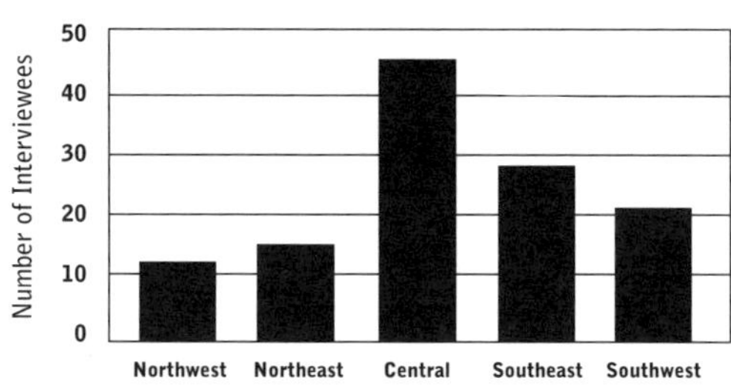

Demographic Profile of Gay Men in Mexico City

the price of two drinks. Most of the gay men interviewed went out accompanied by at least one friend and had to travel a mean time of forty minutes to the predetermined bar, discotheque, or restaurant. Finally, as shown in the last chart, all housing areas of Mexico City were represented in the survey, and the statistics showed a slight predominance of people living in the central neighborhoods.[9]

The Social Spaces of Gay People in Mexico City

According to the results of the questionnaire survey, and based on the assumption that the majority of the men interviewed went out for a variety of reasons,[10] the following are the most important results of this initial look at the patterns of gay socializing in commercial and other public space in Mexico City.

1. Discotheques are the most popular of gay places in Mexico City. Three-quarters of the interviewees went out to socialize in gay discos. This situation is closely linked to the fact that most of the discotheques, both straight and gay, also operate as bars. The most popular discos in the city, El Taller (The Workshop), Le Baron, and Butterflies, had been visited by a large proportion of the gay men in the city. The location of these places shows that the city center is still the most popular area among interviewees who go out, since El Taller and Butterflies are located there. The charms of these places derive from cruising, dancing, drinking, and watching female impersonators, recently augmented by the presence of male strippers and table-dance shows. Most of the discos mentioned by gay men in the questionnaire survey follow the local rules of closing at 4 A.M. However, others remain open far beyond that time. A total of twelve sites were identified as gay discos in the entire Mexico City area.

2. A large proportion of interviewees, roughly 50 percent, preferred cantinas as their primary places for gay socializing. In this respect, it is worth mentioning that there are a smaller number of gay cantinas than gay discotheques in the city. Not surprisingly, according to the answers of the gay men surveyed, we found out that one place is the convergent point in the gay male scene for the whole of Mexico City: a cantina, La Viena, named after the Austrian capital. This place is the hub of the gay scene that revolves around cantinas in the city. One of the main features of La Viena that makes it the most popular among gay men is the absence of an entrance fee and the cheap prices of drinks, particularly beer. Packed on Friday and Saturday evenings, this spot attracts crowds of all kinds, from construction workers to white-collar employees. All social and economic strata gather in La Viena, which is open from midday to midnight. Its convenient location, in relation to other gay places in downtown Mexico City, also increases its popularity among gay men—old and young, rich and poor. Another seven cantina names were mentioned in the survey as socializing places for gay men in the city. Some of these establishments operate as "specialized" cantinas, since most of their patrons are older or members of the Mexican army or hustlers.

Entrance to the gay bar and discotheque Le Baron, Mexico City, 1995. Photograph by Alvaro Sanchez-Crispin and Alvaro Lopez-Lopez.

3. As a distinctive feature of the Mexico City gay scene, half of the people interviewed prefer cafés as social places. Within the Mexico City region, these cafés are mainly located in the Zona Rosa. The most important café of the city for gay men is the VIPS-del Angel. This café is located opposite the statue of Mexican liberty, which is depicted as an angel. Although other chain-cafés are popular among gay men in the city, especially Sanborns and Dennys, the VIPS-del Angel is by far the most frequented and important. Most of the patrons of the café are gay men who enjoy talking and "watching the scene" over a cup of coffee. In spite of the slightly high prices for food, the café is visited often and constantly by gay men of all social and economic strata. The importance of the gay clientele for this café was revealed some years ago when the company decided to refuse service to homosexuals and their profits disappeared. The gay clientele were soon welcomed again.

4. Based on our small number of interviews, we found that public places were less popular among gay men in Mexico City, especially in comparison to other large cities in Latin America. At the present time, parks, plazas, and other public outdoor places were considered less attractive for socializing by the men surveyed. This is due to the lack of green spaces within the city, the air pollution, and the chronic threats of homophobic street violence. Only the Alameda, the "Central Park" of Mexico City, is visited often—by almost one-third of the interviewees. Five parks were mentioned as "cruisey" but they were only rarely visited by the interviewees. In this respect, safety

plays an important role when gay men choose between parks and other, more commercial, public places in the city for socializing. One-quarter of the respondents have been harassed or suffered some sort of physical aggression and/or intimidation, either by uniformed or plainclothes policemen, particularly when these gay men were cruising in parks and other public places. Furthermore, the possibility of bashing exists anywhere in the city, a brutal reality reflected in the opinion of two-thirds of the gay men, who considered all gay places in the city unsafe, both in terms of the physical conditions of the premises and the possibility of being bashed. With regard to the streets preferred for cruising, at least nine names were mentioned. Most of these are located in central Mexico City and in the Zona Rosa.[11]

5. Unlike gay men in many North American and western European cities, gay men living in Mexico City do not often visit bathhouses to socialize. This is true in spite of the relatively cheap entrance fees—in the mid-1990s no more than $1. The two public bathhouses that are exclusively gay and most frequented are located in or near the central part of the city. Many of the interviewees stated that they did not need to visit *specifically* gay bathhouses because all of the bathhouses in the city are cruisey in one way or another. Some key sociological factors of male Mexicans regarding bisexuality, especially involving identities and practices, were explored by Carrier (1985) and become important for understanding bathhouse relationships. Thus, many gay men literally can have fun in any bathhouse of Mexico City.

A hot spot of the gay scene, Cantina La Viena, Mexico City, 1995. Photograph by Alvaro Sanchez-Crispin and Alvaro Lopez-Lopez.

VIPS-del-Angel restaurant, the most popular café for gay men in Mexico City, 1995. Photograph by Alvaro Sanchez-Crispin and Alvaro-Lopez-Lopez.

6. A particularly distinct type of gay space in Mexico City is the labyrinth of underground transportation stations, both the platforms of the stations and their aboveground street areas. There became apparent in the survey an interesting social and spatial phenomenon that had not been recognized in early discussions on gay male public space in the city. The Hidalgo underground station is one of the most popular and visited gay places in the whole of Mexico City, and perhaps in the whole world.[12] Due to its position as a transfer point between the two most congested underground lines, Hidalgo is one of the busiest stations in the whole public transportation system. In spite of the constant presence of police and security agents patrolling the station, there are two platforms continually occupied by gay men, one platform in each of the two stations. In the words of many of the interviewees, Hidalgo is cruisey at any time of the day—in service hours, of course! For many, Hidalgo is "the place" for gay people. Hidalgo is the "miracle station" and "anything goes" in Hidalgo. These were some of the comments gay men made when asked about the significance of Hidalgo in the gay life of Mexico City. Recently, this station has been raided by the metropolitan police on several occasions. Men—gay, straight, or otherwise—have been taken outside the station and threatened with being transferred to the nearest police station and accused of lewd behavior in public places. This charge can lead to a misdemeanor, and corrupt police often use it as a means to extort money from gay

men. Eventually, these men rid themselves of these charges through the *mordida* system, rampant state corruption from police officers to high government officials, which often yields good profits for "raiders."[13] Five other underground stations for cruising were mentioned by interviewees.

7. Prior to the "liberalization" of the social arena in Mexico City, cinemas and theaters were often considered places for gay male contact. Before the recent years of visibility, gay cinemas masquerading as straight porno movie theaters and film festivals were very important meeting places for gay men. Cinemas are still important, as many interviewees stated that they often go to some cinemas to socialize. Of particular significance to the gay life of Mexico City is the Latino Cinema (located in the Zona Rosa); it is one of the most comfortable theaters in town and the site of the International Film Festival. Each year the Festival attracts large gay crowds. Other theaters were mentioned by the interviewees, and some of these appear on the map included in this essay.

Not as numerous as the movie theaters but another important element of the gay landscape of Mexico City are the dramatic theaters. Since many of them are avant-garde places, gay people have often identified personally and socially with particular plays and, consequently, with the location of the theater and its surrounding scene.

Entrance to the well-known underground station, Hidalgo, Mexico City, 1995. Photograph by Alvaro-Sanchez-Crispin and Alvaro Lopez-Lopez.

However, theater prices are a constraint for most gay men of Mexico City, being prohibitive for the many people earning minimum wage.

8. When asked about which neighborhoods could be classified as gay in Mexico City, interviewees mentioned the Colonias Roma, Condesa, and Juárez as most similar to the type of gay neighborhoods in cities such as San Francisco or New York. Another ten names were given as gay *colonias* in the city.[14] It is important to state here that the three major *colonias* are located in the central part of Mexico City and contain some of the most popular gay places in town, including cafés, bars, and streets. However, a really gay neighborhood where the urban land is intensively and constantly used for gay services, businesses, and housing cannot be found in the Mexico City region.

9. With regard to other Mexican cities with gay space recognized by the men interviewed, the results of the research are not surprising: Acapulco and Guadalajara top the list. One-third of the respondents stated that both cities are known as gay. On the Pacific coast, Acapulco is famous the world over as a paradise for tourists, including the international gay scene. Furthermore, Acapulco had openly gay places even before they appeared in Mexico City, transforming this port into a more liberal, more open-minded place than other Mexican cities.[15] No doubt the presence of international tourists has played a profound role in this condition. As a consequence of this liberalizing presence, Acapulco is the most popular destination for gay men from Mexico City, a fact which is enhanced by the easy access between the capital and the port via modern roads and daily flights.

The case of Guadalajara is different and based on the popular belief that *tapatíos*, who are males originally from Guadalajara, are willing to engage in homosexual activities even if they look macho in their appearance. Because of this assumption, this myth, it is not surprising that Guadalajara is a major destination for gay men. Second only to Mexico City in population, Guadalajara has by Mexican standards numerous gay services and businesses and, unlike Acapulco, it caters mainly to local clientele. The interviewees mentioned gay spaces in other Mexican cities, but none as often as Acapulco or Guadalajara.

10. Some of the men surveyed have traveled abroad searching for more liberal environs that offer a wider and more satisfactory selection of gay places within a particular city. Hence, almost 10 percent of the interviewees have been to the United States, particularly to the large cities of California—notably San Francisco, Los Angeles, and San Diego. In these cities, Mexican gay men find cultural and recreational attractions they cannot always find in Mexico City. There is an additional draw for gay people to these American cities: the presence of large, historic Mexican/Chicano communities, as well as recently established, immigrant Latin American populations. These language and cultural elements in the United States, and different social and political context (one that is sometimes more permissive), often make such urban

environments particularly attractive and exciting for gay men visiting from Mexico City. These areas of high gay visibility in the southwestern United States have had a major influence on the emergence of gay networks, enclaves, and communities in Mexico City.

Conclusions

We have drawn several initial conclusions on the socio-spatial interaction of gay men in Mexico City. Gay male places in Mexico City are mainly clustered in the city center and are largely associated with the middle class. Only a few gay male sites are located in either the poorest suburbs or the most affluent areas of the city. The central location of gay male places reflects a general tendency, still present in Mexico City, to find in the central business district the most diversified and numerous offerings of services and businesses of any type in the city. Unlike many North American cities where, more and more, the central city plays a less significant role in the urban economy, the historical center of Mexico City continues to contain the most important commercial and business sites, gay places included. In the last decade, the dynamics of gay places in Mexico City have allowed shifts between one location and another, but much of this mobility has been confined within the perimeter of the city center. Likewise, the number of businesses catering to gay clientele, especially bars, cantinas, and discotheques, have gradually increased in the central area of Mexico City. In this context, it is highly probable that in the next decade a large proportion of the gay men in the city will continue to rely on downtown areas for social contact.

Since the beginning of the 1990s, the official attitude toward the consolidation of gay places in the city has changed. Gay men in Mexico City now enjoy a more relaxed and liberal atmosphere, though this has happened in the context of erratic and often deteriorating economic conditions. The new tolerance has not, however, prevented occasional raids of gay places and this, in turn, has continued to discourage many people from visiting them. Human rights, in this context, are only a distant dream, since intolerance and repression return once in a while to most of the gay places in Mexico City.

As the Mexican capital is spread wide over the Basin of Mexico, the built-up area comprises two administrative entities: the Federal District and the state of Mexico, with different urban programs and policies with respect to land use and licensing businesses. This situation has recently had a particular impact on gay spaces due to the less restrictive laws in the state of Mexico, thanks to the presence of dishonest *políticos,* and this has paved the way for some gay businesses such as bars, bathhouses, and discotheques in the state of Mexico.

For its size Mexico City has very few gay places, many of which are short-lived. According to our survey, gay people in Mexico City tend to go to a particular place rather than to different places. There is one single cantina, one discotheque, one underground station, one park, one circuit of streets, one café more often frequented by gay men than others in the city. As a result, in Mexico City there are no gay places catering specifically to nice-cute-and-clean people, with others for very affluent men. All economic and social strata mix in the same places—sharing the same environs, the same dangers, the same social relationships, the same publications, and the same public demonstrations.

In Mexico City there is a lack of cultural places such as bookstores, help-crisis centers, AIDS-linked information centers, and cultural centers that cater to gay people. No organizations such as a Lesbian and Gay Association or the like are found in the city, enjoying the privilege of using their own premises for cultural purposes. The closest the Mexico City gay organizations can get is the opening of their spaces (mainly bars and discotheques) for afternoon sessions on safe-sex, for coffee breaks, for some informative conference, or the showing of a particular film, as in the case of El Taller. No specialized gay bookstores can be found in town, nor are there card or picture galleries designed to attract a gay clientele.

Finally, in the face of modernity taking place in Mexico, particularly in the context of NAFTA, one wonders what benefits there will be for gay men. More openness? No censorship? Real social acceptance by the predominant straight society in terms of the space used and constructed by gay people? These questions remain as the central topics for future research. At the moment, however, one thing is clear: In the foreseeable future, gay places will continue to be part of the urban landscape in Mexico City —with constant changes in the number of businesses, with a recognizable tendency to be spatially movable within the central area, deeply inserted in the heart of the city, and benefitting an always increasing number of gay men.

Queer and Gendered Housing: A Tale of Two Neighbourhoods in Vancouver[1]

Anne-Marie Bouthillette

The access to and the choices made around housing stock are central factors in the formation of queer enclaves, neighbourhoods, and broader communities. Gay ghettos have never been very homogeneous, and both gender and the gendering of space have been central factors in the identity and distribution of resources and environmental costs. While distinctly gay male and lesbian neighbourhoods exist in most inner cities, the gender-related processes at work in them have seldom been compared. In the case of Vancouver, a metropolitan area of nearly two million people, the two neighbourhoods are the West End, identified with men, and the Commercial Drive area of Grandview-Woodland, called "the Drive," for women.

In this story of two neighbourhoods, my comparative analysis identifies divergences in social relations and culture, as played out across urban space, between gay and queer men and women. I confirm that the historical gay male sexual marketplaces have tended to form the kernel of gay male ghettoisation and territorialisation. However lesbian feminist politics, an early lesbian cultural signifier, have oriented lesbians more towards countercultural enclaves. The presence of a large number of single-occupancy apartments has been a central factor in formation of gay male enclaves, while low-rent spacious family-oriented stock—often semi-detached or detached houses—have typically been sought by lesbian and bisexual women.

The production of these gay-identified spaces reveals that their reinscription on Vancouver's landscape is also determined by different processes. The West End emerges as a landscape that reflects a much more openly sexualised presence, with gay-specific institutions and businesses, events, and several visual cultural cues that inform passersby of its "queer" identity. By contrast, the Drive is more provisional space of sexual minorities, though more likely to be lesbian-friendly. Unable to support lesbian-only institutions, the women have carved their own often-fleeting spaces out of the existing landscape. But in recent years, there have been signs that these boundaries are blurring as more gay men move east to the historically lesbian zone and many single women move into neighbourhoods typical of the more sexualised spaces of single men.

Homosexual men and women have long known that they are more likely to find one another in high-density inner-city settings, that they are more likely to lead a peaceful existence in what is traditionally felt to be more open-minded, urbane, and

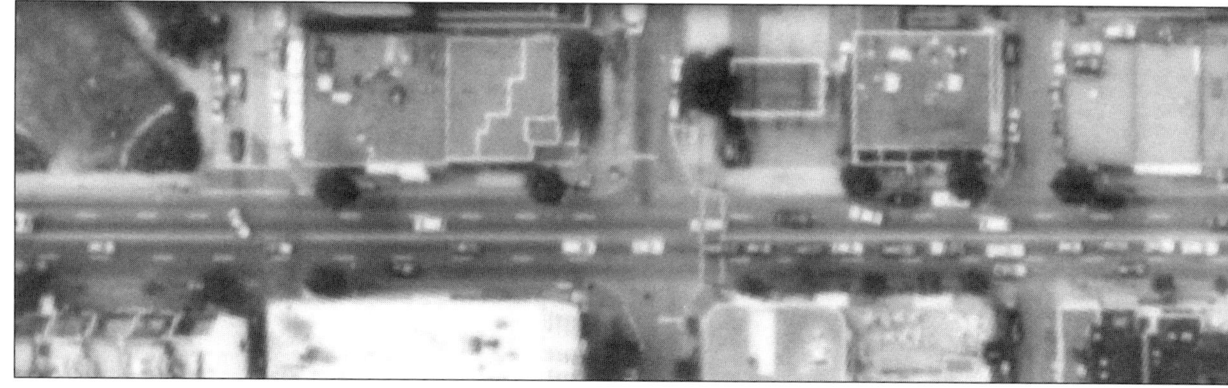

Denman Street near English Bay, one of two queer strips in the West End. Photograph by Selkirk Remote Sensing.

even anonymous surroundings (Harry 1974; Humphreys 1970; Levine 1979). Similarly, social scientists have come to realise this fact: much like turn-of-the-century ethnic minorities, gay male and lesbian communities have developed solid roots and identifiable neighbourhoods in the inner cities of large metropolitan areas, especially in the post-Stonewall era. These neighbourhoods have served many purposes, from being safe places for gay men and lesbians (where they are less likely to be harassed) to constituting stable territorial bases from which rich gay cultures and "institutionally complete" gay communities can develop. Furthermore, newer research and casual observation have concluded that many large cities harbour some spaces that are closely identified with gay men and others that are lesbian-identified. Yet while both types of neighbourhoods have been studied, the two have rarely been compared in terms of the processes that lead to their development and the landscapes they create.

The Lesbian Neighbourhood versus the Gay Male Enclave

Vancouver is an ideal city in which to conduct a comparative study of gay male and lesbian neighbourhoods because, unlike most comparable Canadian and United States cities, Vancouver accommodates two distinct and identifiable gay enclaves—one primarily male, the other female. These neighbourhoods are both the residential and cultural bases for many of the city's gay men and women. Yet, as I hope to show in the following pages, they evolved—and now function—in quite distinctive ways. These ways reflect the inherent socio-economic, cultural, and political differences not only between gay men and women themselves but also between the physical aspects of the neighbourhoods in question.

The two neighbourhoods are the West End and Grandview-Woodland. The former, gay-male-identified, area is located at the heart of Vancouver's downtown, nestled among Stanley Park, English Bay, and the city's central commercial and office districts.

Lesbian-identified Grandview-Woodland—also known as the Drive for its main artery and cultural hub, Commercial Drive—is a large area located east of downtown Vancouver, beyond Chinatown. Much less densely populated and metropolitan than the West End, the Drive symbolises grounded multiculturalism and family living in inner-city Vancouver.

Gay men and lesbians have tended to interact with space in very different ways, although class, cultural, and racial divisions have also been major factors. This difference occurs primarily through two processes. First, gender privilege has meant that women have been constrained in several ways, as compared to men. This has been most obviously true in terms of economic opportunities, but also in terms of family responsibilities, public safety, and political effectiveness. Second, the political and subcultural differences between gay men and lesbians have also had a significant impact on their relative spatial expression. This difference incorporates the second set of factors identified earlier and is manifested in the landscapes that result from gay identification, as well as in the inherent characteristics of the communities that gay men or women might be drawn to. These differences, I contend, play a large part in the way gay men and lesbians choose or are restricted to a certain place. They also help explain how, once appropriated, the space is used and in this way transformed.

Gay male and lesbian neighbourhoods in Vancouver.

Gender in the Geography of Sexual Marginality

When Rose (1984) called for a "rethinking" of gentrification, she argued for a more textured analysis of the phenomenon that would take into consideration the various levels at which this process operated. She believed that gentrification is a household-led phenomenon that occurs for as many different reasons as there are different households. She was intrigued by what she terms "marginal gentrifiers," primarily female-led households whom she perceived as gentrifying for reasons almost entirely unrelated to those typically cited by gentrification theorists such as Gale (1979), Holcomb (1981), Ley (1980, 1981, 1983), and Smith (1979). Her introduction of women as differently motivated agents in this urban process was highly significant and is an argument that sparked other investigations into how nonhegemonic social groups perceive and use urban space.

Not only have we seen increasing amounts of work on the valuing of the places and spaces that are used and experienced daily by women—places such as the family home, the suburbs, the workplace—but we have also seen evidence of the various roles women have played in shaping these and other spaces. Many women's reasons for gentrifying are often so different from the more "typical" upper-middle-class gentrifiers that the women find themselves competing—often unsuccessfully—with these other gentrifiers for community resources. Seemingly then, women's needs with respect to cities are quite different from those once perceived by urbanists to be dominant society's needs. Evidently society is made up of different people and subgroups, each with different concerns, requirements, and powers of agency.

The Production of Queer Territory

Gay culture and its associated material landscape are constantly being produced and reproduced because gay men and women have little tradition to work with, especially concerning the use of space. Unlike ethnic minorities, for instance, the gay individual is not born into the community. Rather, s/he makes a conscious choice to assert a sexual orientation and "come out," to take on a gay identity (Murray 1979). If gay identity itself is in large part a political construction, why then should it come as a surprise that the gay individual's space and culture are, in turn, constructions? Wolfe's (1992) call for a more sophisticated analysis of the production of spaces, echoing Moore Milroy's (1991) framework, inspired Larry Knopp (1995) to develop a framework based on integrating sexuality in the way we understand cities. Knopp categorises ways of knowing and understanding cities as follows: the material centering on the built environment; the ideological or spatial consciousness; and humanism, the lived experience of the city.

Sexuality, like gender and race, is complicit with the production of spaces and with the assigning of hierarchical meanings to these spaces. But Knopp continues to say that spaces are also sexualised on a much more elemental scale: People might use the same spaces, but their experience with a given space might differ a great deal. Different sexual possibilities exist based on differences in class, race, gender, and consequent spatial experiences. In other words, one's sexual potential depends on the private and public places frequented and on the activities undertaken in those places. As a result, for instance, a white middle-class man has very different sexual possibilities available to him than does a black working-class woman. With respect to the creation of gay spaces, Knopp suggests that it is the gendered division of labour, which led to the segregated city forms we know today, that created, in effect, spaces where either femininity *or* masculinity were the norm.

By studying Vancouver's West End and Grandview-Woodland as constructed (homo)sexualised spaces, I had originally hoped to document the gay histories of these districts and to contextualise their construction within the constraints of straight dominance. The ways in which these constraints worked to create these spaces operated in quite different ways for men and women, reinforcing gender-based boundaries and possibilities and thus resulting in significantly different places.

The Production of "Queer" Neighbourhood Cultures

Although problematic by certain more contemporary accounts, the ghetto has been seen in the literature as the logical if not optimal place for gay men and lesbians to reside and socialise. It has been characterised, in turn, as a safe place to retreat to in the face of "an intolerant heterosexual society" (Lauria & Knopp 1985, 158, also Adam 1978; and Levine 1979); an essential material basis from which to develop an institutionally complete community (Harry & DeVall 1978, Murray 1979); a meeting ground or cruising space (Lauria & Knopp 1985; Levine 1979); and a space of personal freedom, where it becomes easy for gay men and women to "come out" and accept or even celebrate their gayness (Harry & DeVall 1978). Levine's (1979) description of the gay ghetto is probably the most germane: ". . . an urban neighborhood can be termed a "gay ghetto" if it contains gay institutions in number, a conspicuous and locally dominant gay subculture that is socially isolated from the larger community, and a residential population that is substantially gay" (364). Broadly speaking, then, the gay ghetto is reducible to being an area that is—and has historically been—a focus for gay existence. While some of its elements are observable and even quantifiable—for instance, gay-oriented businesses and/or institutions—residential populations are somewhat more difficult to ascertain. Indeed, until sexual orientation is an item on the national census, it will continue to be virtually impossible to determine the extent of an area's gay population. As a result, the materiality of a gay ghetto will remain largely unsubstantiated.

The emergence of the West End and the Drive as gay places was a result of existing material conditions coinciding with a set of ideologies associated with each neighbourhood and each sexual subgroup. Specifically, I argue that the type of housing available in each neighbourhood, combined with the area's respective socioeconomic profile and opportunities, and its cultural and ideological attributes, served to attract gay men or women at a very specific time in each community's evolution. Indeed, I maintain that timing was quite significant to the way and the *place* in which each community evolved in Vancouver, just as it was important in other North American cities. As will be shown, changes on the urban landscape were parallelled by, and in fact dovetailed with, the gay revolution and, in turn, gay territorialisation.

Early studies of gay male sociology tended to emphasise the sexually oriented pleasure/leisure aspect of that culture (Harry & DeVall 1978; Humphreys 1975; Levine 1979; Warren 1978)—what Bell (1991) calls "the 'pleasure-geographies' of gay nightlife" (324). As argued by Bawer (1993), we now recognise that a sex-focused identity only applies to a certain proportion of gay men and, arguably, only part of the time at that; however, it must be understood that the sexual component of the gay male identity was a focal point of early gay activism. Moreover, lacking any formal or organised "gay culture" or institutions (Castells & Murphy 1984; Lauria & Knopp 1985; Warren 1974) before the 1950s, sexual activity was the main social bond that homosexual men shared. Long before the emergence of commercial gay areas—let alone full-fledged ghettoes—gay men swarmed to specific areas in the city where they could find or purchase casual sex (Humphreys 1975; Lauria & Knopp 1985). These places—ranging from parks, to public washrooms, bathhouses, and beer parlours—were typically found in the inner city (Edwards 1993; Lauria & Knopp 1985), where anonymity and partner variety were undoubtedly assured.

Gay male and lesbian cultures have often differed significantly, and Altman (1982) and Adler and Brenner (1992) agree that this difference is due in large part simply to the fact that lesbians are women. Being women, lesbians face considerably more restrictions in their locational options. While gay male space is defined by what it has meant to the community's sexual identity, lesbian spaces are where solutions to several social, political, and cultural constraints converge. Indeed, while gay males appropriate and subvert socially accepted sexual (heterosexual) and gender norms, lesbians—as feminists—tend to question these norms altogether. Gay Liberation was a significant force in raising awareness of lesbianism, but it was feminism and the Women's Liberation Movement that gave lesbians a group consciousness. Similarly, Wolf (1979) delineates two distinct periods in lesbian history: first, what she terms "old gay life" centering around bars and dating back to the 1950s and earlier, and then a later period characterised by "a significant shift in lesbian self-image and lifestyle as a result of the influence of the women's and gay liberation movements during the late 1960s and early 1970s" (22). Thus, although gay men and lesbians share the political goal of eliminating prejudice and discrimination on the basis of sexual orientation, their framework and strategies differ profoundly to reflect gender differences. In other words, lesbians carry the additional political and social burden of being women: Their "defined deviance . . . has been and is based on heterosexism and sexism" (Wolfe 1992, 142). This burden is multifaceted, and each of these facets further restricts available urban space for the lesbian community.

Certainly, for many lesbians there is a crucial difference between straight feminism and lesbianism—sexually and culturally. Although some lesbians have argued that "women's culture and lesbian culture are basically the same" (Jay 1979, 51), it is increasingly evident that a separate lesbian culture is evolving with its own literature, folklore, music, and films, and that for many lesbians the difference in sexual orientation between them and heterosexual women is a critical one. Yet certainly, just as gay male culture was founded upon sexual liberation, lesbian culture owes a debt of gratitude to the feminist and the lesbian feminist movements of the 1970s and to the shift in the lesbian self-image, both personal and communal, that occurred then. Lesbianism and feminist politics have therefore had an undeniable mutual relationship that was instrumental in each movement's flowering throughout the 1970s and into the 1980s. Consequently, because feminism evolved as part of the counterculture movement, it can be argued and indeed observed that lesbian culture holds a lot of the same values, priorities, and tastes as did members of the counterculture. I contend, and do others (Adler & Brenner 1992; Altman 1982; Castells 1983; Lockard 1985; and Wolf 1979), that this commonality has been a significant factor in the locational patterns of Western lesbian communities.

Thus lesbian and gay male culture have evolved in different ways, based on different ideologies. While contemporary gay male culture, at least in its beginnings, was very much centred on sexual freedom, lesbian culture has been more inclined to a political feminism. As suggested by Wolfe (1992) and Knopp (1995), gay people like everyone else seek environments that reflect their needs and values. Consequently, we can expect and observe that gay male enclaves will develop around sexual marketplaces, while lesbian neighbourhoods will emerge in areas that were influenced by feminist and countercultural politics in the 1970s—the period when lesbian neighbour hoods began to develop. Furthermore, these neighbourhoods will also fit the socioeconomic profile most accessible to women, especially in terms of cost of housing.

Neighbourhood Identities: Sexualised and Gendered

The differences that emerge between gay men and lesbians—are apparent in the locational choices they make as social groups to assert their sociocultural and material positions. Many Western cities' landscapes have been inscribed with gay male and lesbian values, and definite patterns arise. As will be shown, these patterns are repeated in Vancouver, resulting in the two distinct neighbourhoods that are the subject of this research.

The West End's emergence as a gay male enclave was a result of sheer propinquity. Historically, gay male culture has been defined to a significant extent by the (homo)sexual drive that was the main characteristic shared by most gay men until fairly recently, when a more complex, post-AIDS-hysteria, politically driven gay male culture and practice began emerging. Quite simply, the production of settled gay male places occurred in areas adjacent to the "scene"—the bars and other public places frequented by gay men looking for sexual encounters. And these processes are historically grounded in the late nineteenth and early twentieth centuries. Fairclough (1985) has noted that the West End's beaches, Stanley Park, and the English Bay bathhouse (a public washroom/change room facility intended for the use of beach patrons) have been gay cruising places in Vancouver historically, long before any material gay presence was evident in the area. Furthermore, the coincidence of gay political activism emerging at the same time as the redevelopment in the West End, most notably the sudden increase in rental apartments, allowed gay spatialisation and the formation of a neighbourhood identity to occur quite rapidly:

> Long-time residents suggest that the West End had a small population of self-identified homosexuals as early as the late 1940s, when the area was largely a rooming-house environment. The gay liberation movement of the early 1970s, combined with the rapid expansion of inexpensive one-bedroom apartments in the area, made the West End a focus for gay migration across western Canada. (Fairclough 1995, 96)

As in Toronto (Bouthillette 1994) and Manchester (Whittle 1994), early bars were located in the commercial and industrial districts, away from residential areas. However, as gay settlement began in the West End—the affordable residential area closest to these gay places, in fact located between these "formalised" semipublic places and the more traditional outdoor places—bars began migrating west to Davie, Burnaby, and Robson Streets. Then it is the presence of a large number of apartment buildings in the West End that was a key to the development of a gay ghetto there. Had it not been for that housing, one may speculate that, like Manchester, the neighbourhood's gay identity may have been far less recognised; it is residential concentration that allows gay men to become visible in their everyday lives.

Bars create a nighttime-based set of gay places that can remain largely invisible to those not frequenting the area at those times. A gay residential presence, however, creates a visibility that is evident at all times and in many other everyday places. This is what allows a gay ghetto like the West End to materialise and become part of the local gay or straight consciousness. Indeed, at least from the early 1970s, popular media have noted the presence of gay men in the West End. This population base has furnished the neighbourhood with the essential element needed for further gay institutionalisation to occur in a process of reproduction, given its creation of both a gay market as well as an important symbolic yet rooted gay identity.

This model for the production of gay male places has clearly been repeated in Vancouver. Beginning with a neocolonial and frontier-town landscape of sexual opportunities that drew gay men to the downtown area, there were soon opportunities for settlement in the nearby West End. In the rapidly expanding town, the only feasible residential node for single people in the vicinity of these sexual crossroads was the West End. Similarly, as I will now demonstrate, areas that are known as lesbian districts, in Vancouver and elsewhere, were selected based on this community's particular politics and cultural heritage, although events unfolded in a rather dissimilar manner.

Commercial Drive: Where the Counterculture and the Reconstructed Family Converge

Just as the West End reflected the needs of gay men in the early 1970s, Commercial Drive has embodied for lesbians a distinctive set of politics and material possibilities. In her study of New York's lesbian spaces, Rothenberg (1995) contended that "the timing of Park Slope's gentrification and the women's movement—particularly the directions of lesbian-feminism, cultural feminism and radical feminism—was essential in creating Park Slope as the centre of lesbian population in New York" (175). Closely associated with countercultural values, lesbian-feminist ideals continue to embrace community-oriented living and lesbian feminists seek to (re)construct space to reflect these ideals. As we have seen, Commercial Drive certainly fits this model. A successful combination of countercultural and ethnic institutions, the neighbourhood figured prominently in the "radical" 1960s and 1970s. As observed by one informant, the two Vancouver neighbourhoods that harboured communes in the 1970s were Kitsilano and Grandview-Woodland. However, by the late 1970s and early 1980s Kitsilano had gentrified, while Grandview-Woodland retained its marginal countercultural ambience. Most likely it was the stabilising influence of a diverse ethnic population (*Vancouver Magazine,* 1988, 107) that effectively resisted significant middle-class invasion over the years, as well as the stigma that the 'East Side' bears as the "part of Vancouver where people live only by necessity, never by choice" (White 1980, 103).

Seemingly, this marginal character continued into the 1980s and to a certain extent into the 1990s, when Brad Jackson (1984) identified a "new wave" of people attracted to the Drive, a group composed of "an amorphous and loosely connected group of students, radicals, feminists, gays, artists, and full and marginal professionals, amongst others," whom he saw as having had an impact on changing the Southern

European character of the neighbourhood, on housing and "in the various formal and informal institutions that they have helped to create in the area" (151).

The common perception of the Drive as formerly a mainly Italian area persists, and thus a certain ambiguity arises when one considers that this neighbourhood was especially associated with working-class Latin machismo prior to lesbians' moving in. Cultural diversity, beyond its desirable and often highly marketable cosmopolitan aesthetic, has allowed lesbians to belong, to become a minority within a collection of minorities. Perhaps Rothenberg was correct to observe that lesbians fail to create visible spaces more because of their historical inability to effect local political power than because of essentialist notions of aterritorial femininity, as posited by Castells (1984). If so, then the Drive's grassroots political history would have been yet another attractive feature for lesbians who, at the time of their initial spatialisation, were still very much influenced by feminist praxis. To lesbians in particular, the neighbourhood is especially known for its lesbian-feminist political awareness. According to one resident of the Drive, this has long been the case, for even in 1980 the area was known for harbouring "a lot of political dykes."

As suggested earlier, timing has had a lot to do with the spatialisation of lesbians in Vancouver. While it was the "coming together" of lesbian emancipation and the counterculture that provided lesbians with a culture and a certain sense of spatial control, it was the coming together of these cultural movements and changing social conditions that led to a final spatialisation. The material conditions that existed in Grandview-Woodland in the late 1970s and early 1980s were ripe for lesbian settlement. The presence of cheap suitable housing is perhaps the most often cited locational motivation for lesbians on the Drive, and this is attributed, more often than not, to the fact that lesbians are women. Clearly, gender-based spatial restrictions have affected lesbians in various ways. The first of these has to do with household structure. Even though gay and lesbian households typically include two or more same-sex unrelated people and are equally nontraditional in other respects, lesbian households are further marginalised because lesbians "are far more likely than gay men to carry family responsibilities, to have children" (Adler & Brenner 1992, 26). Because many lesbians do not "come out" until after they are married with children (Wolf 1979) or because, like so many other women, they become single mothers at an early age, they are "more likely than gay men to be primary caretakers of children" (Adler & Brenner 1992, 32). As a result, housing and neighbourhood requirements will include space and facilities for children and an environment that is more conducive to raising a family—more so than, for instance, would be a downtown neighbourhood typical of gay male ghettoes. Family considerations, then, are a further spatial restriction placed on lesbians because they are women.

Contrary to many gay men, women and lesbians face some significant financial constraints. Lesbians, as women, single mothers, and often live-in partners with other women, are at the extreme opposite end of the economic spectrum, with statistically low-average income, being women with family responsibilities. Solutions to such economic constraints have combined both feminist community ideals and the need for affordability (Altman 1982). Women's communes are perhaps the most radical of these solutions, yet communes include many of the elements judged ideal for lesbian mothers, such as sharing facilities, costs of childcare, and household chores. Co-operatives are certainly a more common option, especially since the late 1980s, but perhaps the most common arrangement is the simple sharing of a house by two or more households, often in the form of subdivided flats (Anlin 1989). This scenario is not altogether different from Rose's (1984) theory of marginal gentrification.

The Commercial Drive neighbourhood has always had a family orientation, with a large number of "unconventional" rental units, co-ops, secondary suites, flats in houses, and even communal arrangements that have long had lower rents than the city average. Having resisted widespread gentrification, these conditions therefore offered a secure affordable environment for lesbians fifteen years ago. In addition, the neighbourhood's housing stock is also better suited to households that may include children or several adults in cost-sharing situations.

(Re)producing Queer Places in Vancouver

Key processes in inscribing certain areas as gay male or lesbian spaces are what I define as the "reproduction" of gay spaces. Here, then, I seek to describe the ways in which the gay identity of the neighbourhoods is maintained and recognised by Vancouver's population, gay or straight. In other words, I investigate the material strategies that were adopted in the West End and on the Drive to reinforce the gay ideologies of these spaces. In this way, I am describing the ways in which gay people have modified their environments to reflect their values, needs, and desires. However, this description has an important corollary: Space itself plays a significant role in shaping the cultures that depend on and emerge out of it. Evidently, a process is at work whereby Vancouver's local gay male and female cultures are being reproduced by these environments. This reverse process clearly also merits investigation.

Of the two neighbourhoods, the West End is the most developed as a distinct subcultural place. This situation is undoubtedly a direct reflection of men's higher access to capital, although it also reflects gay men's culture as distinct from that of gay women. Lesbian culture in Vancouver, by contrast, merges to a significant degree with women's culture. Rothenberg (1995) identified "semilesbian or lesbian-congenial spaces" (165) in Park Slope, rather than fully lesbian spaces, and I think this also applies to the Drive.

Several types of gay-friendly or other specific land uses exist in the West End: commercial, residential, institutional, and fleeting and relatively permanent meeting places. Indeed, by most standards (Murray 1979), it would be considered an "institutionally complete" gay neighbourhood. Most, though not all, of these spaces are oriented to gay men as opposed to lesbians, but some are patronised by a variety of people.[2] Furthermore, many non-gay-oriented places also exist in the neighbourhood, including a few supermarkets, a McDonald's, a pharmacy, a number of hotels and offices, and other shops and businesses. Still, the area harbours a significant concentration of gay-oriented places that clearly mark it as a gay neighbourhood.

The places that reproduce the West End as a gay space can be divided roughly into two major categories: the formal ones and the informal ones. The latter, if difficult to isolate or define, are nonetheless the most unequivocally gay in character. These include the more time-specific spaces, such as Stanley Park trails after dark, as well as the streets themselves any time of day. Of course, all the streets are not all gay all the time. Yet it is on the streets that one may witness two men walking hand-in-hand or engaged in a parting embrace on the corner of Davie and Thurlow, and these are the acts that inscribe the neighbourhood as a gay space.

It is also on the streets that gay men live their everyday lives, supported by the network of more formalised spaces that line them. Perhaps the most "visibly gay" of these spaces are commercial ones: gay book/gift stores, gay cafés and restaurants, trendy men's clothing stores. The businesses typically display rainbow flags, stickers, or windsocks—the international gay symbol. And a conspicuous number of patrons are male and sport the gay fashions of the day. These spaces create a "scene" where gay men linger and are recognised by others, and by some straights, as such. They create a network of meeting places, of places to be seen. Recently, gay male enclaves have often created landscapes of consumption—of fashion, food, and coffee, coffee, coffee—where the dubious bar as meeting ground has been replaced by more socially acceptable alternatives. Indeed, the consumption aspect of the neighbourhood is what brings many to its streets, and it can get overwhelming at times.

A central force in the gay male landscape that emerges *is* consumption. Like many people, it is through consumption that gay men socialise, but more importantly, it is through consumption that they are recognised. It is these places of consumption that mark the West End as a gay area to those who are familiar with it, straight or gay. It is by the location of these places, as advertised in the city's gay newspapers, that newcomers to the city or the city's newly "out" can map Vancouver's gay male geography. In this way, the West End's gay character is significantly reproduced through its places of consumption. The predominance of gay-oriented or gay-owned and/or operated services in the neighbourhood also reinforce its gayness.[3] This character is further reinforced as many of the city's major gay events, male or female, take place in the West End.

The lesbian identity of the Drive, though known throughout most of Vancouver, is forged around different elements. Most notably, its reproduction has been some-

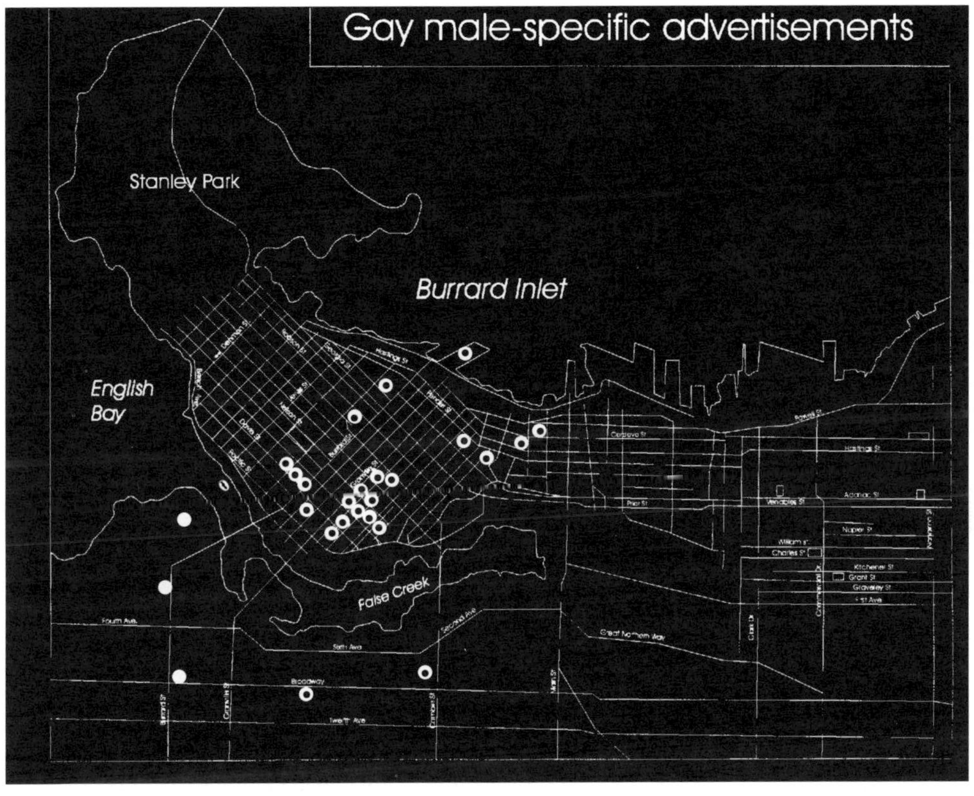

Gay male-specific advertisements. Map by Anne-Marie Bouthillette.

what more subtle than that of the West End because it is less evident as a material culture. First of all there are not as many gay-specific shops or venues, though this is not unusual (Rothenberg 1995). Rather, the strategy of "lesbianising" the Drive has overwhelmingly involved using the spaces that were there and appropriating them, if only temporarily. In this way, one could say that lesbians have come into more direct contact with nonlesbian neighbours, and this is the main process by which the lesbian character of the neighbourhood came to be recognised by the population at large.

The basic elements that have marked the Drive as a lesbian space have largely been feminist or women's institutions.[4] Given lesbianism's link with feminism and women's issues in general, such a place-based focus on women's institutions, at a time when these were a rarity, not only reinforced the area as one open to and active in women's issues but it created a strong lesbian association for the area. Lesbians came to recognise that as the Drive attracted feminist activists, it would also invariably attract other lesbians—women active in the movement themselves, or women expecting the presence of the latter. While the political history of the neighbourhood attracted lesbians in the first place, their presence served to confirm the political awareness of the Drive and keep them there. The leftist political inclination of the neighbourhood has certainly not waned, and the recent relocation of the Greenpeace offices[5] to the Drive continues to reinforce its politics. Furthermore, the celebration of Stonewall 25[6] in Grandview Park, on Commercial Drive, worked to bring neighbourhood politics closer to gay politics; also the Women in View festival, a number of whose venues are in the area, continues to strongly identify the neighborhood with women's politics.

On Commercial Drive, high levels of local "networking" and socialising undoubtedly create a forum within which the lesbian culture and identity can develop. This networking has also undeniably contributed to the area's streets becoming the primary focus of lesbian public life, as mentioned by another informant and confirmed by some of the above observations. This also reflects a creative female use of space, as streets are the most immediately accessible public places. Unable economically to support an array of more formal establishments, lesbians have, unlike their male counterparts, appropriated this most obvious public space.

Formal commercial places do exist in the area, and they have served to reinforce lesbian identities and identifications. However, like the institutions, they are more oriented to women. For instance, the Book Mantel on Commercial Drive was for a long time the only women's bookstore in Vancouver, and it carried books and magazines of interest to lesbians and gay men. Other stores, such as a maternity shop and a couple of women's consignment clothing stores, also create a focus for women, while book and food co-ops including Uprising Breads (an East Vancouver hippie landmark) reinscribe—and to some extent embellish and mythologise—the area's leftist roots. Furthermore, lesbian-owned shops, though not necessarily lesbian-specific, are beginning to take hold. These include a toy/games store and a new women's sex shop, Womyn's Ware, whose owners insist it is open to anyone concerned with female sexuality, whether female or male, gay or straight or bisexual. Like the institutions described above, these commercial spaces mark a lesbian presence on the Drive, while giving the women a further stake in their neighbourhood and increasing their visibility to non-gay residents and visitors.

Perhaps the most effective way by which the area has become known by nongays as a lesbian neighbourhood relates to the integration that has taken place between the lesbians and the neighbourhood's other residents. Unlike the West End, the Drive retains a diverse character within which, as stated by Beaudry's (1988) informant, lesbians are "just another minority." Neighbourhood integration—often on a very small scale—has been significant in exposing the nongay area residents to lesbians, which has both raised awareness of the lesbian presence and lessened misconceptions around lesbianism.

The Not-so-queer Café as Site of Neighbourhood Conflict

While lesbian-specific social spaces have been attempted in the past, with Josephine's "bar/café" being the most notable example, they have failed to survive because, as

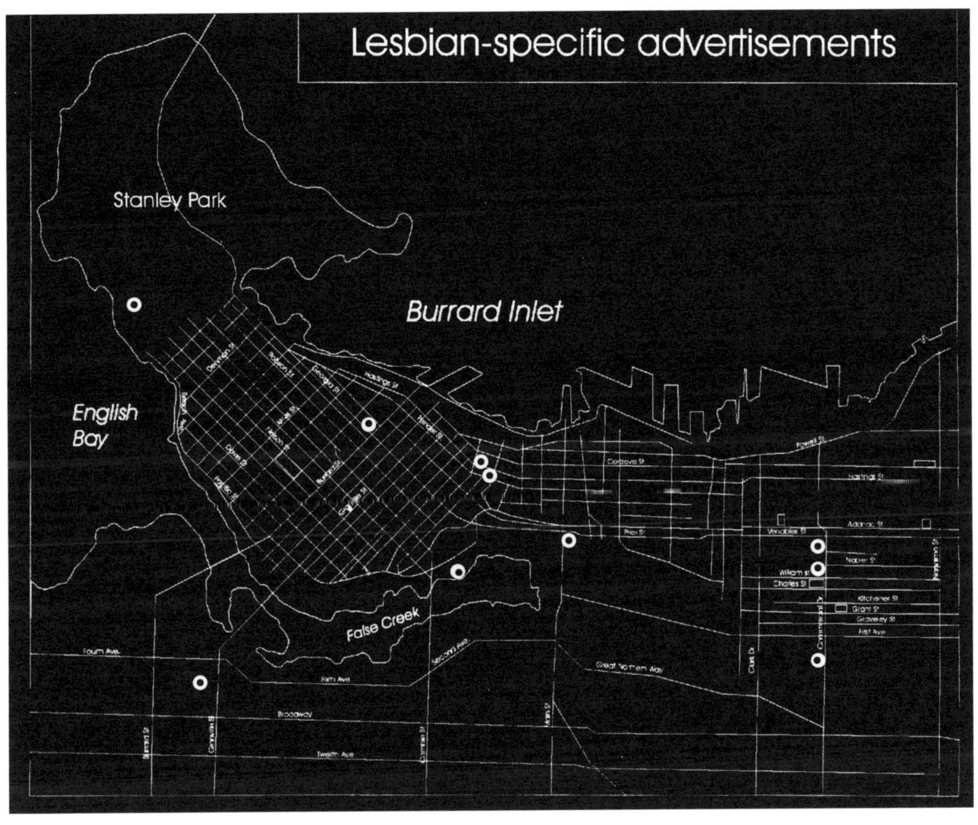

Lesbian-specific advertisements. Map by Anne-Marie Bouthillette.

noted by McNee (1984), lesbians don't have a lot of money and thus find it difficult to support spaces exclusively dedicated to them. Instead, lesbians have used existing places and have made their own space, however ephemeral, within the places. Joe's Café is such an example. A microcosm of the Drive, Joe's has not failed to include lesbians among its clientele. More than this, the coffee bar became an integral part of the lesbian community, although the relationship between Joe and his lesbian patrons remained largely a business association (Serafin 1994, 86). Some lesbians evidently felt close to Joe, and his place and the relationship was fairly respectful.

It is therefore ironic that a betrayal of this respect is what forever inscribed the Drive as a lesbian space. In the summer of 1990, one of Joe's waiters protested the affectionate behaviour of a couple of his lesbian customers. In an effort to support his waiter, Joe sided with him and was perceived as antilesbian. In a matter of hours, the incident escalated to the point where a city-wide boycott of Joe's Café was encouraged. Gay activists picketed the establishment, coming into verbally violent conflict with passersby and Joe's supporters (Serafin 1994; Ward 1990; Wilson 1990). Exchanges between Joe and the protesters precluded negotiation and deteriorated instead to such acts as Joe spraying the protesters with water and the protesters' mooning Joe. It was these symbolic and infamous acts of resistance, pale in comparison to the lesbian activism in other North American cities at the time, that came to inscribe and then to fossilize the Drive as a lesbian-congenial landscape. The misunderstanding was eventually cleared up, and lesbians have returned to patronise Joe's Café once again.

Given Vancouver's importance as the major Canadian enclave for left/lesbian feminism for decades, one of the most striking features of the lesbian community today is its decided lack of visible politics. Like most large North American cities, Vancouver supports a chapter of Lesbian Avengers, but they are not as active as in other cities.[7] Lesbian-specific activism was conspicuously absent; this was not unusual. Rather, lesbian politics in this city are more generally oriented to women's issues, local political concerns, and more broadly queer issues. Consequently, we see lesbians getting involved, for example, in women's housing co-ops, the Vancouver Status of Women office, AIDS Vancouver, the Out on Screen and Women in View festivals, and the pursuit of gay civil rights. I suspect because of the women's physical integration into a very mixed neighbourhood, lesbian culture in Vancouver conveys a very easy-going, tolerant character, in which it takes the place indeed of "just another minority" culture: female, lesbian, queer. That the lesbian community readily identifies with the Drive, itself an eclectic landscape where no one element prevails, is indicative of this cultural association as are the women who testified to their appreciation of the neighbourhood's diversity.

Commercial Drive is remarkable in its absence of lesbian bars and the general lack of emphasis on alchohol consumption. Despite lesbians' financial constraints and different socialisation patterns, even smaller cities support a number of lesbian bars and in some areas in increasing numbers (Wolfe 1992). There is no exclusively lesbian bar in all of Vancouver except for The Lotus, located between East Vancouver and the West End. But there are regular lesbian warehouse parties, most notably those sponsored by Flygirl, which appeal to a wide range of younger and less mainstream lesbians, such as those into leather, and these parties occur within walking distance of the West End.

Moving East/Moving West: The Blurring of Neighbourhood Identities

The boundaries between the gendered gay spaces in Vancouver are being increasingly transgressed by members of both communities, thus diminishing their actual validity. Perhaps the most noticeable trend is gay men moving away from the West End or other parts of the city, province, or country into Grandview-Woodland. The reason cited most often for this migration is financial. Rents in the West End are among the highest in Vancouver, making it more and more difficult for young people to live there. Indeed, the bulk of migrants are perceived to be young gay men who, twenty or even ten years ago, would have sought the West End as a viable refuge from hetero-society. Now, however, they find there a landscape of increasing home-ownership of new and converted condominiums and high rents. Presumably, the older men secured housing while it was still affordable and have a standard of living that comes with age and can support living in the West End. The cultural attraction is still there, but not everyone can afford to live in it. This is changing the demographics of the West End from the "swingers paradise" it was reputed to be in the 1960s and 70s, which continued with a distinctly more gay character into the 1980s, to a "yuppified" landscape of white upper-middle-class professionals.

The West End's marginality made it accessible at one time to those who existed on the margins of society, but like elsewhere, its gentrification produced some gay male displacement. Also, the intense focus on gayness, as noted by an earlier informant, made the neighbourhood intolerable to some. This preference for a more mixed community is echoed by another informant as well. But since the neighbourhood is economically unattainable for seniors and for most families and non-Chinese immigrants, it remains and presumably *will* remain homogeneous.

Another indicator of neighbourhood cultural change concerns the use of bars, and it appears that this may be a change that extends beyond Vancouver. Clearly, the perception that the gay male culture is a bar culture is alive in this city, at least among the gay men that I interviewed. Many of them apologised for not being active in the gay community, fearing they would not be a good interview because they did not go to bars and did not fit the lifestyle. The "lifestyle" is certainly promoted by gay publications such as the recently established *Xtra! West,* which often depicts muscular scantily-clad men in suggestive poses, thus reinforcing the importance of these places within the gay sphere. Yet, the interviewees' comments beg the question: Is this "lifestyle" outdated? It seems rather curious that most, if not all, of these men—who represent various age groups, life situations, and social circles—would be outside popular gay culture.

This changing gay-male social reality has meant that spatial changes have occurred in this community. One of the most obvious options to gay men looking for alternatives has been the Drive. With its still-affordable housing that includes a significant proportion of rental units, its social diversity, and its queer-positive character (thanks to the lesbians who paved the way for them), the Drive and its general vicinity have had an undeniable appeal to gay people from all over Vancouver. For men who don't identify with "the lifestyle," the Drive is a place where they can be gay without the sexually promiscuous image that still pervades the West End.

Evidence of these gendered migrations can be found in the evolving material landscape of the Drive, which includes a gay-male-owned grocery, a gay-male-owned gift and novelty shop, and, most notably, Harry's Off Commercial, the only gay-specific public space on or, in this case, slightly off the Drive. Harry's, which ironically sits in Josephine's old location, is owned by a gay man named Harry Grunsky and employs mainly gay men. It serves a predominantly gay but gender-mixed clientele, and it does not try to hide this from the rest of the community. While retaining its lesbian and gay elements, the Drive continues to emphasise its mixed character. The goal of lesbian and then gay migration has not been to turn the neighbourhood into another gay ghetto but to preserve its multifaceted character. There is little sense of any large-scale gay-influenced displacement taking place in Grandview-Woodland, of a broad-sweeping community or culture taking over the space. Rather, once again, acceptance is fostered and homophobia—already addressed and weakened by the lesbian presence—has the potential to be even further lessened here, too.

This blurring of identity boundaries is also felt in the West End, where gay women are now found in increasing numbers. Not at all excited by the prospect of an all-lesbian apartment building in the West End, one informant stated, "I don't think I'd like to live in that building! [laugh] I don't think so, I think I'd like to stay away from that one!" She was much more content living her life quietly—as a lesbian, yes, but not a radical lesbian. She was hardly apolitical; she was in fact quite active with the Gay and Lesbian Centre which operates out of the West End, volunteering her time on various projects and events. Yet she had not at all enjoyed her time on the Drive (approximately two years), finding the West End much more convenient and much more easygoing in terms of letting gay people express their affection for each other—not "in-your-face," to use her words, but "comfortable." In fact her comments about why she liked the West End echoed quite glaringly those of the men I had spoken with. The kind of space the men had created in the West End conformed to her values much better than the Drive did. This feeling presumably has long been the case for her, yet it was only with the breakdown of gender barriers between gay men and lesbians that she was able to move into that space. Similarly, to gay women who are new to Vancouver, the West End is perceived as a queer space, as opposed to a gay male space, and they move quite readily to this central neighbourhood, supported by the gay male and female network that has developed there and not at all fazed by the area's gay male history. While affordability is still an issue in the West End in general, there remain isolated pockets of relatively affordable housing that are particularly well-suited to lower-middle-income singles. Here again, then, a balance is achieved, evening out male-to-female ratios and reinforcing a cultural identity which, in this case, has been developed by the men but is being shared by the women.

The cultural identity cultivated and reproduced in each area is quite distinct, and although each arose out of cultural experiences historically particular to either gay men or lesbians, they are now sought after by both. Certainly, the areas' respective male or female reputations persist and are still embedded in Vancouver's gay folklore and psyche. It is not possible to erase history. Yet the cultures represented by each neighbourhood have less and less to do with gendered sexuality, and more and more with values and lifestyles that gay men and women can now openly share. In the case of Vancouver, this has meant that the West End continues to be a neighbourhood very much associated with its active material culture—its clubs, cafés, theatres, and shopping—while the Drive has its leftist political street culture—with its alternative theatre,[8] multicultural population, shops and facilities, and its socioeconomic mix:

> Commercial Drive is the future, man . . . Vancouver isn't going to stay middle-class anglo-white forever—the 21st century is just around the corner and it's going to bring some major upheavals to this part of the world. You might as well get used to it now. (Beaudry 1988, 125—quoted from a "self-described neighbourhood sociologist")

The issue of who can subscribe to the ideologies and participate in the experiences embodied in each of these spaces is no longer an issue of gay men versus lesbians. Exchanges between the two populations are now conceivable and do occur. A sense of solidarity between gay men and women is developing, which has everything to do with the right to lead their everyday lives openly, in a manner and with whom they choose. This development clearly brings the men and women much closer to hetero-society and thus it comes as no surprise that a similar kind of open migration and blending between gay spaces and straight spaces is occurring.

Like lesbian-feminist culture, gay male culture is shifting away from sexuality as a defining factor; political ideology and everyday life are becoming increasingly central to gay male identity, thus lessening the need for material spaces that cater to one's sexual needs. Therefore, traditional gay male enclaves such as ghettoes no longer reflect actual gay male life, and new places are sought. Conversely, within lesbian culture, female sexuality is being more and more celebrated, thus mirroring traditional gay male culture. While sexual lesbian material places have yet to establish themselves in any permanent sense, lesbian events in Vancouver are including more sexual content, such as sex shows at the annual International Lesbian Week celebrations or go-go girls at parties. Lesbian erotica books and magazines are flourishing, and two Vancouver-based theatre productions *(Herotica* and *Herotica II)* have featured short and explicit plays about female gay and straight sexuality. Gay male culture and lesbian culture, clearly, are becoming less and less distinct. Consequently, it is logical that their spatial choices should change to reflect these blurring distinctions.

Conclusion

Gay men and lesbians, as men and women with different socioeconomic means and family responsibilities, have (or at least, had, in the context of these initial spatialisations) distinct housing needs that were particularly well met in neighbourhoods that eventually became gay-identified. It was a balance of material housing characteristics and other socioeconomic and cultural attributes, including gay-specific material culture such as the presence of gay public places, that attracted gay men to the West End and lesbians to Grandview-Woodland. However, it is questionable whether, without appropriate housing, the neighbourhoods would have survived and thrived to the extent that they have. Housing is also what drew definite boundaries between male and female gay spaces, as women were less able to afford West End housing or raise their families there, while gay men could afford the more central location's apartments, which also suited them better in terms of their typically smaller households.

Similarly, it is housing that is, again, forcing this shift in spatial boundaries. Specifically, it is the increasing cost of urban accommodations that is most tangibly pushing gay men and women away from central urban areas, and into straight-identified suburbs. While some resistance is evident, and cross-city/cross-gender migration is occurring between the West End and the Drive in an effort to retain a measure of gay spatial identity, the real costs of living in the inner city are becoming too much for some gay people, especially those looking to enter the housing market. Because some of the areas that gay people are moving into are straight-identified and straight-designed neighbourhoods, they may require different neighbourhood concepts, if not different structural housing designs. Also, associated neighbourhood amenities will need to reflect a multiplicity of sexual identities. Certain community services such as health, daycare, and commercial enterprises, for instance, will need to institute policies towards or at least be able to respond to the needs of people in same-sex households.

The Queer Nation Acts Up: Health Care, Politics, and Sexual Diversity in the County of Angels, 1990–92[1]

Ty Geltmaker[2]

Today death, burnout, and the lack of governmental advocacy still overshadow the modest gains made in airing and framing the public debate over AIDS prevention and care. And new grief too easily eclipses recognition of the daily acts of care and survival by individuals and the responses of communities and institutions to the crisis. In Los Angeles in 1996, the epidemic has not "leveled off" and still largely conforms to the epidemiological breakdowns that I reported in 1991. Since Los Angeles County started counting in 1982, some 29,633 men and 1,835 women have been officially diagnosed with AIDS. With 20,748 deaths, 10,720 people are living with AIDS. This does not include the tens of thousands of people living with HIV but not diagnosed with AIDS. While case-fatality rates by year of diagnosis show that people are living longer with AIDS, a recent Los Angeles County AIDS Surveillance Summary[3] reported 3,617 new AIDS cases in 1995. The overwhelming majority of reported AIDS cases are white gay men, followed by Latino gay males.[4] Such information raises as many questions about class, interracial homosexual behavior, and ethnically related religious shame as it does about the historic underreporting in communities that are medically underserved. The current figures for women have some parallels and some key differences from those for men. The largest and most significant increase in cases of women infected is for African Americans.[5] However, in comparison with the number of AIDS-infected African-American women in New York City, the numbers for Los Angeles are comparatively low.

As overt government hostility has declined, an ostensibly more sympathetic Los Angeles County Board of Supervisors, caged by a virulently antitax, anti-immigrant electorate, continues to cut health and public services across the board. The once somewhat generous State of California is now legislatively dominated by an electorate that has returned Governor Pete Wilson, who wants to cut services and build walls to exclude "foreigners" and the full public presence of the majority "minority" population. For example, my electoral district includes East Hollywood, Silverlake, and Echo Park. This district is emblematic of the conditions that make county and suburban domination of the city of Los Angeles possible. This area has the highest percentage of registered voters who vote, and they vote overwhelmingly Democratic and for the

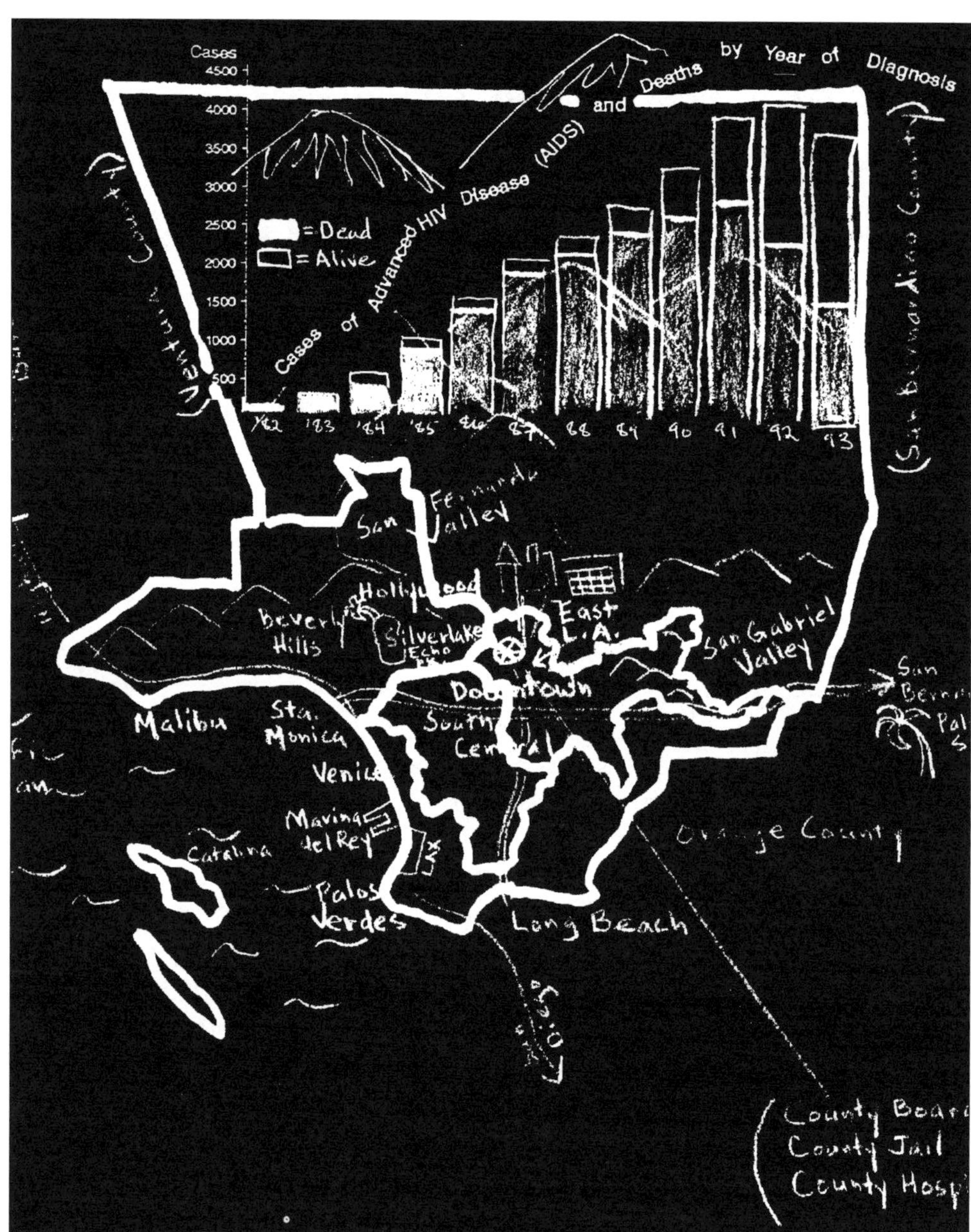

Cases of advanced HIV disease (AIDS) and deaths by year of diagnosis. Collage by Ty Geltmaker.

progressive "left." The area also has the highest percentage of residents in the Los Angeles city limits who cannot vote. These nonvoters are either illegal working people, who have no right to vote even if they wish to participate in local political life, or they are longtime legal aliens who choose not to become citizens because they do not fully identify with the government and culture of the United States. The latter group includes many Mexican-born residents who continue to identify with that country and who experience California as part of Mexico. This alienation from United States electoral life often extends to individuals who are bilingual and to their children.

California's county health care system is in collapse, and the care of people with AIDS has been mercifully farmed out to quasi-public, quasi-private, largely gay-identified service agencies. Foremost among these are AIDS Project Los Angeles, The Gay and Lesbian Community Services Center, and AIDS Healthcare Foundation. These organizations do heroic work, providing levels of care far better than those provided to any disease-identified group served by the Los Angeles County hospital system. But this two-tiered system of health-services delivery points to the quasi-privatized civic polity that continues to dominate Los Angeles. And this situation begs the question of whether this is any way to run a democratic health-care program not based on marginal levels of crisis management. Our service agencies, which are gay-identified and largely white and still effectively race-conscious, cannot adequately reach out to all communities at risk. Certainly the delivery of services remains "un-even" at best. More problematic is the question of why gay people should have to accept the specialized burden that the historically homophobic Los Angeles County elders so enthusiastically unloaded on us. Is this "our" disease?

In "postmodern" Los Angeles, architectonics reflect local politics. The modular 5P-21 AIDS multiservice County-USC clinic, the almost singular focus of early ACT UP/LA's militant efforts and one that drained the energy of so many people, already has been dismantled. The mirrored prefabricated building has been reduced to a ruin in the shadow of the soon-to-be-demolished County-USC hospital. For all of the good done by the current community-based "safety net," I want to scream from my private rooftop that today's nongovernmental emphasis, no matter how politically fashionable, is largely a replication of the balkanized history of Los Angeles's local politics and fiefdoms. For groups without formidable political lobbies, today's system does not offer many workable models for keeping people well and caring for the sick.

As elsewhere, recent "in-your-face" activism in Los Angeles often has been channeled into social service delivery, as it had previously been professionalized into treatment-issue advocacy. A tiny band of aging street activists and more youthful cultural militants continues to engage in occasional public confrontation in Los Angeles. I confess that I have retreated into private anger and grief, doing what I can for friends—living and dead—causing trouble where I can find reason for it.

The emergence of organized political groups of people with AIDS has forced issues of health and illness into public visibility, which threatens traditional assumptions of privacy and public heterosexual privilege. The struggle against the stigmatization of AIDS has forced many gay men and lesbians to reject the relative pleasures of the closet and its legal girdings in discredited notions of constitutional privacy and

Fortress health care. The 1930s County of Los Angeles/University of Southern California Hospital is a teaching institution and a visible icon of community health care access, especially for poor residents of the neighborhoods east of downtown Los Angeles. ACT UP/LA's successful campaign to establish a designated AIDS ward and out-patient HIV/AIDS clinic revealed a system rife with delays of many months for virtually all medical treatments, HIV-related or not. The HIV clinic that was established has since been dismantled, as such services were taken over by primarily gay-identified community agencies. Despite its historic and iconographic importance, the building is slated for demolition, with a new facility to be built farther east in Los Angeles County.

insist on the right to be "queer" on their own terms in public. ACT UP and Queer Nation present a threat not only to prevailing state and church ideologies of power and submission but more importantly to the gendered and sexualized assumptions that define the boundaries of public space itself. People who are ill and people defined as degenerates present a special threat to the historical myths and antiurban morphology of Los Angeles, which those in power still perceive to be an island of private consumption and public piety. The challenge presented by ACT UP and Queer Nation is an integral part of the population densification of the region, feared by old Anglo and new Catholic authorities.

Pain and Pleasure

I would like to ask readers to imagine me speaking these words while stickering myself with the slogans and logos that have made AIDS activism as much a fashion statement as a political vision. I do this not only to remind everyone that AIDS Is Not Over, that Women Die Faster, that I Am A Fag, and that Silence Equals Death, but also to appropriate my body itself as a politically trespassed public space. This reclaiming of the private body as a site of public controversy has everything to do with what I want to infuse into a discussion of health care and sexual diversity in the County of Angels.

I want to talk about visibility and invisibility in the context of human needs and legal rights, expanding the notion of what is acceptably public without surrendering the need for and right to private intimacy. I want to be free to wander through this continuum, emphasizing the particular intensity of such needs and rights on the part of people with illness generally, and people with AIDS specifically. I include all people whose sexuality has been at best tolerated so long as it remains unspoken and unseen, a restraint imposed by conservative privacy legalisms which were held constitutionally nonexistent for homosexuals under the Supreme Court's 1986 *Bowers v. Hardwick* "sodomy" decision.[6]

I also want to suggest that the right-to-privacy defense for private sexual acts is culturally shallow and can easily be employed to silence and closet those who are deemed to be degenerate.[7] And I want to talk about how, in addition to challenging the social inequities that are the real plague for people with AIDS and for self-proclaimed "queers," groups like the AIDS Coalition to Unleash Power (ACT UP) and Queer Nation are consciously subverting entrenched assumptions of power relations, particularly in the arena of public discourse and public space.[8]

Finally, I want to suggest that of all the major North American urban centers caught up in the crisis of AIDS and the challenge of the new queer activism, Los Angeles is historically and morphologically most resistant to the public discussion and representation of death and degeneracy, except perhaps as lurid entertainment in Hollywood films. With so many of us dying of illness and intolerance at society's

Fortress society. Public life in a region known for informality and leisure is increasingly governed by a plethora of rules regulating pedestrian conduct and sociability. These rules of nonengagement stand as a warning to loiterers and lingerers at the entrance to the recessed gardens behind the County Hall of Administration. Such architecturally reinforced restrictions limit options for public presence, including political demonstrations.

pleasure, it should shock no one when we scream: "You Say Don't Fuck, We Say Fuck You" accompanied by the chant "Whose Fucking Streets, Our Fucking Streets."[9]

Since 1987 when, first in New York and then quickly around the country, ACT UP groups came together, the mortally fluid membership has focused on advocating the medical and social needs of people with AIDS, while also fighting AIDS ignorance and bigotry—whether outright homophobia or not. From its emergence in the spring and summer of 1990, Queer Nation—with its tribal ethos of inclusive diversity—has creatively reasserted the notion that safe sex does not mean no sex. Nine years into the epidemic gay men, lesbians, and others who were both drained and emboldened by the battle against AIDS teamed up with younger and older generations of sexual outlaws and formed autonomous Queer Nations across the country. Many of the new Queer Nationals set themselves immediately apart from "assimilationists," who allegedly identified too smugly with a semicomfortable world created out of pre-AIDS gay rights advances. At the same time, some AIDS activists for whom health care and medical research had justifiably become the preeminent issue feared Queer Nation might become "prematurely post-AIDS."

By 1990 ACT UP's town-hall style of debate and open voting, combined with its continued commitment to grassroots agitation, as well as increasing participation in mainstream scientific and political forums, led to factious splits and the founding of splinter ACT UPs in San Francisco, Chicago, Seattle, and elsewhere. This schismatic trend was exacerbated by the tension in all ACT UP chapters between those who would focus strictly on AIDS and those who could not separate AIDS activism from a global politics of radical social transformation.

ACT UP/LA avoided a formal secession, even when it was rocked with similar disagreements over tactics and priorities—particularly regarding whether or not to "negotiate" minimal AIDS funding levels with local government officials. In one such case some members of ACT UP scheduled private meetings with these politicians, intending to tell them not to take "personally" an announced, group-sponsored civil disobedience action. When this was discussed, ACT UP's general body (a corporal metaphor with deep resonance) voted to order a halt to such contacts. This attempt to engage in quasi-official, backroom bargaining by a "responsible" self-styled diplomatic corps—ostensibly backed up by unknowing and obedient troops—was denounced as elitist (no one had elected ACT UP to exclusively "negotiate" for people with AIDS), antidemocratic (the general body had not been informed of or consulted on such specific "negotiations"), and delusional (ACT UP was not an armed force, nor could it go out on strike in the event of failed "negotiations").

Such internal conflicts show ACT UP to be situated in a classically fragile "Jacobin" dilemma of balancing. On the one hand, there is a stated commitment to grassroots democratic procedure and open sharing of information. On the other, there is the countervailing necessity to use almost any means possible in fighting an army of bigots and silent collaborators who present what is perceived to be a mortal threat to individual well-being and the "public safety." But the exigencies of a political coalition united in grief and anger have produced an environment not so conducive to the reception of Robespierrean "leadership" and paranoia as to the steady but tense growth of a Dantonesque willingness to compromise for the common goal of eradicating AIDS.

Now ten years into the epidemic of government hostility and neglect, what is remarkable is the absence of a violent response by activists committed to civil disobedience and humorously postmodern theatrical disruption. A unique synergism of grief, creatively politicized anger, and increasingly specialized scientific expertise is modulated by competing claims to the necessity of secrecy *versus* the imperative of group trust within an atmosphere of radical, democratic debate. In the face of this synergy, it has been difficult for "historic" leaders to manipulate ACT UP's agenda. And the absence of traditional hierarchies has made it difficult for police effectively to infiltrate, despite documented surveillance and harassment.[10]

In this context, Queer Nation was from the beginning dedicated to operating on a more informal, consensual, and ad hoc model of direct action—much as ACT UP itself had done in its earliest years. This distinction no doubt reflects the fact that AIDS imposes an urgency and necessity for sophisticated understandings of science and politics, which not even the compelling fight for gay and lesbian rights can match. One can leave a Queer Nation action feeling good, even if all has not been won. But AIDS is a nonstop drum beating in one's head, and no amount of acting up or gaining progress can assuage it short of the eradication of bigotry and the virus itself. Despite the fact that Queer Nation might be seen as a place for restive people tired of always being angry in the ACT UP mode, the two groups have remained remarkably cross-pollinated and complementary as political engines and personal safe spaces.

As ACT UP came under increasing pressure to "de-homosexualize" its logos and gay-identified style to accommodate the rising numbers of heterosexuals with AIDS, Queer Nation reignited the defused fight for sexual liberation with a gay vengeance, putting gay bashers on notice that "Queers Bash Back."[11] Combining ACT UP's theatrical and persistently gay-identified tactics with a campy commitment to "having the last laugh," Queer Nation's self-proclaimed fags, dykes, faeries, transsexuals, drag queens, witches, and pagans declared war on "homo-hatred" and "compulsory heterosexism in all its cultural manifestations," while calling for a multigendered and multiracial, anticonsumerist society open to "queers of all sexual persuasions."[12] The group's stated refusal to "pander to heterosexual angst" was most forcefully expressed in the 1990 essay "I Hate Straights," plastered across New York and other urban centers. Through marches, kiss-ins, and carnival-like excursions, the new Queer Nationals challenged homophobia as well as hypocritically militarized and commercialized homoeroticism in the government, in the churches, in the entertainment and advertising industries, and in the streets, theme parks, and malls of America.

In Los Angeles and elsewhere this new activism, combined with an increasingly public lesbian eroticism, resulted in the birth of moveable "clubs" with such provocative names as "Fuck" and "Clit." This trend complemented the already established tradition of community-based, safe-sex "jerk-off" gatherings for gay men.[13] Some Queer Nationals even went so far as to argue that the truly subversive act was sex between gay men and lesbians. Others rejected such prescriptions as "pseudo-feminist neo-heterosexuality."[14] All of this took place while the country at-large was titillated with many of the same issues through Madonna's provocations in interviews, videos, and the self-produced feature film *Truth or Dare*—the social bases of which had already been explored in Jennie Livingston's critically acclaimed documentary on New York black and Latino gay youths and "vogue" balls, *Paris Is Burning*.[15]

It can be debated, of course, whether this new activism constitutes a form of liberation or if it is—like Madonna—a self-conscious caricature of social angst and deepest longings to "justify our love." It is unclear whether or not this new culture war—which transcends the traditional defense against homophobic preachers and politicians with the openly stated goal of "promoting homosexuality"—will lead to long-term expanded sexual freedom and public sociability. Some have even suggested that this frenzy of political and cultural activity is, in addition to all else, our battered community's ritual of mourning.[16]

Whatever the temporary analysis or final outcome may be, the losses we have suffered in the meantime will never be exorcised—except perhaps in the minds of those who still embrace Southern California as a place to live in mythic privacy amidst fecal oceans and toxic desert breezes and under rat-infested palms.

Word and Fetish

At the outset I must object to some of the conditions of my discussion. First, I do not have AIDS, nor am I HIV-positive. I don't usually reveal that fact, out of solidarity with my lover, one of my brothers, and everyone else who is HIV-positive. By a fluke, I am not. But I take no solace in that. After having lived, until testing, under the reasonable but false assumption that my results would be positive, I now live with HIV anyway, as one half of a mixed sero-status couple. This gives me a right to speak with some authority even if I also believe that people with HIV/AIDS have a privilege to be heard first and last and to be part of all discussions and policy-making. HIV status does not determine the propriety of one's behavior or the rightness of one's position. But as my lover and I have had to do in our personal life, at least some scientific researchers and health care providers have learned to balance these competing claims to authenticity. Academics and intellectuals need to do so, too. There are already too many AIDS profiteers, carpetbaggers, and critic-cannibals. I don't want to add my name to the list.

Second, even though I have involved myself in every level of ACT UP and Queer Nation work, my concept of grassroots activism requires an anarchically individualist scepticism toward the very groups with which I am affiliated. I share neither the messianic self-congratulatory fervor of some activists nor the safely distant fascination of the observant but removed scholar. While I may appreciate critic Elaine Showalter's recognition of the "stunningly articulate" women and men of ACT UP,[17] I also know that these articulations are occasionally muddled by individuals with unresolved sexual and religious identities, and for whom AIDS activism becomes as much a church/social club as a political movement. In this sense I am typical of most ACT UP and Queer Nation women and men. Most of us simply want to be left alone, alive and well in the combative arms of our lovers, free to be ourselves in a pluralistic society where health care—like speech, education, housing, and food—is a right. We only wish ACT UP and Queer Nation did not have to exist.

Third, as I imply later in this article, with regard to communities defined by race and class, I also cannot speak for people not of my gender. No amount of understanding of shared or analogous experiences of my marginalization as a gay man in a straight society can make my comments those of a woman in an androcentric world. I say this even though I do believe—as a feminist Queer National—that those of us locked out of the burning house of male heterosexual privilege have more in common than not. As James Baldwin put it while speaking of race more than thirty years ago, none of us wants to be integrated back in, and we have the well-suffered advantage of not believing in the myths which sustain those who oppress and exclude us.[18]

But even as I dare not speak for women, or especially for women with HIV or AIDS, I do not wish to gratuitously bash men. I think it is possible—and necessary—to recognize the ways in which men are victimized by race, class, and even gender proscriptions, while rejecting the reductionist conflation of personally experienced injury and officially sanctioned group oppression commonly resorted to by representatives of the so-called Men's Movement. Racism poisons whites, and misogyny and homophobia take their toll even on those who preach the hate. But slaves are not masters, and women and homosexuals do not enjoy the historic social advantages even of heterosexually identified men who thump their neofeminist chests in humble rage. It is also true that some women—organized within groups such as the Traditional Values Coalition, The Concerned Women of America, and Operation Rescue—have acquired a relative sense of power attacking women and men who advocate reproductive and sexual choice.[19] While it may be true historically that such female power roles are fleeting and restricted within a greater male field of control,[20] it is no less true that gay men and lesbians are oppressed by women whose homophobia and heterosexism are not just symptomatic of internalized false male consciousness. The armies of homeless men, with and without AIDS, in the streets and subways of New York City and even Los Angeles also force me to reexamine notions of uncontested male privilege.[21]

Nevertheless, as a man in the midst of an epidemic that has ravaged the community I most identify with, I must never forget to recognize the front-line work of women care providers and activists in the fight against AIDS, public ignorance, and government inaction. Groups like WHAM! (Women's Health Action Mobilization), DAM! (Dyke Action Machine!), and ACT UP's Women's Caucus have forced all of us not only to respond to the "second wave" of AIDS—which is to say, among women—

but also to recognize that the wave has always been there, submerged beneath a health care system that treats women as mothers, sex partners of men, and vectors of disease, but not as individuals.

It has taken far too long for most people to accept the fact that the very definition of which opportunistic infections constitute a diagnosis of Acquired Immune Deficiency Syndrome is the result not only of a large number of male deaths but also of the pre-AIDS history and structure of male-centered clinical trials and privileged access to health care.[22] As the saying goes, Women Don't Get AIDS; They Just Die From It. Indeed, women die of AIDS three to four times faster than men, on average six months after diagnosis—if they ever receive a diagnosis.[23] As Cindy Patton has observed, "from a socio-political viewpoint, AIDS was recognized by epidemiologists because gay men, by the late 1970s, were a visible community."[24] This understanding of the process by which illness is signified and—in the case of AIDS—stigmatized according to perceived commonalities of its "victims" (an archaic and imprecise term which compounds the problem by telescoping all HIV-positive people into an assumed tunnel of rapid helpless death) in no way negates the fact that men who engaged in homosexual activity that we in hindsight can call "unsafe" were and are dying in numbers greater than any other identifiable group. Nor does such an understanding relegate to sexist egocentrism the frantically heroic and lonely first steps taken by gay men in the early 1980s to fight this thing then called GRID (Gay Related Immune Deficiency).

When Mirko Grmek asks the question "Is AIDS really a new disease?" he—like Patton—answers "Yes, AIDS is necessarily new in the sense that it was inconceivable until the 1970s."[25] Grmek cites the historical convergence of culturally and physically identifiable communities perceived to be inherently at risk, and new technologies and "informatics." All of these together permitted the creation of the model of a syndrome of opportunistic infections, each with its own causative agents and facilitated in their destructive work by the breakdown in general immunity related to a single initiatory virus. Arguing that what we now call the Human Immunodeficiency Virus "has been around for a long time in the shadow of other infectious states," Grmek shows how science in effect spatially located and "created" AIDS.[26] In this context, women's demands for expansion of AIDS definitions to include vaginal thrush, for example, not only challenge the male-centered definition by which only oral thrush is an accepted AIDS-related opportunistic infection but they also force reluctant scientists and citizens to confess that illness, like gender and sexuality, is socially constructed and culturally sited across the human body and the body politic.[27]

This brings me to a fourth objection to the terms of my own discussion. I want to argue against abstracting illness or sexuality too far away from excruciating pain and vibrant desire. As a gay man I am resistant to any attempt to deconstruct what gives me honest pleasure, once I have broken down the artifice that had kept me from enjoying and acting out my desires. Similarly, anyone who is sick or dying knows that illness—as Susan Sontag has twice reminded us—is not a metaphor.[28] I want to talk about AIDS and sexual diversity without fetishizing the way we talk about it. And despite my own interest in what we talk about when we talk about AIDS, I will stand mute against language if my conversants are more interested in the discourse of our discourse than in the delivery of health care and human rights. As Sander Gilman has argued, "the pain and suffering of the patient cannot be simply dismissed as a social construction, even though this pain may be understood by patient and health care practitioner alike in a socially determined manner."

Despite my reluctance to embrace Douglas Crimp's learned characterization of AIDS as primarily a "crisis of signification,"[29] I am forced to agree with such an assertion, particularly when I consider the ways in which people with AIDS and sexual "degenerates" have remapped cultural and linguistic space, challenging the ways we talk about people who are ill or different while reclaiming the right to be who we are on our own terms in public. So long as language serves to unleash power and so long as the "crisis of signification" consists of a creative battle for self-definition, then my reservations about my participation in the discourse on AIDS and sexuality fade.

Sick Numbers and Signification

Any discussion of AIDS in Los Angeles County must be prefaced with the reminder that of the eighty-seven independent municipalities within the County's four thousand square-mile territory, only Long Beach and Pasadena operate a public health and hospitals department.[30] San Francisco, where county and city boundaries and functions are fused, is the only other California city in the business of providing health care to its residents. Like the rest of the state, the other eighty-five towns and cities of Los Angeles County—including the city of Los Angeles itself—depend on the County Department of Health Services for public health education and care, as mandated by county charter and state funding mechanisms.

As is true of other vital municipal services, and as most residents who first look to their city governments for assistance and civic identity are loathe to understand, it is the five-member Los Angeles County Board of Supervisors and their nonelected Chief Administrative Officer (CAO) who oversee this health system, setting priorities and approving budgets with a direct impact on the affluent as well as the one-of-every-four Angelenos who cannot afford private health care.[31] This board, which has not expanded since 1852, rules over a population of nearly nine million, with a 1991–92 budget of $12 billion. San Francisco, with a population of less than three-quarters of a million in a contained area of less than fifty square miles and a 1991–92 budget of $1.3 billion, elects eleven representatives to its Board of Supervisors.

With the exception of then-Governor Jerry Brown's 1979 vacancy appointment of African-American former U.S. Representative Yvonne Brathwaite-Burke (which

Fortress government. The Los Angeles County Hall of Administration is the site of the weekly meetings of the five supervisors, which became the focus of ACT UP's political initiatives and demonstrations.

did not lead to her reelection), the board had not counted an "outsider" among its white male ranks since 1875, when the last Latino male served. Accordingly, the spring 1991 election of populist former Los Angeles City Council member Gloria Molina, following the not coincidental retirement of twenty-year veteran progrowth law-and-order supervisor Pete "Pedro" Schabarum and a court-ordered "redistricting" plan to correct historically gerrymandered Latino underrepresentation, was correctly seen as a momentous threat to the board's business as usual.

Reflecting the mind-set of many Angelenos, the supervisors have traditionally viewed their sprawling districts as private fiefdoms, dispensing "discretionary" funds to competing alliances of homeowners and "developers" more concerned with their own backyards and police protection of their personal domains than with overall county-run services such as public health care.[32] So jealous are the supervisors of their special powers and constituencies that the board ultimately paid upwards of $7 million in public funds to private law firms engaged in the unsuccessful fight against the redistricting lawsuit that led to Molina's election. And after years of resisting calls for expansion of the board, the pre-Molina supervisors attempted to dilute the effect of her disruptive presence by suggesting an increase in their number to seven, rather than a more potentially ethnically diverse and representative nine.[33] Additionally, with the exception of Molina and seventeen-year Westside veteran "liberal" supervisor Ed

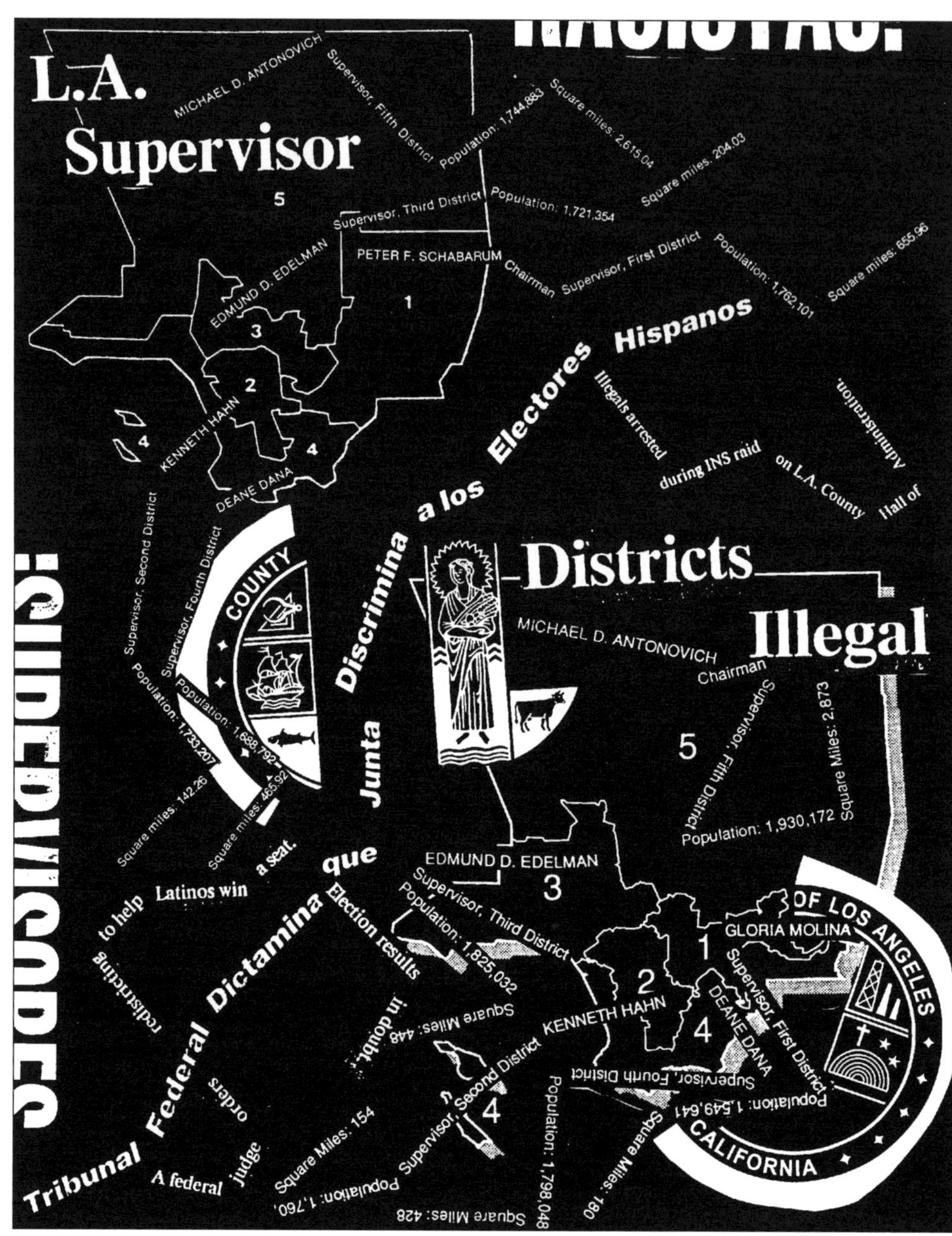

The electoral districts of Los Angeles County—a major factor in the local political economy of AIDS health care and education. Collage by Ty Geltmaker.

Edelman,[34] there is supervisorial resistance to the popular proposal that the Board's CAO—an appointed civil servant virtually unchecked in his packaging of the bulk of the annual budget—be made an elective position.[35]

While the supervisorial positions are by law "nonpartisan," the early 1980s elections of conservatives Mike Antonovich and Deane Dana resulted in a Reaganite board majority led by Schabarum. Against the ineffectual Edelman and with occasional cooperation from thirty-eight-year veteran South Los Angeles supervisor Kenneth Hahn (a populist white New Deal-style politico with a large African American constituency), the conservatives combined a penchant for privatization with a preference for "development" and law-and-order issues, reducing the county's historically mandated commitment to health and welfare services. While actively lobbying for state and national reductions in the same areas, the conservatives excused their budgetary shortfalls as the result not of their own priorities but of reduced funding transfers from Sacramento and Washington.[36]

Until Molina's election resulted in the creation of an ostensibly "liberal" three-person majority of the reinvigorated Edelman, the resuscitated Hahn (whose spirits had dwindled under the combined effects of Schabarum's bullying and a stroke), and the willingly combative Molina herself, the board's AIDS policies had been consistent with its vision of public health and social services in general, infusing the decades-old disregard for the ill and poor with a special contempt for homosexuals and a disease identified with social degenerates.[37]

Despite the fact that Los Angeles doctors Joel Weissman and Michael Gottlieb had been internationally recognized as having first identified in 1979–80 what we now call AIDS, and despite the fact that by 1990 Los Angeles had the second-highest number of AIDS cases in the United States, not one cent of public money was specifically earmarked for AIDS education or care in a county budget until fiscal year 1989–90, nine years into the epidemic.[38] Until that date, minimal services—such as the inadequate and belated HIV outpatient ward established in 1984 at the Los Angeles County-USC Medical Center—were funded internally as a discretionary expense by the Department of Health Services. The County's AIDS Program Office was not established until 1985-86, and the Commission on AIDS was not convened until 1987.[39]

Until activists set out to publicly embarrass the supervisors' political refusal to make the AIDS emergency a county health priority worthy of its own designated funding, one might have lived in a sanitized nonpedestrian Los Angeles of private cars and homes under the impression that AIDS had been miraculously held at bay. Projects like the jocularly effective "Mama Says Play Safe" sex-educational billboards, which gave citizens and visitors to Los Angeles the impression something was being done by the county in the mid-1980s, were in fact funded by a non-county-affiliated physicians group, the Los Angeles County Medical Association. In the absence of a comprehensive county social service plan for people with AIDS, private and volunteer groups like

AIDS Project Los Angeles, Minority AIDS Project, Cara a Cara, Bienestar, Being Alive, and the AIDS Hospice Foundation (now the diversified AIDS Healthcare Foundation), were swamped with simply learning how to take care of the sick and dying.

As the epidemic grew, community-based organizations such as Milagros AIDS Project, Tuesday's Child, and others would proliferate, caring for newly defined epidemiological groups not always best served by pioneering organizations like APLA. On the board, only Edelman advocated for HIV/AIDS programs, as he had traditionally done for gay and lesbian issues. In the midst of a 1988–89 ACT UP campaign of vigils and protests for the establishment of designated, state-of-the-art inpatient and outpatient HIV/AIDS services at the eastside County-USC hospital, Schabarum remarked: "If you were to poll the man on the street, the vast majority of people would not have any interest in AIDS and could care less about funding it." Not to be outdone, in July 1990 fellow conservative Dana reacted to revelations that the wait for a first appointment at the HIV/AIDS clinic had soared to a potentially fatal four months (soon thereafter increasing to twenty weeks), with the exculpation: "There are waiting lists for a lot of other areas, in the children's services, in our county hospital, and everywhere." In addition to betraying a gross ignorance or disregard of the absolute necessity of early intervention against HIV progression, Dana's response showed a willingness to pit the weak against the weak—in this case, people living with a socially stigmatized debilitating disease against children who have access to neither incomes nor the vote.

Indeed, waits for prenatal and other ongoing care at County-USC can routinely reach three or more months, due to understaffing as well as county and state delays in processing patient Medi-Cal entitlements. Reflecting a similar mind-set earlier in the 1990 budget deliberations, Antonovich had blamed what he called "illegal mothers" for draining hospital funds into obstetrics from other worthy areas. Antonovich would persistently answer critics of his divisive pronouncements with evidence of his discretionary funding of shelters for battered women and foster child programs, and his sponsorship of "Child Awareness Month."[40]

The "illegal" or alien "pregnant woman" as scapegoated pariah emerged again in Schabarum's parting resolution at his final board meeting the following March. With no objections to the potential for abuse or to the documented history of coerced sterilization of women at County-USC, the board unanimously approved Schabarum's motion to authorize implantation of the Norplant contraceptive device at county clinics. The resolution also called on the county to provide training in the procedure to physicians not under county employ. Schabarum's apparent last-minute support for reproductive choice might better be understood as a signal to local judges inclined to sentence women deemed unfit for motherhood to court-ordered Norplant implantation, especially since Norplant was approved by the Food and Drug Administration based on clinical trials on poor women at County-USC Women's Hospital, whose staff needed no supervisorial approval for later actual use. Schabarum's motion came one day after the in-court shooting attempt on the life of a Visalia, California, judge who had sentenced a mother appealing a child-abuse conviction to enforced Norplant implantation.[41] HIV-positive status is one of many "conditions" under which women might be ordered or coaxed into "Norplantation" in return for freedom of movement or medical care itself.

This contempt for the bodily autonomy of poor people and the accompanying attempt to divide the most desperate residents of the county did not go unchallenged by ACT UP and other activists whose AIDS demands have always been framed in the context of a respect for "the care of the self" and a call for "universal health care" free to all individuals on demand regardless of citizenship.[42] This demand was repeated at the board's July 31, 1990, budget deliberations, as ACT UP—which had announced it would "storm the death chambers"—noisily called for adoption of the County AIDS Commission's minimal funding recommendations of an augmentation of $9.4 million for AIDS education, early intervention, and care. The commission had noted a real unmet need of $189.4 million beyond the Chief Administrative Officer's tentative allocation of $25.3 million, a paltry figure barely increased from the previous year's budget despite clear evidence of the epidemic's growth.[43]

For the fifth time in just over a year, gloved sheriff's deputies who had hovered ominously over the proceedings with pistols and batons in the full glare of television cameras were ordered to handcuff and remove to the county jail anyone who refused to sit silently. Activists brandishing an American flag and tombstones scrawled with the phrase "Early Intervention/Health Care Is a Right/4-Months Wait=Death" were dragged from the room under the alternately imperious and distressed gazes of Antonovich, Dana, Edelman, and Hahn. Schabarum—who as chairman traditionally gave arrest orders and exited the chambers at the first sign of popular discontent—had avoided this particular confrontation and was said to be fishing in Montana. The same Dana who had pitted children against people with AIDS remarked to a television camera during the arrests: "I'm sure *we're* going to give *them* some money. I can't guarantee they're going to get the nine million they want."[44] The board then slashed every health area except AIDS. But the AIDS budget, already pitifully low, was literally gutted by cuts in related health areas, including gynecological, oncological, ophthamological, psychiatric, and other specialized services and treatments.

The supervisors' 1990 surgical strike conformed to tradition, cutting deep into mental health programs, despite the fact that the county's central jail itself was well on its way to becoming a twenty-first-century insane asylum as the numbers of mentally ill recidivist inmates lacking social services and support in the outside civilian culture of poverty swelled. By the summer of 1991, the central jail would house the largest number of mentally ill people of any institution—punitive or rehabilitative—in the world. While county health services total funds were scheduled to increase by $207 million in 1991–92 (due to expected rises in state and federal revenues), county jail construction was set to receive a massive $150 million boost. Under such conditions the line between health and police budgets was significantly blurred. After years of frontal assaults on mental health programs, the supervisors—including Molina—defended placing in the hands of County Sheriff Sherman Block 1991–92 monies for jail psychiatric treatment most often involving the maintenance of order through the administration of psychotropic drugs. Historians will trace the militarization of the county health budget back to this moment. And geographers will note that the expanse of land east of downtown on either side of the Los Angeles River not only separates a new "world-class" L.A. from an old poor East L.A. but serves also as the vast dumping ground—at the expanding central jail and nearby County-USC Hospital—of this new society's disposable population.

Despite the massive 1990–91 cuts, the supervisors added an extra $3.5 million of the requested $9.4 million augmentation for AIDS programs in that year's budget. Of this amount, $3 million was allocated for home care for the dying (at great savings to the hospital system), and the remaining half million dollars was destined for the construction of the long-fought-for, state-of-the-art HIV/AIDS outpatient clinic at County-USC. But these overdue measures fell far short of recognized needs. Noticeably absent from what the negligent supervisors no doubt felt to be a magnanimous augmentation were any funds for AIDS education or outreach. The board felt comfortable leaving this deadly gap in their local "plan" even though the National Commission on AIDS had met in Los Angeles in April, condemning "the hamstringing restrictions on the use of public dollars imposed by the elected officials" against "efforts that could prevent further spread of the epidemic in a county with the second highest number of reported AIDS cases in the United States."[45]

This deliberate negligence forced much of the immediate problem of educational outreach and housing for people with AIDS onto Mayor Tom Bradley's Los Angeles city administration. Since 1985 the city had operated under a model AIDS antidiscrimination regulation. But not until October 1990 was a formal policy approved by the City Council itself. And because the city has no health-care responsibilities, the new law was largely symbolic, save for the educational programs established for city employees and a provision for bleach and condom kits to be distributed to city jail detainees upon release. Minimal involvement in constructing housing for homeless people with HIV/AIDS would follow.[46] Needle exchange—recommended in the summer of 1991 by the same National Commission on AIDS that castigated the county a year earlier—was and is hopelessly taboo in most city as well as county circles.[47]

Adding insult to injury, the supervisors finessed their 1990–91 AIDS budget by authorizing the County Department of Health Services to contract out the administration of the county's mismanaged West Hollywood early intervention HIV clinic to the respected and willing Gay and Lesbian Community Services Center, but they then cut county funding of the facility from its established operating budget of $1 million to a reassessed need of $750,000.[48]

By the following October, when the wait for an appointment at County-USC remained at twenty-one weeks, emergency efforts by the Commission on AIDS and by Edelman to release monies initially set aside for the still-incomplete "new" AIDS clinic were rebuffed two weeks in a row by Schabarum and Antonovich. During these same October meetings, the board approved a $9.6 million contract for a private firm to develop a computerized fingerprinting system intended to detect fraud among welfare "cheats" in the county's less than generous $312 per month general relief program.[49]

With the spring 1991 arrival of Molina and an eleventh-hour conversion by Hahn, publicly attributed to a personal plea from former County AIDS Commission chair Rabbi Allen Freehling, the much touted "new liberal majority" quickly voted to fund a stopgap bleach and condom distribution program. Not surprisingly, Dana and Antonovich accused Molina of encouraging drug use by removing the threat of HIV infection and voted against the proposal, saying it should be paid for out of the sponsoring supervisors' discretionary funds—as if AIDS were a social club residing in one district and not the whole County.[50] Molina's presence and Hahn's reawakened pleasure in playing to the crowd without being cut off by former chair Schabarum soon emboldened a pent-up public ranging from homeowners protesting neighborhood oil drilling to seasoned AIDS activists. Applause, boos, hisses, and catcalls that would have formerly led to immediate ejection or arrest were begrudgingly tolerated, though warned against, by a ruffled Antonovich at the board's weekly meetings.

This minimal new openness was accompanied by a string of "new majority" policy victories placing the county on record in support of adopting the then-pending state gay and lesbian job and housing rights bill (AB101); favoring the introduction into the United States for research purposes of the so-called "French morning-after abortion pill" (RU486); and urging the lifting of Immigration and Naturalization Service (INS) restrictions on visits to the United States by people with HIV/AIDS. Molina, Edelman, and Hahn also buoyed progressive spirits, bucking the previous majority and settling an expensive five-year-old Los Angeles city lawsuit against the county by raising general relief payments to the ethically reprehensible but then legal maximum of $341 per month. These measures gave the impression of a new concern for human needs and a rejection of the former majority's pattern of hiring high-priced private law firms to defend board hostility to social service spending.[51]

Despite these relative gains, it was quickly obvious that Molina's lone presence on the board could not in itself change embedded priorities and procedures. On the same day the general relief lawsuit was settled, the board—with Molina furiously dissenting—voted to give itself, along with county judges and department heads, a $392 per month "professional development allowance." A public outcry eventually led the supervisors to rescind their veiled pay raise as part of the passage of their 1991–92 budget. But by early 1992 the board, embroiled in scandals over bulletproof cars and gourmet lunches, voted itself a $3,000 pay increase against Molina's objections.[52]

The 1991–92 budget "deliberations" revealed the almost insurmountable odds faced by anyone attempting to rechart the board's traditional course. At the first of just two scheduled budget sessions, CAO Richard Dixon presented the supervisors with a blackboard on which was scribbled the figure "$9.6 million." This was—by Dixon's account—all that was left of available revenues for supervisorial debate after state- and county-mandated entitlement obligations were funded in undifferentiated lump sums to each of the county's departments.[53] In a free-for-all style more appropriate to a Hollywood game show, the veteran supervisors began approving one pet expenditure after another, with the quickly dwindling budget remainder tallied on the board facing the public. When an exasperated Molina demanded the establishment of some procedural order before all the money was frittered away, she was ridiculed by Antonovich and by Dana, who said that as a "newcomer" Molina "should try to learn from the experts."[54] Molina persisted, objecting to the operating assumption that the bulk of the whopping $12 billion budget was untouchable and demanding guarantees from departmental heads that their budget allocations contained no unnecessary expenses, especially for superfluous junkets or ever-popular office redecoration schemes. When Molina demanded to know if this grab-bag approach to the budget was normal, Hahn—as if engaged in a gregarious poker game—said: "Yes, Gloria, go for it."[55] Earlier, Edelman had given credence to Dixon's excuses, saying: "I can understand Ms. Molina's frustration. Unfortunately, we just don't have a lot of revenue that is discretionary to meet the needs." All this was said with no acknowledgement of each of the "veterans'" substantial war chests actively employed to lobby his personal causes from Los Angeles to Sacramento to Washington, and that among these causes none has been the reversal of the very antisocial Reaganite policies of which the supervisors claim to be unwitting fiscal victims.[56]

An undaunted Molina proceeded to introduce cost-saving packages—including a provision requiring top county bureaucrats to take an annual two-day unpaid leave—which would have shored up the gutted hospital emergency-trauma system.[57] Not even Edelman would second the measure. When Edelman proposed a half-million-dollar augmentation of the AIDS budget—for wait-list reductions at the County-USC and three smaller outpatient clinics—Molina, who with Hahn voted for the measure, wondered aloud whether AIDS was receiving more than a fair share of funding while so many other sick people suffered excessive waits as well. Activists were shocked at Molina's willingness to ignore the unique urgency of early intervention against HIV progression, but they recognized that—unlike Dana's remarks of the previous year—Molina was excoriating the collapsed county system, not excusing it.

Aside from Edelman's half-million-dollar appropriation, the board once again ignored its own AIDS Commission's minimal funding recommendations, especially with regard to educational outreach and the increasing need for transportation and housing services for people living longer with AIDS. Operating from an initial Department of Health Services 1991–92 request for $73 million, Chief Administrative Officer Dixon had proposed a county AIDS budget of $32 million. The Commission on AIDS, as well as members of ACT UP and political allies in the "Common Agenda" budget coalition, then literally begged the supervisors for a minimal augmentation of $7.7 million, warning of dire public health consequences down the line if the current bare-bones spending pattern continued. But in the end the supervisors left the AIDS budget at $32.5 million, just $4 million more than the year before, despite significant increases in county AIDS cases as well as certainty that money not spent on early intervention leads to preventable early death for people with HIV.[58]

Nevertheless, the overall budget was the first in memory that did not actually cut the health and mental health sectors. But in an ironic note of justice abused and justice done, less than one month after Dixon had claimed to have pared expenses to a bare minimum, Molina's office received leaked memos revealing that Dixon himself had approved $3 million of unpublicized surpluses to pay "pricey" bonuses to top bureaucrats, including several in health and mental health departments as well as members of his own staff responsible for overseeing his $2 million office renovation. An embarrassed board suspended such bonuses for a year.[59]

Already in July, just as the board was to enter into budget deliberations, Dixon and the county's in-house legal counsel, DeWitt Clinton, had come under similar board scrutiny when activists complained that $7.8 million of federal dollars allocated for local community-based AIDS service organizations under the Ryan White Comprehensive AIDS Resources Emergency (CARE) Act had been blocked by the CAO and counsel since being made available in February. Initially ballyhooed as a national AIDS bailout, once the memory of Ryan White had faded from Congressional agendas the funds for 1991–92 were whittled down from $881 million to $350 million. Nevertheless, while all other local governments had long since authorized the release of their first phase of regional CARE monies (the efficient and timely use of which would be federally monitored to determine phase two follow-up funding), Los Angeles had uniquely and stubbornly argued that the local recipient organizations were in a conflict of interest because they—no differently than the county itself—had participated in the official determination of local priorities and actual disbursements. But this input by the service organizations most experienced in dealing with AIDS was precisely what Congress had mandated. Under severe questioning Dixon was ordered by a unanimous board—amidst uncharacteristically enthusiastic cheers from assembled AIDS activists—to complete phase one allocations of the "emergency" funds by the end of August. Despite the board's belated show of interest, it was clear that contrary to the intent of Congress the supervisors would wash their hands of their local obligations in the name of Ryan White and appropriate the CARE ACT "victory" as justification in minimizing their own 1991–92 AIDS expenses, knowing a little federal help was on the way. Similarly, only after a confrontational meeting with AIDS activists did the county, in February 1992 implement local access to HIV-related drugs that are free under the California AIDS Drug Program, long after Pasadena and Long Beach had done so.[60]

As late as the last week of August 1991, the Commission on AIDS was complaining that its recommendation to the supervisors that the county go on record in support of expanding the Centers for Disease Control definitions of AIDS was being held from the supervisors' agenda by the CAO. The Commission had argued for an AIDS definition expansion to include HIV-positive women suffering certain gynecological disorders as well as all HIV-positive individuals with CD4 (T-helper) cell counts of 200 or below. In fact, the CDC itself had given provisional approval to the CD4-200 count definitional change earlier in the month. But the CAO and counsel were arguing that the county could not afford the increase in officially-counted AIDS cases that such a change would cause, thereby ignoring the obvious fact that by any definition these people are in need of treatment and social services, and that with the new definition the county would be eligible for an increase in federal AIDS funds. Not surprisingly, in July of 1991, San Francisco's supervisors had approved such a policy endorsement without delay.

The Health System Chimera

The long-awaited new County-USC outpatient AIDS clinic finally opened in July 1991. Funded to handle up to 3,500 patient visits per month, the mirrored three-story modular facility is structurally capable of receiving 5,000 such visits, contingent upon the supervisors' largesse. Of the 56 new clinic positions added to the old clinic's 100 personnel, 38 percent were still to be hired two months after the official opening. Similar staffing shortages in the hospital's designated inpatient AIDS ward had reduced patient capacity from 25 to 18, reflecting the county's systemic inability to recruit due to its below-market pay scales, as well as the latest wave of national AIDS hysteria, particularly regarding the testing of health workers.

The summer 1991 establishment of the neighboring for-profit USC-University/National Medical Enterprises Hospital—to which only the privately insured or self-paying affluent may be admitted—has literally split the County-USC medical staff, who are now employed by two institutions with very different, if intertwined, missions. As of early 1992 the public hospital could staff only 1,400 of its 2,000 beds, forcing emergency and other patients to wait from six to fifty hours for initial treatment. Across the street the private hospital counted 221 of its 275 beds empty for lack of paying customers. AIDS specialists further note that when the county hires 5 new doctors, for example, their numbers actually amount to 3.5 full-time physicians because of their necessary work in clinical trial research. These trials—of which County-USC is a national center—provide both supplemental income for the physician and guaranteed primary care and therapeutic options for people with HIV/AIDS who cannot tolerate AZT or ddI, the only two currently legal antiviral AIDS drugs. Without ACT UP's success in opening up the clinical trial process, which created new protocols and "compassionate use" testing programs, and without underground "buyers clubs" where promising trial drugs are illegally available at low cost, people without access to private care would simply be left to waste away, ten years into the epidemic.

Because of staffing shortages and increasing demand, the wait for a first appointment at the new clinic hovers chronically at an inexcusable one month, even though 60 to 80 percent of all scheduled appointments never show up. Indeed, the new clinic 66 percent of whose clients live within ten miles of the facility—is faced with an increasingly "noncontactable" and "noncompliant"[61] population of poor and homeless people with HIV, many of whom discover their sero-status only after admission to the main hospital or emergency room for unrelated injuries or collateral conditions such as tuberculosis.

By the summer of 1991, clinic and hospital staff openly charged that the county's lack of coordinated housing, pharmaceutical delivery, transportation, and other social service programs had resulted in untold numbers of people with AIDS being discharged, often homeless, into the streets around the hospital. In one such case, a homeless man with AIDS was released from a non-AIDS ward despite persistent neuropathy and given a supply of AZT and painkillers along with his medical papers and a slip of paper on which were written the addresses of a downtown skid row flop house, the Social Security Administration, and his next clinic appointment—a full six weeks away. Fortunately for him, the individual wandered into an ACT UP meeting and benefited from the group's outraged intervention the following day with the "noncompliant" board of supervisors themselves.[62]

Incidents such as these have fueled debate among primarily gay AIDS activists over whether community-based organizations ought not attempt to take over all AIDS care from the county, pitting die-hard and benevolent "privatizers" against those who argue that the county must be forced to establish and properly manage a system to which all people, regardless of community affiliation, have an unquestioned right. The July 16 meeting of the board of supervisors witnessed such a split when representatives of community-based organizations making their case for the eventual resolution of the CARE Act fiasco thanked the supervisors for their belated intervention and proceeded to block the planned testimony of other activists who had intended to speak on the County-USC hospital situation and the proposed change of the CDC

AIDS definition to include women's opportunistic infections. After denouncing the community representatives—including City of Los Angeles AIDS coordinator Phill Wilson—on the steps of the County Hall of Administration, the "silenced" activists reentered the board hearing room and after a two-hour wait gave their testimony to an unusually attentive board with only a handful of the public remaining.[63]

These experiences beg the question of who constitutes and speaks for a community, who determines what a community is, as well as how communities of the "insulted and humiliated" come to exist and grow. The issue dividing AIDS activists arrives precisely as county social workers report increasing difficulties in responding to the needs of people with HIV/AIDS who have either no sense of community with anyone or whose existing community affiliations offer no sustained support or understanding for their sociomedical condition.

White self-identified gay men were able to organize around AIDS because their publicly worn sexual marginalization was accompanied by ferocious assumptions of social entitlement and relative access to power and wealth. The new "communities" of AIDS cannot be expected to respond to their diagnoses with such a preexisting sense of common purpose and nascent power. They are either unbound—as with many of the homeless or the intravenous drug users—or tied to communities which are themselves bound by the effects of racism and poverty to diminished social expectations, often accompanied by religious resignation and sexual shame. And then there are the growing numbers of single working mothers, for whom an AIDS diagnosis complicates preexisting gender inequities, not to mention two-parent families learning to cope with the insecurities of HIV.[64]

The lack of a comprehensive federal, state, and county AIDS plan—except to exclude people with HIV from the country and berate those already living here—thus places a constantly shifting burden of cultural awareness and receptivity on existing AIDS community-based service provider organizations who even under the best of intentions may not be able to cope culturally or financially with additional communities with whom they have no contact outside of the crisis context of AIDS. Predictably, the fall 1991 announcement of his sero-positive status by basketball superstar Magic Johnson had not by early 1992 led to increased national leadership or funding for AIDS issues, prompting Johnson to warn he will quit the National AIDS Commission if research and community assistance are not boosted.

As pioneering organizations like AIDS Project Los Angeles began to crack under the weight of bureaucratic "professionalization" and increasing case loads beyond their initially gay-identified AIDS communities, new service groups such as Tuesday's Child (where baby food and diapers are available) emerge in desperate attempts to meet the belatedly recognized other faces of the epidemic. But in Los Angeles, the official "numbers" say the face of AIDS is still primarily white, male, and gay.

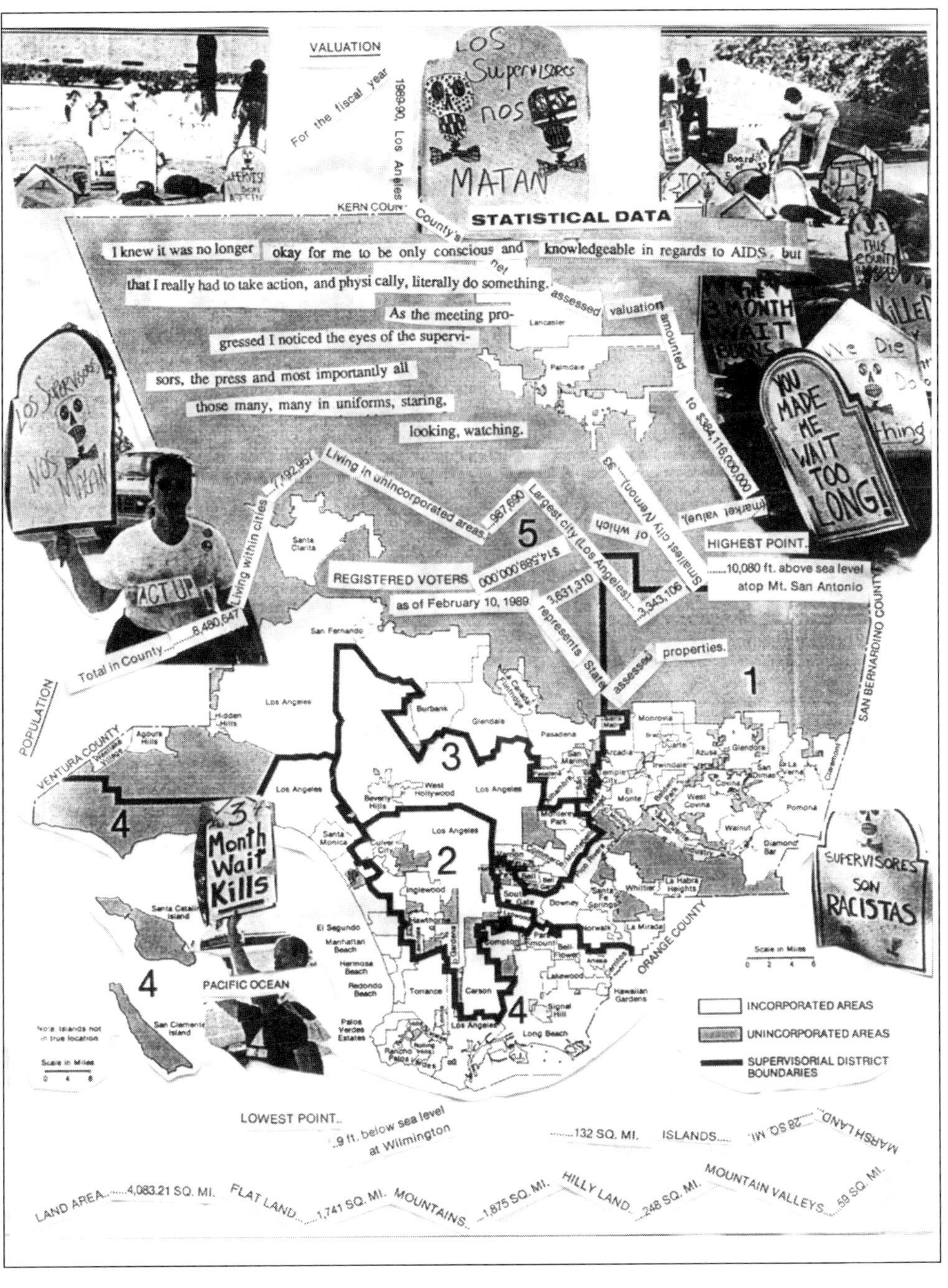

Los Angeles County—some statistics. Collage by Ty Geltmaker.

The County's AIDS Epidemiology Program report for December 1991 reveals that cumulative AIDS cases reported in Los Angeles County ten years into the epidemic stand at 14,114, up 27 percent from the previous year. Cumulative deaths total 9,958, a 31 percent rise over mortality figures through December 1990. The number of new AIDS cases reported in all of 1991 was 2,917, up 16 percent from the year before. Reported cases varied widely from month to month, with a 107 percent increase over the previous year for April 1991, a 23 percent drop for October 1991, and a 42 percent increase (217 cases) for December 1991. The Department of Health Services accompanied its April 1991 figures with a cautionary note that the increase in new cases per month was "due to increased case finding and reporting activities and does not represent a sudden worsening of the AIDS epidemic in Los Angeles County."[65] Whatever its validity, such a disclaimer and the wide variation of new cases reported from month to month forces one to question how many cases are never diagnosed (and thus not reported). Activists who had persistently argued that the county's case figures did not reflect the actual incidence of AIDS in Los Angeles took little satisfaction in the belated admission that "case-finding activity" had been in need of enhancement, especially after the county then announced in June that it was revising its estimates of the number of HIV-positive people in Los Angeles downward from over 100,000 to less than half that amount. The already-cited attempts by the county's CAO to stall supervisorial endorsement of expanded AIDS definitions—out of fear of costs to the county—gives little solace to those who would hope that these numbers reflect reality rather than political will.[66]

By the end of 1991, 71 percent of all Los Angeles County individuals known to have ever been diagnosed with AIDS were dead, a cumulative case fatality rate increase of 2 percent from the previous year. While just barely higher than the equivalent rate for all of California, the Los Angeles cumulative fatality rate is 7 percent higher than for the nation as a whole for 1991.

Despite these grim statistics, there is good evidence that increased early intervention allows people to live longer with HIV/AIDS and not just die of neglect. For the period January–June 1991, 65 percent of individuals with AIDS were alive at least one-half year into their diagnosis. For the second half of the year the figure rose to 82 percent. Seen through the prism of "fatality by half-year diagnosis," these latest figures show "only" 18 percent of people with AIDS died within six months of diagnosis. This index of quick death has fallen from over 90 percent mortality before 1985 to the current low, showing significant and steady drops from a rate of 93 percent in 1986 to 85 percent in 1987, to 78 percent in 1988, and on down to 65 percent in 1989. A significant plunge in this crucial marker—from 55 percent in the first half of 1990 to 46 percent in the second half of the same year, followed by the current figure—is unquestionably the result of early detection and intervention therapies voluntarily entered into by thousands of individuals who decided to test for HIV after the 1989 federal approval of AZT.

The point is not just that AZT—highly toxic and of limited efficacy for many people with HIV/AIDS—is keeping some people alive longer but rather that people have simply identified their "condition" much earlier, and that other antiviral and prophylactic therapies—officially sanctioned in trials or not—have increased longevity. The first of these two points, of course, means that AIDS and our perception of it have been temporally reconstructed, at least once since the "discovery" of the epidemic, even if AIDS is not yet a "chronically manageable" illness over a long time.

It should be remembered that the Los Angeles statistics represent the entire county, including those individuals who can afford private care and keep themselves informed of cutting-edge therapies and research. The figures also beg the question of signification, highlighting the problem of who is privileged to be deemed worthy of an AIDS diagnosis. And even when interpreted with hopeful scepticism, we forget at our peril that these reduced fatality rates are welcome only by those who believe that people with HIV/AIDS do not deserve to die.

Compared to the urban Northeast and western Europe, where female and heterosexually transmitted cases of AIDS represent as much as a quarter of the reported diagnosed total,[67] the official face of AIDS in Los Angeles remains male, white, and gay, with most cases falling in the twenty to forty-nine age span. One would naturally expect to see an upward shift in the age at diagnosis as well as death if early intervention in fact works, reconstructing our idea of AIDS as a "terminal" disease once again. By racial categories, 62 percent of all reported AIDS cases in Los Angeles are classified as white, 20 percent are Hispanic, 16 percent black, 1 percent Asian, with the remainder consisting of either Native Americans or undetermined race. These figures, particularly for blacks and Latinos, may indicate as much about lack of access to health care, and the political marginalization of AIDS and gay issues by traditional minority leaders, as it does about actual incidence of AIDS in these communities.[68]

Of the almost 15,000 locally reported cases of AIDS since counting belatedly began in 1984, Los Angeles reports just 487 women with AIDS. While over three-quarters of the male cases are attributed to homosexual or bisexual relations, of the female cases 34 percent are associated with heterosexual contact, with 28 percent linked to intravenous drug use (IVDU), and 22 percent tied to blood transfusions (against a 1 percent transfusion linkage in male cases). The remaining female cases are related either to "hemophilia or coagulation disorder" (1 percent) or "undetermined" causes (15 percent). There are no reported female cases of transmission through same-sex sexual activity or through "homosexual or bisexual IVDU." Similarly, the case breakdown by sexual orientation lists "Female, heterosexual" as the only female category, while men are listed as homosexual, bisexual, heterosexual, or "unknown."

The only other specific reference to women falls under the pediatric "exposure" from parent to child category. Of the 114 reported pediatric AIDS cases in the County, seventy-two have died. The reported number of teenage AIDS cases stands at a remarkably low thirty-one.

One is tempted to celebrate the relatively low counts of AIDS given by the county for children, teens, and women. Indeed, in the "HIV Seroprevalence Report" attached to the monthly AIDS figures, the county's epidemiologists give evidence culled from county sexually transmitted disease, tuberculosis, methadone, and family planning clinics suggesting at first glance that cases of HIV among women are nonexistent. But these "low" percentages (rarely showing more than 5 percent of any small clinic sampling for one month as HIV-positive, compared to equivalent male figures ranging from 30 percent and more) are likely the most visible of a submerged population with limited access even to "free" county services. How many of the working poor can take a day or two off or find child care in order to endure the long wait for treatment at county facilities, especially if they rely on the region's inadequate public transportation? As shown in previously cited references to the crisis in hospital staffing and emergency rooms, even patients in severe pain abandon hope of treatment and go back to work or home.[69]

Thus the minimal samplings from which the county figures are derived are statistically suspect and do not necessarily represent women in general. Furthermore, many of these women (including one lesbian listed as HIV-positive) show up on seroprevalence reports but are by definition excluded from AIDS diagnosis reports. Indeed, in the AIDS reports, women are subsumed into a morass of male numbers, defined epidemiologically only in relation to their "transmissive" functions as heterosexual partners and as agents of reproduction. As ACT UP's Women's Caucus and other groups have effectively shown, particularly in their work with HIV-positive women imprisoned at the California Institution for Women at Frontera, women are first condemned by exclusion from the Centers for Disease Control AIDS definitions and then sentenced to death by the malign neglect of a system that holds them in contempt except as the sex slaves of money-making men and reproducers of the culture of consumption. Indeed, the lowest socially acceptable standard of medical care is set in women's prisons, especially for HIV-positive women, who are stripped of the "redeeming" status of wife or mother. It is not surprising, therefore, that the one not specifically AIDS-related issue to which ACT UP/LA has consistently committed itself is the physical defense of women's health clinics against the blockades and harassments endured by women clients of every class and race at the hands of groups like Operation Rescue. This is where feminism, gay and lesbian activism, and the politics of AIDS lock arms, defending health care and autonomy over one's own body as inalienable rights.

Gay Blood and The Body of Christ

The battle for individual sovereignty over what Foucault called the "care of the self" is fought by gay men and lesbians each time they simply make themselves visible on the streets.[70] This is true in all of America but even more so in Los Angeles, the least pedestrian and most sprawling of metropolitan regions. Lacking the anonymous bustle and protective gaze of the meandering urban crowd, the privatized organization of space and transportation in Los Angeles places anyone who dares to walk rather than drive at heightened risk of being singled out as "different." In its report "Hate Crime in Los Angeles County, 1990," the County Commission on Human Relations documented a record 45 percent rise in attacks against people perceived to be gay, acknowledging that the 125 verified cases represent "severe underreporting, as many victims are still reluctant to identify themselves to police." In its preliminary report for 1991, the Gay and Lesbian Community Services Center reported a 50 percent rise in physical assault on gays.[71]

Gay bashing and police complicity are not unique to Los Angeles. Densely populated New York City, where police are at least under a more omnipresent public eye and nominal mayoral control, has been wracked by its own epidemic of gay bashings, often at the hands of police.[72] But the Christopher Commission Report resulting from the investigation of the March 3, 1991 beating of Rodney King by Los Angeles city police showed that local law enforcement agencies are awash in officially sanctioned abuse of blacks, Latinos, women, and gays. Gay and lesbian activists have long claimed that one of every six sexual orientation bashings takes place at the hands of the police themselves. As evidence of police ambivalence toward investigating violence against queers, the Human Relations Commission documented only four arrests for gay bashing in the entire county for all of 1990. This pitiful record is not surprising to anyone who has ever reported a gay-related assault to local police, who are all too often either indifferent or of the opinion that violence is part of the territory of risks that comes with being gay. There is also the problem of signification, whereby repeated muggings and assaults on gay men leaving gay bars are listed only as "robberies" because some personal item or cash was taken during the attack.

The Christopher Commission report gave conclusive proof that outright homohatred, tacitly endorsed by Chief Daryl Gates and laced with racist and sexist slurs over cop-car radios,[73] has for years emanated as quasi-official policy from the Office of Operations, overseen by part-time fundamentalist preacher, Assistant Chief Robert Vernon. Under the guise of exercising his personal religious freedom of expression, Vernon has infused the City of Los Angeles Police Department with a theology of heterosexual male domination over gays, women, and children, just as he preaches on tapes sold through his Grace Community Church of the Valley. Vernon was accused by his LAPD critics—including former Assistant Chief Jesse Brewer, now a member of the civilian Police Commission—of running a "God Squad," encouraging and rewarding police personnel attendance at his north San Fernando Valley church. A significant portion of what has come to be seen as Los Angeles's "mercenary" police force lives in the northwest vicinity of Vernon's church—outside of the city limits of "decadent" Los Angeles. Vernon's style of Christian policing enjoys popular support among those who view the city as the cesspool of modern culture, and he has powerful defenders in the county as well. At the height of the public revelations regarding Vernon's mixing of church and state, county supervisor Mike Antonovich—in whose Fifth District Vernon prays—took the unusual step of inserting City of Los Angeles business into the board of supervisors' weekly meeting, declaring support for Vernon's embattled and violated "religious rights." Antonovich's action was not surprising in light of his successful November 1990 bid—backed by Supervisors Dana and Hahn—to officially ally the county with the Boy Scouts in their attempt to fight off a lawsuit challenging the organization's ban on homosexuals.

Vernon's tapes also call on women to be submissive to men and recommend that children "won't die if you use a stick on them. Punishment will keep them out of hell." One can only wonder if this passion to save the weak from the fires of hell was the motivating factor in the beatings of Rodney King and others who have fallen under the batons and bullets of local police. And does a historic reluctance to investigate gay bashings reflect a similar punitive interpretation of salvation?[74] Vernon's boss, Gates—who claims to be agnostic—gave earthly legitimacy to Vernon's claim that homosexuals are "emotionally sick" and unfit for police work, saying of gay and lesbian cops: "Who would want to work with one?"

Such open disregard for the necessity of professional trust and reciprocal assistance among the members of his own force was echoed in numerous allegations of abandonment during situations of duress, as well as outright in-station harassment of LAPD members thought to be gay or lesbian. A decade-old lawsuit by gay former LAPD sergeant Mitchell Grobeson revealed such a pattern of homo-harassment paralleling the intimidation experienced by black, Latino, and female police employees. By the summer of 1991, the police chief's traditional resistance to recruiting and hiring openly gay and lesbian police had been overruled by both the City Council and the Police Commission. Grobeson, who had since joined the San Francisco Police Department, was offered an out-of-court settlement, and gay and lesbian police officers recruited personnel at both the West Hollywood gay and lesbian pride festival and the Sunset Junction street fair. By the time of the Sunset Junction event in early August, queer cops had won the right to recruit in uniform—a significant statement for a largely gay and Latino neighborhood rife with gang violence and gay bashings.

Following the Rodney King beating, Queer Nation played an integral role in the broad based community effort to achieve police accountability. Despite a traditional reticence on the part of some anti-Gates coalition members to associate with fags and dykes, Queer Nation's officially recognized participation in marches and rallies, as well as the "outing" of closeted, progay, pro-Gates city council member Joel Wachs, were instrumental in keeping the issue of gay bashing tied to the more public debate over race and gender.[75] As was true earlier in the year during the protests against the war in the Persian Gulf, Queer Nation fought a double-edged battle against both militarized state violence and homophobia within "progressive" social movements. The overwhelmingly white middle-class antiwar coalition in Los Angeles was less receptive of fags, dykes, and drag queens chanting "Homos for Health Care, Queers for Peace," than was the primarily African-American anti-Gates coalition—which had trouble accepting a bearded self-declared "faggot with AIDS" addressing a downtown rally in a rainbow skirt.

I have focused on the City of Los Angeles police force and not the county because as a result of the Rodney King beating and Christopher Commission inquiry, the city's homophobic policies have been formally unmasked. It is also true that in Los Angeles, just as the county sets the standard for medical care, the city—with its Jack Webb "Dragnet" legacy—sets the standard for police work.

Nevertheless, as of late summer 1991, County Sheriff Sherman Block—who personally led a high-profile 1988–89 attempt to intimidate and criminalize the entire local AIDS movement for its alleged role in the graffiti "vandalism" of a county building —was under increasing pressure to open his department to outside investigators. A wave of killings of unarmed Latino and black males by county sheriff's deputies and charges that sheriff's deputies bilked senior citizens of credit cards forced a reluctant board of supervisors (only Molina called for a fully independent probe) to accede to community demands for a public hearing on county police violence.[76] The initial hearing was stacked with off-duty sheriff's deputies, many of whom openly fraternized with their uniformed colleagues while "privately" videotaping the assembled public. Confronted by aides to Molina, the videotapers ceased their intimidating activity, but a sheriff's spokesman later defended the officers' "first amendment rights."[77]

Protesting citizens sat through two hours of prearranged prosheriff testimony, largely from white suburban community politicians who contract with the sheriff for "protection," before being invited to speak.[78] The same uniformed officers who socialized with their off-duty colleagues frequently hovered menacingly over sections of the public, removing at will anyone suspected of the slightest verbal disruption. An apparently concerned Block sat to Molina's right, taking notes as if he were not the same individual who in late August had casually said: "We've had people who are brutal; in the future I'm sure we will have people who are brutal."[79]

Chair Mike Antonovich dismissed critics with customary aplomb, "Clearly, there is a war raging in our country, and like in any war, there are casualties." He threatened to clear the hearing room even as the assembly gave a standing ovation to the mother and father of fifteen-year-old David Angel Ortiz, who had died unarmed after being shot in the back earlier in the month by zealous sheriff's deputies who "thought" he fitted the description of a car-theft suspect. Witness after witness told of being picked up and summarily beaten in cruising patrol cars, only to be dumped on the streets with a warning to keep quiet—all on the pretext that they fit a generic suspect of "medium height, medium weight, Hispanic, male, with black hair combed back."

Despite Block's surprise announcement that he had appointed a "blue-ribbon panel" to implement Christopher Commission–style reforms (denounced by Molina as an evasive maneuver), the day-long testimony confirmed the widespread belief that deputies involved in the recent killings are repeat offenders, many belonging to racist departmental after-work social "clubs" that rival the Crips and the Bloods in their gang style and violent efficiency.

Ironically, rank-and-file county deputies have perhaps had more immediate contact with queers and people with AIDS than city police, due to the gay presence in county-patrolled West Hollywood, ACT UP protests against Block's AIDS initiatives, and the recurring visits of ACT UP to the board of supervisors and the county jail.[80] But familiarity has bred as much contempt as understanding. Deputies at the county jail—where I was told upon arrival that I had "no rights"—feel free to engage in humiliating body searches, and in one incident forced four black men to strip naked in front of a cell of white and Latino ACT UP inmates. Despite the stated jail policy of isolating homosexuals from the general population, incarcerated members of ACT UP have been taken on "tours" of the jail, with guards announcing that a "faggot with AIDS" is visiting. Confused guards taking jailhouse mug shots have ordered activists to remove their shirts on which were printed "queer," "faggot," and other appropriated deprecations, wondering aloud, "Why do you want to be called faggots?" During our arrest at the board of supervisors in July 1990 my lover and I were told we would have our cuffed wrists broken and our faces smashed by deputies who were enraged at our appropriation of the American flag on which we had attached a pink triangle and our health-care demands. The average citizen who is not black nor Latino nor openly gay, or who has never experienced a strip or body search in the county jail,[81] no doubt holds the popularly reelected sheriff and his loyal deputies in high regard. Like Gates's LAPD, the county's law enforcement agency is highly militarized and technologically advanced, enabling a minimal number of deputies to swoop down on scenes of alleged disorder with maximum force. This reliance on the SWAT approach—developed by Gates himself—means the average "law-abiding" citizen rarely sees the police but only hears their efficient helicopters or sirens from behind walled lawns and locked doors. But by the summer of 1991, the Sheriff was also embroiled in a series of costly and embarrassing lawsuits by former deputies—women and gay males—who charged that an atmosphere of systemic homophobic and misogynous harassment continues under his leadership.[82]

Members of Queer Nation and ACT UP are routinely videotaped by plainclothes agents before, during, and after even the most innocuously peaceful actions. In one such case in the autumn of 1990, two undercover cops filmed members of ACT UP in a West Hollywood park and when confronted, refused to identify themselves or their agency, then trailed the activists' caravan of cars and bus through four distinct municipal jurisdictions—to the California Institution for Women at Frontera, in distant San Bernardino County. Upon arrival at the preannounced, peaceful picket of the prison, the two videotapers flashed badges and were welcomed behind paramilitary riot-police lines, from where they continued their filming. Such surveillance goes beyond traditional quasi-legal intelligence gathering of oppositional political groups, and it reveals ingrained police and civilian-supported perceptions of nonwhites and queers as inherently dangerous "others." When those others are additionally seen as "carriers" of a deadly sexually stigmatized disease, the potential for police—as well as civilian—violence is obviously increased. In Los Angeles, police harassment can also become tragi-comic farcical drama as when in August 1990 a battalion of over fifty baton-toting city cops descended menacingly en masse to monitor Queer Nation's first cross-dressing/kiss-in, browsing tour of the Beverly Center shopping mall and touristy Hard Rock Cafe.

Fortress shopping. When a small group of Queer Nation activists staged a kiss-in at the Beverly Center shopping mall in 1991, a battalion of more than fifty Los Angeles city police arrived and, with batons drawn, made it clear that such public acts would not be tolerated in this sanitized cathedral of consumption.

Documented cases of cops beating gays who were perceived or known to have AIDS—especially when thought to be affiliated with ACT UP—have received less public and press attention in Los Angeles than in New York. In that city the open battle that pits Cardinal John O'Connor and the heavily Catholic police force against ACT UP, WHAM!, and Queer Nation is everyday news.[83] In Los Angeles the traditional absence of a formidable Catholic Church–cop alliance in the O'Connor style has much to do with Southern California's racist history as well as ethnic, religious, and employment demographics.

In Los Angeles the newly installed Cardinal Roger Mahony's burgeoning flock of believers consists in large part of generations of marginalized Latinos who—unlike waves of Irish and other working-class Catholic immigrants in New York—have never been welcomed into the region's police or other socially transformative power bases. Indeed, the masses of local Catholics—native Angelenos and newly arrived refugees—have been locked out of traditional channels of social mobility by the essentially Protestant Anglo forces represented by figures such as Gates, Vernon, Schabarum, and the like. With Mahony's recently enhanced status as a "prince of the Church," it is not surprising to witness him joining O'Connor and other prelates appointed by John Paul II in characterizing critics of Church policy as "Catholic bashers," especially on issues concerning abortion, birth control, sex education, homosexuality, and the hierarchical authority itself.[84] As a relatively young Cardinal with a high profile as leader of the nation's most populous diocese and reputed ambitions for higher Vatican office, Mahony is no stranger to the controversy surrounding these volatile issues. He has formally enforced the 1986 "Ratzinger Doctrine," which labels homosexuality an "intrinsic evil," by forbidding the gay and lesbian Catholic group Dignity from worshipping in the diocese's churches, even while invoking disingenuous Church commands to "love the sinner."[85]

In the weeks immediately following his Vatican investiture, Mahony went into high gear, praying with Operation Rescue clinic blockaders at a "nonblockade" demonstration nonetheless meant to intimidate women from entering the site.[86] The newly red-capped archbishop also smeared the reputation of former "La Placita" pastor and immigrant rights activist Father Luis Olivares—who has AIDS—with accusations that his downtown Los Angeles sanctuary had been a den of homosexuality and murder.[87] In early September, in the boldest move of his new reign, the Cardinal took out ads publicly threatening local Public Broadcasting Service affiliate KCET with an antifunding campaign for its decision to televise the agitprop documentary *Stop the Church,* which mocks ecclesiastical ritual by portraying the December 8, 1989, disruption of O'Connor's Sunday mass at St. Patrick's Cathedral by members of ACT UP and WHAM! The Cardinal likened KCET's decision to air *Stop the Church* to the firebombing of a church or synagogue—something neither ACT UP nor Queer Nation has ever threatened to do—and warned the station it might be held "morally and legally responsible for every future act of terrorism" against religious institutions.

Mahony's presumed power to control the content and tone of public discourse—branding dissenters as sinners, heretics, bigots, and terrorists—conforms to the acknowledged authoritarian vision of O'Connor's wing of the Church which, in the words of conservative theologian Richard J. Neuhaus, "flies defiantly in the face of the predominant cultural orthodoxies of the United States."[88] Indeed, the queerly American "orthodoxy" of self-determination as a lifelong process of working out an individual identity amidst socially constructed choices, free of religious domination, does fly in the face of those authoritarians and conformists whose own affirmation of personal identity requires a regimen of moral condemnation, social isolation, and political exclusion of people defined as the evil "other."

With the much heralded collapse of the "evil empire" of Soviet communism, the political, social, and ecclesiastical need for isolating "sinners" in our midst is intensified. The late twentieth-century bathos of hypocritically prayerful, unrepentant Christian "commemoration" of the Holocaust of the Jews coincides with similarly vulgar fin-de-siècle attempts to simultaneously label lesbians, gays, and people with AIDS as wicked sinners deserving of damnation but loved by merciful believers and their Lord Jesus. Gays, lesbians, and people with AIDS, like Jews, are now subject to grotesque Christian appropriation through prayer of the suffering dealt to them by Christianity itself.

One local manifestation of this pious Christian need to "other" and then "love" those who are "different" is the ongoing, yearlong weekly "outreach" mission to gays and lesbians in West Hollywood by youthful members of the Calvary Chapel of Orange County. When Queer Nation responded to the church's continual harassment of individuals frequenting gay bars and other businesses by descending for a theatrical demonstration at their Orange County campus, we were accused of "bashing Jesus". Claiming the right to harass and "outreach" to gays wherever they choose while hiding behind a wall of preemptive state protection, the fundamentalist and Catholic groups successfully lobbied the state legislature to criminalize with special penalties any "disturbance" of a religious service, as codified in the 1990 Russell Bill.[89] Catholic Church "fathers" have moved closer to the politics of their formerly distant fundamentalist cousins in order to shore up their own flagging hierarchical influence over insurgent lay flocks as much as to maintain their constitutionally questionable temporal privileges.[90]

The hostility of clerics against honestly expressed homoeroticism derives not so much from a belief in classical Church asceticism—which was itself extremely homoerotic—but rather from the impossibility of sustaining the myth of ecclesiastical heterosexual celibacy in the face of both the undeniable evidence of homosexuality in the modern church itself and the latent secular acceptance of homosexuality and women's

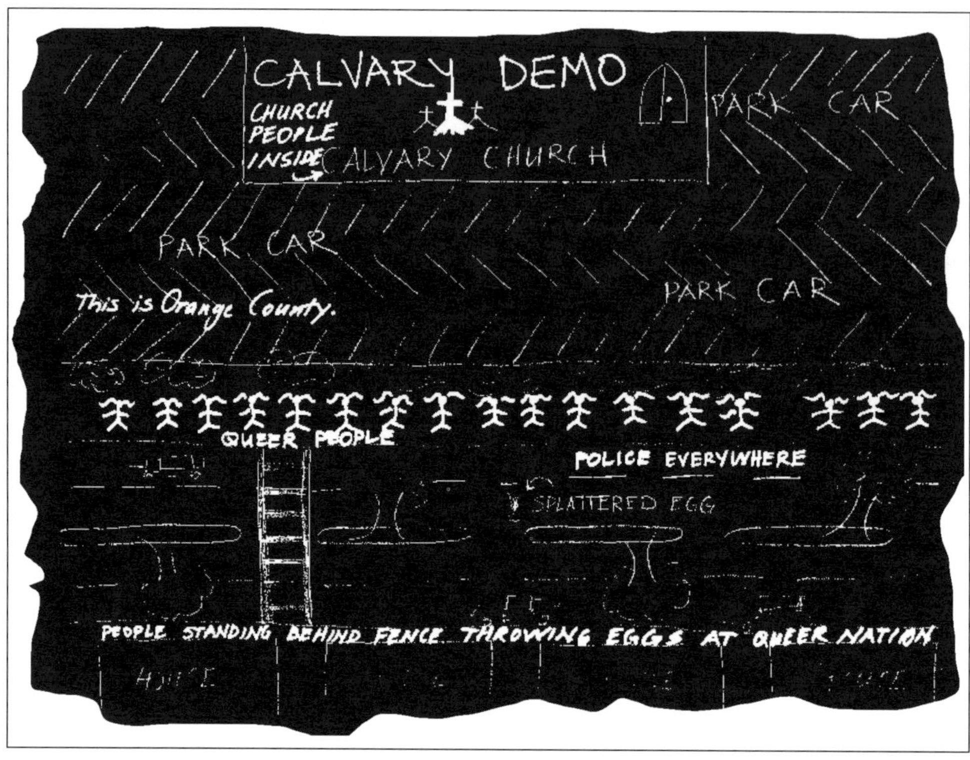

Queer Nation Calvary demo. One of the first Queer Nation LA demonstrations (late 1991) took place outside Calvary Church in Orange County, which had been active in homophobia and AIDSphobia sermoning. The doors of the church were closed to the demonstrators when the sermon started, but about six Queer Nationals had infiltrated the congregation. Halfway through the sermon the Queer Nationals inside demonstrated loudly, disrupting the sermon. Between fifty and one hundred Queer Nationals, along with other groups such as pro-choice activists, were outside in the parking lot. "We were just being fabulous—lesbians eating out barbie dolls and men in drag; neighbors from across the street were throwing eggs at us and police were everywhere." Information from and drawing by Ara Z.[91]

rights as a fact of life in contemporary America. The not-so-secret homosexual life of O'Connor's predecessors, especially Francis Spellman—a Cold War associate of Roy Cohn, J. Edgar Hoover, and other McCarthyite national-security "queens"—as well as the common Italian acceptance of Pope Paul VI's relatively open homosexual existence as Cardinal Montini of Milan, line the walls of today's socially punitive ecclesiastical closet. Not so ironically, this drama unfolds most demonstratively in an America willing to love an emigré Czech tennis star, Martina Navratilova, who is unashamed to say on national television that she is a woman who loves women. Such are the benefits of athletic success, wealth, and presumed female sexual passivity.

While the previously less strident Mahony has never yet been the target of in-church, New York-style disruptions, he has been quietly confronted at the Communion rail and picketed, and the outside walls of some of his churches have been marked with graffiti including "Mahony Murderer."[92] Mahony's attack on KCET and

Stop the Church included the familiar repeated false claim presented as scientific fact that only abstinence protects one from HIV. I happen to be living proof that this is not true, that one can have safe sex in an epidemic. The cardinal's words, however false, reinforce phobias that are eventually taken out on gay men, lesbians, and people with AIDS.

Mahony's fundamentalist Catholicism and increasingly public antihomosexual agenda is directly linked to Los Angeles's changing demographics and politics. As Mike Davis has noted, the Los Angeles that from 1920 to 1960 recorded "the highest proportion of native-born white Protestants of the largest American cities" is "becoming a Catholic town again."[93] Davis convincingly shows that with a rapidly growing Latino-Catholic birth rate, and upwards of 3.5 million parishioners served by over fifteen thousand religious and lay employees, as well as nontaxable churches, rectories, and other real estate valued at billions of dollars, Mahony's church "will be a major arbiter of social and political realignment between old and new status quos," with Olivares's local version of liberation theology losing out.[94]

Gay-bashing in its refined ecclesiastical articulations will be employed out of sincere belief and tactical expediency by Mahony, who is emerging as the anxious would-be successor to the insidious Protestant traditionalists whose control of local health care and law enforcement agencies has finally come under scrutiny. Whether Mahony and his papal absolutists succeed in translating their theocratic vision into public policy is not the only question. Indeed, the prochoice Molina stood up to fierce but ineffective archdiocesan opposition when she successfully gained supervisorial endorsement of local research of RU486, the French abortifacient. And the likelihood that either state senator Diane Watson or former supervisor Yvonne Braithwaite-Burke—both prochoice African-American community leaders—will succeed a retiring Kenneth Hahn in June of 1992 may mean that county government is destined to move even farther from both the old Schabarum and the new Mahony agendas.[95] Similarly, the 1991 election of openly gay Jeff Horton to the Los Angeles Board of Education, as well as the probable 1993 mayoral candidacy of prochoice progay city council member Mike Woo, leaves Mahony as a lone ranger with his work cut out for him.

Precisely in this context, with a public antihomosexual campaign wrapped in pious disclaimers of any intent to harm gay "sinners" whose diseases are a "choice of lifestyle" and whose criticisms of the Church are "bigotry bordering on terrorism," Mahony had a chance to hook into social fear and gain cultural and political leverage—just as televangelist preachers and political crusaders Lou Sheldon and Orange County Congressman William Dannemyer, among others, have successfully done. As the Cardinal strategizes, untold numbers of gay boys and lesbian girls will be taught to hate themselves and others in whom they see the free expression of their own suppressed "sinful" desires. And their heterosexual brothers and sisters will grow up assuming the world is made only for them. Queers—like nineteenth-century children—are to be neither seen nor heard. And those same-sexers who are at peace with their own "care of the self" will be accused by Mahony of practising a "do-it-yourself moral code" that "spreads AIDS."[96]

This deep fear and panic over the public presence of people who are perceived to be different is well documented by the Human Relations Commission's 1990 report, which emphasizes that "blacks, Jews, and gay men were far more likely than members of any other groups to become victims of hate crimes in Los Angeles County." Of the total hate crimes documented, 26 percent were perpetrated against blacks, whose stigmatized racial identity is historically linked to white sexual ambivalence, while Jews and queers each represented 22.7 percent. Of hate crimes based on sexual orientation, 88 percent were against gay men, 8.8 percent against lesbians, and 3.2 percent against mixed gay/lesbian groups. In addition to the well-founded assumption that gay men are bashed by male adolescents struggling with their own socially constructed self-loathing—a situation which can lead to suicide as often as murder[97]—the commission's report suggests that the large number of male victims stems partly from their high visibility as a cultural and economic bloc in gay-identified West Hollywood and Silverlake. Indeed, as the commission notes, lesbian-identified neighborhoods such as Park Slope in Brooklyn suffer epidemic rates of bashing that equal those in gay-male-identified areas.

With regard to gender itself, the commission confessed it was only beginning to collect data on hate crimes against women, stymied by the lack of an agreed-upon definition of just what constitutes such a crime. This shocking admission that such violence has no name illustrates the important work still to be done in making gender a meaningful category of analysis in the law. Los Angeles state assembly representative Lucille Roybal-Allard's pending Bill 1009 would establish rape and domestic violence as hate crimes for the first time in California.[98]

Underscoring the viscerally emotional and physical dependence of the basher on his victims—not unlike Sartre's characterization of the anti-Semite's need for the Jew—the commission report notes that hate crimes based on sexual orientation consist overwhelmingly of assaults intended to cause death or severe physical injury. While 3.3 percent of religiously motivated hate crimes and 27.6 percent of racially motivated hate crimes consist of physical assault, fully 77.6 percent of all sexual orientation hate crimes consist of violence against individuals, rather than graffiti, vandalism, hate literature, or phone calls. White and Latino male adolescents constitute the overwhelming majority of attackers, as reported by their victims. Black adult males are listed in a distant third place, and black male adolescents—stereotyped as the scourge of the urban landscape—show up with only one of their cohort listed as an assailant in a sexual orientation case. Again, the demographics of gay visibility and de facto race segregation in Los Angeles may influence these figures. But it is also likely that marginalized black youths are less socialized into the power ideologies of old-Protestant and new-Catholic Los Angeles manifested by white and Latino boys bashing gays and women on the streets, or in the privacy of Church-sanctified marriage. In an increasingly "sexualized" world of cultural and political discourse, social dislocation, and resurgent antifeminism it is not surprising that the Commission reported four cases of adolescent girls attacking gays and lesbians. In one such case two teenaged girls hurled glass bottles at gay men outside a Silverlake bar while their "boyfriends" screamed "faggot" and other epithets. These are the youthful armies of hate trained by the local church and state.

Myth and Metaphor

Los Angeles is not uniquely homophobic. But it is suffused with a peculiarly local religiosity—now in a state of transition—that overwhelms the expression of diversity through a combination of spatial vastness and boosterist myth. If until 1991 the region was spared the kind of Catholic antigay vitriol previously associated with New York's Cardinal O'Connor, it was nonetheless subjected to a Protestant righteousness that preached a sun-drenched dream of conformist piety and conspicuous consumption.

Los Angeles County is the only jurisdiction in the United States with a municipal seal containing a crucifix. Supervisor Kenneth Hahn, known for offering up extemporaneous Biblical citations during board meetings, designed the seal in the mid-1950s, and he says the crucifix symbolizes the region's Spanish-mission past. But as both Mike Davis and Carey McWilliams have shown, the "Spanish-mission past" is a mythologized history of domination and death recycled as a fairy tale of official "benevolence," "social efficiency," and "tutorial excellence."[99] Kevin Starr has written that transplanted easterner John Steven McGroarty's *The Mission Play,* which was seen in an endless series of outdoor pageants by "an estimated 2.5 million people between 1912 and 1929," comes to an appropriately mythic end when "the dying Spanish heroine, shot accidentally by Indians, tells an American that California's glory will return at such time as the Americans restore a cross to every hill."[100] But one can also read the enormously influential *Mission Play* as a twentieth-century transcontinentally migrated parable of the enduring Puritan vision of God-fearing righteousness established on Earth. This myth persists across all of America, with local variations. The yellow-ribboned righteousness with which Americans have fought their little wars since the ostensibly humiliating defeat in Vietnam, while ignoring the poverty at home, shows a nation still willing to believe (even if unconvinced) in its millenaristic role as a "shining city on a hill," as both the original citizens of the Massachusetts Bay Colony and Ronald Reagan liked to say.

The antiurban pastoral mythologies based on fears of political revolt, social strife, physical illness, and cultural degeneracy that were associated first with European and then East Coast cities are not unique to Los Angeles. Jefferson and de Tocqueville and scores of later commentators have noted that Americans resiliently seek utopian escape from such forces in all periods of history and in all regions of the country, even if the ultimate result is to build bigger, more crowded cities. Los Angeles is unique, though, precisely because it still shakily embodies this quintessentially American tension between private salvation and public righteousness at a relatively late date in the twentieth century.

Since World War II, no other region has experienced such a massive influx of native-born and foreign migrants, transplanting broken dreams and aspirations under the illusion of being in a city that would never let them in. Los Angeles ranks as the American city with the highest per capita number of unlisted telephone numbers. Even loyal Dodger fans are notorious for avoiding crowds at the end of the baseball game by leaving the stadium before the seventh-inning stretch and listening to the game's completion on the radio in the privacy of the car trip home. This premium on privacy and consumption was ironically marketed to all of America through that most collaborative of media: film. But, as the ignominious response of the film industry to AIDS and the plight of HIV-positive actors and technicians in the industry has shown, Hollywood reproduces nothing more than myth for money.[101] Although many of the postwar migrants brought their theology of free enterprise and the good life of private, family consumption with them—memorializing it in crystal cathedrals and shopping-mall churches—the region offered its own Christian civics to those who came in search of full redemption.

In a county with the second-largest Jewish population in America, Board of Supervisor meetings still routinely begin with overtly messianic invocations of Jesus as divine inspiration of local leaders and the land itself, all under an inscription in stone reminding the public that "This Country Was Founded On Free Enterprise." Such state rhetoric is pronounced from behind a metaphorically consistent glass partition separating the anointed governors from the governed.[102] Few Angelenos who have lived here since the postwar years, or before, find this strange, so deeply are these contradictions of officially ordained authority and privacy ingrained in the local culture.

This dominant cultural orthodoxy—including compulsory public heterosexuality—is now in transition and under attack, not because of the importation of any alien or queer ideology, but rather because the region has reached a critical population mass, with a respective threshold threatening life-support processes. These crises, in turn, are unleashing new intrusions and constrictions on both private and public space. As Harold Myerson has noted, the urban density of the largely immigrant low-rise neighborhood around MacArthur Park, just west of downtown Los Angeles, now exceeds that of high-rise Manhattan and rivals the well-documented conditions of New York's teeming Lower East Side a century ago.[103] But this demographic revolution, welcomed by nascent gentrifiers, consumers of world culture, and cultural radicals—variously hungry for profits, exotic food and music, and densely anonymous urban sociability—also offers new opportunities for marginalization and hate against the young jobless newcomers and those old-timers stranded in the crowded rubble. The latter will be forgotten and the former will be scapegoated as illegal, drug-dealing urban "scum."[104]

Survival

The County Hall of Administration, fronted by setback facades that are adorned with warnings against unauthorized public gatherings, is graced on its far side by a sunken plaza of lush vegetation and fountains. But like the fortified elevated Music Center plaza across the street, this urban oasis was not built to encourage public interaction. It is there for the visual pleasure of those who rule, as a stage on which the public is permitted to pass voyeuristically, so long as no one loiters.

Citizens of the new "world-class capital of the Pacific Rim" are expected to go about their productive business under the growing menagerie of mirrored towers built for an illusive downtown monied population. This new downtown is a palimpsest of glitz surrounded by prison cells, junkyards, police garages, helicopter pads, and overcrowded hospital rooms, buffered by vast tracts of razed neighborhoods waiting to be "redeveloped." Uppity queers and people with AIDS are visible reminders to those who have run roughshod over this urban parchment that Los Angeles is filling in its horizontal space, threatening the myths which depend on the old less crowded morphology.

From the top of the County Hall of Administration, it is easy still to believe in the region's history of private speed, uncrowded pleasure, self-justification, inner sanctity, and know-how efficiency. But closer inspection reveals that it is no longer true that Los Angeles's "buildings are the first and only structures on their particular parcels of land."[105] The city and county are busy filling in empty spaces even as they bulldoze the ruins of old communities and disposable architecture, which Banham celebrated as unique to a civilization Carey McWilliams called "an island on the land."[106] Like people washing themselves in the encased concrete channels of the Los Angeles River, queers and people with AIDS disturb the clean illusion that Los Angeles streets are, as Banham claimed, private driveways of personal calm to be smoothly negotiated to and from sleek freeways connecting the beach and the bedroom. Banham's four local ecologies—from the surf to the car—are in permanent tilt and can no longer sustain the myths of *The Mission Play* millenarianism or Chandleresque degeneracy.[107] Queers of all races and sexual persuasions living in Los Angeles know firsthand that the region is not the open-air closet that was said to have offered relative freedom to previous generations of homosexuals willing to keep their vice and their secret to themselves. The late-twentieth-century fin-de-siècle fags and dykes who now populate Los Angeles are no longer living lives like exiled Christopher Isherwood "and his kind," fleeing Nazi Europe and its congestions.[108] Nor are today's L.A. queers much like the anti–Cold War dissident Harry Hay, who organized Mattachine and later "Faerie" resistance to McCarthyite homophobia[109] in hills and canyons above the flat expanse of house-after-private-house, which Banham called the "plains of id."[110] Thanks to the courage of a generation of Isherwoods and Hays, we are out in the open. But we are—whether we like it or not—far removed from the languid decadence of Gavin Lambert's 1950s Hollywood.[111] Our refusal to live in a closet is one way of "just saying no" to a world, a nation, and a region culturally intent on closing borders to those who are different. AIDS has forced us to fight out loud, knowing we risk being labeled terminally rude and criminal.

From the top of the County Hall of Administration, you might not guess that this Hollywood heaven-on-earth is governed as a garrison. By being public, without internalizing someone else's hate and fear, people with AIDS and queers of all races and sexual persuasions show that, at the risk of being called savage, you can raid the encircled wagon trains and rob the bunkered angels of the myths that continue to be used to kill us.

Constructing Manchester's "New Urban Village": Gay Space in the Entrepreneurial City

Stephen Quilley

In the 1980s Manchester emerged as one of the principal centres for gay culture in Britain. The city's "Gay Village" has a spatial coherence that is significantly absent in other comparable urban areas. This development has been closely connected to, and implicated in, a wider explosion of youth culture based on an innovative and energetic club scene: *Mad*chester. Over the same period, in the face of massive and partially orchestrated deindustrialisation, the political culture of the dominant Labour Party has gone through a series of shifts. The emergence of the "Village" has been very much bound up with the changing fortunes of Manchester's new urban left and the transformation of the city's Labour administration under Graham Stringer.

My concern is to document the changing relationship between the Town Hall and the Village. I suggest that from playing a role in a wider discourse of resistance to Thatcherism, the gay presence in the city has, since 1987, been increasingly incorporated into a postmodern narrative of cosmopolitan diversity. At times, and in the face of concerted opposition, the gay community[1] in Manchester has been able to appropriate space. But inscribing its own vernacular into a landscape of power that was constructed largely under the aegis of a property-led redevelopment strategy, the aesthetic of the gay scene has become articulated into a wider reimaging of the city around the familiar theme of European style cafés, pedestrian streets, and arcades, as well as around a central role for leisure and cultural activities. Despite the overt support of the ruling Labour group from 1984, the Village was only recognised as a planning entity, and specifically as a gay place, in 1991. But the Village is now a phenomenon that figures in the calculations of the planners, boosters, and pundits of "The New Manchester: City of Leisure, Pleasure, and Plastic Money."

The Conservative Party's third victory in June 1987 effectively brought an end to the experiment in "local socialism" (Lansley et al. 1989; Cooper 1994). Since then the municipal lesbian and gay project has largely been reversed, as Labour councils have retreated in the face of electoral and financial constraints. However it is my contention that, in Manchester, the apparently small gains made by gay activists during the period of municipal socialism paved the way for the subsequent expansion, consolidation, and commercialisation of the Village. Whilst lesbian and gay issues have, to an extent, been squeezed off the formal agenda of local government, the council continues to sponsor the Village as an enduring and legitimate feature of the emerging

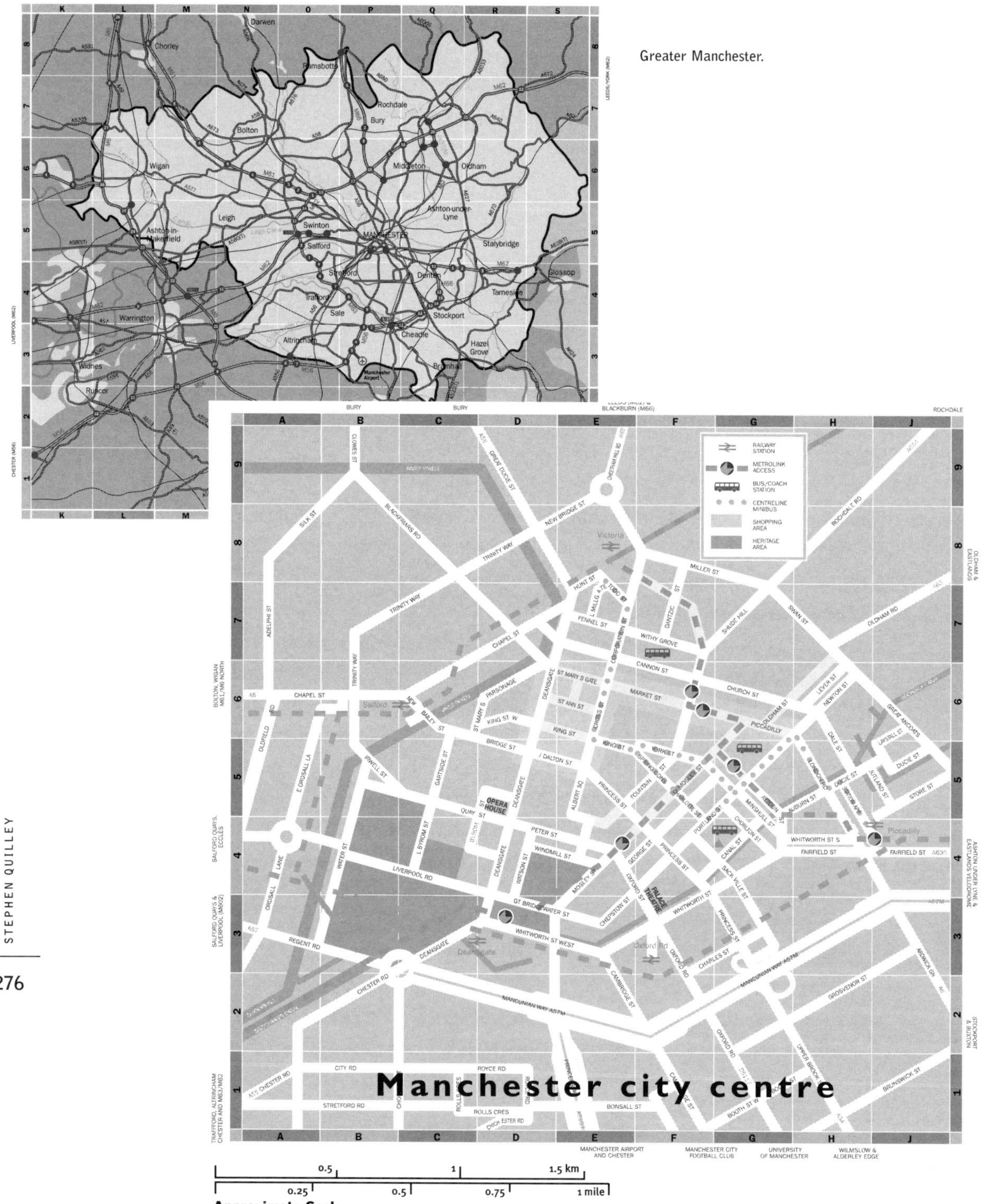

Greater Manchester.

Manchester city centre.

post-industrial cultural-economic landscape. A political-institutional presence in the city has been traded for a more pervasive, cultural-aesthetic presence in which the community is organised as a market rather than a political constituency.

There is a growing literature relating to the role of gay communities in the restructuring of urban space (Castells 1983; Lauria & Knopp 1985; Adler & Brenner 1992). However, in many cases, a narrow emphasis on the "interests, actions and desires" of gay men (Whittle 1994, 43), underplays the broader context of political economy.

The construction of gay places in the partially abandoned space of the inner city is bound up with economic and political processes that extend far beyond the agency of gay men. For instance, an economics of decline can produce opportunities for gay men in terms of gentrifiable stock. The post-Keynesian climate of competition, which pits city against city, can lead to the reevaluation of gay space by policy makers from regulatory problem to marketing asset—a contribution to the leisure economy. Existing commentaries on Manchester's Village do little to specify these "driving economic and social forces" (Hindle 1994, 22). Whittle locates his discussion of the commercial scene in the city, uncomfortably, in terms of a "postcapitalist straight world" and a rather undifferentiated notion of the state (Whittle 1994, 39). My intention is to reassess the development of the Village in terms of the changing economic fortunes, forms, and functions of Manchester as a capitalist city. My main focus is the political and economic project of the local Labour council and its reponses to these changing conditions. I want to argue that the imperatives of the "entrepreneurial city" (Harvey 1987) have had as much to do with developments in the Village as changing aspirations within the gay community.

Before "The Village"

In the 1950s and 1960s gay social life was organised around informal coteries in pubs.[2] The social scene was highly localised, ignored rather than tolerated in any active sense, secretive, and deferential. The relative invisibility of homosexual lives was reflected in the predominant "pregay" homosexual identity: private, individualist, nontransgressive, and rooted in sexual desire. This orientation was reflected in the political campaign during the buildup to the 1967 reform. The reform movement avoided being represented as an abrasive "gay campaign" by focusing instead on issues such as blackmail. This allowed supporters to present homosexuals as victims who needed help and understanding rather than criminalisation.

The Esquire Club's initiative of 1972–73 was the first recognition from within the Campaign for Homosexual Equality (CHE) of the need to move from beyond lifting legal constraints to proactively creating meeting places, an institutionalised social scene.[3] This initiative foundered partly because the breweries were apprehensive about the moral backlash. However, Horsfall associates the wide public debate with the subsequent gradual acceptance of the idea of gay clubs and men dancing with each other: "I think the whole exercise probably changed the police's attitude towards Gay clubs—we didn't have any more of this nonsense about men dancing together . . . so far as I know."[4] The Esquire Club's initiative was a political-institutional attempt to produce gay space. Although it failed, it did pave the way for gay clubs in the commercial scene to become well established by the end of the 1970s. In the emergent gay culture, it was perhaps the first manifestation of the tension between the politics of gay liberation and the commercial scene.

Clearly, over the course of the 1970s, changes in gay identity were symbiotically linked both to the limited legalisation of gay society and the expanding opportunities of the commercial scene, but also to public assertions of collective strength: a visible and overtly transgressive gay politics. However, even by the early 1980s, neither the politics of Gay Lib nor the commercial club scene had effected the transition from institutionalised sociability to institutionalised visibility. Thus Weightman, writing in 1980, characterised the gay bar as a "private place" that "carries few clues declaring its nature." She summarised its architectural features in terms of:

- location in marginal areas—including red-light areas, skid row, and renewal areas
- presentation of an inconspicuous, windowless, and uninviting image
- emphasis on restricting accessibility through the use of internal partitions, notices, and messages (Weightman 1980, 13)

A decade later gay culture in Manchester has appropriated the street, inviting both inspection and participation. The 1994 August bank holiday carnival in the Village attracted over forty thousand people and raised close to £40,000 for the Village Charity. The Village has transformed a marginal area into the fulcrum of the City's night-time economy (Lovatt 1994). The theatrical aesthetic of the café-bar finds its ultimate expression in Manto. Whereas in the traditional pubs favoured by the gay coterie of previous generations, the introverted and cramped privacy of frosted windows, partitions, and intimate corners warded off inspections and intrusions from the censoring eyes of straight society, café-bars such as Manto, with their goldfish-bowl windows magnify and underline a gay presence, inviting scrutiny. They demand attention.

The Emergence of "The Village"

> The great strength of the Village is its compactness. Stand on the corner where Bloom Street crosses Sackville Street and you're within 100 paces of ten gay clubs and pubs, not to mention gay doctors, restaurants, charities, and shops.
>
> —*The Pink Guide,* 1993/94[5]

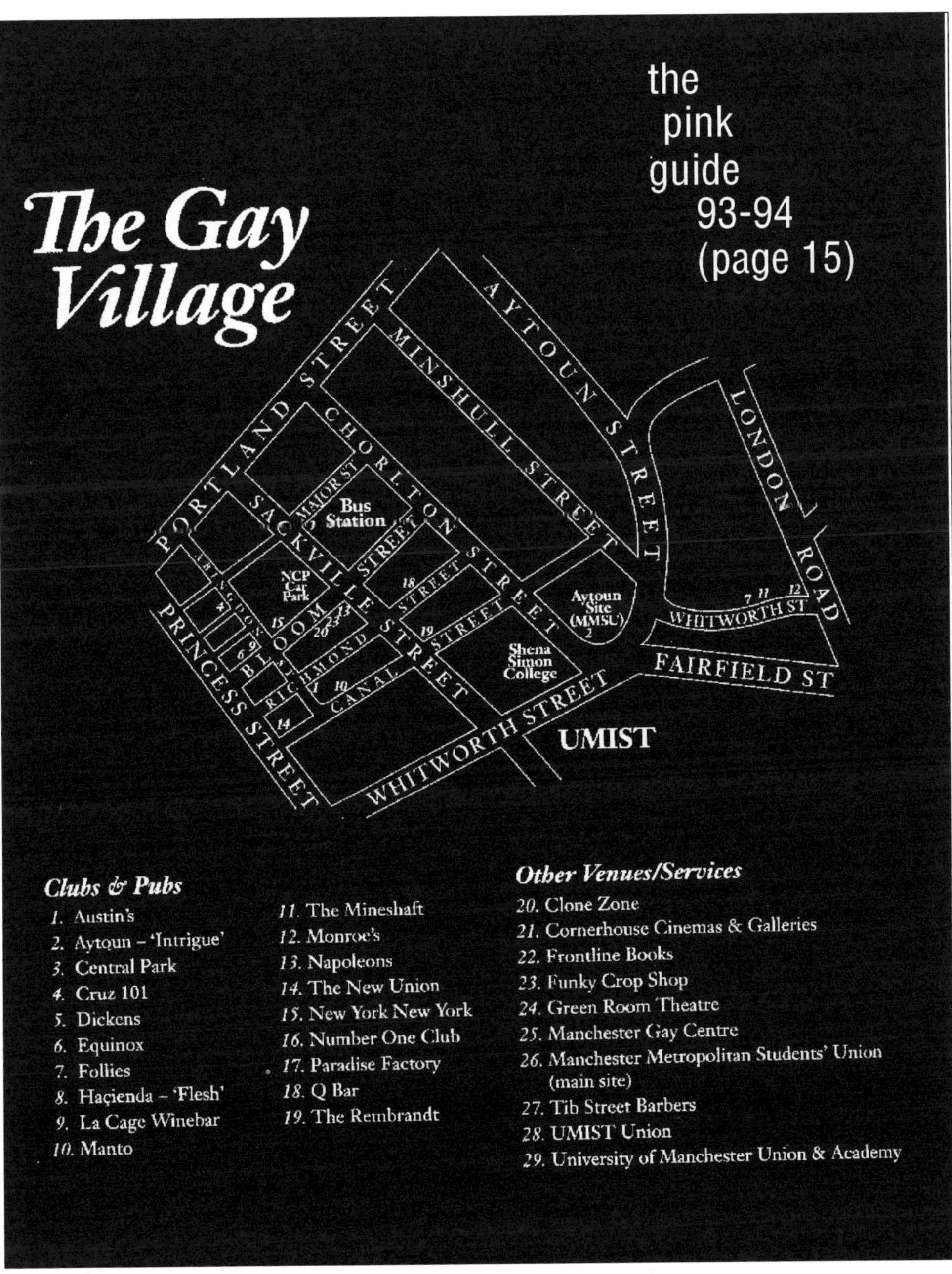

The Gay Village, Manchester. Map © *The Pink Guide 1993/94.*

The Gay Village is not a ghetto. It is rather a "gay developed space" (Fraser & Evans 1993, 12)[6] deliberately constructed as an enclave: a shelter from the intolerance, petty prohibitions, and violence of straight society. The establishment of the Village involved the appropriation of space through the imbrication of a regular pattern of social relations replete with meanings that structure the details of social interaction for gay and straight alike. The uniqueness of the Village lies in the fact that these patterns have moved out of discrete basement bars, onto the street, and into the public space between the bars—creating a bubble in which different rules and conventions are accepted.

This resocialisation of space has not benefitted only gay men. Due to its proximity to the bus station, its lack of street lighting, and its generally sleazy nature, one might have expected nearby Portland Street to inspire routine anxieties in respect to public space. In fact, in a survey of public attitudes, Taylor et al. found that the street was seen to be one of the safest in the city centre, primarily as a result of its proximity to the Village. "A potentially fearful and unsafe area has been made more attractive to others for whom the area was not primarily intended" (Taylor et al., 1993, 32). However this transformation has not been achieved easily. Whilst the Labour Council had funded a gay centre in Bloom Street since the late 1970s, the City Labour Party was hardly a model of progressive thinking.[7] It took a sustained period of lobbying by gay activists, as part of a wider cultural revolution initiated by the municipal left, before the Village became a legitimate element in Manchester's economic and cultural fabric—something the council would advertise as a positive asset.

Gay Activism and Manchester's "New Urban Left"

By the end of the 1970s, gay activity had shrunk, becoming concentrated in just a few locales in central Manchester. The Bloom Street area emerged as the main anchor point for the scene because it had more physical stability and was less commercially volatile. Paradoxically, the recession of the early 1980s increased this stability. As in other major industrial cities, the conflict between the Labour-controlled local authority committed to contesting and reversing the dramatic deindustrialisation that had ravaged the local economy and a central government wedded to real estate and finance interests resulted in a policy vacuum. The local authority resisted government initiatives but did not have the resources to implement an alternative strategy. The deadlock simply resulted in stagnation. Central Manchester seemed locked into a downward spiral of economic decline. With only a negligible residential population, with companies and businesses closing down and moving out (Peck & Emmerich 1992, 1993), and shunned by both the government and large-scale capital, the decaying downtown area became increasingly abandoned. It was subject to a haemorrhaging of the social relations and consequently of the meanings through which places constitute themselves in space (Smith in Thrift & Williamson 1987). Unoccupied by capital, central Manchester was thus "decentred" and open to colonisation.

However, whilst consolidation around the Bloom Street area had begun, there were still major obstacles to any significant institutionalisation. Police harassment combined with a general atmosphere of intolerance meant that clubs were ephemeral.

Furthermore gay culture had yet to become fashionable and trend-setting in popular youth culture. Given problems with security, policing, and in some cases the local authorities—such as with respect to licensing applications—gay clubs were often a commercial liability.

The commercial scene only really began to take off in the mid-1980s. At that time the emergence of a Labour administration, more sympathetic to gay rights, coincided with Manchester moving centre-stage, as a showcase for pop music and youth culture in general. Politically, this period started with a "revolution" in the Town Hall in 1984—in reality, a successful left-wing coup against the dominant right wing of the Labour Party, led by Graham Stringer who remains at the helm in 1994.

In the three years prior to the takeover, rebel left-wing councillors ran a vociferous campaign against the cuts being implemented by the leadership and twice had the whip removed.[8] Stringer himself places a great deal of emphasis on this period:

> During our three–four years in opposition we made alliances at all sorts of levels with all sorts of people who put feminist politics and the politics of the lesbian and gay movement onto the agenda in Manchester. If we had not been fighting the cuts with them, these issues would have dropped from most agendas. (Quoted in Lansley et al., 1989, 14)

Thus the ascendance of the "New Urban Left" created a window of opportunity for lesbian and gay activists to push a municipal agenda. This coincided with changes in the lesbian and gay movement itself. Cooper notes the shift away from the 1970s revolutionary strategies, such as separatism, and the movement towards identity politics: "The 1980s saw a renewed interest in affirming gay identity, developing political alliances, particularly between men and women, and working within the state" (Cooper, 1994, 23). Demands for affirmation and antidiscrimination initiatives marked a move away from an exclusive emphasis on sexuality and gender as motors of social change. Cooper argues that the reasons for this shift lay in the increasing size and strength of gay communities, the growing commercial scene, and expanding possibilities for gay lifestyles, as well as the recognition among feminists that differences in experience and relations of power made any simple unity based on gender increasingly problematic: "Identity affirmation rather than sexual deconstruction became the priority." As a result of these shifts, lesbian and gay activists increasingly became involved in the city Labour Party, in the National Association of Local Government Officers (NALGO), and in the work of the council—either as employees or council members.

Institutionalised Sexual Politics: Tensions and Contradictions

In Manchester, as elsewhere, the point of entry was the existing formal commitment of the Labour Party to equal opportunities policies. From the beginning, the lesbian and gay municipal project was severely compromised by the liberal pluralist assumptions of this policy framework. The implicitly essentialist view of homosexuality conveniently dovetailed with the prevailing paradigm of multiculturalism. However, as Cooper points out, this made it very difficult to move beyond a simple acknowledgement of equality and acted to undermine more radical approaches to sexuality which sought to problematise heterosexuality and its relation to the dominant institutions. The resulting "ideological steer" consistently constrained the agenda and weakened policy commitments. More radical policy innovations were nearly always organised out: "filtered and reshaped through a complex process of self-censorship, consultation, and monitoring" (Cooper, 1994, 81).

The problems associated with the gender blindness of the equal opportunities paradigm were clearly manifest in the different municipal experiences of gay men and lesbian women in Manchester. Gay activists identified quickly with the male-oriented structures of the Town Hall and with a number of out gay councillors.[9] Consequently the Gay Men's Sub-Committee[10] was able to intervene much more quickly and effectively in the policy process. For lesbian activists the relationship with the Town Hall was always more problematic. Many of the initial meetings were taken up with issues raised by that relationship, such as whether to hold meetings in the Town Hall.

The obstacles in the way of an institutionalised sexual politics were compounded by the more general bureaucratic inertia plaguing experiments in "local socialism" from the start. Failure to transform the bureaucratic traditions and structures of local government meant that radical policy innovation resulted in policy indigestion as initiatives were diverted, bogged down, and stifled at the implementation stage (Lansley et al., 1989, 11). Despite these problems, the municipal lesbian and gay project in Manchester did prepare the way for the subsequent expansion and consolidation of the Village. However limited, the commitment of the municipal left to establishing the legitimacy of the homosexual presence in the city was real, and it has been sustained in the face of much criticism, for nearly a decade.

1984–87 Policy, Planning Struggles for the Legitimacy of Gay Space

Prior to 1984, Graham Stringer was chair of the city Labour party, unchallenged spokesperson for the Left, and an obvious choice for group leader. He came to power on the back of a wave of determined opposition to the rather modest package of cuts drawn up by the right-wing Labour leadership in 1983. As part of this package, the gay centre on Bloom Street, one of twenty-three projects funded under the Urban Aid programme, had its funding slashed by 25 percent. The new administration was quick to restore the funding to its previous level.[11] This action exemplified the rainbow-alliance politics of the new regime. The municipal left saw lesbians and gay men as part of their natural constituency and allies in a shared struggle against the Conser vative government. The struggle for lesbian and gay rights became implicated in a much wider challenge to the central state. Thus in Manchester the Gay Sweatshop Theatre Group was approached to do a benefit for the miners.[12] The Campaign for Nuclear Disarmament advertised regularly in the pages of *Mancunian Gay* and whereas the Gay Centre was allowed its first stall at the Manchester Show in September 1984, the military were banned for the first time.

The council provided material as well as symbolic support. Throughout the period, the local gay press benefitted and was to some extent sustained by advertising revenues from the City Council. Increased funding for the gay centre culminated in the eventual move to new premises on Sidney Street. Perhaps more importantly, the new political influence of gay activists allowed the gay community to start defending itself against the low-level guerrilla war waged periodically by the Greater Manchester Police Force. Issues relating to policing and police harassment were and still are a constant preoccupation for the gay community. Thus in 1984 the gay press was full of stories relating to the use of plainclothes "pretty cops," agents provocateurs, to trap gay men in the act of cottaging. Whilst the practice had been disowned by the Manchester Force in 1982 and was against Home Office guidelines, the Manchester Police were obviously continuing the practice.[13] The problem was heightened in Manchester by the presence of James Anderton who, as chief constable, carried out a religious crusade against those whom he famously claimed to be "swirling around in a cesspit of their own making."[14] Thus in Manchester the police took a meticulous and highly obstructive interest in licensing applications in general and gay clubs in particular. Clubs were raided frequently, and owners and customers were subjected to intimidation.

In 1981 the Police Committee had refused to make any specific effort to avoid discriminating against gay men and lesbians. That same year the gay community had been specifically excluded from the newly established Community Liaison Panels. However, while they could not get rid of Anderton,[15] constant political pressure did lead to limited recognition of the legitimacy of the scene. Thus even by the end of Anderton's reign as chief constable, the Sub–Committee was having periodic discussions with the local police on matters relating to the policing of the Village. They requested specific officers, sensitive to the issues, to be available to deal with cases reported by gay men and lesbians.[16] Also in 1990 "Scene Out" worker Chris Payne was selected as a lay visitor for Bootle Street Police Station, specifically to deal with lesbians and gays taken into custody in the vicinity of the Village.[17] Similarly, although periodic bouts of harassment have continued, it is significant that senior policemen were willing to talk to members of OutRage.[18] By 1992 Anderton's replacement, David Wilmot, was willing to issue a statement relating to the need for equal opportunity for lesbian and gay police officers. Wilmot's *glasnost* has yet to fully overturn the legacy of the Anderton regime: Recidivist elements recently indulged in a gratuitous raid on the Mineshaft Club, resulting in thirteen arrests.[19] However since then the chief constable has visited the Village to meet local gay entrepreneurs, and a more senior and sympathetic superintendent has taken over liaison duties.

For marginalised groups seeking to appropriate space, a real index of success is when local authorities accept the *local* self-definitions of place. Thus acceptance of Chinatown as a planning entity, as a place, should be seen as an important if limited affirmation of legitimacy for the Chinese community's place in Manchester. By this logic the council bureaucracy has moved some way towards formally acknowledging the Village. Whilst NALGO had been supportive for many years, it took several years for the department to move beyond a vague commitment to equal opportunities. Thus in 1985 the Chief Planning Officer and the Equal Opportunities Committee (EOC) rejected the suggestion that there was a need for research and general information on the lesbian and gay Communities in Manchester—a point of view contested vigorously by the Gay Men's Sub–Committee.[20] However by 1990, after pressure from the community led to the rejection of an application for a multistory car park on Bloom Street, the Highways and Planning Committee agreed that the community should be consulted on all further planning applications. At the same time, the Sub-Committee was putting forward proposals for public-notice boards in the Bloom Street area, showing details and locations of facilities in the area. This was less about information than the desire for public recognition of the scene by the council. It was the first time that the area as a whole had been claimed as a gay space. The increasing confidence of the community can be seen also in deliberations about the possible new gay centre which stressed the need for visibility: ". . . it's no accident that [hitherto] gay premises of all kinds have ended up in dark dungeon-like basements hidden away from the world" (EOC minutes, 28 August 1985). However, whilst political pressure and influence in the Labour Party certainly made a difference, the final 1991 conversion of council officers to the idea of the Gay Village as a unitary entity significant in planning terms was due more to the recognition of the area's economic importance in marketing the city. Thus whilst the first reference in the gay press to the idea of a Village was in 1984, it was not until three years after the imposition of the Central Manchester Development Corporation in 1991 that *City Planning News*[21] referred to the Gay Village as a planning entity.

From Municipal Socialism to "City Chauvinism"

> They completely changed course. . . . It was a conscious thing. They decided to do that. (Interview with Dick Pickering, Manchester GMB)

After the third Conservative general election victory in 1987, there was a waning of both the political influence of the new left in the Labour Party and the grassroots activism that sustained it. Left councils were faced with a choice between grim but futile resistance or a political U-turn. The defeat meant the implementation of cuts in local government expenditures. However 1987 also marked the qualitative defeat of municipal socialism as the exemplar of a possible alternative to Thatcherism.

The political implications of Labour's defeat were not lost on Graham Stringer. He quickly came to the conclusion that accommodation and cooperation with the Tory government represented the only way forward for the council. Of all the radical councils, Manchester has adapted to the new political climate most successfully. Indeed whilst the level of party activism has plummeted, and whilst many disillusioned activists have left the party, many of those people involved in the pre-1984 struggle against cuts, including Stringer, are still prominent in the 1994 council leadership.

Abandoning the model of municipal socialism, Stringer also moved away from the politics of the rainbow alliance. Gradually, references to "people based" and "bottom-up" economic policies were replaced by a managerial emphasis on getting things done. In place of "defending jobs and improving services," the new corporate slogan was Manchester City Council: Making it Happen. The political imperative was no longer resistance to Thatcherism. Rather, the council began to follow a single-minded strategy of city chauvinism: getting the best for Manchester. Most of the time "getting the best" simply meant attracting the most investment from the EEC, from central government, and from private corporations.

Since 1987 the Labour group has abandoned any serious idea that the process of deindustrialisation could be reversed. Cooperating with the Central Manchester Development Corporation (CMDC) and government initiatives such as the City Challenge, the council has become actively implicated in a process of property-led urban regeneration. It has accepted an economic vision for the city based on its status as a regional capital and financial centre. The future is seen to depend on the service sector, with a central position accorded to leisure and cultural consumption. The central theme in the new economic strategy has been the reimaging of the city around these themes. Those involved in marketing the city refer to these themes as the Euroscript. The strategy has coalesced around a succession of hallmark events that have provided platforms upon which to rehearse this script ad nauseam: the Olympic bids, City of Drama, global forum, and so on. In the marketing pamphlets and publicity videos of the city's new boosters, Manchester is being actively reinvented as a "progressive European city . . . cosmopolitan and culturally rich" (Manchester City Council, 1994). The Gay Village, along with other cultural quarters such as Rusholme and Chinatown, is being harnessed as an exotic proof of the city's cosmopolitan and progressive credentials. This script serves to underline the transition away from a more homogeneous, if somewhat fictive, past based on production. The future is postindustrial (CMDC 1990) and culturally diverse.

In line with this shift away from purely oppositional politics, the political-institutional structures that had served the alliance politics of resistance were gradually wound down. By 1992 the EOC, with its separate gay and lesbian subcommittees, had been submerged into the Policy and Resources subcommittee. Instead of a formal structure involving co-optees from the community, there is an open invitation for various groups to bring up issues informally with lead members such as Pat Karney and Clare Nangle. But the dissipation of the municipal lesbian and gay project should not be seen simply in terms of the defeat of the left and the adoption of a radically different political strategy. After 1988 the wider movement was subject to a process of demobilisation. This was in part related to the more general weakening of the extra-parliamentary left, but it owed just as much to shifting priorities within gay society. "James "Cesspit" Anderton may have gone, but so has the late eighties radicalism which mobilised so many thousands against Section 28." (*The Pink Guide*, 1993/94:9). Thus by July 1990, the Organisation for Lesbian and Gay Action—established in the aftermath of Clause 28—had been wound down due to a lack of interest. There was also widespread disillusionment within lesbian and gay communities relating to the failure to turn access to the political-institutional system into a radical sexual politics. The Equal Opportunities framework, which aimed to treat all homosexual relations equally, could not address difficult issues and struggles within the community (Cooper 1994, 179). Another reason for the widening gap between lesbian and gay activists and the officers working in local government and the wider community was the alternative focus for gay activity offered by the burgeoning commercial scene. Political involvement was no longer trendy or transgressive. Disillusionment was exacerbated by boredom, and Manchester's commercial scene was particularly diverting (Cooper 1994, 170). Here it is worth examining the emergence of postgay identities that were, in part, a reaction to the collectivist and monolithic political identity of "gay liberation." The "queer diaspora" is also seen to be a creative response to the tragedy and loss experienced by the post-AIDS generation. In this context, institutional links with the Town Hall seemed increasingly irrelevant. Thus when Paul Fairweather left his post in June 1989 there was a period of four months when none of the four subcommittee positions were filled. The Gay Men's Sub–Committee gradually lost the confidence of the community.[22] By contrast, the Village flourished, in part reflecting an efflorescent "diasporic queer culture" more comfortably expressed through the commercial scene. Emergent postgay identities were more easily articulated with the leisure/consumption-oriented strategy of property-led regeneration adopted by Stringer after 1987.

Marketing "The Scene": Confirming Narratives of Cosmopolitan Diversity

Whilst formal institutional links between gay activists and the council were being eroded, the commitment to gay rights was not abandoned. However it was reformulated and is no longer framed in terms of an anticonservative anticapitalist discourse of resistance. The Village and its gay entrepreneurs have become exemplars of the new economic strategy which, it is hoped, will bring jobs back to the city. According to councillor Pat Karney: "One of our main concerns [in supporting the nighttime economy . . . and the Village] is to bring jobs and investment back to the city." Thus when Stringer posed for a photo-call in Manto, a café-bar in the Village, and expressed support for reducing the age of homosexual consent,[23] he also implicitly articulated the links between the Village and Manchester's new leisure/service economy. Along with Chinatown and the Northern Quarter, the Gay Village is being included in the government's *City Pride* initiative. It is being incorporated into a marketing exercise in which Manchester is presented as a progressive, tolerant, and above all interesting patchwork of diverse districts and quarters.[24] These cultural quarters function, almost by definition, as exotica. Gay culture is increasingly seen as a lure for the city's rapidly growing tourist industry. This much is frankly acknowledged by the Greater Manchester Visitor and Convention Bureau.

> GAY MANCHESTER: A major factor in the city's unique sense of style is the predominance and excitement generated by "Queer Culture" and gay lifestyle. In the heart of the city, Manchester's Gay Village bulges with some of the best eateries, drinkeries and danceries around—the atmosphere is happily mixed with the warm welcome.[25]

The upbeat commentary continues: "Remember, if it's happening and hip, it has to be the life and soul of Manchester." "Queer Culture" may be subject to a process of relegitimation, as it finds a place in the official representations of the city. But it remains in inverted commas, defined as a spectacle and an asset, from the perspective of a very specific economic project.

With this economic agenda in mind, since the late 1980s Stringer's clique has had an increasing amount of contact with gay entrepreneurs in the Village. On one occasion in 1992, Pat Karney led a group of doubtful councillors around the clubs to press the cause for a more liberal licensing regime and to underline the economic possibilities of the nighttime economy. Rather than being seen in terms of ethical-political commitment to a political ally, the Village has increasingly been recognised as an asset—highly relevant to Manchester's postindustrial future in Europe. The commercial scene has become more compatible with the Manchester Euroscript: a postindustrial service-based economy with a world-class reputation for clubs and pop music; capital of a major European region; a significant cultural and sporting centre; a twenty-four-hour city.[26] A new axis developed between the Village and the Town Hall. But this time it was the entrepreneurs[27] rather than the activists who increasingly sought out Stringer and Karney et al.—not only in their role as sponsors of this Euroscript but also as advocates of the Village. As Karney said: "We know the owners and managers . . . They come to us for advice. The council is now very supportive . . . [if anything, it is becoming a bit of a problem] . . . too many people come to see us." The political space provided during the early years of the Stringer administration allowed the city's gay culture to develop such that it could now lead the way in developing a European-style street ambience as well as the club culture necessary to make the twenty-four-hour city a reality. Gay activism has increasingly concentrated on issues around HIV/AIDS.[28] The fund-raising events associated with these campaigns are easily compatible with the notions of vibrant street life and public space that are increasingly in vogue with the visionaries of *Manchester 2000*. Thus the street market referred to above is now a three-day fund-raising carnival that involves closing part of the city centre to traffic: "a major North West event."

> I think that he [the Lord Mayor] was a bit pissed off because two months previously he had thirty-eight floats in the Lord Mayor's parade and we had managed thirty-two in the first go at a gay parade . . . [The carnival has] an Australian Mardi Gras type atmosphere. (Interview with Rob Jackson, Director of the Village Charity, March 1994)

The success and increasing importance of the *Madigras* in the civic calender is the most visible aspect of a new symbiotic relationship that is developing between the increasingly commercialised gay scene and the city's new entrepreneurial economic project. The extent to which the Village is becoming increasingly mainstream is evident in the gay-club-scene references that now appear in tourist brochures and press commentaries. For instance, in its special issue on Manchester, British Rail's Inter-City Xcursions refers to the Paradise Factory as: "situated [on the edge of] the Gay Village, club nights here can be camp and colourful."[29]

In these small ways, the city is able to reposition itself as a cosmopolitan (European) metropolis on a par with Amsterdam or Melbourne. There is more than an element of the urban spectacle in this "commodification" of gay culture. Along with Chinatown, Rusholme's Curry Mile, and the youthful verve of *Mad*chester, the Village is increasingly conscripted into a municipal narrative of vibrancy and theatricality. Thus, in the glossy pamphlet accompanying an exhibition on architecture and the city's new café society (*Café Bars*, Manchester, 1994), we are told that: "Manto is the stage in the urban theatre. Its steel frame facade, the proscenium. Its balcony, the gods. Its clientele both players and audience."[30] It is perhaps no accident that Manto is one of the most youthful and mixed gay venues, playing host to a significant number of straights who are happy to adopt, if only for a night, the mores and public conventions of gay society. The venue indeed plays host to both players and audience.

Liberation '91 Gay Festival, April 13, 1991, The Gay Village, Manchester. Courtesy of News Team International Ltd.

Conclusion

I have identified two overlapping phases in the development of the Village.

1. Between 1984 and 1988 a dominant political-institutional dynamic working on an axis linking mainly left-wing gay activists based around the gay centre in Bloom Street and the Town Hall. The formal point of contact in the bureaucratic structure was the EOC, specifically the Gay Men's Sub–Committee.

2. From 1987: A market dynamic, in which the expansion of the commercial scene was actively facilitated by the same group in the Labour Leadership—led from the front by Stringer himself. The dynamic axis moved away from the gay activists and the Sub–Committee whilst the EOC was gradually downgraded. Instead personal and informal contacts developed between the Labour group and the gay entrepreneurs.

The point of continuity was Stringer's leadership and unwavering commitment to gay rights. The changing way in which this commitment was manifested reflected the political shift in the Labour Party and the new strategy of critical cooperation with central government and the CMDC. Stringer's new friends in the media and local businesses shared a commitment to Manchester and getting what they could out of the new national regime for the city. As David Plowright[31] put it: "A few of us got together with the City Council and began to say let's stop dabbing our eyes at the loss of these manufacturing industries and see whether we can't do something to get to terms with what Madam called the enterprise culture."

The commitment to gay rights was no longer wrapped up in a discourse of popular resistance to Thatcher. Rather it was woven into a clever Mancunian version of enterprise culture. The Village has a place in the script of those intent on marketing the city because it exemplifies the transition from the homogeneous working-class identity of Manchester's industrial past to the metropolitan diversity of its post-industrial future.

At the same time, within the gay and lesbian communities, there were reactions against the left-wing gay activism associated with Town Hall politics (Cooper, 1994). The commercial scene offered an increasingly vibrant alternative focus for social life, which diverted attention and interest away from institutional politics. Increasingly the link between the "scene" and gay activism was articulated as a celebration of sexual identity and sexual diversity—as with the carnival. The Village Charity has emerged as a focus for gay activism separate from the Gay Centre. Perhaps significantly, the charity has new offices in the centre of the Village, whereas the new Gay Centre is now somewhat isolated away from the Village in Sidney Street. The Charity's newsletter, *Village Voice,* betrays a wider leadership role that was formerly the prerogative of political activists. Full-time worker Rob Jackson describes himself as politically conservative, but he is full of admiration for Stringer's leadership in Manchester.

During the 1980s the gay community was able to consolidate a presence in Manchester, at first by taking advantage of the temporary economic abandonment of the central city. Subsequently the Village has become an important element in the revitalization of the downtown area. By adapting to the changing political and economic climate, gay culture has insinuated itself into the Euroscript: Manchester's version of a rejuvenated postindustrial city. The Village has led the way in reappropriating the street for pedestrians and flaneurs: for a mode of urban experience that is central to European notions, in which positive ambience in public space is the result of social face-to-face vibrancy and participation. This ambience is best experienced through the act of strolling (de Certeau 1984). Gay gentrification in the neighbouring Granby Village development has contributed to this project in the vicinity of Canal Street.

However this success is ambiguous. The Village is central to the reinvention of a city-living tradition absent in Manchester for nearly two hundred years (O'Connor 1994). But this invention is part of a wider political and economic project. Stringer's Mancunian version of enterprise culture was constructed in the face of municipal socialism's defeat. The new project has required the Council and the city's Labour Party to abandon any hopes for a serious revival in Manchester's fortunes as an industrial city. Instead, Stringer has chosen to cooperate actively with a strategy of property-led regeneration. The enthusiasm and political acumen that he has brought to this endeavour has won him a circle of unlikely admirers, including Michael Heseltine and many of Manchester's leading businessmen. The strategy has undeniably transformed Manchester's economic prospects by attracting millions of pounds into the city for a string of flagship projects. However it has also contributed to a widening gulf between rich and poor in the city: between those with the money to take advantage of the new leisure and cultural opportunities, and those who either service this new economy or who are marginalised and excluded from it. The much-vaunted dynamism of Manchester's economy depends increasingly on a labour market that has seen a dramatic increase in the numbers of low paid, part-time nonunion workers with insecure jobs.

In so far as the Village has been incorporated into this economic project, marginal sexualities have become involved in a "sexual accumulation project" (Evans 1993). This is true in that the Village is central to the general reimaging of the city, and also specifically in that it generates considerable revenues for the nighttime economy. But commercialisation has brought its own tensions. Sexual transgression has been recuperated, but not on its own terms. As Steve Whittle points out: "Most gays are not rich, young, white, and beautiful and the scene is starting to exclude them."[32] The Village has institutionalised a visible gay presence in the city. But involvement in the wider cultural economy has meant that, to an extent, gay sexuality is being exploited as an urban spectacle. There has also been some concern among lesbians and gay men about the increasing number of straight people using the Village and undermining its primary significance as a safe place (Whittle 1994).

Whittle is pessimistic about commercial development and asks rhetorically whether the Village developed to service the needs of gay people or whether, on the contrary, it was a ploy to render gay culture amenable to exploitation and sanitization (Whittle 1994, 31). But is it useful to make a reading of the Village as simply good or bad? The articulation of gay culture within the emerging landscape of power has clearly created great opportunities. For a council-sponsored gay carnival to have established itself as *the* public event in the city centre over the August bank holiday is an index of the changes that have taken place over the last fifteen years. The presence of ostensibly friendly police officers, both men and women, sporting red ribbons indicates a significant change in relations between the police and the gay community, even if they are yet to be regarded as Village Bobbies!

At the same time one cannot ignore the undeniable problems that this mode of legitimation entails. By recognising the way in which the development of the Village is intertwined with the construction of a particular cultural-economic vision for Manchester's future, these tensions can be better understood and placed in a wider context. For example, Whittle highlights patterns of economic and racial exclusion in the Village. But in this respect the Village is simply a microcosm of a mode of economic and social development that affects the whole city. It seems that a gay vernacular will have a permanent place in Manchester's new cultural and economic landscape. It is one element among many in the city's attempt to market itself as a truly heterogeneous and culturally diverse, European metropolis. Thus, at least to some extent, its continued success depends on the sustainability of that economic model.

Part 4—Queer Sites

Preceding page: The *Homomonument* in Amsterdam, 1995.

Placemaking and the Dialectics of Public and Private

Gordon Brent Ingram, Anne-Marie Bouthillette, and Yolanda Retter

Queer places are always formed by a mixture of accidental and purposeful (though often unevenly articulated) forces. In this century, sites[1] of queer presence ambiguously overlap the public and the private. These intermediate zones survive by their populations' consciously chosen strategies of invisibility and visibility, defense, and expansion. The construction of queer sites, both unstructured spaces for spontaneous contact and key institutions, has many facets: social, cultural, economic, and political. In Part 4 of *Queers in Space*, we examine a range of placemaking strategies and tactics, some more historical, others more contemporary.

How sexual minorities come to placemaking says much about social networks and relationships to local political economies.[2] The space occupied by refugees from repression, such as gay ghetto bars before Stonewall, is profoundly different from a contemporary sex club that emphasizes maximum opportunities for diverse and safe(r) pleasures. Just as queer identities are constructed within the context of heteronormativity, queer places have been forged within spaces not originally intended for gay use. Identifying a place as queer is a deliberate action parallel to "coming out." Although certain sites have been the focus of gay activities for many years, the nature of these queer places changes, just as identities and modes of contact do. Without a conscious effort to constantly reinvent the queerness of such places, heteronormative forces in society often overwhelm and push out networks of sexual minorities.

In Part 4 of *Queers in Space*, we explore the relationships between queer presence, visibility, claiming of sites, and placemaking. We are especially concerned with the shifting dialectics of public and private arenas and their relationship to how same-sex and "degendered"[3] sexualities and communalities express themselves and are, at least, partially tolerated. Queer sites are usually characterized by contradictions and ambiguity, allowing for a wide range of erotic and other forms of social contact. Rather than constructing sites explicitly for homoerotic communality and expression, much formation of queer space has concentrated on transcending heteronormative constraints. In times of repression and culturally enforced conformity, the least constraining places are those that are neither totally public or private, containing rich striations within short physical distances. These queer spaces offer more room to move than do the places that are the outgrowths of heteronormative relationships and consumerism. The resulting labyrinths are the products of both random conditions, such as lack of accessibility and competing demand, and adaptive collages, combining kitsch, high- and lowbrow aesthetics, and a hodgepodge of desires. The resulting establishments have sometimes bonded in queer coalitions for activism.

The Stonewall riots transformed queer sites forever. They fueled a new cohesion, perhaps even a kind of militarization, that has aggressively contested and reappropriated places and public resources, though sometimes only for short periods. The ritual power of these demonstrations to groups long culturally and emotionally ghettoized cannot be overestimated. Placemaking has achieved more than the temporary assertion of control over points and territories. These experiences continue to transform how we view ourselves and our inherent rights, as well as how we move within our communities and across neighbourhoods and landscapes. The Stonewall riots signalled that the status of sexual minority does not automatically lead to the loss of all political and economic rights.

Sites of public and semipublic sexuality, political activity, and remembrance have remained contentious issues within both our communities and broader society. Today, in virtually every neighbourhood in North America and Europe with sizable lesbian and gay male communities, there has been at least one major controversy about safety, another about sexuality, and another about the placement of sculptural

The AIDS Memorial Grove, Golden Gate Park, San Francisco, 1996.

and pictorial information at queer public sites. Displaying art that explicitly explores queer sensibilities in the arena of public outdoor space has begun to emerge as a trend over the past decade.[4] Presence, visibility, political activism, policy, design, and art are transforming places.

Boundaries separating public and private realms have shifted radically over the past three centuries. There have always been exceptional sites that escaped police detection and served as refuges for communality and sexual contact for sexual minorities. But to assume that today there is more queer space just because there is less repression is simplistic. Today, in much of the world, commercial spaces for limited public contact appear to be expanding, whereas areas of hidden queer "public" life, such as parks for sex, are expanding to a comparatively lesser degree. Queer private space, such as bedrooms and apartments, continues to grow because of increased access to housing through improved economic conditions, declining pressures to participate in heteronormative families, and employment-related relocation.

What factors shape today's spatial distribution of queer life between public and private? Certainly, the interrelationships of population densities, demographics, and housing influence the amount of private space available to different individuals and classes. Expensive square-footage costs for housing often push many activities into parks, cafés, and public meeting areas. The influence of consumerism in malls and renovated urban villages provides new forms of public space. But higher levels of crime and homophobic harassment, along with partial privatization of previously public space, can push communality into semiprivate and private spaces, particularly commercial establishments. But many queer networks continue to work for increased public presence and improved opportunities for contact and subsequent eroticism, such as various forms of cruising.

Individual and communal access to queer places, both public and private, remains variable and is still often related to gender, race, ethnicity, language, and disability. In much of North America, women, people of colour, people wanting to speak languages other than English, the disabled, and sexual minorities effectively have less access to any kind of place. The situation in Europe is only slightly better because of greater language diversity and a more developed culture of outdoor open space. But British urban theoretician Elizabeth Wilson has suggested that for women, the public/private divide may well be continuing to intensify.[5] Today's divisions of public and private space are still tied to gender, and perceived transgressions against the status quo often result in violence or threats.[6]

Such class boundaries are reflected in the forms, textures, and markers of the gay male, lesbian, bisexual, and transgendered placemaking, making them clearly different. The construction of any kind of space is in large part a response to what is scarce, and each class experiences different lacks. For example, for women in patriarchal contexts, basic security often has been of paramount concern. Although options for sexual minorities other than middle-class white men still remain limited, great strides in placemaking have occurred over the past decade. But for groups who are marginalized economically, most of these places are inaccessible, and infrequent, ephemeral events such as street fairs and parties form their main experiences of queer space. Still, queer public and private places are becoming "decolonized," and women and other marginalized groups, though often constrained by poverty, are creating new communal and commercial space.

The essays in this section offer four examples of sexual minorities who are claiming and reconstructing space to create refuges, sites of greater freedom of expression, nodes of communality, and community-based institutions. Such placemaking processes involve disputes over interpretations of history and hierarchies of uses for resources. By documenting these places, these essays affirm the continuity of homosexual acts and the connectedness of cultures of resistance.

In "Invisible Women in Invisible Places: The Production of Social Space in Lesbian Bars," Maxine Wolfe interviews witnesses to trace how bars developed as lesbian social spaces and their role as both "sites of domination and sites of resistance." In "Lesbian Spaces in Los Angeles, 1970–1990," Yolanda Retter outlines a typology of lesbian placemaking, particularly related to service delivery, cultural events, and politics, that developed in Los Angeles after Stonewall and before the formation of Queer Nation. Her research confirms the existence of a pattern of lesbian housing and public spaces that is scattered rather than clustered.

In "Leather Nights in the Woods: Locating Male Homosexuality and Sadomasochism in a Dutch Highway Rest Area," gay activist Maurice van Lieshout examines public sex as placemaking in a time and place of relative, though far from complete, tolerance. He describes patterns of irregular nodes of public sex that have persisted well into the current proliferation of less overtly sexualized queer institutions. Many of the sites in this forest, at specific times, were associated with specific desires, and Lieshout's descriptions suggest the shifting nature of queer placemaking as networks form and desires are articulated. The author sheds light on one of the most taboo and reviled aspects of male homosexuality: outdoor labyrinths for public sex. Lieshout's microgeography is cathartic in beginning to represent the richness of intermingled communal and sexual transactions.

In "Queer Spaces in New York City: Places of Struggle/Places of Strength," Betti-Sue Hertz, Ed Eisenberg, and Lisa Maya Knauer of the REPOhistory Collective relate contemporary public art theory and community activism to reinscribing gay heritage on the broader historical narrative of New York City. In the contest over "The Stonewall Legacy,"[7] plaques and walking tours selectively highlight and revise particular aspects of lesbian and gay history.[8] Members of REPOhistory, a public art group, memorialized sites of gay activism in lower Manhattan. By installing pink triangles on lampposts, they hope to firmly establish these historical queer landmarks in the current "memory crisis"[9] concerning the extensive activism unleashed by the Stonewall riots.

REPOhistory Collective, *Queer Spaces* installation with luminary David Welch. Julius's Bar, lower Manhattan, 1995.

Invisible Women in Invisible Places: The Production of Social Space in Lesbian Bars[1]

Maxine Wolfe

Though invisible in our literature as "environments for women," lesbian bars exist in small towns and in large cities all over the United States and the world. This paper traces the history of their development in the United States, their uses and meanings for lesbians in different communities, as well as their relationship to lesbian culture and to the emergence of the modern lesbian and gay political movement, and to the larger communities of which they are a part. A perspective called the "social production of people/environment relationships" is used, one in which historical analysis provides the link between existing macro- and microlevel approaches to understanding people/environment relationships at the present time. This perspective explores the relationship between environmental change and social change and leads to questions about assumptions, concepts, and methods in current work in our field.

Introduction

Existing approaches to understanding the relationship between people and environmental settings include those at the micro- (i.e., environmental, architectural, and psychological) and macro- (i.e., political, cultural, and social) levels of analyses. The former typically decontextualize people/environment relationships from the larger societal context; the latter either focus on abstract space/social categories or eliminate individual/group experience and interpretation. The approach taken in this paper—the social production of people/environment relationships—uses an interpretative and contextualized historical method to show the relationship between micro- and macrolevel processes in creating and transforming people/environment relations (Manzo & Wolfe 1990).

Yet historical analysis, as a method for understanding people/environment relationships, can inhibit change if the past is seen as a set of "facts" leading directly to the only "true" story. The present approach, by contrast, is based on questioning whose interpretations are available and why; whose past is made visible and whose invisible (Davidson & Lytle 1982; Lerner 1979). It has as its premise understanding what Foucault called a "history of the present" (Dreyfuss & Rabinow 1983). It seeks to clarify and relate the historical interplay among forces at the present moment and at other times, looking for differences and similarities, discontinuities and continuities, changes in language, use, and meaning as well as physical form.

However, many analyses based on Foucaultian concepts, or growing out of other neo-Marxist approaches, focus exclusively on the history of normatively identifiable building types and assume that dominant discourses reveal the story of their production, uses, and meanings. Yet this leads to only a partial story of people/environment relationship—a story of domination. In contrast, the current perspective focuses on the "marginalized discourses," seeks to hear the voices of "ordinary" individuals, to recognize the importance of daily experiences, and to account for forces larger than the individual but not to artificially inflate their dominance (Diamond & Quinby 1988). Its premise is that people are active creators of their own identities and environments, rather than mere bearers of dominant social relations or passive absorbers of dominant ideology.

By focusing on settings other than mass-produced normative-built forms—in this instance, lesbian bars—and on uses for and meanings of existing forms that were never intended, either by those who created them or who currently manage them, I am seeking to clarify the relationship between environmental change and social change brought about by other than dominant groups—in this instance, lesbians. Yet existing attempts to understand environmental/social change as a process of consciousness and contestation still privilege economic explanations. Of particular relevance to the present paper is Castell's approach to understanding the role of the "gay" community in affecting urban change in San Francisco (1983). While on the surface his analysis appears to use a "cultural" explanation, he focuses only on gay men, claiming that lesbians could not be identified in the landscape of San Francisco because they did not own property. Yet lesbians in San Francisco do have a culture and a known geography as part of it—neighbourhoods they live in, places they frequent—despite their lack of economic power. And they have played a role in the social/environmental change in that city. The present approach, while drawing on some of Castell's concepts, attempts to deal with the social production of people/environment relationship by focusing on the intersection of class, gender, and race, as well as sexuality, in understanding the creation, uses, and meanings of the sociophysical world and its relation to social change and to definitions and transformations of culture.

The concept of culture, in environmental social science as well as other disciplines, is often used in a static fashion and as a barrier to change. "Tradition" is frequently cited as a basis for continuing oppressive ways of living. We need to question whose traditions are being continued, who defines what constitutes a "culture" as opposed to a "subculture," who benefits from such definitions, and why (Grahn 1984; Ladner 1973). Culture is also premised on the idea that any set of social practices is in a continual process of creation, maintaining parts of the past while being transformed as well. As a lesbian, I have a particular interest in documenting and understanding various aspects of lesbian culture, agreeing with Grahn (1984) that:

> What gives any group of people distinction and dignity is its culture. This includes a remembrance of the past and a setting of itself in a world context whereby the group can see who it is relative to everyone else. I have always been bothered by the definition of homosexuality as a behaviour. Scratching is a behaviour. Homosexuality is a way of being, one that can completely influence a person's life and shape its meaning and direction. (xii-xiv)

Though lesbians and gay men, as well as aspects of our culture, have existed for thousands of years in every known society and nation, our existence, history, and transformations are rarely represented in any work in the social sciences field or fields such as environmental design. Our culture has been trivialized as "lifestyle" and our places, spaces, and geography are unknown and invisible to most people.

This invisibility reflects and is reflected in the heterosexist biases in our literature, including the literature on "women and environments," in which lesbians are rarely, if ever, mentioned and then only in passing. We are neither part of the generic category of "women" nor are we identified as a particular group of women with particular needs. Yet we are not the only people who are made invisible (Bradley & Wolfe 1987). In our case, an unravelling of heterosexist bias raises particular questions. Some may be applicable to invisible others; some may be specific to who we are and how we lead our lives. In our case, heterosexist bias has led to a consideration of women primarily in relation to men and children, most often in nuclear family arrangements. Apparently we are neither the housed nor the homeless, we neither use public transportation nor work inside or outside the home. This bias has led to an understanding of the "home" as the primary site of identity formation and place attachment and to a lack of focus on environments outside the home that are not workplaces. It has also desexualized people/environment relationships. The current research speaks to these biases and demonstrates how consciousness about them can change the understanding of people/environment relationships.

Finally, in relation to all unrepresented people there is the issue of accessing and interpreting information. Existing literature is often bigoted and hateful, especially if written by people with overt antilesbian and gay political agendas. It is also likely to be stereotyped and inaccurate if writers have not examined their heterosexist biases or consulted diverse members of lesbian and gay communities or the literature. Historical information is more difficult to locate since most of it has been deliberately destroyed either by governments,[2] by families, or by lesbians themselves. And much written material, whether archival or current, is about middle- and upper-class white people. We have little information, except from dominant media, about others. Much of our information must come from fiction and oral history, sources generally not considered to be "hard" or "acceptable" data in the social sciences. We have to dig hard and do a lot of interpreting. In the current paper I have used a wide range of sources, some archival and some current. Much of the information I have gathered comes from the Lesbian Herstory Archives Bar Project. We mailed out a request for information, disseminating it through lesbian organizations, events, and individuals. We asked women to write to us and give us the names and locations of bars they knew about, to describe them and their experiences. Women gave incredibly detailed and rich descriptions, remembering the physical appearance and specific addresses of bars, the names of women they met, and so on—often forty to sixty years after their experience.

In summary, in this paper I use the concept of the social production of people/environment relationships to focus on particular aspects of some lesbian lives in the United States—lesbian bars. I use historical analysis, linking micro- and macrolevels to understand their development, sociophysical characteristics, meanings and uses, the role they play in lesbian lives and culture, and their relationship to social change within and outside of lesbian and gay communities. I conclude with implications for understanding all people/environment relationships.

Lesbians, Identity, and Cultures in Context

One of the most significant controversies for lesbians today is whether individual "lesbian" identity, or group identity and lesbian culture, existed prior to the end of the nineteenth century in the Western world (Vicinus 1989). This controversy is partly due to the dearth of historical information. Yet, more importantly for my purposes, it reflects the historic period we are living in, which has its own form of sanctions. For example, in the eighteenth century and continuing throughout the nineteenth century, "romantic friendships" between women,[3] two women living together for life and being treated as a "couple," were found in upper-middle-class circles (Cott 1977; Faderman 1980). Some scholars argue about whether we can prove these women were "lesbians," a term that in the current historical period describes women who have sexual relationships with or erotic desires toward women and a self-conscious "lesbian identity." The argument stated this way is impossible to resolve, given the historic suppression of the public expression of female sexuality (Vicinus 1989). Thus while these women expressed passion for one another and often shared the same bed, neither they nor others described their sexual behaviour.

It is the existence of the argument itself, rather than its resolution, that is significant. Heterosexuals never have to prove sexual activity in order to be considered to have a heterosexual identity. Thus the argument reflects the profoundness of the still-remaining stigma attached to being labeled "a lesbian" in 1992—even one hundred years after one's death. It also reflects the reality of having to confront legal actions for "slander" brought by living relatives of the deceased.[4]

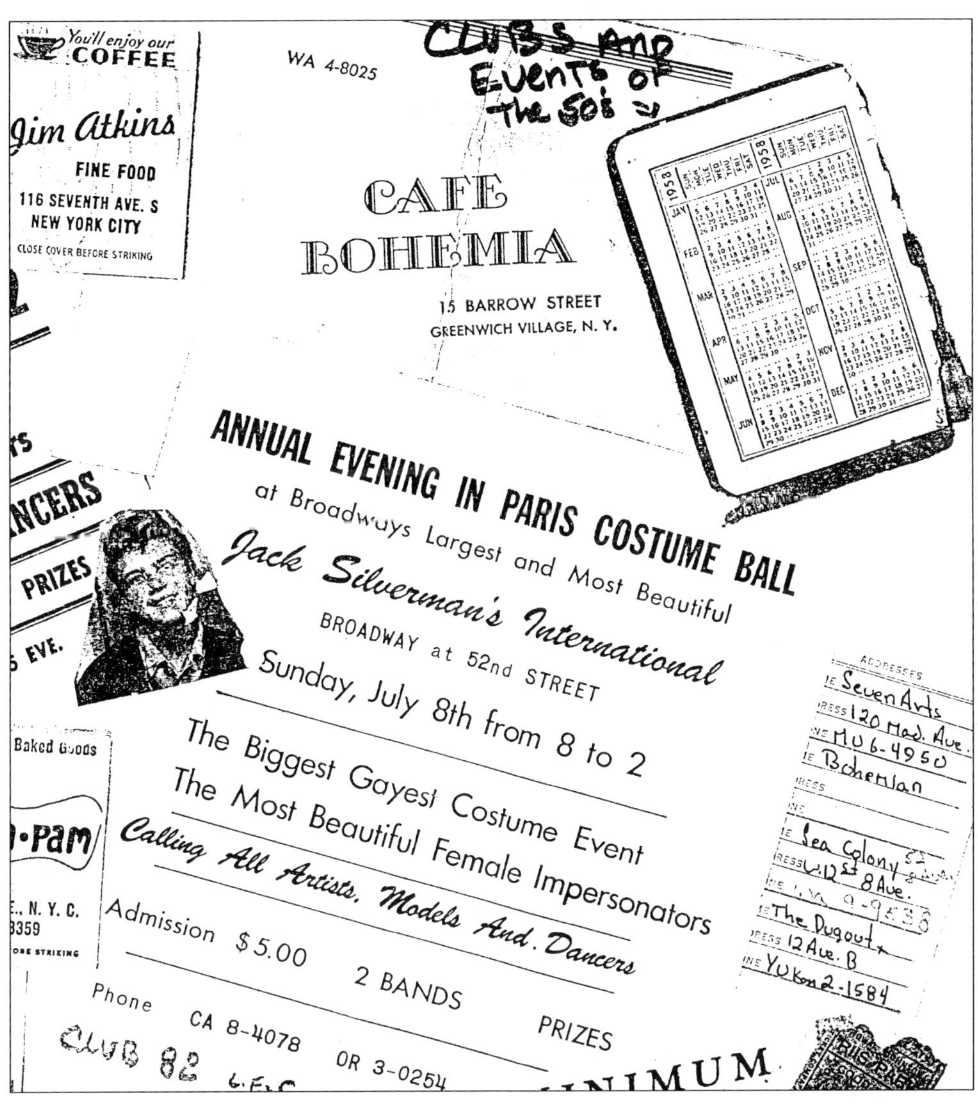

Memorabilia from United States lesbian bar culture, 1950's to the 1980's. Collage by Maxine Wolfe. Courtesy of the Lesbian Herstory Education Foundation, Inc./ Lesbian Herstory Archives, Brooklyn, New York.

It is within this current context that recent research clarifies some issues while raising new questions. For example, it is clear that although it was in nineteenth-century public discourse, such as medical texts, that the idea of "homosexuality" began to be applied to individuals rather than to sexual acts, some kind of organized "gay culture" existed much earlier. Using police records, Trumbach (1987, 1989) has documented that "minority Gay culture" was "fully established by 1750 at least in northwestern Europe, that is, in the Netherlands, France, and England" (Trumbach 1989, 150), and their forefathers appeared even earlier in urban Italy. In France court records show that twenty or thirty of these "sodomites" would gather together at particular taverns. In fact they were arrested simply for being there at certain times because authorities used this as evidence that an individual was a "sodomite" (Rey 1987).

Much less specific information exists about women known to have engaged in same-sex sexual relationships and to have formed social groups or networks on this basis. Court and police records, rich sources of archival information about early gay male experience and transformation, hardly mention lesbians. There were "communities of women," religious and nonreligious, far earlier than the nineteenth century (Bennet et al. 1989), and women both inside and outside of these communities consciously acknowledged and acted upon their erotic desires for other women (Brown 1986; Whitebread 1992). Yet, the extent to which they consciously grouped themselves, conceptually or physically, with other women on that basis is unknown, but possible. For example, "passing women," women who dressed in men's clothing, took male roles, and were thought to be men, existed in early-modern Europe (Dekker & van der Pol 1988). Some had sexual relationships with other women; some married and lived together for years. Some passing women hid their gender from their partners, but in other relationships both women consciously lived together despite religious condemnation and the threat of severe secular/legal sanctions. Since most were poor, it is possible that there existed some kind of network for obtaining the necessary male clothing, given a world where owning a set of clothes was a luxury.

Some writers have maintained that lesbian identity and, therefore, a lesbian culture, could only have developed in the nineteenth century because the ability for women to live independently necessitated changes in the larger economic and social structure (Ferguson 1981). However as Vicinus (1989) points out, from the eighteenth century some working-class and professional women earned their own money and lived independent of their families, often with other women. Yet public discourse prior to the nineteenth century, while documenting different types of lesbian foremothers (i.e., passing women, wandering groups of "flamboyant actresses" and vagrants, powerful political figures, and "romantic friends") did not treat them as cohesive conscious social groups of women with same-sex desire, i.e., lesbians who were part of a lesbian culture. Vicinus (1989) concludes this was the result of men controlling public discourse and interpreting women's same-sex desire either with condescension, amusement, or curiosity, or as despicable but rare sexual aberrations that required horrible punishment or expulsion.

There is much more to unravel about lesbian life and culture prior to the nineteenth century, its continuities/discontinuities with modern lesbian culture, and the ways in which it did or did not overlap with gay male cultures. Yet as Grahn (1984) points out, aspects of modern lesbian and gay culture clearly have a long history in different parts of the world:

> The [Lesbian] and Gay culture . . . is old, extremely old, and is continuous . . . a result of characteristics that members teach each other so that the characteristics repeat era after era [for example, the use of the colour purple] . . . [it] is sometimes underground, sometimes above ground, and often both. (xiv)[5]

Today there exist lesbian and gay cultures that reach from Chile to Soweto, from Canada to Kenya, from the United States to Russia. While there are specific cultural expressions in different countries, there is also an international culture with an array of links, often passed on from person to person as well as through international organizations (i.e., the International Lesbian and Gay Association). In the United States (but elsewhere, as well) there are lesbian and gay community centres, retirement villages, travel guides, hotels, bookstores, arts, literature, health services, religious organizations, and more. But one of the first collective "public environments" to emerge, and which still remain in the United States and elsewhere, was bars.

Though invisible in our literature on "women and environments," lesbian bars exist in small towns and large cities in the United States and in many countries in the world (Ferrari 1992; Zoe 1991). I can trace lesbian use of bar environments in the United States to the late 1800s (Katz 1976) and the existence of bars used exclusively by lesbians to the 1920s. The development of lesbian bars must be viewed in light of the role that science (particularly social science and medicine) and secular law played in defining some women as "deviant" during that time, as well as the role of media in publicizing lesbian existence. Yet I agree with Chauncey (1988) and Weeks (1991) that the public discourse did not create an individual lesbian identity or a lesbian culture. Most writers described what they saw, and they used language already in use of the streets, i.e., "pansy" and "queer." And in fact, doctors were surprised that their "cases" did not consider themselves to be "perverts." This discourse did, however, provide some of the parameters within which, and outside of which, lesbians could create a meaningful world and survive, a world in which bars became a significant sociophysical environment for some.

The Emergence, Transformation, and Legacies of Dominant Views of Lesbian "Deviance"

The defined deviance of lesbians has been and is based on heterosexism and sexism—the ideas that heterosexuality is the only "normal" and, indeed, "natural" form of sexuality, that all women want to be or are bonded to a man; and if they don't want to be or aren't, they hate men, have been rejected by men, or want to be men. The unnaturalness of homosexuality began to be codified in the early 1800s, after the American Revolution, when medical and legal professionals began to take over the church's role in defining sin and morality. Prior to the nineteenth century, sodomy statutes used religious language. But at the beginning of the 1800s, "the phrase 'crimes against nature' increasingly appeared in statutes, implying that acts of sodomy offended a nature order rather than the will of God" (D'Emilio & Freedman 1988, 122). According to Vicinus (1989), at this time there was much more public commentary by men about lesbian sexual relationships, especially in relationship to Bohemia, where

> women who were not necessarily wealthy . . . could choose to live a sexually free life-style. At the same time, some middle-class working women began to wear simple and practical clothing, though it was described as "masculine." They entered previously all-male public arenas, i.e., medicine, art, literature, and travel. "The active mannish woman from the middle classes can be found throughout Europe and America by the mid-century." (184)

Working-class and poor lesbians were more likely to be part of a "passing" relationship during the early part of the century (Bérubé 1979) or working as prostitutes (Bérubé 1979; Everhard 1986; Vicinus 1989); both were roles which received some media attention. By the end of the 1800s, since women were being defined as "asexual" (which they weren't), physicians began defining lesbians as "inverts" and "perverts"—women who were manlike in their sexual desire, were "masculine" looking, but who hated men. Their "madness" was ascribed to congenital physical, physiological, and mental abnormality (D'Emilio & Freedman 1988). Lesbians who did not look "masculine" or dress in male attire were made invisible since they were considered to be behaving appropriately for their sex, i.e., playing the female role. If women didn't look manly but were unmarried, they were "spinsters"—a term which began to be used pejoratively at the turn of the century to refer to women who were rejected by men. Previously it had described women who were not married and who devoted their lives to good works and social pursuits.

After 1900 the term "homosexual" also began to be used, and between 1900 and 1920, medicine and social science began to define lesbians by their supposedly deviant sexual-object choice. This could now include women who did not look or dress in a "masculine" fashion. This shift occurred at a time when women's sexual and erotic desire and behaviour were being acknowledged publicly. Yet despite research which showed that sexual behaviour between women was not uncommon (described below), it was seen as "deviant" nevertheless. The attempt to separate inversion from homosexuality so as to include "nonmasculine" looking women was not totally successful. For example, Havelock Ellis, though separating transvestism from male homosexuality, could in 1915 still describe "lesbian transvestites" and even noted that those lesbians "who wore female attire usually showed some traits of masculine simplicity in their dress" (quoted in Chauncey 1989). The notion of sexual-object choice as being significant was solidified by Freud who classified "children, animals, and persons of the same sex deviants 'in respect to the sexual object'" (Chauncey, 1989).

By the end of the 1920s, the public image of lesbians was as dangerous man-hating "mannish" women, who were morbid and pathological. Remnants of all of these attitudes and definitions exist today. In addition, during and after World War II, the development of psychiatry solidified the pathological aspects of lesbianism and saw it as something that could and should be cured. This was codified in the psychiatric classification system. It was not until 1973, after extreme pressure from the lesbian and gay liberation movement, that this was changed so that homosexuality was not automatically considered pathological. As possible pathology, however, it still remains a ground for exclusion from immigration, and in March 1992 a well-known psychoanalyst led workshops about lesbianism based on its pathology and described methods for curing it. Furthermore, today, even in New York and San Francisco, places supposedly "free" for lesbians and gay men, when a woman and a man engage in behaviours in public that have an erotic sexual/sensual component—holding hands, hugging, dancing together, kissing—they can do this with impunity. Yet two women holding hands, hugging, dancing, or kissing in public in the same fashion—that is, with a clear or even suspected erotic component—are at best tolerated as "flaunting their lifestyle" (we apparently do not have a life) and in most cases are putting their lives at risk. How did these definitions and attitudes arise, and how do they relate to the emergence and development of lesbian bars?

The Emergence of Lesbian Bars in Context

The changes in law and new definitions of "female deviance" came in the wake of political movements dominated by or being about women, including the abolition movement, the union movement, and the suffrage movement. Middle-class women entered the universities and professions and demanded a voice in the political system. They created the all-woman environments of settlement houses. At the same time, published writings began to claim that women were negatively affected by intellectual life (D'Emilio & Freedman 1988). Yet by the end of the nineteenth century, more middle-class women were following in their footsteps. Public pressure increased. There was a definite counterdevelopment in public discourse aimed specifically at the middle classes. It denigrated the concept of "separate spheres" for men and women, which had supported the existence of all-female environments and organizations, and pushed instead for a heterosexual-family definition of life. D'Emilio and Freedman quote G. Stanley Hall, the psychologist, as writing in 1904 that "higher education threatened to produce women who were functionally castrated. . . deplore the necessity of childbearing . . . and abhor the limitations of married life" (190). And, indeed, the number of never-married women in the late 1880s was the highest it has ever been in the United States (until the last few years), and the number of children per married household was decreasing despite the passage of antiabortion laws and regulations that prevented the dissemination of contraceptive devices. After 1900 some writers made a direct connection between politically active middle-class women and lesbianism (D'Emilio & Freedman 1988). Despite these attacks, research conducted by Kathryn Davis (a well-known Progressive Era researcher and lesbian) and published in 1929 found that sexual relationships between unmarried college women were not uncommon. She found that, of the twelve hundred unmarried women college graduates she interviewed, 28 percent of the women who attended all-women's colleges and 20 percent of those from coeducational institutions reported intimate relationships with other women that were of a sexual nature; 50 percent reported having erotic feelings for other women (Davis 1929).

Throughout this time (and up to the present), there were still many women "passing" as men, several of whom came to public attention (Bérubé 1979). And a group of passing black women, none of whom were ever discovered, worked for the New York Central Railroad in Buffalo and formed a secret social group. In the mid-nineteenth century the word "dike" meant a well-dressed man or a full set of male clothes; by the turn of the century, "dyke" came to mean a "masculine" lesbian (Bérubé 1979). By 1908 new slang appeared in these circles to describe lesbians—"bulldykers." And after 1920, women who occasionally wore men's clothing and those who passed as men began to socialize more openly in cafés and night clubs (San Francisco Lesbian and Gay History Project 1989).

The largest group of women who did not engage in the traditional domestic role, beginning at the turn of the century, were poor and working-class women who entered the public sphere working as low-paid labourers. In 1880 there were 2.6 million women known to be in the paid labour force; by 1930 the number grew to 10.8 million, far greater than the increase in women of working age in the population. Described by Progressive Era reformers as "women adrift," they lived apart from their families, in boarding houses, YWCAs, cooperative apartments, and furnished rooms. In 1900 in urban areas, one in five women in the paid-labour force lived "adrift." They were a heterogeneous group, although all were poor. Most were young and had never been married; some were older women who were separated, widowed, or divorced. They were black and white women from small towns and rural areas, and immigrants from Europe and Canada (Meyerowitz 1988).

At the end of the nineteenth century, these "women adrift" were often described as symbols of moral decay. Middle-class reformers saw them as exploited victims. At the same time, heterosocial (mixed male/female) leisure environments were developed and geared specifically toward working-class women and men (dance halls, amusement parks, and so on: Peiss 1986). By the late 1920s those who were still "adrift" were described as "symbols of modern urban individualism"; "a self-seeking woman who shunned the constraints of family" and was a sexual experimenter (Meyerowitz 1988, xix). From 1900 on there is evidence that some of these women were lesbians, and by the 1920s lesbian communities were apparent in both the black and white furnished-room districts of Chicago (Meyerowitz 1988). Zorbaugh (1929) described lesbians meeting in tearooms in those areas and cited one woman who described lesbian parties in boarding houses.

The 1920s have been described as the time of the "heterosexual revolution," when heterosexuality was socially enforced as the only normal way of life for white middle-class women. Many white women's organizations (clubs, union groups, and so on), which had flourished between the mid-1800s and World War I, lost strength after women won the vote in 1920. There was political repression, especially against women who had been active in the antiwar pacifist movements (Rapp & Ross 1981); "lesbian-baiting" was combined with "Red-baiting," a pattern that would repeat itself during the anti-Communist McCarthy Era in the 1950s. The image of the fun-loving "Flapper" was accompanied by a consumer campaign geared to women, which the *Ladies Home Journal* called the "cosmetics revolution" (Rapp & Ross 1981). A massive literature on sex and marriage directed at a popular audience "redefined female freedom within the context of heterosexual "'fulfillment' and male control" (Duggan 1981, 80) and presented the idea of the "companiate marriage." This literature appeared liberal, for example judging sex for pleasure (within marriage) as good. However all-women's institutions were denigrated, feminist views of female independence were attacked as "extreme," and "individual feminists, female friendships, celibacy, or 'spinsterhood,' 'lesbianism,' and 'frigidity,' were judged as deviant, pathological, misguided or pathetic" (Duggan 1981, 80). Statistics show the movement had some effect on women, in that marriage rates increased. Yet women's participation in the paid-labour force increased. And lesbians of different social classes started to form their own communities.

Bullough and Bullough (1977) describe one such community in Salt Lake City, Utah, in the 1920s. These women, both middle- and working-class, met often and even read and discussed Freud's views of homosexuality. Kennedy and Davis (1989) identified an upper-class community in Buffalo, New York, during the 1920s, and black and white working-class communities during the 1930s that they suggest began even earlier.

Beginning in the 1920s, as it became more acceptable for women in general to be in bar environments, the use of bars by lesbians also increased, and the first known bars used exclusively by lesbians came into existence, appearing in many large and small cities. The "butch-femme" style of dress became part of this milieu.[6] The bars were used predominantly by working-class lesbians, both black and white. In Harlem, black lesbians and gay men "in the life" met in cabarets, which also attracted a white lesbian and gay male clientele. Many black lesbians became part of the entertainment world, for example as chorus dancers, creating a safe space for themselves in a largely female environment. They often held parties in apartments, which were safer in terms of the police; others met in "Buffet flats," apartments where sexual performances would take place and where Prohibition liquor was available (Garber 1989). Prohibition probably increased bar use by lesbians because speakeasies, illegal clubs where liquor was served, were already a partly "hidden world" where the lesbians could exist freely among heterosexuals who were also breaking the law and moral convention. Garber documents that several Harlem speakeasies catered to what they called the "pansy trade." Lait and Mortimer (1946), in an otherwise bigoted and right-wing book, describe the transformation of Greenwich Village during Prohibition into a place for speakeasies that catered to lesbians and gay men, claiming that the Village shared with Harlem the appropriate physical prerequisites of being off the beaten track and having narrow and dimly lit streets.

Significantly, then, lesbian communities and lesbian bars as "public places" to gather developed in a time of backlash—a time when lesbianism was being publicly denounced as pathological. Bérubé (1979) suggests that though much of the public discourse was negative, the existence of public discussion allowed individual lesbians and gay men to know that they were not alone in their erotic desires. Bérubé describes the impact in the late 1800s of the publicity about the Oscar Wilde trials in England: gay male culture was pushed further underground and a stereotype was created, but isolated gay men came to be aware of the existence of others like themselves and of an existing urban homosexual culture of which they could become a part.[7]

Thus the evidence points to the use of bars by lesbians as early as the late 1800s, but it was in the 1920s that they emerged as coherent sociophysical settings and took on many of the characteristics they still have today. Evidence from the 1930s is sketchier and suggests that they continued to function but in the more sombre fashion of the Depression (Davis & Kennedy 1989; Gray n.d.). During World War II the number of bars expanded dramatically in urban areas and in towns around military bases (Bérubé 1991), as millions of men and women found themselves in a homosocial environment together. They continued to increase during the 1950s and 1960s, despite the anticommunist McCarthy Era purges of thousands of lesbians and gay men from the military and despite unrelenting police raids and arrests of patrons. Again, the media publicity about these events created great fear and anxiety, but it also broadcast the existence of lesbians and gay men and, in the latter case, provided others with the names and locations of bars. And, although not all lesbians used them, until the late 1960s they were the only "publicly" identifiable places for lesbian life. However, lesbian bars, lesbians' experiences of bars, and their uses of them, from their inception to the present, have always been framed in at least two ways: (1) by the profound experience of being able to be who we are in a social space shared by others like ourselves; and (2)

The Continental Hotel, site of a lesbian bar, Toronto, 1940's. Photograph by E. R. White. Courtesy of the City of Toronto Archives.

by the ways in which we were and are viewed and treated within these places and by the larger society.

The Meanings, Uses, Sociophysical Environments, and Experiences of Lesbian Bars in Context

Lesbians' experiences in lesbian bars were framed by definitions and attitudes about lesbian "deviance," codified into law or evidenced by selective applications of generic laws only to lesbians and gay men (Editors of the Harvard Law Review 1989). Secular laws against women dressing like men, which dated back to early-modern Europe, had their counterparts in the United States. They formed one of the bases for police raids on bars. In the 1950s and 1960s, when bars were raided, women who did not have on at least three pieces of women's clothing were arrested for impersonating a man. One lesbian from New Orleans describes her response: "I wore lace on my socks so the cops wouldn't have any problems seeing they were women's socks. . . ." (Impact 1980) Similarly, laws against "sexual misconduct" and "lewd and lascivious acts" were used to arrest women found holding hands or dancing together; "no visible means of support" was another law applied selectively. Until the late 1960s, when organized lesbian and gay groups brought and won lawsuits, it was illegal for lesbians and gay men to gather in a public place where liquor was served (D'Emilio 1983).

Today, sodomy laws still exist in twenty-four states and the District of Columbia. These laws often do not distinguish between heterosexual and homosexual sodomy, but they are applied selectively to gay people.[8] In Georgia in the mid-1980s, a gay man was arrested under this law by a police officer who came to deliver a summons on some other matter and found him having sex in his own home. In 1986, in ruling on this case, the U.S. Supreme Court, the highest court in the United States, upheld the Georgia law as constitutional. We were found to have no rights to privacy, even in our homes, under the U.S. Constitution. The majority opinion stated:

> To hold that the act of homosexual sodomy is somehow protected as a fundamental right would be to cast aside millennia of moral teaching.
>
> —(*Bowers v. Hardwick,* 1986)

The "tradition" of the Bible was cited as precedent for this ruling in a country that is supposedly predicated on the separation of church and state.

These types of laws, the mentality behind them, and their selective application have meant that lesbian bars, as "public" meeting places for "deviant" women, have been subject historically to police raids, closings, and arsons, and their users to humiliation, arrests, rapes, beatings, and other forms of violence by the police as well as by heterosexual men who are not the police.[9] Bar raids occur unpredictably. They are frequently a governmental response to criticism about laxity of law enforcement, relying on the bigoted attitudes of heterosexual citizens and their lack of sympathy towards lesbians and gay men for their political currency. Other crackdowns on lesbian and gay bars occur when conservative and right-wing political factions control local and national government. Bar raids were prevalent in the 1950s during the anticommunist McCarthy Era. In the late 1970s and early 1980s, they began again in the wake of Anita Bryant's antihomosexual "Save Our Children" campaign, focused on repealing lesbian and gay antidiscrimination laws, and when the Reagan government took power and started promulgating overt antilesbian and gay hatred and bigotry. The governmental response to the AIDS crisis threatened to close all gay establishments, including bookstores, but an organized political response prevented that overtly, except in the cases of gay bathhouses, many of which were raided and closed even though they were the major venue for the distribution of safer-sex material.

In 1958 one bar was raided seventy-eight times in a year and a half. Women arrested had their names published in the newspaper and even had their employers notified (Impact 1980). Attitudes of the police and media were reflected in newspaper reports, including an article titled "That Was No Lady, That Was. . ." A patrolman involved in the raid was quoted as saying: "The establishment is frequented by many sexual degenerates . . ." (*San Francisco Chronicle,* Sept. 1, 1958).

These incidents and attitudes continue. In 1979 off-duty policemen and some friends attempted to enter a lesbian bar in San Francisco, shouting, "Let's get the dykes." When they were told they could not enter, they replied, "We are the police and we can do what we goddam well want to."

Several women were injured before they could push the men out and lock themselves in (*San Francisco Bay Guardian* and other articles, various dates). Earlier that year, when two women were leaving another San Francisco lesbian bar, they were abused, beaten, and arrested by the police and charged with resisting arrest and failure to present identification (*San Francisco Bay Guardian* and other articles, various dates).

The publication of names or a criminal arrest record may seem to have been more threatening in the 1950s than today. However most lesbians and gay men are still not "out" on their jobs or to their families.[10] The felt need to "be in the closet,"[11] even in 1992, is because one can still be fired from one's job, lose one's housing or children, be discharged from the military, or thrown out of one's family if one's identity as a lesbian or gay man is known. Only three states and sixty cities have even limited antidiscrimination legislation,[12] and there is none on the national level. Fighting discrimination, even in states with these laws, requires a costly and lengthy lawsuit. And laws do not protect lesbians against rejection by their families or violence from others. In the United States, antilesbian and gay violence increased over 300 percent in the last five years; increases in different cities ranged from 17 percent to 202 percent last year. In 1991 there were eight known antigay murders, compared with three the year before (*New York Times,* March 19, 1992). In New York State, with a large and politically active lesbian and gay population, there is no statewide antidiscrimination legislation and the Republican-controlled state Senate has, for five years, defeated a Hate Crimes Bill, refusing to allow sexual orientation to be included as a bias category.[13] Violence and discrimination occur with little recourse, legal or political, even today. It is still a risk for a woman to be in a lesbian bar in the United States in 1992. This is also true in other countries. For example, in November 1988, a lesbian bar in Guadalajara, Mexico, was raided by the police, who took the women to a secluded part of the city and raped them (Letter to lesbian organizations, 1989).

Yet, women continue to go to lesbian bars all over the world. That more lesbians go to bars than to women's centres, and that the women who use them are more diverse in terms of age, race, and economics emphasizes the major role they still play in lesbian life. Their continued existence speaks to a complicated set of issues, including the needs of lesbians to have places to go that validate the reality of their world and their lives as social and sexual beings. Yet this validation today, as in the past, occurs in places that, in most cases, we neither own nor control and in which illegality takes its toll.

That lesbian bars came into existence or continue to exist, even though their users and their existence were (and still often are) illegal, has been because the owners, overwhelmingly heterosexual men, had and continue to have agreements with police, with governments, and with organized crime. The owners and the police use the situation to make money, but also to reinforce dominant definitions of "normality" and "deviance" and to keep all women "in their place." Lesbians, like heterosexual women, rarely own their own businesses because they command fewer economic resources than men.[14] In an illegal business it is even rarer. When a heterosexual owner does not run the bar himself, he rents it to lesbians. He has the money for bribes to get a liquor license and for payoff to the police for protection from the police themselves and from other men. Yet in the 1950s and 1960s, even when the police were paid off, often they would raid bars just to frighten the women. They would notify the owners in advance, who would then alert customers to stop dancing or holding hands and would also turn the lights on brightly. The police would arrive, walk through the bar harassing the women with questions and comments, and then leave (Nestle 1987).

Lesbians operating a bar someone else owns get a percentage of the entrance fee and of the drink sales. If a bar becomes a popular meeting place, and because there is a captive audience, owners raise the rent. Since research shows that most lesbians come to bars to socialize, to dance, shoot pool, and so on, and not to drink (Levi 1980), in order to pay the increased rent, either the entrance fee or the price of drinks must be raised. The lower discretionary income of women compared with that of men usually means the patronage drops. Eventually the bar closes (often reopening as a heterosexual bar). This is one of the reasons for the short existence of most lesbian bars in New York and other cities.

When lesbians attempt to own a bar, it is often more than they bargained for in terms of the violence and harassment. One lesbian owner describes her attempts to run a bar in St. Louis, Missouri, in the late 1970s:

> Women's cars were frequently vandalized and/or burglarized. Two women were beaten up. Our windows were broken, we were robbed twice. . . . Many nights I risked a gun or knife in my gut by threatened angry men who couldn't get in.

She finally closed the bar and then attempted to open another bar in a better, less isolated neighbourhood. The windows were broken and shot at. The police did not respond to a bomb threat, and "four men frequently harassed women on the streets and in their cars. . . . [I] discovered that three of the four men were in the police academy about to graduate" (*The Trouble with Women's Bars*, 1979). People in the neighbourhood then petitioned to have the bar closed, and her liquor license was revoked. Then a judge reinstated it temporarily. But the bar was firebombed while they were preparing to fight the closing in the courts.

The combination of laws, their use, concepts of deviance, ownership, and the prospect and experience of violence affect the location, stability and actual physical environments of lesbian bars, as well as lesbians' experiences of being in them. Judy Grahn (1984) describes the first gay bar she went to in the 1950s:

> It was on a sleazy street of pawnshops, clubs featuring women dancers pushing watered-down drinks on a quota system between dances, tattoo parlours, rundown hotels, and hamburger counters. . . . The street had a permanently dislocated look, unwashed and untended, a look of transience and worn-out baggage. (29)

Here is a description from 1979:

> They're all across the street from the Pepsi Cola Bottling Company or Joe's Electrical Heating Service or right next door to the Climax Lounge where loud women kiss on loud men right out front of God and everybody then stare at you when they realize you're not going into their bar but into the "other one".
>
> —(Waters, 1979)

This is as true today as it was then. During a recent Environmental Design Research Association Conference in Champaign-Urbana, Illinois, I decided to go to a local bar with a friend. We could not locate it by the address we had, and we were told at a heterosexual bar that it was located on the "other side of the tracks." It was just a couple of blocks away from the police department. Location in some deserted place raises the likelihood of rapes and beatings; location near the police department insures surveillance and control, though not necessarily safety. The bar was across the street from a

Union House, Queen Street, with spaces for lesbians and sex-workers, 1947-1965. At other periods, this was a gay male bar and lesbians entered as escorts to men. Courtesy of the City of Toronto Archives, Gilbert Milne Collection.

pool hall used by heterosexual men, which raises the likelihood of harassment and violence. An isolated location often means that lesbians who do not have cars have to use public transportation or taxis. Lesbians in Champaign-Urbana told us they have taxis pick them up in front of the heterosexual bar because they have been attacked by drivers when picked up in front of their bar. While locations vary from industrial areas to downtown office areas, these places are usually deserted at night when bars open.

To insure continued patronage and to protect their premises (or if lesbian-owned, their users) from men passing by who might break the windows, or who come in to "beat up women" or to assert their male prerogatives to go anywhere they want, most lesbian bars have no windows or cover up their windows. The lights are generally very dim to protect their users from recognition should unwanted people enter purposefully or unknowingly. Lesbian bars generally don't have signs or names or other distinguishing outside physical features that might give them away to nonlesbian citizens. In the 1950s there was often a back room where dancing took place. Even today, generally the dance floors or even the entire bar are not visually accessible from the entrance. At many bars you are buzzed inside after you have entered a closed-in foyer, where you pay an entrance fee to a person who is in a closed-in "box office." This was my experience in Ashville, North Carolina, and even in 1990 in Rotterdam, in a country supposedly tolerant of gay people. I was also questioned as to how I found out the bar's location.

Many lesbian bars are not "places" in the sense of a consistent physical location that one could design or decorate permanently. Often they are "women's nights" at other bars. A few years ago in London, the "lesbian bars" moved on different nights of the week (being held in the private, usually basement, party spaces in heterosexual pubs) to protect women from being beaten up.

In the last few years gentrification has taken its toll: The location of lesbian bars in industrial areas or older commercial areas in cities has meant that as condo-conversions occur, lesbian bars are pushed out either by huge increases in rent or by legal manoeuvres. One New York bar located in a downtown commercial area and operated as a restaurant during the day and a lesbian bar at night for thirty-four years had to close in 1984 when the building owner created apartments in the industrial space above and threatened eviction. A judge prevented the eviction but ruled that no music could be played after 11 P.M.—the time when most lesbian bars start filling up. A heterosexual bar opened in its place (Pickett 1984; Letter to Lesbian Herstory Archives, 1984).

That lesbian bars continue to exist is because lesbians use them. In most areas, they are the only places outside of private homes where lesbians feel they can be who they really are—socially and sexually. Here are how some women described this in relation to the bars in the 1950s and 1960s:

Rear of Union House. Courtesy of the City of Toronto Archives, Gilbert Milne Collection.

> We needed the lesbian air . . . to breathe the life we could not see anywhere else, those of us who wanted to see women dance, make love, wear shirts and pants . . . we found each other and the space to be a sexually powerful butch-femme community.
>
> —(Nestle 1987, 37)

> Bars were the places we could be together. . . . That's where I could be open, where I could totally be who I was.
>
> —(Barrett 1990, 167)

And a lesbian says about bars today: "I can flirt and be flirted with. (Barrett 1990, 176)

In a world where most of us cannot openly exist, lesbian bars provide a momentary safe separate place to meet other lesbians. They can be the place where people thrown out of their families can create a new support network or where lesbians can do things they might get hassled for somewhere else, such as playing pool or dancing with other women (Levi 1980). Yet they are not really private in the sense of autonomy, or of controlling the environment, or for many, of choosing them over some other place where we can be "out." Often married lesbians come to lesbian bars to meet and be with other women because they wouldn't risk going somewhere more open (Barrett 1989).

The bars function as "public places" for lesbians to meet other lesbians, the only lesbian "public places" in most of the United States or the world. And lesbian bars are the places where, most often, lesbians "come out" (that is, make a statement to themselves and to others that they are lesbians):

> From the minute I entered the doors . . . and gaped in thrilled shock at the self-assured, proud lesbians, I ceased then to be a nice white Protestant girl with a tomboy nature who had once had a secret and very loving lesbian relationship with another nice girl who was attending college to become a teacher. That definition no longer applied, as I stepped into my first Gay bar to become a full-fledged dike, a more-than-a-lesbian.
>
> —(Grahn 1984, 30)

One lesbian says: "Where is the young lesbian supposed to get her notions about what it can be like to be a lesbian if she doesn't go to college?" (Bulkin 1980, 42) and another lesbian talking about bars today, says: ". . . people come out through the bars because they are the most accessible places" (Barrett 1990, 63).

Yet lesbian bars are not legally or socially "public," since they are not open to everyone and one cannot be open about going to them. Their dual status has repercussions and reveals that, in some instances, a law that seems positive for heterosexual women can be negative for lesbians. In 1980 in New York, and undoubtedly spurred on by the real estate–connected mayor in New York and the push for gentrification, a lesbian bar centrally located in Greenwich Village had its liquor license revoked by the State Liquor Authority. Two undercover investigators attempted to enter and were discouraged and then overcharged as a way of pressuring them to leave. The city filed suit on the charge of sex discrimination, based on statutes passed in the 1960s and used successfully in the 1970s by heterosexual women seeking access to all-male clubs. As a result, at the present time in New York, it is illegal to have a lesbian-only bar. Yet lesbian-only bars exist as a refuge from a homophobic society, where experience shows that heterosexual men try to enter only to harass or gawk at lesbians. In one case a woman was raped by a heterosexual man at a mixed lesbian and gay bar; contrary to stereotype, you can't always tell a gay man from a heterosexual one. In some cities keeping men out has meant that lesbian bars operate as private clubs with memberships. A member has to bring you with her, making it very difficult for young lesbians to use them as places for "coming out."

Conclusion: Lesbian Bars as Sites of Domination and as Sites of Resistance

The fact that we could not and still cannot have open and visible places that we control, and in which we can be who we are with impunity, takes its toll. The bars in the 1950s and 1960s, controlled by others treating lesbians in a humiliating way and operated illegally, added to some women's sense of unworthiness and deviance. In the 1950s many women felt alien to the butch-femme culture, yet felt compelled to be part of it in order to have a community. This "rigidification" of sex roles within the bars mirrored the heterosexual world of the 1950s. Similarly the androgynous world of the 1960s that affected heterosexual culture (i.e., unisex) was made into a norm for lesbians in the wake of Second Wave feminism and also caused some women to feel alienated from it. The bar culture, although integrated racially in some places, also mirrored the larger racist society of which it was a part. During World War II most bars were segregated, even in urban areas. Subsequently, even today, black lesbians can have difficulties at bars that serve a predominantly white clientele. Similarly, there were and are some bars that catered to an "upscale" clientele. However as a rule, wealthier lesbians are more likely to meet in private homes. Thus these upscale bars have been few in number, although guidebooks make class distinctions, i.e., describing some as "Ivy League," "sophisticated," or "rough." In smaller places, if lesbians want to be in a bar, they learn to mix with different classes and often with gay men. In larger cities, class, race, and sex segregation is more easily implemented by owners and sometimes chosen by clientele. And the constant stress of the homophobic society—of leading dual lives then as now, in a context where there is alcohol, along with constant pressure from management to buy drinks even when women don't come for that purpose—has led many women to become alcoholic. It also created a volatile atmosphere, especially in the 1950s and 1960s, where fights would start between customers.

Yet these sites of domination also became sites of resistance. In the 1950s constant fear and experience of arrests loomed large, and many women finally retreated, under pressure, into the closet; i.e., they got married. Others, at the end of the 1950s, who wanted a different way of life and some who had clear middle-class biases, formed social organizations such as the Daughters of Bilitis. At the time this group had an assimilationist perspective, attempting to prove they were just like heterosexuals. They had dress codes that required members to wear "feminine" clothing. Unlike their counterparts in similar male organizations, they didn't think that fighting bar raids was a women's issue. They eventually identified with liberal feminist organizations in the mid-1960s and did not survive after the beginning of the lesbian and Gay Liberation movement.

Women who remained in the bar environments in the 1950s and 1960s had a conscious sense that they were risking a great deal to be there and decided it was worth it. In that sense, lesbian bars served a function neither their owners nor the government wanted. They became sites of resistance because they demonstrated the social validity of lesbian sexual desire and existence, as well as the operation of male domination, homophobia, and the political rather than individual nature and effects of oppression. Joan Nestle (1987) describes this experience. To use the bathroom in

The Times Square Lounge, King Edward Hotel, Toronto, 1955, a bar frequented by gay men and lesbian dates. Photograph by E.R. White. Courtesy of the City of Toronto Archives.

these bars lesbians had to wait in a line, a line that wove throughout the entire bar. To reinforce the view that the lesbians were "sexual deviants," the owners had someone watching them at the bathroom door, and only one woman at a time was allowed inside. This created the line. Each woman was given a specific amount of toilet paper as she entered:

> Buried deep in our endurance was our fury. That line was practice and theory seared into one. We wove our freedoms, our culture, around their obstacles of hatred. Every time I took a fistful of toilet paper, I swore eventual liberation. It would, however, be liberation with a memory.
>
> —(Nestle 1987, 39)

David and Kennedy (1989), using oral history, document the role that bars played in the transformation of lesbians' confrontations with a hostile heterosexual world. In the 1940s, ". . . women braved ridicule and verbal abuse, but rarely physical conflict . . . In the fifties, . . . the street dyke emerged" (427–28). These lesbians dressed as they wanted to outside of the bar, took jobs that allowed it, and fought back when harassed. The street dyke was a "full-time 'queer' . . . ready at any time to fight for her space and her dignity" (428). Visibly "butch" or in "butch-femme couples," using the streets and public transportation to get to the bars even on weekday nights, "participants in bar life were engaged in constant, often violent, struggle for public space" (429). Here is what one of their narrators said about that experience:

> Things back then were horrible . . . [but] even though I was getting my brains beaten up I would never stand up and say, "no, don't hit me, I'm not gay." I wouldn't do that (428).

The Civil Rights and Black Power movements of the 1960s created the context in which this bar experience could be transformed into the beginnings of an overt political movement. In 1969 at a police raid on a Greenwich Village bar, it was a "street dyke" who refused to go with the police when they tried to arrest her and whose resistance was the final straw that triggered what is called the Stonewall Rebellion. This violent confrontation between the lesbians and gay men and the police is considered to be the beginning of the modern lesbian and gay liberation movement (Truscott IV 1969). In describing what patrons said motivated their actions, Truscott (1969a) reported that most understood that "what was and should have always been theirs, what should have been the free control of these people was shown up for what it really was, an instrument of power and exploitation" (2). There have been many changes in the lesbian and gay community and political movement since the Stonewall Rebellion. At the end of the 1960s, lesbian and gay community centres emerged as other "public" spaces. (I am currently investigating their development.) Yet lesbian bars continued to exist. In the 1970s lesbians began to picket and boycott bars with racist admission policies. And in the 1980s bars became the site of the prosex lesbian movement, a reaction to the emergence of the conservative right-wing, antigay, and antisex Reagan government and to some parts of lesbian-feminism, which some believe desexualized lesbianism to make it more acceptable to heterosexual feminists. The AIDS crisis has brought lesbians and gay men together in direct-action groups like the AIDS Coalition to Unleash Power (ACT UP), they have pushed for a "queer" identity once again, and they socialize in bars more often together. This part of the story needs to be told at another time.

Implications for Environmental Social Science Theory, Research, and Action

Jeffrey Weeks (1991) wrote, in relation to identity:

> It is striven for, contested, negotiated, and achieved, often in struggle of the subordinated against the dominant . . . . It is put together in circumstances bequeathed by history, in collective experiences as much as by individual destiny. (94)

The same can be said for the sociophysical world and for people/environment relationships. Theories of people/environment relationships, as well as research and action based on it, must incorporate the existence of both domination and resistance and must bring together the micro- and macrolevels of analysis. Regardless of the people, environments, or environmental issues we are concerned about, we have to seek to understand the nature of systems and values (including our own) that create certain types of environments and not others, for certain people and not others, and how and why this happens. Then, and only then, can we understand why people living under certain circumstances view the world and act in the world in the ways they do, and how and why they create environments for themselves in order to survive and make life meaningful. A process of change and its end products can only be understood and evaluated in relation to a set of values as to what constitutes a better world and for whom. This requires understanding the nature of and relationship between the past and present, and a serious consideration of whether our work continues an oppressive past or helps to change it. In doing this we raise questions about the very basic nature of the categories we use to describe the world and our work within it, categories which influence the nature of our work and its outcomes. As this research has shown, people will create changes in the physical, social, and political world in pursuit of their own survival and liberation. Our choice is whether or not we will be part of those changes and learn from them or whether we will, even if by errors of omission, be an added barrier against them.

Lesbian Spaces in Los Angeles, 1970–90

Yolanda Retter

> So they created a . . . community by living in certain neighborhoods, operating businesses, by meeting in bars . . . by inventing fests and celebrations; in short by organizing socially, culturally and politically.
>
> —Manuel Castells[1]

In Los Angeles (L.A.), as in other large cities, lesbians established "community"[2] through social and personal networks and locational "anchors," "places . . . such as bars, organizations, buildings, etc.—that focus the community's life" (Richard Herrell).[3] As the gay and lesbian movements grew in many urban locations, so did the number of anchors. According to Castells, "In 1969 there were fifty gay organizations, in 1973, there were over eight hundred."[4] Although lesbian spaces are found in specific geographic locations and certain areas have been known to be good places for lesbians to live (such as Venice and Silverlake), residential enclaves similar to gay West Hollywood or the Castro Street area in San Francisco were not discernible in L.A. between 1970 and 1990. The patterns of lesbian spaces led one researcher to conclude that

> Lesbian communities are not territorially based . . . they exist in the context of their urban environments . . . which provide the settings where activities take place and members and organizations meet.[5]

More recently, researchers such as Rothenberg (1995) in *Mapping Desire,* and Bouthillette in this anthology, have identified more visible lesbian enclaves such as Park Slope in Brooklyn, New York, and Commercial Drive in Vancouver, British Columbia. While such areas may constitute the beginnings of lesbian neighborhoods, these researchers confirm that such tentative areas exist within the unstable and often hostile contexts of broader neighborhoods and urban environments. This article is meant as a preliminary record of spaces meaningful to segments of the activist lesbian community in L.A. during a specific period of time—from soon after the emergence of lesbian feminism to just before the advent of queer nationalism.

In this chronicle I describe and reflect on the formation of lesbian public spaces in Los Angeles, particularly the construction of lesbian feminist institutions. I have also lived through many of the events described and knew these spaces and their social dynamics. After the emergence of lesbian feminism in Los Angeles circa 1970, lesbian homes and public meeting spaces continued to be scattered throughout the city's diverse neighborhoods.[6] This discussion is about the processes of forming lesbian spaces within a large, highly diverse, and at times contentious, metropolitan area.

My central argument is that lesbian "territorialization" was and continues to be significantly different from that of gay men. Further, without more careful examination of the often less-visible placemaking dynamics of women, notions of "queer space" and territory will remain profoundly male-oriented. Thus we will miss the full implications of new notions of queer place and placemaking for understanding the formation of communities defined by gender, race, class, age, and erotic difference, and their impacts on local political economies. My additional argument is that spaces that have been gendered by women, and used and inhabited by marginalized groups, require new research methods and "intersectional archaelogies" such as those now being articulated by women of color, in order for us, in the present, to fully understand the historical functions and relative importance of these spaces.

Spaces as Sites of Politicization and Community-Building

Before Stonewall, public lesbian spaces were limited to a small network of bars, home parties, softball fields, and in some areas, discrete strips of beaches such as Venice and Fire Island. Lesbian bars were the primary public spaces frequented by pre-Stonewall lesbians. Although these sites have often been dismissed as oppressive and apolitical, research on pre-Stonewall Buffalo, New York, working-class bars shows that lesbians in these bars interacted in a resistant "prepolitical" manner and that these collective interactions laid part of the foundation for a collective lesbian identity and community (Kennedy & Davis 1993). Lockard noted that an "institutional base" of lesbian-defined places and organizations is necessary in order for a group to develop this sense of community. Without this base, "what exists in any given city is more properly a social network of lesbians, not a lesbian community."[7] Assertions about community-building in the bars are confirmed by Joan Nestle, a veteran of the 1950s butch/femme culture in New York.[8] Although the phrase "lesbian community" did not emerge until the 1970s, pre-Stonewall lesbians did create rudimentary forms of community in bars and other gathering spaces. Under inhospitable circumstances, they carved out what Lyman and Scott call "free territory," or spaces that offer deprived groups, "opportunities for freedom of action with respect to normatively discrepant behavior and maintenance of specific identities."[9]

Thus it seems fair to acknowledge that our foresisters, without benefit of political theory or public support, identified with and defended territories where they could assert and maintain their resistant behavior and emerging collective consciousness.

After Stonewall, the "politicized" lesbian community in L.A.[10] generated a whirlwind of activity as it developed its institutional base. Whereas before Stonewall, bars had been the main public space where one could affirm one's identity and perhaps find a relationship, now the emerging political lesbian movement offered a number of alternatives. To attend a Tuesday night Lesbian Feminist meeting at the Crenshaw Women's Center was to immerse oneself in a universe of politicized lesbian activity and intentional community-building that included centers, "rap" groups, political groups, lesbian businesses, concerts, dances, marches, demonstrations, conferences, publishing endeavors, and personal relationships. Although small in total numbers,[11] these activists were highly energetic and projected a presence larger than their true size. Whether in a small group or as part of the "lavender menace," what motivated those second-wave activists was the heady feeling of new possibilities realized through collective endeavors.

Communitas and Public Spaces

As lesbian activism increased and lesbian spaces proliferated, there were moments when activists in those early movement years experienced, and today recall, a sense of "communitas." Joan Cassell noted that communitas,

> can be experienced at rallies and "actions," when a woman is marching with other women, surrounded by indifferent or hostile spectators; it may appear late at night when a small group of exhausted feminists is racing against a deadline to complete a project. This feeling of intense intimacy and trust, this "communion of mutually supportive women," can be an intoxicating experience.[12]

Throughout the decades, the lesbian civil wars notwithstanding,[13] lesbians in L.A. have had their moments of communitas including:

- the Lesbian Conference at UCLA (1973);
- the Margie Adam, Chris Williamson, Vickie Randle Embassy Theatre concert (1974);
- the International Women's Year conference in Houston (1977);
- the defeat of the Briggs initiative (1978);
- the first March on Washington (1979);
- the Lesbians of Color Conference in Malibu (1983);
- the second Annual Dyke March in West Hollywood (1995).

Types of Lesbian Spaces

I define urban lesbian spaces as physical sites where lesbians congregate for a variety of purposes and where we feel a range of comfort and safety. These sites (re)affirm lesbian identity and visibility in a heterosexual society and homosexual culture that has intentionally and by omission tried to render lesbians invisible (Castells 1983, 140; Cavin 1990; Weisen Cook 1979). This network of spaces constitutes the "institutional base" of the community. It offers multiple points of entry into the community and provides both an information network and an element of continuity and structure (Lockard 1985). Both the ongoing and changing concerns of the lesbian movement and the diversity of its various communities inform the nature and character of our spaces. Generic types of lesbian spaces include cultural venues, service centers, places in which to socialize, private homes, and places of business. For financial reasons, many lesbian spaces are rented or borrowed as needed and therefore come under the category of "temporary lesbian spaces." In Los Angeles, as in many other cities, lesbian spaces that were intended as permanent sites closed due to lack of funding or internecine fighting.

Public and Private Spaces

While public spaces may be recorded through listings in community publications and directories, private ones often remain invisible and are lost to history. Attaching a lavender triangle to certain houses around the city, thereby identifying them as homes we have lived in, would provide proof that "we are (indeed) everywhere" and that some houses and apartments qualify for "lesbian heritage site" status, having been passed from lesbian to lesbian. There were also a number of collective lesbian living spaces in cities in the 1970s, and there is an ongoing tradition of such spaces, including separatist[14] ones in rural settings (Cheney 1985). More recently, lesbians have solved the paradox of community *cum* autonomy by buying or leasing separate spaces within a larger lesbian compound. Examples include The Pagoda in Florida and a mobile home park near Phoenix.

The category of lesbian spaces, which includes private homes, also includes a type that I call "politicized home spaces." For example, *The Lesbian Tide,* which started as the L.A. Daughters of Bilitis (DOB)[15] newsletter in 1971 and was L.A.'s first "out" lesbian periodical, was published at the home of Jeanne Cordova on Ogden Street. Jeanne was a key organizer in the lesbian and gay community and her house tripled as a living space, a place of business, and a political meeting space.

Service Centers

These spaces were organized to serve the diverse needs of the diverse lesbian community —an impossible goal. Their mission was to provide needed services in a safe lesbian space. Examples include the Gay Women's Service Center (1971–72) and Connexxus Women's Center/Centro de Mujeres (1984–90). The organizations running these centers always struggled to raise monies needed for operating expenses. Outside funding was generally unavailable, as lesbian issues have never been "ideas in good currency."[16] One exception was the Alcoholism Center for Women (ACW). Since its inception in 1974 ACW has, due to the nature of its mission (prevention, education, and recovery), been adequately funded. The original grant for ACW was obtained by lesbians working with the Gay Community Services Center, and soon after, ACW spun off to its own turn-of-the-century houses on Alvarado Street, where it has continued as lesbian space offering an invaluable service to both lesbians and nonlesbians. Throughout the years it has also offered meeting space for community groups. Lesbians of Color, which was organized in 1978, first met in members' homes and then at ACW into the mid-1980s. In the L.A. uprising of 1992, ACW was spared while many buildings/ businesses in the immediate neighborhood were destroyed.[17]

Lesbian-friendly Spaces

These sites were not lesbian-focused but had lesbians on staff and made room for lesbian groups, programming, and concerns. They included the Women's Center on Crenshaw Boulevard, the Westside Women's Center, and the Woman's Building. Some nonlesbian sites were also inferred "safe spaces" for all women. I once extricated a woman from a heterosexual battering situation taking place on an L.A. street, and I took her to a house belonging to The Feminist Women's Health Center. When I explained the situation to the woman who answered the door, she readily accepted the woman into the safety of the house.

Event Spaces

I divide these spaces into "unique event spaces" and "recurring event spaces." The former are sites where lesbians gathered perhaps only once, but which hold symbolic and historic meaning for us. Examples are Janns Steps at UCLA, where Robin Morgan gave her keynote speech at the West Coast Lesbian Conference in 1973—for many an unforgettable event. Another event space is the L.A. County Museum of Art (LACMA), site of the 1973 First National Lesbian Kiss-In. A later example is Cottontail Ranch in Malibu, site of the 1983 National Lesbians of Color Conference. Recurring event spaces include Friendship Auditorium on Riverside Drive in L.A. and Veterans Auditorium in nearby Culver City, where dances and other cultural events are still held. A variety of recurring but temporary event sites frequented by L.A. lesbians are located outside the city.

They include(d):

- ships (Olivia Cruises);
- parks (The annual Women's Music Festival at Yosemite);
- camps (Califia's week-long retreats at Camp De Beneville); and
- resorts (The Dinah Shore Golf Tournament/Weekend in Palm Springs).

Businesses

The final type of lesbian space discussed in this article is lesbian-identified businesses, which by the early 1970s had begun to proliferate. Past examples include a licensed contracting company (Building Women), Z Budapest's Wicca, and a travel agency owned and operated by a Latina (Womantours). In 1974 the Womantours premises offered meeting space to the first Latina lesbian group in Los Angeles. The one long-lasting example of a lesbian-owned business is Sisterhood Bookstore, established in 1972, which also serves as a distribution point for community information as well as a venue for readings by lesbians and other authors. Presently there is a wide variety of lesbian-owned businesses in L.A. offering services ranging from accounting to health care to travel. Several community-business directories attest to the variety and varied geographic locations of lesbian businesses. Although the Community Yellow Pages, founded in 1982, makes a disclaimer as to the implied sexual orientation of those listed in their book, one can read between the lines. The same applies to many listings in the L.A. Women's Yellow Pages, which was started in 1977 by four lesbians. Although these business spaces in general do not proclaim their lesbian orientation, they signify a lesbian presence on an economic level.

Historical Examples

> Gay culture is inseparable from gay politics.
>
> —Manuel Castells[18]

The lesbians of L.A. responded with great enthusiasm to the Stonewall uprising of June 1969. By early 1970 L.A. had its first "in your face" gay organization, the Gay Liberation Front (GLF). A handful of women and scores of men attended GLF meetings at several locations.[19] By late 1970 lesbians who had developed a feminist analysis about power differentials felt their agendas were not a priority in the co-gender groups then extant (Martin 1970). New cognitive spaces required new physical spaces, and lesbians worked to create them. While their activism was now lesbian-focused, it did at times intersect with the efforts of groups such as heterosexual feminists in the National Organization for Women (NOW), gay males at The Gay Community Services Center, and antiwar activists.

As the lesbian and gay movement grew, lesbian-focused spaces proliferated. DOB opened an office and meeting space on South Vermont Avenue in 1971. It was one of the first semipublic nonbar lesbian spaces in L.A. Meanwhile, in 1971, more political lesbians found a friendly home at the Women's Center on Crenshaw Boulevard and formed Lesbian Feminists. This was a high-energy group that held well-attended weekly meetings; sponsored a Saturday night coffeehouse, a "Sisters Give Rides to Sisters" campaign, and gay-straight dialogues; worked with NOW to get its historic prolesbian resolution passed; and participated in coalition events such as the annual Gay Pride Parade (Christopher Street West) and antiwar marches.

In 1971 Del Whan and others opened what is believed to be the first lesbian services center anywhere—the Gay Women's Service Center (GWSC) on Glendale Boulevard in Echo Park. Two stores down from the GWSC's second location was another friendly space, Gina's, a resale shop run by lesbians. The GWSC, which was the first in L.A. to have the word "gay"[20] blatantly visible on the sign outside its building, helped women find housing, hosted rap groups, and provided referrals. Rap groups provided needed support and information to lesbians coming out to themselves and others. Using data from a voluntarily taped group at the GWSC, Sharon Raphael wrote an early dissertation on the lesbian coming-out process (Raphael 1974). At the time, coming out to others was often a prelude to a stint as a lesbian activist. Thus these spaces often served a dual purpose—support and politicization.

In late 1971 the Gay Community Services Center (The Center) opened on Wilshire Blvd. The "L" word was added nearly a decade later, in 1980. Since its inception, The Center has had difficulty attracting and keeping a radical lesbian presence. Some attribute this to a combination of gender-centrism and the need of some lesbians to work in and from their own separate spaces. Since it opened, The Center has offered support groups for women and, over the years, a number of lesbian-focused programs and projects. In 1972 the Sisters Liberation House on South Oxford was opened by women working with The Center in coalition with other L.A. lesbian and feminist groups. During the ten months that it was in operation, Sisters housed lesbians newly arrived in town, heterosexual women on disability, young lesbians with limited resources, and women newly arrived in Lesbian Nation. The demographics of the house cut across class, ethnicity, and generations. Although neighbors complained about noise, the number of residents, the unmowed lawn, and the "gayly colored rags" that served as curtains, Sisters blithely persevered in its mission to provide affordable housing and space for community meetings and political gatherings. This was also a space for personal meetings, as more than one lesbian romance blossomed on the site.

In 1972 lesbian and heterosexual feminists living on the west side of town, near the Pacific Ocean, f(o)unded the Westside Women's Center (WWC) on Venice Boulevard. A former staff member described twelve-hour days during which center staff struggled in true feminist tradition to provide everything to everyone, with next to no funding. Services at the WWC included a self-help clinic and rap groups. One "gay-straight dialogue" drew a crowd that filled all the rooms in the center.[21] Eventually the WCC relocated to The Church at Ocean Park on Hill Street. This church hosted many lesbian gatherings, including dances and The Los Angeles Women's History Day (1983). Just north of the church, at 237 Hill Street, stands a "lesbian heritage site." In that small house, the L.A. Women's Center reopened briefly in 1974, and it was also used at different times by the WWC, the Radical Therapy Collective, Fat Underground, and *Sister Newspaper*. Its final lesbian reincarnation was as Womonspace in 1977.

Also located on the West Side was the Venice Pavilion, where Evan Paxton and others produced the Great Lesbian Talent Shows in 1974 and 1976. Near the Pavilion, in front of the Westwinds gay bar, was the site of a cogender "gay beach." In 1974, in nearby Santa Monica, the YWCA provided space for "Lesbian Night," but made it clear that this was not an officially sponsored YWCA event. The Santa Monica Bay Women's Club on 4th Street was the site of a number of memorable lesbian events, including the opening concert of The Los Angeles Women's Community Chorus, which had many lesbian members in 1977, and the founding conference of the National Lesbian Feminist Organization (1978).

Large Gatherings

As the movement grew, so did the need for spaces in which large numbers of lesbians could gather. These gatherings symbolized our resolve to be proactive, celebratory, and visible. The West Coast Gay Women's Conference in 1971 drew approximately 350 women. It took place at the Metropolitan Community Church's original site on Union Street. The West Coast Lesbian Conference at the University of California's Los Angeles campus (UCLA) in 1973 attracted approximately fifteen hundred lesbians. The site was secured for us by then UCLA staff person and now California state assemblywoman, Sheila Kuehl. Meanwhile UCLA's sports arch-rival USC (University of Southern California), which has a reputation as a conservative institution, was in the 1970s the site of NOW's annual and well-attended Lesbian Task Force Conference. In 1995 USC offered rent-free space to The ONE International Gay and Lesbian Archives and to the June Mazer Lesbian Collection.[22]

In addition to conferences, many marches and demonstrations were held in public spaces considered temporarily "liberated" for lesbian/gay gatherings and celebrations. The Annual Gay Pride parade (Christopher Street West) was held on Hollywood Boulevard until it was moved to Santa Monica Boulevard in West Hollywood. In 1994, following the lead of other cities around the United States, lesbians organized the first L.A. Dyke March on the Friday before the Gay Pride Parade. The march, which wends its way along Santa Monica Boulevard in West Hollywood, has grown in its second and third years and promises to be a popular annual event for lesbians from a variety of generations and ethnicities.

Bars and Restaurants

The emergence of the "politically correct" lesbian liberation movement did not signal the end of lesbian bars. These hardy perennial spaces, which were the sites of pioneer lesbian resistance, continued to cater to various segments of the community. Throughout the decades, some bars hosted political meetings and fundraisers. In the early 1970s the Seventh Circle on Van Ness Street was frequented by both lesbian feminists and lesbians who did not consider themselves "political." The Catch One on Pico Boulevard was established in 1972 by an African-American lesbian and still functions as both a social and political meeting space. The long-lasting Club 22 on Lankershim Boulevard in nearby North Hollywood changed owners and names throughout the decades but remains a lesbian space. In West Hollywood another garden-variety bar,

The Palms on Santa Monica Boulevard, has survived fluctuating economic times and political climates, including a picket by Lesbians of Color in 1980.

In addition to bars, Los Angeles briefly supported one lesbian-owned restaurant. The L.A. Women's Saloon opened in 1975 on Fountain Avenue and was soon faced with neighbors' complaints about its beer and wine license and condemnation as a "devil's workshop" by a Baptist Church across the street. Complaints and condemnations notwithstanding, The Saloon was a space where many experienced a sense of communitas. One activist described it as

> . . . a place a woman can go after marching and speeching . . . and not feel depleted and overwhelmed by the abundant incongruities of the patriarchy. Instead she can go to the Saloon and feel energized and "whelmed," trusting and well-fed.[23]

Along with food and drink, the Saloon offered meeting space and hosted cultural events. The Saloon was affected by one lesbian civil war[24] and experienced ongoing financial troubles before it closed in 1976. Another restaurant that will live on in L.A. lesbian lore is Papa Choux's. In 1984 two lesbians of color, Deborah Johnson and Zandra Rolón, legally challenged the restaurant's "heterosexuals only" policy for its private "couples booths." The lesbian couple won the lawsuit; Papa Choux closed its booths, and later went out of business.

Cultural Events

> . . . concerts, festivals and conferences serve as geographical gathering places where we foster lesbian culture and community.
>
> —Zimmerman 1990[25]

Since most lesbian groups did not and do not have the money to buy cultural spaces, they rented them for the evening or the week, and occasionally leased them for longer periods of time. In these spaces lesbians sang, danced, painted, read, wrote, performed, and publicly shared a developing lesbian aesthetic.

Lesbian or "women's music," as it was euphemistically called, was celebrated in nonlesbian venues such as the Robert Frost Auditorium and the Veterans Memorial Auditorium, both in Culver City, the Wilshire Ebell Theatre in Los Angeles, and McCabe's Guitar Shop in Santa Monica. Dances were held at churches, schools, and a union hall. Lesbian literature emerged from its long night of sad endings and self-hatred as readings at Sisterhood, Page One, and other L.A. area women's bookstores celebrated lesbian relationships, identity, and community. Such spaces also offered crucial new opportunities for lesbian authors to dialogue publicly with a lesbian audience.

Lesbian artists also found(ed) spaces in which to develop what Arlene Raven (1977) called a "lesbian sensibility in art." Toward that end, in 1973 Arlene cofounded a feminist art space (Womanspace) on Venice Boulevard. During its second month of operation Womanspace hosted Lesbian Week, which included slide shows, films, and a gay-straight dialogue. Bee Ottinger's photography thesis, done with subjects at Sisters Liberation House, was also exhibited at Womanspace. Later in 1973 Raven cofounded the Woman's Building (WB). At the WB, lesbians created projects such as "An Oral History of Lesbianism" (1979), a collaborative "experimental theatre art work," and The Great American Lesbian Art Show (1980). A constant moving force in these lesbian productions was artist and writer Terry Wolverton. The WB, first located on Grandview Avenue and then in an industrial area on Spring Street, closed in 1991.

Co-gender Groups and How They Diversified

Lesbians have a history of attempting to work in alliance with both gay men and heterosexual women. These efforts have had mixed results (Cavin 1990), one of which was the emergence of a number of lesbian groups derived from cogender organizations. In 1976 lesbians associated with Whitman-Brooks formed Southern California Women for Understanding (SCWU). Beginning in the 1980s, lesbians of color split off from various cogender groups and formed their own lesbian groups including Lesbianas Unidas (1984) and Asian Pacific Lesbians and Friends (1985). In 1990 African-American women from various groups came together to form Uloah (United Lesbians of African Heritage). These groups hold meetings and events at members' homes and in public spaces. Examples of long-lasting cogender groups and spaces are The Metropolitan Community Church, which was founded by Troy Perry in 1968; Temple Beth Chayim Chadasim founded in 1972; and Dignity, a Catholic group founded in 1969.

At another cogender organization, the Gay (and Lesbian) Community Services Center, lesbian space was often in a tenuous position. Advocates of lesbian space frequently found themselves justifying its importance to those who questioned its purpose in a cogender organization. The same questions were asked, albeit more discretely, when people of color requested separate spaces and programs. In 1982 Lesbian Central became the official lesbian space at the Center. The program was funded until 1989, when community politics (re)shifted to cogender programming. The Center now provides meeting space but no permanent and separate space for a variety of lesbian interests.

Throughout the decades lesbian frustration with cogender groups has waxed and waned. In 1983 when the Center declined to hire a Latina as their CEO, lesbians created Connexxus Women's Center/Centro de Mujeres. Connexxuswas located in West Hollywood and, at its peak was a $200,000-a-year operation. Its programs included support groups, social events, a counseling program, and referrals. Lesbians familiar with the more humble accommodations of other lesbian spaces were pleased with the more upscale environment provided first on Santa Monica Boulevard and then at more moderate quarters on La Cienega Boulevard. Unfortunately, a single lesbian center could not possibly meet the needs of such an ethnically, socioeconomically, generationally, politically, and geographically diverse lesbian community as the one extant in Los Angeles.

The needs and interests of one particular class of lesbians, lesbians of color, have been—and too often still are—lost within white-dominated groups and organizations, and so one of the ongoing battles in the lesbian civil wars has been over racism. Connexxus attempted to address this split. From its inception in 1984 until its demise in 1990, the Connexxus board of directors was chaired by women of color, and the organization made serious efforts to create programming relevant to lesbians of color. It was most proactive in the Latina community. Connexxus funded an outreach program in East L.A. at El Centro Human Services Corporation, and after Connexxus closed, Latina lesbian support groups continued to meet at El Centro. Connexxus sponsored photographer Laura Aguilar's Latina Lesbian series, portions of which traveled to various exhibition spaces including Los Angeles's City Hall. Connexxus also provided meeting space for other women of color groups. Asian Pacific Lesbians and Friends met there briefly in 1988, as did an African-American women's support group. Attendance at the Connexxus dances came to reflect the center's relatively successful results of efforts to reach out to a cross-section of the L.A. lesbian community.

The 1990s

In 1976 an editorial in the Lesbian News noted that "there is no organization in the Los Angeles area that caters exclusively to Lesbian interests."[26] By 1995 we had almost come full circle. The one surviving lesbian-focused nonbar public space in L.A. is the June Mazer Lesbian Collection. Although public lesbian spaces of the 1970s genre are now scarce, the contemporary lesbian institutional base, albeit in different guises, is strong. Although lesbian residential enclaves may be variously emerging and merging (Bouthillette, *Queers in Space*), contemporary public lesbian spaces still reflect a lack of physical "territorializing." Whether due to economic, pragmatic, or essentialist factors, lesbian public spaces are now more often signified by events and networks that represent a wide(r) variety of interests. This trend toward multiplicity and a nomadic style may clash with the sensibilities of older generations used to more stationary, sequential, and separatist patterns.

Aside from a few institutions, lesbian public space in Los Angeles seems less stable than it was two decades ago. Currently, generations of lesbians from a variety of backgrounds, with varying interests, causes, and styles can choose from a plethora of groups and events listed in the *Lesbian News*, in various local "zines," and in cyberspace on the World Wide Web. In the polyphonic milieu of late twentieth-century United States urban culture, Lesbian Nation persists in spaces where lesbians live and where we publicly gather to assert our existence, express the diversity of our communit(y/ies) and sometimes even experience a sense of communitas in the context of broader historical processes as we attempt to negotiate and overcome a variety of social and economic inequities.[27]

Map of Lesbian Spaces in Los Angeles, 1970–1990.

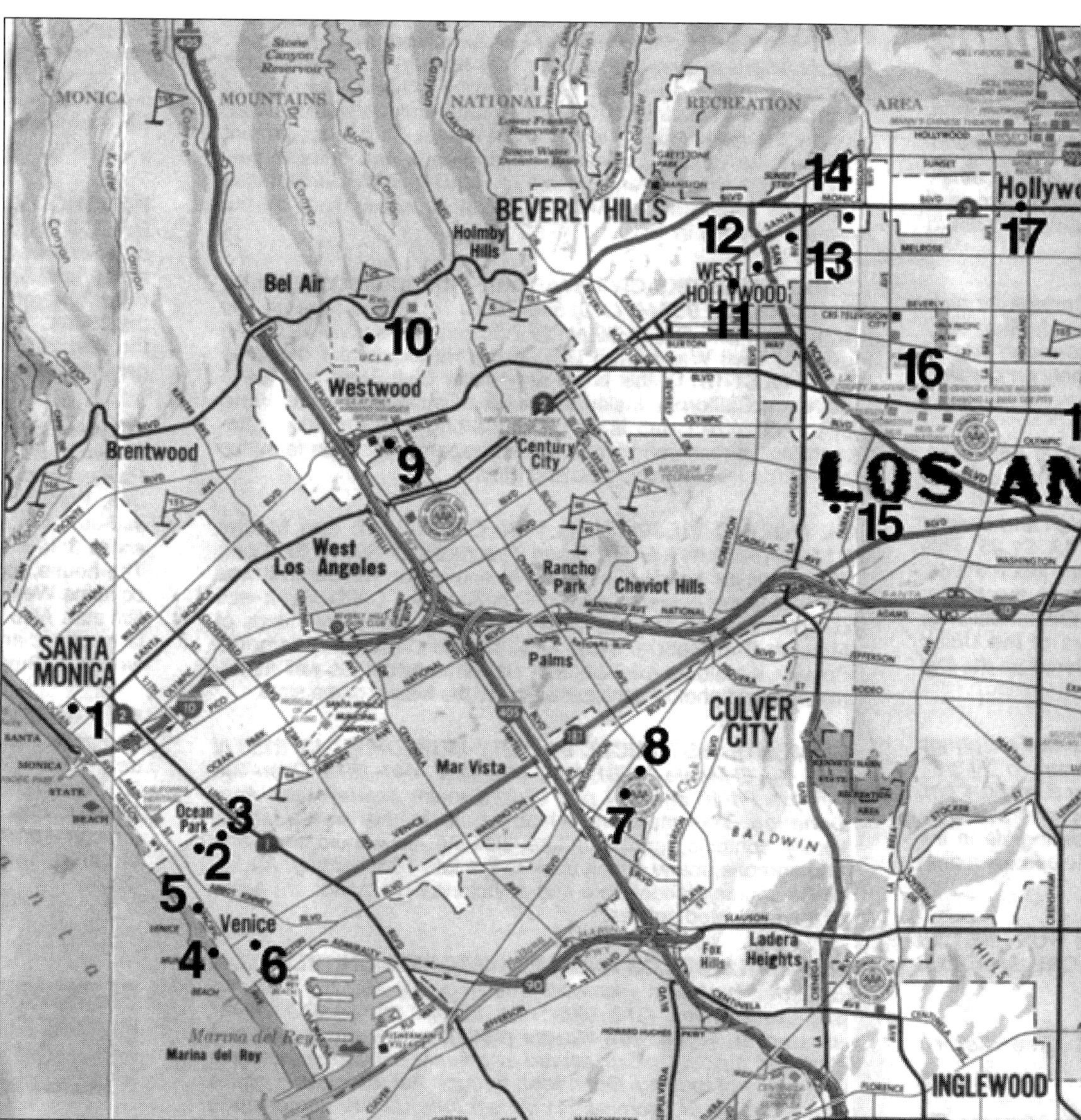

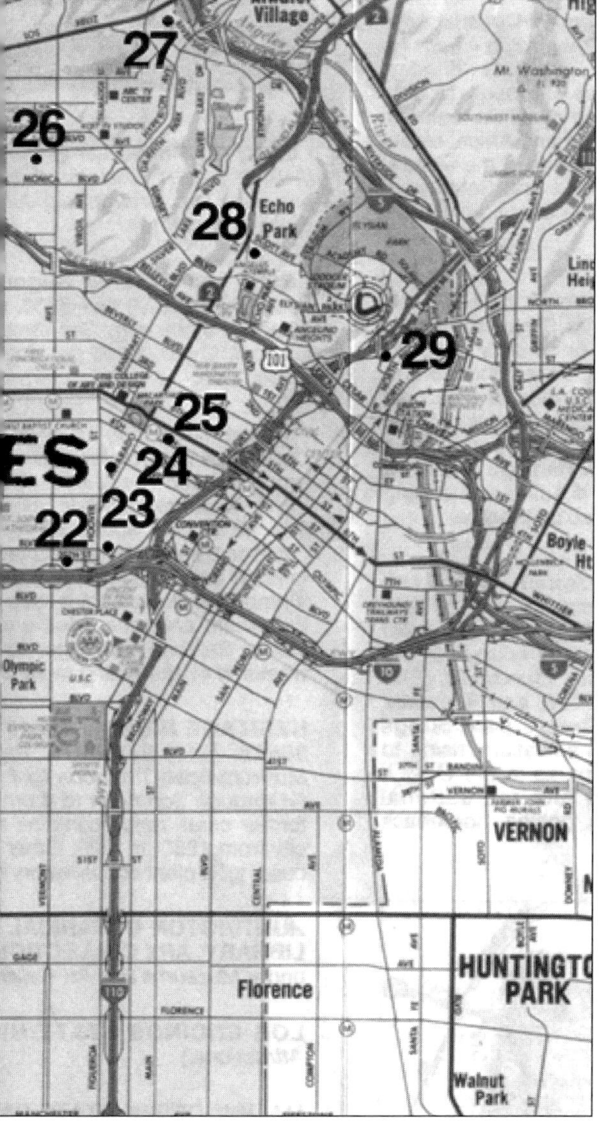

Key

1. Santa Monica Bay Women's Club—4th Street
2. Church at Ocean Park—Hill Street
3. Womonspace—Hill Street
4. Venice Pavilion—Venice Beach Boardwalk
5. Gay Beach—Venice Beach
6. Westside Women's Center—Venice Boulevard
7. Robert Frost Auditorium—Elenda Street
8. Veterans Memorial Auditorium—Overland Avenue
9. Sisterhood Bookstore—Westwood Boulevard
10. Janns Steps—University of California Los Angeles (UCLA) Campus
11. Connexxus Women's Center—Santa Monica Boulevard (site 1)
12. June Mazer Lesbian Collection—Robertson Boulevard
13. The Palms—Santa Monica Boulevard
14. Holistic Health for Women—Santa Monica Boulevard
15. Beth Chayim Chadasim—Pico Boulevard
16. Los Angeles County Museum of Art (LACMA)—Wilshire Boulevard
17. Gay and Lesbian Community Services Center—Highland Avenue (site 2)
18. Seventh Circle Bar—Van Ness Avenue
19. Women's Center—Crenshaw Boulevard
20. Catch One Bar—Pico Boulevard
21. Sisters Liberation House—Oxford Avenue
22. Daughters of Bilitis Center—Vermont Avenue
23. Metropolitan Community Church—Union Street
24. Alcoholism Center for Women—Alvarado Street
25. Gay Community Services Center—Wilshire Boulevard
26. Women's Saloon—Fountain Avenue
27. Friendship Auditorium—Riverside Drive
28. Gay Women's Service Center—Glendale Boulevard
29. Woman's Building—Spring Street (site 2)

Leather Nights in the Woods: Locating Male Homosexuality and Sadomasochism in a Dutch Highway Rest Area[1]

Maurice van Lieshout

This article describes a constellation of sites for homosexual encounters that existed, until recent years, in a highway rest area called "the Mollebos" near the centre of the Netherlands. The focus of my research was on the microgeography of specific gay male sexualities and was only carried out on Monday evenings and nights. These were the so-called leather nights, which attracted a specific group of patrons: men into leathersexuality and sadomasochism (S/M). Participant observation, informal conversations, and in-depth interviews made it possible to analyze the spatial strategies used by men while cruising[2] and the specific meanings individual participants attached to outdoor leathersexuality. In the Netherlands, cruisers are no longer members of "a silent community." The leather nights in the woods proved to be an important supplement to the Dutch gay leather and S/M scene. For many visitors, these "leather nights in the woods" served as major sexualized space for the realization of erotic fantasies.

> Monday evening. After dinner Peter, a forty-two-year-old civil servant in a small town in the Dutch province Noord-Holland, changes clothes. He puts on his motorcycling wear: black leather jeans, heavy boots, black leather jacket. Nothing unusual for a biker. Some extras are less common: a cockring round his balls and penis, a black leather shirt, and a chain on the left shoulder of his jacket. Peter also takes along a black leather cap. At 9:00 P.M. he sets off in the direction of Arnhem. Near Driebergen, some fifty-five miles and fifty minutes from home, on the A12 highway he bears off to a rest stop.
>
> At the moment Peter brings his motorbike to a stop in the parking lot, a man leaves his car. He is called John, a twenty-seven-year-old cook, working and living in a village in the province Noord-Brabant. He left home at 8:30 P.M. and travelled seventy-five miles. John is wearing tight jeans, boots, and a white T-shirt. He opens the trunk of his car and takes out some leather clothing. On top of his jeans he puts on chaps, and he hangs a jacket on his right shoulder. He looks around and walks slowly to the right, to the fence that separates the rest stop from the woods. Where

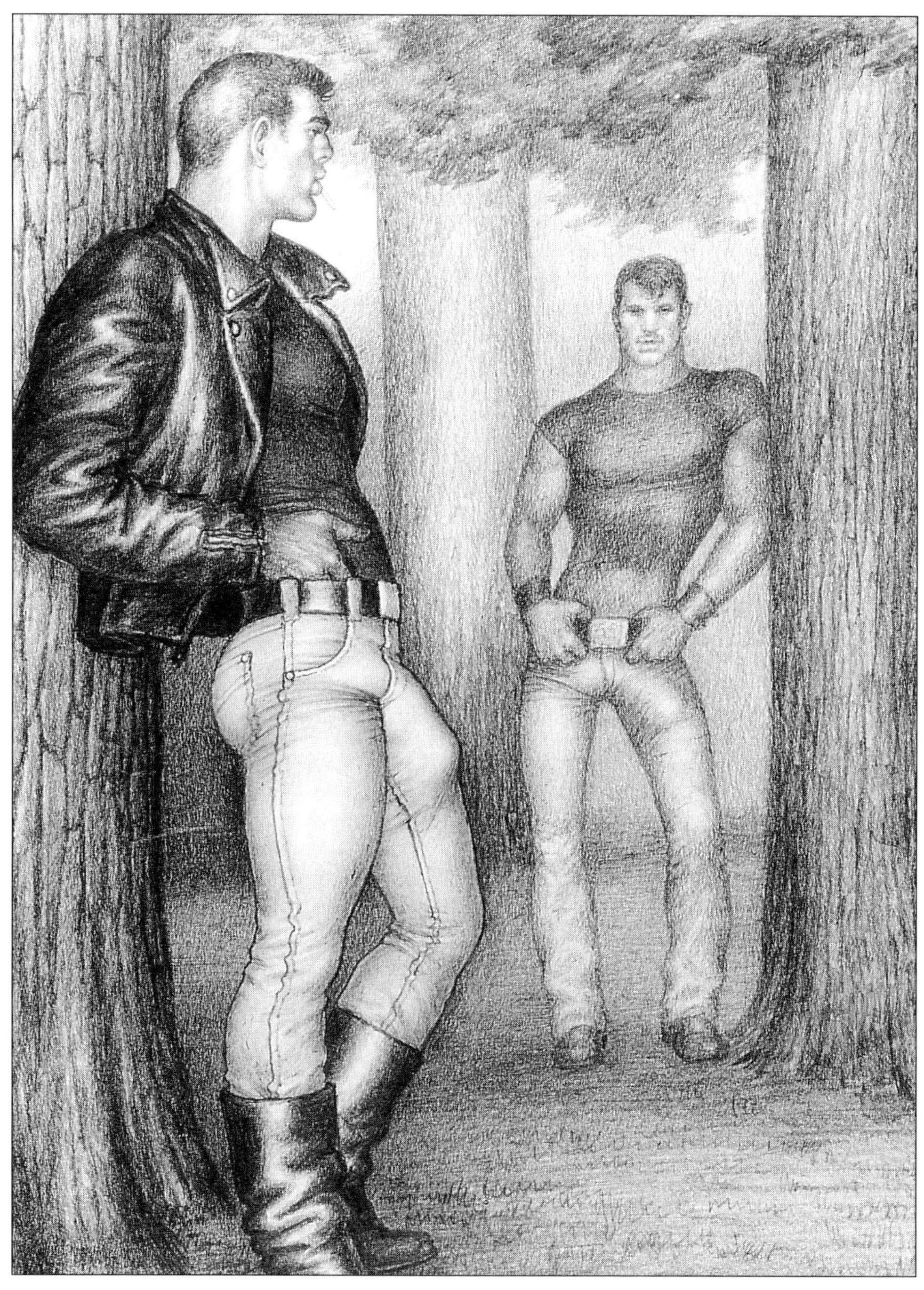

Park cruising and sex. Tom of Finland, *Untitled,* 1968. Drawing courtesy of the Tom of Finland Foundation, Los Angeles.

the wire has been cut through, John disappears in the woodland. Meanwhile Peter locks his bike and chains his crash helmet. He puts on his leather cap, greets another biker, and follows John into the woods.[3]

Until recently, men from many areas of the Netherlands visited a highway rest stop and the bordering woods, both called *het Mollebos,* searching for other men with whom to have sex. The rest stop was closed by the Department of Public Works in December 1991.[4] For many years, the Mollebos was used by men as a place for meeting and cruising.[5] As a cruising area located in the center of the Netherlands, it was one of the most popular sites in the country. Cruising and sexual activities took place throughout the year, twenty-four hours a day. Visitors came from all over the country.[6] On Monday evenings and nights, participants were mainly men devoted to leathersexuality and sadomasochism.

In this article I describe research carried out during the so-called leather nights. After a short review of literature on public homosexual encounters, I give an analysis—as far as the Netherlands is concerned—of the two subcultural phenomena that become fused during the leather nights: cruising for largely impersonal sex in public places, and gay leathersexuality and S/M.

The last part of this study is an account of my research in the Mollebos. I pay special attention to my role as participant and researcher and to the methodological problems with which I was faced. This report is concentrated on three sets of questions:

1. The patrons of the leather nights,
2. The way that these men used the layout of the cruising area, and
3. The individual meanings that participants attached to outdoor leathersexuality and S/M.

1. Research on Impersonal Public Homosexual Encounters

From Deviancy to Variety

Recent research on public homosexual encounters is scarce. Most investigations were carried out in the United States between 1965 and 1975 and published between 1970 and 1978 (Humphreys 1974; Ponte 1974; Troiden 1974; Corzine & Kirby 1977; Delph 1978).[7] This research largely belongs to a tradition of sociological study of "deviant" behavior.[8] Researchers especially wanted to know what kind of people these sexual deviants were, where they frequented, and which sexual activities they performed. We must bear in mind that, in most cases, investigations were concerned with illegal criminal acts. The acts researchers registered were seen as forms of "'impersonal' sex," a concept still generally used to characterize a wide range of less-sanctioned sexual behavior, be it considered casual, public, or perverse (Lee 1990, 577–78).

Most researchers adhered to "the objectivist tradition of depersonalized, decontextualized report-writing" (Walsh-Bowers & Parlour 1992, 107). All of them emphasized the fact that they are outsiders, and most of them first had to become familiar with the gay subculture in general. Ponte (1974) and Corzine and Kirby (1977), who investigated the sexual marketplace in parking lots, never witnessed any of the sexual acts that took place at those sites. The latter researchers used an informant to determine what was going on between truckers and other men. Ponte almost never got out of his car and cut short conversations when males approached him. For the contemporary reader, his research makes an awkward and fainthearted impression. Humphreys's study was from the limited vantage point of being a "watchqueen," a man who acts as a lookout while others are having sex. His work in "tearooms," such as washrooms and other public conveniences, is still impressive, although his methodology was, from an ethical point of view, fiercely criticized.[9] His research gave many Americans a startling perspective on perversions and deviant behavior, especially since Humphreys ascertained that 54 percent of tearoom visitors that he witnessed turned out to be "decent" married men living with their wives.

Changing Attitudes Towards Impersonal Sex

"Impersonal," "casual," or "anonymous" sexual contacts had and still have a bad reputation among the majority of people. It is the kind of sex that offends notions of romantic love, steady relationships, or long-term commitment—ideas that are widespread in modern Western culture. Many people consider "impersonal" sex a way of compensating for a lack of personal sex. Furthermore, it means practicing promiscuity. That this kind of sex is pursued and enjoyed as an end in itself often seems shocking. The fact that sexual acts often take place, not in private but in public, adds greatly to state hostility and controversy.

Participating in impersonal sex means ". . . adopting the same attitude to the consumption of sexual pleasure which one would normally adopt to eating" (Lee 1990, 579). This means enjoying a wide variety of settings, duration, sexual scripts, tastes, and partners. In many cases, however, impersonal sex is restricted to one or two favorite sexual activities, for instance only gay sex and only leathersex.

Public (homo)sexual encounters are contrary not only to conventional morality, but in many cases also to legal rules. In most countries, participating in public (homo) sexual encounters can lead to a charge of indecent assault. It is not surprising that the early Dutch gay movement condemned cruising and public homosexual encounters. This was not only because these encounters created the chance of violating clause 248 bis of the Netherlands criminal code but also because they damaged the desired image of the "decent" homosexual citizen.[10] This attitude changed in the mid-1970s.

The expansion of indoor gay facilities, particularly bars, discos, and baths, in the 1970s and 1980s offered many new opportunities to have impersonal sex. The Dutch gay male subculture followed the development started in the United States. "The 1960s and 1970s were the modern 'golden age' of impersonal gay sex, since they came after penicillin and before AIDS." (Lee 1990, 579) In this period moral and legal attitudes towards promiscuity and impersonal sex began to become more tolerant across Dutch society.

Gay activists initially had a negative view of the use of public settings such as parks, parking lots, and rest areas for having sexual encounters. Men using these facilities were considered to be "closet queens." A standard image was that of the middle-aged married man, a nondescript and unattractive figure. More radical views of sexuality in the mid-1970s advocated room for all kinds of lust and sexual satisfaction. These views gradually received more support. However the rise of AIDS in the second half of the 1980s led to a renewed, by no means general, appreciation for monogamous relationships.[11]

Nowadays the gay movement and many, possibly most, homosexuals in the Netherlands consider impersonal sex and sexual encounters in public places as two possibilities in a wide range of means for erotic and sexual expression. They do so without expressing moral condemnation. Among themselves, most gay men no longer have to conceal that they participate in a sexual subculture. But in communication with others, such as their biological families, heterosexual friends, and colleagues, they will be less frank.

Cruising in the Nineties

Changing attitudes towards public homosexual encounters affect manners in cruising areas. Cruisers in the Netherlands no longer are the "silent community" described in research carried out in the 1960s and 1970s (Delph 1978; Humphreys 1974). It is no longer necessary to keep your mouth shut and to stay anonymous. Visiting a park or rest area also can be a social event to talk with acquaintances and friends and to be introduced to others. For many gay men, cruising areas are just one of many places to meet other men. And if you actually have sex there, concealing identity is as inconsequential as, in most cases, are the processes of verbally revealing personal information. Spatial limitations that served as protection, as was the case in tearooms where Humphreys operated, can now be redefined where there is less repression and threat of violence. For example, a public convenience with only one entrance or exit was and is a very bad place to be when queerbashers arrive.

Even the attitude of authorities, including the police, has changed in the last ten years. In the Netherlands, police academy students and practicing officers receive education on homosexuality and the gay subculture. Victims of queerbashing are in many cases treated as victims of sexual assault and are encouraged to inform anonymously. It is no longer a matter of course that patrolling a cruising area means harassing cruising men. On the contrary, patrolling is aimed at protecting them from violence.[12]

The Dutch Gay Leather and S/M Scene

Some gay men have a distinct preference for very masculine appearances. Their "impression management" is aimed at looking tough and cool. In many cases they wear leather clothing, have a short haircut, and try to look very macho. Their style is derived from the mostly American images of toughness and masculinity personified in the cowboy and the motorbike rebel (Lieshout 1989). Those images are not copied exactly, but rather added and reworked. By adding and combining new items, such as cockrings as signs to announce S/M preference, and emphasizing certain characteristics, such as very tight leathers that accentuate the penis and buttocks, a distinct gay macho style emerged (Blachford 1981). For many gay men, leather is not only a style item but also, and especially, a sexual fetish. Wearing leather can have different sexual meanings, particularly in an S/M setting (Kamel 1983). Being gay and being a man are integrated in a subcultural and overtly sexual style that perhaps is strange, repulsive, or ludicrous to outsiders but very meaningful to men who identify themselves with such an image.

Many, but certainly not all, leathermen like sadomasochism. Many, but not all, S/M-lovers like leather. The leather and S/M scene overlap and in places where you find gay leathermen you can be sure to find S/M devotees. In the United States and many European countries like the Netherlands, leathermen know "a group cohesiveness of sufficient strength to generate shared [. . .] contact norms, action norms, and relationship norms" (Kamel 1983, 168). Sexual risks typical of casual and S/M sex are minimized by shared rules of behavior (Lee 1983).[13]

Although a gay leather scene already existed in the 1950s, the great breakthrough came in the 1970s, first in the United States and later in Europe. The growing popularity of the macho style coincided with the expansion of subcultural facilities. An important characteristic of the leather and S/M scene, in contrast to the gay subculture in general, is the limited value attached to youth. Maturity and experience, and a well-built body, can make men over thirty or forty years attractive partners.

Dutch gay men who are devotees of leather and/or S/M nowadays have many facilities to make contacts. Amsterdam is known for its leather bars, of which several have a "backroom" or "orgy room." Leather bars can be found in other big cities, too. "Leatherguys" can participate in parties and other activities organized by gay associations and motorclubs. At least two S/M associations have special branches and organize special meetings for gay men, including meetings to "play" and a weekend for outdoor activities in a private woodland. Individual contacts can be made by putting ads in a national newspaper, gay magazines, or specialised sex magazines. A more direct way is calling a gay box, such as a telephone sex service, or visiting a porn cinema. Some street hustlers, professional prostitutes, and call boys specialise in leathersexuality and S/M. But opportunites to meet other leathermen in outdoor cruising areas were remote[14] until the leather nights in the Mollebos developed. Those Monday nights were a new "facility" in the Dutch gay leather and S/M scene.

2. Leather Nights in the Woods

On Monday evenings and nights, the Mollebos attracted a specific category of patrons: (gay) men into leathersex and sadomasochism. It is not exactly known when and how these leather nights started. My interviews with regular visitors revealed that they have existed at least since 1987.[15] Leather nights never started before dusk, which meant they began earlier in winter than in summer. The leather nights in summer were more inviting, not only because of better weather conditions, but also because of a larger number of potential sex partners concentrated in a two- or three-hour period.

Research Methods and Problems

Before I paid my first visit to this cruising area, I already knew that leatherguys were not to be expected in daytime. I nevertheless went there in daytime once and saw that "normal" cruising was going on. My visit was in order to survey the setting. In 1990 I visited the Mollebos seven times and in 1991 fifteen times. All of my visits took place on Mondays between 9:00 P.M. and 1:30 A.M., varying in length from ninety minutes to four hours, with a mean time of two hours and thirty minutes.

My first visits to the Mollebos in 1990 were as a participant. I was curious to know what this cruising area had to offer as a new facility in the Dutch gay leather and S/M scene. In that respect I was not disappointed. But that was not the only reason that I returned to the Mollebos many times. The mere fact that this facility for leathermen existed interested me as a researcher in gay studies. I decided to systematize my observations of cruising and courting practices. The same applied to the information I obtained from informal conversations with Mollebos cruising men about the use of other facilities to get sex and about the individual meaning they attach to these leather nights. On my fourth or fifth visit, my role became a mixed one. For part of the evening and night, I was an observing participant and for some time a participating observer. For approximately 80 percent of the time that I spent in all of my visits to the Mollebos, I focused on my role as "participant observer."

My experience in leather bars and cruising areas made it possible to feel at ease almost immediately. It made me an insider from the moment I knew the ground plan of the area and could find my way to the spots where the action was going on. I think my investigation is a good example of what is called an "opportunistic research strategy" (Riemer 1977). Riemer makes a plea for research in which sociologists take advantage of "unique circumstances or timely events, familiar social situations, [and] special expertise." An opportunistic research strategy facilitates "entry into research setting, rapport between the investigator and the persons being studied, [and] . . . accurate interpretation." Riemer mentions disadvantages to this mode of research, including emotional involvement with the members being studied "to the point that one's objectivity may be affected," and the difficulty or sometimes impossibility of replicating the research results.

I experienced all the advantages and disadvantages Riemer mentions. For an outsider, it must be extremely difficult to construct a clear and broad picture of this leather cruising scene.[16] Some of my informants told me that they wanted to cooperate only because they considered me as "one of them." First of all, they looked upon me as a participant with a positive attitude towards their activities, and only secondly did they perceive me as a researcher.[17]

During seventeen leather nights in the Mollebos, my attention was largely fixed on observation. With several cruising men, I conducted short informal conversations. I learned that sometimes a special skill is required to avoid the impression that a conversation is started as a cautious invitation to have sex. Questions like "Where are you from?" and "Do you come here often?" belong to the international repertoire of opening gambits in conversation between cruisers.[18] Answers do not have to be truthful. In those cases where I could check the answers, I often found that my conversation partners were telling facts and not lies.

Asking some guy what he regards as exciting in leather cruising implies you also have to be able and willing to share your own experiences. Again, this is difficult or impossible for an outsider. Only when the conversation lasted longer than a few minutes did I tell something about my investigation. Not until I returned home did I make some notes. I did not register precisely the number of men I saw and what sexual activities they were involved in. Those statistics were not my main interest.

The closing of the Mollebos parking lot was announced only two weeks beforehand. At that moment, I was not sure whether I could consider my field research as completed. A worse problem was that there was no opportunity left to ask cruisers to agree to an extended interview in another location. I had planned some interviews for a better and more complete understanding of the significance that visiting the leather nights has to individual participants. A new research strategy was needed to obtain that information. I could contact some patrons of the leather nights I knew from other places. This resulted in two interviews. In addition, I put a personal ad in a daily newspaper with many gay ads in the personal column, a gay magazine, and two gay leather and S/M magazines.[19] I did not expect to get many reactions. I received only four serious letters, which led to three more interviews.

Leather Night Participants

The number of men on the leather nights I attended varied from fifteen to forty, with an average of twenty-five. Most of them arrived by car, some on motorbike.

The majority were single; some men shared a car but operated independently in the woods, others stayed together. I witnessed a few master-slave couples who liked to execute an outdoor S/M scene or were looking for an audience. One "master" regularly took out his "slave" like a dog: He led him around on a leash attached to a neck collar. The slave was allowed to walk on two feet. There were other familiar faces, such as one guy in an army officer's outfit giving orders to a boy in a soldier's uniform with full kit.

For some patrons, their occupation on Monday evenings was fixed. If weather conditions were not too bad, you could be sure to meet them in the Mollebos. I observed ten participants at least ten or more times and three at least fifteen times. Because of the size of the area, it is possible that several participants stayed unnoticed. Only on one occasion did I see "suspect" visitors: three boys about twenty years old who arrived together—a fact which is in itself reason for suspicion—talked too loud, and were not familiar with the layout of the area. They seemed impressed by the number of cruising men and soon left.[20]

Some 50 to 70 percent of the men on Monday evenings wore leather. Some were in black leather from head to foot, a few with additional metal studs and chains. The Mollebos cruising site is one of few areas where gay leathermen can make this kind of identity statement without being embarrassed. The other sites in the Netherlands are leather bars, motorbike meetings, and certain streets and specific times in the city centre of Amsterdam. Knowing other leather guys are around not only creates opportunities for favorite sexual acts but also means receiving vital recognition and support in this expression, creating a "mutual bond of identity support and conviction." (Delph 1978, 112) As one of my informants told me:

> It gives me a special thrill to see other guys with a similar image, to know I'm part of this group of horny leathermen. You know you feel the same about masculinity and what is exciting in leather. It has this macho presentation but most of us only play a role as a tough guy. Did you ever hear two heterosexual macho men talk about their addiction to opera or their way to prepare a fish salad?

Some leather-night patrons indicated S/M preferences by means of a chain or metal ring, most often a single or double cockring, attached to the right (M) or left (S) shoulder of their leather jacket. A bunch of keys or handcuffs hanging on an often-studded belt could have the same function.

I met several men interested in S/M who did not wear any signs of their preferences. They shared experiences by indicating a specific role one can restrict the chances of meeting interesting sex partners. They said that they prefer to make certain sexual preferences clear during a contact. This is certainly the case when someone is not restricted to either the S role or the M role but likes both sides of S/M.

Most Monday night patrons were attracted to leather. That preference gave a safe basis to start sexual communication if they saw someone attractive. It was not unusual for cruising contact that started around leather to end in S/M play. Such contact is initiated not only by nonverbal signs but also by simply asking, "Do you also like S/M?" and "What do you like?" Through these verbalizations, partners obtain key information that can be used to enhance sexual fulfillment. When S/M preferences are absent or do not fit, sex partners can stick to more regular sexual activities.

The leather nights were visited not only by leathermen and lovers of army uniforms. Some participants liked to see their partners in leather but did not wear leather clothing themselves. A masochist once told me he felt only masters should wear leather clothing. For some other men, the Mollebos provided an opportunity to get an idea of the leather subculture in which they had more limited interest. In a leather bar, this group would not feel at ease. Some gay men who visited the Mollebos just did not know beforehand that Monday night "meant" leather night.

I met several patrons I knew from other settings, including Amsterdam leather bars and a cruising area in my hometown, as well as individuals with whom I had already had personal contact. From my conversations and interviews with regular visitors, I learned that most of them make use of several facilities in the leather and S/M scene, especially leather bars. Fred (thirty-six, living in the eastern part of the Netherlands) said,

> If you like cruising in a park or elsewhere and you are into leather or S/M, mostly you won't find many potential partners. Where I live there are no leather bars nearby and I don't have the opportunity to go to Amsterdam every weekend. So this really supplies a need.

For many of the men who come on Monday night, the Mollebos also supplies a social function. They see acquaintances and friends with whom they can exchange news and information. And they talk about more than just the leather scene.

Action in a Cruising Area

Participants at the Mollebos appear to engage in sexual activities similar to those performed in other locations. Sex during the leather nights tends to be more rough or aggressive, but every leatherman can also tell you about and show you "soft sex" such as hugging and kissing. Only on two occasions did I witness or suspect unsafe sexual acts. But again, I was not there to count and register sexual acts.[21] Leathersex, and especially S/M, are, in most cases, less penis-oriented than regular gay sex in public places.[22] More body parts are involved and the sexual act is not, by definition, focused solely on orgasm. Richard, a twenty-seven-year-old leatherguy, said,

> When I spend two or three hours in the Mollebos I like to have sex with several men. That gives me a special thrill. I let them come but prevent myself from coming. It can be very exciting to control your sensual lust in such a way. With the last partner I then feel so hot that I can't hold it any longer. It really gives great satisfaction.

Leathersex that is a bit aggressive can turn into S/M, with roles defined by the particular situation in which two men are engaged. A sexual contact can also be defined in terms of "top" and "bottom" roles from the start. This is often the case when someone presenting himself as a masochist approaches a sadist, or vice versa.[23] In such a contact, the S takes control and determines what the M is allowed to do. Most "top" men try to find out what the M likes. Once or twice, I heard about an S in the Mollebos who did not seem to know the rules of the game. He immediately started to treat his partner in such a rough way that the latter broke off contact after less than one minute.

S/M sex in the Mollebos occasionally was quite rough. Nevertheless, hard S/M, for example extended whipping, was scarce, and in most cases, was only performed by a master who brought his own slave. In encounters between partners who were new to each other, most people were very cautious. Bondage, as used in private settings, was therefore not very common. To get yourself tied to a tree by an unknown man can be exciting in fantasy but turns into a nightmare in reality. Most S/M in the Mollebos was limited to some form of discipline, for instance licking boots, or to tormenting sensitive body parts.

3. *The Mollebos as Erotic Space*

The Mollebos rest area is located in the woods on the southern lane of the A12 highway. The rest area consists of two parking lanes; there are some picnic spots but no other facilities. The highway is separated from the rest area by a strip of woodland fifty to seventy yards wide. The entrance to the woods, on the south side, was and is blocked by a fence. This fence was repeatedly cut and breached by cruising men (Leeuw 1991, 1). People who used this passage to enter the woods had to first cross an asphalt cycle track to get into the cruising area. This woodland is crisscrossed with footpaths and narrow tracks. The main part consists of coniferous wood. North of Driebergen, it can be legally entered on foot or on bike. In the daytime the woods are visited by tourists and residents of a nearby camping site. Some problematic encounters between members of the two groups, cruisers and holidaymakers, have been reported (Leeuw 1991, 3). In general, however, "the taken-for-granted functions of this setting as perceived by the population at large" served as "a cloak of concealment for homosexual activity" (Delph 1978, 60). During the evening and night, the area was almost exclusively the territory of cruising men. Possibilities of walking around unself-consciously, and opportunities to allocate specific functions and acts to different parts of the area, were much greater than during the daytime.

In most respects this cruising area met conditions that favor the pursuit of "impersonal" or "casual" sex (Weinberg & Williams 1975):

1. A more or less safe setting with low public visibility;
2. A field of attractive potential partners available for the desired sexual acts, at minimal expense;
3. The existence of a known and shared intent and of clear and simple rules for transforming the intent into interaction; and
4. A congenial atmosphere.

Opinions will differ on another condition mentioned by Weinberg and Williams: the level of comfort afforded by the physical setting. I expect most conditions at the Mollebos were better fulfilled after sunset than in the daytime.

Spatial Strategies on Leather Nights

Different parts of the territory of the parking lot and the woods appeared to have different functions. The parking lot (P) and the picnic ground on the southern side constituted the first exploration zone (number 1 on map). Most leather night participants parked their cars or motorbikes at the rear end of the parking lot, nearer to the exit than to the entrance.

Other visitors who only came to "rest" tended to have no special preference in where they parked their cars. Their numbers were small, and most only stayed there for a short time. For cruising men, the parking lot and picnic ground was the first area in which to form an impression of the number of leathermen and the presence of outsiders. This zone was also used for social contact and for breaks from cruising. This was especially the case for motorbikers who tended to gather there.

Functions of the different zones were not strictly separated. Before 1990 the strip of woodland between the highway and parking lot was the main sexual zone. (Fours on the map denote sexual zones.) Thus, cruising was concentrated in the parking lot and on a footpath across this woodland. In the last few years of the Mollebos as a cruising area, the bulk of the action moved to the woods behind the fence.

During my observations, most men usually went to the gap in the fence in order to enter the woods. After crossing the cycle track diagonally, they arrived at the main access to the sexual zone (number 2 on map). This access point is at the beginning of a wide and dark path where participants tried to adjust to the darkness. Some cruising took place at the beginning of this path—especially between new arrivals and men who seemed to be leaving. For the former, immediate action was needed if one was

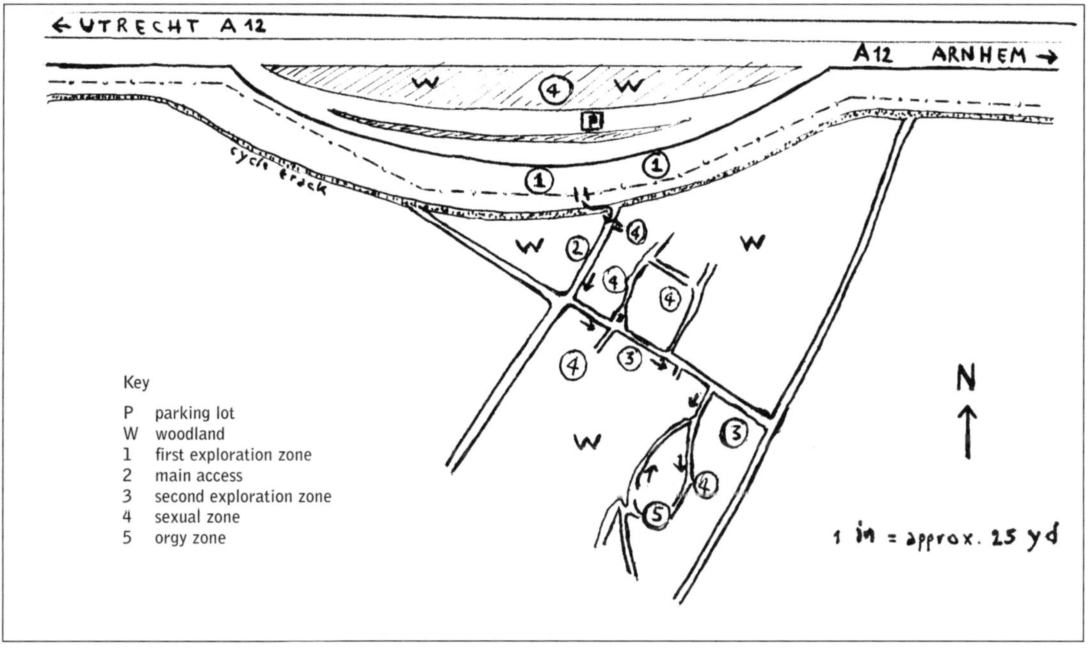

Ground plan of the Mollebos area. Map by Maurice van Lieshout.

interested in someone who was leaving and on his way to the parking lot. For the latter, contact in this portal zone often meant giving oneself a last opportunity to get in touch with someone. On several occasions, I saw men on their way to the exit turn around to follow an arrival. A recent arrival who wanted to cruise someone leaving submitted to an almost desperate task. It meant cutting short all cruising ceremonials, immediately catching someone's attention, having some visual confirmation related to interests, and curtly enticing the one about to leave to follow him into the bushes. The same ritual also took place at the end of the access path where participants had to turn left to get into the main cruising and sex zones.

The small path on the left had a short, very dark, and tunnel-like entrance. Farther down this path, the cover on both sides is low. This meant that on this path patrons could get the best visual impression of potential sex partners. This path functioned as a second exploration zone and the main artery of the cruising area on leather nights (number 3 on map). On this path, there was usually a lot of traffic. During their stay in the Mollebos, most men walked up and down this path many times. It served as a conduit from more social to explicitly sexual activities. It was the place in which to have a chat with an acquaintance without losing opportunities to make more overtly sexual contact. A passerby could easily show interest in a person who was talking to someone else. If the attraction was mutual, the men speaking would wind up their conversation in order for the initially "cruised" man to follow the cruiser.

The conduit path provided entrance to several more sexualized zones. The first of such areas was on the left and also was used for cruising. The next area was mostly used for actual sex between people who had already made contact. The last sexual zone, along the right of this conduit path, was the main sexual area. There was a path in this zone that lead into a thickly wooded area. This path got narrower and darker and ended in a pitch-black space. This area was used as a backroom or orgy room (number 5 on map). At night it is very difficult to see anything there, and it was necessary to use other senses in order to track other people. In trying to manoeuvre in the darkness, often the best thing to do was to walk until you bumped another guy. Hands grasping at you, sensual sounds, the smell of poppers,[24] and a vague visual sense of moving figures made it clear you were not alone. On this spot, patrons could have truly anonymous sex, often with more than one partner at a time. With arms forward to avoid further crashes with men and trees, it was possible to leave this outdoor orgy room through the other side. From that point, one could return to the main path and start the circle, or circuit, all over again.

Cruising and sex were not restricted to the above-mentioned areas. Within a one-mile range you could come across leathermen, including some who purposely retired to quiet places. However, most of the action was found in the area described above. Entering this zone had the meaning of being available for sex.

Excursus: A Comparison with Spatial Strategies in Backrooms

The similarities of the spaces in the Mollebos area and the spatial strategies in leather bars with backroom facilities are striking. In Amsterdam, leather bars like Argos, the Eagle, the Web, and the Cuckoo's Nest have the same segmentation with an exploration or social zone and a sexual and orgy zone.[25] The exploration zone generally consists of two rooms: the actual bar in the front and a second room or segment in the back. For example, the Web and the Cuckoo's Nest have on the border of this area a billiard table that is covered on weekend nights. A television monitor showing porn videos is available in three of these bars. Although borders between the two exploration segments are fuzzy, the second functions as an obvious transitional area to the sexual zone. Less talking and more "eyeing," gazing, and cruising is going on here than in the front area. Many patrons in this zone are not engaged in conversation but are looking intently at the crowd in order to find a sex partner. This area serves the same purpose as the main artery in the Mollebos cruising area. This area is also used as a rest area or room in which to "chill out" between repeated visits, in the course of a night, to the sexual zone.[26]

The sexual zone also consists of two areas: an often circular cruising area and a sex area with some cabins in which to retire. On crowded nights, sexual activities take place everywhere in this zone. Generally speaking, the further one penetrates these leather bars, the less talking takes place, the less lighting is installed, and the more sexual activities can be expected.

Courting Practices

Courting practices are in general the same in both settings. Cruising means catching the attention of a guy to whom one is attracted and then seducing him in one way or another to lead to sex acts. It is also possible to restrict oneself to being cruised, which means to only respond to initiatives by others. In most cruising situations, participants perform both roles.

In the Mollebos area, cruising demands more walking around than is usual and possible in leather bars. The size of the woods also means more exercise than in other outside cruising areas. In both situations, however, eye contact is essential. Arriving in a cruising site demands a brief examination of those present. Many patrons prefer to explore the area first. Guys who are appealing get an initial glance. Walking past someone more than once or turning the head in the direction of a passing guy are means of indicating interest. Following a passerby can serve the same function.

In many cases the best way to attract someone's attention is to place oneself nearby and then try to make eye contact. One can then give the pursued a glance that is a holding or penetrating shot directly into his eyes. Then wait, but not too long, for a reciprocal glance. If it is not given, one can try again, but in most cases such repeated attempts will prove to be useless. In cases where there is mutual attraction, potential partners can approach each other and start body contact—or one can wait till the other does so. In the Mollebos, the next step after making eye contact is to retire to a spot to have sex. One man takes the initiative, glances once more at the chosen one, and starts walking—expecting to be followed.

In other situations, especially when visibility is poor, as is the case in orgy zones, initial contact is made by groping, mostly through putting a hand in the groin. If the hand is removed immediately, this means "I am not interested in you (at this moment)."

In cruising situations, "No" always means "No." A negative response is most commonly given in a nonverbal way, such as nodding or removing a hand, and it must not be taken personally. It is not insulting or humiliating if one gets a negative response to an advance—on the condition that occasionally there are successes.

Individual Meanings in Visiting the Mollebos Leather Nights

From the five men who frequented the Mollebos and whom I interviewed, I learned that taking part in the leather nights had a special meaning to each of them. They all had tried to make their sexual fantasies come true. The outdoor setting in the woods was important to most of them. Richard (twenty-seven) said,

> Woodland in the dark has a promise of adventure. Perhaps it is the combination of fear and expectation. Behind each tree you may expect something or someone frightening or tempting or both. For me it is a very erotic scenery. When I have sex in the Mollebos I am always very aware of the surroundings. I also like other settings, but leathersex and a scenery like these woods belong to each other.

James (thirty-four, into leather and soft S/M) is reminded of his boyhood:

> I really liked to play in the woods. We had these games we called "police and villain" or "cowboy and Indian." You had to overpower members of the other party. That meant a lot of physical contact. In some cases a boy was tied to a tree. These games excited me, gave me feelings I later learned were erotic. The leather nights evoke similar feelings. Boys playing together in a game that is all about power and submission. On the other hand, the entire situation is very different; how many men share my fantasy when visiting the Mollebos? I pretend they do.

The woods is a favorite topos in leather and S/M fiction and pornography. For example, it is often the scene in which to be captured, tortured, and raped by a gang of motorbike boys. In many stories, pictures and drawings of a forest suggest a masculinized setting, as do the mountains. Many drawings by Tom of Finland—the most famous artist portraying leathermen—are situated in a woodland. His fantasy men, with their enormous oversized cocks, are often engaged in S/M and group sex scenes. Finland's images are extremely popular among gay leathermen.[27] John (twenty-seven) has had recurring fantasies about being captured by several leathermen.

> I know such a situation can only happen if staged. Once I experienced this fantasy come true on a weekend with other leathermen in a private woodland. It was one of my best sexual experiences. In the Mollebos, I must complete the scene with my own fantasy. Sometimes I imagine guys in a role of which they are not aware. But that doesn't matter.

But it is not important to everyone that the leather nights take place in woodland. Robin (thirty-nine, loves leather but not S/M) visited the Mollebos as a place to meet other motorbikers. But he was disappointed to find out that the majority of visitors arrive by car.

> I went several times to a highway rest area near Münster, just over the Dutch-German border. That meant a three-hour ride (190 miles). There you can meet many bikers, also on Monday nights. I like sex more when I know my partner is a biker. The presence of a motorbike is not necessary but I think it's nice if a bike is nearby.

Conclusion

The Mollebos area proved to be a facility for many men to make contacts with other men interested in having sex. Leather and S/M men had confiscated, for one night a week, a small portion of public territory. The leather nights were an important supplement to their more ongoing scene. The existence of these nights, although stopped in December 1991, indicates a development in the Dutch gay male subculture that occurred in indoor facilities much earlier: an ongoing diversification to supply various desires and needs.

A few months after the closing of the Mollebos area, leathermen "conquered" a new highway rest area, continuing the Monday evenings.[28] The short history of the Mollebos area makes it clear that, in spite of all the tolerance and openness towards public homosexual encounters, in Dutch society maintaining cruising areas has not been a major agenda item either for the gay movement or government institutions.

The Mollebos proved to be exciting for gay men, as an outdoor facility as well as a wooded territory. It served for many as a sexual *Fantasia Land* where dreams could come true. The woods met conditions for exciting leather and S/M meetings: an erotically experienced space that suggested adventure, hazard, and heightened sensation. Of course, nights in the Mollebos could also be boring and cold. Nevertheless, many leathermen turned out to be regular visitors, on every occasion hoping that the woods would redeem their promise.

The meanings that individual (gay) men attach to visiting places such as the Mollebos and participating in sex acts in outdoor spaces seem to have some elements in common and to differ in other, more personal, aspects. Investigations of the experiences and behaviours of regular visitors to leather nights and among patrons of an indoor cruising area for leathermen, through observation and interviews, can tell us much about the individual meanings that these men attach to their sexual activities, to their gender roles and gender identities, and to the public spaces and landscapes to which they are drawn.

QUEER SPACES

In 1888, financier James Everard converted an old church at 28 W. 28th Street into a Turkish bathhouse. By the onset of World War I, the clientele was primarily gay men. For more than half a century, until it burned to the ground in 1977, the Everard was the most famous and enduring of a network of gay bathhouses that were an integral part of the sexual life, folklore and economy of New York's gay community. In 1985 the city ordered the baths, including a rebuilt Everard, closed down due to the risk of AIDS transmission.

PLACES OF STRUGGLE PLACES OF STRENGTH

REPO HISTORY

9

REPOhistory Collective, *Queer Spaces* installation #9, 1994. Courtesy of Storefront for Art and Architecture, New York, and sarabande digital communication services, New York.

Queer Spaces in New York City: Places of Struggle/Places of Strength

Betti-Sue Hertz, Ed Eisenberg, and Lisa Maya Knauer[1]

In June 1994 REPOhistory, a multimedia artists' collective based in New York, installed a series of street signs about overlooked gay and lesbian histories at nine locations in lower Manhattan. The signs—pink tempered masonite triangles installed on lamp posts—declared these previously unmarked sites on New York City streets to be "queer spaces" and reclaimed them as important landmarks in the City's history. Installed just before the annual Pride Week festivities and in commemoration of the twenty-fifth anniversary of Stonewall, they were officially maintained through the end of August 1994. (However, a July 1995 visit to City Hall and the Christopher Street Pier confirmed that at least two of the signs were still up a year later.)

The Queer Spaces Sign Project—initiated in response to a call issued by the Storefront for Art and Architecture, for an exhibition called "Queer Space"—is part of a larger movement to make visible and validate gay and lesbian presence in the city and in public space. In this case, remembrance is significant for the construction of "public memory."[2] The signs[3] mark specific locations and inform the public about what occurred there, and historicize everyday spaces. They raise questions about public landmarking, territoriality, and problematics of the public and the private. They challenge history's dominant narratives and its forceful silences. A double-edged response to the resistance of public embrace of gay and lesbian presence and visibility is implied in the border text that frames each sign: "*places of struggle/places of strength.*"

History of REPOhistory

REPOhistory began in the spring of 1989, when a group of artists, educators, and activists came together to discuss a collaboration on site-specific public art dealing with historical themes. We spent several months developing some common critical and theoretical ground before embarking on a specific project. Our intent was not to replace the dominant culture's history with a monolithic alternative but to offer a plurality of voices, issues, and ideas. Reading Eduardo Galeano's *Memories of Fire,* a collage of fragmentary but interrelated narratives on the history of the Americas, allowed us to imagine a kind of "magical realist" or multilayered approach that would encourage viewers to imagine their own alternatives and directly engage them.

Our first collective undertaking, the Lower Manhattan Sign Project, was a series of thirty-nine 18-inch × 24-inch metal signs with images and text silkscreened on both sides. The signs were installed on lamp posts throughout the Financial District for a year beginning in June 1992. The area is saturated with official historical demarcations, from the American Express Heritage Trail to Landmark District signs. Our project simultaneously appropriated and critiqued the visual language of these official markers. It reframed several centuries of local history, ranging from the original "sale" of Manhattan island to Nelson Mandela's triumphal visit to New York in 1990. The signs were dispersed over an area approximately one mile square.

Initially conceived as a guerrilla art action—signs installed in the dead of night, replaced as necessary, and hopefully documented before they eventually disappeared—the project was eventually installed under a permit from the Department of Transportation[4] and with full approval of the local Community Board. It was created over a period of two years and combined both collaborative and individual work styles. A total of forty-nine artists, activists, and scholars participated in the creation of the signs. A core group of fifteen to twenty people participated in the initial conceptualization of the project and developed lists of possible sites and themes. But artists were not limited to these lists. The core collective developed overall guidelines such as size, maximum amount of text, range of type sizes, and number of colors, while allowing individual artists or teams much freedom in designing their signs. They edited and proofread the text for all the signs. Because the content and design was extremely heterogeneous, we created a common visual element to unify the project. On the bottom of the back of each sign was a box containing a logo, a number corresponding to a map, and a series of two or three provocative, perhaps rhetorical, questions directly addressing the viewer: Is this a historic site? Is this history part of your history?

Our second undertaking was "Choice Histories: Framing Abortion" a more fully collaborative multimedia installation at Artists Space, a nonprofit gallery in New York City, also in 1992. Small groups of six to eight artists worked together to create tableaux that examined a specific aspect of the history of reproductive rights in America. "We broke into working groups based on four broad areas of interest: law and morality; race and class; the history of medicine; and issues of sexuality. We agreed to share information in order to compile a linear chronology. Each group, then, has collaboratively created a tableaux or vignette that raises a particular set of questions and that also—in varying degrees—accommodates individual work. Our source material has included personal accounts, mythologies, and imaginative works in addition to historical information. We are concerned with subjective and internal responses to both real and fictional accounts of the history of abortion."[5]

Queer Spaces of Manhattan

In late February 1994, when Todd Ayoung brought Storefront's open call for its Queer Space exhibition to REPOhistory's attention, the group was going through a period of relative inactivity. So when Todd told us that the Storefront curators had indicated

REPOhistory Collective, *Queer Spaces* installation #7, lower Manhattan, 1994. Photograph © Jim Costanzo. Courtesy of REPOhistory Collective and Storefront for Art and Architecture, New York.

interest in our sign project and were eager to see what we would propose, several members saw this as an opportunity to refocus the group's energies. We thought we could devise a quick street intervention. With the deadline for proposals a little more than a week away, a group met several days later and proposed three possible themes for a minisign project: gaybashing, cruising, and red-light districts. Of these, a consensus appeared to coalesce around the proposal to mark sites of antigay violence. More than a year earlier, the group had, in fact, considered a citywide project to document sites of bias-related acts of violence against various social groups. Although we had never actively pursued the project, it had not faded from our memory. The Queer Space exhibition offered an opportunity to execute a slice of the idea as a prelude to a possible larger project against all forms of bias. Soon, however, it became clear that our consensus was illusory. One member, who had missed the meeting at which the idea was proposed, raised the objection that signs on gaybashing would present gays and lesbians simply as victims. She suggested that we focus instead on resistance to violence, highlighting the work of groups like the New York City Gay and Lesbian Anti-Violence Project. By late March, this critique had led the group to settle on a more open-ended project: the recent history of gay activism and its roots around the Stonewall period. But as often happens in the collective process, some members argued for not limiting the project to the Stonewall era. They suggested that we broaden our historical scope to include the pre-Stonewall era, to reclaim the older

QUEER SPACES

PLACES OF STRUGGLE PLACES OF STRENGTH

The first gay rights demonstration in New York City occurred on September 19, 1964 in front of the Whitehall Street Induction Center. A dozen brave men and women formed a picket line and handed out leaflets protesting the U.S. Army's policies of giving less-than-honorable discharges to homosexuals, and revealing information about draftees' sexual orientation to other government agencies. The demonstration was organized by Homosexual League of N.Y. and co-sponsored by the N.Y.C. League for Sexual Freedom.

REPO HISTORY

1

REPOhistory Collective, *Queer Spaces* installation #1, 1994. Courtesy of Storefront for Art and Architecture, New York, and sarabande digital communication services, New York.

and more deeply hidden parts of the history. Individual signs would recall social and political actions at specific locations and mark recreational sites of significance to the developing identity and increasingly public aspect of gay life.

Several REPOhistory members were involved in the Queer Spaces project. Because many of the project's participants had long been involved with the collective, we had come to rely on each other for the perspectives and skills we had demonstrated in the past. And our process for Queer Spaces developed out of both the material and the form of previous experiences. Several active members would prove to be important informants on gay history and culture as the project evolved. As earlier projects embodied the voices of African Americans or reproductive rights specialists, in this project the experience and opinions of the gay members were noted with special interest. However the interest and willingness of all members to engage in discussions and research was absolutely necessary to the success of the project. Many members also had the opportunity to speak with activists in the gay and lesbian community about ideas for signs, and they asked individuals for feedback on how we were approaching the material. Members of REPOhistory active in the Queer Spaces Project included Lisa Maya Knauer, Mark O'Brien, Ed Eisenberg, Tom Klem, Jim Costanzo, Todd Ayoung, Betti-Sue Hertz, and Megan Pugh. Other members, including Kara Lynch, Ayisha Abraham, and Lise Prown, helped out in one way or another during the process.

The Stonewall twenty-fifth anniversary, a major Gay Pride Parade, and the Gay Games saturated the city with more queer imagery and media coverage than the public had ever seen before. But most of that imagery promoted and advertised specific events. There was little on the streets that asked the general public to reflect on gay and lesbian history, other than the Stonewall riot itself. (However, several historical books and maps on gay New York, most notably George Chauncey's *Gay New York: Gender, Urban Culture and the Making of the Gay Male World, 1890–1940* and *Stonewall,* by Martin Duberman, first appeared in bookshops around this time. The "Becoming Visible" exhibit at the New York Public Library was to be the most comprehensive presentation thus far of archival material about the gay and lesbian movement.)

What could be our unique contribution within the energized moment of the Stonewall anniversary? The process of mythologizing the Stonewall riots is well under way. Indeed the fictionalized film version of the event may soon become most people's reality. This mythical Stonewall exists independent of a historical view of a gay activist context. Yet it was the extraordinarily brave activism prior to the riot that made it possible and the liberation movement Stonewall sparked that made the riot itself into such a significant event. The history of early gay rights activism and the gay liberation and lesbian feminist movements is still largely unknown and unmarked. To date, no book has been written that documents the history in its entirety, even as many of its key participants steadily die.[6]

The twenty-fifth anniversary of Stonewall was an appropriate occasion for commemorating its history rather than another, such as the period of 1890–1940, which has been documented by George Chauncey. By publicly acknowledging several key developments in the emergence of a politically conscious gay and lesbian community, REPOhistory's Queer Spaces sign project sought to counter the decontextualized mythologizing of Stonewall that was in full swing during the anniversary celebrations. Three of our sites also turned up on OLGAD's (Organization of Lesbian and Gay Architects and Designers)[7] map of Greenwich Village in its *Guide to Lesbian and Gay New York Historical Landmarks.*[8] Most of our other sites fall outside the domain of those maps. Had we been able to do more signs, we could have fleshed out this history more fully: documenting educational reforms and the proliferation of community organizations, and addressing issues such as lesbian separatism, self-organizing by lesbian and gay people of color, and the emergence of radical sex for which the Mineshaft, a sex club operating from 1976 to 1985, would have been the best location.[9]

QUEER SPACES

The Daughters of Bilitis, one of the earliest lesbian political organizations, had offices at 30 Charlton Street for several years, beginning in 1963. Due to the political climate of the era, many members used assumed names to protect their jobs and families. But the very existence of Daughters of Bilitis was a challenge to invisibility. Together with the Mattachine Society, an early gay men's group, the Daughters of Bilitis were in the vanguard of pre-Stonewall gay and lesbian organizing.

PLACES OF STRUGGLE PLACES OF STRENGTH

REPO HISTORY

5

REPOhistory Collective, *Queer Spaces* installation #5, 1994. Courtesy of Storefront for Art and Architecture, New York, and sarabande digital communication services, New York.

While we were aware of the significance of the "gay ghetto" of the Village/Chelsea/Soho area as a site where activist history is made, we also wanted to expand our scope geographically to less obvious areas. But while the idea of a citywide project was appealing, limited resources dictated that we would be able to produce at most eight to ten signs, and we felt the impact would be too diluted if they were spread throughout the five boroughs. For example, we researched the site of a gay bathhouse in Harlem, the Mount Morris Baths at 125th and Madison, which has been a popular spot since the early part of the century, and is still open.

In the end some of us felt uneasy about putting a sign that might be controversial in a community where we were primarily outsiders. REPOhistory members worked hard at the issue of inclusion. For some this meant actively imagining and identifying with subject positions that were not their own. In conversation, straight and gay members would discuss various topics to ensure that a range of gay subjects were represented, and they questioned any exclusion. We were also conscious of the need to represent gay men and lesbians from various racial, gender, and sexuality groups. A week into April, needing to get started on some signs, we voted (each person casting eight ballots) to do six specific signs from a list of twenty-five possibilities. We left two, eventually three, additional signs undetermined at that time. Ed, Lisa, and Mark researched and wrote the text for all six of the initially selected signs, and in the course of further research, each of them came up with a site for an additional sign. Thus we eventually installed nine signs.

Up until the Queer Spaces project, our efforts to include gay and lesbian histories had been relatively minor. There had been no signs on queer history in the first sign project, although the Queer Spaces sign at the ACT UP demonstration was originally researched for that project. The Choice Histories installation only sketchily examined the social construction of sexuality, including homosexuality, in the United States—as part of the history of reproductive rights. The Queer Space exhibition provided us with a needed focus for developing a project about queer public history in New York City.

We frequently checked in with gay friends, gay and lesbian organizations, and research centers. An invaluable resource was Ken Lustbader, an urban planner who worked at the city's landmarks commission. He had written a master's thesis based, in part, upon our original sign project and had researched several gay sites for hypothetical "landmarking." He was extremely supportive of our efforts and generously

REPOhistory Collective, *Queer Spaces* installation #8, lower Manhattan, 1994. Photograph © Jim Costanzo. Courtesy of REPOhistory Collective and Storefront for Art and Architecture, New York.

shared much of his research with us. We talked with him frequently, and he also put us in contact with OLGAD, which was producing a queer history map of New York for the Stonewall anniversary. Staff at the Lesbian Herstory Archives contributed personal memories of the pre-Stonewall era, and provided us with the addresses of the first several headquarters of the Daughters of Bilitis.

This project encouraged gay members to take on leadership roles within the group. Ed was especially important to the evolution of the Queer Spaces project. He was able to draw on both his own experiential knowledge and his encyclopedic memory of recent gay events. His memories and experiences, as well as narratives of gay, bisexual, and straight members, from personal memory and knowledge of the periods under review led us to interesting bits of gay history in Manhattan. Conversations amongst the members helped to educate those who had little contact with gay activism. They were brought into closer contact with the history through the "I was there" accounts. Readings, as well as our increased contact with gay and lesbian activists, shed light on what events or sites might be considered important to the gay community. REPOhistory's membership ranges in age from mid-twenties to late forties, and this age span has worked in our favor. A variety of historical perspectives emerged through our intergenerational dialogue. Discussions on language and ways of telling became especially important as we finalized the texts for the signs.

"Visibility" was fast becoming an activist buzz word, especially as exemplified in the work of the Lesbian Avengers whose parades, street actions, and manifestoes became real trendsetters for 1990s activism. Selecting which histories we would represent was our most serious challenge. Two ideas prevailed in the initial lists: visibility and rights, and social spaces for sexual expression and freedom. Both expressed a form of gay resistance and activism. We chose to mark public establishments such as public baths and bars, the civil rights struggle, and organizations involved with those struggles. However we danced around the question of the closet without defining it. In the final selection we were unable to include materials reflecting some key developing areas of public activism: feminism, the role of theoretical intellectuals who were redefining queer language and identity, new sociologies, and literary and poetic voices that had indeed enabled the growth of the gay movement.

The Queer Spaces project represented a new stage for our collective work process. While each person took on specific tasks, there is no sign that represents a single artist's work. We decided to design the signs collectively, and suggestions were made for different images that might accompany the texts. These images included silhouettes of same-sex kissing, photos of Wigstock, an annual drag event in Manhattan, and adaptations of Gay Pride button designs. Megan and Lise submitted designs that were then discussed, redesigned, and reworked with the group. The final decision to eliminate the images was due partly to the difficulty of creating a cohesive two-color

QUEER SPACES

New York City's Gay and Lesbian Civil Rights Bill was introduced in the City Council on January 6, 1971. It was the first bill in the nation's history to prohibit discrimination on the basis of sexual orientation in employment, housing and public accommodations. However, it took fifteen years, numerous hearings, demonstrations and the selection of a new council majority leader for the legislation to finally pass on March 20, 1986 and become law.

PLACES OF STRUGGLE PLACES OF STRENGTH

REPO HISTORY

3

REPOhistory Collective, *Queer Spaces* installation #3, 1994. Courtesy of Storefront for Art and Architecture, New York, and sarabande digital communication services, New York.

design in the triangular format within our budgetary limitations. We were also very committed to stating historical facts on the signs. The text-only final design did create a striking presence on the street, although the lack of imagery was a source of disappointment to some of the group's members. The consistency in approach and tone created a coherent cumulative reading from one sign to another. The pink triangle could be seen from a great distance; its obvious reference as a gay indicator did not, however, convey its role as a historical marker. Our approach would later be criticized by one person for being too "codified" in content and writing style, and too predictable in the sites that were selected. Was it enough to represent the history within movement politics? Only a piece of the history? Arguably, it was precisely because of this traditional left identification that these sites were most valued by the group, whose most active members trace their ideological lineage to movement politics.[10]

Because the signs were fairly dispersed, a passerby might happen upon only a few of the signs. It is unlikely that anyone who had not picked up a project map at

Storefront and then consciously set out to visit each location would see all the signs on site. This could only be assured at the Storefront exhibition,[11] where all of the signs were displayed. Seeing the pink triangle and its unexpected information out on the street had a very different impact than seeing the same triangles in a group show at a gallery. The signs proved to be a powerful intervention in the routine lexicon of the street. As indicators, they formed a dialogue among history, place, and community and reminded the viewer of a particular site's value. Unlike monuments, the signs called attention to themselves first, in order to encourage the viewer to think about the meanings of the space around them. They educated by using small bits of history and became a metaphor for the larger picture in scattered increments.

Since we sought and received official permits, we saw the signs as ironically blending into the accepted typology of public signage. Tom had developed an excellent relationship with the New York City Department of Transportation during our first sign project, which helped him smooth our way for Queer Spaces. The distinction between signs and posters has proved to be very important for REPOhistory. The presentational shift toward the look of permanence, although none of our projects have been permanent thus far, has come to be understood as being important when reviewing the status that the work has achieved. This status suggests that we have actually effected a different reading of the site, which would not have been taken as seriously if we had approached it with more ephemeral material—both in terms of its physical and psychological weight. This imprint, the surprise of its seeming permanence combined with its illuminating historical content, hovers between a No Parking type of sign and a historical marker. Yet the Queer Spaces signs weren't either of these things. What would happen if we were to put up signs with similar subject matter in bronze? Would this further the presence of our histories?

Because our work is in the vulnerable arena of the street, we knew that simple factual information could cause a wide range of reaction and response by the audience. A few of the signs were taken down right away. We suspect, for example, that the sign commemorating Bonnie and Clyde's, which was across the street from an active firehouse, was taken down by the firemen. On the other hand, when putting up the sign by the Everard, we were eyed suspiciously by the owner of a small family luncheonette. Assuming that he or his regular customers would be offended by the reference to a notorious bathhouse and pull the sign down, we decided to try and gain his sympathy by showing him our permit and explaining our "art project." To our considerable surprise, he not only remembered the Everard but reminisced fondly about how much safer the street was late at night, and how much brisker his father's business, when the Everard's gay clientele was drawn to the neighborhood. And while we were installing the sign in front of Julius's Bar, patrons of the bar came out and were glad to see that the bar was getting some recognition amidst all the attention being

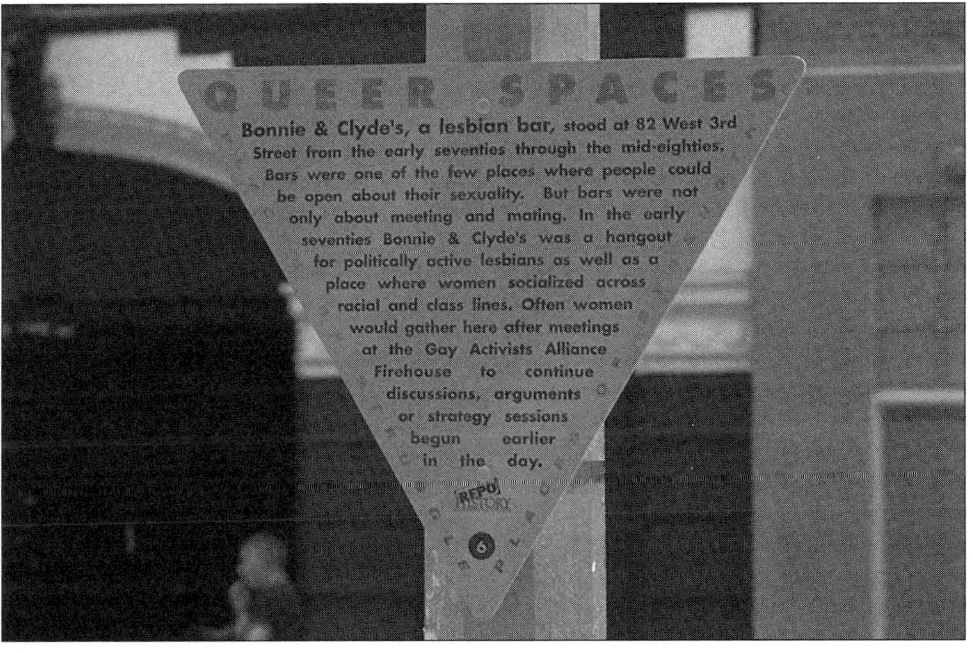

REPOhistory Collective, *Queer Spaces* installation #6, lower Manhattan, 1994. Photograph © Jim Costanzo. Courtesy of REPOhistory Collective and Storefront for Art and Architecture, New York.

showered on the Stonewall Bar around the corner. The signs remained up throughout the summer.

What Did We Want to Accomplish, and How Successful Were We?

The stake that individual members of REPOhistory take in certain projects has been underanalyzed by the group thus far. The relationship between an individual's wish and will and those of the group is always debated and weighed. Also the personal reason an individual has for making a suggestion for a project or a subject may not be fully expressed. Nonetheless, these more private agendas often get played out in the group process and dynamic. The following anecdote illustrates this point—as some readers of this essay's early drafts have remarked, "I didn't know that was what he was thinking." One of the reasons Todd suggested that the group participate in the Queer Space show was to encourage REPOhistory as a whole to consider the importance of queer theory in recent cultural studies discourse. He felt that we were still functioning within a traditional left/movement paradigm and that participation in the Queer Space exhibition would encourage queer-theory readings that were functioning in important ways to define feminist and postcolonial theory, areas of investigation of interest to Todd. He wanted to use readings and discussions of contemporary queer theory and how theory reconfigures our future present to expand the theoretical underpinnings for how projects got developed and implemented. This reconfiguration forces "movements" to question and rearticulate their actions as histories in the making, as opposed to history as a given. Todd's motivation was in fact twofold, because he was starting to feel alienated from some of the paradigms that were operating as a primary and (he thought) predictable force in the group. He wanted to take a more active role in introducing new paradigms, because his own analyses had shifted in the five years since the group formed. He had come to consider the center-versus-margins model outdated. However Todd did not impress upon the group his original private reasons for promoting the project, and ultimately he was unable to either more clearly articulate his own biases or redirect the group. Clearly history from a more traditional left perspective, and not contemporary theory, was our driving force.

Several members expressed disappointment that we were not able to attract new individuals to work on Queer Spaces. We tried to reach out to groups such as Fierce Pussy, a lesbian postering collective, and the New York City Gay and Lesbian Anti-Violence Project. We wanted (gay) permission and support, as well as information and resources. However many small progressive groups are overextended and operate with a small membership, suggesting that a collaboration on a sign, for example, proved to be too difficult, especially in our short time frame.

REPOhistory often operated on its own, and we had done few projects that were part of something larger—or, if they were, they were exhibited without a strongly linked context.[12] This project had moved us into new dialogue with members of the gay, architecture, and urbanist communities. We took a closer look at how we had been influenced by their work. We linked our efforts with others working toward similar goals of claiming public space as contested territory for the construction of history and the meaning of space and site. We were able to see how our strategy overlapped and intersected with those of other artists in the exhibition, and we spoke with them about purpose, process, and outcomes. We became more aware of how our project dovetailed with groups such as Fierce Pussy, the Gay and Lesbian Anti-Violence Project, Lesbian Avengers, OLGAD, and the Lesbian Herstory Archives. Jane Moore of the Empire State Pride Agenda was so excited that she suggested reviving the goal of a citywide antibias project, as part of a lobbying effort to pass a statewide hate-crimes bill. The reviews of the show brought REPOhistory to the attention of a broader audience.

Moreover, our contribution to gay visibility on the public street must not have gone unnoticed. Did those few who are "in-the-know" in terms of the local history of the struggle for gay identity and civil rights cheer (the recognition) or yawn (at the obvious)? Many visitors and New Yorkers (and that includes large parts of the gay community) are not aware of the sites and their significance. The specific nine signs were symbols for the myriad sites we couldn't mark. At the very least, they were reminders of a complex past that cumulatively effected change through community-

REPOhistory Collective, *Queer Spaces* installation #4, lower Manhattan, 1994. Photograph © Jim Costanzo. Courtesy of REPOhistory Collective and Storefront for Art and Architecture, New York.

building actions and an increased sense of ownership of place. We were pleased we could contribute to this historic moment, the twenty-fifth anniversary of the Stonewall Uprising.

Signs Installed in 1994

∇ The first gay rights demonstration in New York City, held on September 19, 1964, protesting antigay policies of the U.S. Army (Whitehall Street)

∇ Julius's Bar, a Greenwich Village hangout that won a landmark 1967 court case over "decency" standards, which helped bring an end to the legal harassment of gay and lesbian establishments (West 10th Street and Waverly Place)

∇ The Gay Activists Alliance Firehouse, an early site of post-Stonewall political organizing (99 Wooster Street)

∇ The Daughters of Bilitis, one of the earliest lesbian organizations in the U.S. (30 Charlton Street)

∇ Bonnie and Clyde's Bar, representing lesbian culture and women's spaces (West 3rd Street)

∇ The Everard, one of New York City's most famous and enduring gay bathhouses, which was eventually shut down by the health commissioner in 1985 due to the threat of AIDS (28 W. 28th Street)

REPOhistory Collective, *Queer Spaces* installation #2, lower Manhattan, 1994. Photograph © Jim Costanzo. Courtesy of REPOhistory Collective and Storefront for Art and Architecture, New York.

- ∇ The introduction of New York City's gay civil rights bill, on January 6, 1971, and its passage after fifteen years of political and legal struggle (City Hall)
- ∇ The first ACT UP demonstration, targeting AIDS profiteering by drug companies, held on March 24, 1987 (Wall Street & Broadway)
- ∇ The legendary transvestite Marsha P. Johnson, whose July 1992 death by drowning may have been the result of homophobic violence (Christopher Steet pier)

Part 5—Queerscape Architectures

Preceding page: Nick Trubenbach, apartment plan, *Media Mavens* series, 1996.

Making Room: Queerscape Architectures and the Spaces of Activism

Gordon Brent Ingram, Anne-Marie Bouthillette, and Yolanda Retter

> Through the erection of partitions that divide space, architecture colludes in creating and upholding prevailing social hierarchies and distinctions.
>
> —Joel Sanders, *STUD*[1]

Architecture, as both a field of culture and a discipline of social science, has sustained a growing interest in confronting the underlying heteronormative rules that constrain much of residential building design,[2] in cities, suburbs, and rural zones. If the architectural design is an artifact of heteronormative social politics and purpose, embellished or obscured by political economy, what are the actual signs of constraint on eroticism, outright repression, marginality, and resistance? The building itself? The plan? The interactions between the designer and the client? The subsequent habitation and reconstruction of the space? The interplay with surrounding neighbourhoods and landscapes? How can this institutionalized prejudice be confronted and overcome?

In Part 5 of *Queers in Space,* we consider strategies for exposing the sexual politics behind architectural designs and buildings. First we look at structures that embody public, semipublic, and private space. Although buildings have represented the safety of privacy and home for sexual minorities, a shift is now occurring. As architecture theoretician Beatrix Colomina has observed, "The private is . . . now more public than the public."[3] And buildings are often the sites where lines between public and private are most clearly drawn and where the attempts to concretize those boundaries are the most in earnest.

The first two essays in this section explore designed space as a regulator of the public and the private realms. The divisions between public and private space have been contested throughout the history of class conflict; most recently, women and sexual minorities have attempted to shape more livable communities that reflect their identities and concerns. But private space has often been closely tied to patriarchal and heteronormative notions of sexuality and intimacy. These problems have cast shadows on the field of architecture for well over a century.

The constructed privacy of the room, especially the bedroom, has codified, and in some cases fossilized, mythologies concerning race, gender, and sexuality.[4] It was

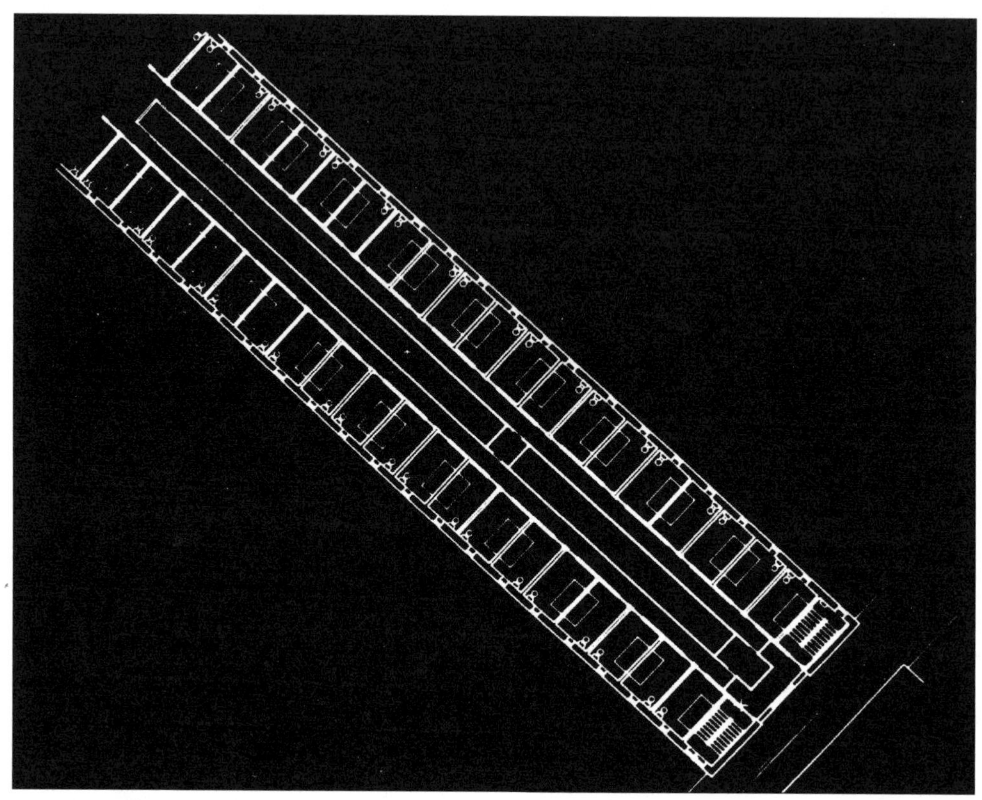

Blake Goble and Robert Ransick, floor plan of Jean Genet's prison, installation from *The Walls Speak: Passages from Queer Places,* Storefront for Art and Architecture, New York, 1994.

not until the great nineteenth-century expansion of public institutions, particularly schools, hospitals, and prisons, that the social engineering of architecture became overt, particularly as related to notions of gender and morality.[5] Paradoxically, this same period fostered greater appreciation of the need for well-protected intimate space, "the home," to safeguard and enhance production. This concern for social programming resulted in houses and apartments designed for married heterosexuals, although other social and erotic configurations would eventually dwell in and reconstruct them. The collusion of architecture in this ruse of heterosexual mythology is now well recognized and has contributed to the aesthetics of camp, kitsch, and drag.

Over the last century, the fields of architecture, interior decorating, landscape architecture, and urban design have often welcomed, or tolerated, the presence of sexual minorities and women. Although the stereotypes of the "fag decorator" and the nineteenth-century lesbian landscape architect are reductive and insulting, the role of sexual minorities in environmental design has indeed been curious. By propping up the mythology of the heteronormative home—the North American house and garden with white picket fence—homosexual designers often have been more complacent than subversive in their design. The gay decorator and designer have often exemplified gay roles in heterosexual societies, though ironically, architecture has had a central role in maintaining "the grid of control"[6] so central to the Victorian patriarchy and to heteronormative life. Deleuze and Guattari's concept of the "smooth" spaces that existed before civilization, contrasted with the "striated" space[7] where hierarchies are more obviously concretized, in part through design, is useful here. For most groups of sexual minorities, designed spaces both inside and outside "the home" remain a minefield of contradictions. As Kenneth Silver has argued in his examination of the culture and aesthetics of gay male bedrooms, "the point at which home ceases to be the container for a family, and yet still shelters a family that is not the name, the symbolic weight of that physical place called home increases exponentially."[8]

Bernard Tschumi has proposed three ways to explore "the impossible relation between architecture and program," including "crossprogramming" (displacing one programmed use with a use programmed for another space), "transprogramming" (combining two programs, regardless of their incompatibilities), and "disprogramming" (allowing two programs to contaminate and destabilize each other, to create a new synthesis).[9] But this theory has been little explored in terms of the design of buildings used and inhabited by sexual minorities—which, after all, includes most buildings.

In this century myriad strategies for undermining heteronormative controls have evolved to confront the narrow programming of domestic spaces.[10] It would be simplistic to envision a queer architecture that simply "deconstructs"[11] or negates heteronormative design. To reduce lesbian and gay establishments and institutions to centres, bars, baths, resorts, and memorials would limit diverse experiences and initiatives. However, certain styles are associated with visibly and invisibly queer

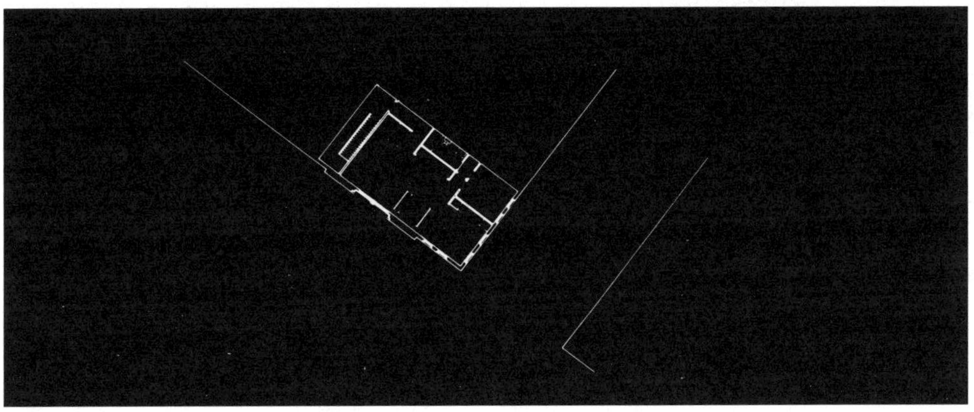

Blake Goble and Robert Ransick, floor plan of David Wojnarowicz's apartment, installation from *The Walls Speak: Passages from Queer Places*, Storefront for Art and Architecture, New York, 1994.

establishments, whether the 1970s bathhouse, now increasingly rare, or overdesigned "pre-decon" and pre-AIDS lofts. Although the relationships between building architectural space and "the dark, private space of sexuality"[12] are important, to emphasize eroticism at the expense of domesticity would limit the full set of queer opportunities both in social relationships and impacts on landscapes and urban space.

In "Having Something to Wear: The Landscape of Identity on Christopher Street," James Polchin examines the increasing commodification of desire in defining gay male streetscapes. He highlights the curious relationships between historicized gay resistance and communality, embodied in 'Stonewall,' and contemporary emphasis on the body and how gay male consumer culture can produce feelings of alienation and set parameters for social life. The sidewalk and facade—part spatial, part commercial, part epistemological—mediate interior fantasies and commercial exchanges.

In "The Meaning at the Wall: Tracing the Gay Bathhouse," Ira Tattelman examines the design of one of the most reviled institutions of homoerotic contact and "promiscuity" in North America. While Tattelman emphasizes pre-AIDS institutions, this lineage of design, part fantasy kitsch and part public institution, continues to thrive and diversify, particularly with the advent of private sex clubs. He traces the roots of gay male bathhouse culture and designs in cultures less influenced by Victorian morals, which built bathhouses to promote hygiene and communality. Many of these bathhouses were queered in the first half of the twentieth century, partly because better plumbing and larger bathrooms in private homes caused heterosexual presence to decline, and partly because of the sexual cultures that were formed as longstanding North American puritanism began to wane. These trends have reshaped the social textures of both queer and nonqueer communities.

Finally, we look at a range of confrontational tactics for asserting minority sexualities in public space. Such acts of courage often occur in the face of state-sanctioned terror or malevolent indifference. This "ghetto-busting" represents the ongoing struggle over public space that continues to have a profound impact on communities. A dimension of this struggle exists within specific populations of sexual minorities themselves. Much of the activism of the now largely defunct ACT UP and Queer Nation has often functioned to challenge complacency and paralysis within gay and lesbian communities, rather than to reconstruct and open up 'the ghetto.'

New forms of activism focus on subversion, critical (re)habitation, and reexperiencing of public space.[13] To implement these goals, three sets of interrelated tactics have emerged over the past decade: choreography, urban design, and public art. The Situationists (of the 1957–72 movement to disrupt the psychogeographies of the city) first recognized that social relationships were being increasingly mediated and structured by imagery. But they were somewhat naïve in their hope of subverting these alienating processes by means of "the spectacle."[14] In contrast, the attempts of the many

David, Los Angeles, King of Hearts, 1983. Photography © 1997 by Mark Chester.

ACT UP chapters to appropriate media attention through spectacle were motivated by the immediate and personal experience of people dying. The Situationists explored and played with spectacle; AIDS activists and queer nationalists used related street tactics because community and individual survival was at stake.

Gaining more public space, even for a short time, is probably one of the most important functions of contemporary activism and of queerscape architecture. Using tactics that unmask the closeted hostility and cultivated indifference of the state, oppositional demonstrations and staged media events have created a kind of "anti-architecture" to make a few points. Much of the cultural iconography of gay liberation, the struggle against AIDS, and queer nationalism has involved the aggressive "reappropriation" of public space, often involving "choreography" including riots, demonstrations, and "zaps." Making space both for resistance and for new communal and erotic relations is at the root of these radical actions.

Sites of public art often become "points of exchange between public and private space."[15] The prototype of contemporary and activist queer public art production was the now defunct group Gran Fury,[16] which was based in New York City. Together with other collectives of gay and lesbian "cultural workers," Gran Fury increased the focus on topics such as AIDS, relied on broader confrontational tactics, and employed bold imagery in making pointed, often emotion-laden statements on public policy.

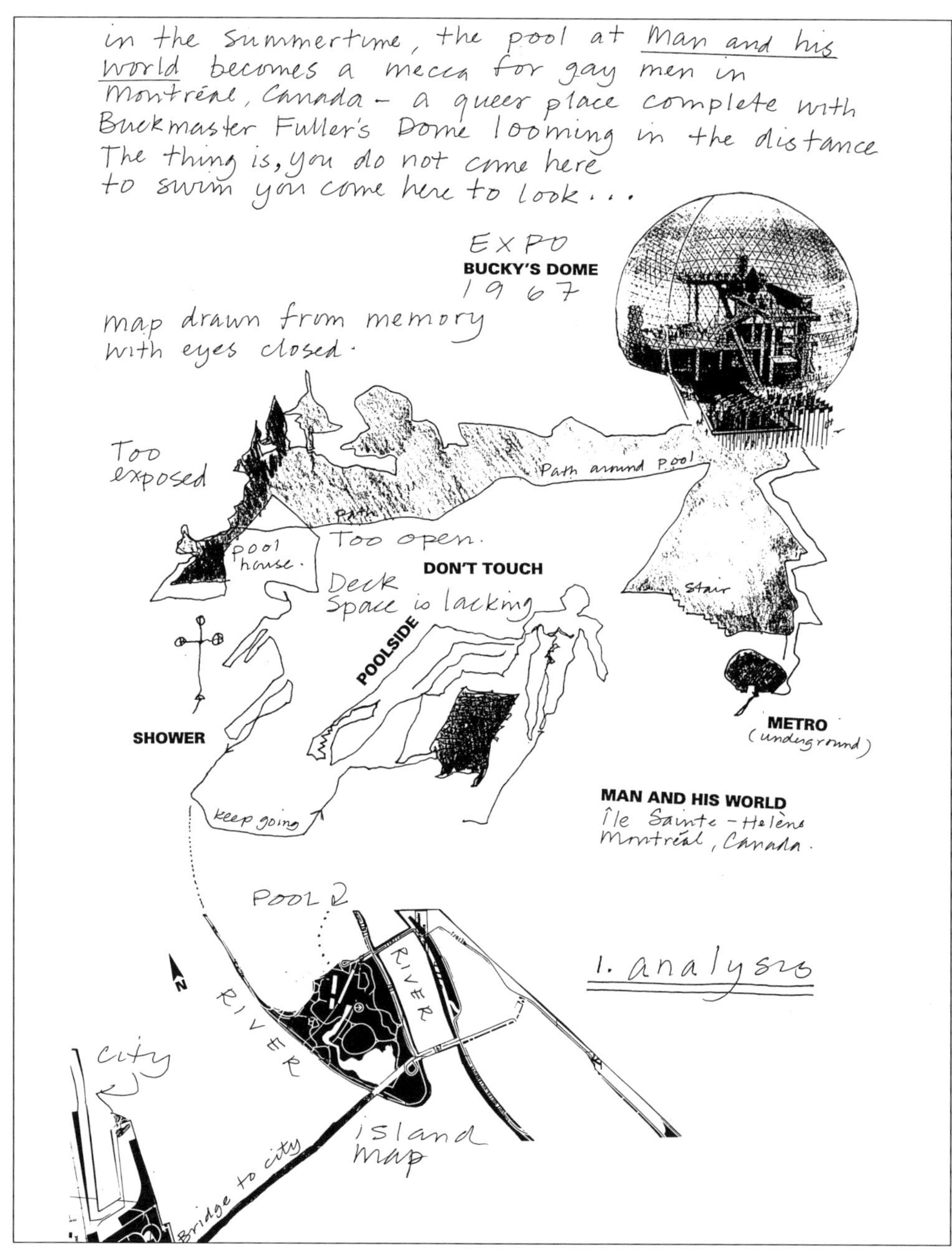

Michael Carroll, *1. Analysis, man and his world,* Montréal Expo '67/Ile Sainte-Helene.

In "This Is about People Dying: The Tactics of Early ACT UP and Lesbian Avengers in New York City," Laraine Sommella interviews Maxine Wolfe on the formation and early tactics of those organizations, which have creatively and often desperately confronted misogyny and homophobia through expanded presence in the public

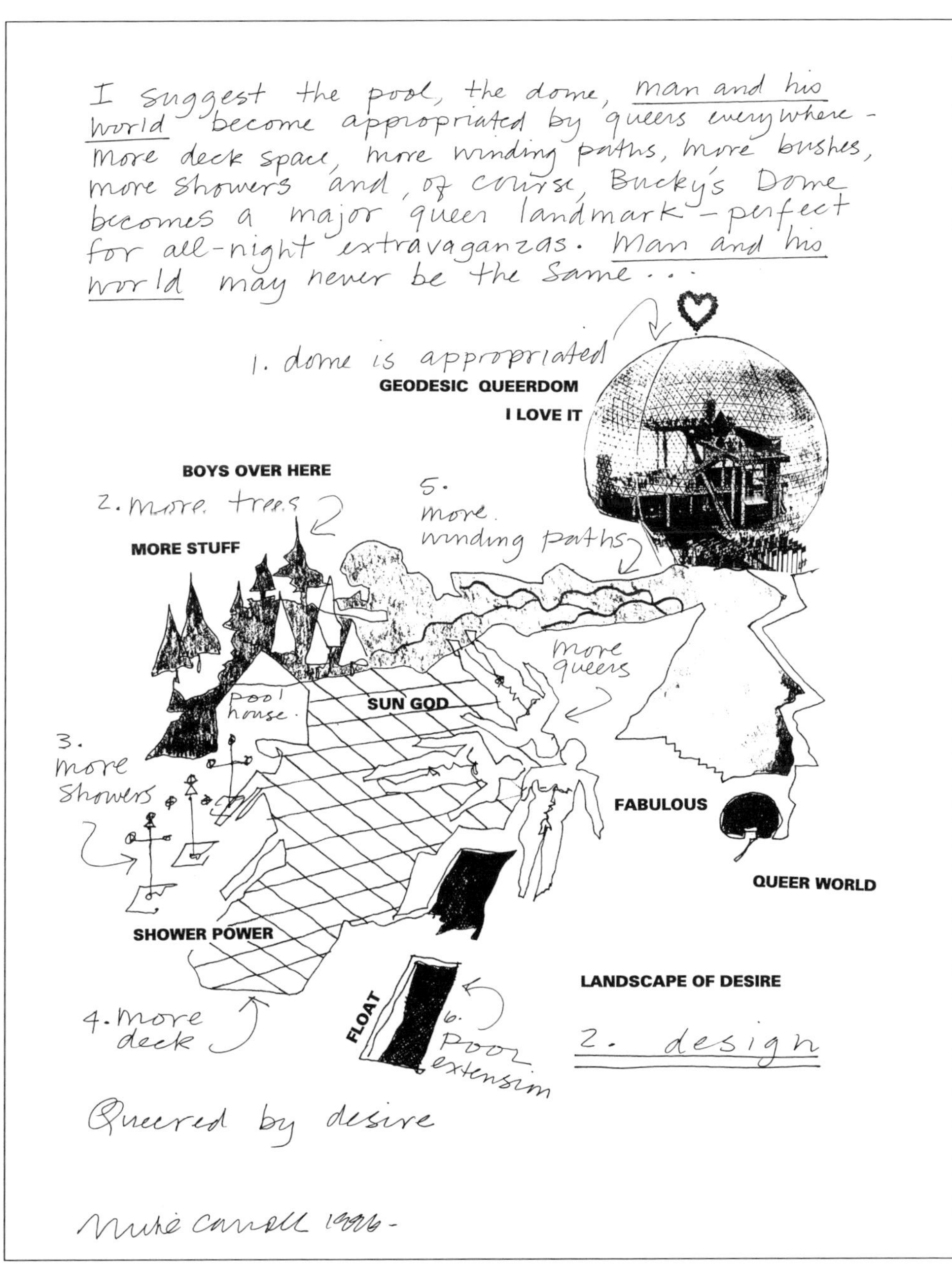

Michael Carroll, *2. Design, landscape of desire,* Montréal Expo '67/Ile Sainte-Helene.

realm. Groups such as Lesbian Avengers have most recently expanded and radicalized notions of "visibility"[17] and have confronted inequities such as enforced invisibility in only partially queered public space. The professional urban designer has not yet found the solutions to such problems. The field of environmental design is only slowly considering the implications of social science and cultural studies in the shaping of public space.

The tactics described in "Do You Love the Dyke in Your Face?" by Carrie Moyer and Dyke Action Machine! use lesbian public art to confront patriarchal and heteronormative violence, intimidation, and erasure. And in this struggle, humour, parody, and sarcasm make very effective weapons.

The essays in this section reveal two goals that must be accomplished before queerscape architectures can at last fully develop and flourish. First, the heteronormative currents that have shaped both indoor and outdoor space must be unmasked and challenged. Second, this challenge must be brought into the public arena through well-planned attention-getting activism and other means of increasing visibility, such as public art. Raising awareness of homophobia, discrimination, and complacency can pave the way for changes in planning and design, policy, and attitudes that have, up to this point, greatly limited queer self-expression, community building, and use of space.

Toronto AIDS Memorial, 1995.

Having Something to Wear: The Landscape of Identity on Christopher Street

James Polchin

I stand at the corner of Christopher Street and Seventh Avenue in New York City loading my camera, when an older man approaches and asks, "Would you like me to take your picture?" I smile and say, "No, actually I'm taking pictures of other people along the street." We talk a bit and I tell him about the project I am doing on Christopher Street, to which he replies, "I have a project we could both work on and you could make some money off of it." I know what is happening. I smile, laugh, and say no thanks. He asks with a surprised tone, "You've never hustled before?" I say no. He says, "Really?" Then he starts to talk about the decline of America and how the whole country is going to hell with all these immigrants and soon there will just be chaos. I leave him standing on the corner.

I start with this story because it speaks volumes about how place and social relations play out within urban landscapes. I am interested in the types of identities that places produce and in the types of memories that rise up around places, sites, and streets. I am also interested in how the urban culture of Christopher Street provides a space where collective memory and individual activities emerge from the commercial and social life of the street. My encounter with the aging man brought together the possibilities of both commercial and sexual transactions, of both being and being a part of the street's landscape. The street corner provided the stage for a buyer and a seller, two queers making a private connection in the public realm. My body for his money; two white queers on Christopher Street. I ask myself: How is it that this street could produce this exchange between us? What is it about this street, its structure and character, that allows certain social interaction? And how is it that Christopher Street not only produces types of experiences but also history, memory, and symbols of queer resistance? Such concerns led me to other questions about Christopher Street, questions that brought both queer political and social identity together with commercial culture. I outline a way of conceptualizing the relationship between the urban landscape and the emergence of queer political and social identity. While some historians have documented the development of gay and lesbian communities in large and small cities, my task here is to explore ways in which gay communities have affected the urban culture: configuring a vision of queerness through a mediation between commercial culture and urban geography.

Billboards targetting gay men on Christopher Street.

Edmund White ends his 1987 novel, *The Beautiful Room is Empty,* on June 27, 1969, the night drag queens and other queers protested the police raid on the Stonewall Inn, located near Seventh Avenue on Christopher Street. "The night was hot," writes White,

> We gay guys had taken over all of Christopher Street; even the shops were gay. Although the bars were owned by the Mafia, we somehow thought of them as ours. Just as this street, this one street in a city of ten thousand streets, felt like ours.[1]

For White's story of Stonewall, the power and importance of the landscape of Christopher Street is intimately connected with the eventual political and social identities that emerged in the post-Stonewall years. The claiming of a street by gay men becomes a claim on a sense of self, the projection of an identity within the public space of urban culture. The novel ends with a brief narrative of Stonewall's significance that resonates within the collective memory of gay men and lesbians today, reenacted each year through the performance of Pride Parades.

More importantly, the ending of *The Beautiful Room is Empty* presents a gay community based on men's activities in the public realm and whose sense of self is configured through street life, commercial culture, and protest. The claiming of an urban space, the formation of a community, provides a means for creating a vision of identity, a vision that, like most identities in the twentieth-century United States, relies on commercial culture. Today, gay and lesbian identity on Christopher Street is such a highly marketable product that the street increasingly reflects an almost themed environment for tourism. For the gay and lesbian tourist, Christopher Street produces a historical sense of sexual liberation within a contemporary landscape that mixes queerness with social and consumer spaces. The street becomes a space where production and consumption of gay identity and gay community is visualized and made possible on many levels. The highly masculinized aesthetics that dominate the street's commercial and social milieux produce a landscape that reflects male desires.

If Christopher Street is a queer space, which I believe it to be, such queerness emerges from the ways the male body is displayed, performed, desired, and consumed within the street scenes, whether commercial or social.[2] The sidewalks provide spaces to mediate between these two realms and suggest the larger mediation that gay and lesbian identities have maintained within society. Like the experience of many immigrant groups in the United States, whose process of acculturation was manifested through a participation within consumer culture, gay and lesbian identities emerge, in part, through an intersection between social and consumer realms. I focus here on the ways Christopher Street functions as a space of mediation, suggesting the limitations the street's social and commercial landscapes produce, as well as the potential of such landscapes in the formation of queer political and community life. I slice out a segment of Christopher Street, what I consider the street's "shopping district" between Sixth Avenue on the east and Hudson Street on the west. This section best reflects the street's social and commercial dynamics.

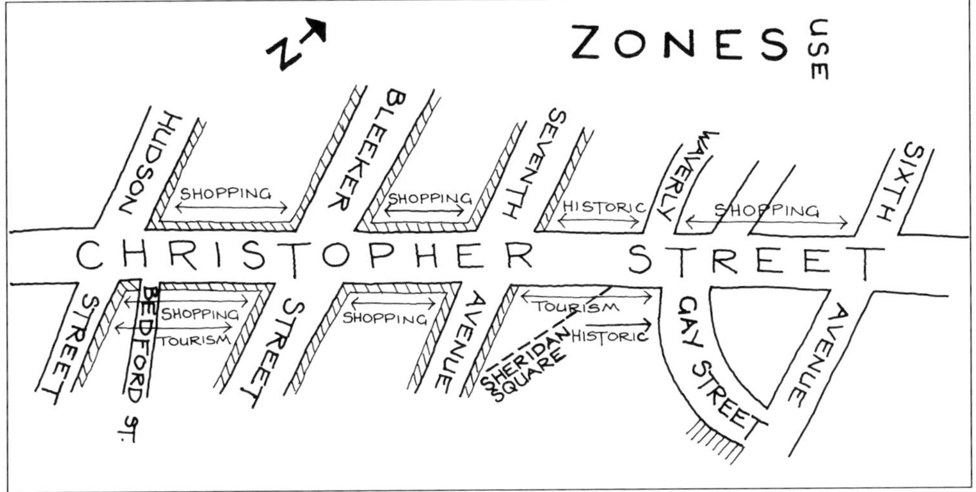

Map by James Polchin and Gordon Brent Ingram.

"Success on this street is merchandising, merchandising, merchandising," said one store owner, who changes his window displays frequently.[3] The narrow sidewalks of Christopher Street keep shoppers close to the store windows, creating narrow spaces between the commercial interiors and public street life. Walking along the street produces a historical sense of place through nineteenth-century tenement architecture that frames the street experience. The working-class history of the area is written on these buildings and weighs down upon the commercial life that dominates the space today.[4] On the narrow sidewalks, the storefronts dominate the vista of the street with images of eroticized masculinized male bodies or highly refined merchandise. The large windows reflect your image in the glass—you see yourself in the window, in the store. As William Leach suggests, "the pictures behind the glass enticed the viewer. The result was a mingling of refusal and desire that must have greatly intensified desire."[5]

In this sense Christopher Street is a shopping street in a city known for such avenues of consumption. The street participates in the city's larger social exchanges between production and consumption, between desire and economics. But here the terms of desire center on the male body. In a culture that consistently regulates the behavior of the queer body, Christopher Street provides a space where queer sexuality can be viewed, displayed, expressed, and consumed. The represented bodies are not the Foucaultian idea of the "docile bodies," ones which under the weight of social discipline are devoid of power, but rather ones that exhibit a physical eroticized strength where the body pushes beyond the clothes.[6] However idealized these bodies may be, they suggest a certain transgression against the social and political power that attempts to contain queer sexuality.

The Leatherman's window display constantly re-creates the gay male leather aesthetic. The store constructs a sense of masculinity through leather accoutrements and clothing, and it deconstructs the very stability of such masculinity. The window presents the intersection of commodity and identity. Almost anyone could enter the doorway to the side of the window, buy the leather, and construct a similar self, just as easily as one could buy some glass lamps across the street to adorn a living room in a certain style. Hence the plastic male bodies in the storefronts, while highly masculinized, present a possibility that can be changed and altered through the process of consumption. Such possibility allows an active gay consumer to construct himself as he desires, providing for a certain agency that is of course dependent upon economic viability. Ironically, within this notion of possibility, images of the male body become such constructed variations of gay sexual aesthetics that, while everything appears highly masculine, the representation of masculinity in general becomes suspect. The exaggeration of hypermasculinized bodies within the commercial and social landscape of the street exposes the instability of cultural expectations surrounding bodies, gender, and desire—expectations that attempt to organize identity upon the body.

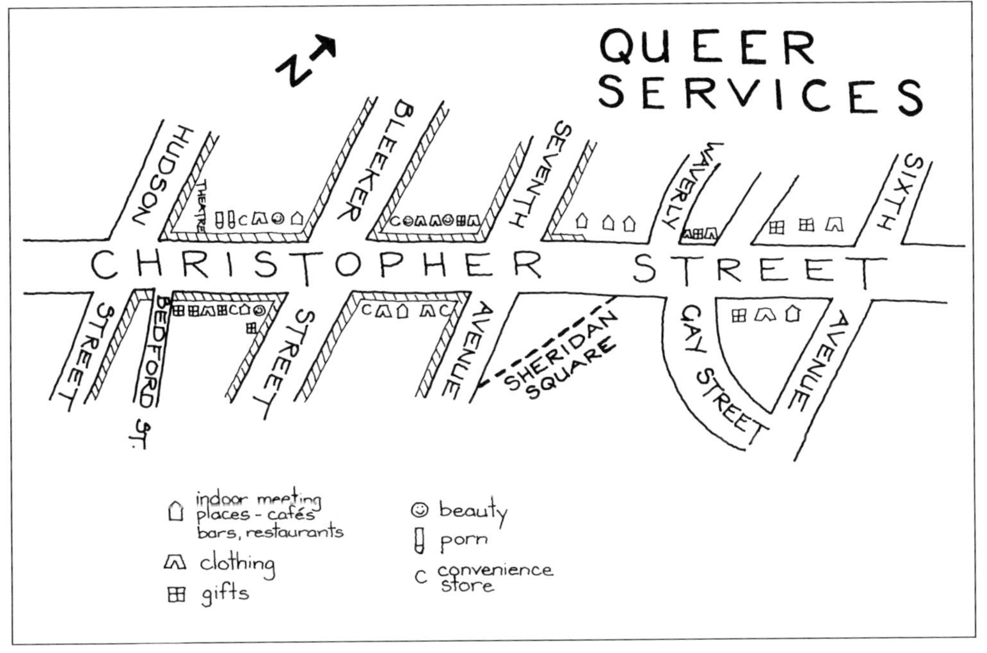

Map by James Polchin and Gordon Brent Ingram.

To continue this point, consider the gay male video store between Bleecker Street and Seventh Avenue. Here gay erotic film stars display themselves, some almost nude and others dressed in officer, cadet, or police attire. The product is the body and visual representations of gay male sexual experiences, emphasizing the voyeurism inherent in the shopping experience, on this street and other retail streets in the city. The male bodies underscore the larger dynamic of the street—a site where the activity of shopping is a process of visual desire. The models stare out at you and display themselves for what they are. As John Berger has noted, "To be naked is to be oneself. To be nude is to be seen naked by others and yet not recognized for oneself. To be naked is to be without disguise. Nudity [on the other hand] is a form of dress."[7] Thus the dressed male nude reflects a form of masculinity, a construction of desire that merges with other images and plays with the social expectations of the male body. This window creates a certain interest and desire by representing "dressed nudes" in much the same way as the other storefronts represent their products.

The representation of the body becomes central to the political and social development of queer protest. The pre-Stonewall raids pushed the queer bodies from the darkened bars onto the street, making the body visible for humiliation. The queer body made public produced anxieties about gender roles and, more importantly, frustration over social relations in public spaces. The call for visibility is a call to be public. This relationship between the queer body and public spaces is the basis for the formation of a collective memory within the contemporary gay and lesbian movement. The performance of the annual Pride Parade enacts and reenacts a political expression of visibility within the public realm, and asserts a sense of self by locating the queer body within a particular social environment—namely, the street. Such visibility reacts against the confined space of the "closet," which has been perhaps the most compelling metaphor for visibility and identity within gay and lesbian narratives in the past twenty-five years. The closet symbolizes the space of denial, darkness, confinement. To come out depends upon emerging from the spatial structures of the closet and into the public, onto the street. Therefore the process of attaining an authentic gay identity relies on a movement from one space to another—from the closet to the street.

In an angry *New York Times* letter to the editor, a writer bemoans that the 1993 Gay Pride Parade was "really nothing more than a rather offensive display of flesh . . . Christopher Street and gay bars thrust out for the masses to choke on."[8] This critic's disdain for the body made public unwittingly suggests the essence of producing queer spaces: the act of visibility. Queer space cannot be located within a particular place because it does not necessarily represent defined boundaries, but rather it exists through a presentation of queer bodies and desires. In this sense, Christopher Street projects a desire in which male bodies perform in the street and the storefronts. Queerness here emerges along narrow spaces in social life. To talk about queer identity is to talk about forms in which the body can reconsider itself within the cultural codes of gender and

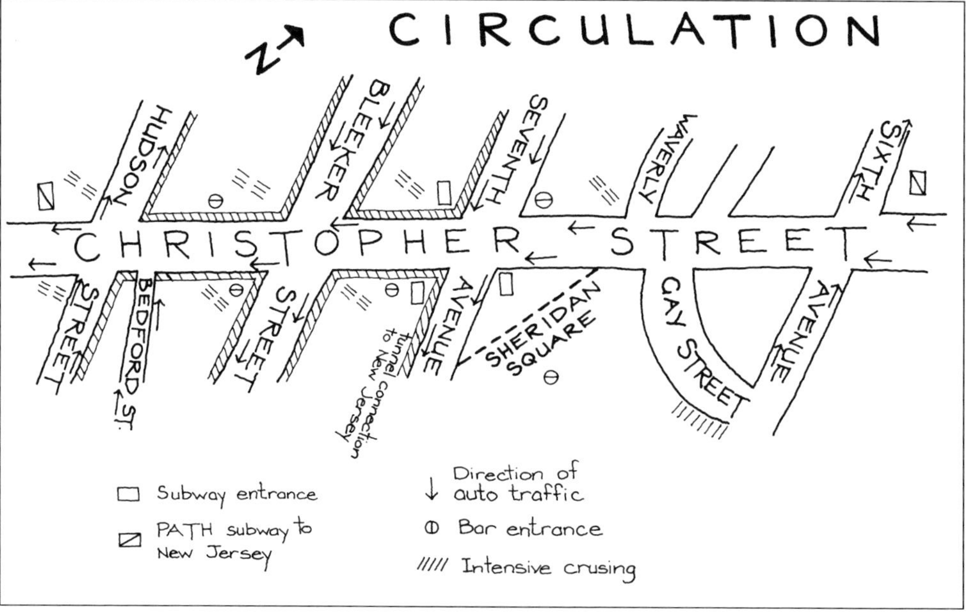

Map by James Polchin and Gordon Brent Ingram.

sexuality—reconsiderations made possible in the spatial realm between social relations and commercial structures. What I am suggesting is that queer communities have emerged in the twentieth century amidst the rapid development of the urban landscape and, with it, the cosmopolitan character of commercial culture.

John D'Emilio, in his influential essay "Capitalism and Gay Identity," suggests that the development of industrial capitalism fostered economic independence from the structures of the family in the late nineteenth century. The emergence of a free-wage labor system, according to D'Emilio, had allowed large numbers of men and women to form communities and social and political subjectivities outside familial ties. The changes in economic structures gave men and women opportunities for independent employment and lifestyles. Such independence provided a means of experiencing and expressing erotic lives outside of the social norms based on familial responsibilities.[9] To push D'Emilio's idea further, I want to suggest that not only the means of free-wage labor but also the rise of consumerism, the ability to create and re-create oneself, has played a significant role in the development of gay communities within the urban landscape. In other words, the emergence of industrial capitalism, with its focus on mass production, created the marketplaces of consumption, and therefore both components—free-wage labor and consumerism—have been significant to the development of a type of gay community over the past several decades in the United States. Christopher Street thus represents an aspect of queer identity that has emerged from the confluence of urban life, queer communities, and commercial culture over the past century. As Chauncey notes, in the interwar period the Village, like Harlem, became a type of liminal space where visitors were encouraged to disregard some of the social injunctions that normally constrained their behavior—behavior that in other settings, particularly their own neighborhoods, they might consider objectionable. In this sense, "The dance halls, clubs, bars, and other commercial spaces were important sites where freedoms from sex and gender codes were enabled.[10]

Admittedly, there are many "invisible" bodies on Christopher Street. The lesbian body and bodies of color only nominally appear in the storefront aesthetics and the heart of the street life. Christopher Street, with its specialty stores and gay bars, reflects the economic strength of gay men. Though Manuel Castells has suggested that "When gay men try to liberate themselves from cultural and sexual oppression, they need a physical space from which to strike out,"[11] the ability to stake a claim over land relies on economic factors as well. Creating a landscape for sexual or political purposes requires, like all landscapes, a certain amount of capital. As Sy Adler and Johanna Breener contend, "To take over urban space requires also the control of residential and business property."[12] Christopher Street, then, reflects the economic strength of a certain strata of the gay male community. "This is a gay mecca," claims one store owner. "Sooner or later every gay man in America will pass in front of my store."[13] As both owner and consumer, the lesbian body and bodies of color recede into the background of the economic landscape of the street.

On the margins of the street at night, on the fringe of the street's shopping district, you will find people like Wade Henley, a twenty-one-year-old resident of Harlem. "We can't really hang out on the corner where we live, so we come here," says Henley. "This is where I feel comfortable."[14]

On this street the place of such individuals, is outside the shops and bars, outside the economic foundations of the street. In this way, the street reflects a larger national displacement of individuals from the marketplace. Yet Henley and others come to Christopher Street to feel comfortable—to find a place, a site, where experience and desire can be expressed and realized, as opposed to the communities and streets where they live. And in this sense Christopher Street produces a symbolic place of queer identity—a place where the body and its desires can exist, resist, and be comfortable in public. The raid on the Stonewall Inn was just as much an attack against a bar as it was an attempt to reconfigure the social landscape of Christopher Street. Such attempts to reshape the street produce the political symbolism that the street maintains in the collective memory of gays and lesbians. To participate in the lived experience within the narrow sidewalks is to mediate between the social and the commercial.

In June the street swells with queer tourists taking photos and buying T-shirts and other body attire that proclaims a sexual identity. In the larger sense, the street is a symbol that reflects a historical narrative of ownership over one's sense of self—one's body—on the street. The street is imagined, re-created, and consumed through

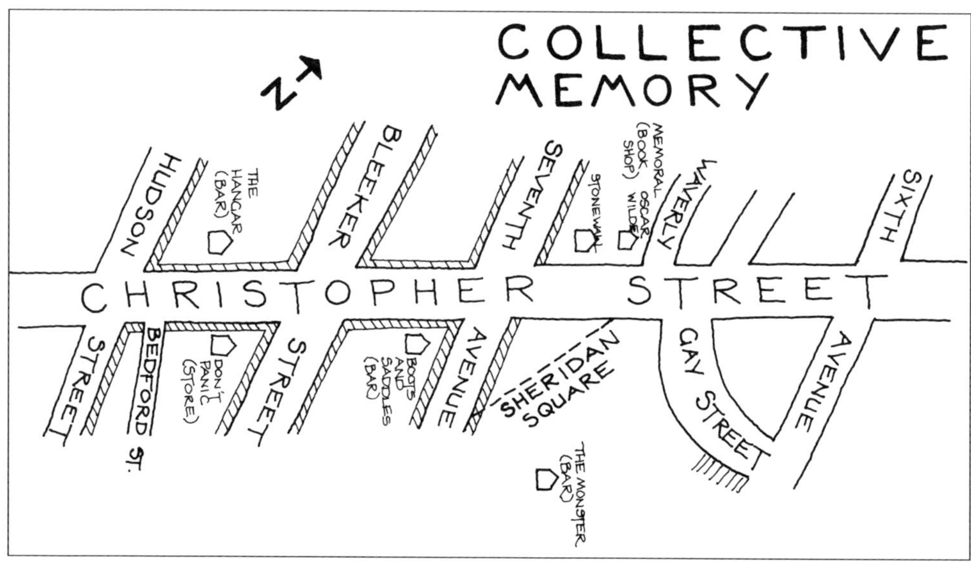

Map by James Polchin and Gordon Brent Ingram.

The consumer landscape of Christopher Street.

the narratives of collective identity. It functions as a historical site, grounded on spectacle and consumption, and it provides a sense of being part of history through the experience of place.[15] The politics of Christopher Street emerge through the complexities of representation and urban form. The intersections between commercial interests and personal identity, between consuming and producing, are realized within the street's urban landscape. Along the narrow spaces of the sidewalk, one experiences the complexities of identity and desire, positioned between the fluid social relations in the public realm and the urban form of commercial storefronts. Within such spaces, both real and imagined, a certain expression of desire is attempted.

The points I want to conclude with are more beginnings than endings. How can we begin to conceptualize the role that queer communities have played in affecting the character of the urban landscapes? More importantly, what connections can be drawn between the commercial culture and queer identity in the twentieth century? What is the relationship between sexual expression and commercial desires? Ultimately, I want to question the current popular idea that "gay ghettoes" are spaces of limitations and suggest the larger significance of such spaces in the production of urban social and commercial life. Any consideration of queer identity within the urban landscape of such places as Greenwich Village or the Castro needs to engage with the development of commercial culture—a development that has reshaped the contours of social life in the United States over the past one hundred years. And finally, I want to suggest that urban gay and lesbian communities represent spaces of mediation between social life and commercial life and, as such, play integral parts in forming and reforming American cultural identies.

The Meaning at the Wall: Tracing the Gay Bathhouse[1]

Ira Tattelman

> The ideal conditions of the bathhouse:
>
> 1. Include features that protect the participant.
> 2. Provide ample access to good sexual partners and setting at a reasonable cost.
> 3. Promote a known, shared, and organized reality within the opportunity structure.
> 4. Bound the experience.
> 5. Include a congenial atmosphere.
> 6. Include physical settings that promote relaxation and convenience.
>
> —Weinberg, 1979, 166

In this discussion of "interior" queer space, I explore the phenomenon of the gay bathhouse—especially in the United States just before and, now in, the age of AIDS. Everyone seems to remember something about the baths, but this collective memory has been influenced by many readings and misreadings. My intention is to understand how bathhouses, as gathering spaces, became places for overt sexuality. As their popularity grew, the social organization inside the baths began to influence the organization of gay men in the city. When many city governments closed gay baths in the mid-1980s, the bathhouse became disreputable, and the gay men who inhabited them were displaced. By understanding the behaviors, practices, and situations within the baths, associations outside the baths can be interpreted.

I am interested in the proliferation of gay male bathhouses in the 1970s and early 1980s. My area of research concentrates on urban North America, most frequently New York City. By tracing the development of baths from ethnic enclaves to gay male spaces, one can understand the important function that gay baths served as social institutions that allowed for casual encounters, communication with like-minded individuals and sensual, as well as sexual, intercourse. While the baths offered space for both individual activities and collective encounters, they also fostered an environment of anonymity. As a consequence, patrons felt safe exhibiting a broad range of behaviors that the world outside the baths was less likely to tolerate.

Tracing the Gay Bathhouse

Bathhouses have long been places where shared activities occur. In Greek, Roman, Islamic, Japanese, Finnish, and Turkish cultures (among others), they have acted as

James Everard's Russian and Turkish Baths—1893 Marketing Brochure. Courtesy of a private collection.

spaces for gathering, repose, and communal, ritual, and physical stimulation. As a building type, they have historically been adaptable to the changing communities that used them; they are open to the layering of activity and interpretation.

New York, as a city of immigrant groups, has a unique bathhouse history because of its built-in constituency. Public bathhouses gained popularity at the beginning of this century (as they did in other cities), but only for a brief period of time. A change in health standards and economics motivated landlords and builders to bring bathing functions into the private homes of all classes. By mid-century, the public baths had closed or were renovated for other uses.

Private baths developed as commercial ventures. Some developed as an urban counterpart to the country club, a private space for gentlemen to gather. The Everard Baths, for instance, were located on New York's 28th Street, easily accessible from big hotels and the main arteries of travel. Other bathhouses developed into places where the surrounding ethnic communities gathered, familiar spots for washing, relaxation, and recreation.

Through the years, many of the baths began to attract and cater to homosexuals. In time, some began to serve homosexuals exclusively. In *Gay New York,* George Chauncey writes:

> The safest, most enduring, and one of the most affirmative of the settings in which gay men gathered in the first half of the twentieth century was the baths. . . . Gay bathhouses had appeared in New York by the turn of the century and by World War I several of them had become institutions in the city, their addresses and distinctive social and sexual character known to almost every gay New Yorker and to many gay Europeans as well. (1994, 207)

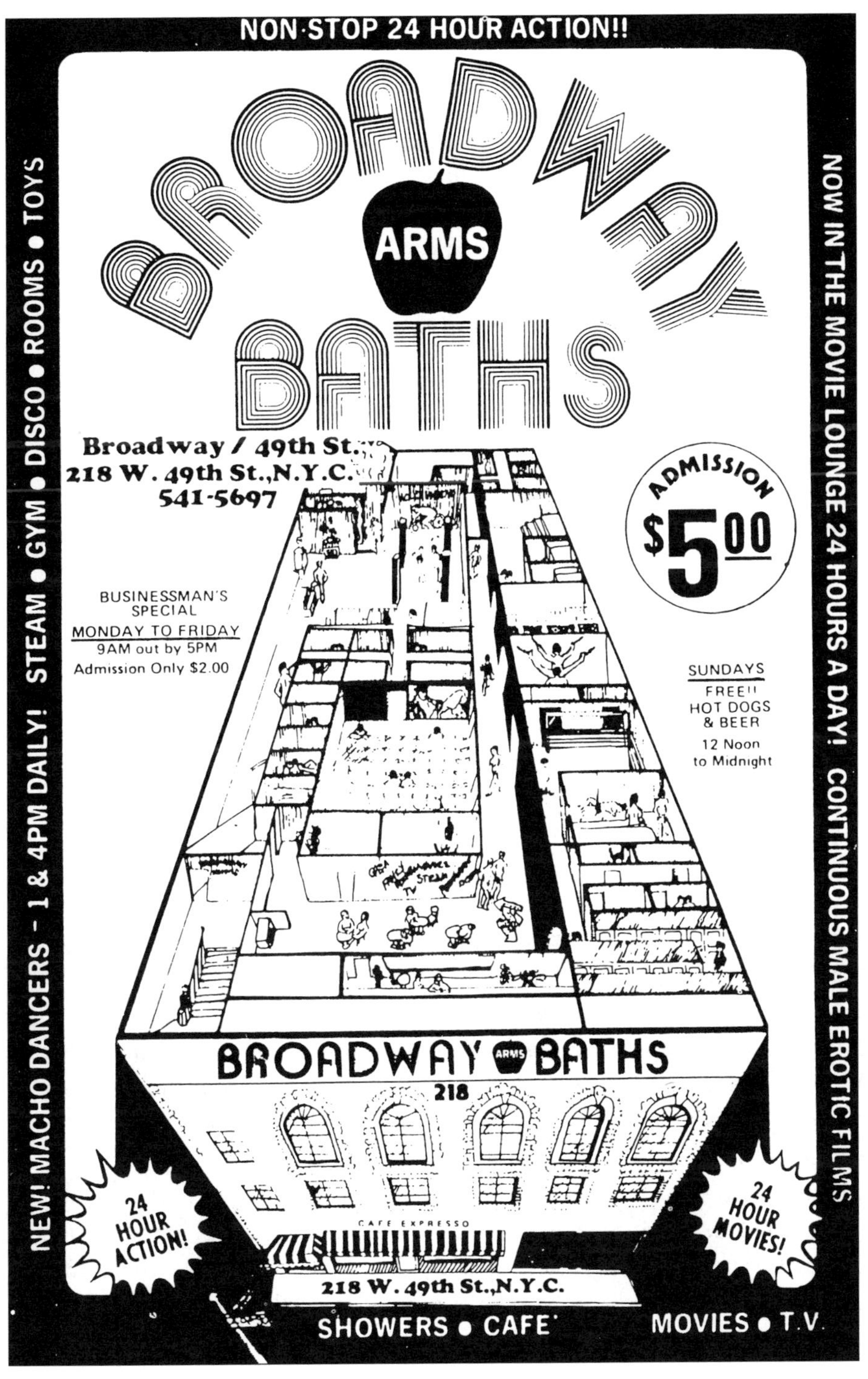

Advertisement for The Broadway Arms Baths. Courtesy of a private collection.

Gay men had always been attracted to the baths, spaces of male bonding and homoerotic undertones. While a gay presence had been evident for many years, the bathhouses developed into primary sites for gay male affiliation.

By the 1970s the bathhouse became a magnetic force for many because they perceived the baths to be without limits or prohibition. The strategy of the bathhouse was to prioritize sex over all else; in this place of congregation, any fantasy had the possibility of being played out. This exploration opened up new relations between men; the authority of a straight society was displaced. Instead the authority of desire was brought forward and, with it, the proposition of repetition and multiplicity. Everyone was here together, and everyone seemed willing to participate.

While sexual relations may have been the main reason people went to the baths, not everyone took advantage of the situation. There were other ways to participate in one of the few spaces that openly catered to gays. For some the goal of social contact and proximity was enough. Conversations with strangers or acquaintances, while kept to a minimum, included pleasantries, tourist tips, or campy humor; occasionally, long-term relationships developed. In this enclosed space, safe from homophobic attacks, community and identification flourished.

The principle of the bathhouse was that you brought nothing inside with you. Ideally the bathhouse tried to erase the boundaries that divide people; clothing was removed, and issues of class were left at the lockers. By stripping bare, new experiences became possible. When you left, you took those things you had learned from participating in the bathhouse, by communicating with your body, back out into the world. While institutions such as bars, discos, churches, publications, theaters, and professional associations supported the development of a "gay identity," the bathhouse became the evidence of this new freedom and an assertion of the right to be.

The success of this "world of pleasure" may have resulted from the fact that the bathhouse was virtually invisible to those who did not support its practices. That situation began to change, however, with the discovery of HIV and the government's reaction to AIDS. The existence of bathhouses and press coverage of them made the baths mythic. HIV was transmitted through some of the sexual activities that took place in the bathhouse, and AIDS as a condition formed outside the bathhouse was used to interrupt the activities within the bathhouse.

After the closure of the baths, displacements occurred. Some of the men who might have found sexual satisfaction in the bathhouse now found sex in more public locations, such as bathrooms and parks. These sites are often dangerous; men become prey to attackers and have no access to safe-sex items unless they bring them. While danger and fear can be exciting, the vulnerability of gay men in public space can also be emotionally debilitating.

The last ten years have also seen an increased visibility in gay and lesbian institutions. Unfortunately, part of their bid for acceptance resulted from marginalizing the

Patrick Angus, *A Corridor in the Baths,* from *Strip Show: Paintings by Patrick Angus.* Reproduction © Douglas Blair Turnbaugh. Courtesy of the Estate of Patrick Angus.

display of sexuality within the community. The response to the radical right's use of sexualized images in antigay messages has been to hide or suppress our differences rather than express them.

Today, out of nostalgia, the possibility of profit, and the desire to reclaim sexual expression, a variety of sex clubs and sex parties have appeared to fill the gap left by the disappearance of bathhouses. Sex clubs are often located in large open warehouses with few amenities. Sex parties often occur in rented spaces or in people's apartments. Backrooms, darkrooms, and jack-off rooms have also been reintroduced to bars and discos in major cities. The ideals of these spaces of occupation are familiar:

> As bodies of desire, individuals forfeit their subjective selves and are reconstituted as parts of a collective assemblage in which personal identities are exchanged for anonymous positions within a multiplicity of desiring bodies.
>
> —(Ricco 1994–95, 28)

Increasingly popular among younger queers who never experienced the bathhouse in its heyday, these sex spaces represent a hipper alternative to the stigmatized baths. Mark Thompson, member of Black Leather Wings, a group that seeks to blend radical sexuality with spiritual ritual, summarized one of the current movements:

> I am after the notion of discovering something finer in all this—sex as a path toward knowing, toward manhood, individualization, initiation. I shudder to think that we would be re-creating the activity of the 1970s in a 1990s package.
>
> —(Sadownick 1993, 26)

While these spaces represent a new interest in sexual exploration, they are not as diverse and open as bathhouses; most people remain clothed and exhibit more personal boundaries. There is a lot of groping but far less sexual exchange. Designed for "getting off," the sex clubs of the 1990s offer fewer possibilities for intimacy and sensuality.

The Public Bath[2]

> Bathhouses and public showers were plentiful in major urban centers during a period when people could not afford private washing facilities. Although they were not, by and large, the gay sexual institutions of the pre-AIDS 1970s and 1980s, a few baths in New York City were notorious as meeting places for sex.
>
> —(J. Weinberg 1993, 19)

The public bath movement developed out of a desire to upgrade the city standards of public health and morality. Reformers believed that a reciprocal relationship existed between character and clean environment. W. L. Ross, manager of Philadelphia's Gaskill Street Baths, stated, "The object is not only to promote bathing facilities, but to elevate taste and morals" (Glassberg 1979, 9). Like the museums, libraries, and parks that were also developed at the turn of the century, the baths were built to embody and promote "Victorian" propriety to the working class and immigrants. Proponents hoped they could Americanize these people by teaching them mainstream values that would enhance their lives. They also hoped to create a community center, with the respectable bathhouse as a replacement for the vice-laden bar.

While most middle- and upper-class apartments had bathtubs, few tenements were equipped with one. The first successful indoor public bathhouse opened in New York City on the Lower East Side in 1891. An inscription above the doorway proclaimed, "Cleanliness is Next to Godliness." By 1902 there was one municipal bath open year-round, fifteen floating baths that were open during the summer, and several smaller ones under the sponsorship of private organizations. By 1912 no less than twelve municipal baths were in operation year-round. The inclusion of bathtubs in all new tenements, however, slowed the public bath movement. By 1934 only 11 percent of the apartments in New York City were without baths and showers, and most public baths had closed their doors. The bathhouse building was designed to contrast with neighboring tenements. It generally had a light colored facade, which separated it from the worn and dark surroundings. Compared to other public buildings, however, the plain exterior of the baths was deliberately modest. Dr. Baruch of the New York Association for Improving the Condition of the Poor recommended quiet styling in 1907 "so as not to repel the poor by its architectural pretensions" (Glassberg 1979, 14). The interiors of the small buildings were designed for speed and sanitation. The shower and dressing chambers were divided by partitions and screens. Men were kept separate from women, not only in the baths but also in the waiting rooms and lobbies.

The baths were scattered throughout the city to cater to individual neighborhoods. This not only brought baths directly to the people, but insured that different ethnic, racial, and class groups would not mix. Homosexuals, however, are not physically identifiable nor did they congregate in one neighborhood. Their "difference" could be masked and then unveiled to specific people at certain times.

The bathhouses were open to a broad range of social interaction. Several of the baths in New York "could not be utilized, then and there, for homosexual practicalities. They were merely establishments for anatomic inspections" (Katz 1983, 330). After meeting in these public spaces, spaces appropriated by homosexuals for a period of time, men often made appointments to see each other in more private locations.

The Russian and Turkish Baths

The Russian and Turkish baths used the principle that supplying heat to the surface of the body had hygienic, remedial, and curative powers. Food, conversation, games, and sometimes sexual pleasure became part of the bathhouse experience. Because users spent long hours at the baths, the owners needed to promote a sense of ease for their patrons. The sites were easily located and accessible, and the layout and program offered efficiency, comfort, and cleanliness.

The bathhouse also relied on its physical setting; the artistry of the space had commercial value. Decorations and fittings, while rarely extravagant, were desirable and necessary features. From glazed tiles, painted murals, and mosaic floors to stained glass domes, ornamental wooden partitions, and brass waterspouts, the owners paid attention to spatial design and social arrangement by creating the illusion of foreign luxury. A 1893 marketing brochure for the Everard Baths reads:

> The most complete and beautiful bathing establishment in the world was opened to the public on May 3d, 1888 . . . at a cost of over $160,000. Nothing was left undone to render it the most complete and elegant institution of its kind.
>
> —(Moses Ackerley, 1893)

Bathhouses offered a sense of historical continuity to many of the people who used them. They also established a sense of solidarity and pride within the communities where they were located. The features and advantages of these places included the chance to see other men without clothes; the attention of attendants for scrubbing, massaging, and drying; and the physical grooming provided by chiropodists, manicurists, or barbers. The baths also offered an intensity and timeliness that could be found in few other locations.

The Gay Bathhouse

> Gay patronage and sexual activity were concentrated at two kinds of baths: baths visited by straight as well as gay men, but whose management tolerated limited homosexual activity, and baths that catered to gay men by excluding nonhomosexual patrons and creating an environment in which homosexual activity was encouraged and safeguarded.
>
> —(Chauncey 1994, 209)

Gay baths have a long history in New York. In the 1950s the Penn Post Baths accommodated the rush-hour traffic near the train station. In the early 1970s the Continental Baths in the Ansonia Hotel offered a swimming pool, saunas, orgy rooms, and Bette Midler. The Mount Morris Baths, located in Harlem since 1927, was one of the few places where black gay men could connect with other men.

The St. Marks Baths, on the Lower East Side in Manhattan, provides a good example of the gradual change in patrons. Built in 1913 as the St. Marks Russian and Turkish Baths, the establishment catered to businessmen in the area. As businesses began to move, the baths became popular with neighborhood residents. In the 1950s it served older Jewish men during the day and gay men at night. In the 1960s it became exclusively gay, but was considered unclean and uninviting. Bought and refurbished by Bruce Mailman in 1979, the baths were redesigned for gay sexual expression in all its variety. In 1985 the bathhouse was closed by the city, due to the AIDS crisis. The building has been boarded up ever since.

> At its peak, the St. Marks Baths was the hotbed of a revolution in public sex that crystallized for many homosexual men the very essence of what it meant to be gay in America in the late 1970s and early 1980s.
>
> —(Peters 1994, 80)

In 1982, prior to the discovery of HIV, there were at least 160 homosexual baths located in most major cities.[3] Additional spaces, although sometimes called baths, operated without the wet areas of saunas, hot tubs, or steam rooms that first gave bathhouses their name. In 1994 a similar listing in *Steam* magazine had a total of sixty-one baths.[4] This figure does not include the sex clubs and sex parties that came into being during the late 1980s. *Steam* lists a total of seventy-five places. (*Steam* 1994, 118–20.)

In its time the bathhouse offered gay men the safety and freedom within which to explore a multiple set of interrelationships. While the interactions were social as well as sexual, sensual pleasure was predominant, relying less on the orgasm and more on the multiplicity of senses, the erotic potential of the whole body, and the promise that almost any fantasy could be fulfilled. As such, the bathhouse became a place of difference. Assumptions and beliefs were questioned by the disparate mix one could find and the possibilities of unrestricted sexual activity.

> The primary function of the establishment is to provide a place, free from harassment, where gay men can meet and fulfill any and all sexual urges, provided, of course, that they can find compliant partners.
>
> —(Brook 1985, 96)

The practice of taking risks, of experimenting, sustained the baths. One participated in activities that offered a variety of connections, a broad association of sounds, touches, tastes, and smells. The imagination of the space offered a continuous experience; seeing and being seen was only one of its many attributes.

In New York City alone, a total of sixteen gay bathhouses operated. Today, six have been torn down. Five have been converted to other uses, including a restaurant, a wholesale market, a dance club, and a personnel office. Two, although closed, still retain the remnant of the bathhouse. Only three remain open, and they operate very differently now as a result of AIDS. Yet even though the bathhouse structures still standing are in disuse, disrepair, or are unoccupied, their sites are not empty of history or meaning. The bathhouse still has something valuable to say.

The Meaning at the Wall

Often located in nonresidential areas, the gay bathhouse, from the outside, was muted in appearance. Visibility represented risk. Closed to the streets, its windows covered with wooden boards or steel shutters, the baths remained rather inconspicuous. For the uninitiated, the building was hard to find.

The facade acted as a mask, to hide the bathhouse within the neighborhood, providing no external indication of what was happening inside. Unlike other commercial establishments, most bathhouses did not advertise themselves with street-level signs or a list of services. Like a shield keeping out those who were not wanted, the front of the building protected the identity of those who entered. The baths were only open to people who already knew about them—through guidebooks, other gay meeting places, or police-raid listings in the local newspaper.

Entering the baths often involved some sort of screening; no one entered the system unannounced. Patrons, who looked for protection from public embarrassment or legal harassment, appreciated the security of engaging in sexual activity in a relatively safe private space. Many baths operated as private membership clubs to keep their patrons secure. In 1973 there were close to a half-million members nationwide in the Club Baths chain, making the Club Baths the largest national gay organization.[5]

One entered the building by pushing open a solid door. Usually, a front door is the only threshold between inside and outside, but in the bathhouse, there was a series of thresholds. A number of locked doors delayed possible intrusion by an unwanted guest.

The admissions desk was often behind bars or thick glass. Anyone entering had to show his card and sign his name twice: the first for registration and the second for valuables, which were put into a locked safety deposit box.[6] After the attendant handed over a towel and key, a buzzer opened the heavy inner security door that separated anticipation from the promise of pleasure. This spatial disjuncture from a more public space to a more private space, from outsider to participant, established one of the clearest boundaries in the baths.

The police were well aware of the baths and the sex that took place inside, but they did not often raid bathhouses. Unlike the parks, toilets, and certain bars, the baths were bounded defined spaces out of public view. An unsuspecting person was unlikely to find him/herself inside. When a police raid did occur, it was usually prompted by public pressure or notoriety. To point the light on the bathhouse, to make the bathhouse visible, was to jeopardize the survival of an institution that depended on its ability to operate without attracting public attention. The exclusivity of the baths and their unobtrusive presence revealed their unspoken nature.

10th Street Baths, still operating as a Russian and Turkish bathhouse on the lower East Side, New York City, 1995.

Propositioning the Host

Gay men are not static; they are all too familiar with movement and the longing to participate. Socially and politically, they have been put in motion by being kicked out, turned away, and kept behind closed doors. Often unwelcome in spaces considered mainstream, gay men found themselves in spaces abandoned by everyone else.

Like the area in which it is situated, the bathhouse, even though it looked deserted from the outside, never closed. The world of the bathhouse was revealed every second of every hour of every day, including holidays, to those who could afford to enter.

The bathhouse brought sexual activity from the city parks and public restrooms indoors. The anonymity of those spaces was maintained, as well as a sense of mobility. In place of the city grid, the uniformity of bathroom stalls, or the labyrinth of a wooded park, the bathhouse provided the corridor path lined on both sides with small doors. By providing a self-contained order in which unrelated bodies could come together, the bathhouse created a new social network.

The collection of spatial forms and interactions available to the gay male community was multiplied and magnified. In a place where one could meet the man of one's dreams or the man of the moment, the stage set was carefully planned. The notion of masculinity was heightened by using the imagery of prisons or the paneled walls of Victorian places. City spaces were replicated with truck cabs in darkened alleys or glory holes carved into the walls of bathroomlike stalls. The high school gymnasium and YMCA showed up in the locker and wet rooms. The baths choreographed almost any and all sexual urges; the requirement was that one found one or more willing partners, spectators, or performers. On a good night, there were plenty around so the search never took too long.

The constant movement through the maze of halls carried a presumption of availability; the design of the baths encouraged cruising. With few markers to orient one's position, the bath neutralized typical reference points. Instead the individual body became prominent.[7] Circling through the spaces became a deliberate search, a fluid series of meeting and wanderings. It could also be a demeaning and humiliating experience—trying to find someone before one's time was up.

While the bathhouse defined a social network, it also limited, excluded, and separated the community from those who could not or did not want to enter. The place reinforced some of the biases of the outside world. As Leo Bersani writes, the bathhouse was "ruthlessly ranked, hierarchized, and competitive," bringing racist and phobic social relations from outside into the baths (Bersani 1988, 206). Women, whether lesbian or not, were also kept out of the baths. As a result, the baths only allowed for a certain kind of self-discovery.

Increasing Complexity

> The city's form and structure provide the context in which social rules and expectations are internalized or habituated in order to ensure social conformity, or position social marginality at a safe or insulated and bounded distance (ghettoization).
>
> —(Grosz 1992, 250)

When the city organized family, social, and sexual relations, gay men were left with few places in which to make connections. The bathhouse filled a void. Inside, the boundaries of a sanctioned value system were constantly being tested and threatened. Gay male promiscuity happily emerged from centuries of repression.

The actions of the men who visited the baths celebrated their difference from the mainstream even if, outside the bathhouse, they helped make up the mainstream. As an example, some married men used the bathhouse as an anonymous outlet for homosexual experimentation. They entered the baths purely for the sex and had "no interest in having any social contact with any of the people in the baths other than the most casual of conversations" (Hoffman 1968, 51). One of the attractions of the baths, of course, was the formalized, silent, and (some would say) impersonal sexual opportunities. Men could act on their homosexual desires and experience "homosexual satisfaction without becoming involved in the social and interpersonal aspects of the homosexual community" (Hoffman 1968, 51).

The baths generated a multitude of relations. Two views regarding the effects of these relations emerged. One is that the baths became an extension of homosexual repression, continuing to hide the community and suppress political and social action. The second view is that the opportunity to interact with others in a ritualized setting was positive; that the baths created a place where it was possible to find and experience commonality.[8]

The first view realizes the power of institutions; they are more powerful than the individuals who inhabit them. In a way, the baths were designed so that no one ever got past the moment of want. The gay male body was inscribed with sexual desire and little else. By surrendering to the power of an enticing distraction, the patron remained isolated in a forbidden world. In a space of fantasy, the overabundance of stimulation became deprivation; the prevalence of consumption has the power to depersonalize. As a result, the bathhouse became an extension of the closet. The collective orgasm, the intensity of sexual pleasure, made the community powerless to pursue any other goal. Only when the bathhouse closed, when the men inside were forced out of hiding, was visibility possible.

The second assessment argues that the bathhouse did not silence the community; instead it allowed an emerging community to express itself outside the language of a homophobic society. Patrons moved away from the spoken word and innuendo to sex as performance, technique, and mutual satisfaction. Inside these shelters, patrons followed a uniform dress code, wearing a single white towel and, through the dimness of lights, favoring the other senses over sight. Behavior was coded by location, posture, eye contact, and hand gestures. Water was used for relaxation and sensuality of the skin. Music was continuous, without announcers or station breaks. Although I have heard of bathhouses playing local radio stations, the norm seemed to be a more universal, nonspecific form of aural atmosphere.

The structured environment of the baths, with the symbols that only the initiated could understand, formed a community that was hard to find outside the bathhouse walls. In the context of an uninhibited reality, people moved in relation to one another. There were shared effects and cognitions. By defying the conventions of the world outside and respecting the established rituals of the baths, individual and communal expression was orchestrated in rich and varied ways.

The Glare of the Spotlights

> We all knew people who had the most magical experience very late one night in the Everard Baths with a man they never saw again, but of whose embraces they would think of periodically for the rest of their lives.
>
> —(Holleran 1978, 154)

Bathhouses survived on a structure of consumption, control, and community. When passing through the security doors behind the darkened entrances and windows, a sense of understanding with those who had walked through before was reassuring. Appearing timeless and secluded from the world, the bathhouse attempted to loosen long-imposed restraints; as the individual retreated behind the door, one's street identity disappeared. Entering the building, one accepted a position in the performance of the space.

When the bathhouses came under attack, many bathhouse owners and gay activist leaders viewed the government interference as misplaced. Health inspectors and the media might have been more effective focusing on the type of sexual activity that spread the HIV virus rather than on the sites where those activities occurred. Because public parks and private residences, other places where gay sex happens, could not be closed, the bathhouse became a symbol of government action. The backrooms at bars also closed under threat of health officials.

The bathhouse, with its broad mix of straight, closeted, bisexual, and openly gay men, could have become a site for AIDS education, demonstrations, workshops, and videos.[9] In countries such as Germany and Holland, the bathhouses were never closed. Instead, while remaining important sites for community support and social gathering, they became sites for safe-sex education and practices.[10] In the United States, a conservative social agenda and the reaction against multiple sexual encounters prevented policy-makers from focusing on the virus and disease. Many people found it difficult to think that gay male sexuality and the prevention of HIV transmittal could happen at the same time and in the same place.

As queers come out of the overprecaution toward sex, with the need to claim their own sexuality, they are regaining the celebration of sex and the pleasure of

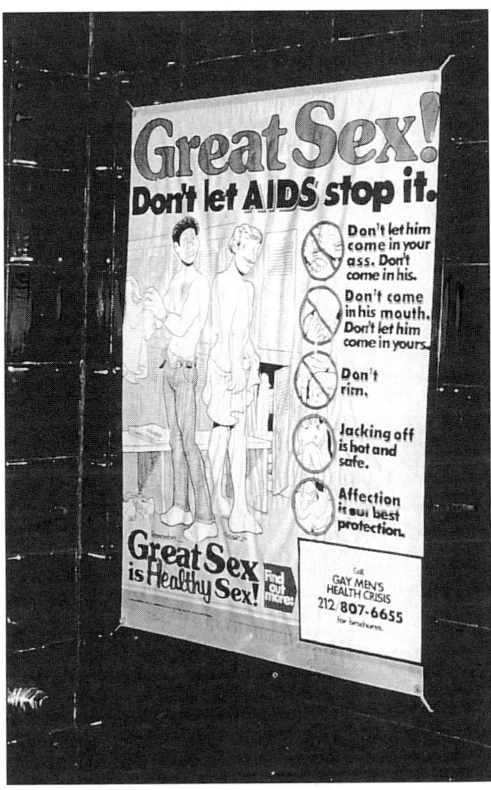

Safer-sex poster inside the St. Marks Baths. Photograph by Ira Tattelman.

multiplicity, release, and abandon. Some people remain offended by this promiscuity in light of rising HIV transmission among young men. Recent articles, however, have stated that "not a single study has shown that the second wave of AIDS can be traced to sex clubs. Most risk happens in the bedroom, not the backroom" (Warner 1995, 34).

What queers are rediscovering is that sex can operate as a form of cultural critique. While the baths may have replayed power dynamics and mirrored the dominant masculine script of mainstream society, they also helped reconfigure and redefine that power. The erotics of gay sex use irony and simulation. The roles of top and bottom, even the divisions between heterosexual and homosexual were often mobile in the baths. These reversals began to subvert forms of domination. Acts of masculinity became eroticized so that they stopped being analogous with straight society and became something else. By isolating the sexual and social structures of the outside world and playing with them, some of the infrastructures were made visible. This visibility demystified the originals. When one left the baths, the world looked different. The traditions of society could be understood more clearly, and then questioned.

In Closing

Bruce Mailman died in June of 1994, at the age of fifty-five. In Mailman's obituary, the *New York Times* described his St. Marks as a "gay bathhouse and meeting place that was closed in 1985 by the New York City Health Department as a public health hazard." Mailman had tried for a number of years to reopen the baths; he sued the city, but the courts upheld the city's decision. After his final unsuccessful attempt, he became interested in selling the building with the hope that a commercial venture would take over and erase its former use. When I asked to photograph the interior, the

The former St. Marks Baths. Photograph by Ira Tattelman.

"landscape" of the St. Marks Baths, Mailman refused. He wanted the baths to be remembered by those who had experienced it. To photograph the empty remnants would destroy those memories. A bathhouse without men filling it is no longer a bathhouse.

Just after his death, the building was sold to a video chain. It is scheduled to open as a video store, record store, café, and production facility.

This Is about People Dying: The Tactics of Early ACT UP and Lesbian Avengers in New York City

An interview with Maxine Wolfe by Laraine Sommella

The following is a compilation of excerpts from telephone interviews recorded in 1995 by Laraine Sommella. In 1994 informal discussions with Brent Ingram in Maxine Wolfe's garden in Park Slope, Brooklyn, on the early tactics of ACT UP New York City[1] led to these interviews with lesbian scholar Laraine Sommella. Passages that function as background are included in the notes for this essay.

LARAINE SOMMELLA: I was just reading a review of Sarah Schulman's *My American History*[2] in the *Nation*. It was by Jan Clausen,[3] and she makes reference to "the [Lesbian] Avengers' particular brand of organizing." Have you seen that?
MAXINE WOLFE: No. How does she [Clausen] know anything about it?
LS: Well, she doesn't really say. She's talking about the Avengers' "energetic protests" but wonders "really how far can we go in the current climate?" Some interesting issues that she raises.
MW: She certainly doesn't come to Avenger meetings. One of the Avengers confronted Tory Osborne at the National Creating Change Conference of the National Lesbian and Gay Task Force (NLGTF). Never having spoken to any one of us or done anything with us, saying how our entire strategy was totally wrong in the *Advocate*,[4] which has never seriously covered the group. She actually apologized. Everyone just wants to bash anyone who is doing anything. I've never seen such negativism. Recently, at a women's studies conference, someone who none of us had ever heard of gave a paper, and she had had nothing to do with the Avengers and totally bashed the Avengers. Who is this person? Did she ever talk to anybody? No. You know what I'm saying? Like, don't be an Avenger. . . . If you're not part of it, you're not doing anything else, you come to an academic conference, and you tear some group apart when you have absolutely done nothing about the issue yourself . . . and haven't even spoken to anyone. Many people basically assume that anyone who does visible creative public actions that are "energetic"—what a condescending word—and "catchy" are empty-headed idiots with no political strategy. They think that we don't think. Apparently the only people who think—in their view—are those who lobby, who are not "energetic." The U.S. left has always been suspicious of anyone who gets mainstream coverage or who looks and acts "nonintellectual."

Maxine Wolfe. Photograph © Morgan Gwenwald.

LS: Before we talk about your more current work in the Avengers and the evolution of tactics for taking and remaking of public space, I would like to ask you about the activism that lead up to ACT UP New York. What was the chronology that foreshadowed the formation of ACT UP New York[5] and what other groups were involved in direct action that perhaps you were involved in or knew about?

MW: Everyone sort of thinks that ACT UP came out of the blue and in fact, there's a certain mythology that Larry Kramer gave this talk one night at the Lesbian and Gay Community Center and everyone went "Oh my God" and then they formed ACT UP and nothing had been there. As usual, that's not true. That's a discontinuous history.

LS: Yes, people don't necessarily think in terms of development.

MW: In 1986 I was at the first public meeting of what was called the Lesbian and Gay Antidefamation League, which became GLAAD, and which was held in the New York City Community Center. I went with a lesbian friend, and we were in this room with about three hundred gay men and four lesbians, and we were sitting next to these two guys and one turned to the other and said, "Wow, this is the first thing that's happened in fifteen years." And I turned to her and said, "Where have these people been?"

A brief overview—with the last two years leading up to the formation of ACT UP New York being the most important. After the first few years of the Gay Activist Alliance (GAA) and especially after the firehouse was arsoned in 1974, most of the gay male community in New York and a few Democratic Party dykes focused on getting the gay rights bill passed in New York City and New York State. Basically they became part of the Democratic Party organization, whether formally or informally, and attempted to orchestrate passage of bills behind the scenes. At the same time, in the gay male mainstream, "the community," certain professional, business, and religious groups formed. While those organizations and networks were totally reformist, if political at all, they enabled the Gay Men's Health Crisis (GMHC) to form in the early 1980s. There was a new basis to get money, to know where people were, to create an infrastructure. That was not there before. But for a lot of that period, from the mid-

1970s to the early 1980s, that is what gay men were doing. Most lesbians were not involved with gay men in activism and were basically either in the antirape or antiviolence movement or lesbian-feminist groups, forming their own organizations and doing political work. But this work was not necessarily focused on lesbians and gay men and rather much more on women.[6] Activism was focused on either women's issues, generically defined, or other global ones against racism and nuclear technology. For example, there was the Women's Pentagon Action, which did not have an analysis of homophobia nor a focus on lesbians. But in New York City, in 1984 and 1985, when the whole issue of closing the bathhouses came up, there were a lot of spontaneous actions. These had similarities to actions in 1981 and 1982 when there were raids on black and Latino transvestite bars and the demonstrations against the viciously homophobic film, *Cruising*.

In terms of a specific AIDS focus early in the 1980s, there were the People With AIDS Coalition (PWA) and the GMHC. Right away, people in GMHC got more and more pissed because the organization was unwilling to take political stands. Part of it was that they were looking for money and government funding, and so, as it happens in those kinds of formalized institutions, GMHC became less and less political. They did not want to alienate the people who are going to give them money. But the PWA Coalition formed in 1982 in Denver with principles that focused on empowerment, which really came out of the feminist health movement.

Fierce pussy, Dyke March, Stonewall 25, New York City, June, 1994. Photograph by Saskia Scheffer.

LS: There's a link.

MW: In New York City, there was a huge uproar over the closing of the bathhouses and many people went to hearings at the City Council. They showed up on the steps of City Council, almost spontaneously I would say, and started chanting when David Summers, who was there to testify and who was a person with AIDS, was arrested when he tried to go in to testify. The police were so crazed. People nearly rioted outside, shouting, "We won't go until you let him go." That is where GLAAD started, the Gay and Lesbian Alliance Against Defamation. They called a community meeting and I went to it. It was pretty tame, as far as I was concerned, and very much in the image of earlier kinds of generally progressive organizations. There was already a board. They already had an idea about what they were doing. And basically, they wanted an army of soldiers. It was a very hierarchical organization. The first meeting that I went to was the marshaling committee. One of the guys who was running it, Marty Robinson, was one of the founders of GAA and basically told all of the men sitting there that they did not have to worry and that they had talked to the cops already, and they were doing an action against the *New York Post* because of its homophobic coverage of AIDS. He basically told them that the marshals were a kind of barrier between the police and the protesters, which is certainly not my idea of what a marshal does; and the idea of wanting to get a permit from the cops to demonstrate—quite amazing.

There was a group of us in 1983 at the City Council hearings on the gay rights bill, including a lesbian-feminist group that I was in at that time called Women For Women, along with some women from Women's Pentagon Action, and two gay men. After years of trying to negotiate the bill through the back doors of the Democratic Party and having it never even getting out of committee for a vote, we decided that when the bill was coming up to that committee for a vote on whether it should even come out of committee that it was time to "fuck the people who are telling everybody to be nice, we weren't gonna be nice." We formed this very ad hoc group that ended up at the end of the council meeting when they did not vote it out of committee that year, sitting in at the City Council and having to be dragged out and arrested. Our banner said "Lesbian liberation, we won; go away."

GLAAD soon formed and immediately became a bone of contention because it started doing these very orchestrated demonstrations. By "orchestrated," I mean they negotiated with the cops, they basically told you when to show up, when to go home, and there was absolutely no input from anybody into what was going to be done. The board of directors made the decisions. Women coming to their meetings eventually just stopped because they were huge meetings and no one would even get a chance to get up and speak.

At that point, I just decided there wasn't anything I was going to be able to do about this shit because coming from the lesbian community, I wasn't a gay man. Most of the gay men with whom I had worked in the left were not around, and nobody was doing anything very much. Who was I to tell gay men how to do stuff about AIDS? So I just sort of kept looking for stuff to do. I helped form a group of faculty and students at City University of New York (CUNY) just to keep my hand in. I worked at the Lesbian Herstory Archives, "The Archives," and then one day a friend of mine said, "There's this new group that's meeting. Do you want to go to their meeting the Monday after Gay Pride Day?" and I said "Yes" and we went to ACT UP.

LS: When was this?

MW: ACT UP started in March of 1987, and I started going in June of 1987. The people who came to the first meeting of ACT UP included individuals from GMHC who had become totally disaffected by its unwillingness to do any political stuff. There were people from the PWA Coalition who wanted to get out on the streets, and they already had this image of a feminist take on the health establishment because of Michael Callen who was very much influenced by the feminist health movement. There was also the SILENCE=DEATH Project, which was a group of men who had started meeting a year and half before, including Avram Finklestein, Oliver Smith, and Chris Lione. They were a whole group of men who needed to talk to each other and others about what the fuck were they going to do, being gay men in the age of AIDS?! Several of them were designers of various sorts—graphic designers—and they ended up deciding that they had to start doing wheat-pasting on the streets, to get the message out to people: "Why aren't you doing something?" So they created the SILENCE=DEATH logo well before ACT UP ever existed, and they made posters before ACT UP ever existed, and the posters at the bottom said something like, "What's really happening in Washington? What's happening with Reagan and Bush and the Food and Drug Administration? It ended with this statement: "Turn anger, fear, grief into action." Several of these graphic designers were at that first evening that Larry spoke.

The other group that was represented at the first meeting of ACT UP in March 1987 was the Lavender Hill Mob. The Lavender Hill Mob included Marty Robinson, who had left GLAAD because the organization had become much more focused on not holding public meetings and not wanting to do big actions. Marty had run their "Swift and Terrible Retribution Committee" and was one of the founders of GAA. He felt totally strangulated by GLAAD's agenda. Marty got together a few friends including Bill Balhman, who was also from GAA, Henry Yaeger, and a young dyke who was seventeen at the time, Jean Elizabeth Glass, along with a couple of other people. They formed this thing called the Lavender Hill Mob. Not only did they start doing zaps[7] but they also started meeting with government officials around AIDS policy issues. They had been going to government conferences, had started leafletting, their message being: "What the fuck are you doing in Washington?" and "Why aren't you finding treatments?" etcetera. The first article that was in the *New York Native* about ACT UP, that everyone thinks was the first public presence of ACT UP, the Wall Street Action in March 1987, had the headline "Kramer, Mob, and others call for traffic blockade."[8]

So the night when Larry came to speak, in March of 1987, there was a very particular audience in that room. The person who was originally supposed to read was Nora Ephron. Now, I would never go to hear Nora Ephron read. It's definitely more a gay male focus. But she couldn't come and Larry Kramer spoke instead. When I came into ACT UP, I did not even know who the fuck Larry Kramer was. He was irrelevant in my life. I had vaguely heard people say that he had written a book called *Faggots,*[9] but why would I ever read that? For me, he was not an icon at all. But for the people in that room, he spoke to them. He had been screaming for years and nobody had done anything. From my point of view, there was a whole group of people there ready to do something. They were looking for a kick in the ass and needed an event to be at together, that would lead to that, and that was it. At some point he yelled, "What are you gonna do?" and somebody in the audience said, "Why don't we revive the AIDS Action Network?"[10] Then people said, "Let's have a meeting and let's do something." They called a meeting and about seventy people showed up. Soon after, they did their first Wall Street Action. They did not have a lot of people coming to their meetings until after Gay Pride that June and the March on Washington in the fall of 1987. If you did not read the *New York Native,* you wouldn't know that they existed.

LS: Was the Wall Street action covered in the mainstream press?

MW: I think the April one they did about taxes might have been because they were charged by horses. But I do not remember ever seeing it. When someone said to me, "We should go meet this group," I had no idea who they were except that I had marched behind them at the Gay Pride March and saw this incredible "thing," which was a concentration camp with wire all around and people inside. There were people outside the wire dressed in masks and military gear and handing out flyers and people were selling ACT UP T-shirts with the SILENCE=DEATH logo,[11] which the SILENCE=DEATH project had given them permission to use. I went up to this guy and I said, "Are there any lesbians in your group?" and he said, "Yeah," and the next day I showed up and there were four visible women and two of them were straight. It had that kind of impact. If you can imagine, there is always this tension in the Gay Pride March in New York because the majority come to it for a celebration and they do not want it to be anything political at all. And this was 1987: We're already five years into the crisis, loads of people had died, the community was in a state of shock, and Gay Pride was supposed to be a way to get away from all of this. And ACT UP had the *chutzpah* to build a concentration camp float.

LS: It was an "in-your-face" move and very dramatic.

MW: When I came to the meeting the next night, there were three hundred people in that room.

The alternative, controversial march on Pride Day, 1994. Protesters marched up Fifth Avenue without a march permit. Photograph by Saskia Scheffer.

LS: And you directly connect that parade presence with that turnout?
MW: Absolutely.
LS: This was what people needed. They saw something that they were enthused about.
MW: Yes. AIDS really knocked people for a loop. It's hard for people to understand if they aren't part of it. Larry Kramer and I disagree on almost everything, especially on his use of holocaust imagery, but he lost an entire life network. He would say that he had five hundred friends and acquaintances who had died. If you think about it, that's the size of a small town in Germany. For gay people who did not have close relationships with their families, and especially if they were Larry's age, in their late fifties, they had to go through finding themselves and new friends. There was no one around to form this new group of people, your village, and so many were dead—suddenly, in a very short time. At the beginning of the epidemic, you would go into the hospital on Monday and be dead on Tuesday. People were dying left and right, horrible deaths, and nobody knew why. The shock was incredible. People were trying to figure out so hard how to take care of the people they cared about, how to take care of themselves, how not to get sick, how to prevent people from dying, how to get services to people in every way, shape, and form. The idea of doing anything else was overwhelming. ACT UP took that leadership role in that Gay Pride march and marched in the middle of a "space" that is apolitical and often commercial. The political groups are usually in the back, and nobody pays any attention to them. Instead, ACT UP marched up there, basically in your face, saying people want to quarantine us and tattoo us and saying, "Get with it folks, we have to do something." The imagery was so stark that people said, "Got It." The same thing happened in the fall of 1987 at the March on Washington.
LS: What happened in Washington?
MW: ACT UP got there late. The SILENCE=DEATH Project[12] had made incredible posters. One was a Ronald Reagan poster in dayglo green that said "AIDSGATE." We had another poster that said "SILENCE=DEATH." ACT UP member Michael Miles was a stage designer, and he designed an incredible contraption with these posters—a snake formation. Each poster was held by an individual person but was connected and we used those in Washington and they went way up above your head and we all wore SILENCE=DEATH T-shirts. We also had these huge banners that were of the late eighties order of things—black with huge white letters—very stark, very black. ACT UP had become very well known for these banners. Everyone else had purple banners with flourishing letters but our posters were very striking, very stark, with very clean lines. This was very graphic-design-oriented kind of stuff and had a tremendous impact. Many ACT UP groups started after that march.

The New York ACT UP style was wonderful—writing leaflets that you could read and I think, more importantly, not relying only on the written word but also visual media. Although the ages of people in ACT UP have always been quite diverse, there were a lot of young people. ACT UP people were always "classified" as young sexy people. The friends I had in ACT UP tended to be older and more literate. But they were visual: people in theater and art. Other younger men and women, who were not part of that scene, were totally willing to go with it. They were media generation people who had grown up with television and multimedia. They were well aware, any time we did a demo, that there would be TV cameras present and what these cameras would be looking at.

LS: How do you utilize that?

MW: We focused on what would stand out, what would show up. This was in a way that no one I ever knew had done before. It was easy to learn stuff. What color do you make banners when you use them at night as opposed to day? And what size does something have to be to show up? How will this move through space? And I think that was very important because in fact that's exactly what caught the media's attention. Not just that we did things that other people did not do, but that the way that we did them, we were very present. We did not just picket around the front of a building, which is totally boring; we broke into the building [laughter]. We dressed up in costume. Half the time we would go to dinners that were held by Republicans, we'd go in drag to get in. And we would pretend to be most anything if we could to get in somewhere. There was this whole idea that you would do what you had to do to get in somewhere, and that you would get into it; you wouldn't be on the outside looking in, asking people to take your leaflet but you would be demanding that people pay attention to what you had to say and taking over spaces where people would not expect that you could get in.

LS: You said that a group of AIDS activists came together in Washington, D.C., during the 1987 March on Washington? Who were they? Were they both newcomers to political action and others with a history or herstory of activist tactics?

MW: That meeting had been arranged mostly by gay men, and some lesbians. They had been working on the left for years and obviously wanted to do something about the AIDS crisis. They called ACT UP and said they wanted to hold this meeting and they called themselves ACT NOW. So on the Monday after the march, some of us stayed in D.C. and went to the meeting. It was horrifying. These people had arranged the whole day—the agenda had been planned. There were various "lefty" groups involved, who of course had already come with proposals and started putting them out. Several proposals were in opposition to each other. One was The Nine Days of Action (or Nine Days of Rage)—to do actions for nine days in a row that spring, all over the country, and each day would deal with a different AIDS issue. But they were stuck in a rut. They said things about doing a day on "AIDS in the Barrio and the Ghetto," a sort of "lefty version" of politics that was outdated in language and style. They had no day for AIDS and homophobia! I was with a lot of men from ACT UP who had been very excited about the idea that there would actually be a national network of activist AIDS groups.

Forget even imagining that it would be ACT UP groups; just people who were willing to do something about this crisis in a grassroots way. They were freaked by the ACT UP approach. They couldn't believe that this is what people were doing. I got up to the microphone and I said, "I don't get why you don't have a day on AIDS and homophobia," and one of the guys said to me, "Well, you know, I mean, gay men aren't gonna come out for anybody else." I said, "Fuck that; they're dying, they'll come out for themselves and then you can worry about getting them out for somebody else." This is an example of the homophobia of the left. Other issues such as those of "poor people or people of color" were always more important and there were still some very chauvinist illusions, on the part of some people, that none of the people in these "more oppressed groups" were gay or vulnerable to AIDS, and that they, the "lefties," were the "unusual" gay men who were progressive, while every other white gay man was horrible.

The people affected by the crisis, at that point, were overwhelmingly gay males. People were dead and dying and the majority of them were, and still are, gay males. But if they knew the statistics, even then, they would have seen that a lot of them were gay men of color. But many of the lefty white gay men, even as late as 1987, had completely divorced those categories from one another and wanted people to do actions only about people of color and not about gay men. Although groups did start after that, they weren't necessarily the groups that came to those early meetings. They were people who had come to the March on Washington and had seen ACT UP and we had made twenty thousand leaflets to hand out. That is the other thing that ACT UP used to do. We would go to a Gay Pride march even in New York with twenty thousand leaflets and hand them all out. They would be very straightforward leaflets. It wouldn't take you three days to read them. And these leaflets were very political, very clear, and to the point. They would say something like "Racism and Homophobia started the AIDS crisis." But they wouldn't go on and on. They would always be in a very catchy kind of style and comprehensible. So the impact of ACT UP was from the combination of the visual imagery and the accessibility of everything that was produced in terms of language, and the fact that we were out on the streets in places where people did not want us and without asking their permission. In terms of going to places where people did not expect us, one of the first things of course was the Wall Street Action where people blocked traffic and got arrested, and it had been many years in the gay male community since they had seen anybody do that. To explain the evolution of ACT UP's particular orientation around direct action, it is necessary to go back a few years.

Soon after GLAAD New York was formed, they had the "Swift and Terrible Retribution" Committee. This was right around the time of the *Hardwick* decision. The U.S. Supreme Court upheld the Georgia sodomy law.[13] Everyone headed down to Sheridan Square.[14] The word gets around, and people just show up. A huge mob congregated at Sheridan Square spontaneously that night. It was, by the way, the night after the Gay Pride March. The decision was well timed in Washington not to be on the day of the Gay Pride March. But it was four days before the Statue of Liberty Centennial in 1986, July 4th, and they were expecting a million visitors to New York City, and so a couple of thousand people gathered in Sheridan Square. The people from GLAAD came, and they were trying to get everybody to go home. "Go home, go home, go home, you're gonna get into trouble." But nobody would go home and people ended up spontaneously blocking traffic on Sixth Avenue and 8th Street in the heart of the Village for hours, and then finally people said, "Let's meet tomorrow night at the church near the community center, and let's figure out what we're gonna do."

A dyke that I know showed up there with a flyer already made that said "Storm the Statue of Liberty; Meet at Sheridan Square on July 4th," and the people from GLAAD were horrified. They really did not want this to happen. They did not want anyone to fuck up this party. They said things like "People are coming here and it's a big holiday, and you don't want to fuck it up for people; you're gonna ruin their party; you're not gonna get your point across." Nobody listened to them. People put out these flyers. And it's the beginning of the summer. . . . On the 4th of July weekend, five thousand showed up with a couple of day's notice! When I got there everyone was whispering "Battery Park, Battery Park." GLAAD had negotiated with the cops for a permit to march to Federal Plaza, about ten blocks north of where the Centennial Celebration was happening and to rally there. But people were determined to go down to Battery Park—to be a presence in the midst of the tourists at the Centennial. After the rally at Federal Plaza, GLAAD stationed marshals to block the demonstration from going downtown. This was just a totally spontaneous act of about five thousand people, who were communicating by passing the word back; these people broke through the marshal line. The cops formed a barricade around Trinity Place with cars and horses and were basically telling people that they weren't gonna let them go through. There were some people from GLAAD who were standing up and saying, "Break it up now, you don't want to do this stuff." So everybody basically decided that we would split up and then meet in Battery Park; we would break up and go to Battery Park and in twos and threes. About two thousand people showed up in Battery Park, right in the middle of Middle America visiting the Statue of Liberty Centennial, and people gave speeches and took over statues and marched again to the New York Post, and this thing went on for seven hours. It was making a statement that people were not going to stay contained in the area of the city that everyone said you had to be in. One of the things that I always felt in my years in the left in New York is that people always stayed where they were supposed to. People would hand out leaflets in Greenwich Village; what's the big deal? Who are you talking to? And I remember having huge fights when I was doing abortion stuff because the group of lesbians that I was working with in CARASA New York wanted to go and give out stuff in Fordham Road in the Bronx, and Flatbush Avenue in Brooklyn—to go to various ethnic and cultural neighborhoods. Everyone panicked. The difference between ACT UP and those earlier groups was twofold. First, ACT UP was about organizing the unorganized. It wasn't a lefty coalition where there's one person from this group and one person from that group and one person for the other group and you claim you have a coalition but you really have three people. It was about mobilizing a community that had not been organized to do this kind of direct action in at least twelve or fourteen years. Secondly, ACT UP was about people doing stuff for themselves. We weren't being philanthropists. We weren't a vanguard. We were trying to save our own lives and the lives of people we knew. We were very materially affected.

LS: That material-interest issue reminds me of the stake early antiwar activists had in their political work.

MW: ACT UP definitely draws from that kind of perspective. It works. ACT UP has always been called a gay white male group, and I once gave a talk that everyone calls gay white males rich "*bougie*,"[15]worse than "*bougie*," upper middle class. ACT UP, the group of people who started ACT UP initially, included women and people of color. There have always been people—lesbians and gay men of color and straight women. About the only group not really represented in ACT UP were straight men, and there have been a couple of those too.

LS: And the lesbians were a significant force?

MW: Even though we were a small group, we were the people who had done politics. We were the people who did the civil disobedience training. We have always been the marshals. We have always been the logistics people because we came out of that kind of background. The men have always been the graphic artists and we do the xeroxing and typesetting. There are things that everyone has access to. Gay men have access to graphics; we have access to reproduction.

LS: They utilize the male gaze. [laughter]

MW: The group of lesbians who were in ACT UP, from early on, were grown-up in a way because we had come through the lesbian-feminist wars and because we knew we were in a gay male group. We knew we wanted to work on AIDS issues; we did not come in there to work on women and AIDS. Because we had learned a few things, thankfully, from the years previous, someone could get up and say, "We need people to man this table," and we wouldn't stand up and say, "You sexist, chauvinist pig." We would say, "Staff the table," and they would go, "Oh, staff the table," and then people would go on.

LS: You did not have to walk out. You had maturity.

MW: Well, there were a couple of reasons. The truth is that we were not in the raw state of pain in which you should never be if you are in a mixed group like that. And the men were, most of them, badly trained but not ill intentioned. There were some misogynists who never could be trained, some men who were incredibly feminist, and some—the majority—were just badly trained like we all are. And we women who were there were grown-up enough to understand being badly trained. We weren't in the state of rawness where we thought everyone was a misogynist to the core or thought to ourselves, "Kill them, get rid of them." It actually worked out very well, and I think that the women became a very strong force because we were also very gutsy about the kinds of things we did. The first huge action was at Shea Stadium, and it really scared the men in the group.[16]

In the spring of 1988, activist AIDS groups across the country called for the Nine Days of Action. In New York we actually called them the "Nine Days of Rain" because it rained on almost every one of the days. The only two days it did not rain was for the women's action, which was at Shea Stadium, and an action that we did at the Harlem Office Building, about prisoners and AIDS. Afterwards we decided that God must be a Black Lesbian.

As a women's committee, we were trying to figure out what we were gonna do because it was supposed to be a day on women and AIDS. We were sitting around one night trying to figure out what to do, and we threw out all these ideas like driving up to some big political event in a horse-drawn carriage that looked like part of a wedding. We were just drawing out the craziest ideas we could think of, and one of the women asked, "What is the goal of what we want to do?" Part of this was about the difference in status between women and men at the very beginning of the AIDS crisis, even though they were both sick. Women were erased totally and also pictured as vectors to men getting infected, and all the advertising on the subways in New York was about women taking condoms with them in their purse. It would say "Don't forget *these* when you go out," as if women wore condoms. It sort of reminded me of my own growing up, and it was the woman who always had to be the one responsible. We said that we wanted to get the message out that heterosexual men are responsible; that they're the only people being let off the hook in this epidemic by the media. Gay men are being put down; prostitutes and women are being told they have to take condoms along. What is anyone asking from straight men in the world? Nothing. So we decided that we wanted to go to a venue that in people's minds was heterosexual, and male heterosexual, to the core. And the Nine Days of Action were in the spring—May 4th—and we were trying to figure out what venue would fit this, and all of a sudden, one of the women said, "Baseball games! The Mets game!" and everyone in the room just went crazy.

We began to throw around crazy ideas like jumping on the field, wearing hats with two frankfurters sticking out and so on. One woman was absolutely panicked. She had absolutely never had anything to do with sports. But everybody else in the room was taking off on it. Two of the women were baseball nuts, so we finally decided this was the best idea we ever had, and we sat down and really worked out a plan. We

AIDS IS NOT A BALL GAME.

MEN! DON'T ENDANGER THE WOMEN YOU LOVE.*

AIDS is the leading cause of death among women between the ages of 25 to 34 in NYC.

HERE'S THE SCORE:

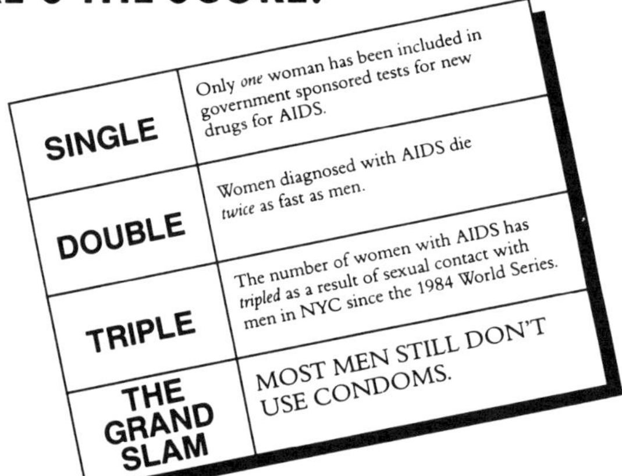

USE CONDOMS. NO GLOVE, NO LOVE!

*And if you can't be with the one you love, protect the one you're with.

SPRING AIDS ACTION '88—Nine Days of National AIDS Related Actions and Protests.

The AIDS Coalition To Unleash Power (212) 533-8888

ACT UP is a diverse, non-partisan group of individuals united in anger and committed to direct action to end the AIDS crisis.

Leaflet by ACT UP New York, 1988. Courtesy of the Lesbian Herstory Education Foundation, Inc./ Lesbian Herstory Archives, Brooklyn, New York.

were gonna get tickets in blocks. Shea Stadium is U-shaped. We planned to get seating in blocks in the three different areas of the "U" and that we would do "call-and-response" like you do at college football games. Originally we were gonna have each person hold a card and the cards would spell out messages. And then we called up Shea Stadium and found out that in fact there was a ball game that night and that we could get blocks of seats and that if you bought sixty seats, you could even get a message on the message board! And we thought, "Wow, this is fucking amazing!"

And then we really got into it; we made up leaflets that used baseball terminology: "AIDS is not a ball game," "Here's the score," and then it had a scorecard. And it said: "Single: There's not a single woman in a clinical treatment trial in the United States of America," "Double: The number of cases of women with AIDS has doubled since x years ago," and at the bottom it said, "No glove, no love." Our idea was that we would get there before the game started. We'd make up ten thousand flyers and bring condoms, and we'd stand at every entrance at the ball park and we'd give a condom and a flyer to any man we saw coming by. And then we would go inside with these banners and do this call-and-response thing. We came up with these banners that said things like "Don't balk at safer sex," "Strike out AIDS," and "No glove, no love," and in between we had "Aids kills women—Men use condoms." And in the center we had "SILENCE=DEATH" and this huge triangle.

So we come to the floor of ACT UP and we presented it as our Nine Days of Action thing and the room becomes like dead silent. Panic is in the air, absolute panic. So people start standing up and speaking. First, we got the "class" stuff. "We're gonna get beaten to death there," and we're standing there very calmly saying, "Do you know who goes to Shea Stadium? We go to Shea Stadium. Kids go to Shea Stadium on Friday nights to pick each other up. Queers go to Shea Stadium." And in the room all of a sudden the closet baseball queers start standing up. All these gay men who wouldn't tell anyone they were baseball nuts because it's not the "thing to be," and they started saying, "Yeah! I go to Shea Stadium." So we finally got people to go.

So we went and it was really funny how we even knew how big to make things because, for example, we had to measure the seats to know how big to make the banner. A woman, Debbie, and I went to buy the first sixty seats, and we had to get people to pay for them because we did not have that much money in ACT UP then, and what we decided to do was to buy sixty at a time and sell them and then get sixty more. Our goal was to get sixty in each section. At that point one of the guys from the SILENCE=DEATH Project, Chris Lione, correctly assessed that we should not make up individual cards because if people did not show up, we wouldn't have the letters. So we went to Shea Stadium to measure the seats so we could make the banners. All you needed was a person at each end. So we went to make banners. We bought the first sixty. We asked this woman if we could go and see where the seats were located exactly and she said, oh, they were constructing in Shea Stadium that day and we couldn't go in. We said, "Oh, really?" and she said, "Really, you really can't." We said okay, but as we were walking out we saw an entrance into the park and decided that we'd try to go through. We started to walk through it and this guy comes, a security guard comes from the office, and he says, "Excuse me, girls, what are you doing?" But it was really easy. If you're a woman, especially a "femmy" woman, you can get away with so much. We just said, "Oh, you know, this is our very first baseball game and we're coming here with a whole bunch of friends and they sent us to get the tickets and we don't know anything about it and now we wanted to go see the seats and they won't let us do it and we're so worried because we don't know anything about it and don't you think we could go inside and just look?" and he said, "What I don't see, I don't know."

We went in, found the seats we had just bought, measured them all out. We had rulers so that we could make banners that were exactly the right length. We also went to a night game to check out the lighting and to figure out how big the letters would have to be to be seen.

Word of this got out. In the beginning we could hardly get anybody to buy seats. By the last day, I was getting phone calls from people I hadn't heard from in years from the left because the word had gotten out that this was gonna be the most amazing thing that had ever happened, and people were acting like I was their connection for a seat in the orchestra. They'd say, "Do you have seats at Shea Stadium?" and I'd say, "No, I don't." So it actually turned out to be quite amazing because we ended up selling around 400 tickets.

At Shea Stadium we had people spread in three different sections and there was also a whole big issue about standing outside and handing out these leaflets. Because Shea Stadium is owned by the City of New York, but the Mets rent it. Anything that happens *in* Shea Stadium is in relationship to the Mets. The parking lot is owned by Kenny or was then. That's private property. They can decide what happens in the parking lot. But there's a whole space that is not really either publicly or privately owned or leased—almost like a street or plaza that goes around the entrances to the stadium, that looks like a sidewalk but a big sidewalk and that is not the parking lot and is not the stadium. We could not find out for weeks who it belonged to. We wanted to know, if we were going to get arrested, what it was we would be getting arrested for. Were we on private property or public property? Who knew? And we kept trying to get in touch with Shea Stadium. We also wanted to get in touch with them because we wanted the Mets to declare this National Woman and AIDS Day, and we left them many messages and they never called us back. And by that time, ACT UP had a reputation for doing things. Especially the women, because we had just done another demonstration in January, and the police nearly went crazy because we did not ask the city and the police for permits.

We had coming up on the LED screen a message that said "Welcome the National Women and AIDS Day Committee," and we did not think we'd have any trouble getting in because we had tickets. But giving out these flyers outside, that we thought we would end up getting arrested for. About a week and a half before this whole thing was going to happen, some guy wrote a story in the *Village Voice* about ACT UP that mentioned we were going to Shea Stadium. A friend of mine who was actually working with Shea Stadium on a totally different thing—she was working with them on a performance art thing that was going to be happening in their parking lot, and they did not know that she had anything to do with ACT UP—was there one day when the guy she was working with was talking to the community/police liaison. The officer was saying, "Did you hear? These crazy people are coming to the ballpark next week—these ACT UP people—and they're going to rip up the turf and they're going to do this and we're going to do that." And we thought, "Holy Shit, we're going to show up, and they're going to be in riot gear!" And we weren't even doing anything that provocative, from our point of view. I mean we saw this as an educational action. There was nothing we wanted from Shea Stadium. So we actually thought of this as a lighthearted but hard-hitting educational action because it would be in a place where no one would ever expect us to be.

So we got one of the women to call up the cops—not to ask for a permit. She said, "You know, we've been trying to get in touch with Shea Stadium for three and a half months and nobody has called us back. We just wanted to let you know that we're going to be out there on Wednesday night, and we just did not want you to maybe get freaked that we were coming." And of course, when he started asking questions like "How many?" she just said, "Well, I don't know, but we just wanted you to know." So it wouldn't be this kind of riot gear kind of thing. When we got there, they had spoken to the people at Shea Stadium, and the head of their public relations department came out and put our leaflets in every one of their press packets, and he made sure that we could stand at every single doorway and give out all of our stuff. It was great, but we hadn't negotiated; we just went.

It was the most amazing thing because we had made these banners with a black background and white lettering. We had six long rows in each area and each row had a set of banners, and we only opened them up when the visiting team was up because we did not want to upset the New York Mets fans. At a certain point, I do not remember what inning it was, the first banners opened up. They started at the top of the group and they were always three lines. And the first one opened up and it said "Don't balk at safe sex." And then across the stadium, opposite them, in the seats above the other field, three banners rolled open and they said "Aids kills women," and then in the center, behind home plate, the next three opened up and they said "Men! Use condoms."

And then, people in ACT UP got so into having these banners that people started swaying back and forth, up and down, and the visual effect was incredible. Because it was at night, totally dark, and the lighting from the ballpark totally reflected the white letters of the banners. An inning and a half later, we opened the next set of banners. They said "Strike out Aids," "No glove, no love," and the final one said "SILENCE= DEATH" and it had a huge triangle and ACT UP! This was on C-Span. We not only got to the twenty thousand people who were in the ballpark, but it was televised around the country and we gave out leaflets. We reached an incredible number of people in an audience that we'd otherwise never have been able to get to. Most of the people came from ACT UP, but many people from other groups got wind of it and thought it was the most exciting thing. So there was one whole section of non-ACT UP people.

LS: In early ACT UP New York, what was the attitude toward conventional rather than alternative science or AIDS treatment? What role did the women play in moving ACT UP beyond framings of treatment solutions in terms of conventional medicine? Was there a switch in emphasis at some point from conventional to alternative treatments?

MW: The switch to the more alternative treatment wasn't just a women-versus-men thing. I think that's the one thing that people shared initially or that the men got that the women already had was that the health care system was political and the research system was political and it wasn't just a matter of good and bad science. It was a matter of who did they care about and what were they going to do and that you couldn't separate politics and science.

LS: So this was a feminist perspective that had already been developed by the women's movement.

MW: Yes, it was from the women's health movement. And many gay men in ACT UP knew firsthand already because the initial ravages of the epidemic were happening to them. But gradually a particular set or subset of people in ACT UP starting thinking that the problem was not the structure of science. Rather, it was a problem of who was doing it. A major issue was that the people doing the research were kind of divorced from the people who were being affected by the research.

LS: Which is a political issue and not a science issue?

MW: Right. But they did not have any critique of the way that science gets done in any other sense. In effect, they moved to a point where they did not have an analysis of the fact that the government only tests drugs that drug companies can make money from, and those decisions in science are being determined by profit and advancement through the university system and not by what will save people's lives. At that point there was a very decided split, with people leaving ACT UP to form the Treatment Advocacy Group (TAG). They told everyone that they represented the people who had AIDS and that everybody else in ACT UP was seronegative, which was a total lie. If you were talking about women, it was a social thing, while if you were talking about treatment, it was a male issue. You could not talk about women's stuff with that group of people without them believing that it was a social issue associated with AIDS instead of a treatment issue. In that way they were no different from the government people that we were confronting. If science does not include everyone, it's not really science; it's white male science, and that's a very specific kind of science. A lot of the people who left to form TAG were more allopathically oriented, like traditional U.S. medicine, and they had far more faith in the capitalist system of profit. They even thought it was going to work for them. Eventually.

LS: It sounds like most of the people who eventually became involved with ACT UP were not politicized in terms of their gay identity.
MW: Not originally; no, not at all.
LS: That was something that developed over time, then.
MW: Right. They were . . . some of the people were very strong from the beginning. But the majority of gay men coming to ACT UP, really I would describe it as "hiding their gayness behind AIDS." In other words, they were coming out only to fight the AIDS crisis. And then they discovered the kind of experience of working with the gay community when you're gay and being able to be out in that place and the electricity of it and of people feeling good about themselves—really experiencing it firsthand—and became totally out. People changed their career paths; people dropped corporate jobs.
LS: Their consciousness got raised.
MW: Yes. And there's no way to go back.
LS: In light of this issue we've just been discussing, how did Lesbian Avengers develop out of ACT UP?
MW: It did not develop out of ACT UP. In a couple of instances I've tried to correct this impression. Actually, there were six lesbians who started the Avengers.
LS: When was that?
MW: Our first public meeting was in July 1992, but our first meeting to talk about the Avengers was in May 1992. In 1982, when we were kicked out of CARASA,[17] Sarah Schulman and myself and some other women started a group called Women For Women, which was a lesbian-feminist group. We called it "a lesbian-feminist group fighting for women's liberation with warmth and a sense of humor." And we told everybody they could spell Women For Women anyway they wanted to. So it was incredible, because some people spelled it Wimmin and some people would spell it Womyn and some would spell it Women.
LS: Pure anarchy.
MW: Yes. We wanted to say, "Why are we operating on that level?" Anyway, we were the people who sat in at that gay-rights hearing that had the big banner that said "Lesbian liberation, we won't go away." Then that group kind of fell apart, around antiporn versus anticensorship, and people began getting panicked about being lesbians out on the street. It was okay when we did stuff about reproductive rights, but when it was about lesbians there was a whole bunch of younger women who just panicked to be out on the street. It began to devolve into them discussing coming out and what not. Anyway, it died. And then also, about a year before we started Lesbian Avengers, Sarah Schulman and I always used to talk about how are we going to get more lesbians out on the street. And then with the resurgence of the stuff around abortion we said, "Come on, all these dykes are going to be fighting for abortion again, and none of these people have ever come out to do anything for us. Still. Yet. Never." And we were over the top

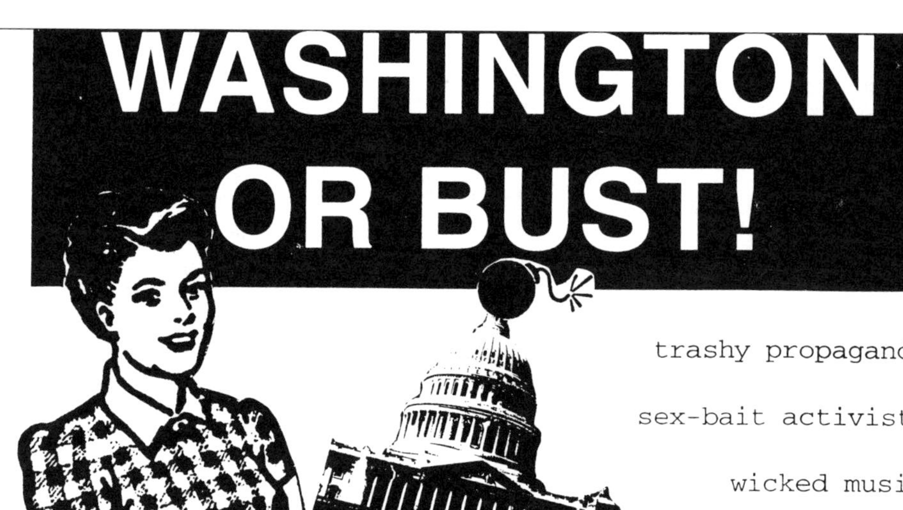

Fundraising flyer for Lesbian Avenger participation in the second March on Washington. Flyer by Lesbian Avengers New York. Courtesy of the Lesbian Herstory Education Foundation, Inc./ Lesbian Herstory Archives, Brooklyn, New York.

on abortion stuff because we'd done it for so many years and had gotten thrown out as soon as we'd mentioned lesbians.

So Sarah said she was going to call a community meeting to get together whatever lesbian groups there were, just to come together to talk about what they were doing and what things we could do together. But I said to her, "Sarah, this is the wrong time." And she said, "Well, I'm going to try it." And I said, "Well, go ahead. I don't feel like it's the right time." So she went ahead and she called every single group up in New York

personally and said, "You don't have to agree with each other, you don't have to come to agree with each other." Over one hundred women showed up at this meeting. Some of them were younger dykes from ACT UP and Dyke Action Machine! (DAM!), which was originally part of Queer Nation/New York, and some had been doing organizing for years. But it dissolved into a parody of why people stopped doing stuff years ago. While going around the room, one woman stood up and claimed that we should be doing work on animal rights, and somebody else got up saying we should do something else. As this is happening, Sarah was getting more and more crazed because she has this style which is that she wants things to go the way she wants them to go. And she was there to find out what actions we could do, and people weren't talking about that. At one point, as this was starting to happen, it got to me and I stood up and I said "I can't believe that I'm sitting here and there's not one person in this room who is talking about what a lesbian issue is. Are you all out at your workplaces? Are you all getting decent health care?" I mean, they were living in another world, and the only person who had spoken about this was June Chan, who we had worked with in Women for Women who had started Asian Lesbians of the East Coast. She was organizing with this whole other group a protest against Lambda Legal Defense, who refused to stop their fundraiser at *Miss Saigon*.[18] I said, "Now, do you want to know why *that's* a lesbian and gay issue? Because an organization that says "lesbian" in its title is holding a fundraiser there. Otherwise, I don't hear anybody doing anything." Sarah was desperately trying to rein these people in and I said, "Sarah, let it go because if you keep trying to tell them they can't argue about this, you're going to get massacred."
LS: In fact, it wasn't the time, as you said.
MW: It wasn't the time, and it wasn't the way to go about it. So, I kept wanting to do this but I was very tied into ACT UP stuff, and Sarah is friends with Ana Simo, who is a lesbian who ran the first lesbian performance space in New York called "Medusa's Revenge." She's a writer and translator, a Cuban dyke, and she was very upset about what was going on in New York around the AIDS curriculum and the Rainbow curriculum. Sarah told Ana that she should talk to me because my idea was that we should just arbitrarily, without asking anybody, make up leaflets that said "Are you being harassed at work?" and other examples and then to say "Call the Lesbian Direct Action Hotline. We'll do an action for you." And she thought that was a great idea. She and I went out to have a drink and she said she really wanted to do something and this was January and I said, "Ana, I can't do anything until May," and she said, "OK, in May I'm going to invite people to my house for dinner." I said, "OK, you do that in May and I'll come." And damned if she did not remember. In May she called me and said, "OK, it's time to do something."

We ended up calling a lot of different women who we had worked with in different ways over the years. The people who ended up at that meeting included Marie Honan and Anne Maguire, who were two of the lesbians who started the Irish Lesbian and Gay Organization, Sarah, Ana, Anne D'Adetsky and myself.[19] And we sat and had dinner and talked about whether starting a lesbian group was a possibility. In forty minutes we had a name. The group had to be a fait accompli, and no one could have a say in whether or not the group could exist because then it would never exist. We had to have a name and a group and an action and, basically, we had to figure out a way for lesbians to come to this action and to become part of planning for it. Ana had noticed what was in the newspapers at the time about the AIDS curriculum and the Rainbow curriculum and the right-wingers on the New York City School Board. After about two days, the issue of the Rainbow curriculum had disappeared and all the focus was on AIDS and not on lesbian and gay issues.

So we decided that night that our first action would be in September of 1992 against one of the school boards that refused to implement the Rainbow curriculum. We decided on Lesbian Avengers[20] as a name. We decided that we would give out club cards at Gay Pride, which was coming up in June. We each chipped in thirty-three dollars to pay for the making of eight thousand club cards. Sarah and someone else wrote the original text of the club card, which said something like "Lesbians, dykes, gay women: Cold-blooded liars like George Bush in the White House—what did they ever do for us? Religion. The State. Who cares. We want revenge and we want it now. What have you got to lose?" And then we put down the phone number of the telephone in the upstairs part of my house and set up a tape machine. When you called the number, the tape said "You have reached the Lesbian Avengers. We're planning our first action for the first day of school in September against the community school boards that have refused to accept the Rainbow curriculum. If you want to be part of the planning, come to our first meeting on July 6th." Ana was looking for a logo, and she went into the graphics file in her computer and her son said, "What about this funny bomb logo?" And she loved it—we all loved it, so we took the bomb. And then we gave the cards out only to lesbians who were not in the March. We did not want women who were already committed to nine thousand other groups. We wanted to reach women who were new. Seventy lesbians showed up for the first meeting.[21]

LS: Where was this?

MW: Our first action was in Queens, in a totally almost suburban area of Queens, which was almost totally white. Middle Village. There's never been a public demonstration in Middle Village. Basically, we decided that the only way to do anything about this was to do something that nobody else would do.[22] The women who came to the first meeting were all willing to do this. They were risk-takers. They had called a number they knew nothing about that they got from a card handed to them by someone they did not know. They knew that they were coming to a meeting about doing something on the first day of school about the Rainbow curriculum. Then word-of-mouth kicked in, and every week new women would show up. And what were their biggest issues? Their biggest issues were, "Aren't we using children, who are going to school on the first day, when it's already so chaotic and so upsetting to them already, and isn't this going to be terrible for kids?" And I said, "As someone who has two kids, this is what's going to happen. The first day of school is going to be great. The first day of school, these kids are going to get balloons and marching bands. They're going to think, 'Wow! This is fantastic!' And then the second day of school we're not going to be there and they're going to think, 'Oh my God. This is so boring. I can't believe it.'"

LS: "Where are those women?" [laughter]

MW: The other issue was that we had come up with this idea to make balloons that said "Ask about lesbian lives." People were really upset about that—these new women who would come in later weeks to the planning meeting. And we would have to go through the same argument again and again. They said "How can you give those balloons to children? That's really manipulating them." And I would then say, "What if the balloons said 'Save the Whales'?" The trademark of what the Avengers wanted to do was to be in a place and confront the issue that is the "no-no." Gay people connected to kids. That's where everyone falls apart—especially in Queens suburbs where no one ever goes. So we ended up doing it. We had seventy women show up on the first day of school. We had to go to the end of the train line, and then we marched. We were lucky when we picked out the school district that it ended up being the district of this totally right-wing woman who then gave us a lot of publicity. We wheat-pasted the neighborhood for weeks beforehand saying we were coming. And the Queens police showed up panicked but very nice because they have never ever had this happen to them. And we marched down this main street and then went over to the school. And when we got to the school, the police tried to tell us that we couldn't walk in front of the school. And we said, "That's not the law; the law says that if there's voting here, we can't give out literature within fifty feet of the voting site, but this is a city street and we're allowed to walk here." So we actually marched around the school and the kids were coming in for the first day of school and we handed out balloons and we had a marching band and sang songs like "We Are Family."

LS: How did the children and the parents respond?

MW: Well, there were a couple of parents who took the balloons and gave them to the kids, and there were other parents who were just horrified. They said things like "Let that balloon go! Don't you take that balloon!" And we thought that was fine, too, because then the kid is going to ask "Why? Why can't we say the word 'lesbian'?" So in the end none of us got arrested. We got a good amount of publicity for the issue, for ourselves, and that became our trademark—to do cutting-edge kind of stuff—out in places where people do not want us to be out. I think that a lot of that kind of attitude is not just a direct descendent from ACT UP because ACT UP's tactics were already an appropriation of those tactics from Gay Activist Alliance and feminists. Sarah

Early Lesbian Avengers flyer for actions around school curriculum and Public School 87, Queens, New York, 1993. Flyer by Lesbian Avengers New York. Courtesy of the Lesbian Herstory Education Foundation, Inc./ Lesbian Herstory Archives, Brooklyn, New York.

Schulman had been arrested in 1991 for busting up the East hearings in Congress. It is not as if these tactics had directly evolved from ACT UP. Not everyone originally in the Avengers had anything to do with ACT UP. Nor were the Avengers even in opposition to ACT UP. It was simply that, and this is the way several of us have felt for many years, lesbians have always been at the forefront of all movements for social change and most often in the leadership, especially in the women's movement, but they've been closeted. We wanted to be out, and we wanted to do something for ourselves because no one ever does anything about lesbians. No one.

LS: Were the Avengers formed as a reaction to political differences with "the boys"?

MW: No. Not at all.

LS: So that it wasn't because of political differences with the men in ACT UP?

MW: No. In fact Anne and Marie started the Irish Gay and Lesbian Organization and have and still do work in ILǴO, the International Lesbian and Gay Organization. Anne D'Adetsky has worked in ACT UP and in TAG. I've worked in mixed groups all my life. We did want to be able to be in a group where we did not have to deal with either the homophobia of straight women or the sexism of gay men. But that's not because we don't work with men. *We wanted to work on lesbian issues.* It was proactive. It became clear to us that nobody could even articulate what that was anymore. We wanted to work with women, with lesbians, around those issues and not have to worry about that other stuff. And I still work in ACT UP, for example, and Anne and Marie are still in the Irish Lesbian and Gay Organization, and the Avengers have done the marshaling and logistics strategy for the Irish Lesbian and Gay Organization for the last two years.

LS: So there's lots of crossover between and among the memberships.

MW: Yes. Going back to what Jan Clausen said about "energetic" . . . somehow people think that if you are visible and do media-grabbing events, then all it is about is frivolity. For example, our "signature," so to speak, is the fact that we eat fire. Lots of people think that this is a circus stunt to open or close events. But eating fire has great significance for the Avengers, as does the frequent use of fire, and we refuse to simply go somewhere and do it as a stunt. We started fire-eating as part of our actions against the Oregon antilesbian and gay amendment.[23] In September 1992 an African-American lesbian and a disabled white gay man, Hattie Cohens and Brian Mock, were burned to death in their apartment in Salem when neo-Nazi skinheads threw a molotov cocktail through their window. This was in the middle of the Citizen Alliance's first (unsuccessful) campaign, which was filled with hate, to pass the amendment. There had been no national media attention paid to the murders. And even our side in Oregon had not made the murders widely known. When we heard about it, we decided that we could focus on making it known widely, both within New York City and nationally. We sent press releases around the country, held a press conference at City Hall. Eventually, Anna Quindlan picked it up in the *New York Times*.[24] Quindlan's article was photocopied and put in mailboxes in Oregon. When the Anti-Violence Project in New York asked us to be one of the groups doing "something" on a street corner during the annual Take Back the Night March, which took place on the night before Hallowe'en, when there is the highest level of antilesbian and gay violence in New York City, we came up with the idea to focus on the Oregon murders. We were ambitious—not only did we plan something for the march but something we could do leading up to the day of the vote three days later. We created a huge shrine to Hattie and Brian—a triptych—with their photos and the words—"Burned to Death for Being Who They Are." We took the corner of Sixth Avenue and Bleecker Street as our place. This is where two dykes had been badly bashed a few months earlier. We camped out there for three days and nights and handed out leaflets about the murders and about the antilesbian and gay initiatives around the country. Our kickoff was the antiviolence Take Back the Night March. Jennifer Monson, who had been a fire-eater in Jennifer Miller's Circus Amok, came up with the idea of us eating fire and taught

Lesbian Avengers shrine in memory of Hattie Mae Cohens and Brian Mock, victims of homophobic violence at the hands of neo-Nazis in Oregon, 1992. Photograph by Saskia Scheffer.

everyone to eat fire who wanted to learn. Lysander Puccio, who was studying theology, wrote a eulogy. When the March got to our corner, she gave her eulogy—it sounds corny but it was incredibly moving because she spoke about our fears and about the real hatred against us, using as an example not only Hattie and Brian but about the two dykes who had been bashed on that corner. Then, she basically said that we could not let their fire consume us; instead we had to take it and make it our own, letting it give us the energy to fight back. At that point about ten dykes got into a circle in front of the crowd and lit their torches from one another's tongues and then ate the fire while the rest of us chanted "Their fire will not consume us; we take it and make it our own." The crowd roared! We stayed on that corner for three days and nights; it was freezing and raining. Passersby started bringing us food and blankets. People came and lit candles in front of the shrine and brought mementos of friends who had died of physical violence, from AIDS. And so fire-eating and the use of fire became a way of expressing our purpose and still is. And we refuse to do it unless we can tell the story. A couple of weeks later, after the votes in Oregon and Colorado were in, we staged a march down Fifth Avenue during rush hour. A group of women had made torches to light the way down from the Plaza Hotel to Rockefeller Center, our symbol of the major media that had not covered the murders nor other violence against us. To march without a permit was against the law. But the women with the torches persisted, and when the flames were lit and they wrestled them away from the cops, everyone was empowered. We ended that demo by burning replicas of the Oregon and Colorado amendments there, in front of Rockefeller Center, while everyone chanted "Their fire will not consume us; we take it and make it our own." We also ate fire in front of the White House during the dyke march we organized, again without a permit, the night before the 1993 Lesbian/Gay March on Washington.[25]

The Dyke Marches are another example of taking over public space for our own ends. It began in October 1992, when we realized that lesbians would blend invisibly into the massive numbers of gay men who would come to the 1993 March on Washington, and the message would be all about assimilation and the military. We sent an announcement to the *Lesbian Connection,* a newsletter that goes to thousands

Lesbian Avengers eating fire in front of The White House, Washington, D.C., April 24, 1993. Photograph © Morgan Gwenwald.

of lesbians around the country, saying there would be a dyke march. Lesbians from Los Angeles and Philadelphia, from ACT UP New York and the Avengers, had conference phone calls during January and solidified plans. The New York Avengers came down to D.C. and handed out eight thousand palm cards on Friday in the day and at night, and on Saturday during the day. First we thought no one would show up. Then we realized that thousands would and that there was no way that we could actually marshal this, except to trust that enough dykes in the crowd had done it and would take care of each other. As the time approached, hundreds of dykes started to show up at Dupont Circle. It was overwhelming, and the excitement was extraordinary. There were about twenty thousand dykes at the "nonpermitted" march and we marched past the White House, where the Avengers ate fire, and onto a grassy part of the mall for a closing ceremony. Amazingly, the gay press hardly covered it. There was an article in the *Nation,* which said that all of the media except the *Washington Post* had not covered the most important event of the weekend that was not assimilationist and not about the military, the Dyke March.[26] We always have that problem, even with the gay media, and it happened again during Stonewall 25 when we organized the International Dyke March. All the papers covered was the Stonewall Committee's arguments with Guiliani about whether they could march down Fifth Avenue, which they did not, and ACT UP saying they would anyway, which they did. Meanwhile, we organized a nonpermitted International Dyke March for Saturday evening. It began at Bryant Park, on 42nd Street, between Fifth and Sixth Avenues, and marched downtown on Fifth Avenue all the way to Washington Square Park, where we had a rally. Although the March was not slated to begin until 5:30, by 3:30 dykes were already showing up at the park, and by 5 P.M., it was totally a dyke space—dykes chatting in groups, sitting on benches reading, a dyke saxophone quartet playing music. And then the drum rolls began at 5:30, and the banner went up in the air. The effect was electrifying. There were thousands of dykes marching down 42nd Street to Fifth Avenue, they were willing to risk arrest, and *boom* we were on Fifth Avenue, and a huge roar went up, not only from the marchers but from a couple of thousand dykes and fags sitting and waiting for us on the main library steps on Fifth. The cops kept trying to keep us to two lanes, and then they started to push on us and tried to have vehicles drive on the side of us. We just stood there chanting—not moving—and told them it would get worse if they did not let us march. We had two or three standoffs like this, and then they just gave up.

Again, the gay media hardly covered this but the straight media did. But the lesbian grapevine still exists and now there are dyke marches all over the country and in some places they are seen as *the* alternative marches in the Stonewall celebrations in late June. Because there are no contingents, you do not have to be in a group to have a place in the march; you do not have to dress or act in a certain way. Fag friends stand on the sidelines and cheer us on. In some cities gay men march along. Lots of dykes feel that this is the real event of the weekend.

LS: What are the Lesbian Avengers doing now? What kinds of actions are you involved in, and what kinds of missions are you undertaking?

MW: Well, we're still going where no one wants us to go. I'll give you two examples. The first is that we have a Lesbian Avengers civil-rights organizing project. This is our second year of doing it. This year we sent eight full-time organizers and ten part-time organizers to live and work in rural northern Idaho to do "out" organizing against

The first annual Dyke Pride March in New York City, June 1993. Photograph by Saskia Scheffer.

Proposition One there[27]—much to the chagrin of the mainstream lesbian and gay campaign there, who were once again going to do a campaign that did not mention lesbians and gay men, even though the right wing mentions us all the time. We were incredibly successful in every place that we worked, including extreme right-wing areas where the Aryan Nation shows up at Human Rights Tasks Force events in Nazi regalia. We actually won by far larger percentages in every area in which we worked than the mainstream campaign or in comparison to the statewide vote.

LS: What kinds of actions did you do?

MW: We did everything from wrapping a ribbon around a Unitarian Church to help the minister declare it a "hate-free zone" to going to the Latah County Fair and holding a Lesbian and Gay Freedom Picnic and handing out Hershey's Kisses, with a little card that said “Last year at this Fair fifteen lesbians and gay men were harassed. Wouldn’t you like a kiss instead?” We did door-to-door out canvassing. We wrote literature that was about lesbians and gay men. There were some independent northern campaigns like Voices for Human Rights which, while they weren’t as radical as we were, were perfectly willing to not use the closeted literature of the mainstream lesbian and gay campaign in Boise and used ours instead. We made lawn signs that, instead of saying “No on One,” said “No lesbian bashing, No on One” and “No Gay Teen Suicide, No on One.” We actually worked with some people in Lewiston, Idaho, and we helped them to form the Lewiston Lesbian and Gay Society, and they held a public town meeting at which five lesbians and gay men who had grown up in that town came out. That’s the kind of stuff that we’ve been doing there. And in that campaign, people went out and lived there for four months, and I was out there for ten days in November.

In New York City, we just did a series of coalition actions Ana organized with Las Buenas Amigas, which is a Latina lesbian group, and African-American Women United for Societal Change about this radio station called “Mega K Q,” which is one of only two radio stations in New York and the only one on AM that does Spanish music and programming. Their major morning program is also in Los Angeles and several other parts of the country and is the most racist homophobic sexist dialogue you’ve ever heard—like “Women want to be raped” and “Latina lesbians and gay men should be eliminated.” It’s horrifying. So we started out a few months ago with an Avenger action in which we did a small picket outside the station calling it “hate radio,” and six women got inside and actually took over their microphones and said “Enough. Stop this. Stop the Hate. Hate isn’t funny,” and then walked out without getting arrested. Then we came back and did another action. In that one we wheat-pasted in Latin neighborhoods saying “Stop the Hate. Call Mega K Q.” We called their advertisers and got them to put pressure on them. Then, last week, we did this joint action with Las Buenas Amigas and African Ancestral Lesbians for a march that went down 57th Street and across Sixth Avenue and down 56th Street to their building, chanting. We had a huge piñata that was made like a radio, and it had two monster heads coming out of it. We had a drum corps drumming Latin music, and we had made up songs. We do a lot of stuff like that.

We also do very visual actions, and we go to places where no one wants us to be. We did an action on Staten Island. We went to the Alice Austin House, which is a National Historic Landmark. Alice Austin was a dyke photographer at the turn of the century, who actually produced one of the most incredible collections of photographs of lesbians and gay men. But the people who run the House refuse to admit that she was a lesbian and that she lived in it for thirty-three years with her lover. Everyone knows this. We went out there when they had a “Nautical Day” dressed as turn-of-the-century lifeguards and carrying big life preservers that said "Dyke Preserver" on them. And we had rewritten songs like "Ho Ho Homosex Homosexual/Alice and Gertrude were lesbians and we are as well." We did a whole performance thing out there—in Staten Island.

LS: That's a scary thing to do, Maxine. I know people on Staten Island. [laughter]

MW: We do serious politics. For example, when we worked in Idaho, we lived out there for four months—eight organizers living in northern Idaho and really getting to know the people and working with the people and being part of what was going on there and just helping people express it in ways that are unusual.

Do You Love the Dyke in Your Face?[1]

Carrie Moyer and Dyke Action Machine!

In 1990 I joined Queer Nation, New York, a few months after its founding. I had never been in an activist group, though I certainly was a prime candidate for one. Since coming out in high school, I had felt progressively more angry and alienated from straight mainstream culture. I had gone to many ACT UP demos but never had "joined." From the beginning I was very taken with Queer Nation—volunteering to design the press kit at my first meeting. Queer Nation was starting to get some media attention, coordinated by a few of the men who had ties to the industry. As I later learned, media access available to gay and lesbian organizations is almost always the sole province of men—men who, in the "straight" world, are commonly publicists or in advertising. If women play a part at all, they are usually spokespersons—not media contacts or strategists.

Before joining Queer Nation, I had been working as a graphic designer for major consumer advertising and design firms for five years. So by the time I hooked up with two other Queer Nationals, Masha Gessen and Charles Welz, to form the working group "Truth In Advertising," I had been totally immersed in the language of the industry for quite some time. I was more than ready to use my training to promote queer causes. Personally, I had also been greatly affected by the work of Gran Fury,[2] Barbara Kruger,[3] and the Guerrilla Girls,[4] and was eager to incorporate their tactics into our aesthetic attack. *Truth in Advertising* was based on a very simple premise: to include gay people in the visual environment that surrounds New Yorkers every time they set foot outside. Our work was a foreseeable product of gay and lesbian activism of the time: trying to get straight culture to accept us, to "like" us, by becoming more visible to *them,* by being out. One of our first campaigns was a takeoff of the New York State Lottery campaign—"All you need is a dollar bill and a dream." Our version, which was wheat-pasted over the actual ads on the street and in subway stations, stated "All you need is a three-dollar bill and a dream." Some of the posters merely transposed the gender of the speaker, making the ad queer ("I'd tell every man I ever loved—who's sorry now?" states Jeff Smith, Queer plumber) while others reclaimed queer-baiting slang by using it to describe the speaker's ultimate fantasy ("I'd start my own cigarette company and call it 'Fags.'").

Not surprisingly, Queer Nation, the group that was supposed to unite gay *and* lesbian activists to agitate for an agenda common to both, rarely—if ever—focused on lesbian issues. So Dyke Action Machine! (DAM!) began as the lesbian working group of Queer Nation. Our first events were primarily visibility actions, such as usurping straight or neutral spaces by staging kiss-ins at malls, (straight) singles bars, and on the Staten Island Ferry. After attending the first-ever National Lesbian Conference in Atlanta in 1991, DAM! lost momentum and finally died out due to a lack of leadership and political experience. Before the group completely expired, photographer Sue Schaffner and I started doing poster campaigns using the *Truth in Advertising* model —we provided lesbians on the street with the pleasure of seeing their own images in professional, well-designed public art. We wanted to create facsimiles of the very images that ignored our existence.

As DAM! the activist group died out, DAM! the lesbian graphics project[5] thrived. Sue and I have continued to do our public art/poster campaigns. Our first, in 1991, was a spoof of the GAP ads, then ubiquitous throughout New York City. These ads featured minor or underground celebrities modeling T-shirts and jeans—the only *out* celebrity ever featured in their campaign was Tony Kushner. DAM!'s posters addressed how lesbians were not, at that precise moment in the history of advertising, considered either celebrities or even general consumers and showed images of chic downtown dykes (former DAM! members all). It is important to note that when lesbian celebrities were later used to sell products—such as L.A. Eyewear (Melissa Etheridge) or the *New York Times* (Martina Navratilova)—the women had all become famous while closeted and later came out. Lesbians who had *always* been out are still not considered to be celebrities by either the gay or straight media. The captions on our first campaign read "Anti-violence whistle blown by Samantha, Pink Panther. Photograph by Girl Ray." Our work acknowledged that a basic requirement for being recognized in American culture is a person's participation in a consumer group. At the time, we had no insight into the dangers to gay people of niche marketing.

From the start, our means of getting the message out was to plaster anything or any place in sight. During the first three years, DAM! relied heavily on a small pack of friends who led our midnight wheat-pasting attacks, often having to return to the same sites night after night as the phone company diligently undid our work. As with any public campaign, our most successful hits were in well-trafficked areas next to the ads we were satirizing, or at least in the right context—the lesbo-erotic images of companies such as Kikit and Banana Republic provided perfect foils. In 1992 *Family Circle* magazine launched a campaign positing "family values," a phrase popularized at that time by the Religious Right as a hip new trend. The ads showed flexed biceps with lawn-mower tattoos and hunky dreadlocked men snuggling babies. Our project that year, "Lesbian Family Values," was a set of three diptychs presenting the family tradition in lesbian culture, while at the same time critiquing the crass revisionist marketing of the family. Predating the mainstreaming of the gay family, gay marriage, and the lesbian baby boom, the work dissected the Reagan/Right-wing connotations

DAM!, *Lesbian Family Values* campaign, installed posters, Manhattan, 1992. Photography courtesy of Carrie Moyer.

by evoking lesbian families with such slogans as "Dykes were family, by golly, before families became trendy."

Calvin Klein's underwear campaign, featuring homophobic rapper Marky Mark, served as our inspiration in 1993. While staying stylistically close to the actual Klein ads, our message functioned not only as a lesbian response aimed at other lesbians but also as a query to straight people. The question posed by the poster, "Do You Love the Dyke in Your Life?" presumes that everyone has a dyke in her/his life, and people's treatment of the lesbian(s) in their lives might be less than universally loving. The poster was also a direct hit on the homogeneous white gym body so beloved by both heterosexual and gay male cultures.

Straight to Hell[6] is the movie DAM! would like to see made but never will. In 1994 we created the poster for this faux film and had it plastered all over Manhattan for Stonewall 25, right next to posters for *The Lion King* and *Sleepless in Seattle*. Increasingly, the images of gay men and lesbians are being manufactured and controlled by the straight media—from the momentary craze, "lesbian chic," to movies such as *Philadelphia,* in which the "life" of a PWA is depicted by a straight director, to coming out as a career move for a wide array of "stars" and has-beens: k.d. lang, Janis Ian, and even Boy George! *Straight to Hell* aimed to cross that line dubbed by *Newsweek* as the "limit of tolerance." In a twist on the gays in the military issue, a lesbian is expelled from the army and returns for blood, with her stone-butch posse

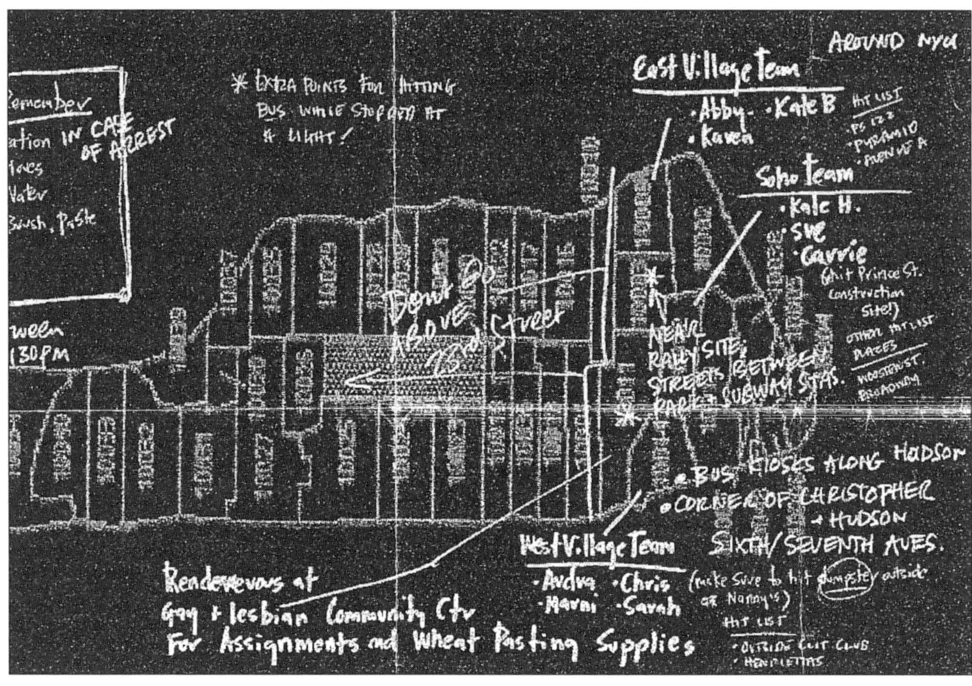

DAM!, street installation plan from the 1992 *Family Circle* campaign, Manhattan, 1992. Courtesy of Carrie Moyer.

DAM!, *Do You Love the Dyke in Your Life?* campaign, installed posters, Manhattan, 1993. Photography courtesy of Carrie Moyer.

in tow. The text reads: "She came out. So the Army kicked her out. NOW SHE'S OUT FOR BLOOD." The poster advertises a lesbian revenge film, and the iconography and the language are identitical to those used to position a Steven Segal or an Arnold Schwarzenegger film in the pop-culture universe. Only this time the enemy is straight people. The three protagonists tower over the viewer, their collective shape coming to a phallic point at the top of the poster. The folded arms and stoic faces evoke the gangsta-rapper. The righteous anger colossal enough to wreak havoc on corrupt institutions, to right all wrongs, or to save the planet is never the prerogative of women—let alone lesbians. Women who get revenge are either psychos with pickaxes or stalkers, as in *Single White Female*. The subtext of *Straight to Hell* is that lesbians are not groveling for the acceptance of straights but are a posse of powerful dykes who will protect their own.[7]

Starting with the faux film poster, DAM!'s position in relation to popular imagery has been to move away from reactive art or appropriation art (with a twist) and to address underlying conventions common to all marketing strategies, whether they are used for selling clothes, magazines, or movies. After having spent entire lives being marginalized by the official heterosexual culture and again by official gay (male) culture, DAM!'s greatest pleasure has been to construct a visual/textual bridge from our community to the "real" world, the public world. Our graphic language articulates and represents a lesbian reality that dominating visual images ignore, deny, and repress. Because the posters are wheat-pasted throughout the city, the great sea of viewers is intoxicating for us as artists, while politically it negates the exclusionary perception of "audience" that public displays anticipate.

As lesbians and gay men, we are still unused to being the targets for mainstream advertising. Just as perceptive marketing managers expect, we unquestioningly project ourselves onto each and every sexually-ambiguous or possibly "gay-friendly" advertising scenario that comes into our field of vision. (See especially campaigns for Johnny Walker, Diesel Jeans, and almost anything advertised in *Out* Magazine.) We are ever straining to identify with the ad industry's newly imposed representations of us. Because of this false public representation, we tend to be overly grateful when some mainstream company actually does advertise specifically to us; Virgin Airlines received over 200 letters of thanks from readers after they advertised in *Out* Magazine. Mulryan/Nash, an ad agency that focuses exclusively on the gay and lesbian market, has obliquely noted that, since many gay people are geographically separated or driven away by their homophobic families, the buying patterns learned from parents are not in place.[8] So when a company actually "reaches out" to the gay or lesbian consumer, it can expect a certain amount of brand loyalty. Mom and Dad might not like me, but I know Absolut Vodka does! Yet even within the corporate movement to contain and

DAM!, *Straight to Hell* campaign poster, 1994. Courtesy of Carrie Moyer.

homogenize the gay and lesbian community, consistent with some niche marketing techniques, lesbians are still unrecognized and invisible.

DAM!, always eager for new venues for agitprop, rode the wave of the World-wide Web in 1995 when we launched our interactive promotion for a fantasy lesbian television network on the Internet. Web surfers could download our site, "The Girlie Network,"[9] check out the prime-time schedule, and open up glossy teasers for selected shows. Our lineup featured such Sapphic classics as "Leave Us The Beaver" and "The Snip Squad," as well as promo for four additional shows. Since going online in the summer of 1995, our website has received over fourteen thousand "hits" or visits by Net users per month and has generated hundreds of responses. The project has become most gratifying for us (the makers), as we now have a direct contact with our audience. One troubling aspect of making public art that exists only on the Internet is the inherent elitism of the medium. While it lets us know for a fact that significant numbers of people notice our work, in many ways we don't like our new audience. Our viewers are much more homogeneous—more male, more middle-class, more academic (since most Internet users are based in colleges). For this reason DAM! has decided only to use cyberspace as a place to post information on future real-world projects.

In 1996 DAM! went slumming with D.A.M. S.C.U.M., creating several lo-tech incendiary devices sure to offend just about everyone. Our multifaceted project—consisting of matchbooks, wallet cards, and a magazine page, all promoting an interactive phone line—envisions a lesbian militia of which Valerie Solanas would have been proud. Male callers are offered the chance to listen to the S.C.U.M. Manifesto, and female callers a description of DAM!'s self-defense products for the "separatist-on-the-go." The magazine portion of D.A.M. S.C.U.M. debuted in the September 1996 issue of *Art Journal*. Over the summer, ten thousand wallet cards and matchbooks appeared at ATMs, bars, and building foyers. Part homage to Valerie Solanas, part feminist foray into the Waco phenomenon, part loving tribute to low-budget marketing, D.A.M. S.C.U.M. is a hybrid which makes *Soldier of Fortune* finally take that dive.

Because DAM!'s projects react to transitory public advertising campaigns, their life spans are relatively short. By necessity, they have to be cheap and fast. They must be oppositional and seductive. To appeal to the lesbian viewer, the posters must refer to elements of lesbian culture from an insider's perspective, but at the same time be empowering to the lesbian observer by placing those images within the vocabulary of "the world," thereby not re-creating the obscurity of her existence. These posters become quintessential antiobjects. They are intended to be disposable, not precious, while subverting the permanence of architecture by altering the visual/spatial environment. Yet women seize upon these images, giving them a second life. Long after the campaign is over, these posters still hang on refrigerators or in bedrooms, become memorabilia in scrapbooks, and are mailed to other lesbian communities across the country. Often these images will appear months or years later on another continent, after having traveled the underground railroad by which lesbians communicate, despite being excluded from the commercial media.

Our next challenge as a public art/agitprop outfit is to find a new way of surprising our viewers into action. What uncharted media avenues remain for making an impact within image-saturated urban sites? Could more humble lo-fi/lo-tech projects become a means of addressing an audience already jaded by slick cynical representations of queerness? Stay tuned for DAM!'s exploits in the quotidian world of budget advertising, and don't be surprised when you find a message on a matchbook, business card, frisbee, coffee cup. . .

Strategies for (Re)constructing Queer Communities

Gordon Brent Ingram, Anne-Marie Bouthillette, and Yolanda Retter

> Love-making and home-making, eroticism and domesticity, sexual delight and the assiduous nurture of children—these are among the highest human goals of genuine biotechnic planning. Everything from the distribution of open spaces to the heights of windows is affected by this program, and the sooner the architect and planner faces these facts of contemporary life and evaluates them intelligently, the quicker will he throw off the clichés of old-fashioned design.
>
> —Lewis Mumford, 1938[1]

We complete this discussion of the physical spaces of marginalized sexualities with a review of why it is so important, at this point in history, to consider the various possible relationships between communality, community, and environmental design. For many of the contributors to *Queers in Space,* the 1993–97 period has represented an odyssey beyond queer nationalism and opaque vague queer theory back to the "village," and home. But the social forces and ignorance that pushed sexual minorities out of their villages are not gone, and our hard-won ghettos, no matter how tacky and brimming with alienation, may be only a temporary refuge. Here we revisit some of the book's main concepts and finish by presenting an expanded spatial lexicon and the visions, strategies, and tactics necessary to improve peoples' lives. While respecting differences within queer communities, a common language and vision for the future are prerequisites to imagining, and then planning, architectures that expand freedom of expression, reappropriate androcentric, ethnocentric, and commercial queer spaces, and sustain far deeper forms of community.

Naming the Terrain: Constructing a Queers-in-Space Lexicon

People often mean different things when they use the same words. We suggest the following tentative definitions that have emerged as we completed this project:

[queer] site

> A point in physical space where there is contact and exchange involving at least two people and where there is positive or impartial relationship to homoeroticism within a broader environment that includes some kind of homophobia; sites can exist for a moment or can be more stable

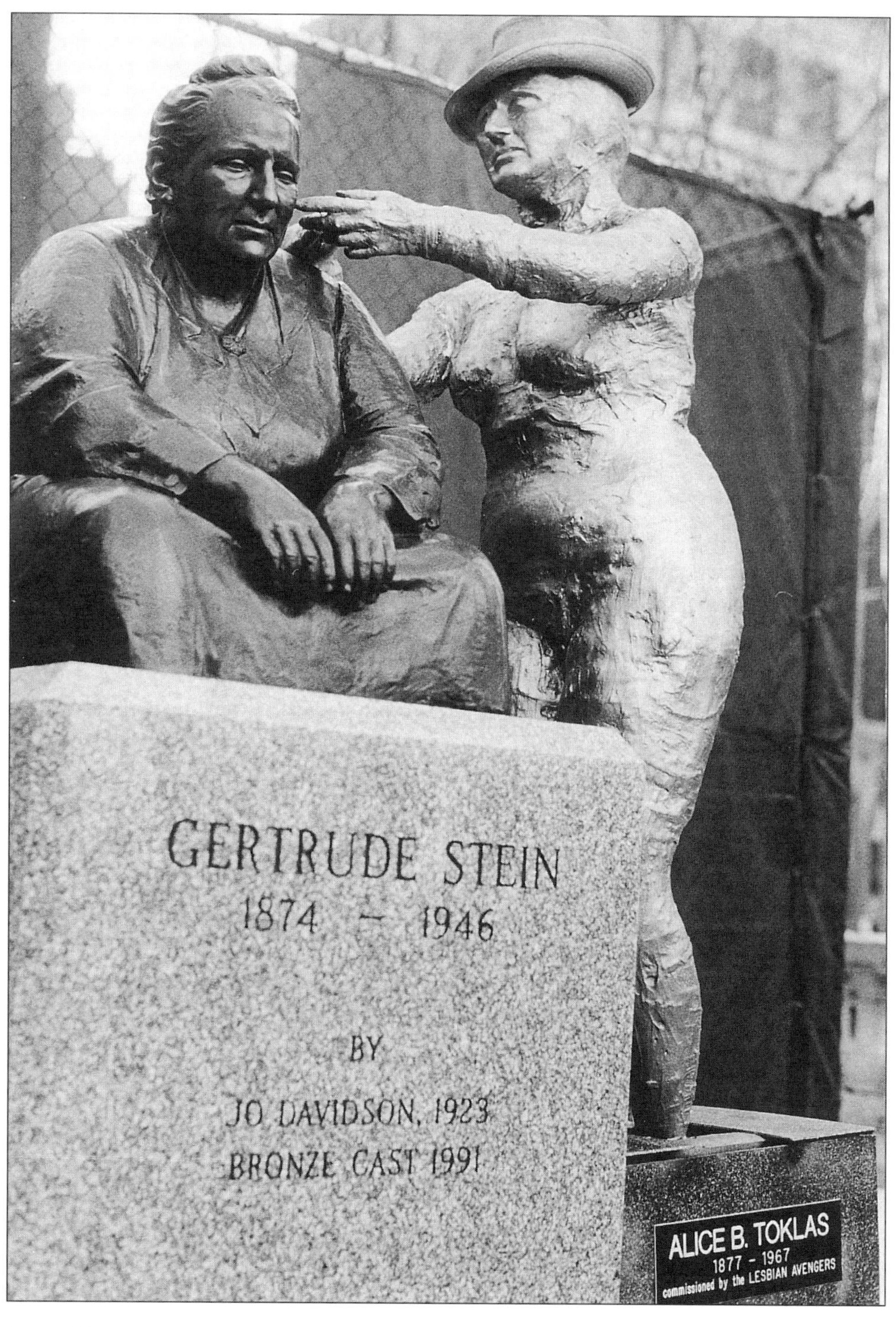

Statues of Gertrude Stein and newly installed Alice B. Toklas, Bryant Park, New York City, 1993. Photograph © Morgan Gwenwald.

[queer] space

An expanding set of queer sites that function to destabilize heteronormative relations and thus provide more opportunities for homoerotic expression and related communality

[queer] network

A shifting set of relations and exchanges, involving more than two people, with a positive or impartial relationship to homoeroticism within a globalizing political economy that includes some kind of homophobia; networks can be defined by combinations of identities, desires, sensibilities, interests, locations, and proximities

[queer] node

A set of particularly important or strategic queer sites for the ongoing functioning and contact of some of the networks marginalized in heteronormative political economies

queerscape

A physical landscape that harbours queer sites and queer space, where resistance to heteronormative constraints and a diversity of homoerotic relations intensify, cumulatively, over time

[a queer] community/communities

A full collection or select subset of queer networks for a particular territory, with relatively stable relationships that enhance interdependence, mutual support, and protection

[queer] placemaking

The use and casual or purposeful modification of a site or set of sites by queer networks, which marks their irregular or ongoing presence

[queer] appropriation [of space]

The transformation of formerly homophobic and heteronormative social and physical space (whether public, private, or derived from the electronic media) for social relations that support or enhance opportunities for homoerotic and allied communality and eroticism

[queer] territorialization

Relatively secure placemaking across landscapes that cumulatively challenges constraints on queer communities, homoeroticism, and the dominance of heteronormative relations and cultures

Mark Robbins, *Utopian Prospect*, permanent installation at Byrdcliffe Art Colony, Woodstock, New York, 1988.

deterritorialization [of queer groups]

The loss of identifiable queer sites and nodes, and thus substantial portions of a local queerscape, through homophobia, capital, or environmental deterioration

delocalization

The indefinite replication of the configurations of key relationships associated with one queer site or node at another, possibly distant locale—a sort of multiple placemaking[2]

Ongoing Debates

This anthology was conceived to deepen engagement and continue the debate on queer communities and landscapes; we have both illuminated commonalities and articulated theoretical differences. A telling flashpoint is the variety of interpretations and uses of Manuel Castell's discussion of San Francisco, *The City and the Grassroots,* which presents his interpretations of the differences in lesbian and gay male place-making. Although influential and considered almost paradigmatic throughout much of the 1980s, his generalizations appear today as somewhat simplistic, if not essentialist. Yet for many, Castell's vision is still the one that makes the most sense.

Other debates will require entire books to explore; they include differences in communalities and communities that exist in developing and developed contexts (such as North and South) and the ambiguous role of the liberal state.

Reconstructing Community: Strategies, Tactics, and Interventions

> I predict a series of homosexual cities, small, compact, carefully planned areas, will soon be blatantly advertised and exist from coast to coast.
>
> —Criswell 1970[3]

The neat little homosexual enclaves envisioned a year after Stonewall by the professional psychic Criswell have not materialized, largely because there has been no demand for them. They would have been deathly boring. Instead, queer presences and markers proliferate, entailing sites, buildings, neighbourhoods, regions, and cyberspace. Most members of sexual minorities have little interest in living in separate communities or even ghettos. But expanding the social and cultural relations necessary to enrich a wide range of communalities and communities definitely requires material changes shaped by both public policy and design of the physical environment.

Within the range of subtle social and aesthetic amenities important to service economies, queer space is one of several competing planning paradigms based on recognition of "difference" and the resulting need for "place."[4] This new dynamic exposes and skews the purposes of conventional planning and design, confronting its biases and inequities related to sexuality and social relations. Concerns for eroticism and the communalities of desires and aesthetics will diminish once we achieve environmental designs that minimize all forms of inequity and marginalization.

Paradoxically, the notion of queer space has emerged at a time when lesbian and gay culture, theory, and politics are being increasingly recognized in many university curricula, while at the same time the influence of the humanities in planning continues to decline.[5] Thus queerscape architecture represents an example of "the return of aesthetics to city planning."[6] Intensified flow of information and growing access to electronic images have inevitably increased media representations of minority sexualities.

But the social fragmentation unleashed with globalizing capital tends to limit the sites of minority sexual cultures to redefined ghettos and a few corners of cyberspace. These constraints make the inhabiting and defending of physical queer space more immediately important than the planning and function of the sites themselves.

New forms of planning and approaches to forging civic alliances are already taking form. Rather than shaping space based on contests between groups with relatively static identities, more subtle differences can categorize a range of social and social-environmental relationships and related desires and needs. Underpinning these fluid groupings are more "objective," or at least shared, political economic realities. Political organizing and planning related to public space, housing, and other aspects of landscape need to involve various levels of "communicative action"[7] that recognize commonalities and differences. Yet certain caveats must be observed whenever planning is carried out. As Sophie Watson and Katherine Gibson put it, "Planning for difference, where difference is constructed as a threat to social order, means recognizing that planning as a tool for reform can shift to planning as a tool for control and repression."[8]

The beginnings of queerscape architecture have been based on asserting desire and exposing homophobia. Continuing efforts are needed in confronting the mythologies of liberal democracy and identifying political and institutional relationships that

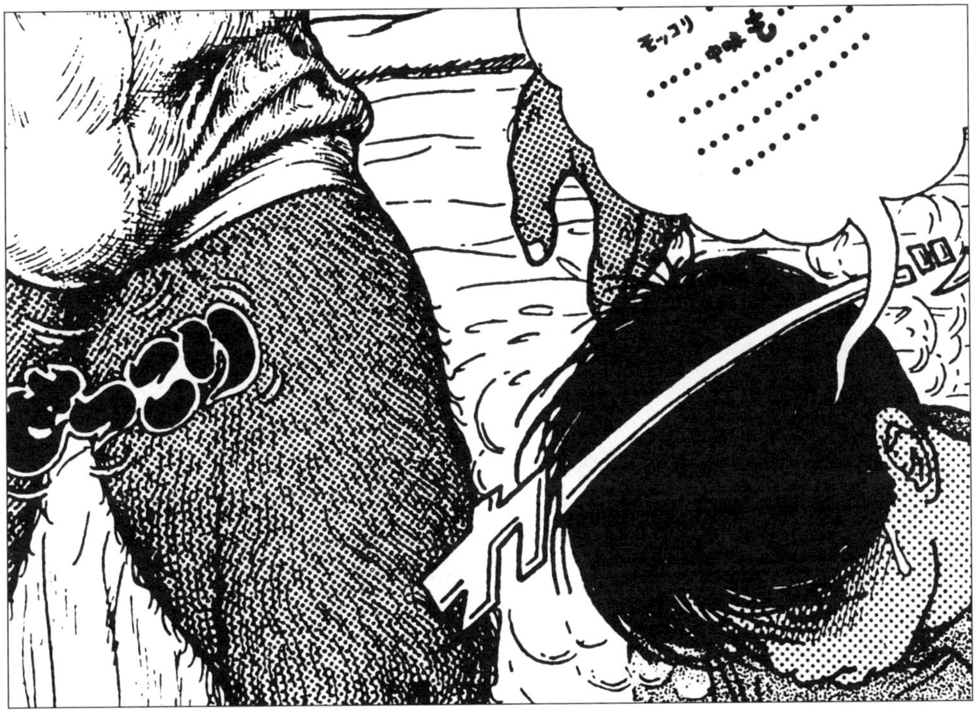

Mark Robbins, *Borrowed Landscape: 36 Views,* Museum of Modern Art, Saitama, Japan, 1994.

complacently allow heteronormative hegemony. This means uncovering the internalized heteronormative influence on gay culture itself. Planning, politics, and economics, no matter how democratic their patinas, must be reconsidered critically.

Today, few spaces are specifically "programmed" and designed for queer life. Many that do exist are expensive, overly cute, and crowded. Most of these sites quickly feel outmoded. It is time to conceive of programmes and designs that provide space for sexual minorities and marginalized sexualities. Lack of acknowledgment, except in the most patronizing and chauvinistic terms, in urban design and landscape architecture has for too long been the experience of queer people. As Clare Cooper Marcus quoted C. M. Deasy, "The purpose of planning or design is not to create a physical artifact, but a setting for human behavior,"[9] and with it, greater individual growth, social contact, and liberation. This social or "functionalist" position contrasts sharply with formalist impulses to reduce public space to reflect the aesthetic impulses of an elite.

Emerging recognition of queer space in planning and design is also another sign of the modernist/postmodernist "divide."[10] The modernist dream of comprehensive "master" plans has been supplanted by the hope of "muddling" forward by small increments of progress. For example, if a plan is far from comprehensive but helps prevent gay bashing, it is worth the effort. The totalizing effort is being replaced by a varied piecemeal (re)eroticization of everyday life to create queer space. As Elspeth Probyn said, "The local is only a fragmented set of possibilities that can be articulated into a momentary politics of time and space."[11] But when constellations of identities, affinities, sensibilities, desires, and acts are "linked" by proximity, sometimes enough social pressure is generated to have a large-scale impact.

Most cities have set forth utopian discourses, invariably with erotic aspects, that have produced spaces for new social relations and enhanced collective communication and contact. These "urban practices"[12] can be further developed and applied to rural and suburban settings.

Sexual minorities have often attempted to transform landscapes to create spaces for self-protection, for pleasure, and for building homes and refuges for healing.[13] In recent decades this movement has increased in momentum because of greater mobility in populations and more communication links. Queer activism in politics, public space, and art is increasing at a time of conflict concerning "participation" in design for public space.[14] Queer tactics can extend from creating an ephemeral presence, such as lesbian and gay parades, to concretizing queer interpretations of events, such as AIDS memorial sites. New levels of coordination and planning will be needed to implement reforms in policies and laws to lessen homophobic and economic constraints on the use of designed and natural open space. The needs and interests of specific groups must be analyzed to effect greater social inclusion. Such intervention falls into several categories: legislation, the court system, planning, finance, information access, civic participation, and culture.

The Trouble with Guidelines

The 1960s urban open-space movement attempted to flesh out modernist generalizations[15] based on vague liberal guidelines, such as those for parks and streets;[16] these oversimplifications, no matter how well-intentioned, can be easily misused. The homophobic narratives of modernist design provided little space for "difference," for marginality, for anyone who could not easily conform to a homogeneous consumer image—least of all for "queers" and other "perverts." Even the design guidelines for open space articulated in the 1990s, in a more tolerant climate, tend to ignore not only the thorny questions of public sex and gender equity in access but also the design issues related to cruising, socializing, camaraderie, and contact, which form major functions of neighbourhood parks for many queer enclaves and networks.[17] Today, much of the setting for our daily lives reflects this unsuccessful, if not cynical and hypocritical, attempt at making democratic space. Modernism has left in the landscape many psychological and social land mines.

Decades ago the progressive urban designer Donald Appleyard proposed some principles for the reclamation of streetscapes as public space: the street as a community, as neighbourly territory, as a place for play and learning, as a green and pleasant environment, and as a unique site of historical importance.[18] These principles could be queered, though with the following warning: It would be easy to make a new set of dogmatic generalizations that, though avowedly antipatriarchal, anticolonial, antiracist, sex-positive, and queer, might stand in the way of a more fundamental, authentic opening of public space. Such guidelines too often merely serve as blunt instruments for the construction of artifacts that might be as crude as those they are meant to replace.

Few recipes have been offered for the design and maintenance, let alone the recognition, of queer space. One early exploration by Michael Immel in the early 1980s, though often mired in essentialist notions, concluded that "gay identity and gay space is historically and cultural specific."[19] He made guidelines for settings such as parks[20] and streets. After a decade and a half of the ravages of AIDS, his prototypes seem quaint and naïve (thus proving his axiom). But any guidelines, like identities and even acts, are informed by specific experiences based on gender and race and embedded in the political economies of particular times. We need self-reflexive guidelines limited to particular time periods, places, and problems. "Defining gay design"[21] will elude modernist impulses to generalize and totalize; it will be accomplished by specific groups to serve specific sites and regions, often for fleeting periods of time.

Towards Queerscape Architecture

> New city forms and spaces will depend . . . on the creation of innovative tactics and plays to deal with uncertainty and disorder in this city of lost narrative forms.
>
> —Christine Boyer, 1994[22]

At a time of persistent homophobic violence and higher than necessary rates of death in most queer communities, as well as biophysical deterioration in public space and public lands, most queerscape architecture will arise from efforts to make areas safer, to construct public art (such as memorials) to confront erasure of queer experience, and to protect and restore vulnerable natural ecosystems. In *Queers in Space,* our intent has not been to fetishize physical space or to suggest an instrumentalist form of architecture that subverts other designs for social change. The opposite is true. But we are materialists, recognizing that tolerance of sexual expression requires room—places to meet, bedrooms, and updated "lovers' lanes," to name only a few spaces. Yet design decisions that stifle opportunities for contact between members of sexual minorities are being made every day. Many physical aspects of our communities reflect only incomplete adaptations of spatial archaeologies of repression. New forms of intervention, many of them necessarily architectural, will emerge in the coming years. Although concerns for safety from attacks, equitable access, and more truly public art are legitimate, they should not be viewed as reductive "element plans" but rather as broader questions that should inform all stages of the programming and subsequent use of public and private space.

Architecture, including landscape design and urban policy, has often been employed to "stabilize"[23] social contexts, rather than to spark creative forms of social change. But queerscape architecture, especially when based on modified forms of constructionist queer theory, can have almost the opposite effect. It takes nerve, a sense of humour, and dedication to envision and advocate for viable places that foster old and new ways to enjoy each other in the face of crowding, environmental degradation, and the continued hostility of the state. But these new queerings, no matter how quickly outmoded, are not only ethical in terms of promoting greater social equity and security, increased options for contact and expression, and deepened relationships—they are also a lot more fun.

Del LaGrace Volcano, *Sophie and Lulu: Editors of QUIM*, London, 1992.

Notes

Lost in Space, pages 3–16

1. Deutsche, *Evictions,* 269–327.
2. Valentine, Out and about, 105.
3. Young, The ideal of community and the politics of difference, in *Feminism/Postmodernism,* 301.
4. Pringle and Watson, Introduction, *Postmodern Cities and Spaces.* The notion of "constructing interests" was attributed to a paper by these writers especially for issues related to women in the city.
5. Rich, *Blood, Bread, and Poetry,* 210–31.
6. Deutsche, Men in space and Boys towns, in *Evictions,* xi–xii.
7. Haraway, *Simians, Cyborgs, and Women,* 157.
8. The architectural theorist, Manfredo Tafuri, spoke of using theory for recognition of conflictual and dialectical relationships in environmental design. See Tafuri, *Architecture and Utopia,* 1–49.
9. Boyer, *City of Collective Memory,* 3.
10. Tenhaaf, Mysteries of the bioapparatus, in *Immersed in Technology,* 51–71.
11. Boone, Queer sites in modernism, in *Geography of Identity,* 244–45.
12. The phrase "lost in space" was first used in George O. Smith's 1959 *Lost in Space.* For the initial set of stories for the television series, see Dave Van Arnam and Ron Archer, *Lost in Space.* Since then there have been numerous books on the series. See the web site http://www.lookup.com/Homepages/47451/space/trivia.html as of April 1996. In recent years the "lost in space" phrase and metaphor has been used to describe suburban North American culture of the 1960s and 1970s, the discontent of which has had such a bearing on contemporary North American lesbian and gay culture. Marleen S. Barr's anthology, *Lost in Space,* blazed the trail for this exploration though her claim of a feminist, lost-in-space "paradigm" may be premature.
13. Slagle, In defense of Queer Nation, 93.
14. "Queer" as in "queer theory" has been transformed in the last decade from a pejorative to a signifier of a female-male homosexual coalition. In contrast, "queers" still connotes hostility and homophobia. We use "queers" in this anthology because it is the shortest term for indicating the collectivity of marginalized consensual sexualities: lesbian, gay male, bisexual, transgendered, transvestite, and specific erotic networks such as those involving sadomasochism. We also recognize that while use of the term queers in 1997 makes many of us uncomfortable, it is often because the plural invokes recognition of the persistence of homophobic hostility—violence and threats of violence that are still very much with us today.
15. Relph, *Place and Placelessness,* 2-28.
16. Delany, *Dhalgren,* 372. See also Delany, *Tales from Nevèrÿon.*
17. Habermas, *Structural Transformation,* xi. Many of our notions of constructed public space are based on Jürgen Habermas's paradigmatic discussion of how "the emergent bourgeoisie gradually replaced a public sphere in which the ruler's power was merely represented *before* the people with a sphere in which state authority was publicly monitored through informed and critical discourse *by* the people."
18. Bhabha presents a broader framework for lesbian/gay/queer theory to be situated within decolonization along with various forms of internationalism and transculture, as well as a theory of "the other," in *Location of Culture,* 19–39.
19. Duggan and Hunter, *Sex Wars,* 1–14. "Sex Wars" refers to the conflicts that raged in many North American and European lesbian and gay communities from the late 1970s to the early 1990s around divergent positions on pornography, sadomasochism, possible links between male sexuality and misogynist violence, and censorship.
20. Boyer, *City of Collective Memory,* 4.
21. Drucker, In the tropics there is no sin, 75–109. Drucker began to construct an analytical framework to account for the extent and the diversity of sexual minorities in the developing world and the South that would recognize the impacts of both imperialism and the persistence of "indigenous sexualities" on difference and strategies for activism (77–78, 85–86). While his review is a step towards a more global theory of sexual minorities at a time when such a notion is increasingly suspect, there is only a limited recognition of the more contemporary impacts of the increasing globalization of capital and the rise of Third World middle classes. In this context, his notion of persistent indigenous sexualities might be better conceived as "localized sexualities" where there is persistent resistance to Eurocentric framings of gender and sexualities—including many that include strong elements of homoeroticism.
22. Gare, *Postmodernism and the Environmental Crisis,* 6–8.
23. Boyer, *City of Collective Memory,* 343.
24. Deutsche, *Evictions,* 74.
25. Ibid., 52. Deutsche argues that "Spatial forms are social structures" and that under late capitalism "Space, severed from its social production, is thus

fetishized as a physical entity and undergoes, through inversion, a transformation."

26. Hoff, Gender as a postmodern category of paralysis, 443–47.
27. Jeffreys, The queer disappearance of lesbian sexuality in the academy, 459–72.
28. Zita, Gay and lesbian studies, in *Tilting the Tower,* 258–76.
29. Anzaldua, *Making Face/Making Soul,* xvii.
30. Smith, *Home Girls,* xxxii.
31. Kennedy and Davis, *Boots of Leather, Slippers of Gold,* 16–17. An example is how these two writers try to account for the lack of African-American lesbians in their Buffalo study.
32. Wigley, *The Architecture of Deconstruction,* 59–95 and 177–204, especially 184–85. For a review of the multiplicity of physical and cultural spaces, see Tschumi, *Architecture and Disjunction,* 26–51.
33. Probyn, Travels in the postmodern, in *Feminism/Postmodernism,* 178.
34. Ibid., 187.
35. Fanon, *Black Skins, White Masks,* 183.
36. Duggan and Hunter, *Sex Wars,* 170.
37. Ibid., 168.
38. Ibid.
39. Grosz, *Space, Time, and Perversion.* While nearly all of these discussions employ or at least borrow from "feminist" social and geographical analyses, we are reminded of Grosz's cautionary: "A test is feminist or patriarchal only provisionally, only momentarily, only in some but not in all its possible readings, and in some but not all of its possible effects."
40. Ibid., 39–43.
41. Deutsche, *Evictions,* 74–77. See especially p. 76.
42. Ibid., 106–107.
43. "Sex-negative" is a phrase coined by opponents of positions such as those of Andrea Dworkin. In *Queers in Space,* we are not interested in evaluating these divergent positions but rather in exploring their implications for queer alliances, communities, and territorialization for the coming years.
44. Lechte, (Not) belonging in postmodern space, in *Postmodern Cities and Spaces,* 99.
45. For the emergence of notions of site-specificity, see Owens, The allegorical impulse, in *Beyond Recognition,* 55; Crimp, *On the Museum's Ruins,* 17 and 150–86. For a more critical discussion of site-specificity, see Deutsche, *Evictions,* xiii–xv, 67–70, 90–93.
46. Boyer, *City of Collective Memory,* 476.
47. Delany, *Dhalgren,* 14.
48. Foucault, Other spaces, 9–10.
49. Tafuri, *Architecture and Utopia,* 5. Manfredo Tafuri confronted the notion of the "original purity of the act of designing the environment" that has permeated much of modern design and planning.
50. Contemporary notions of "territorialization" and "reterritorialization" are largely derived from Deleuze and Guattari's, *A Thousand Plateaus* (originally published in 1972 as *Capitalisme et Schizophrenia*). Elizabeth Grosz's 1995 essay, Architecture from the outside, in *Space, Time, and Perversion,* 124–37, provides the most careful consideration of gendered and queer(ed) space in terms of those Deleuzean concepts. See also Patton, Marxism and beyond, in *Marxism and the Interpretation of Culture,* 123–39, and Chauncey, *Gay New York,* 23.
51. Morrill, Revamping the gay sensibility, in *Politics and Poetics of Camp,* 110–29.

Queer Space, pages 17–26

1. Diederich Diederichsen, Culture is a metaphor for "it's their problem": The German left and its revolutionary allies. (Paper presented at The Contact Zone Symposium. Moderated by René Green, Drawing Center, New York, April 9, 1994.)
2. From Civil Wars: Queer theory and the arenas of activism symposium (Organized by Juli Carson and Matthew Ehrlich, The New School for Social Research, New York City, May 1994).
3. "Queer" has also been embraced by some people, due to its more inclusive nature, whereas "gay" has come to connote white homosexual male.
4. Mohr, *Gays/Justice,* 98–100.
5. Homophile was a term used in the 1950s by early American activists precisely because it eschewed the narrow focus on sexual acts.
6. Rosario, Sexual liberalism and compulsory heterosexuality, 271, 272, 276.
7. This does not preclude the oscillation from one to the other, or the self-identifications of "bisexualities" or "transgendered" peoples.
8. Doty, *Making Things Perfectly Queer,* xv–xvi.
9. Municipal legislation and other public laws may be the place where such values can be reinforced. These parameters may create queer-friendly or hostile climates.
10. Barthes, *A Lover's Discourse,* 73.
11. Harris, Revenge of a snow queen, 8–9.
12. 1crew@andromeda.rutgers.edu—Louie Crew 4 July, 1994 17:43 hr from The E-Directory of Lesbigay Scholars.
13. *Wired Magazine,* August 1994:104.
14. Genet, *Querelle,* 97.

Marginality, pages 27–52

1. Mumford, *Culture of Cities,* 431–33.
2. Jackson, *A Sense of Place; A Sense of Time,* viii–ix.
3. In terms of the relationship between marginalized social groups and their use of the "margins" of landscapes and urban space, I am most influenced by H. P. Winchester and P. E. White's The location of marginalised groups in the inner city, 37–54.

4. For the most respected discussion of sexual acts and identities that are marginalized, see Rubin, Thinking sex, in *Pleasure and Danger,* 267–319. See her diagram of the "sex hierarchy" on p. 281.
5. An increasingly rich body of narrative describes sexual minorities as immigrants, and lesbian and gay ethnic immigrants as outsiders, even within communities of sexual minorities. For a recent example, see Manalansan, Search for the community—Filipino gay men in New York City, 59–73.
6. The "landscape" emerged both as a concept and a "way of seeing" in the fifteenth and early sixteenth centuries. See Cosgrove, Prospect, perspective and the evolution of the landscape idea, 46.
7. Luke, Placing power, siting space, 613–28.
8. The first two uses of the term "queerscape" were in my 1994 essay, Lost landscapes and the spatial contextualization of queerness, 4–9; and months later by Mays, Cities/The controversial concept of "queer space" breathes new life into the arid subject of city planning, redefining urban space.
9. Duberman, *Stonewall,* 192–208.
10. Delaney, Public space or publicity? 2–4.
11. de Certeau, *Practice of Everyday Life,* xvi–xvii. My framework for examining marginality includes Michel de Certeau's notion of "marginality of the majority," and bell hooks's 1990 essay, Choosing the margin as a space of radical openness, 145–54.
12. The culture of "transvestites" has changed greatly, including more viable options for the transgendered and a slight increase in the acceptance of cross-dressing. The two most influential discussions that have focused on cross-*dressing* more than questions of body and sexuality are in Newton, *Mother Camp;* Bullough and Bullough, *Cross Dressing, Sex, and Gender;* Garber, *Vested Interests.* As for the classic interior spaces of drag, Newton provides some plans of performance sites from the 1960s on pp. 71 and 89.
13. For a description of the origins of the Gay Liberation Front, in New York City, see Duberman, *Stonewall,* 211–12, 214–44.
14. For a discussion of recent queer nationalism's confrontation of "public and private," see Slagle, In defense of Queer Nation, 90–91.
15. "Scape" is used as in "the whole uneasy scape" (Delany, *Dhalgren*). "Landscape" is derived from the German *landschaft,* (Cosgrove, Prospect, perspective, and the evolution of the landscape idea, 56–57) and the Flemish *landschap,* words that were coined as commercial exchange and travel increased across and between the regions. Given the key role of Flanders in expanding European trade at the time when the word began to be popularly used, I have focused on the Flemish root. The suffix *schap* suggests a district or combination of places as well as the portions of a body. (Woordenboek, *Eigentijds Nederlands,* 684; Verhoeff-Schot and Cauberghe, *Thieme's Handwoordenboek Nederlands Engels/Engels Nederlands,* 492 and 1013). There was an early Dutch gay journal from the 1950s called *Vriendscap,* as in "friendscape." See the magazine's announcement in *One* 1(2) (February 1958): 8.
16. Fone, *A Road to Stonewall,* 116–27. My notion of culture in this discussion includes commercial advertising and pornography. In terms of the latter, Byrne R. S. Fone's 1995 discussion of the initial identification of homoerotic pornography as desires and acts unacceptable to emerging state and cultural bureaucracies, often perceived as being threats to "the public" (space), is useful.
17. For an analysis of the more liberal state, still very much an exception in government consideration of sexual minorities, see Whittle, Consuming differences, in *Margins of the City,* 27–41.
18. Tafuri, *Architecture and Utopia.* Manfredo Tafuri described the metropolis as "the place of absolute alienation." He related this alienation to capitalism. I argue that even with some recent liberalization in the corporate world, capitalism is still intrisically bound to patriarchy and homophobia.
19. Haraway, *Simians, Cyborgs, and Women,* 127–48.
20. For one of the most relevant frameworks for understanding constructions of "race" in terms of dislocations and territorialization, see Hess, Black and front and black again, in *Place and Politics,* 162–82.
21. For two recent discussions on the impact of class, on struggles around it, on queer identities and relations—ones that have direct impacts on communities and physical environments—see Field, *Over the Rainbow,* and Gilmartin, We weren't bar people, 1–51. Gilmartin explores some relationships between class and location, as in the "politics of location" with their inevitable physical spatial aspects.
22. Gay and lesbian establishments, such as cafés and bars, are often no more accessible to disabled people than less friendly and more homophobic spaces. For example, the Cafe Flore, a particularly important and for many of us "sacred" meeting place for San Francisco's queer communities, has violated several city guidelines. Its crowdedness, combined with bolted tables and steps, makes disabled access difficult if not impossible. Two of the few discussions of "ableism" and lesbian communities (none found for gay men), are Hearn, A woman's right to cruise, in *Out the Other Side,* 47; Hearn, Oi! What about us? in *Radical Records,* 116–27; and Appleby, Disability and "compulsory heterosexuality," 502–5.
23. The discourses of "difference" have expanded greatly in recent years, and there are numerous frameworks now being articulated. For an example of the kind of conception of difference employed in this essay, see Haraway, Situated knowledge, in *Simians, Cyborgs, and Women,* 200. For two of the many recent discussions on queer theory and difference, see Terry, Theorizing deviant historiography, 54–74; and the cautionary note in footnote 6 on page xxix of Warner, Introduction, in *Fear of a Queer Planet,* vii–xxxi.

24. For one review of the impacts of increased globalization of capital from the standpoint of formerly colonized areas, see Shiva, Homeless in the "global village," in *Ecofeminism,* 98–107.
25. Butler, *Gender Trouble,* 35–78.
26. Berlant and Freeman, Queer nationality, in *Fear of a Queer Planet,* 197.
27. Appleyard, *Livable Streets, Protected Neighborhoods,* 24.
28. For three discussions of the positions of bisexuals in relationship to "queer" identities, see Evans, Dual citizenship? Bisexuality, in *Sexual Citizenship,* 147–73; George, Towards a definition of bisexuality, in *Women and Bisexuality,* 157–83; and Hemmings, Locating bisexual identities, in *Mapping Desire,* 41–55.
29. Transgendered people confront highly unstable identity constructs, which have direct implications for their use of public space. For a discussion that begins to link transexuals with biography, with implications for use of place, see Stone, The empire strikes back, in *Body Guards,* 280–304. On pp. 298–99, the author argues that "transsexuals must take responsibility for *all* of their history, to begin to rearticulate their lives not as a series of erasures in the service of a species of feminism conceived from within a traditional frame, but as a political action begun by reappropriating difference and reclaiming the power of the refigured and reinscribed body."
30. For one of the better documented chronicles of the marginalization of transvestites in gay and lesbian activism, see Duberman's chronicle of Sylvia Ray Rivera in *Stonewall,* 235–39, 246, 251–55, 259, 262–65, and 276.
31. For overviews of some of the more marginalized sexual practices, see Mains, Urban aboriginals and the celebration of leather magic, in *Gay Spirit,* 99–117; Thompson, ed., *Leatherfolk,* xi–xx; and Truscott's essay in the same volume, S/M: Some questions and a few answers, 15–36. See also SAMOIS, *Coming to Power* and Chancer, *Sadomasochism in Everyday Life.*
32. For a description of the formation of a visible lesbian presence in a neighborhood, see Rothenberg, "And she told two friends", in *Mapping Desire,* 165–81.
33. Butler, *Bodies That Matter,* 3. This term was used in Judith Butler's phrase, "the regulation of identificatory practices" as directly related to constructed notions of gender and "sex." My usage is focused on an auxiliary aspect of gender and sexual identities related to passing through and identifying (and disidentifying) with specific points in geography.
34. Felshin, Introduction, in *But is it Art?,* 8–29.
35. Harvey, *The Condition of Postmodernity.*
36. Wilson, *The Sphinx in the City,* 135–59. Also see her 1988 memoirs and mappings of being a lesbian in London in the sixties, Memoirs of an anti-heroine, in *Radical Records,* 42–50.
37. Crimp, On the museum's ruin, in *On the Museum's Ruins,* 44–64.
38. Owens, The allegorical impulse and The discourse of others, in *Beyond Recognition,* 52–69, 166–90.
39. Thanks to Haris Metaxa of Florence for sharing her ideas and manuscripts in 1994–96.
40. Keith and Pile, eds., Introduction. The politics of place, in *Place and Politics,* 1–21.
41. Jackson, The idea of "race" and the geography of racism, in *Race and Racism.*
42. One notion of "marginalized" nationality goes back to the Roman word *natio,* which referred to the tribes that had been conquered. See Mies, Women have no fatherland, in *Ecofeminism,* 116–31.
43. Hayden, *Power of Place,* 2–13. On p. 23 Hayden notes that "The territories of the gay and lesbian communities can be mapped."
44. Forest, West Hollywood as symbol, 135–37.
45. Tschumi, *Architecture and Disjunction,* 152–68.
46. Duncan and Duncan, (Re)reading the landscape, 117.
47. Chauncey, *Gay New York,* 2.
48. While the term "the homosexual community" was employed in a number of discussions in the 1950s, it was in Hooker, The homosexual community, in *Personality Research,* 40–59, that the term came into broader usage in North America.
49. For one of the earliest sociological studies of "the homosexual community," in this case of Montréal, see Leznoff and Westley, The homosexual community, 257.
50. Wolf, *The Lesbian Community.*
51. D'Emilio, *Sexual Politics, Sexual Communities.*
52. Lauria and Knopp, Toward an analysis of the role of gay communities in the urban renaissance, 152–69.
53. Di Augelli and Hart, Gay women, men and families in rural settings, 79–93.
54. Murray, Components of gay community in San Francisco, in *Gay Culture in America,* 107–45.
55. See Almgren, Community with/out pro-pink-uity, in *Margins of the City,* 45–63.
56. For a discussion of communality and computer networks, see Stone, Agency and proximity, in *War of Desire and Technology,* 99–121.
57. Warner, Introduction, in *Fear of a Queer Planet,* vii–xxxi.
58. Ibid., xxv.
59. West, Beyond eurocentrism and multiculturalism, 10–19.
60. Within the framework of Benedict Anderson's *Imagined Communities,* a "nation" (7) is somewhere between a divinely ordained sovereignty and a community based around comradeship. In this sense, much of "queer nationalism" is more of an expanding networked form of queer municipalism,

particularly when so many different kinds of networks of sexual minorities are involved. And the kinds of "territorialization" (170–78) that have emerged so far are more consistent with operations within munipalities rather than discreet states.

61. Pieterse and Parekh, Shifting imaginaries, in *Decolonization of Imagination,* 6–14.
62. For a discussion of spatial "containment" as based on race, see Agyeman, Black people in a white landscape, 232–36.
63. One of the better documented lesbian and gay subcultures in North America, built around non-European racial and cultural identities, was Harlem in the 1920s. See Garber, A spectacle in color, in *Hidden From History,* 318–31.
64. Boone, Queer sites in modernism, in *Geography of Identity,* 244.
65. Brossard, Green night of Labyrinthe Park, in *Sexy Bodies,* 128–36.
66. Jagose, Way out—The category lesbian and the fantasy of the utopic space, 264–87.
67. Goonatilake, The self wandering between cultural localization and globalization, in *Decolonization of the Imagination,* 225–39.
68. For one of the more influential discussions on confronting persistent sexism and racism, within and outside of an activist group, see Saalfield and Navarro, Shocking pink praxis, 341–69.
69. Habermas, *Structural Transformation,* 5.
70. Ibid., 7.
71. Ibid., 65–70.
72. Debord, *Society of the Spectacle,* 154.
73. One of the first theoretical discussions of gay and lesbian space is Weightman, Commentary: Towards a geography of the gay community, 106–12.
74. For an overview of the concept of "queer space," see *Manifestos: Queer space* (New York: Storefront for Art and Architecture, June 1994), 254 and *Queer Space* (New York: Storefront for Art and Architecture), 4 large newsprint pages. Herbert Muschamp (1994) notes, "'Queer space' is a catchy term, but what does it mean? Don't ask, don't tell, one is tempted to say." In what is probably veiled reduction of queerness to sexual acts, Muschamp notes, "Queer space can be ghettoized social or sexual playgrounds." (Muschamp, Designing a framework for diversity, 32). Henry Urbach has noted the dynamic and contradiction embedded in the term as queer with "same-sex-sex," on one hand, and "queer" as estranged and marginalized on the other hand. He sees a corollary contradiction with space (Panel discussion "Queer Space 1," Storefront Art and Architecture/Cafe Architettura, New York City, June 19, 1994). At the same meeting, Mark Wigley noted that the identification and commodification of "queer space" holds the danger of a fixed architecture and noted the need to use more subversive conceptions of "architecture" to counter "underlying hegemonies."
75. Herdt and Boxer, Introduction: Culture, history, and life course of gay men, in *Gay Culture in America,* 1–28. See p. 2, where they relate the notion of homophobia to the gay liberation movement.
76. Bell, Binnie, Cream, and Valentine, All hyped up and no place to go, 32.
77. Herek and Berrill, eds., *Hate Crimes.*
78. My use of "decentered" is in the sense of diverse and always marginal in terms of attempts at a totalizing ideology. For example, Arlene Stein (Sisters and queers, 33–55) outlined the diversification of "local" identities (53), in contrast to more centrist ideologies such as lesbian feminism, "Younger women today are trying to carve out lesbian identities at a moment when many of the apparent certainties of the past have eroded—the meaning of lesbianism, the relationship between lesbianism and feminism, and the political potential of identity politics. They recognize that while marginalized groups construct symbolic fictions of their experience as a means of self-validation, and that compulsory heterosexuality necessitates the construction of a lesbian/gay identity, identities are always simultaneously enabling *and* constraining." See pp. 52–53.
79. Smith and Katz, Grounding metaphor, in *Place and Politics,* 67.
80. For an example of differences in access to open space, consider the current debates on "cruising" for women. There are few such sites in spite of a growing number of urban women who desire casual contact. In recent years there has been considerable discussion of this issue, notably by the late Tessa Boffin of London but, so far, there have been few written discussions.
81. One example of these relationships is Paul Shimazaki's description of Tokyo's gay neighbourhood, Nichome, in Tokyo: Sexopolis, 22–27.
82. Panel discussion "Queer Space 1," Storefront Art and Architecture/Cafe Architettura, New York City, June 19, 1994.
83. The term "body space" was used by Elizabeth Grosz in Bodies-cities, in *Sexuality and Space,* 249–50.
84. Habermas, *Structural Transformation,* xvi and 3.
85. Wilson, Bodies in public and private, in *Public Bodies—Private States,* 12.
86. Boyer, *City of Collective Memory,* 18.
87. Tschumi, *Architecture and Disjunction,* 174.
88. Betsky, *Building Sex,* 65–67. Betsky argues that heterotopias were some of the first space "in which women would exercise power."
89. Foucault, Other spaces, 11.
90. Soja, Heterotopologies, in *Postmodern Cities and Spaces,* 15.
91. Tschumi, *Architecture and Disjunction,* 16.
92. In recent years the *heterotopia* "industry" in postmodern geography has applied the term to a wider range of spaces with various types of mirroring and disorientation. The concept remains contradictory and open to wide interpretation as related to

particular purposes. See Genocchio, Discourse, discontinuity, difference, in *Postmodern Cities and Spaces,* 35–46. I use the term specifically for those spaces that, from a variety of socially related and cultural processes, challenge or subvert the hegemony of the current configurations of heteronormativity, patriarchy, and neocolonialism. In this sense heterotopia allows some form of queering of an environment and a social milieu.

93. For a tentative discussion of one highly constructed space of disorientation that emerged soon after Stonewall, see Bredbeck, Troping the light fantastic, 71–107.
94. Henri Lefebvre's *Production of Space* provides a basis for considering the key role of public art in the creation of queer space in his outline of "representational spaces" (39). Michel de Certeau noted that the "implantatation of memory in a place" is a central function of art (*Practice of Everyday Life,* 86).
95. Tafuri, *Architecture and Utopia,* 143.
96. Delany, *Dhalgren,* 702.
97. Hay, Parallels between love relations and our relations to place, 256–59.
98. Boyer, *City of Collective Memory,* 467.
99. Reyes, Queer spaces, 93.
100. McDonough, Situationist space, 77.
101. Debord, Introduction to a critique of urban geography, in *Situationist International Anthology,* 5.
102. Ibid., 6.
103. For an overview of the theoretical contributions of the Situationists to contemporary activism, see Wollen, Bitter victory, in *On the Passage of a few people through a rather brief moment in time,* 20–61; and Burch, Situationist poise, space and architecture, 12–13.
104. For a chronology of the early years of ACT UP and what led to the creation of this activist group, see Maxine Wolfe, in *Queers in Space;* and The AIDS Coalition to unleash power, in *AIDS Prevention and Services,* 217–47. Also see Crimp and Rolston, *AIDS demo graphics;* and Saalfield and Navarro, Shocking pink praxis.
105. According to Maxine Wolfe, Queer Nation had links to an ACT UP Affinity Group, founded in a 1989 action at New York City Hall. See The AIDS Coalition to unleash power, 218–19. Most Queer Nation chapters did not last for much more than two years. For examples of their antihomophobic interventions, see Martin, Gays form patrols to battle hate crimes (Queer Nation), *Los Angeles Times* 110 (December 3, 1991): B1, and Presley Noble, Gay group asks accord in job dispute; meeting is requested with gift-store chain (activists from Queer Nation seek end to anti-gay employment policies at Cracker Barrel Old Country Store Inc.), *New York Times* (November 25, 1992): C4, D4.
106. Both "zaps" and "kiss-ins" date back to the Gay Activist Alliance (GAA) of New York City, in 1970. See Evans, How to zap the straights, in *The Gay Liberation Book,* 110–15. Zaps probably originated from the pre-Stonewall "going wrecking" in which straights were taunted. See Duberman, *Stonewall,* 83. Also see Duberman's descriptions of the early GAA zaps on pp. 232–33.
107. For a discussion of the kiss-in as a tactic by Queer Nation since 1991, see Berlant and Freeman, Queer nationality, in *Fear of a Queer Planet,* 208.
108. Derbyshire, A measure of queer, 45.
109. Rey, Parisian homosexuals create a lifestyle, 1700–1750: The Police Archives. In this 1987 essay, Michael Rey noted that, "at least as far back as 1714, the Paris police were actively involved in the surveillance of popular rendezvous sites of gay men. In fact, what is known today of such early queer sites is often based on accounts associated with subsequent homophobic repression."
110. Chauncey, *Gay New York,* 9.
111. Kepner, Gay beach, 5–10.
112. See Joan Nestle's essay in *Queers in Space.*
113. Egerton, Out but not down, 75–88. In considering the impacts of increasing options for "singles" housing in the post–World War II period, gender has remained a major factor with lesbians having much less access well into the 1980s.
114. Grube, Queens and flaming virgins, 14–17.
115. Deleuze and Guattari, *A Thousand Plateaus,* 112 and 133. Much of Deleuze and Guattari's treatise on capitalism and schizophrenia is on reterritorialization.
116. At the 1995 conference "Queer Frontiers" at the University of Southern California, John Rechy noted that in 1965–69 in Los Angeles there were a number of organized confrontations with police in public open space such as Griffith Park, but that these were not well reported in the mainstream media.
117. By "Stonewall riots," I mean not only the initial riot on June 27, 1969 but also the subsequent period of confrontations with police punctuated by the August 29–30, 1970, riots. See anonymous, 1000 gays riot in New York, 1–10.
118. Teal, *The Gay Militants,* 24.
119. Kissack, Freaking fag revolutionaries, 104–34.
120. Teal, *Gay Militants,* 26–27; Duberman, *Stonewall,* 216 and endnote #3, 303; and Bird, Trees in a Queens park cut down as vigilantes harass homosexuals, *New York Times* (July 1, 1969): 1, 29. Bird quoted a vigilante who stated that "the harassment tactics had worked at first against the homosexuals but that later when they began to insist that they had had a right to be on public land, firmer action was "needed." The police gave tacit consent to the destruction at Kew Gardens, which actually occurred a week before the Stonewall riots, which in turn were a response to gay resistance to homophobia earlier that spring. Also see Bird, Queens

resident says the police stood by as park trees were cut, *New York Times* (July 2, 1969): 38.

121. Fraser, "Gay ghettos" seen as police targets, *New York Times* (August 31, 1970): 28.
122. One example of the extra hidden costs of creating semi-public, privately owned queer space is the bribes that have been paid to police and other officials, especially in the times before homosexuality was decriminalized.
123. For the most important discussion of "appropriation" of space, see Lefebvre, *Production of Space,* 164–68. "Reappropriation" is barely a word in English and is best represented by the related word used by the Italian Left, *riappropriazione.*
124. By "architecture," I refer to efforts to "reinscribe the movement of bodies in space" (Tschumi, *Architecture and Disjunction,* 3). I make this, along with social functions, central to any process of design and related decision-making about inhabited environments. I also acknowledge Manfredo Tafuri's notion of architecture as often constituting "spaces of domination" (*The Sphere and the Labyrinth,* 2).
125. In the early days of ACT UP, there was considerable shock value in the "turning right side up" of the pink triangle. For another perspective on the appropriation of the pink and black triangle symbols used by the Nazis, see Elman, Triangles and tribulations, 1–11.
126. Duggan and Hunter, *Sex Wars,* 168.
127. For one discussion of the insertion of imagery and information, in essence "art," into public places, as a political act, see Gott, Where the streets have new aims, in *Don't Leave Me This Way,* 186–211.
128. Foucault, Other spaces, 9–10.
129. For an initial overview of the early theoretical discussions and controversies around gay "public sex," see Weeks, *Sexuality and Its Discontents,* 219–23; and David Bell's 1995 discussion, Perverse dynamics, sexual citizenship and the transformation of intimacy in *Mapping Desire*; plus his discussion in this volume. Controversies over public sex have raged publicly in the gay communities since at least the activist decade leading up to Stonewall. For example, Larry Carlson edited a lively debate with rather atomized notions of sex and privacy in 1967 in San Francisco (Open forum: Sex in public places, 14-15). And just before the recognition of AIDS as an epidemic, there was a debate in response to Califia, The issue of public sex, 18–20.
130. For an example of environmental art that functions either to transmit queer content or to "queer" a site, see Robbins, Utopian Prospects, in *Angles of Incidence,* 38–41.
131. Davis, The diversity of queer politics, in *Mapping Desire,* 284–303.
132. Harvey, From space to place and back again, in *Mapping the Futures,* 3–29.
133. Knopp, Sexuality and the spatial dynamics of capitalism, 662.
134. Davis, *City of Quartz,* 221–64.
135. Debord, *Society of the Spectacle,* 12.
136. Boyer, *City of Collective Memory,* 51.
137. Henry Urbach (Spatial rubbings, 90–95) talked of a "nomadic queer culture whose carnal activities are elsewhere taboo" (90) and noted "Nomadic space—indefinite, open, and smooth—exceeds and disrupts the realm of stable social forms marked by borders and enclosures" (93).
138. Guattari, *Regimes, pathways, subjects* 19: 26–27.
139. Virilio, *Speed and Politics,* 133–51.
140. For one of the earliest discussions of the post-Queer Nation wave of street patrols, see Miles, The fabulous fight back, 54–59.
141. Central to queerscape architecture, therefore, is the excavation of attempts to impose or maintain certain social hierarchies, such as homophobia, or assertion of a more egalitarian and sustainable social "program." See Tschumi, *Architecture and Disjunction,* 101–52.
142. Boyer, *City of Collective Memory,* 66–67. Collective memory for queer groups has involved many different types of events and experiences. In the last decade mentions of the past have often touched on a number of metanarratives such as the Nazi deportations in World War II, the 1969 Stonewall riots, and the first wave of the AIDS pandemic. But historical interpretations, as with memory of specific events and their significance, are always contested and denied by some. Such processes of grieving and remembrance, like those of the Nazi deportees, can explore the nature of place as part of the healing from homophobic violence. See Seel, *I, Pierre Seel, Deported Homosexual,* 133–37.
143. Cooper, *Sexing the City.* This book is a discussion of municipal strategies for promotion of gay and lesbian rights and expansion of services in the left Labour Party city administrations in Britain over the last decade. See p. 13.

Narratives of Place, pages 55–60

1. Lefebvre, *Production of Space,* 3–7, 28.
2. Varela, When is a map cognitive? in *The Evolution of Cognitive Maps,* 99.
3. Thomashow, *Ecological Identity,* 192–99.
4. Marcus, Environmental autobiography.
5. Gärling, The role of cognitive maps in spatial decisions, 269–78.
6. Boyer, *City of Collective Memory,* 203–91.
7. Cosgrove, Prospect, perspective, and the evolution of the landscape idea, 45.
8. Ibid., 46.
9. Gould and White, *Mental Maps,* 16.
10. Ibid., 157–164.

11. Orlean, Differential cognition of urban residents, in *Image and Environment,* 115–30.
12. Ibid., 116. "They may be described as *lateralizations,* as semiorganized aggregates of individuals who participate in a way of life which is different from the various communities through which they pass."
13. Appleyard, Notes on urban perception and knowledge, in *Image and Environment,* 110.
14. Hillier, To boldly go where no planners have ever. . ., 89–113.
15. Haraway, *Simians, Cyborgs, and Women,* 147.
16. Tschumi, *Architecture and Disjunction,* 10–11.
17. Haraway, *Simians, Cyborgs, and Women,* 183–201.
18. Sadie Plant uses the term "radical subjectivity" in discussing Vaneigem, *The Revolution of Everyday Life* (*The Most Radical Gesture,* 38). "The radical subject demands the right to construct the situation in which it lives."
19. Haraway, *Simians, Cyborgs, and Women,* 194.

Restriction and Reclamation, pages 61–67

1. Nestle, *Restricted Country.*
2. In the 1950s and 1960s, women who acted out of line could be taken to the Women's House of Detention, near The Sea Colony, on 6th Avenue (at 8th Street near the Jefferson Market Library). It was a common sight to see lovers calling to each other between the few tiny windows that looked toward the street.
3. Nestle, *Restricted Country,* 37–39.
4. The Sea Colony was a working-class lesbian bar in New York City. I was part of its world from 1958 until the mid-sixties.
5. Nestle, *Restricted Country,* 46–48.

The Interim Photographs, pages 69–76

1. Arbus, *diane arbus.*
2. Aukeman, Bill Jacobson, 95.
3. Part of the Interim Photographs series exhibited at Grey Art Gallery in New York City in 1993. See Watney, Bill Jacobson, 101.

People and Their Streets, Places, pages 77–80

1. The characters in this story were later developed into Schulman's *Rat Bohemia.* The story in *Queers in Space,* as well as that in *Rat Bohemia,* focuses on an almost mythic, though increasingly gentrified, area of the Lower East Side of Manhattan—just west of the "renovated" Tompkins Square Park.

One-Handed Geographies, pages 81–87

1. Jarman, *Modern Nature,* 98. As this quote immediately establishes, my discussion of sexscapes is site-specific: the "Heath" to which Jarman refers is Hampstead Heath, a famous London cruising ground. My entire discussion is focused on Britain, although I use material from elsewhere. Of course, this means that I take for granted certain configurations of sex in space that are founded at least in part on the British legal system's construction of the public and private spaces of sex and sexual identity. We remain governed largely by a piece of legislation from the 1960s, the so-called Wolfenden Act, which decriminalised sex between two men of over 21 years of age and in private. In early 1994 the minimum age was reduced to 18. There was no mention of lesbians. Sex between more than two men, sex outside of a very narrowly defined "private" space—indeed any show of (homo)affection "in public"—is open to censure if not prosecution. Even winking at another man or holding hands can be arrestable offences. The rather vague charge of "promoting homosexuality" makes institutions think twice before showing gay art or publishing gay books. For example, one British university press used this ruling to deny publication to an academic text on gay men's politics. Obscenity laws can deem even a leather jacket obscene, and sadomasochism is effectively outlawed—thanks to a test case involving a group of consenting same-sex sadomasochists. For a fuller discussion, see Bell, Perverse dynamics, sexual citizenship and the transformation of intimacy, in *Mapping Desire,* 304–17.
2. For examples, see Bell, Erotic topographies, 96–100; Colomina, ed., *Sexuality and Space;* Douglas and Rasmussen, *The Nude Beach;* Keogh, Public sex: Spaces, acts, identities (presented at the Sexuality and Space Network conference, London, 1992); Woodhead, "Surveillant gays," in *Mapping Desire,* 231–44.
3. For a working example of sexual psychogeography, see Hallam, *The Book of Sodom.*
4. The phrase "polymorphous decentred exchange" is taken from Singer, *Erotic Welfare,* 122. I take it to mean sex acts freed from what she calls an "ejaculatory teleology"—sex with scripts that move beyond the standard scenarios of foreplay, penetration, orgasm. In S/M scenes, for example, the orgasm may not even be part of the script, which may instead involve fantasies, tit-torture, fisting, bondage, and so on. I appropriate the phrase "polymorphous decentered" to apply also to landscapes, since it seems to embody many of the tropes currently used to refer to what we might call the postmodern landscape. For work considering urban

landscapes and sexualities, see, for example, Henning Bech, Citysex: Representing lust in public (presented at the Geographies of Desire conference, Amsterdam, 1993); Jon Binnie, Fucking among the ruins: Postmodern sex in post-industrial places (presented at the Sexuality and Space Network conference, London, 1992); Sue Golding, The excess, 23–28; and Quantum philosophy, impossible geographies and a few small points about life, liberty and the pursuit of sex (all in the name of democracy), in *Place and Politics,* 206–19; Knopp, Sexuality and urban space, in *Mapping Desire,* 149–61.

5. The oral histories that make up such a queer archaeology can be found in, among others, Hall Carpenter Archives Lesbian Oral History Group, *Inventing Ourselves;* Hall Carpenter Archives Gay Men's Oral History Group, *Walking After Midnight*; Hutchins and Ka'ahumanu, eds., *Bi Any Other Name;* Kennedy and Davis, *Boots of Leather, Slippers of Gold;* National Lesbian and Gay Survey, *Proust, Cole Porter, Michelangelo, Marc Almond and me; What a Lesbian Looks Like;* Newton, *Cherry Grove, Fire Island;* Off Pink Collective, *Bisexual Lives.*
6. Pfohl, Venus in Microsoft, in *The Last Sex,* 189.
7. National Lesbian and Gay Survey, Grant, in *Proust, Cole Porter, Michelangelo, Marc Almond and me,* 114.
8. For public sex, see Bell, Citizenship and the politics of pleasure (presented at the Institute of British Geographers annual conference, London, 1992); Perverse dynamics, sexual citizenship and the transformation of intimacy, in *Mapping Desire,* 304-17; and Pleasure and danger, 139-153; Weeks, *Sexuality and its Discontents;* and Changing sexual and personal values in the age of AIDS (presented at the Forum on Sexuality conference, Amsterdam, 1992).
9. It was in this language that the British *Sexual Offences Act* (1967) expressed its feelings about the decriminalisation of adult male homosexuality; see Wilson, Which equality?, in *Activating Theory,* 171–89.
10. My use of the phrase "heteronormativity" is most influenced by Eadie, Activating bisexuality, in *Activating Theory,* 156; for the sexed body in space, see Bell, Binnie, Cream, and Valentine, All hyped up and no place to go, 31–48; Cream, Out of place (presented at the Association of American Geographers annual conference, San Francisco, 1994); and Re-Solving riddles, in *Mapping Desire,* 31-40; Geltmaker, The Queer Nation acts up, 609–50; Grosz, Bodies-cities, in *Sexuality and Space,* 241–54; Johnson, Embodying geography: Some implications for considering the sexed body in space (presented at the New Zealand Geographical Society conference, Dunedin); Longhurst, The strange case of the missing body in geography (presented at the Association of American Geographers annual conference, San Francisco, 1994); Rose, On being ambivalent, in *New Words, New Worlds,* 156–63; and Rose, *Feminism and Geography.*
11. From Prof. Sturlason (pseud.), Fatuous joyriders, *Fatuous Times* 3 (1993): 4. Joyriding was/is one in a series of moral panics centred on youth culture in the U.K.; teenage boys stealing fast cars to drive round the city, taunting the police, and sometimes crashing, killing or injuring themselves and others. Joyriding has been widely interpreted as signalling some kind of crisis in contemporary (working-class) masculinity; see Campbell, *Goliath.* The classic text on car fetishism and car sex remains Ballard, *Crash.*
12. For queer performativity, see Butler, Critically queer, 17–32; Sedgwick, Queer performativity, 1–15; and Sedgwick, *Tendencies.*
13. See Cresswell, The geography of transgressions: Its limits and uses (presented at the Association of American Geographers annual conference, San Francisco, 1994), for a discussion of ACT UP, among others. See also Crimp and Rolston, *AIDS demo graphics.*
14. See Bell, In bed with the state, 445-52; Bell and Valentine, The sexed self, in *Mapping the Subject,* 143-57.
15. For debates on transgression, see Bell, Binnie, Cream, and Valentine, All hyped up and no place to go (note 10); Wilson, Is transgression transgressive? in *Activating Theory,* 107–17.
16. For definitions and explorations, see Debord and Wolman, Methods of detournement, in *Situationist International Anthology,* 8–14.
17. For a way to draw these maps, see Ingram, Queers in space (presented at the Queer Sites conference, Toronto, 1993); for fictions that map out possible queer utopias, see, for example, Zimmerman, *Safe Sea of Women.*
18. Sturlason (pseud.), note 11, p. 5.
19. Munt, The lesbian *flâneur,* in *Mapping Desire,* 125.
20. What place is there in the queer city, for example, for sadomasochism, bestiality, or paedophilia? See SAMOIS, ed., *Coming to Power;* Dekkers, *Dearest Pet;* O'Carroll, *Paedophilia.* For a crucial discussion of "sexual hierarchies" see Rubin, Thinking sex, in *Lesbian and Gay Studies Reader,* 3–44.
21. A recent British legal case around male same-sex sadomasochism, known as Operation Spanner, has brought these issues out into the open. Crucially, the defence of privacy and consent was ruled immaterial, and the men were convicted of assault charges, including "aiding and abetting assault on oneself." The legal battle and public debate around Operation Spanner continues and has expanded. For the current status of the case see the Spanner Defense Group website: *http://www.skintwo.co.uk.* See Bibbings and Aldridge, Sexual expression, body modification, and the defence of consent, 356–70; Gange and Johnstone, Believe me, everybody has

something pierced in California, 51–68; Stanley, Sins and passions, 207–26.

22. See, for example, the many debates from the early and mid-1990s on "outing," such as Johansson and Percy, *Out*, and Mohr, *Gay Ideas*.
23. This might be thought of as a central element of queer citizenship; see Cooper, An engaged state, in *Activating Theory*, 190–218.
24. Golding, Sexual manners, in *Pleasure Principles*, 80.
25. Jarman, *Modern Nature*, 83.
26. See Bell, Perverse dynamics, sexual citizenship, and the transformation of intimacy.
27. The notion of "sex talk" as used here comes from Cooper (note 24), p. 208; the phrase "creative and wild possibilities" I borrow from Sue Golding, Quantum philosophy (note 4), p. 217.
28. Sedgwick, *Tendencies* (note 13), is among the most inspirational texts to encourage such a task.
29. Jarman, *At Your Own Risk*, 80.

Surveying Territories and Landscapes, pages 91–94

1. For the more cultural and psychological aspects of the notion of the commons, see Thomashow, *Ecological Identity*, 67–102.
2. Francis, The making of democratic streets, in *Public Streets for Public Use*, 28–29.

"Open" Space as Strategic Queer Sites, pages 95–125

1. This research began in San Francisco in 1979 as an academic study, with nonvoyeuristic photographs, of gay male use of Buena Vista Park. I shared information and photographs, which a fellow Berkeley student and member of Gays and Lesbians of Wurster Hall worked into his own research (Immel, Gay urban open space in San Francisco, 33). Because of the hysteria around AIDS and gay male "promiscuity" in subsequent years, I did not publish on this topic and moved on to other questions of public space and lands, and "marginality."
2. Weeks, *Sexuality and Its Discontents*, 223.
3. Wilson, *Public Bodies—Private States*, 9–10. In her 1984 essay, Bodies in public and private, Elizabeth Wilson noted that the notion of the "open city," with its large component of relatively egalitarian public space, always involved a element of surveillance, particularly by the state.
4. Crouch, The historical development of urban open space, in *Urban Open Space*, 7–8.
5. Boyer, *City of Collective Memory*, 133. Also relevant is the eighteenth-century work of Abbé Laugier whom Bernard Tschumi quoted as stating "Whoever knows how to design a park well will have no difficulty in tracing the plan for the building of a city according to its given area and situation." (Tschumi, *Architecture and Disjunction*, 85; and Tafuri, *Architecture and Utopia*, 4.) Laugier was a central figure in the formation of modern design practice based on principles of eighteenth-century Enlightenment.
6. Boone, Queer sites in modernism, in *Geography of Identity*, 253.
7. Boyer, *City of Collective Memory*, 183–84. Boyer suggests the key relationship between open space and communal and neighbourhood identities.
8. Habermas, *Structural Transformation*, 1.
9. Kenney, Strategic visibility.
10. I use the term "essentialize" as a verb, derived from the school of essentialism that looks for fixed patterns of behaviour, relationships, and "nature"—particularly for social groups with some different biological manifestations as to gender, race, or interest in particular sex acts.
11. For three discussions on the positions of bisexuals in relationship to queer identities, see Evans, Dual citizenship?, in *Sexual Citizenship;* George, Towards a definition of bisexuality, in *Women and Bisexuality;* and Hemmings, Locating bisexual identities, in *Mapping Desire*, 41–55, as well as Hemmings's discussion in *Queers in Space*.
12. Cream, Re-solving riddles, in *Mapping Desire*, 33–34.
13. Architectual theorist Henry Urbach, once outlined the activistic nature of architecture and noted that "Architecture not only represents a stage of social relations but is also a politicized protagonist." (Panel discussion "Queer Space 1," Storefront Art and Architecture/Cafe Architettura, New York City, June 19, 1994).
14. In using this widely used phrase "open space," one of the notions closest to my own is that of Iris Marion Young who said, "A public space is a place accessible to anyone, where people engage in activity as individuals or in small groups . . . The unoppressive city is thus defined as openness to unassimilated otherness." See Nicholson, ed., The ideal of community and the politics of difference, in *Feminism/Postmodernism*, 319.
15. In this way I reject the argument that the notion of public space provides the basis for a new normative theory of politics harking back to modernism, no matter how supple a framework informed by space. See Howell, Public space and the public sphere, 303–22.
16. Weightman, Gay bars as private places, 10–13.
17. One of the few case studies of the "use" of landscape architecture to minimize homoerotic contact was the work of Michael Immel on Buena Vista Park. See Immel, Gay urban open space in San Francisco, 37–44.

18. Lynch, The openness of open space, in *City Sense and City Design,* 396.
19. Chauncey, *Gay New York,* 9. In his recent book on the formation of gay male subcultures in New York, George Chauncey argues that "gay life in New York was *less* tolerated, *less* visible to outsiders, and *more* rigidly segregated in the second third of the century than the first, and that the very severity of the post–World War II reaction has tended to blind us to the relative tolerance of the prewar years." This pattern was similar to those in many other North American cities.
20. Jacobs, *Death and Life of Great American Cities,* 92. See her use of the term "pervert park," where she states "Several decades ago Washington Square became Philadelphia's pervert park, to the point where it was shunned by office lunchers. . . ."
21. Golding, Quantum philosophy, impossible geographies and a few small points about life, liberty and the pursuit of sex (all in the name of democracy), in *Place and Politics,* 213–14.
22. Jacobs, *Death and Life,* 79.
23. Rubin, (interviewed by Judith Butler), Sexual traffic, 76 and 78.
24. Lynch, Open space, in *City Sense,* 413.
25. Heckscher, The management of open spaces, in *Urban Open Space,* 19–20.
26. Chauncey, *Gay New York,* 2. While the record of sites of homosexual activity now extends back to the Renaissance (Giovanni Dall'Orto, 1994), this essay will only go as far back as eighteenth-century Europe.
27. Deleuze and Guattari, *A Thousand Plateaus,* 503.
28. Cory, *The Homosexual in America.*
29. Ibid., 114.
30. "Cruising" is a complex set of codes, alliances, and practices, which have varied greatly among sites, regions, and times. Cruising practices are often highly site-specific. For one portrayal of cruising by a white man in Washington, D.C., between World Wars I and II, see Russell, ed., *Jeb and Dash.* In those memories Jeb used the term in 1923 (66). Other descriptions of well-established cruising sites in the early 1920s in Washington are on pp. 31, 41, 61, 62, 63, 64, 65, and 66. The emergence of cruising as part of a more "global" culture of sexual dissidence began after World War II. See Marshall, *Beginner's Guide to Cruising.*
31. Leznoff and Westley, The homosexual community, 257–263. The mention here of the timing of government support is because the resulting research was used by a federal government for RCMP surveillance that intensified in the late 1950s and 1960s.
32. Ibid., 261–62.
33. Ibid., 257.
34. Delph, *The Silent Community,* 159.
35. Sex-negative attitudes internalized in the gay male community have even lead to cooperation with police entrapment efforts. See pp. 18–22 in Tucker, Gender, fucking and utopia, 3–34.
36. Sociologist Peter Nardi reviewed the controversy around the book and its significance in The Breastplace of Righteousness, 1–10.
37. Humphreys, *Tearoom Trade: Impersonal sex in public places,* 14.
38. Ponte, Life in a parking lot, in *Deviance: Field studies and self-disclosure,* 3–29.
39. Valentine, Out and about, 105.
40. Crimp, *On the Museum's Ruins,* 150–86.
41. Patton, Tremble, hetero swine! in *Fear of a Queer Planet,* 174.
42. I conceive a queerscape ecology related to "landscape ecology" as in Forman and Godron, *Landscape Ecology.* Recognitions of social factors and respective impacts in these landscapes that were recognized as being inherently "cultural" were central to the modern inception of this field, as in Dansereau's 1966 essay Ecological impact and human ecology, in *Future Environments of North America,* 425–64. Most contemporary inventories of local ecologies are based on natural ecosystems, through there are some examples of more "hard-surfaced" urban studies such as Appleyard's The ecology of the street, in *Livable Streets,* 29–40.
43. Imafuku, Glass made of water, in *Transculture La Biennale di Venezia 1995,* 56.
44. Forman and Godron, *Landscape Ecology,* 159–68.
45. Delany, *The Mad Man.*
46. In 1993 Chip Delany kindly engaged in three long conversations on public sex, while in Toronto and New York writing *The Mad Man.* Along with this information, he kindly loaned me a revised marked version of Delany, *The Motion of Light in Water,* which was to be reprinted with the changes.
47. Delany, *Mad Man,* 72–77, 190–96, 220–23, 435, and 499–501.
48. Ibid., 190–92.
49. Grosz, *Space, Time, and Perversion,* 141–54.
50. Grace, *Love Bites.*
51. Stamps, Doing battles with censors, 70–73.
52. Adams, The three (dis)graces, 130–38.
53. I had extensive conversations with Della Grace in 1979 and 1980 in San Francisco, in 1993 in Toronto, and in 1994 in Rome.
54. Grace, Xenomorphisis, 124.
55. Pettinger, Why fetish?, 87 and 88.
56. This discussion on open space is focused on the following photographs in *Love Bites:* Lesbarados, pp. 38 and 39; the images in The Ceremony, particularly pp. 44–49; the images in Cold-store Romance, especially pp. 57–59 and p. 62.
57. Griggers, Lesbian bodies in the age of (post)mechanical reproduction, in *Fear of a Queer Planet,* 187.
58. Grosz, *Space, Time, and Perversion,* 151.

59. Immel, Gay urban open space in San Francisco, 31.
60. Rechy, *The Sexual Outlaw*.
61. Ibid., 22.
62. Ibid., 140.
63. The "script" of the hypermasculine man often responds to and replicates "his dangerous, adversarial world of scarce resources." See Mosher and Tomkins, Scripting the macho man, 60.
64. I am endebted to Leo Bersani's early essay Is the rectum a grave? in *AIDS: Cultural Analysis, Cultural Activism*, 197–222, especially 203–9, 220. It explored the relationship between portrayals of "machismo" and more profound forms of homophobia, particularly as related to AIDS discourses.
65. One of the first discussions about Tom of Finland in the mainstream gay press was in Reed, Repression and exaggeration, 16–21.
66. As a teenager, Tom of Finland began to have sex with men in public places. He has said that some of his partners were German troops occupying Finland under the Nazi regime.
67. Blake, Tom of Finland—An appreciation, in *Out in Culture*, 350–51.
68. Ibid., 351. Tom of Finland removed from circulation his early Nazi fantasies.
69. Ibid., 350.
70. Tom of Finland Inc. (P. O. Box 26716, Los Angeles, California 90026) distributes catalogues and materials. The archives of his work are at the Tom of Finland Foundation (P. O. Box 26658, Los Angeles, California 90026).
71. Tom of Finland, *Kake Pleasure Park*, 1.
72. Deleuze and Guattari developed the concept of the plateau, as based on Gregory Bateson's work on Balinese culture, as "a continuous, self-vibrating region of intensities whose development avoids orientation towards a culminating point or external end," in contrast to more ephemeral episodes such as parades, street fairs, and demonstrations. See Deleuze and Guattari, *Thousand Plateaus*, 22.
73. Fatona and Wyngaaden, *Hogan's Alley* (colour, English language, 32:30 minutes, distributed by Video In, 1965 Main Street, Vancouver, Canada, fax: 1(604)876-1185). Both Fatona and Wyngaaden provided additional information from their research on the project in conversations in 1994 and 1995.
74. Knopp, Sexuality and the spatial dynamics of capitalism, 651–69. See p. 665, where Knopp attributes this phrase to Tim Davis and his 1991 paper "'Success' and the gay community: Reconceptualizations of space and urban social movements" (presented at the First National Graduate Student Conference on Lesbian and Gay Studies, Milwaukee, Wisconsin, April 1991).
75. Thanks to Don Hann for the transcripts of his talk, The lesbian and gay civil rights struggle in British Columbia, 1971–1980, a talk given at Harry's Off-Commercial on October 14, 1995, as a benefit for Little Sisters Bookstore.
76. Boone, Queer sites in modernism, in *Geography of Identity*, 259.
77. Deleuze and Guattari, *Nomadology*, 4.
78. My relationship to this new city is that my paternal grandparents both moved to Vancouver from southern Ontario and a nearby area of upstate New York, in 1890 and married in 1891. My father was born in the Kitsilano neighbourhood in 1905, and I took many trips with him back to Vancouver in the years 1960–71, while growing up on southeastern Vancouver Island. My father's family was highly skeptical of what Vancouver had become and what was articulated by some as a betrayal of Arcadian promises. One of my father's brothers, less than a year older, died from a homophobic assault in Stanley Park in 1970.
79. Fung, *Dirty Laundry*, videotape (Toronto: Fungus Productions).
80. For a mid-1970s discussion of the emergence of lesbian feminism in the region, see Rand, Interview with lesbian feminist, 4–5, 11.
81. Kinsman, *Regulation of Desire*, 31–34, 66–67, 81–98.
82. McLaren, Sex radicals in the Canadian Pacific Northwest, 527–46.
83. For a discussion on British Columbia, see Ingram, Landscapes of (un)lawful chaos, 242–49. Perhaps the most heated discussions on contemporary interpretations of nature and its implications for perception and use of landscapes, have been the reactions to Donna Haraway's *Simians, Cyborgs, and Women*, such as the 1995 anthology *Reinventing Nature?* In Pacific Canada, there has been a more regional discussion of the aesthetics of decolonization that Watson (1994) alluded to.
84. Berelowitz, From factor 15 to feu d'artifice, 32–37.
85. Howard, The Library, the park, and the pervert, 166–87.
86. For one of the best documented urban chronicles of surveillance of gay men in public outdoor space, see Chauncey, Privacy could only be had in public, in *STUD*, 234–48.
87. Adam, Winning rights and freedoms in Canada, in *The Third Pink Book*, 25–37.
88. Even after partial decriminalization, legal statutes were used by the police to harass cruisers. For an overview of the legal instruments of the 1970s, see Tide, Laws used against us, *Gay Tide* 16: 6–7 and Cruise with care, *Gay Tide* 18: 10.
89. See the following articles from *Gay Tide*, the Vancouver paper that most carefully monitored police harassment of gays in the 1970s: Editorial, Police entrapment on upswing 2(4) (August 1, 1975); Anonymous, Gay victim speaks out 3(3) (August, 9, 1976); David Rand and Robert Cook, Community unites to voice anger 16 (1977): 1; No

liaison with police 16 (1977): 2; Editorial, A breakthrough 16 (1977): 3; Don Hann and Rob Royce, City police record: Smash hit 16 (1977): 4; Police harassment: Three responses 17 (1977): 4 ; Stop police attacks 18 (1978): 1.

90. Hann and Royce, City police record, *Gay Tide.*
91. There was some discussion on continuing RCMP surveillance as late as 1980. See Loos, Opening the mounties' closet, 9. However, earlier surveillance of a much more coordinated nature has been confirmed. For example, "By 1963, the RCMP started a project of attaching red dots to a map of Ottawa to identify homosexual hangouts. It became so awash with dots that a second, much larger map was purchased. It too became covered in a sea of dots, and attempts were made to locate an even larger map" (Hannan, 1994) with additional correspondence with Gary Kinsman in 1994. Also see Kinsman, *Regulation of Desire,* 120–23. The extent of the RCMP surveillance of lesbians and gay men in Vancouver is still unclear.
92. McLeod, *Lesbian and Gay Liberation in Canada,* 278.
93. "Ask supported law reform and sponsored public lectures and discussion groups, coffee parties (Gab'N'Java), social events and outings, a lending library, and, eventually, a drop-in and community centre." See McLeod, *Lesbian and Gay Liberation in Canada,* 7, 10. Also see Kinsman, *Regulation of Desire,* 147–58.
94. Ibid., 11, 12.
95. Ibid. 3, 26, 29.
96. Batten, The homosexual life in Canada, 28, 32.
97. Ross, *The House That Jill Built,* 24.
98. Ibid., 61.
99. Vancouver's public space still very much reflects the liberal, government interventionist urban vision of Ron Basford.
100. The GLF shared a storefront office in Vancouver's Gastown district with the Yippies (Youth International Party). See McLeod, *Lesbian and Gay Liberation in Canada,* 54–55, 69. Few if any descriptions of Vancouver GLF and its relationship to the Yippies have been recorded. Martin Duberman provides a description of the strained relationships between the New York City GLF and the Yippies in his 1993 *Stonewall,* 129–37, 178–79.
101. Ibid., 102.
102. Ibid., 106, 109.
103. Ibid., 113.
104. Ibid., 127.
105. Ibid., 134, 135.
106. Ibid., 181–82.
107. In the late 1980s and early 1990s, there appears to have been a fairly coordinated movement by neo-Nazis in Canada and the United States to target gay men in public places. The most notorious case that has come to media attention so far involves a Winnipeg "skinhead" who was accused of killing a gay man in a cruising area there. The skinhead then fled and successfully joined a Canadian military regiment that was sent to the United Nations operations in Somalia, where four Somalis were tortured and murdered, involving the same individual. The scandal highlighted the neo-Nazi movement and the racist nature of the murders, and led to the greatest disgrace to the Canadian military in its history and the disbanding of the regiment. For one of the hundreds of articles on this scandal, see Roberts, Skinheads charged in slaying: Investigation of 1991 beating nets four suspects, one of whom served in Somalia, *The Globe and Mail* (Toronto, March 2, 1996): A4.
108. Samis, Homohate queeried, 1.
109. Delany, Vancouver as postmodern city, in *Vancouver,* 1–24.
110. Boddy, Plastic lion's gate, in *Vancouver,* 25–49.
111. Like most large cities on the west coast of North America, the population of those of British descent in Vancouver was rarely the majority. Soon after the turn of the twenty-first century, the total of non-European groups will be more than half of the population of the entire metropolitan area.
112. Fatona and Ingram, Scattered at the margins, 30–31.
113. It is always difficult to map use of open space, particularly by social groups that are not clearly visible and to whom privacy is a huge issue. The background information for the discussion of queer outdoor space in Vancouver is based on personal observations from 1970 to present, the 1973 Cook and Scythes map that included cruising areas, and information, discussions, and interviews. A 1995 map of strategic sites for Vancouver's "bisexual, gay, and lesbian communities" (*Angles* 13(11): 11) indicates many more indoor private sites and no longer maps important outdoor sites because there are now too many and their functions have diversified.
114. Anonymous, Pacific gays and lesbians rally to combat rising street violence, 8, 15.
115. Anonymous, Vancouver's pre-election surprise, 7.
116. Sanders, Constructing lesbian and gay rights, 102.
117. Homosexuality was somewhat decriminalized in Canada in 1968, and in the debate in Parliament, Canadian Prime Minister Pierre Trudeau stated, "The state has no business in the bedrooms of the nation."
118. In a 1982 essay from Toronto, describing a similar Canadian context for "public" and "private" space, Ken Popert suggested that the public/private dichotomy itself was homophobic and proposed the notion of "collective space."
119. Brown, Ironies of distance, 160.
120. Significantly, the huge amount of female street prostitution in Vancouver is associated with heroin addic-tion, while the male and transsexual prostitution "scenes" are not dominated by pimps or drug use.

121. Brown, Sex, scale and the "new urban politics," in *Mapping Desire,* 245–63. See p. 255.
122. Stanley Park is one of the largest fragments of remaining forest in the Vancouver area, though it was selectively logged between 1860 and 1880. See Oke, North, and Slaymaker, Primordial to prim order, in *Vancouver and Its Region,* 166.
123. The Vanport Hotel was at 645 Main Street, Vancouver.
124. Box and Harrison, Natural spaces in urban places, 231–35.
125. Chauncey, Privacy could only be had in public, in *STUD,* 224.

"No More Shit," pages 127–45

1. The histories and destinies of gay male communities in Toronto have been and will continue to be extricably linked to those of lesbians, bisexuals, and other sexual minorities. While most of the public sites and respective demonstrations and business areas serve women and men—and other sexual minorities than gay men—this essay and its background research is limited to gay men and the public spaces strategic to them.
2. I am assisted in chronicling gay male communities by Miller, Lesbian and Gay Heritage of Toronto; Crawford, *Homosexuality in Canada;* and McLeod, *Lesbian and Gay Liberation in Canada.*
3. Rocke, Sodomites in fifteenth-century Tuscany: The views of Bernardino of Siena, 7–31. The author states "In 1512 a group of youths demanded that the government release men recently jailed for sodomy" (31, note 70).
4. For a recent synopsis of those raids and the responses to them see Hawkes, 15 years after the raid, *XTRA West!* 66 (February 22, 1996): 13.
5. Chauncey, *Gay New York,* 1–29.
6. Much of my analysis for the 1950s in Toronto is based on work about Montréal in Leznoff and Westley, The homosexual community, 257–63. The classic study of Toronto's later, above-ground gay community is in Murray, The institutional elaboration of a quasi-ethnic community, 165–77.
7. As part of an oral history project, I interviewed thirty-five gay men in the mid-1980s, men who could remember Toronto's pre-Stonewall gay community from the 1950s and 1960s. A more extensive discussion of these interviews is in Grube, Queens and flaming virgins, 14–17, and Grube, Natives and settlers, 119–35.
8. White native English-speakers born in Canada have comprised a declining portion of the gay male community in Toronto. With demographic trends this group may well become a minority in Toronto.
9. Kinsman, *Regulation of Desire.*
10. For an example of the first gay liberation agenda that emerged in Toronto soon after decriminalization, see Waite and De Novo, We Demand, 4–7.
11. Gibson, *More than an Island;* and Gibson, Portrait of the Toronto Island community, 24–28.
12. Turning drag into a public spectacle was not without resistance. See Salsbery, Witchcraft and faggotry, 8–9; and Anonymous, Near-riot at drag contest, 8.
13. The Body Politic, Gay Toronto, *The Body Politic* 14 (1974): 19.
14. Unless otherwise noted, all quotations are from personal interviews. This material is available to legitimate researchers for verification purposes as long as anonymity is guaranteed to the interviewees.
15. Mays, Green passages, A13.
16. Public sex was established in David Balfour Park well before partial decriminalization, though use probably increased in the 1970s. See Hannon and Lewis, I Know a Place . . ., 43; The Body Politic, Gang homophobic violence in Balfour Park, 12; Bearchell, Shoot-up in David Balfour Park; and Mays, Green passages.
17. Lesk, Aimless development threatens gay beach, 10–11; and Patterson and O'Connor, Beach bylaw bingo, 47.
18. Anonymous, What do you say to a guy after you've blown him in the park, 13–14.
19. Much of this section is taken from the 1993 article "No more shit," 21–28, which was based on a paper of the same name read to the 1992 International Gay Studies Conference, *La Ville en Rose,* in Montréal, November 15, 1992.
20. Hannon, Taking it to the streets, 9.
21. Hannon, Loss, Mahoney, Patterson, and Spalding, Who is next? Me?, 9–11.
22. The Body Politic, Toronto cops raid gay bath, charge 28 men, 12–13.
23. Brittan, Getting off, 27–30.
24. At the time, the Progressive Conservative Party had controlled the government of Ontario for three decades but lost power in the next election.
25. For one discussion of the problem in discerning "public" and "private" space that emerged out of an experience of resisting the bathhouse raids, see Popert's 1982 essay Public sexuality and social space, 29–31. Popert argued that the simple dichotomy was no longer viable. He proposed a grey zone called "collective space."
26. Bearchell, Putting on the pressure, 8–10.
27. The Body Politic, Police stepping up park and bathroom busts, 13.
28. Bearchell, Lesbian Pride March is a first for Canada, 10.
29. Bearchell, Another park, another politician, 9.
30. In 1984 there was still a concentrated gay neighbourhood on Church Street and there were still more gay sites scattered along Yonge Street as based on the map, The Body Politic's Summer '84 Key to Toronto, *The Body Politic* 105: 29.
31. Some of these statements are expansions on a paper, Are you now or have you ever been an essentialist? given at the International Gay Studies Conference in

Amsterdam—Homosexuality, Which Homosexuality? in 1987.

32. The maps in this essay were drawn by Kathleen Morrisey and first appeared in Gay Toronto, *The Body Politic* 14: 19.

From Landmarks to Spaces, pages 147–62

1. What I mean by the term "spaces" will become clear in the course of this essay.
2. Organizing sexualities: Gay and lesbian movements since the 1960s, International Conference, Amsterdam, June 22–24, 1994. The conference was the result of a collaboration between four Dutch institutions: the Department of Politics and Public Administration, Free University of Amsterdam; the Department of Lesbian and Gay Studies, University of Amsterdam; the Department of Lesbian and Gay Studies, University of Utrecht; the Department of Lesbian and Gay Studies, University of Nijmegen.
3. Matthias Duyves, Framing Preferences, Framing Differences: The invention of Amsterdam as a gay capital.
4. The spaces framing lesbian identity are not as well documented as those framing gay male identity. Documentation that does exist is mostly in a U.S. or U.K. context. See, for example, Faderman, *Odd Girls and Twilight Lovers;* and more recently, Munt, The lesbian *flâneur,* in *Mapping Desire.* See also articles by Joan Nestle and Pat Califia in this volume.
5. When I say temporary I mean that while there are bisexual "special events" and bisexual meetings, there are (as far as I know) no identifiable public bisexual cultural spaces such as bars, clubs, restaurants, cruising areas, et cetera—no concrete bisexual spaces to ground oneself in and through.
6. Mead, Bisexuality: What's it all about?; Wolff, *Bisexuality—A study;* Klein, *The Bisexual Option.*
7. This is not to say that there were no writings on bisexuality, but none that had a widespread readership or effect. Other writings include: Fast and Wells, *Bisexual Living;* Blumstein and Schwartz, Bisexual women, in *The Social Psychology of Sex;* Bode, *A View from Another Closet.*
8. Barnes, *Nightwood;* Stekel, *Bisexual Love.*
9. The increasingly close political relationship between lesbianism and feminism certainly has a lot to do with this "disappearance" in relation to bisexuality in women in the late 1970s.
10. This bisexual "explosion" has been particularly noticeable in the U.S. The most notable works in this area are: Klein and Wolf, eds., *Two Lives to Lead;* Geller, ed., *Bisexuality;* Hutchins and Ka'ahumanu, eds., *Bi Any Other Name;* Weise, ed., *Closer to Home;* George, *Women and Bisexuality;* Tucker, ed., *Bisexual Politics;* Rose, ed., *Bisexual Horizons;* Hall and Pramaggiore, eds., *RePresenting Bisexualities;* Bi Academic Intervention, ed., *The Bisexual Imaginary.*
11. In the U.K. in 1994 there were eighteen bisexual groups, organising on a local level and coming together at national events such as the annual National Bisexual Conference and London Lesbian and Gay Pride (now London Lesbian, Gay, Bisexual, and Transgender Pride). National bisexual networks or organisations include a recently established Bisexual Resource Centre and a National Bisexual Phoneline. *Bifrost*—the U.K. national bisexual magazine—was founded in 1991 and was replaced in 1995 by *Bi Community News.* In the U.S. there are local bisexual groups in almost every large city; a national bisexual network (BiNet); and since the First National Bisexual Conference in the U.S. in San Francisco in 1990, regular national gatherings. Bisexual space has also been created on the internet, with user-lists such as "bisexual activism" (biact-L), "bisexuality" (bisexu-L), and "bisexual females" (bifem-L) distributing an increasing number of posts daily.
12. The course was repeated in 1993 and 1995.
13. Däumer, Queer ethics, or the challenge of bisexuality to lesbian ethics, 91–106. This article swiftly became one of the most frequently quoted by British bisexual researchers, as it was the first publication to theorize bisexuality in a queer theory and feminist context.
14. Bi-Academic Intervention was cofounded by Clare Hemmings and Ann Kaloski, and runs from the Centre for Women's Studies, University of York, U.K. The group produces a regular newsletter and mailing list and holds biannual dayschools that focus specifically on bisexual theorising. It is worth noting that a significant number of members of the list are graduate students or junior academic faculty.
15. Hall and Pramaggiore eds., *RePresenting Bisexualities.*
16. Bi-Academic Intervention, ed., *The Bisexual Imaginary.*
17. These tentative networks were set up by a group of bisexual feminist activists and researchers after the queer theory conference in Iowa City in November 1994. (Inqueery/Intheory/Indeed: The Sixth North American Lesbian, Gay, and Bisexual Studies Conference, November 17–29, 1994, The University of Iowa, Iowa City, Iowa, U.S.) In February 1995 the Queer Studies list (QStudy-L) hosted a discussion on bisexuality and sexual fluidity that moved beyond the usual "should we or shouldn't we include them" kind of debate. Posts ranged in content from those saying that they would never have sex with a bisexual (Mon, 20 Feb 1995 02:15:24 EST), those interrogating the political usefulness of the term, those looking at personal reasons for the discomfort with bisexuals ("If I do have any problems concerning bisexuality, the source is no more

complicated than a broken heart experienced during the formative period of my gay identity," David Anderson, Tue, 21 Feb 1995 20:00:00 PST), to those examining the relationship between desire for particular sexes and desire for particular genders ("identifying as 'bisexual' often expresses little of my queer desire for fems (of whatever sex)" Lynne Degitz, Wed, 22 Feb 1995 17:02:21 -0500).

18. One of the first queer volumes to address bisexuality is Bristow and Wilson, eds., *Activating Theory*. Other recent anthologies to include articles on bisexuality are Weisser and Fleischner, eds., *Feminist Nightmares;* Bell and Valentine, eds., *Mapping Desire;* and of course, this one. The new *Journal of Lesbian, Gay, and Bisexual Identity* (edited by W. Blumenfeld) includes articles on bisexuality and has bisexual researchers on the editorial board.
19. Garber, *Vice Versa*.
20. Garber, *Vested Interests*.
21. Kermode, *New York Times Book Review;* White, *New Yorker;* McFarquhar, *The Nation*. Recent articles on bisexuality in the *New York Times* and *Newsweek* also mention *Vice Versa*.
22. Sedgwick, "Bi," Queer Studies List. <*QSTUDY-L@UBVM.cc.buffalo.edu*> (Wed, 17, Aug. 15:49:34 -0400).
23. Personally, I am skeptical of theorising bisexuality as a changing gender position in relation to sexual object-choice. This is because I am wary of collapsing bisexual desire into androgyny, of confusing sexuality and gender when they are already confused enough, and because I think that our gendered sense of self is less fluid than we might like to imagine. However, I cannot ignore the fact that a large number of people I have met who behave bisexually, or have some sense of themselves as having bisexual desire, also say that they shift gender positions in relation to gender of object-choice. For example, one friend tells me that femininity and masculinity in a sexual partner (regardless of sexed body) bring out the "opposite" gender in her—sometimes she may be butch, sometimes femme. An interesting factor in this fluid gendered sexual position is that people commonly feel that the "other part of themselves" (the femme or butch that they are not currently "performing") does not disappear but remains dormant, presently untapped. This, of course, brings us back to a Freudian notion of bisexuality as potential, as the basis of human sexuality from which we can (and are expected to) go one way or another. For the development of Freud's position on bisexuality, see Masson, ed., *Freud S.;* Richards, ed., Three essays on the theory of sexuality, in *The Penguin Freud Library Volume 7;* and Hysterical phantasies and their relation to bisexuality and A child is being beaten, in *The Penguin Freud Library Volume 10;* Freud, Psychogenesis of a case of homosexuality in a woman, in *Collected Papers, Volume II;* and The ego and the id, in *The Standard Edition of the Complete Psychological Works of Sigmund Freud*. For a thorough analysis of Freud's views on bisexuality see Marjorie Garber's chapter "Freud and the Golden Fliess," in *Vice Versa*. For an analysis of "Psychogenesis" from a bisexual perspective see P. Davidson, *Her Libido Flowed in Two Currents . . .*.

    On a personal level, my discomfort with the notion of a gender- fluid bisexual desire comes from the difficulty of being accepted (and accepting myself) as a bisexual femme. "Do bisexuals do butch/ femme?" one skeptical butch asks, as if it were an impossible concept that a bisexual might have a particular gender identity.
24. Eve Sedgwick highlights this tendency within contemporary theorizing (particularly within queer, women's, and cultural and critical studies) to eschew writing about the body for fear of being labeled essentialist: "the distance of any . . . [theoretical] . . . account from a biological basis is assumed to correlate almost precisely with its potential for doing justice to difference (individual, historical, and cross-cultural), to contingency, to performative force, and to the possibility of change." (Sedgwick, Shame in the cybernetic fold, 496)

    It seems highly ironic that queer theory, which was born from "in-your-face" bodies that had had enough, has moved towards denying the bodies that gave it life and urgency. Queer theory is often everything about transgression but nothing about the bodies we transgress with.
25. Experience is a contested term that is no longer seen as the expression of truth or identity (Scott, *Experience*). Following Scott, Steven Angelides remarks—in an article that argues for the theoretical usefulness of bisexuality—that "[i]t is not . . . experience that reveals the truth of identity, but identity which constructs the truth of experience" [The economy of (hetero)sexuality]. The tendency has been to see experience either as the *truth of identity* or as completely subjective. My own view is to read experience as expressing truth both on a subjective and collective or historical level, in that there is nothing more true than experience, even if that truth is always partial. If experience is constructed by identity, as Angelides suggests (and, more particularly, linear narratives of identity), then experience also expresses the formation and structure of identity, re-creates it through and leaves traces on the individual body. I also want to suggest that experience doesn't only signify identity but also desire and a history of the body. A (self-identified or by default) heterosexual man's experience of same-sex desire may be constructed as contingent, as false in relation to his overriding identity as heterosexual or, in the earlier understanding of experience, as revealing his true homosexuality. Whichever

reading is accepted, the man's experience of same-sex desire is part of the history of his body, his acts and desires. The experience cannot be erased.

26. Whereas in straight, gay, and lesbian sexualities, the sex or gender of object-choice is perceived to define the identity, bisexuality is never the result of such a consistent object-choice. An individual's final or resultant sexual identity is always defined by the sex and gender of the sexual object-choice made, never by other factors that might influence an individual's sense of his or her sexuality. So, for example, although power relations are implicit in the structures as described above, this is never said to be the defining factor of sexual identity. Sexualities such as fetishism, S/M, or sexualities primarily focused on intergenerational relations, race/ethnicity, or class may be understood as secondary within this framework, or as perversions, but cannot be accounted for as primarily influencing sexual identity. Freud discusses some of these in "Deviations in Respect of the Sexual Aim," acknowledging that some degree of, for example, fetishism is "habitually present in normal love," that it becomes pathological only "when the longing for the fetish passes beyond the point of being merely a necessary condition attached to the sexual object and actually takes the place of the normal aim." (Freud, Deviations in respect of the sexual aim: Three essays on the theory of sexuality, 66–67.) Within contemporary lesbian and gay politics and theory, it is only in the last decade—with the U.S. and U.K. "sex wars" and the attack on S/M practices by the British legal system in 1990—that S/M and fetishism have been taken on as sexual identities by some practitioners of those acts. Such moves help to expose the fallacy that the sexual self is formed through sex and gender alone. See Bell, Perverse dynamics, sexual citizenship and the transformation of intimacy, in *Mapping Desire,* 304–17.
27. The sex or gender of sexual partner does not equal bisexuality. Because of this lack of consistency, the gender of the bisexual is also impossible to "assign correctly" in order for masculinity and femininity to be seen as the only possible sexual complements. It is possible to attempt such reassignment with lesbian or gay sexuality through terms such as "mannish lesbian" and "effeminate man," but what about a "sometimes mannish bisexual woman"? It doesn't have quite the same ring to it. The only way of producing bisexuality through this structure is as hermaphrodite, as androgyne, or as the potential that precedes adult sexual choice. (M. Bowie, Bisexuality, in *Feminism and Psychoanalysis.*) Curiously, bisexuality becomes stripped of sexuality in itself, while being seen as the "tie that binds" both the two (supposedly) oppositional structures of heterosexuality and homosexuality together, and the binary components of male/female, masculine/feminine.This contradiction—hypersexual/asexual—is reflected in the Kinsey scale. Bisexuality binds the opposite poles of heterosexuality and homosexuality, ensures their relationship to one another, yet in itself is a range rather than a fixed position. The closer to one end of the scale one is, the more heterosexual or the more homosexual one is: This is determined by the relative sexual object-choices one makes. The sex and gender base of sexual identity is not challenged. To be a Kinsey 3 is to be equally attracted to men and women (and one could also read, equally masculine/equally feminine), i.e., completely bisexual, and it is also to be equally unattracted to men and women (and an equal absence of gender identity?), i.e., completely asexual. Bisexuality is never about two, only about one—asexual or self-fulfilling—or three, continuously and equally attracted to both men and women. (Kinsey, Pomeroy, and Martin, *Sexual Behavior in the Human Male,* 636–59; and *Sexual Behavior in the Human Female,* 468–76.)
28. In terms of chronology, bisexuality does not structurally display the requisite consistency of object-choice over time. The formation of sexual identity requires not only that one make a particular gendered and sexed object-choice, but that this be consistent. The present can only be validated by the anticipated future, which can only be validated by a past that is retrospectively given meaning according to the present. The actual events of the past are less important than the retrospective meaning they are given. One is allowed "mistakes," as long as they are seen as mistakes or as an interruption to the narrative of one's true sexual identity. This makes the structure of sexual identity and desire highly precarious because it only makes sense if and when it is repeated, and so is always anticipating that moment of repetition, always failing to consolidate its permanence.
29. Card, Lesbian attitudes and the second sex, 213. A similar view of bisexuality in women as lacking the requisite loyalty for a valid sexual and political identity is expressed by Marilyn Frye when she says that "Loyalty and identity are so closely connected as to be almost just two aspects of the one phenomenon" (Frye, History and responsibility, 216). Both articles combine psychoanalytic frameworks with contemporary political frameworks (where one's relationship to oppression marks the validity of one's identity). The articles are discussed by Fraser in *Framing Contention.*
30. In the same way as lesbians and gay men construct narratives that lend consistency to their lives before the moment of "self-realisation", bisexuals strive to create a "before" and "after" that lends validity to their present self-perceptions and their (consistent) desire for people of more than one sex. A cursory glance at recent bisexual anthologies highlights the desire for such "coming out" narratives. "'For the

first time I felt like a whole person'" (Gregory, The case for a feminist bisexuality, in *Sex and Love,* 150). There is an authentic sexuality, and therefore a whole self, that has not previously been allowed expression: "My sexuality has caused me problems because it was too broad to be acceptable to me, as I was trying to force it into narrow definitions—first heterosexual, and second, lesbian" (Gregory "Feminist bisexuality," 150). It has always existed in more or less the same form and can be charted as being reenacted over time—an authentic chronologically-validated bisexual self. The need to mention one's lasting attractions to people of both sexes also figures prominently in bisexual self-narratives. One of the contributors to the volume *Bisexual Lives* begins (and ends) her story with a list of her current lovers, with the time that she has been seeing each of them in parentheses; for example, "Amanda (for two and a half years), Paul (for four and a half years)" (Clare, *Bisexual Lives,* 27) and the list goes on. The impression that is hard to shake is that here is a real bisexual, dedicated to multiple object-choices of both sexes, steadfast in her endlessly mutable, never-satisfied bisexual desire.

31. Foucault's history of sexuality, while attempting to problematise the notion of identity, still tells the story from that perspective, still writes around a point of identity that is privileged. For Foucault that moment is the end of the nineteenth century with the intelligibility of a white male homosexual identity. That moment is written, rewritten, reinscribed as the moment, the monomoment of the history of sexuality (M. Foucault, *The history of sexuality).* This is paradoxical because also in Foucauldian terms those moments where a clearly defined sexual identity/body/existence emerges are less interesting and tell us less about the formation of the categories of sexual identity than the moments that are more subtly defined, more liable to open interpretation (Foucault, The discourse on language, in *The Archaeology of Knowledge,* 215–37; Lecture one: Jan 1976, Two lectures, power/knowledge: Selected interviews and other writings 1972–1977, 82, 85). And one might also suggest that because of this, the "emergence of an identity", or the telling of the history of that identity as real, is less a narrative of resistance necessarily, but more a narrative of the dominant, which to my mind, has already been told and only gains strength through its repetition.

32. Rewriting history in this way focuses on substitution rather than reevaluation of our understanding of sexual identities and the ways in which we write history in the first place. To give you some idea of the strength of this "reclaiming" in bisexual circles—both Fritz Klein and Marjorie Garber highlight Oscar Wilde's relationships with both men and women, Klein in 1978 (*The Bisexual Option*), Garber in 1995 (*Vice Versa*). Klein is unequivocal about his view of Wilde as bisexual; Garber is well enough aware of the theoretical problems of "reclaiming" from a contemporary standpoint (see Faderman, *Surpassing the Love of Men)* to qualify her documentation of Wilde's erotic life by saying, "since Wilde's genius lay in inventing himself as an apostle of perversity, of transgression as such, to 'reclaim' him as bisexual instead of gay would be merely to repeat the gesture of fragmentation and compartmentalization, the gesture of essentializing, that is contrary to his own practice and thought." (354–55)

    This is rhetoric, however. Since Garber considers pretty much any desire or behaviour that is not either exclusively focused on one sex or exclusively determined by the sex and gender of object-choice to be "bisexual," and since she does not adequately or consistently distinguish between behaviour and identity, Wilde is, according to her definition, bisexual. A more pragmatic (and I hope accurate) view of the significance of figures such as Wilde (and Sackville-West and Virginia Woolf) would be to say that—however he identified in his lifetime—he is now an important part of the histories of more than one sexual minority group. I elaborate on this view in an article on the complex relationships between transgender, bisexual, and lesbian and gay histories, theories, and politics (Hemmings, From lesbian nation to transgender liberation).

33. As far as I know, the first place where "monosexual" is defined as being the opposite of bisexual is in Hutchins and Ka'ahumanu, *Bi Any Other Name.* The glossary defines monosexual as "a term used for both heterosexuals and homosexuals—i.e., all people who love only one gender and take for granted the sexual dichotomy set up by the patriarchy. Bisexuality calls this system of categories and divisions into question." (370)

    Here gender is being used instead of "sex." I assume it is being used incorrectly, given that lesbians, gay men, and heterosexuals commonly have, express, and act on desire for more than one gender, even if they do not have, express, or act on (though some do) desire for more than one sex.

34. As a theoretical tool the term monosexual creates a boundary around bisexuality (that only the most enlightened and gender-free may cross?), misrepresenting complex desires and communities that make up the history of bisexuality. The choice is monosexual or bisexual (or polysexual). The implications of this are bizarre to say the least. If a lesbian has sex with men does that make her bisexual? What about her self-definition? If she only has sex with women, but does not "take for granted the sexual dichotomy set up by the patriarchy" (Hutchins and Ka'ahumanu, 370)—the second test for identifying monosexuals, which clearly does not make her bisexual, is she then a nonmonosexual lesbian?

What kind of test can be used to determine someone's acceptance of sexual dichotomies? Is a self-identified bisexual who thinks that sexual dichotomies are just fine and/or only has sexual relations with one gender a monosexual bisexual? As a femme bisexual whose desire is currently fueled by masculinity (in men or women—one gender, but in more than one sex), am I monosexual?

35. Of course, neither do the majority of gay, lesbian, or straight people. The difference is that a bisexual cannot as a rule go somewhere (other than to bisexual support or political groups) that is specifically for bisexuals. The lack of self-recognition differs in type as well as degree.
36. Access to social and political spaces (particularly in lesbian and gay subcultures) is granted by default; if you're with a same-sex partner or with same-sex friends, you must be a lesbian or gay man. Your sexuality is what is most visible, is again formed by association. You are "read as" lesbian, gay, or straight. Even in spaces that include the term bisexual (as is happening more and more often), how to be "read as" bisexual?
37. Amanda Udis-Kessler argues that bisexuals should not focus so much on inclusion within gay and lesbian communities, stating that "Post-Stonewall lesbian and gay groups got on fine for more than a decade without bisexuals insisting on inclusion, and bisexuals presumably got along fine during that period without needing to seek inclusion." (Udis-Kessler, Identity/Politics: A history of the bisexual movement, paper presented at Inqueery/Intheory/Indeed, 2) What Udis-Kessler fails to note is that positive inclusion and "default presence" are separate issues. Bisexuals have always been involved in lesbian and gay communities, but are seeking recognition rather than "entrance." Where were these elusive bisexuals, and of what did their "getting along fine" consist?
38. Upton, White and black landscapes in eighteenth-century Virginia, in *Material Life in America,* 357.
39. Northampton came to the eyes of the ever-curious U.S. public with a feature article called Strange town where men aren't wanted, in the *National Enquirer* (April 21, 1992). The sensationalist article dubbed Northampton "Lesbianville, U.S." and gave the impression that a third of Northampton's population is lesbian. (It's large, but it's not that large!) The article fueled a number of almost identical articles across the country: Northampton was featured in articles in the *LA Times* and the *Associated Press*, and was covered on *CNN* and *20/20* in September 1992.
40. Already we can see the difficulty of defining what is butch/femme, what is heterosexual, and what is FTM/femme. Even as someone who is acutely aware that how one dresses or whom one is "with" does not necessarily denote who one is or how one identifies, I am more likely to read certain signs as butch/femme than FTM/femme, or obviously male/female couples as straight than as bisexual. This is partly due, of course, to the fact that this is a predominantly lesbian bar but also due to what one expects to see and how one is acculturated into reading things in certain ways.
41. Jane knows that she gets read as straight and as fag hag, because she has been told this by people who first read her this way.
42. In my experience bisexual men do not talk as much about relationships with men, which cause them to challenge their sense of themselves as bisexual. This may happen more in men-only groups.
43. Obviously these scenarios are complicated when issues of monogamy or nonmonogamy are introduced.
44. Lani Ka'ahumanu is a bisexual activist and writer, coauthor with Loraine Hutchins of *Bi Any Other Name.*
45. There is a new wave of people who are identifying as bisexual from a much earlier age, in part due to increased visibility of the bisexual movement. The feature story on bisexuality in *Newsweek* in July 1995 proclaims Bisexuality: Not gay. Not straight. A new sexual identity emerges (July 17, 1995). While, of course, bisexuality is hardly a new sexual identity, the brash declaration marks the recent confidence of a bisexual movement.
46. In 1987, following the success of the Bisexual Contingent at the March on Washington for Lesbian and Gay Rights in October and the Fourth Annual Conference on Bisexuality organised by the East Coast Bisexual Network in May, a flyer asking "Are You Ready for a National Bisexual Network?" was circulated. The North American Bisexual Network-in-Formation was born. When it proved too difficult for the coordinators in San Francisco to network effectively with everyone who had expressed an interest, plans began for a national conference to bring people together to discuss, amongst other things, the function, aims and organisation of the national network. The information on the First National Bisexual Conference discussed here is drawn from archive material on the conference and from interviews with key participants. Many thanks especially to Lani Ka'ahumanu, who allowed me to root through the boxes of archive material stored in her basement, and who kept my caffeine levels high!
47. The final site was agreed upon just weeks before the conference. It was the Mission High School on the corner of 18th and Delores. (Steering Committee Minutes, May 5 1990, future references denoted by SCM.)
48. The large San Francisco Lesbian and Gay Pride Parade took place on the Sunday after the conference.
49. The People of Color Caucus first met on March 11, 1990. (SCM: March 3, 1990.)

50. SCM: January 21, 1990.
51. SCM: June 5, 1989.
52. An article in the *Bay Area Bisexual Newsletter* in February/March 1990 outlined the reasons "why feminism is part of the statement of purpose of this upcoming June conference" (Tucker, Smith, Feminism and the conference). The reasons given were inclusion, the centrality of feminism to fostering community among bisexual men and women, and the necessity of making the links between different forms of oppression (in this case sexism and bi- and homophobia). The letter was fueled by disagreements within and outside the steering committee about the role feminism should play in a bisexual conference (and by implication a broader bisexual movement). Responses on both sides were printed in the following issue of the newsletter (2(3), April/May/June/July 1990).
53. The transgender movement in the U.S. makes a point of including partners of transgender people in its definition. This is partly because partners of transgender people may also find themselves without a clear sense of community. For example, a lesbian may find herself ostracised from the lesbian community if her partner is an FTM. People involved with bisexuals may also find themselves having to explain their sexual choice to members of their community. It is not unknown for lesbians to be given a hard time by other lesbians for having bisexual lovers.
54. For example, Garber's chapter "Erotic education" argues that sexual dynamics between tutor and student are bisexual desire, because they are not primarily determined by gender (*Vice Versa,* 317–44). Anything from fetishism to intergenerational sex could, on this basis, be classed as bisexual desire.

Domestic Dykes, pages 163-68

1. Massey, Questions of locality, 142–49.
2. As discussed by Sy Adler and Joanna Brenner, Gender and space, 27.
3. Castells, *City and the Grassroots.*
4. Lauria and Knopp, Toward an analysis of the role of gay communities in the urban renaissance, 152–69; Knopp, Social theory, social movements and public policy, 253–61; Knopp, Some theoretical implications of gay involvement in an urban land market, 337–52; Knopp, Sexuality and the spatial dynamics of capitalism, 651–69.
5. See Kitzinger, *The Social Construction of Lesbianism;* Ponse, *Identities in the Lesbian World;* D. G. Wolf, *The Lesbian Community;* Kennedy and Davis, eds., *Boots of Leather, Slippers of Gold.* A more recent work that highlights differences between lesbians is Stein, *Sisters, Sexperts, Queers.*
6. Such as S. J. Wolfe and Penelope, *Sexual Practice/Textual Theory.*
7. Bell, Insignificant others, 323–29; Valentine, Desperately seeking Susan, 109–16; Adler and Brenner, Gender and space, 24–34.
8. Adler and Brenner, Gender and space; Valentine, Insignificant others.
9. Such as Ross, The house that Jill built, 75–91; Egerton, Out but not down, 75–88.

Queer Zones and Enclaves, pages 171–75

1. For North America, some of the best indications of the beginnings of a rural gay men's "movement" were the first twenty issues of *RFD,* a formerly collective journal.
2. The most important work on gay male gentrification has been by Knopp, Some theoretical implications of gay involvement in an urban land market, 337–52, and Exploiting the rent-gap, 48–64. Also see the earlier Lauria and Knopp, Toward an analysis of the role of gay communities in the urban renaissance, 152–69.
3. Knopp, Sexuality and the spatial dynamics of capitalism, 651–69.
4. Anderson, The shifting stage of politics, 140–41, 145.
5. Smith and Katz, Grounding metaphor, in *Place and Politics,* 67.
6. Davis, The suburban nightmare; while older suburbs experience many problems of the inner city, "edge cities" now offer a new escape, *Los Angeles Times* 113 (October 23, 1994): M1.
7. Delany, Vancouver as a postmodern city, in *Vancouver,* 3–7.
8. Groth, San Francisco, 29.
9. Drucker, In the tropics there is no sin, 93–94.
10. National pages, Protesters call for more help for homeless who have AIDS, *New York Times* 139 (October 8, 1989): 31.
11. Specter and Gladwell, Protesters take over AIDS event; chanting drowns out speech by Sullivan as conference ends, *Washington Post* 113 (June 25, 1990): A1.
12. Henderson, Activists take to streets to fight spread of AIDS, *Washington Post* 115 (August 23, 1992): B3 and The best anti-AIDS tool ever, in *Los Angeles Times* 111 (September 10, 1992): B6.
13. Davis, Who killed LA, 3–29; and Who killed LA: Part two, 29–64. Also see Davis, In LA, burning all illusions, 743–46; and Davis, The LA inferno, 57–80.
14. Patton, *Inventing AIDS,* 28.
15. Ibid., 131.
16. Soja, Heterotopologies, in *Postmodern Cities and Spaces,* 13–34.

17. For an analysis of Manchester as such a liberal city state, still very much an exception in government consideration of sexual minorities, see Whittle, Consuming differences, in *Margins of the City,* 27–41.

San Francisco, pages 177–96

1. Thanks to Dorothy Allison for her November 1986 lecture at the National Leather Association Convention in Seattle on the zones in the city of literature, and to Wendy Chapkis for her suggestions.
2. This compilation of the writings of Pat Califia is published by Cleis Press of Pittsburgh and San Francisco. See pp. 205–13.
3. Califia, A personal view of the history of the lesbian s/m community and movement in San Francisco, in *Coming to Power,* 243–81.
4. Rubin classed "good sex" as heterosexual, married, monogamous, reproductive. She put the following in the "major area of contest": unmarried heterosexual couples; promiscuous heterosexuals; masturbation; long-term stable lesbian and gay male couples; lesbians in bars; and promiscuous gay men at the baths or in the park. Under the category of bad sex she places transvestites, transsexuals, fetishists, prostitution, and cross-generational contact. See Rubin, Thinking Sex, in *Pleasure and Danger,* 282. On p. 281 she also posits the duality of "the charmed circle" versus "the outer limits."
5. Bawer, *A Place at the Table.*
6. Rubin, Thinking Sex, 296–97.
7. Ibid., 302.
8. For an overview of the feminist censorship movement and feminist opposition to it in the United States, see Duggan, Censorship in the name of feminism, in *Sex Wars,* 30–42.
9. Rubin wrote a history of this space in a 1991 essay, The Catacombs, in *Leatherfolk,* 119–41. Pat Califia's debut is mentioned on p. 130.
10. Califia, Dangerous tongues, in *Forbidden Passages,* 9–24.

Gay Male Places of Mexico City, pages 197–212

1. For instance, this situation is indirectly depicted in the case of West Berlin in an article by Cockburn (1988) on the location of districts within that city where prostitution is practised and on their link with the diffusion of the AIDS pandemic.
2. At the same time, from 1992 onward, many American gay magazines (published in a Spanish version in Spain, like *All-Man, Honcho,* and others) began to be sold in the newsstands all over Mexico City, at lower prices than their Mexican counterparts. For instance, the price was $8 (U.S.) for a copy of *Hermes* at the beginning of 1994, and $7 for one of *All-Man.*
3. Until now, the influence of the AIDS pandemic on the spatial mobility of gay men in Mexico City has not been examined. However, it is clear that some places frequented by gay men, such as cinemas, bathhouses, and cruisy parks or streets, have been experiencing a reduction in the number of regular customers after the appearance of AIDS.
4. These two "bookstores" actually sell all kind of paraphernalia for both gay and nongay people.
5. These newly developed businesses catering to gay men are located in the central districts of Mexico City, such as the Zona Rosa, the historical city center and the outskirts of both areas. In spite of their recognizability within the urban space, these businesses are visited less frequently than they are asked to send "professionals" to the addresses of gay men. Hence it is safe to say that no intense or constant flows toward these companies' premises have been generated, in part because many of the affluent gay men who can afford to buy these services may fear being ripped off when visiting the places.
6. It is important to mention that the general response of the gay men surveyed was enthusiastic and very helpful. Out of 138 gay men contacted, only 7 refused to complete the questionnaire. No aggressive attitudes toward the interviewers were found; this is remarkable since one-half of the answers came from strangers intercepted in the streets and under-ground stations.
7. The questionnaire survey also included items such as marital status, type of relationships of the interviewee, religion, opinion on local political issues, housing conditions, number of people depending on the salary of the interviewee, and the number and kind of his material possessions; general features of the gay men interviewed are not examined in this paper.
8. Roughly 70 percent of the interviewees were born in the Mexico City region.
9. This division of the city into five major sectors was arbitrarily done. From the *Circuito Interior* (or Inner Ring), which encircles the old historical city center and consequently defines the central area of Mexico City, the other four sectors were drawn. First the northeast, containing the airport area, some industrial districts and poor neighborhoods of East Mexico City such as Nezahualcóyotl, one of the largest shantytowns anywhere in the world. The northwest contains most of the industrial sections of the city, as well as some middle- and upper-middle-class *colonias* (housing neighborhoods). The affluent southwest comprises most of the fashionable districts in the city, such as Coyoacán and El Pedregal, the University main campus, and many other attractive *colonias.* Finally, the southeast spreads over some semirural areas, such as

Xochimilco, and includes poor and unconsolidated housing sectors of the city.

10. Attending to the results of the questionnaire survey, most of the gay men interviewed go out for many reasons, particularly to have some fun in the places visited (44 percent) and to meet friends and to get to know new people (26 percent). Only 2 percent of the men surveyed reported they do not go out at all.
11. By the time the questionnaire survey was completed, the "European-trip" quadrangle had not yet appeared in the urban gay arena. There is a neighborhood on the southwestern outskirts of the Zona Rosa, which has been recently taken over by hustlers, where streets are named after European cities: Hamburg, Liege, Bourdeaux, Seville, and so on. This is a square-shaped area, whose perimeter can be used as a travel circuit, that has become popular among gay men who own and drive a car. The metaphor is clear: A "tour of Europe" with the benefits of cruising. However, in the last year or so, this area of the city has become unsafe, as police have constantly harrassed hustlers and nonhustlers in these streets.
12. The station is named after the leader of the Mexican political independence movement, which eventually freed the country from the Spanish Crown at the beginning of the last century. One wonders whether the active gay life that takes place at Hidalgo underground station has any association with the idea of freedom or if it is purely coincidental.
13. The cost of evading a misdemeanor charge related to cruising, or even a suggestion of public sex, can exceed $100 (U.S.) in payoffs to police.
14. In reference to these other, less visible and possibly emerging *colonias*, there was no reference to any district or sector in particular. Nor was any reason given to define why these were considered gay neighbourhoods.
15. So important is Acapulco to the gay life in Mexico that, when the most reactionary right-wing groups deterred the opening session and works of the ILGA conference in July 1991 (originally to be held in Guadalajara), the municipality of Acapulco and other Mexican authorities allowed the conference to be changed to that port.

Queer and Gendered Housing, pages 213–32

1. This article is a condensation from my 1995 QUEER SCAPES: Patterns and Processes of Gay Male and Lesbian Spatialisation in Vancouver, B.C. (a thesis submitted in partial fulfillment of the requirements for the degree of Master of Arts in The Faculty of Graduate Studies, Department of Geography, The University of British Columbia, Vancouver). Funding was from the Central Mortgage and Housing Corporation of the government of Canada (Housing needs of gay men and lesbians September 1994–December 1995) and the Geography department of The University of British Columbia. I am grateful to the following individuals for their support, guidance, comments, and interview contributions: Michael Brown, Janelle Allison, Trudi Bunting, and my thesis committee members David Ley and Geraldine Pratt.
2. Indeed, with the West End being such a popular tourist sightseeing destination (with its beaches, Stanley Park, and viewpoints, not to mention its central location), it is hardly surprising that certain shops, restaurants, and cafés will have a quite varied clientele—gay, straight, male, or female.
3. When one surveys *Xtra! West*, one finds that 20 percent of service ads are for professional services—including lawyers, financial advisors, counsellors, insurance agents, and so on, but not including medical, real estate, or travel services (which, added to the above total, raise the percentage to 51 percent). These personal services, excluding the last three categories, are mostly located in the West End (59 percent of ads, 57 percent of advertisers). The same is true of medical professionals (64 percent of ads, 82 percent of advertisers) and real estate agents (53 percent and 50 percent), while travel services include agencies (67 percent of which are in the West End) as well as destinations such as hotels and B&Bs, which are typically out of town. Other services include nonprofit agencies such as AIDS Vancouver or Meals on Wheels, which are all located in the West End (except the Vancouver Lesbian Connection and AIDS Vancouver Island), as well as personal services such as those related to beauty and fitness, which are also located primarily in the West End (61 percent of ads, 55 percent of advertisers). The West End definitely gets the lion's share of advertisers (50 percent), a proportion that increases noticeably if out-of-town advertisers are removed from the total (to 57 percent). Thus from these sources, the West End clearly emerges as Vancouver's premier gay area.
4. There are only a small number of neighbourhood institutions, such as the Vancouver Lesbian Connection and the Gazebo Connection, two lesbian networking groups, that are aimed specifically at gay women. The majority of them are grassroots organisations aimed at women in general, as well as visible minorities and low-income families. These include the Vancouver Status of Women Office (established in 1976), the Women's Health Collective, MOSAIC —a multicultural integration service organisation, and the REACH community clinic.
5. Greenpeace was originally founded in Vancouver in the early 1970s, but in the 1980s, after a bitter power

struggle, the organization's headquarters and funds were transferred from Kitsilano, adjacent to the West End, to Amsterdam. Nonetheless, the large Greenpeace office on the Drive supports numerous "alternative" jobs and services in the neighbourhood.

6. Stonewall 25 was a festival commemorating the twenty-fifth anniversary of the Stonewall riots. It included several parties at West End bars, but its crowning event was the celebration in Grandview Park, a music festival and rally aimed at reinforcing gay solidarity.
7. Aside from Lesbian Visibility Week and the lesbian-led Queer Patrols against homophobic violence, few incidences of activism have been reported, and a spokesperson for the Vancouver Lesbian Connection, where the group met until 1994, could not recall any recent Lesbian Avengers event. The group actually disbanded that year and has just recently started up again. While the protest at Joe's Café was over antilesbian sentiment, the protesters were a mishmash of gay men, lesbians, young students—even some of Joe's waiters quit their jobs and joined them (Serafin 1994).
8. Vancouver's 1995 Fringe Festival was held at ten East Vancouver venues on and around the Drive. Organizers felt that the neighbourhood's character and amenities (such as funky cafés and late-night spaghetti houses) were particularly well suited to the alternative theatre festival and hoped that it could become its permanent home.

The Queer Nation Acts Up, pages 233–74

1. This version was first delivered at the University of Southern California (USC) in March 1991 with an initial article published in 1992 as The Queer Nation acts up: Health care, politics, and sexual diversity in the County of Angels, *Environment and Planning D—Society and Space* 10: 609–50. This version of "The Queer Nation acts up" has been reworked as a historical document of that time of euphoric fear without the extensive citations made in the original article.
2. I was particularly active in ACT UP/LA and Queer Nation/LA from 1990 to 1992, and this discussion is limited to that period and not to those organizations at other times. Many thanks to Barrie Thorne and Michael Dear, who encouraged me to write the initial essay so long ago.
3. Los Angeles County Department of Health Services, March 1996, Public Health Week '96: AIDS Update—Gender and age group of persons reported with AIDS in 1994: Differences between Los Angeles County and the United States (1 page table); Comparison of 1987–1990 and 1991–1994 cumulative AIDS rates (per 100,000) by city and area in Los Angeles County (1 page table); and Adult/adolescent AIDS cases reported in 1994 by HIV risk group: Differences between Los Angeles County and the United States. On file HIV Epidemiology Program, County of Los Angeles, 600 S. Commonwealth Ave., Suite 805, Los Angeles, California 90005. Fax: (213) 487-9386.
4. Of the AIDS cases reported for men, 55 percent are white gay, 24 percent are Latino, and 18 percent are African American.
5. Of women in Los Angeles reported with AIDS, 28 percent are white, 36 percent are African American, and 33 percent are Latina.
6. See the following articles in the *Los Angeles Times* 110 (hereafter noted as *LAT*): Philip Hager, A dissenting voice: Blackmun disputes ruling on homosexuals, *LAT* (May 18, 1991): B1. *Editors' note*: Except where noted, all issues of the *Los Angeles Times* articles cited are in Volume 110 and all issues of the *New York Times* cited are in Volume 140.
7. In addition to the *Hardwick* decision's rejection of homosexuality as a meaningful legal category, AIDS has compounded inequities of spousal, hospital visitation, insurance, housing, health, child custody, inheritance, and other rights taken for granted by individuals who enjoy the marriage option. The rage over unequal status and fear of violence, destitution, and death felt by gay people in this regard became apparent when, just after this article was completed in the fall of 1991, unprecedented thousands of previously politically inactive gay men and lesbians took to the streets of Los Angeles protesting Republican Governor Pete Wilson's surprise veto of Assembly Bill 101, which would have banned job discrimination based on sexual orientation.
8. See Crimp and Rolston, *AIDS demo graphics;* Patton, *Sex and Germs,* 144–58. For a related analysis of early activist challenges to the prevailing scientific and epistemological paradigms at the time, see Epstein, Democratic science?, 35–64. On the alliance of activists and scientists against political and religious claims to authority see Wachter, *The Fragile Coalition;* and my Why I shouted Louis Sullivan down, *ACT UP/LA Newsletter* 3(4) (August–September 1990). See also the film documentaries by Phil Zwickler, *Positive* (1990); Testing the Limits Collective, *Voices from the Front* (1991); Stuart Marshall, *Over Our Dead Bodies* (1991); and Graham Henman, *The Silent War* (1991); Rosa von Praunheim's 1989 docu-performance *Silence=Death;* Marlon Riggs's *Anthem* (1990); and John DiStefano's, *Tell Me Why: The epistemology of disco* (1991). Also see David Wojnarowicz's Post cards from America: X-rays from hell (reprinted in his 1991 *Close To The Knives,* 111–123).
9. For an understanding of the anger behind the phrase, see Larry Kramer, Ten years of plague, *The Advocate* 580 (July 2, 1991): 62–65 and Robert

Massa, The age of AIDS: The slippery slope, *Village Voice* 36(32) (August 6, 1991): 18–19.

10. See Esther Kaplan, ACT UP under siege, *Village Voice* 36(29) (July 16, 1991): 35–36 and comments regarding Los Angeles police and sheriff's deputies later in this article.
11. The phrase was first popularized as a front page headline of the sensationalist tabloid *New York Post* after members of Queer Nation chased down hecklers taunting them with antigay epithets and circled an unsuspecting former New York mayor Ed Koch during a "Take Back the Night" march through Greenwich Village on the Saturday before the 1990 San Francisco Sixth International Conference on AIDS. See Jack Curry, A gay parade protesting violence turns violent, *NYT* 139 (June 18, 1990): A12, B3; and Robin Hardy, Die harder: AIDS activism is abandoning gay men, *Village Voice* 36(28) (July 2, 1991): 33–34.
12. From Queer Nation/LA's founding statement, August 1990. In that period, I argue that Queer Nation/LA was the least separatist and factionalized, though still not fully racially mixed, of the larger Queer Nations. This situation, which was also true of ACT UP/LA in comparison to other ACT UP groups, may have had as much to do with the distances members lived from one another as well as the absence in Los Angeles of compact urban group cultures of identity more readily created and reproduced in the denser metropolitan areas. Indeed, visitors to the Los Angeles meetings of each group remarked at the relative absence of such cliques and factions so visible—in word and fashion—in cities such as New York and San Francisco. In this sense the morphological exceptionalism I have tagged to Los Angeles may in fact be the spatial norm for most of North America outside of the Eastern corridor and San Francisco Bay. What passed as a "laid-back," more compromising, or less uniformly stylized way of dressing and doing things among Los Angeles activists suggested a less tightly connected community of individuals, who literally found some of their few experiences of community at these meetings and actions. While Angelenos may both enjoy and suffer the heightened isolation that our lower density both imposes and permits, similar activists in New York or San Francisco may well crisscross each others' paths constantly, creating both distinct intragroup subcultures and rivalries as well as a critical sociopolitical mass particularly suited for large street actions impossible to imagine in Los Angeles, at least until the fall 1991 anti-(Governor Pete) Wilson marches.
13. See Lily Braindrop, The art of Amazon cruising and Sapphic sexual etiquette, *The Advocate* 582 (July 30, 1991): 60–63; Karen Ocamb, Lust for life: Our changing sex scene, *Lesbian News* (September 1991): 1.
14. See Doug Sadownick, The birth of a queer nation and the death of "gay" and "lesbian," *LA Weekly* (May 17, 1991): 20–27, and my and other letters in *LA Weekly* (June 7, 1991): 6 and (June 14, 1991): 6.
15. See Jeffrey Hilbert, The politics of drag, *The Advocate* 575 (April 23, 1991): 42–47. Besides challenging traditional "left" paradigms of the interstices of race, class, and gender, the new queer and AIDS activism was more rooted in a sensation of euphoria, defined as a giddy hybrid of sadness, fear, and defiant celebration of community well-being, in the face of so much violence and death in the wake of the AIDS pandemic.
16. One can, of course, organize for survival and mourn creatively at the same time, as most of ACT UP's colorful demonstrations have shown. The same point has been made locally by performance artist Tim Miller and others affiliated with the Highways performance space, including the Sodomy Players' 1991 production of *AIDS! The Musical!*, which proclaims: "You've had the disease, you've been to the demonstration, now see the musical!" See AIDS! The musical!: Reflection of anger, *LAT* (August 1, 1991): F9–10. A similarly ironic treatment of AIDS was Rosa von Praunheim's farcical mid–1980s film *A Virus Knows No Morals*.
17. Showalter, *Sexual Anarchy*.
18. Baldwin, *The Fire Next Time*.
19. See Richard Simon, Gay charges bias in vote for board's presidency, *LAT* 109 (June 20, 1990): B1, B8.
20. See Koonz, *Mothers in the Fatherland: Women, the family, and Nazi politics* for a thorough investigation of the circumscribed but crucial role played by women in the implementation of repressive social policy.
21. See Bly, *Iron John;* Brod, ed., *The Making of Masculinities: The new men's studies;* and Peter Marin, The prejudice against men (chronic homelessness essentially problem of single adult men), *The Nation* 253(2) (July 8, 1991): 46, which falls short of a thorough analysis of class and gender, much less homosexuality and AIDS, which are not even mentioned.
22. See Marlene Cimon's, GAO cites bias in health research, *LAT* 109 (June 19, 1990): A20.
23. See T. V. Ellerbrock, T. J. Bush, M. E. Chamberland, and M. J. Oxtoby, Epidemiology of women with AIDS in the United States, 1981 through 1990—A comparison of heterosexual men with AIDS. *JAMA/Journal of the American Medical Association* 265(22) (1991): 2971–75; Mireya Navarro, Dated AIDS definition keeps benefits from many patients, *NYT* (July 8, 1991): A1; Marcia Ann Gillespie, HIV: The Global Crisis (Women and AIDS), *Ms.* 1(4): 17; Peg Byron, HIV: The national scandal, *Ms.* 1(4): 24; Kathryn Anastos and Carola Marte, Women—The missing persons in the AIDS epidemic, *Health/PAC Bulletin* (winter, 1989): 6–13, reprinted in Nancy F. McKenzie, ed., *The AIDS Reader: Social, political, ethical issues*, 190–99; and Anastos and Marte, Women—The missing persons in the AIDS epi-

demic, Part II, *Health/PAC Bulletin* (spring, 1990): 11–18; and Wendy Chavkin, Preventing AIDS, targeting women, *Health/PAC Bulletin* (spring, 1990): 19–23.

24. Patton, *Inventing AIDS*, 27. See also Altman, *AIDS in the Mind of America*.
25. Grmek, *History of AIDS*.
26. This analysis owes much to Foucault's *The Birth of the Clinic*.
27. In this respect, the August 8, 1991, announcement by the Centers for Disease Control that it would "redefine" AIDS to include people with T4 helper-cell counts of 200 or below, regardless of the presence or absence of opportunistic infections, was a welcome event even though it did not address the issue of differences in types of opportunistic infections between women and men. See Marlene Cimons, Federal government to expand definition of AIDS, *LAT* (August 9, 1991): A37.
28. Sontag, *Illness as Metaphor*, and *AIDS and Its Metaphors*. For a provocative dissent, see Jan Zita Grover, The necessity of metaphor, in *Taking Liberties*, 152–59, especially regarding the necessity of conceptualizing and articulating a war against AIDS and AIDS bigots.
29. See Gilman, *Disease and Representation*, 10. See also Crimp, *AIDS: Cultural analysis/cultural activism*, 3.
30. For Pasadena's official response to AIDS see Kevin Ulrich, Group vows to oppose city AIDS funding, *Pasadena Star-News* (June 10, 1991): A3.
31. See Irene Wielawski's slightly mistitled, Society's ills put burden on city hospitals, report says, *LAT* (June 12, 1990): A3.
32. See Bill Boyarsky, Running for supervisor: Cash over qualifications, *LAT* 109 (May 27, 1990): M5. For the most celebrated but city-of-Los-Angeles-centered overview of power relations in Los Angeles, see Mike Davis, *City of Quartz*. For one of his assessments of L.A. for the 1990–91 years see Mike Davis, The dark side of development: Without real planning, LA borders on chaos. *LAT* (September 29, 1991): M1.
33. See *Los Angeles Times* editorial, Why five just isn't enough (August 2, 1990): B6; and Ruben Martinez, County lines, *LA Weekly* (July 19, 1991): 10–12.
34. On supervisor Edelman and what passed as liberal moderation on the Board see Joe Domanick, Save for his seat, the passion was missing, *LAT* 109 (July 3, 1990): B7.
35. For the CAO's relatively unchecked power to disburse funds see Richard Simon, County gave $3 million in bonuses, *LAT* (Aug. 23, 1991): B1 and LA supervisor districts illegal, *LAT* (June 5, 1990): A1..
36. See Joe Domanick, L.A. turns its back on its people, *LAT* 109 (June 20, 1990): B7. On privatization see Bob Pool, Going commercial; County wants to rent space for ads on its vehicles, other property, *LAT* (Feb. 27, 1991): B1; and Amy Pyle, Rental fees urged for county departments, *LAT* (Aug. 8, 1991): B3.
37. See Bill Boyarsky's A strong case for AIDS funds, *LAT* 109 (July 11, 1990): B2 and The task that awaits the liberals, *LAT* (March 15, 1991): B2.
38. On Weissman and Gottlieb see Mirko Grmek, *History of AIDS*, 4. On Los Angeles' national AIDS ranking, see David E. Kanouse, et al., *AIDS-Related Knowledge, Attitudes, Beliefs, and Behaviors in Los Angeles County.* For the telling blank column for specifically appropriated AIDS spending in years preceding 1989–90 see *County of Los Angeles 1990–1991 Proposed Budget*, Health Services-AIDS Programs, 25(12). *Editors' note*: Except where otherwise noted, County of Los Angeles reports, minutes, and other documents are thought to be on file in respective departments.
39. Funding mechanism and dates confirmed in personal conversation (and are on file) with Robert Frangenberg, director, AIDS Program Office, County of Los Angeles, Aug. 23, 1991.
40. For Schabarum's comment on AIDS funding, see Victor Merina, 15 seized in AIDS sit-in at board metting, *LAT* (May 17, 1989): B2. For Dana's comment on waits, see interview with Penny Griego, KCBS-TV, July 24, 1990. For County waits and delays in processing entitlements, see Irene Wielawski, Cutbacks at hospitals to add agony for the poor, *LAT* 109 (Sept. 1, 1990): B1.
41. For Schabarum's motion see Agenda for the Board of Supervisors of the County of Los Angeles, March 5, 1991 (item no. 6, listed as CRON No. 91043LAC0037, and the audiotape of the meeting).
42. See ACT UP/LA's statement distributed at the July 31, 1990 board of supervisors meeting.
43. See letters dated April 20, April 23, and May 8, 1990, from Judge Rand Schrader, chair, Los Angeles County Commission on AIDS, to each of the supervisors.
44. For Dana's quote see interview with Penny Griego, KCBS-TV, July 31, 1990. See 27 urging help with AIDS are arrested in Los Angeles, *NYT* 139 (May 23, 1990): A14; Victor J. Fernandez, Piden 9.4 milliones para la lucha contra el SIDA, *La Opinion* (August 1, 1990): 2; 38 AIDS activists arrested in protest, *LAT* 109 (August 1, 1990): B2.
45. See editorial Epidemic that won't go away (National Commission on AIDS report), *LAT* 109 (April 29, 1990): M6.
46. See Shawn Hubler and Victor F. Zonana, AIDS adds misery to homeless ranks, *LAT* 109 (April 25, 1990): A1, A18.
47. See National Commission on AIDS, June Osborne, chair, The twin epidemics of substance abuse and HIV (Washington, D.C., July 1991; released Aug. 6, 1991); and John J. Goldman, Study indicates clean syringe program cuts spread of AIDS, *LAT* 110 (Aug. 15, 1991): A5.
48. See Victor F. Zonana, County, gay-led coalition begin talks on HIV clinic, *LAT* 109 (May 15, 1990): B3.

49. On the refusal to fund the emergency "wait" measure see unsigned *LAT* Metro Digest articles, Edelman's try to release AIDS money is blocked, *LAT* 109 (October 26, 1990): B2.
50. See Amy Pyle, AIDS bleach condom program ok'd, *LAT* (March 26, 1991): B1 and Doug Sadownick, County AIDS flip-flop, *LA Weekly* (April 5, 1991): 14.
51. On California State Assembly Bill (AB)101, see *County Agenda* (July 2, 1991, item 72-B, CRON No. 91179LAC0088); for RU486 see *County Agenda* (July 9, 1991, item 6, CRON No. 91183LAC0059); for INS HIV/AIDS restrictions see *County Agenda* (July 16, 1991, item 38-B, CRON No. 91193LAC0040); and the audiotaped testimony of ACT UP member Dale Griner (July 16, 1991). For the general relief settlement see Richard Simon, County ready to enact hike in AID payments, *LAT* (June 11, 1991): B3.
52. See Richard Simon, Supervisors vote to hike own benefits, *LAT* 111 (Jan. 15, 1992): B1.
53. See County of Los Angeles 1991-1992 Proposed Budget; and Richard Simon, County's $11.1 billion budget plan contains widespread cuts, *LAT* (May 18, 1991): B5.
54. See Richard Simon, Supervisors ok $12-billion budget, reject unpaid 2-day leave, *LAT* (July 24, 1991): B3.
55. This was personally heard by this author. Also consult audiotape of budget session, County of Los Angeles board of supervisors (August 23, 1991).
56. See Richard Simon, Supervisors cancel pay 'allowance' but Stir Molina's anger, *LAT* (July 23, 1991): B1.
57. See, for example, Irene Wielawski, Patients giving up on emergency rooms, *LAT* (Aug. 28, 1991): A3, and Claire Spiegel, 21 local emergency rooms bar neurological patients, *LAT* (Aug. 7, 1991): A1.
58. See the Los Angeles County Commission on AIDS July 24 memo to each supervisor for the minimal unmet needs recommendations, along with the two-and-one-half-inch-thick County of Los Angeles Proposed Budget, 1991–1992, 26(17). Also see audiotaped testimony of AIDS commission chair Judge Rand Schrader and members of Common Agenda at the June 7, 1991, board meeting, and audiotaped testimony by ACT UP members Connie Norman, James Rosen, Jan Speller, and Mary Lucey at the July 16 board meeting.
59. See Richard Simon, "County gave $3 million in bonuses."
60. See Doug Sadnownick, AIDS bottleneck, *LA Weekly* (July 26, 1991): 14–16 and Rick Harding, Prospects for a rise in federal AIDS funds are slight, most say, *The Advocate* 580 (July 2, 1991): 25.
61. The nineteenth-century characterizations were made by AIDS outpatient clinic nurse manager Tammy Kramer at the May 13, 1991, meeting of the County-USC AIDS Community Advisory Council. Despite her language, Kramer and the overworked clinic and inpatient staff, in their free time, delivered pharmaceutical supplies to clinic patients' homes and carried out other services the county political administration had refused to fund.
62. See previously cited audiotaped testimony of Connie Norman and James Rosen, Board of Supervisors, July 16, 1991. Rosen and Norman chastised the board for its own "non-compliance" demanding that each of the supervisors hire an HIV-positive staff member in order to understand the urgency of living with HIV.
63. See previously cited audiotaped testimony of Norman, Rosen, Speller, and Lucey, Board of Supervisors, July 16, 1991.
64. Insights provided by County-USC AIDS social work staff. See also Kathleen Teltsch, Custody help for mothers with AIDS, *NYT* (August 30, 1991): A15.
65. County of Los Angeles Department of Health Services AIDS epidemiology program letter of May 14, 1991.
66. See Robert Steinbrook, Data on county's HIV cases revised to lower figure, *LAT* (June 20, 1991): B1.
67. See previously cited *Health/PAC Bulletins* and Carlo Gallucci, Giovanni Maria Pace et al., Rapporto: Dieci anni di Aids, *L'Espresso* 37(24) (June 16, 1991): 128–37.
68. See McBride, *From TB to AIDS;* Clarence Page, Blacks, latinos: Dying in their own "closet," *LAT* (June 19, 1991): B7; Sheryl Stolberg, Surgeon general exhorts latinos to talk about AIDS, *LAT* (Sept. 7, 1991): B1; and Kanouse et al., *AIDS-Related Knowledge.*
69. See the previously cited article by Irene Wielawski, Patients giving up on emergency rooms.
70. See Comstock, *Violence Against Lesbians and Gay Men.*
71. See Los Angeles County Commission on Human Relations, *Hate Crime in Los Angeles County, 1990,* 5; and Karen Ocamb, Violent anti-gay crime up 50 percent, *Update* (Jan. 29, 1992).
72. See David Treadwell, 3 N.Y. officers charged in unprovoked pistol-whipping, *LAT* (March 22, 1991): A36.
73. See Richard A. Serrano, LAPD stays suspensions of six officers, *LAT* 110 (August 3, 1991): A1.
74. See Seth Mydans, Videotape of beating by officers puts full glare on brutality issue; aberration or not, violence is caught on camera, (white police officers in Los Angeles beat black man . . .) *NYT* (March 18, 1991): A1 and Seth Mydans, Brutality issue remains as Los Angeles trial nears (Los Angeles, California Police Department, Rodney King beating case) *NYT* 141 (February 3, 1991): A1, A10.

75. See Karen Ocamb, LA's queer response, *OutWeek* 97 (May 8, 1991): 40; and Doug Sadownick, Daryl Gates, Joel Wachs, and Queer Nation, *LA Weekly* (May 17, 1991): 22–23.
76. See Dean E. Murphy and Victor Merina, Calls mount for probe of sheriff's department, *LAT* (August 18, 1991): A1; Richard Simon, Supervisors order public hearing on sheriff's department, *LAT* (Sept. 4, 1991): B8.
77. Personal observation, and discussion with Officer Erickson of the Sheriff's Community Relations office, September 10, 1991.
78. See Bill Boyarsky, Stacking up support for Sheriff Block, *LAT* (Sept. 13, 1991): B2.
79. Testimony of Dr. Gloria Romero, September 10, 1991, citing August 30 edition of *LAT*.
80. Block's inadequate departmental AIDS educational policies had been denounced by AIDS activists in a March 1988 disruption of the Sheriff's Academy graduation ceremonies. See Paul Feldman, AIDS protesters carted out of sheriff's academy rites, *LAT* 106 (March 5, 1988): Part II/p. 10 and ACT UP/LA Archives summary entries of March 3, 1988; Oct. 31, 1988; and July 25, 1989.
81. Personal experience of the author. See also Charisse Jones, Transsexual alleges abuse by law officers, *LAT* (August 2, 1991): B7.
82. See unsigned article, Patt Morrison, Women still finding bias in sheriff's dept., *LAT* (Aug. 13, 1991): B1, B8; and Susan Bouman Paolino, My dream of enforcing the law became a nightmare, *LAT* (Aug. 18, 1991): M3.
83. See previously cited article by David Treadwell; Jerry Gray, Gay group and Irish parade at Loggerheads, *NYT* (March 14, 1991): B1.
84. See Thomas B. Rosenstiel, O'Connor renews issue of bias against catholicism, *LAT* (April 4, 1991): A5; Amy Kuebelbeck, Under fire, *LAT* (Sept. 9, 1991): E1.
85. On the Ratzinger Doctrine, named for Pope Paul II's official guardian of faith and morals, Cardinal Josef Ratzinger of Germany, see Don A. Schanche, Vatican warning seen against liberal views on sexuality, *LAT* 105 (Oct. 31, 1986): 10.
86. See Tracy Wilkinson and Jane Fritsch, Rallies try to put abortion issue back in spotlight, *LAT* (August 25, 1991): B1.
87. See Ron Curran, Final sanctuary, *LA Weekly* (September 6, 1991): 22–27.
88. See Thomas B. Rosenstiel, O'Connor renews issue of bias against catholicism, *LAT* (April 4, 1991): A5.
89. See Scott Harris and Lynn Smith, Gay activists disrupt Christian service, *LAT* (Orange County edition), (Sept. 9, 1991): A1, A22.
90. From a June 1996 interview with Ara Z, Berkeley, California.
91. See, for example, Penelope McMillan, Mahony gets mixed feedback on feud with KCET, *LAT* (September 9, 1991): B1.
92. See Ronald Soble, Four catholic churches defaced in AIDS protest, *LAT* 108 (Dec. 4, 1989): B1, B8.
93. Davis, *City of Quartz,* 326.
94. Ibid., 329 and the entire chapter New Confessions, 325–72.
95. See Richard Simon, Sen. Watson will run for supervisor Hahn's post, *LAT* (September 6, 1991): B1 and Historic change seen as filing begins today, *LAT* 111 (February 10, 1992): B1.
96. See Sharon Bernstein, KCET unworthy of public support, Mahony declares, *LAT* (September 1991): B1.
97. See Gary Remafedi, J. A. Farrow, and R. W. Deisher, Risk factors for attempted suicide in gay and bisexual youth, *Pediatrics* 87(6) (June 1991): 867–69 and Shira Maguen, Teen suicide: The government's cover-up and America's lost children, *The Advocate* 586 (September 24, 1991): 40–47.
98. See Lieutenant Governor Leo McCarthy's letter, Swift action required, *Bay Area Reporter* 21(6) (June 27, 1991): 7.
99. McWilliams, *Southern California*, 37, and Davis, *City of Quartz*, 26–30.
100. Kevin Starr, *Inventing the Dream,* 89.
101. See previous discussion in section 1, as well as Victor Zonana, Profile in courage, anger: Brad Davis battled AIDS, Hollywood indifference, *LAT* (September 11, 1991): F1.
102. Molina vowed to remove the barrier, installed—according to Antonivich aide Dawson Oppenheimer — to protect the supervisors, in their public meetings, from a new and increasingly unruly population.
103. Harold Myerson, Latter-day Lower East Side, *LA Weekly* (August 2, 1991): 12.
104. See Frank Clifford, City's planners see more crowding as cure for LA, *LAT* (August 25, 1991): A1; Robert A. Jones, On California: A fertile land for growing hate groups, *LAT* (August 28, 1991): A3; and Susan Paterno, Young and alone, *LAT* (September 10, 1991): E1.
105. Banham, *Los Angeles,* 21.
106. McWilliams, *Southern California.*
107. See Davis, Sunshine or noir? in *City of Quartz*, 17–97; and Banham, *Los Angeles,* 213.
108. See Isherwood, *The Berlin Stories*, *Christopher and His Kind,* and *A Single Man.*
109. See Timmons, *The Trouble With Harry.*
110. Banham, *Los Angeles*, 161–77.
111. Lambert, *The Slide Area.*

Constructing Manchester's "New Urban Village," pages 275–92

1. By "gay community" I refer mainly to gay men, although I am aware that lesbians use and have been involved in developing the Village scene.

2. Much of this information is drawn from the full transcript of an interview with Allan Horsfall included in the appendix of Corton, Anal Treat: Manchester's Gay Village—Dissection of a "Community." Horsfall was a founder, in 1964, of the North West Homosexual Law Reform Committee. (All interviews were conducted by Stephen Quilley between May and August of 1990. They were conducted in confidence but aspects of the transcripts can be made available through the Manchester International Centre for Labour Studies, Manchester University, M13 9PL.) See also Horsfall, Battling for Wolfenden, in *Radical Records.*
3. The idea was to create a network of small social clubs covering the smaller towns as well as major cities. It was hoped that they could be used as a base to provide counselling services, lists of "like minded people," and a bar.
4. Corton, Anal Treat, Appendix 4,13. In fact, James Anderton did try unsuccessfully to use a nineteenth-century law against licentious dancing to close down gay clubs again at the end of the 1970s.
5. *Manchester Pink Guide 1993/94 (Manchester: Pink Guide),* 2. It should be remembered that although the Village is the first phenomenon of its kind in Britain, it is tiny compared to similar areas abroad—most notably in America and Australia. Just by way of comparison, by 1980 the San Francisco scene boasted 234 bars and controlled up to a quarter of the vote in local elections (see Castells, *City and the Grassroots,* 143–145).
6. In San Francisco, gay men talk about "liberated zones" to make the same distinction (see Castells, *City and the Grassroots*).
7. Thus, even as late as 1978, the Hulme Labour Party banned a gay disco (*Mancunian Gay* 1 (1978): 3). By 1991 Hulme had selected a gay candidate for the local council elections. This illustrates the changes that had occurred in the Labour Party as well as in the ward of Hulme itself (*Scene Out,* Hulme gay candidate, *Scene Out* 22 (1991): 9). (Back issues of *Mancunian Gay* and *Scene Out* are on file at the Manchester Central Library, St. Peters Square, Manchester M1.)
8. The Manchester Fightback campaign brought together rebel councillors, the trade unions, and community activists. It was modelled on a similar campaign in Lambeth (Interview with Dave Carter).
9. Interview with Pat Karney.
10. The Gay Men's Sub-Committee is a subcommittee of the Equal Opportunities Committee of Manchester City Council. These committees are made up of elected local councillors, sometimes with "cooptees" from the community, and are responsible for drafting policy and making routine administrative and managerial decisions where these are not delegated to Council Officers.
11. *Mancunian Gay,* Gay centre grant, *Mancunian Gay* 35 (1984): 13.
12. Minutes of the Gay Men's Sub-Committee, February 21, 1985, City of Manchester. All minutes of this Sub-Committee are on file in the Archive of the Manchester City Council in the town hall, Manchester M1.
13. *Mancunian Gay,* Manchester gets gay police watchdog, *Mancunian Gay* 39 (1985): 4. See also *Mancunian Gay* 33 (1984): 3 and 35 (1984): 3.
14. This is legendary and very well known in Britain, but it was and is so often repeated that I do not know when he originally said it—nor to whom. The phrase is quoted in a song "Mission from God" on a floppy disc by Dan Gooch, released by Red Herring, London, in 1987 and again, in a different version, on a tape entitled, "Why not?" by Wild Bill Harzia and the Malarial Swamp Dogs, produced and released by Phil Salmon, London, in 1989.
15. The Sub-Committee did call for Anderton's resignation after he recommended the criminalisation of homosexuality in 1987 (Gay Men's Sub-Committee: December 14, 1987).
16. Minutes of the Gay Men's Sub-Committee, February 1, 1990, City of Manchester.
17. *Scene Out,* Lay lay lay, *Scene Out* 14 (May, 1990): 7.
18. Inspector Anderson (Chief, Plainclothes) is said to have promised to take complaints about the use of "pretty police" to trap gay men. Over a three-month period, fifty-four men were said to have been cautioned by police in the Oxford Road area *(Scene Out* 24 (March 1991): 10).
19. 105 people attended an angry public meeting the same evening (Editorial, *All Points North* 44 (1994): News Section).
20. Gay Men's Sub-Committee minutes, October, 1985, City of Manchester.
21. From issue 2:4 of City Planning News of the City of Manchester (summer 1991): 1.
22. *Scene Out,* Open grievances, *Scene Out* 15 (June 1990): 7.
23. Ian Craig, We'll fight for lower consent age, say gays, *Manchester Evening News* (February 22, 1994): 2.
24. Manchester City Council, City Pride Challenge (on file, Archive of the City of Manchester, 1994). This was a planning document giving details of the Council's development plans in the wake of its success in winning urban regeneration funding under the conservative government's competitive City Challenge scheme.
25. From "Manchester—Club Capital" press release (on file, Archives, City of Manchester, 1995). The convention bureau is supported by all the local authorities, as well as the development corporations and various other "quangos" (government and government-related corporations).
26. The gay entrepreneurs in the Village were at the centre of an experiment with liberalised licensing hours in 1993. See Lovatt, The 24-Hour City: Selected papers from the first national conference on the night-time economy.

27. This included individuals such as Carol Ainscow of Manto, and Paradise Factory.
28. The Village Charity was set up in February 1991 to raise money for issues relating to HIV and AIDS. It started as a street sale organised by local businesses.
29. This quotation was from a British Rail brochure for its 1995 InterCity X-Cursions (on file, British Rail, London). In this case, the perception of mainstream legitimacy is encouraging the world of corporate capital to target gay consumers more overtly with both advertising campaigns and gay-specific products. Thus, Allied Domecq, the international drinks group, is opening a series of gay pubs in a number of British cities, including Manchester. Rival brewer Bass also plans future investment in gay venues. (Meg Carter, Raising a glass to gay pubs, *Financial Times* (July 27, 1995: 14). Meanwhile the 1995 Gay Pride in London attracted £100,000 sponsorship from companies, including Levis and Virgin (the figure in 1994 was only £15,000). However it is not simply the overhyped pink pound that is attracting corporate attention. Also important is the perceived trendsetting momentum of gay fashion. This, more than the lure of specifically gay consumers, lies behind Guinness's planned TV advertisement featuring a gay couple in the July 22, 1995 issue of the *Financial Times*.
30. This quotation is from a 1994 brochure produced by Mathew Thompson of Matt Publications for an exhibition hosted by the Royal Institute of British Architects Bookshop, Portland Street, Manchester M1.
31. At the time he made this statement, David Plowright was director of Granada TV and member of the self-proclaimed "Manchester Mafia."
32. Steve Kingston, C'mon out and meet the Village People, *Manchester Evening News Magazine* (June 8, 1994): 23.

Placemaking and the Dialectics of Public and Private, pages 295–99

1. Luke, Placing Power, Siting Space, 613–28.
2. Relph, *Place and Placelessness*, 63–78.
3. "Degendered" sexuality refers to relations where binary gender lines have been destabilized by transsexual identities, intersexuality, or bisexuality.
4. For an example of queer environmental art see Robbins, Utopian prospects in *Angles of Incidence*, 38–41.
5. Wilson, Bodies in public and private, in *Public Bodies—Private States*, 11.
6. Namaste, Genderbashing, 225–27.
7. Murphy, Walking the queer city, 195.
8. Ibid., 196.
9. Boyer, *City of Collective Memory*, 26–27.

Invisible Women in Invisible Places, pages 301–24

1. An earlier version of this discussion was published as Invisible women in invisible places: Lesbians, lesbian bars, and the social production of people/environment relationships, *Architecture and Behaviour* 8(2) (1992): 137–58.
2. For instance, the National Socialists burned the archives of Magnus Hirshfeld, which contained material about lesbians and gay men pre-1900.
3. These relationships, some of which were effectively marriages, were called "Boston Marriages" in the nineteenth century.
4. Two years ago, a black gay British filmmaker, Isaac Julien, had to cut out portions of his film about black gay male experience, "Looking for Langston," in order to distribute it in the U.S. The surviving family of Langston Hughes, a well-known black poet of the Harlem Renaissance, threatened a lawsuit.
5. Grahn uses the term "gay" to include "lesbian and gay"; similarly, some lesbians call themselves "gay women."
6. Refers to women who dressed in male attire (suits) and women who dressed in female attire (dresses). In different time periods it also referred to a way of behaving publicly. It does not refer to women who believe they are men or who re-create a heterosexual relationship between women.
7. In 1929 there were similar public controversies about a Broadway play that had a lesbian theme and about the U.S. censorship trial of Radclyffe Hall's *The Well of Loneliness*, which Bullough and Bullough (1977) describe as being hotly debated in the Salt Lake City community.
8. Even when sodomy laws are not used legally for their intended purposes, they provide a basis for other legal decisions, i.e., evaluating lesbians and gay men as unfit parents, de facto, because of their sexuality.
9. *San Francisco Bay Guardian* and other articles, various dates.
10. Most lesbians and gay men do not fit stereotypes and are not easily identifiable. Therefore they are often expected and pressured to conform to heterosexual behavior unless they let other people know about their sexuality. This is called "coming out."
11. Not letting others know one's sexuality, most frequently kept hidden to avoid repercussions. Many lesbians and gay men, for example, are married for this reason. Due to societal pressure and negative images, some lesbians and gay men do not even admit to themselves they are lesbians and gay men, or they are out to some people and not to others. "Coming out" is an ongoing process as one meets new people.
12. Prohibits discrimination against lesbians and gay men in some forms of employment, in the use of

public accommodations (hotels, restaurants), and in some cases, housing. However religious organizations can still discriminate, and only housing with a certain number of units is covered.

13. This law would add specific penalties for a crime shown to be motivated by bigotry based on race, sex, religion, physical or mental ability, or sexual orientation.
14. In every city there are many more gay male bars than lesbian bars.

Lesbian Spaces in Los Angeles, pages 325–37

1. Castells, *City and the Grassroots,* 143.
2. The lesbian "community" is made up of many different communities divided along the intersections of race/ethnicity, age, socioeconomic status, politicization, erotic practices, et cetera. Community in this article is defined less as an entity and more as a project. When Castells used the phrase "gay community," he noted that he meant ". . . a deliberate effort by gay people to set up their own organizations and institutions in all spheres of life" (Castells, 161). Although Castells was referring to gay (male) communities, the observation can be applied to efforts by lesbians to set up an institutional base, whether or not various sectors interacted across the intersections.
3. Herrell, The symbolic strategies of Chicago's Gay and Lesbian Pride Day parade, in *Gay Culture in America*, 231.
4. Castells, *City and the Grassroots,* 142.
5. Lockard, The lesbian community, 88.
6. For example, mailing lists belonging to Lesbians of Color and Connexxus Womens' Center show home addresses in a variety of zip code zones.
7. Lockard, The lesbian community, 88.
8. Nestle, *Restricted Country*, 100.
9. Lyman and Scott, *Social Psychology Through Symbolic Interaction*, 215.
10. In the first decade after Stonewall, the politicized, visible, and recorded lesbian community membership was generally white, under forty, and, depending on the organization, from various classes and educational backgrounds.
11. "Only a minority of the lesbian population of a city are active members of the community at one time" (Lockard, The lesbian community, 85).
12. Cassell, *A Group Called Women,* 153.
13. Over the years, differing agendas in the diverse lesbian community have sparked interest, ignited debate, and sometimes exploded into intracommunity conflicts. Class, race, separatism, butch/fem roles, S/M, monogamy, identity politics, transsexuals in lesbian groups, and gay male gendercentrism are some of the issues that have been at the heart of what I call the "lesbian civil wars."
14. As Shugar noted: "Perhaps nothing is more out of fashion in feminist critical theory today than the discourse of lesbian separatism." Separatism here refers to a position that advocates for lesbian-only spatial and/or cognitive territories in which lesbians can further a lesbian-focused agenda. Separatism's complexities and controversies have been treated in several works including S. Hoagland and J. Penelope, *For Lesbians Only;* and D. Shugar, *Separatism and Women's Community.*
15. DOB, the oldest of the early North American lesbian organizations, was founded in 1955.
16. "Ideas in good currency" are issues that get funded; they are ". . . ideas powerful for the formation of public policy, they change over time, obey a law of limited numbers and they lag behind changing events . . ." (Schon, *Beyond the Stable State,* 123).
17. After what many felt were lenient verdicts brought in against the police officers who beat Rodney King, parts of L.A. erupted. Many businesses were looted and burned. Susan Chacin, ACW's current director, is of the opinion that ACW's neighbors have a positive regard for the work of the organization and that that is the reason the firestorm passed ACW by. Since ACW is a nonprofit enterprise with a residence next door to its offices rather than a retail operation, it may have benefited from a combination of factors.
18. Castells, *City and the Grassroots,* 163.
19. See the December 1969 Statement of Purpose—Gay Liberation Front, Los Angeles, California, in Harry Hay, *Radically Gay,* 176–78. The statement reflected what was to become an all too common lack of concern and/or awareness about the issues of those who were not white or male. Women are mentioned only once in "We support the demands of Blacks, Chicanos, Orientals *[sic]*, Women, Youth, Senior Citizens and others demanding their full rights as human beings" (177).
20. In the early 1970s, the word "gay" was the umbrella term for both lesbians and homosexual males. At that point many lesbian activists used the term "gay women" to mean lesbians. As lesbians grew impatient with their invisibility in the gay liberation movement, "gay" was redefined to mean male homosexual. Eventually, long-lasting organizations like the National Gay Task Force added the word "lesbian" to their titles as a politically correct way to promote lesbian visibility. Today, for lesbian activists of the 1970s genre, there is a sense of déjà vu with the term "queer."
21. Sherna Gluck, interview, June 1995.
22. Under the auspices of Connexxus, this invaluable lesbian history archive moved from Oakland to Southern California in 1987. It was first housed in

a private home in Altadena and then moved to Robertson Blvd., into a building owned by the city of West Hollywood. In 1995 there was a split on the Board between those who wanted to maintain the Mazer as a separatist space and those who believed that in order for it to thrive it should affiliate with USC and take advantage of the benefits that come from being associated with, but not appropriated by, an affluent academic institution. ONE, a cogender archive, will be moving to USC and has set up the Lesbian Legacy Collection and separate space for its lesbian materials.

23. Doczi, "Whelmed" by the women's saloon, *The Lesbian Tide* (February 1975): 20.
24. Beers, "Gunfight" at the LA saloon, *The Lesbian News* (September 1997): 1.
25. Zimmerman, *Safe Sea of Women*, 160.
26. Beers, New lesbian center, *The Lesbian News* (January 1976): 1.
27. Some questions regarding methodology and positionality: How do we define parameters? Does the map of the "territory" that I have identified convey an accurate picture of spaces important to the politicized lesbian community in L.A. during a certain time period, or is it simply a geographic/historical record of my own political activities in that community? Is it a record of spaces that, in general, were defined by white lesbians of various classes and political agendas, and by those lesbians of color who were active within this geographic area during this time period?

Leather Nights in the Woods, pages 339–55

1. This article was reworked from van Lieshout's Leather nights in the woods: Homosexual encounters in a Dutch highway rest area, *Journal of Homosexuality* 29(1) (1995): 19–39.
2. For an illustration of outdoor cruising, see Tom of Finland, *Tom of Finland Retrospective* (Los Angeles: Tom of Finland Foundation, 1989: unnumbered pages "1966" and "1968").
3. In this article all names of persons have been changed. Peter and John are prototypes of Monday evening cruising visitors in this rest stop. I want to thank all leathermen who were willing to cooperate in this investigation.
4. The rest stop was made inaccessible by barricading the entrance and repairing the fence at the side of the woods (Observation, March 1992). "Official" reason: the parking lot had become superfluous because of the opening of a new rest stop and recreation area nearby. (It includes a gas station, which makes the area unattractive for cruising.) As my observation area can no longer be used for cruising, there is no reason to conceal its real name and location.
5. "Cruising is the deliberate, active, and usually mobile search for sexual partner(s) in a social setting" (Lee, The social organization of sexual risk, in *Studies in Sadomasochism*, 284).
6. The fact that the Mollebos attracted cruising men from all over the country is confirmed by a report of the national police force (de Leeuw, *Het mollebos, een homo-baan*, 2).
7. A notable characteristic in Delph's research is the assumption that men looking for impersonal sex contacts initially try to find out whether a potential partner has a "homosexual identity." As far as my experience and study of literature teaches, the main touchstone is someone's interest in homosexual activity independent of his sexual identity.
8. As far as I know, there has been little comparable ethnographic research on public homosexual encounters in other parts of western Europe.
9. Humphreys gathered a sample of tearoom participants by tracing—with some help of policemen—the license plates of their cars. This sample was added to the overall sample for a social health survey. Thanks to this strategy, fifty tearoom visitors were interviewed. Their results were later compared to fifty from the overall sample (Humphreys, *Tearoom Trade*, 30–44).
10. Clause 248 bis—introduced in the Netherlands in 1911 and revoked in 1971—penalized homosexual contacts between an adult and a minor (under 21).
11. In Holland the rise of AIDS has not led to the closing of gay baths and backrooms. Gay subculture facilities are used to give information on AIDS prevention and safe sex.
12. In the case of the Mollebos cruising area, a police squad leader has recommended some measures aimed at *improving* cruising conditions. He argues that homosexuality as such is not to be discussed. If the landed proprietor continues to tolerate cruising and sexual activities, it is advisable in this policeman's opinion to place litter baskets, to give entrance to the woods by means of something like a turnstile, to set up a notice board in the rest area, and to improve contacts between police officers and visitors (de Leeuw, *Het mollebos*, 4–5). Only a few months later this squad leader was—like many others—surprised by the announcement that the Department of Public Works was going to close this highway rest area (*Gay Krant*, November 30, 1991).
13. Lee mentions four specific issues concerning this behavior: protected territories, screening a potential partner, negotiation of the S/M "scenario," and control of interaction during the sex act. I identified these sets of rules during my observations in the Mollebos area.

14. It seems that some cruising areas in the Netherlands enjoyed temporary popularity among leathermen. But the leathermen always were a minority among cruisers.
15. Why these leather nights took place on Monday, the most prosaic day in the week, I don't know. I can only give some speculations. On Monday most leather bars are closed. Monday evening seems to be safe: it is not the most popular day for queerbashers to set out. Compared with other evenings, the Monday evening is quiet and therefore easier to "claim" by a specific group of patrons.
16. A role comparable to the role of "lookout" or "watchqueen" that Humphreys and Troiden performed in their studies on sexual encounters in public conveniences (Humphreys) and in a highway rest stop (Troiden) was not available in this situation (Humphreys, *Tearoom Trade,* 26–30; Troiden, Homosexual encounters in a highway rest stop, in *Sexual Deviance and Sexual Deviants,* 216).
17. Most men who knew about my "special mission" didn't think it worthwhile to tell others. Most guys who were or seemed sexually interested in me (and vice versa) were excluded from my investigation. Giving information could function as a means to get sex. Such a transaction disturbs the reliability of the data. To give a simple example: if someone wants to have sex and you ask him (before or after) "How old are you?" you can almost be sure he doesn't mention his real age if he thinks that fact harms his sex appeal.
18. Other questions like "Do you have the time?" and "Got a match?" are more ambiguous. They often represent a code message meaning "Are you (sexually) interested in me?" A negative answer is not humiliating; a positive answer leaves open the possibility to stay on a noncommittal level. It is my experience in Dutch cruising areas that these are favorite questions among street hustlers to track prospective customers. See also Troiden, "Homosexual encounters," 214; Corzine and Kirby, Cruising the truckers, 180–83.
19. The text of this ad read: "Do (Did) you regularly visit the leathernights in the Mollebos? Academic researcher/journalist is interested to hear about your experiences. Absolute serious intentions; information is dealt with confidentially and anonymously."
20. I never noticed a police car in the parking lot. In the last few years police in some districts have patrolled cruising areas, not with the intention of disturbing cruising men but of protecting them against aggression from queerbashers. Until recently, harassment by policemen was more common. The fact that I only once saw (potential) queerbashers doesn't mean the Mollebos was a safe place. Some informants reported queerbashing two years before, and police reports show acts of violence against Mollebos visitors did occur other times in the week (de Leeuw, *Het mollebos,* 2–3).
21. The report by a police squad leader mentions "condoms" as one of several items that make the woods filthy. This suggests—as I witnessed myself—that condoms are used for anal intercourse (de Leeuw, *Het mollebos,* 2).
22. In tearoom sex, as described by Humphreys, all sexual activity is concentrated on the penis, which is in most cases fellated. Other body parts are ignored (Humphreys, *Tearoom Trade*). In the Netherlands there are almost no public conveniences that can serve for this kind of anonymous sex. As I point out further in this article, developments in outdoor cruising have also led to a reduced need for tearoom sex.
23. Some "S"s (sadists) will never approach an "M" (masochist) because they feel it is inappropriate to their role. For the same reason, some S's restrict cruising to loitering on one or two fixed spots to avoid the impression they have to seek out a sex partner.
24. Poppers refers to a drug consisting of butyl and volatile nitrites. It is kept in a small tube and inhaled through the nose. Users say that it heightens sexual intensity and the duration of orgasm. Others say it has no effect on them, and some people think the only effect is the smell of dirty socks.
25. Although some of these bars recently have changed their layout, they still have a comparable segmentation. The same segmentation can be found in less-frequented bars and was to be found in some leather discos closed several years ago (Steps, LL-Pakhuis). An analogous zonal division existed in illustrious American leather and S/M facilities like the Mineshaft in New York (Brodsky, A retrospective ethnography of the Mineshaft) and the Catacombs in San Francisco (Rubin, The Catacombs, in *Leatherfolk*).
26. In both settings (Mollebos and leather bars) some visitors head directly for the sexual zone to find a sex partner (in the dark orgy room, a completely anonymous partner).
27. It could be very interesting to investigate the influence of his iconography on the image of gay leathermen.
28. This rest area was already in use as a cruising site.

Queer Spaces in New York City, pages 357–70

1. All three coauthors are members of REPOhistory, a collective of artists and writers. Thanks to editorial comments from Mark O'Brien and Sarabande Press of New York City for graphics support.
2. Hayden, *The Power of Place,* 44–62 and Boyer, *City of Collective Memory,* 1–29.

3. These strategies were first explored by REPOhistory in 1991 in The Lower Manhattan Sign Project. See the catalog REPOhistory, *The Lower Manhattan Sign Project*, especially the essay by Lucy Lippard, Anti-Amnesia, 4–7 (reprinted from the December 1992 issue of *Z Magazine*). See also Elise Harris, No choice, 42 and Lynette Holloway, Art and history prove a volatile mix, B3.
4. New York City Department of Transportation (DOT) Permit Art Work. Signed by Tom Klem, REPOhistory Permittee and Elliot G. Sander, Commissioner of Transportation, City of New York (doc. 2752Y/p. 148, on file DOT and REPOhistory).
5. Tess Timoney, Introductory essay, On choice histories, in *Choice Histories: Framing abortion. An artist's book by REPOhistory*. Produced in conjunction with the exhibition "A New World Order: Part One," guest-curated by Connie Butler at Artists Space, New York City (New York: REPOhistory, June 11–July 11, 1992): 4–7.
6. Ed notes that it was the unexpected death in 1993 of Jim Owles, founding president of Gay Activists Alliance and later the first openly gay candidate for public office in New York City, that made him particularly aware that this history is not adequately documented.
7. OLGAD, Box 927, Old Chelsea Station, New York, New York 10113. tel. (212) 388-9881.
8. OLGAD, *Guide to Lesbian and Gay New York Historical Landmarks*.
9. The events and sites that were also considered but which did not have signs installed included: the Mount Morris Baths (125th St. and Madison Ave.); the first AIDS discrimination suit in the United States, brought by Lambda Legal Defense and Education Fund on behalf of Dr. Joseph Sonnabend, a doctor who faced eviction for treating patients with AIDS at his office (West 10th Street); the Central Park "ramble," a cruising area; and the original site of the Harvey Milk Academy, New York City's public high school for lesbian and gay youth.
10. Betti-Sue has asked a series of questions about the definition of activism put forth by the group. She contends that activism may have been defined too narrowly and without reflection of the broadening of its powers as it is currently defined. Was the mostly straight group comfortable with our final selections because we had targeted activism as a publicly demonstrable act that didn't interrogate the private aspects of public space and behavior? Could we make visible on the street what we do in the bedroom and claim it as activist? Did we circumvent the question about if and how to make public what is queer? What did we miss by foregrounding public events, spaces, and memory? The subjective experience of queering space, the transmutable moment of public sex on the pier, the backrooms of the gay bars were alluded to but left in the shadows. Where were feminism's personal emotional and familial issues? Was documented history easier to deal with and less questionable as representations of a movement? In the realm of the sexual there was little that was daring about the signs' content. No outright sex or bad words or naughty images accompanied the rather straightforward "reports." Ed has answered Betti-Sue in several different accounts. He writes, "I would say no, just that an activist history is more appropriate to a commemoration of Stonewall. An interrogation of the private could be more appropriate in a different context (e.g., Valentine's Day). As a person who is subject to most of these experiences, I chose sites of greater importance to me. The GAA Firehouse was just such a site. . . . To silence the histories leading up to, including and following Stonewall, a history of seminal importance to the gay and lesbian community, on the grounds of some queer theory (or multiculturalism, i.e., to diminish its significance because it was carried out primarily, but hardly exclusively, by European-American men and women although all cultural subgroups benefitted), is itself oppressive." For a personal Manifesto (non-REPOhistory) included in the Manifestos/ Proposals publication for the "Queer Space" exhibition, Ed proposed an idea different from straightforward activism. "The notion of queer space implies the existence of a nonqueer space. Such nonqueer space is (beside the sanctum of "straight" privilege—reproductive sexuality), desexualized space. The desexualization of space goes back to the fundamental myth of western civilization: Eve and Adam covering their nakedness with fig leaves. Thus, to make space queer, it must be resexualized. Such sexualized space currently exists only in limited circumstances such as queer bars, clubs, and private residences. Public space in general remains nonsexual. In a move to begin to sexually reclaim these public spaces as queer, I propose that, on June 26, 1994, as participants in Stonewall 25 march pass the United Nations building in New York City, they remove all their clothing and proceed the rest of the way to Central Park in the state of nature."
11. For relevant reviews of the June and July 1994 exhibition at the Storefront for Art and Architecture, New York City, see Muschamp, Designing a framework for diversity, 32; Butler, Queer space, 83-84; and Sullivan, Design community celebrates gay rights, 24-25.
12. REPOhistory presented *Entering Buttermilk Bottom*, a site-specific outdoor installation about an African-American neighborhood in Atlanta that was destroyed in the early 1960s by urban renewal. It was presented as part of the 1995 Arts Festival of Atlanta. See Bo Emerson, Uncovering Buttermilk Bottom, D1; Catherine Fox, "City site works" successful in some spots, isn't in others, C7, and Rob Walton, Bottoms up—REPOhistory exhumes Buttermilk Bottom, 32, 38.

Making Room, pages 373–80

1. Sanders, Introduction, in *STUD,* 13 and 17.
2. Gianni, Weir, Sedgwick, and Moon, Queerying (single family) space, 69–77. This was a review of the "House Rule" exhibition in Ottawa in 1994.
3. Colomina, *Privacy and Publicity,* 8.
4. Scott, Jungle fever—Black gay identity politics, white dick, and the utopian bedroom, 299–321.
5. For a discussion of the programming of power relationships that include gender and "morality," see Markus, *Buildings and Power.*
6. Betsky, *Building Sex,* 30.
7. Deleuze and Guattari, *A Thousand Plateaus,* 23–24.
8. Silver, Master bedrooms, master narratives, in *Not At Home,* 221.
9. Tschumi, *Architecture and Disjunction,* 205.
10. Gianni, et al., Queering (single-family) space, 54–57.
11. Wigley, *The Architecture of Deconstruction,* 35–57.
12. Silver, Master bedrooms, master narratives, in *Not At Home,* 208.
13. Watson and Gibson, Postmodern politics and planning, in *Postmodern Cities and Spaces,* 255.
14. Plant, *The Most Radical Gesture,* 31.
15. Duggan, Queering the state, in *Sex Wars,* 179–93.
16. Christopher Knight, Fury + political attack = graphic AIDS message, *Los Angeles Times* 110 (March 6, 1991): F1.
17. Peter Freiberg, Angry lesbians with a sense of humour, *Washington Blade* 24(22) (May): 3, 24 and Dave Saltonstall and Michael S. C. Claffey, Hearts are proud and gay, *Daily News* (June 26, 1994): 8.

Having Something to Wear, pages 381-90

1. White, *The Beautiful Room is Empty,* 224.
2. Christine Boyer has edited a useful history of the social landscape of the street entitled, Straight down Christopher Street: A tale of the oldest street in Greenwich Village, in *Greenwich Village,* 36–53. A short paragraph notes the Stonewall riots in June of 1969, adding, "Christopher Street quickly became emblematic of the Gay Liberation Movement and a focal point for subsequent marches," (51). The street remains solely "emblematic" in this history, for the significance of queer desires and experiences historically in the shaping and reshaping of the street's landscape go unexamined in this "straight" walk down the street.
3. Martin, Strictly business: Christopher Street rebounds as thriving "Gay Mecca," *New York Times* (21 June, 1993): B3.
4. Chauncey, *Gay New York,* 232. Chauncey notes that after World War I "rapid commercialization of the Village . . . altered its character. The construction of the subway routes along Seventh Avenue in 1917 and along Sixth Avenue in 1927–1930 and simultaneous widening and extension of both avenues transformed the Village from a remote self-contained backwater into one of the most central and easily reached of the city's neighborhoods."
5. Leach, *Land of Desire,* 63.
6. For a seminal discussion of the notion of "docile bodies" see Michel Foucault, *Discipline and Punishment.* Reprinted as Docile bodies in *The Foucault Reader,* 182.
7. Berger, *Ways of Seeing,* 54.
8. Jonathan F. Alex. Letter to the editor—Gay Pride March should have made a more positive statement, *New York Times* (6 July, 1993): A16.
9. D'Emilio, Capitalism and gay identity, in *Lesbian and Gay Studies Reader,* 467–76.
10. Chauncey, *Gay New York,* 236.
11. Castells, *City and the Grassroots,* 140.
12. Sy Adler and Johanna Brenner, Gender and space, 24–34.
13. Martin, "Strictly business," B3.
14. Randy Kennedy, Christopher Street: Changes sweep the Gay Mecca, *New York Times* (19 June 1994).
15. During the "Stonewall 25" events of the summer of 1994, the National Museum and Archive of Lesbian and Gay Culture mounted a series of storefront exhibitions on Christopher Street entitled "Windows of Gay Life." As Keven Murphy (Walking the queer city, 195–201) suggests, "The 'Windows' exhibit asked passersby to look at a queer neighborhood in new ways by linking familiar sites of contemporary commerce and social life to the cultural and historical richness of gay and lesbian experience" (195).

The Meaning at the Wall, pages 391–406

1. Earlier versions of this paper appeared in *The Harvard Gay & Lesbian Review* 2(2) (spring 1995).
2. This section is heavily based on the 1979 article by David Glassberg and on Marilyn T. Williams's book, *Washing "The Great Unwashed."*
3. Gayellow Pages. Note: Baths are located in thirty-one states plus Washington, D.C., and Puerto Rico.
4. *Steam,* 111–17. Note: Baths are located in eighteen states plus Washington, D.C., and Puerto Rico. Fifty-two of the baths are also listed in the 1982 Gayellow Pages. Only nine are new, in new locations, or newly listed.
5. *Gay* (April 23, 1973): 14.
6. The signing of one's name often resulted in a series of aliases. Bruce Mailman at the St. Marks Baths tried to change that. "I got excited about doing something so people could be honest. At the gay baths, people wouldn't sign their own names. They

were embarrassed to see someone they knew on the street." (Peters, The sexual revolution Mailman delivered, 81)

7. Even though snatches of conversation and their vocal inflections could help place the class and education levels of the patrons, some suggest that the baths, in their attempts at equalization, became focused on vanity. "Inside the baths, looks are all that matter and nobody cares what you've done, how much money you have, or who your daddy was. Gay men can be especially vicious in rejecting older men or men with even the slightest deformity." (Young, So you're planning to spend a night at the tubs, 50)
8. Larry Knopp has pointed out these conditions when writing on urban space and sexualities. The density and cultural complexity of cities has led to frequent portrayals of sexual diversity and freedom as peculiarly urban phenomena. On the other hand, the concentration of these movements and subcultures in urban space has made it easier to both demonize and control them and to sanctify majority cultures and spaces (Knopp, Sexuality and Urban Space, 149).
9. Safer-sex education performed by Man-to-Man, a Vancouver AIDS organization, targets gay men in the locations where sex takes place. One volunteer said, "I think mainly what the function is, is to make sure that condoms are distributed. We don't talk a lot. We just make it a point to walk around and hand people condoms. We don't talk to them or acknowledge them, though we usually get a "thank you" in return." (Brown, Sex, scale, and the new urban politics, 251). Regarding the HIV testing that takes place in the baths, a nurse with Man-to-Man remarked, "The idea is strike while the iron is hot. It's there. It's anonymous. So it's acceptable." (Brown, Sex, scale, 252)
10. A recent paper based on data collected in the late 1980s indicates that sauna users in Belgium do not constitute a high-risk segment of the gay population. Sauna clients are more likely than nonclients to practice safer sex. This finding suggests that saunas may be safer sexual venues than the alternatives. Therefore closing or restricting sauna operations may actually increase HIV transmission, an effect just the opposite of the one anticipated by the advocates of restrictions (Bolton, Vincke, and Mak, Gay baths revisited, 269).

This Is About People Dying, pages 407–37

1. *Editors' note*: For articles in the mainstream media that often contradict Wolfe's experience at the actual events and that convey the concern on the part of the state about ACT UP activism, see Cynthia Crossen, Shock troops: AIDS activist group harasses and provokes to make its point, *Wall Street Journal* (December 7, 1989): A1; Jason DeParle, Rash, rude, and effective. ACT UP helps change AIDS policy, *New York Times* 139 (January 3, 1990): A12, B1; Editorial, AIDS and misdirected rage (ACT UP disrupts sixth annual International AIDS Conference), *New York Times* 139 (June 26, 1990): A18, A22; James Barron, Prosecutor's appeal dropped on police beating of protester, *New York Times* 141 (October 17, 1991): B4; Debbi Wilgoren, 74 AIDS activists arrested in Capitol protests, *Washington Post* 114 (October 2, 1991): A24; David W. Dunlap, FBI kept file on Act Up in protest years; dossier appears to be mainly news clippings, *New York Times* 144 (May 16, 1995): A15, B3.
2. Schulman, *My American History.*
3. Jan Clausen, Review, *My American History,* 583.
4. In a one-page opinion at the back of an issue of *The Advocate,* Tory Osborne stated that "some of our vibrant activist groups need to get real: Sending the Lesbian Avengers into Lewiston, Me., last fall during the city's ballot struggle was about as effective as it would be to send the '60s group the Yippies into factories to organize against the Vietnamese War." (Up against the wall, 80).
5. The discussion in this interview augments a more structured chronology of ACT UP NY already published. See Maxine Wolfe, The AIDS Coalition to unleash power, in *AIDS Prevention and Services,* 217–47.
6. I worked in a lesbian and gay male leftist coalition in the early 80s called CRASH—Committee against Racism, Sexism, Antisemitism, and Heterosexism. There was a group called DARE—Dykes Against Racism Everywhere. There was a group called DONT—Dykes Opposed to Nuclear Technology. But a lot of that stuff was not necessarily focused, especially after the early years, on lesbian issues.
7. They dressed up and then busted up a dinner that Cardinal O'Connor was at, the Alfred E. Smith Memorial Dinner, which the Catholic Church holds in New York every year.
8. Kramer, Mob, others call for traffic blockade, *New York Native* (March 30, 1987): 1.
9. Kramer, *Faggots.*
10. The AIDS Action Network was basically a group of the Democratic Party made up of politically oriented people who had started meeting early on, in 1981 and 1982 Vivian Shapiro was part of it. They wanted to see if they could do anything in Albany about getting money for AIDS treatment. But it really fizzled.
11. Patton, *Inventing AIDS,* 126–31.
12. The SILENCE=DEATH Project may have renamed itself Gran Fury by then, but I think that it was still referred to as the SILENCE=DEATH Project.
13. For two discussions of the implications of the *Hardwick* decision, see Lisa Duggan, Banned in the

U.S.A, 80–84 and Nan D. Hunter, Life after *Hardwick*, in *Sex Wars*, 84–100.

14. Sheridan Square is in the "West Village" and was the site of the 1969 Stonewall riots.
15. "*Bougie*" was a New Left adjective roughly equivalent to "bourgeois," when used in the same way.
16. For a background overview on the work of ACT UP NY, leading up to the 1988 Shea Stadium action, see David France, ACT UP fires up, *Village Voice* (May 3, 1988): 36.
17. CARASA stood for Coalition for Abortion Rights and Against Sterilization Abuse.
18. A coalition of Asian American groups protested against the performance of Miss Saigon. There were different organizational responses. The Asian Lesbians of the East Coast (ALOEC) tried to pressure two community groups who were holding fundraisers with that show. They successfully pressured the Lesbian and Gay Community Center to drop their plans. Lambda Legal Defense refused to drop it saying it was their major fundraiser of the year. So on the night of their fundraiser ALOEC organized a picket at the theater and handed out flyers—lots of community people came to that demonstration.
19. Anne D'Adetsky often came to ACT UP meetings, but I would not say that she was a central person in ACT UP. But she had never been in the Women's Caucus.
20. Some of the early history of the Lesbian Avengers in New York City is recounted on their homepage: *www.cc.columbia.edu/vk20/lesbian/avenger.html* (as of June 1996).
21. See the description of the September 9, 1992 action on the New York City Lesbian Avengers homepage (see n. 20).
22. Faye Penn, Avenging angels or diabolical dykes? Lesbian direct-action group is targeting school kids, *QW* (September 2, 1992): 26 and Gary Terracino, When dykes met Queens—Gary Terracino on the Lesbian Avengers' first day at school, *QW* (September 20, 1992): 26–27.
23. Jennifer Monson, Moving dyke bodies, 8.
24. Anne Quindlan, Putting hatred to a vote. Presidential candidates should decry Oregon's anti-homosexual Ballot Measure 9, *New York Times* 142 (October 28, 1992): A19, A21.
25. Some of these events are also recounted on New York City Lesbian Avengers homepage (see n. 20).
26. Andrew Kopkind, Editorial, Paint it pink, March on Washington, *The Nation* 256(19) (May 17, 1993): 652–53.
27. Sara Pursley, With the Lesbian Avengers in Idaho, *The Nation* (January 23, 1995): 90–94.

Do You Love the Dyke in Your Face? pages 439–46

1. This paper is an excerpt of a speech given at Design Pride, the *First Lesbian and Gay Design Conference* held at the Cooper Union in New York City, June 1994.
2. Gran Fury is a collective of AIDS activists formed in January 1988 that appropriates dominant media techniques to provoke viewers into direct action. Some of their many public art projects include: *Kissing Doesn't Kill*, a poster campaign that appeared on the sides of buses in New York City, San Francisco, and Chicago from 1988–90 and *Welcome to America*, a billboard project produced in conjunction with the Whitney Museum of American Art for *Imageworld: Art and Media,* 1989. Some artists who have worked with Gran Fury include Avram Finklestein, Tom Kalin, John Lindell, Loring McAlpin, Marlene McCarty, and Donald Moffett.
3. Barbara Kruger is one of the most influential artists of the last fifteen years. Her unforgettable red, black, and white images combine ominous pronouncements in heavy sans serif type with noir-ish industrial photographs from the 1950s and 1960s. The graphic impact of her work derives its power from the anxiety Kruger is able to produce in the viewer, revealing how advertising contains us, heightening our insecurities and reinforcing "normalcy."
4. The Guerrilla Girls is an anonymous collective consisting of women artists and art professionals and was founded in 1985. Hiding their identities behind gorilla masks, the group keeps the New York City art public humorously informed on the rampant sexism of the art world with clever classy poster campaigns.
5. Dyke Action Machine!, the lesbian graphics project, has two members: Carrie Moyer and Sue Schaffner.
6. *Straight To Hell* was a column and later a collection of true-to-life sex stories by Boyd McDonald. The poster image appeared in the Scene and Heard section, *Village Voice* 2(23) (June 7, 1994).
7. For another interpretation of the *Straight To Hell* poster, see Collier Schorr's article on Dyke Action Machine! Poster girls, 13–14.
8. Reaching the gay market, on file, Mulryan/Nash, New York, New York. 1994, 10.
9. To access Dyke Action Machine!'s home page: *http://www.echonyc.com/~dam*

Strategies for (Re)constructing Queer Communities, pages 447–57

1. Mumford, *Culture of Cities,* 433.
2. This multiple placemaking can also be highly monotonous and have the blandness of franchises and chain stores.
3. Quoted from Criswell Predicts to the Year 2000, A gay "nation" in the Sierras? *The Advocate* 4(19) (November 11–24, 1970: 1, 14): 14.
4. Fahriye Hazer Sancar, Paradigms of postmodernity and implications for planning and design review processes, 317–21.
5. John Dakin, Inhumanities of urban planning, 437.
6. Boyer, The return of aesthetics to city planning, 49–56.
7. Forester, *Critical Theory, Public Policy, and Planning Practice,* 24–30.
8. Ibid., 259.
9. Marcus, Preface, *People Places,* x.
10. Irving, The modern/postmodern divide and urban planning, 474–487.
11. Probyn, Travels in the postmodern, in *Feminism/Postmodernism,* 187.
12. de Certeau, *Practice of Everyday Life,* 93.
13. The celebrated "queer" garden of recent years was Derek Jarman's in Dungeness, on the south coast of England, which he acquired and created while living with AIDS. See Jarman, *derek jarman's garden.*
14. Moughtin, *Urban Design,* 11–18.
15. Rudofsky, *Streets For People.*
16. Marcus and Francis, Introduction: Public places and design guidelines, in *People Places,* 1–7.
17. The lack of any mention of eroticism, sexual minorities, and related conflicts in the user inventory and guidelines of Clare Cooper Marcus's 1990 Neighborhood parks, in *People Places,* 69–118 is one of the most surprising and late examples of a sort of "homophobia by omission" in landscape design.
18. Appleyard with Gerson and Lintell, *Livable Streets, Protected Neighborhoods.*
19. Michael Lee Immel, Gay urban open space in San Francisco, 56.
20. Ibid., 30–37.
21. Philip Arcidi, Defining gay design, 36.
22. Boyer, *City of Collective Memory,* 68.
23. Tschumi, *Architecture and Disjunction,* 19.

Bibliography

Lost in Space, pages 3–16

Anzaldua, G. 1990. *Making Face/Making Soul: Haciendo caras.* San Francisco: Aunt Lute Foundation Books.

Barr, M. S. 1992. *Lost in Space: Probing feminist science fiction and beyond.* Chapel Hill, North Carolina: University of North Carolina Press.

Bhabha, H. 1994. *The Location of Culture.* New York: Routledge.

Boone, J. 1996. Queer sites in modernism: Harlem/The Left Bank/Greenwich Village. In *Geography of Identity.* Edited by Patricia Yaeger. Ann Arbor: University of Michigan Press.

Boyer, M. C. 1994. *The City of Collective Memory: Its historical imagery and architectural entertainments.* Cambridge, Massachusetts: MIT Press.

Chauncey, G. 1994. *Gay New York: Gender, urban culture, and the making of the gay male world 1890–1940.* New York: BasicBooks.

Crimp, D. 1993. *On the Museum's Ruins.* Cambridge, Massachusetts: MIT Press.

Delany, S. R. 1979. *Tales from Nevèrÿon.* New York: Bantam Books.

———. 1996. *Dhalgren.* Hanover, New Hampshire: Wesleyan University Press/University Press of New England.

Deleuze, G., and F. Guattari. 1987. *A Thousand Plateaus: Capitalism and schizophrenia.* Translated by Brian Massumi. Minneapolis: University of Minnesota Press. Originally published in 1972 as *Capitalisme et Schizophrenia.* Paris: Editions de Minuit.

Deutsche, R. 1996. *Evictions: Art and spatial politics.* Cambridge, Massachusetts: MIT Press.

Drucker, P. 1996. In the tropics there is no sin: Sexuality and gay-lesbian movements in the Third World. *new left review* 218.

Duggan, L. and N. D. Hunter. 1995. *Sex Wars: Sexual dissent and political culture.* New York: Routledge.

Fanon, F. 1991. *Black Skins, White Masks.* Translated by Charles Lam Markmann. New York: Grove Weidenfeld.

Foucault, M. 1986. Other spaces: The principles of heterotopia. *Lotus International* 48/49.

Gare, A. E. 1995. *Postmodernism and the Environmental Crisis.* New York: Routledge.

Grosz, E. 1995. *Space, Time, and Perversion: Essays on the politics of bodies.* New York: Routledge.

Habermas, J. 1991. *The Structural Transformation of the Public Sphere: An inquiry into a category of bourgeois society.* Translated by Thomas Burger. Cambridge, Massachusetts: MIT Press. Originally published in 1962 as *Strukturwandel der Öffentlicheit.*

Haraway, D. J. 1991. *Simians, Cyborgs, and Women: The reinvention of nature.* New York: Routledge.

Hoff, J. 1994. Gender as a postmodern category of paralysis. *Women's Studies International Forum* 17(4).

Jacobs, J. 1961. *Death and Life of Great American Cities.* New York: Random House.

Jeffreys, S. 1994. The queer disappearance of lesbian sexuality in the academy. *Women's Studies International Forum* 17(5).

Kennedy, E. L., and M. D. Davis. 1993. *Boots of Leather, Slippers of Gold: The history of a lesbian community.* New York: Routledge.

Lechte, J. 1995. (Not) belonging in postmodern space. In *Postmodern Cities and Spaces.* Edited by Sophie Watson and Katherine Gibson. Cambridge, Massachusetts: Blackwell.

Morrill, C. 1994. Revamping the gay sensibility: Queer camp and *dyke noir.* In *The Politics and Poetics of Camp.* Edited by Moe Meyer. New York: Routledge.

Owens, C. 1992. The allegorical impulse: Toward a theory of postmodernism. In *Beyond Recognition: Representation, power, and culture.* Edited by S. Bryson, B. Kruger, L. Tillman, and J. Weinstock. Berkeley: University of California Press.

Patton, P. 1988. Marxism and beyond: Strategies for reterritorialization. In *Marxism and the Interpretation of Culture.* Edited by Cary Nelson and Lawrence Grossberg. Chicago: University of Chicago Press.

Pringle, R., and S. Watson. 1995. Introduction. In *Postmodern Cities and Spaces.* Edited by Sophie Watson and Katherine Gibson. Cambridge, Massachusetts: Blackwell.

Probyn, E. 1990. Travels in the postmodern: Making sense of the local. In *Feminism/Postmodernism.* Edited by Linda J. Nicholson. New York: Routledge.

Relph, E. 1976. *Place and Placelessness.* London: Pion.

Rich, A. 1986. *Blood, Bread, and Poetry: Selected prose, 1979–1985.* New York: W. W. Norton.

Slagle, R. A. 1995. In defense of Queer Nation: From *identity politics* to a *politics of difference. Western Journal of Communication* 59 (spring).

Smith, B. 1983. *Home Girls: A black feminist anthology.* New York: Kitchen Table/Women of Color Press.

Smith, G. 1959. *Lost in Space.* New York: Ace Books.

Tafuri, M. 1976. *Architecture and Utopia: Design and capitalist development.* Translated by Barbara Luigia La Penta. Cambridge, Massachusetts: MIT Press.

Tenhaaf, N. 1996. Mysteries of the bioapparatus. In *Immersed in Technology: Art and virtual environments.* Edited by Mary Anne Moser and Douglas MacLeod. For the Banff Centre for the Arts. Cambridge, Massachusetts: MIT Press.

Tschumi, B. 1996. *Architecture and Disjunction.* Cambridge, Massachusetts: MIT Press.

Valentine, G. 1995. Out and about: Geographies of lesbian landscapes. *International Journal of Urban and Regional Research* 19.

Van Arnam, D., and R. Archer. 1967. *Lost in Space.* New York: Pyramid Books.

Wigley, M. 1993. *The Architecture of Deconstruction: Derrida's haunt.* Cambridge, Massachusetts: MIT Press.

Young, I. M. 1990. The ideal of community and the politics of difference. In *Feminism/Postmodernism.* Edited by Linda J. Nicholson. New York: Routledge.

Zita, J. G. 1994. Gay and lesbian studies: Yet another unhappy marriage? In *Tilting the Tower.* Edited by L. Garber. New York: Routledge.

Queer Space, pages 17–26

Barthes, R. 1978. *A Lover's Discourse: Fragments.* Translated by Richard Howard. New York: Hill and Wang.

Doty, A. 1993. *Making Things Perfectly Queer: Interpreting mass culture.* Minneapolis: University of Minnesota Press.

Genet, J. 1974. *Querelle.* Translated by Anselm Hollo. New York: Grove Press.

Harris, L. A. 1991. Revenge of a snow queen. *Out/Look* 4(1) (summer).

Mohr, R. D. 1988. *Gays/Justice: A study of ethics, society, and law.* New York: Columbia University Press.

Rosario, V. 1992. Sexual liberalism and compulsory heterosexuality. *Contemporary French Civilization.*

Marginality, pages 27–52

Agyeman, J. 1990. Black people in a white landscape. *Built Environment* 16(3).

Almgren, H. 1994. Community with/out pro-pink-uity. In *The Margins of the City: Gay men's urban lives.* Edited by Stephen Whittle. Brookfield, Vermont: Ashgate Publishing Company.

Anderson, B. 1983, 1991. *Imagined Communities: Reflections on the origin and spread of nationalism.* London: Verso.

Anonymous. 1970. 1000 gays riot in New York. *The Advocate* 4(16) (September 30–October 13).

Appleby, Y. 1992. Disability and "compulsory heterosexuality." *Feminism and Psychology* 2(3).

Appleyard, D., M. S. Gerson, and M. Lintell. 1981. *Livable Streets, Protected Neighborhoods.* Berkeley: University of California Press.

Bell, D., Binnie, J., Cream, J. and Valentine, G. 1994. All hyped up and no place to go. *Gender, Place, and Culture* 1(1).

Betsky, A. 1995. *Building Sex: Men, women, architecture, and the construction of sexuality.* New York: William Morrow.

Berlant, L., and E. Freeman. 1993. Queer nationality. In *Fear of a Queer Planet: Queer politics and social theory.* Edited by Michael Warner. Minneapolis: University of Minnesota Press.

Boone, J. 1996. Queer sites in modernism: Harlem/The Left Bank/Greenwich Village. In *Geography of Identity.* Edited by Patricia Yaeger. Ann Arbor: University of Michigan Press.

Boyer, M. C. 1994. *The City of Collective Memory: Its historical imagery and architectural entertainments.* Cambridge, Massachusetts: MIT Press.

Bredbeck, G. W. 1996. Troping the light fantastic—Representing disco then and now. *GLQ* 3(1).

Brossard, N. 1995. Green night of Labyrinthe Park: *La nuit verte du Parc Labyrinthe.* In *Sexy Bodies: The strange carnalities of feminism.* Edited by Elizabeth Grosz and Elspeth Probyn. New York: Routledge.

Bullough, V. L., and B. Bullough. 1993. *Cross Dressing, Sex, and Gender.* Philadelphia: University of Pennsylvania Press.

Burch, J. 1995. Situationist poise, space and architecture. *Transgressions* 1(1).

Butler, J. P. 1990. *Gender Trouble: Feminism and the subversion of identity.* New York: Routledge.

———. 1993. *Bodies that Matter: On the discursive limits of "sex."* New York: Routledge.

Califia, P. 1982. The issue of public sex. *The Advocate* (September 30).

Carlson, L. 1967. Open forum: Sex in public places. *Vector: Journal of the Society for Individual Rights* 3(6). On file University of California at Berkeley, Microfilm 33693—NRLF storage facility.

Chancer, L. S. 1992. *Sadomasochism in Everyday Life: The dynamics of power and powerlessness.* New Brunswick, New Jersey: Rutgers University Press.

Chauncey, G. 1994. *Gay New York: Gender, urban culture, and the making of the gay male world, 1890–1940.* New York: BasicBooks.

Cooper, D. 1994. *Sexing the City: Lesbian and gay politics within the activist state.* Concord, Massachusetts: Paul and Company.

Cosgrove, D. 1985. Prospect, perspective and the evolution of the landscape idea. *Transactions of the Institute of British Geographers* 10.

Crimp, D. 1993. On the museum's ruin. In *On the Museum's Ruins.* Cambridge, Massachusetts: MIT Press.

Crimp, D., and A. Rolston. 1990. *AIDS demo graphics.* Seattle: Bay Press.

Davis, M. 1992. *City of Quartz: Excavating the future in Los Angeles.* New York: Vintage Books.

Davis, T. 1995. The diversity of queer politics and the redefinition of sexual identity and community in urban spaces. In *Mapping Desire: Geographies of sexualities.* Edited by David Bell and Gill Valentine. London and New York: Routledge.

Debord, G. 1981. Introduction to a critique of urban geography. In *Situationist International Anthology.* Edited and translated by Ken Knabb. Berkeley, California: Bureau of Public Secrets.

———. 1994. *The Society of the Spectacle.* Translated by D. Nicholson-Smith. New York: Zone Books.

de Certeau, M. 1984. *The Practice of Everyday Life.* Translated by Steven F. Rendall. Berkeley: University of California Press.

Delaney, J. 1994-95. Public space or publicity? *a|r|c* 5.

Delany, S. R. 1996. *Dhalgren.* Hanover, New Hampshire: Wesleyan University Press/University Press of New England.

D'Emilio, J. 1983. *Sexual Politics, Sexual Communities.* Chicago: University of Chicago Press.

Derbyshire, P. 1994. A measure of queer. *Critical Quarterly* 36(1).

Di Augelli, A., and Hart, M. M. 1987. Gay women, men and families in rural settings: Toward the development of helping communities. *American Journal of Community Psychology* 15(1).

Duberman, M. 1993. *Stonewall.* New York: Dutton.

Duncan, J., and N. Duncan. 1988. (Re)reading the landscape. *Environment and Planning D—Society and Space* 6.

Egerton, J. 1990. Out but not down: Lesbians' experience of housing. *Feminist Review* 36.

Elman, R. A. 1996. Triangles and tribulations: The politics of Nazi symbols. *Journal of Homosexuality* 30(3).

Evans, A. 1973. How to zap the straights. In *The Gay Liberation Book.* San Francisco: Ramparts Press.

Evans, D. T. 1993. Dual citizenship? Bisexuality. In *Sexual Citizenship: The material construction of sexualities.* New York: Routledge.

Felshin, N., ed. 1995. Introduction. In *But is it Art? The spirit of art as activism.* Seattle: Bay Press.

Field, N. 1995. *Over the Rainbow: Money, class, and homophobia.* London: Pluto Press.

Fone, B. R. S. 1995. *A Road to Stonewall: Male homosexuality and homophobia in English and American literature, 1750–1969.* New York: Twayne.

Forest, B. 1995. West Hollywood as symbol: The significance of place in the construction of a gay identity. *Environment and Planning D—Society and Space* 13.

Foucault, M. 1986. Other spaces: The principles of heterotopia. *Lotus International* 48/49.

Fraser, C. G. 1970. "Gay ghettos" seen as police targets. *New York Times* (August 31): 28.

Garber, E. 1989. A spectacle in color: The lesbian and gay subculture in jazz age Harlem. In *Hidden from History: Reclaiming the gay and lesbian past.* Edited by Martin B. Duberman, Martha Vicinus, and George Chauncey. New York: New American Library.

Garber, M. 1992. *Vested Interests: Cross-dressing and cultural anxiety.* New York: Routledge.

Genocchio, B. 1995. Discourse, discontinuity, difference: The question of "other" spaces In *Postmodern Cities and Spaces.* Edited by Sophie Watson and Katherine Gibson. Cambridge, Massachusetts: Blackwell.

George, S. 1993. Towards a definition of bisexuality. In *Women and Bisexuality.* London: Scarlet Press.

Gilmartin, K. 1996. We weren't bar people: Middle-class lesbian identities and cultural spaces. *GLQ* 3.

Goonatilake, S. 1995. The self wandering between cultural localization and globalization. In *The Decolonization of Imagination: Culture, knowledge, and power.* Edited by Jan Nederveen Pieterse and Bhikhu Parekh. London: Zed Books.

Gott, T. 1994. Where the streets have new aims: The poster in the Age of AIDS. In *Don't Leave Me This Way: Art in the age of AIDS.* Compiled by Ted Gott. Canberra, Australia: National Gallery of Australia.

Grosz, E. 1992. Bodies-cities. In *Sexuality and Space.* Edited by Beatriz Colomina. New York: Princeton Architectural Press.

Grube, J. 1986. Queens and flaming virgins: Towards a sense of gay community. *Rites* 2(9).

Guittari, F. 1992. Regimes, pathways, subjects.

Habermas, J. 1991. *The Structural Transformation of the Public Sphere: An inquiry into a category of bourgeois society.* Translated by Thomas Burger. Cambridge, Massachusetts: MIT Press.

Haraway, D. J. 1991. *Simians, Cyborgs, and Women: The reinvention of nature.* New York: Routledge.

Harvey, D. 1989. *The Condition of Postmodernity: An enquiry into the origins of cultural change.* Cambridge, Massachusetts: Blackwell.

———. 1993. From space to place and back again: Reflections on the condition of postmodernity. In *Mapping the Futures: Local cultures, global change.* Edited by Jon Bird, Barry Curtis, Tim Putnam, George Robertson, and Lisa Tickner. London: Routledge.

Hay, R. 1991. Parallels between love relations and our relations to place. *Area* 23.

Hayden, D. 1995. *The Power of Place: Urban landscapes as public history.* Cambridge, Massachusetts: MIT Press.

Hearn, K. 1988. Oi! What about us? In *Radical Records: Thirty years of lesbian and gay history.* Edited by Bob Cant and Susan Hemmings. London: Routledge.

———. 1988. A woman's right to cruise. In *Out the Other Side: Contemporary lesbian writings.* Edited by Christian McEwen and Sue O'Sullivan. London: Virago.

Hemmings, C. 1995. Locating bisexual identities: Discourses of bisexuality and contemporary feminist theory. In *Mapping Desire: Geographies of sexualities.* Edited by David Bell and Gill Valentine. London and New York: Routledge.

Herdt, G., and A. Boxer. 1992. Introduction: Culture, history, and life course of gay men. In *Gay Culture in America: Essays from the field.* Edited by Gilbert Herdt. Boston: Beacon Press.

Herek, G. M., and K. T. Berrill, eds. 1992. *Hate Crimes: Confronting violence against lesbians and gay men.* Newbury Park, California: Sage Publications.

Hess, B. 1993. Black and front and black again: Racialization through contested times and space. In *Place and the Politics of Identity.* Edited by Michael Keith and Steve Pile. London: Routledge.

Hooker, E. 1962. The homosexual community. In *Personality Research.* Copenhagen: Society for Personality Research.

hooks, b. 1990. Choosing the margin as a space of radical openness. In *Yearnings: Race, gender, cultural politics.* Boston: South End Press.

Ingram, G. B. 1994. Lost landscapes and the spatial contextualization of queerness. *UnderCurrents: Critical environmental studies.* York University Faculty of Environmental Studies, Toronto.

Jackson, J. B. 1994. *A Sense of Place; A Sense of Time.* New Haven, Connecticut: Yale University Press.

Jackson, P. 1987. The idea of "race" and the geography of racism. In *Race and Racism: Essays in social geography.* Edited by P. Jackson. London: Allen & Unwin.

Jagose, A. 1993. Way out—The category lesbian and the fantasy of the utopic space. *Journal of the History of Sexuality* 4(2).

Keith, M., and S. Pile, eds. 1993. The politics of place. In *Place and the Politics of Identity.* London: Routledge.

Kepner, J. [Frank Golovitz]. 1958. Gay beach. *ONE Magazine* 6(7).

Kissack, T. 1995. Freaking fag revolutionaries: New York's Gay Liberation Front, 1969–1971. *Radical History Review* 62.

Knopp, L. 1992. Sexuality and the spatial dynamics of capitalism. *Environment and Planning D —Society and Space* 10.

Lauria, M., and L. Knopp. 1985. Toward an analysis of the role of gay communities in the urban renaissance. *Urban Geography* 6(2).

Lefebvre, H. 1974, 1991. *The Production of Space.* Translated by Donald Nicholson-Smith. Cambridge, Massachusetts: Blackwell.

Leznoff, M., and W. A. Westley. 1956. The homosexual community. *Social Problems* 3(4) (April).

Luke, T. W. 1994. Placing power, siting space—The politics of global and local in the new world order. *Environment and Planning D—Society and Space* 12(5).

Mains, G. 1987. Urban aboriginals and the celebration of leather magic. In *Gay Spirit: Myth and meaning.* Edited by Mark Thompson. New York: St. Martin's Press.

Manalansan, M. F. 1994. Search for the community–Filipino gay men in New York City. *Amerasia Journal* 20(1).

Mays, J. B. 1994. Cities/The controversial concept of "queer space" breathes new life into the arid subject of city planning, redefining urban space. *The Globe and Mail* (Toronto) (October 1).

McDonough, T. F. 1994. Situationist space. *October* 67.

Mies, M. and V. Shiva. 1993. *Ecofeminism.* Halifax, Nova Scotia: Fernwood Publications.

Miles, S. 1992. The fabulous fight back: On the streets after dark to confront gay bashers. *Out/Look* 5(1).

Mumford, L. 1938. *The Culture of Cities.* New York: Harcourt Brace and Company.

Murray, S. O. 1992. Components of gay community in San Francisco. In *Gay Culture in America: Essays from the field.* Edited by Gilbert Herdt. Boston: Beacon Press.

Muschamp, H. 1994. Designing a framework for diversity. *New York Times*, June 19, 1994.

Newton, E. 1972, 1979. *Mother Camp: Female impersonators in America.* Chicago: University of Chicago Press.

Owens, C. 1992. The allegorical impulse: Towards a theory of postmodernism (Part 1) and The discourse of others: Feminists and postmodernism. In *Beyond Recognition: Representation, power, and culture.* Edited by S. Bryson, B. Kruger, L. Tillman, and J. Weinstock. Berkeley: University of California Press.

Pieterse, J. N., and Parekh, B. 1995. Shifting imaginaries: Decolonization, internal decolonization, postcoloniality. In *The Decolonization of Imagination: Culture, knowledge, and power.* Edited by Jan Nederveen Pieterse and Bhikhu Parekh. London: Zed Books.

Reyes, E. E. 1993. Queer Spaces: The space of lesbians and gay men of color in Los Angeles. A thesis submitted in partial satisfaction of the requirements for the degree of Master of Arts in Urban Planning, University of California, Los Angeles. UCLA University Research Library LD791.8 U7R33.

Robbins, M. 1992. Utopian Prospects. In *Angles of Incidence.* New York: Princeton University Press.

Rothenberg, T. 1995. "And she told two friends": Lesbians creating urban social space. In *Mapping Desire: Geographies of sexualities.* Edited by David Bell and Gill Valentine. London and New York: Routledge.

Rubin, G. 1984. Thinking sex: Notes for a radical theory of the politics of sexuality. In *Pleasure and Danger: Exploring female sexuality.* Edited by Carole S. Vance. New York: Routledge.

Saalfield, C., and R. Navarro. 1991. Shocking pink praxis: Race and gender on the ACT UP! frontlines. In *Inside/Out: Lesbian theories, gay theories.* Edited by Dianna Fuss. New York: Routledge.

SAMOIS. 1987. *Coming to power: Writings and graphics on lesbian s/m.* Boston: Alyson Publications.

Seel, P. 1995. *I, Pierre Seel, Deported Homosexual: A memoir of Nazi terror.* Translated by Joachim Neugroschel. New York: BasicBooks/Harper Collins.

Shimazaki, P. 1988. Tokyo: Sexopolis. *Out/Look: National lesbian and gay quarterly* 1.

Shiva, V. 1993. Homeless in the "global village." In *Ecofeminism.* Written by Maria Mies and Vandana Shiva. London: Zed Books.

Slagle, R. A. 1995. In defense of Queer Nation: From *identity politics* to a *politics of difference. Western Journal of Communication* 59 (spring).

Smith, N., and C. Katz. 1993. Grounding metaphor: Towards a spatialized politics. In *Place and the Politics of Identity*. Edited by Michael Keith and Steve Pile. New York: Routledge.

Soja, E. W. 1995. Heterotopologies: A remembrance of other spaces in the Citadel-LA. In *Postmodern Cities and Spaces*. Edited by Sophie Watson and Katherine Gibson. Cambridge, Massachusetts: Blackwell.

Stein, A. 1992. Sisters and queers: The decentering of lesbian feminism. *Socialist Review* 22(1).

Stone, A. R. 1991. The empire strikes back: A posttranssexual manifesto. In *Body Guards: The cultural politics of gender ambiguity*. Edited by Julia Epstein and Kristina Straub. New York: Routledge.

———. 1995. Agency and proximity: Communities/CommuniTrees. In *The War of Desire and Technology at the Close of the Mechanical Age*. Cambridge, Massachusetts: MIT Press.

Tafuri, M. 1976. *Architecture and Utopia: Design and capitalist development*. Translated by Barbara Luigia La Penta. Cambridge, Massachusetts: MIT Press.

———. 1987. *The Sphere and the Labyrinth: Avant-Gardes and architecture from Piranesi to the 1970s*. Translated by Pellegrino d'Acrierno and Robert Connolly. Cambridge, Massachusetts: MIT Press.

Teal, D. 1971. *The Gay Militants*. New York: Stein and Day.

Terry. n.d. Theorizing deviant historiography. *Differences: A journal of feminist cultural studies* 3(2).

Thompson, M. ed. 1991. *Leatherfolk: Radical sex, people, politics, and practice*. Boston: Alyson Publications.

Tom of Finland. 1984. *The Men by Tom of Finland*. Los Angeles: Tom of Finland Inc.

Truscott, L. 1991. S/M: Some questions and a few answers. In *Leatherfolk: Radical sex, people, politics, and practice*. Edited by Mark Thompson. Boston: Alyson Publications.

Tschumi, B. 1996. *Architecture and Disjunction*. Cambridge, Massachusetts: MIT Press.

Urbach, H. 1993. Spatial rubbings. *Sites* 25.

Virilio, P. 1986. *Speed and Politics*. Translated by Mark Polizzotti. New York: Semiotext(e).

Warner, M. 1993. Introduction. In *Fear of a Queer Planet: Queer politics and social theory*. Edited by Michael Warner. Minneapolis: University of Minnesota Press.

Weeks, J. 1985. *Sexuality and Its Discontents: Meanings, myths, and modern sexualities*. London: Routledge and Kegan Paul.

Weightman, B. A. 1981. Commentary: Towards a geography of the gay community. *Journal of Cultural Geography* 1.

West, C. 1994. Beyond eurocentrism and multiculturalism. *Public* 10.

Whittle, S. 1994. Consuming differences: The collaboration of the gay body with the cultural state. In *The Margins of the City: Gay men's urban lives*. Edited by Stephen Whittle. Brookfield, Vermont: Ashgate Publishing Company.

Wilson, E. 1984. Bodies in public and private. In *Public Bodies—Private States: New views on photography, representation, and gender*. Edited by Jane Brettle and Sally Rice. Manchester, England: Manchester University Press.

———. 1988. Memoirs of an anti-heroine. In *Radical Records: Thirty years of lesbian and gay history*. Edited by Bob Cant and Susan Hemmings. London and New York: Routledge.

———. 1991. *The Sphinx in the City: Urban life, the control of disorder, and women*. Berkeley: University of California Press.

Winchester, H. P., and P. E. White. 1988. The location of marginalised groups in the inner city. *Environment and Planning D—Society and Space* 6(1).

Wolf, D. G. 1979. *The Lesbian Community*. Berkeley: University of California Press.

Wolfe, M. 1994. The AIDS Coalition to unleash power, New York (ACT UP NY): A direct action political model of community research for AIDS prevention. In *AIDS Prevention and Services: Community-based research*. Edited by Johannes P. Van Vugt. Westport, Connecticut: Bergin and Garvey.

Wollen, P. 1990. Bitter victory: The art and politics of the Situationist International. In *On the Passage of a few people through a rather brief moment in time: The Situationist International, 1957–1972*. Edited by Elisabeth Sussman. Boston, Massachusetts: The Institute of Art/MIT Press.

Narratives of Place, pages 55–60

Appleyard, D. 1973. Notes on urban perception and knowledge. In *Image and Environment: Cognitive mapping and spatial behavior*. Edited by Roger M. Downs and David Stea. Chicago: Aldine Publishing.

Boyer, M. C. 1994. *The City of Collective Memory: Its historical imagery and architectural entertainments*. Cambridge, Massachusetts: MIT Press.

Cosgrove, D. 1985. Prospect, perspective and the evolution of the landscape idea. *Transactions of the Institute of British Geographers* 10.

Gärling, T. 1989. The role of cognitive maps in spatial decisions. *Journal of Environmental Psychology* 9(4).

Gould, P., and R. White. 1986. *Mental Maps*. Boston: Allen & Unwin.

Haraway, D. J. 1991. *Simians, Cyborgs, and Women: The reinvention of nature*. New York: Routledge.

Hillier, J. 1993. To boldly go where no planners have ever . . .. *Environment and Planning D—Society and Space* 11.

Lefebvre, H. 1991. *The Production of Space*. Translated by Donald Nicholson-Smith. Cambridge, Massachusetts: Blackwell.

Marcus, C. C. 1979. Environmental autobiography. Berkeley: Institute of Urban and Regional Development of the University of California. Working paper number 301. On file, University of California, Berkeley: College of Environmental Design Library HT393.C2C25.W6.

Orlean, P. 1973. Differential cognition of urban residents: Effects of social scale and mapping. In *Image and Environment: Cognitive mapping and spatial behavior*. Edited by Roger M. Downs and David Stea. Chicago: Aldine Publishing.

Plant, S. 1992. *The Most Radical Gesture: The situationist international in a postmodern age*. London: Routledge.

Thomashow, M. 1996. *Ecological Identity: Becoming a reflective environmentalist*. Cambridge, Massachusetts: MIT Press.

Tschumi, B. 1996. *Architecture and Disjunction*. Cambridge, Massachusetts: MIT Press.

Varela, F. 1993. When is a map cognitive? In *The Evolution of Cognitive Maps—New paradigms for the twenty-first century*. Edited by Ervin Laszlo, Ignazio Masulli, Robert Artigiani, and Vilmos Csanyi. Luxembourg: Gordon and Breach.

Restriction and Reclamation, pages 61–67

Nestle, J. 1987. *A Restricted Country*. Ithaca, New York: Firebrand Books.

The Interim Photographs, pages 69–76

Arbus, D. 1972. *diane arbus*. Millerton, New York: Aperture.

Aukeman. 1995. Bill Jacobson: Coming together and letting go. *ARTNEWS* (October).

Watney, S. 1995. Bill Jacobson: Photographer's Gallery. *ARTFORUM* (April).

One-Handed Geographies, pages 81–87

Ballard, J. G. 1973. *Crash*. London: Jonathan Cape.

Bell, D. 1994. Erotic topographies: On the sexuality and space network. *Antipode* 26(1).

———. 1994. In bed with the state: Political geography and sexual politics. *Geoforum* 25(4).

———. 1995. Perverse dynamics, sexual citizenship, and the transformation of intimacy. In *Mapping Desire: Geographies of sexualities*. Edited by David Bell and Gill Valentine. London and New York: Routledge.

———. n.d. Pleasure and danger: The paradoxical spaces of sexual citizenship. *Political Geography* 14(2).

Bell, D., J. Binnie, J. Cream, and G. Valentine. 1994. All hyped up and no place to go. *Gender, Place, and Culture* 1(1).

Bell, D., and G. Valentine. 1995. The sexed self: Strategies of performance, sites of resistance. In *Mapping the Subject: Geographies of cultural transformation*. Edited by Steve Pile and Nigel Thrift. London: Routledge.

Bibbings, L., and P. Alldridge. 1993. Sexual expression, body alteration, and the defence of consent. *Journal of Law and Society* 20(3).

Butler, J. 1993. Critically queer. *GLQ* 1(1).

Campbell, B. 1993. *Goliath: Britain's dangerous places.* London: Methuen.

Colomina, B., ed. 1992. *Sexuality and Space.* New York: Princeton Architectural Press.

Cooper, D. 1993. An engaged state: Sexuality, governance and the potential for change. In *Activating Theory: Lesbian, gay, bisexual politics.* Edited by J. Bristow and A. Wilson. London: Lawrence and Wishart.

Cream, J. 1995. Re-solving riddles: The sexed body. In *Mapping Desire: Geographies of sexualities.* Edited by David Bell and Gill Valentine. London and New York: Routledge.

Crimp, D. and Rolston, A. 1990. *AIDS demo graphics.* Seattle: Bay Press.

Debord, G., and G. Wolman. 1981. Methods of detournement. In *Situationist International Anthology.* Edited by Ken Knabb. Berkeley: Bureau of Public Secrets (originally published 1956).

Dekkers. M. 1994. *Dearest Pet: On bestiality.* London: Verso.

Douglas, J., and P. Rasmussen. 1977. *The Nude Beach.* London: Sage.

Eadie, J. 1993. Activating bisexuality: Towards a bi/sexual politics. In *Activating Theory: Lesbian, gay, bisexual politics.* Edited by J. Bristow and A. Wilson. London: Lawrence and Wishart.

Gange, J., and S. Johnstone. 1993. Believe me, everybody has something pierced in California: An interview with Nayland Blake. *New Formations* 19.

Geltmaker, T. 1992. The queer nation acts up: Health care, politics, and sexual diversity in the County of Angels. *Environment and Planning D—Society and Space* 10(4).

Golding, S. 1993. The excess: An added remark on sex, rubber, ethics, and other impurities. *New Formations* 19.

———. 1993. Quantum philosophy, impossible geographies and a few small points about life, liberty and the pursuit of sex (all in the name of democracy). In *Place and the Politics of Identity.* Edited by Michael Keith and Steve Pile. London: Routledge.

———. 1993. Sexual manners. In *Pleasure Principles: Politics, sexuality and ethics.* Edited by V. Harwood, D. Oswell, K. Parkinson and A. Ward. London: Lawrence and Wishart.

Grosz, E. 1992. Bodies-cities. In *Sexuality and Space.* Edited by Beatriz Colomina. New York: Princeton Architectural Press.

Hall Carpenter Archives Gay Men's Oral History Group. n.d. *Walking After Midnight: Gay men's life stories.* London: Routledge.

Hall Carpenter Archives Lesbian Oral History Group. 1989. *Inventing Ourselves: Lesbian life stories.* London: Routledge.

Hallam, P. 1993. *The Book of Sodom.* London: Verso.

Hutchins, L., and L. Ka'ahumanu, eds. 1991. *Bi Any Other Name: Bisexual people speak out.* Boston: Alyson Publications.

Jarman, D. 1992. *At Your Own Risk: A saint's testament.* London: Hutchinson.

———. 1992. *Modern Nature: The journals of Derek Jarman.* London: Vintage.

Johansson, W., and W. Percy. 1994. *Outing: Shattering the conspiracy of silence.* New York: Harrington Park Press.

Kennedy, E. L., and M. D. Davis. 1993. *Boots of Leather, Slippers of Gold: The history of a lesbian community.* New York: Routledge.

Knopp, L. 1995. Sexuality and space: A framework for analysis. In *Mapping Desire: Geographies of sexualities.* Edited by David Bell and Gill Valentine. London and New York: Routledge.

Mohr, R. 1992. *Gay Ideas: Outing and other controversies.* Boston: Beacon Press.

Munt, S. 1995. The lesbian *flâneur*. In *Mapping Desire: Geographies of sexualities.* Edited by David Bell and Gill Valentine. London and New York: Routledge.

National Lesbian and Gay Survey. 1992. *Proust, Cole Porter, Michelangelo, Marc Almond and me: Writings by gay men on their lives and lifestyles.* London: Routledge.

National Lesbian and Gay Survey 1992. *What a Lesbian Looks Like: Writings by lesbians on their lives and lifestyles.* London: Routledge.

Newton, E. 1993. *Cherry Grove, Fire Island: Sixty years in America's first gay and lesbian town.* Boston: Beacon Press.

O'Carroll, T. 1980. *Paedophilia: The radical case.* London: Peter Owen.

OffPink Collective. 1988. *Bisexual Lives.* London: OffPink Publishing.

Pfohl, S. 1993. Venus in Microsoft. In *The Last Sex: Feminism and outlaw bodies.* Edited by Arthur Kroker and Marilouise Kroker. New York: St. Martin's Press.

Rose, G. 1991. On being ambivalent: Women and feminisms in geography. In *New Words, New Worlds: Reconceptualising social and cultural geography.* Edited by Chris Philo. Lampeter: Social and Cultural Geography Study Group.

Rose, G. 1993. *Feminism and Geography: The limits of geographical knowledge.* Cambridge: Polity Press.

Rubin, G. 1993. Thinking sex: Notes for a radical theory of the politics of sexuality. In *The Lesbian and Gay Studies Reader.* Edited by H. Abelove, M. Barale, and D. Halperin. New York: Routledge.

SAMOIS. 1982. *Coming to Power: Writings and graphics on lesbian s/m.* Boston: Alyson Publications.

Sedgwick, E. 1993. Queer performativity: Henry James's The Art of the Novel. *GLQ* 1(1).

———. 1994. *Tendencies.* New York: Routledge.

Singer, L. 1993. *Erotic Welfare: Sexual theory and politics in the age of epidemic.* New York: Routledge.

Stanley, C. 1993. Sins and passions. *Law and Critique* 4(2).

Weeks, J. 1985. *Sexuality and Its Discontents: Meanings, myths, and modern sexualities.* London: Routledge and Kegan Paul.

Wilson, A. 1993. Which equality? Toleration, difference or respect. In *Activating Theory: Lesbian, gay, bisexual politics.* Edited by J. Bristow and A. Wilson. London: Lawrence and Wishart.

Wilson, E. 1993. Is transgression transgressive? In *Activating Theory: Lesbian, gay, bisexual politics.* Edited by J. Bristow and A. Wilson. London: Lawrence and Wishart.

Woodhead, D. 1995. "Surveillant gays": HIV, space and the constitution of identities. In *Mapping Desire: Geographies of sexualities.* Edited by David Bell and Gill Valentine. London and New York: Routledge.

Zimmerman, B. 1990. *The Safe Sea of Women: Lesbian fiction, 1969–1989.* Boston: Beacon Press.

Surveying Territories and Landscapes, pages 91—94

Francis, M. 1987. The making of democratic streets. In *Public Streets for Public Use.* Edited by Anne Vernez Moudon. New York: Van Nostrand Reinhold.

Thomashow, M. 1996. *Ecological Identity: Becoming a reflective environmentalist.* Cambridge, Massachusetts: MIT Press.

"Open" Space as Strategic Queer Sites, pages 95—125

Adam, B. D. 1993. Winning rights and freedoms in Canada. In *The Third Pink Book: A global view of lesbian and gay liberation and oppression.* Edited by Art Hendriks, Rob Tielman, and Evert van der Veen. Buffalo, New York: Prometheus.

Adams, P. 1993. The three (dis)graces. *New Formations* 19.

Anonymous. 1979. Pacific gays and lesbians rally to combat rising street violence. *The Body Politic* 56.

Anonymous. 1982. Vancouver's pre-election surprise. *The Body Politic* 89.

Appleyard, D., M. S. Gerson, and M. Lintell. 1981. *Livable Streets, Protected Neighborhoods.* Berkeley: University of California Press.

Batten, J. 1969. The homosexual life in Canada: Will Trudeau's change in the law make any difference? An answer from the gay world. *Saturday Night* (September).

Berelowitz, L. 1994,1995. From factor 15 to feu d'artifice: The nature of public space in Vancouver. *a|r|c* 5.

Bersani, L. 1988. Is the rectum a grave? In *AIDS: Cultural Analysis, Cultural Activism.* Edited by Douglas Crimp. Cambridge, Massachusetts: MIT Press.

Blake, N. 1995. Tom of Finland—An appreciation. In *Out in Culture: Gay, lesbian, and queer essays on popular culture.* Edited by Corey I. Creekmur and Alexander Doty. Durham, North Carolina: Duke University Press.

Boddy, T. 1994. Plastic lion's gate: A short history of the postmodern in Vancouver architecture. In *Vancouver: Representing the postmodern city.* Edited by Paul Delany. Vancouver: Arsenal Pulp Press.

Boone, J. 1996. Queer sites in modernism: Harlem/The Left Bank/Greenwich Village. In *Geography of Identity*. Edited by Patricia Yaeger. Ann Arbor: University of Michigan Press.

Box, J., and C. Harrison. 1993. Natural spaces in urban places. *Town & Country Planning* 62(9).

Boyer, M. C. 1994. *The City of Collective Memory: Its historical imagery and architectural entertainments*. Cambridge, Massachusetts: MIT Press.

Brown. M. 1995. Ironies of distance: An ongoing critique of the geographies of AIDS. *Environment and Planning D—Society and Space* 13

———. 1995. Sex, scale and the "new urban politics": HIV-prevention strategies from Yaletown, Vancouver. In *Mapping Desire: Geographies of sexualities*. Edited by David Bell and Gill Valentine. London and New York: Routledge.

Chauncey, G. 1994. *Gay New York: Gender, urban culture, and the making of the gay male world, 1890–1940*. New York: BasicBooks.

———. 1996. Privacy could only be had in public: Gay uses of the streets. In *STUD: Architectures of masculinity*. New York: Princeton University Press.

Cory, D. W. 1951 (1960). *The Homosexual in America, A Subjective Approach*. New York: Castle Books.

Cream, J. 1995. Re-solving riddles: The sexed body. In *Mapping Desire: Geographies of sexualities*. Edited by David Bell and Gill Valentine. London and New York: Routledge.

Crimp, D. 1993. *On the Museum's Ruins*. Cambridge, Massachusetts: MIT Press.

Crouch, D. P. 1979. The historical development of urban open space. In *Urban Open Space*. Edited by Lisa Taylor. New York: Rizzoli.

Dansereau, P. 1966. Ecological impact and human ecology. In *Future Environments of North America*. Edited by F. Fraser Darling and J. P. Milton. Garden City, New York: Natural History Press.

Delany, P. 1994. Vancouver as postmodern city. In *Vancouver: Representing the postmodern city*. Edited by Paul Delany. Vancouver: Arsenal Pulp Press.

Delany, S. R. 1990. *The Motion of Light in Water: East Village Sex and Science Fiction Writing: 1960-1965*. London: Paladin/Grafton Books.

———. 1994. *The Mad Man*. New York: Richard Kasak Books.

Deleuze, G., and F. Guattari. 1986. *Nomadology: The war machine*. Translated by Brian Massumi. New York: Semiotext(e).

———. 1987. *A Thousand Plateaus: Capitalism and schizophrenia*. Translated by Brian Massumi. Minneapolis: University of Minnesota Press.

Delph, E. W. 1978. *The Silent Community: Public homosexual encounters*. Beverly Hills, California: Sage Publications.

Evans, D. T. 1993. Dual citizenship? Bisexuality. In *Sexual Citizenship: The material construction of sexualities*. New York: Routledge.

Fatona, A., and G. B. Ingram. 1995. Scattered at the margins. *FUSE* 18.

Forman, R. T. T., and M. Godron. 1986. *Landscape Ecology*. New York: John Wiley.

George, S. 1993. Towards a definition of bisexuality. In *Women and Bisexuality*. London: Scarlet Press.

Golding, S. 1993. Quantum philosophy, impossible geographies and a few small points about life, liberty and the pursuit of sex (all in the name of democracy). In *Place and the Politics of Identity*. Edited by Michael Keith and Steve Pile. London: Routledge.

Grace, D. 1991. *Love Bites: Photographs by Della Grace*. London: Gay Male Press.

———. 1993. Xenomorphisis. *New Formations* 19.

Grosz, E. 1995. *Space, Time, and Perversion: Essays on the politics of bodies*. New York: Routledge.

Griggers, C. 1993. Lesbian bodies in the age of (post)mechanical reproduction. In *Fear of a Queer Planet: Queer politics and social change*. Edited by Michael Warner. Minneapolis: University of Minnesota Press.

Habermas, J. 1991. *The Structural Transformation of the Public Sphere: An inquiry into a category of bourgeois society*. Translated by Thomas Burger. Cambridge, Massachusetts: MIT Press.

Hann, D. 1995. The lesbian and gay civil rights struggle in British Columbia, 1971–1980. Transcripts of a talk given at Harry's Off-Commercial on October 14, 1995, during a benefit for Little Sisters Bookstore.

Haraway, D. J. 1991. *Simians, Cyborgs, and Women: The reinvention of nature*. New York: Routledge.

Heckscher, A. 1979. The management of open spaces: Who runs them, and with what aim? in *Urban Open Space*. Edited by Lisa Taylor. New York: Rizzoli

Hemmings, C. 1995. Locating bisexual identities: Discourses of bisexuality and contemporary feminist theory. In *Mapping Desire: Geographies of sexualities*. Edited by David Bell and Gill Valentine. London and New York: Routledge.

Howard, J. 1995. The Library, the park, and the pervert: Public space and homosexual encounters in post–World War II Atlanta. *Radical History Review* 62.

Howell, P. 1993. Public space and the public sphere: Political theory and the historical geography of modernity. *Environment and Planning D—Society and Space* 11.

Humphreys, R. A. L. 1975. Enlarged edition with initial book published in 1970. *Tearoom Trade: Impersonal sex in public places*. Chicago: Aldine.

Imafuku, R. 1995. Glass made of water. In *Transculture La Biennale di Venezia 1995*. Curated by F. Nanjo and D. Friis-Hansen. Tokyo: The Japan Foundation.

Immel, M. 1983. Gay urban open space in San Francisco: The landscape of liberation. Thesis for the partial fulfillment of a Master of Landscape Architecture. On file University of California at Berkeley, College of Environmental Design Library. NA25.5.I332.

Ingram, G. B. 1995. Landscapes of (un)lawful chaos: Conflicts around temperate rain forest and biological diversity in Pacific Canada. *RECIEL: Review of European Community & International Environmental Law* 4(3).

Jacobs, J. 1961. *Death and Life of Great American Cities*. New York: Random House.

Kenney, M. R. 1994. Strategic visibility: Gay and lesbian place-claiming in Los Angeles, 1970–1994. Ph.D. dissertation, University of California at Los Angeles. UCLA University Research Library LD 791.9 U7K395. University Microfilms International order number 9507348 tel. 1-800-521-0600.

Kinsman, G. 1987. *The Regulation of Desire: Sexuality in Canada*. Montréal: Black Rose Books.

Knopp, L. 1992. Sexuality and the spatial dynamics of capitalism. *Environment and Planning D—Society and Space* 10.

Leznoff, M., and W. A. Westley. 1956. The Homosexual Community. *Social Problems* 3(4) (April).

Loos, B. 1981. Opening the mounties' closet. *The Body Politic* 77.

Lynch, K. 1991. Open space: Freedom and control. In *City Sense and City Design: Writings and projects of Kevin Lynch*. Edited by T. Banerjee and M. Southworth. Cambridge: MIT Press.

———. 1991. The openness of open space. In *City Sense and City Design: Writings and projects of Kevin Lynch*. Edited by T. Banerjee and M. Southworth. Cambridge: MIT Press.

Marshall, G. 1964. *The Beginner's Guide to Cruising*. Washington, D.C.: Guild Press.

McLaren, A. 1992. Sex radicals in the Canadian Pacific Northwest, 1820–1920. *Journal of the History of Sexuality* 2(4).

McLeod, D. W. 1996. *Lesbian and Gay Liberation in Canada: A selected annotated chronology, 1964–1975*. Toronto: ECW Press/Homeward Books.

Mosher, D. L., and S. S. Tomkins. 1988. Scripting the macho man: Hypermasculine socialization and enculturation. *Journal of Sex Research* 25.

Nardi, P. 1995. The Breastplace of Righteousness: Twenty-five years after Laud Humphreys' *Tearoom Trade: Impersonal Sex in Public Places*. *Journal of Homosexuality* 30(2).

Oke, T. R., M. North, and O. Slaymaker. 1992. Primordial to prim order: A century of environmental change. In *Vancouver and Its Region*. Edited by Graeme Wynn and Timothy Oke. Vancouver: University of British Columbia Press.

Patton, C. 1993. Tremble, hetero swine! In *Fear of a Queer Planet: Queer politics and social change*. Edited by Michael Warner. Minneapolis: University of Minnesota Press.

Pettinger, A. 1993. Why fetish? *New Formations* 19.

Ponte, M. R. 1974. Life in a parking lot: An ethnography of a homosexual drive-in. In *Deviance: Field studies and self-disclosure*. Edited by Jerry Jacobs. Palo Alto, California: National Press Books.

Rand, D. 1977. Interview with lesbian feminist. *Gay Tide* 15.

Rechy, J. 1977. *The Sexual Outlaw: A documentary*. New York: Grove Weidenfeld.

Reed, D. 1980. Repression and exaggeration: The art of Tom of Finland. *Christopher Street* 4 (April).

Ross, B. L. 1995. *The House That Jill Built: A lesbian nation in formation*. Toronto: University of Toronto Press.

Rubin, G. Interview by Judith Butler. Sexual traffic. *Differences* 6(2–3).

Russell, I. ed. 1993. *Jeb and Dash: A diary of gay life, 1918–1945*. Boston: Faber and Faber.

Samis, S. 1995. Homohate queeried. Bashing and abuse in our own backyard. *Angles* 13(9) (September).

Sanders, D. 1994. Constructing lesbian and gay rights. Canadian Journal of Law and Society/Revue Canadienne Droit et Société 9(2).

Soulé, M., and G. Lease, eds. 1995. *Reinventing Nature?* New York: Routledge.

Stamps, W. 1991. Doing battles with censors. *The Advocate* 582 (July 30).

Tafuri, M. 1976. *Architecture and Utopia: Design and capitalist development.* Translated by Barbara Luigia La Penta. Cambridge, Massachusetts: MIT Press.

Tom of Finland. 1984. *Kake Pleasure Park.* Los Angeles: Tom of Finland Inc.

Tschumi, B. 1996. *Architecture and Disjunction.* Cambridge, Massachusetts: MIT Press.

Tucker, S. 1991. Gender, fucking and utopia. *Social Text* 27.

Valentine, G. 1995. Out and about. Geographies of lesbian landscapes. *International Journal of Urban and Regional Research* 19.

Weeks, J. 1985. *Sexuality and Its Discontents: Meanings, myths, and modern sexualities.* London: Routledge and Kegan Paul.

Weightman, B. A. 1980. Gay bars as private places. *Landscape* 24(1).

Wilson, E. 1984. *Public Bodies—Private States: New views on photography, representation, and gender.* Edited by Jane Brettle and Sally Rice. Manchester, England: Manchester University Press.

Young, I. M. 1990. The ideal of community and the politics of difference. In *Feminism/Postmodernism.* Edited by Linda J. Nicholson. New York: Routledge.

"No More Shit," pages 127–45

Anonymous. 1968. Near-riot at drag contest: Fire-bomb found. *Toronto Telegram* (November 1).

Anonymous. 1976. What do you say to a guy after you've blown him in the park. *The Body Politic* 27.

Bearchell, C. 1980. Shoot-up in David Balfour Park: Cops use bullets to arrest five, *The Body Politic* 67.

———. 1981. Putting on the pressure. *The Body Politic* 74.

———. 1981. Lesbian Pride March is a first for Canada. *The Body Politic* 79.

———. 1981. Another park, another politician. *The Body Politic* 83.

The Body Politic. 1974–1985. Gay Toronto. *The Body Politic.*

———. 1979. Gang homophobic violence in Balfour Park. *The Body Politic* 56.

———. 1979. Toronto cops raid gay bath, charge 28 men. *The Body Politic* 50.

———. 1982. Police stepping up park and bathroom busts. *The Body Politic* 86.

Brittan, A. 1979. Getting off. *The Body Politic* 56.

Chauncey, G. 1994. *Gay New York: Gender, urban culture, and the making of the gay male world, 1890–1940.* New York: BasicBooks.

Crawford, W. 1984. *Homosexuality in Canada: A bibliography.* 2d ed. Toronto: Canadian Gay Archives.

Gibson, S. D. S. 1984. *More than an island: A history of the Toronto Islands.* Toronto: Irwin Publishing.

———. 1986. Portrait of the Toronto Island community. *Landscape* 29(2).

Grube, J. 1986. Queens and flaming virgins: Towards a sense of gay community. *Rites* 2(9).

———. 1991. Natives and settlers: An ethnographic note on early interaction of older homosexual men with younger gay liberationists. *Journal of Homosexuality* 20(3/4).

———. 1993. "No more shit": Toronto gay men and the police. *SLOGAN* (16)3.

Hannon, G. 1986. Taking it to the streets. *The Body Politic* 71.

Hannon, G., and B. Lewis. 1979. I know a place . . .. *The Body Politic* 53.

Hannon, G., B. Lewis, E. Mahoney, C. Patterson, and R. Spalding. 1981. Who is next? Me? *The Body Politic* 72.

Hawkes, B. 1996. 15 years after the raid. *XTRA West!* 66 (February 22).

Kinsman, G. 1987. *The Regulation of Desire: Sexuality in Canada.* Montréal: Black Rose Books.

Lesk, A. 1985. Aimless development threatens gay beach. *The Body Politic* 111

Leznoff, M., and W. A. Westley. 1956. The Homosexual Community. *Social Problems* 3(4) (April).

Mays, J. B. 1994. Green passages/Examining the different meanings in urban territory—Queer space. *The Globe and Mail* (Toronto) (September 21): A13.

McLeod, D. W. 1996. *Lesbian and Gay Liberation in Canada: A selected annotated chronology, 1964–1975.* Toronto: ECW Press/Homeward Books.

Miller, A. V. 1982. *Lesbian and Gay Heritage of Toronto.* Toronto: Canadian Gay Archives.

Murray, S. O. 1979. The institutional elaboration of a quasi-ethnic community. *The International Review of Modern Sociology* 9.

O'Connor, A. 1985. Beach bylaw bingo. *The Body Politic* 117.

Popert, K. 1982. Public sexuality and social space. *The Body Politic* 85.

Salsbery, L. 1967. Witchcraft and faggotry. *Varsity Review* 3 of the University of Toronto (November).

Waite, B., and C. De Novo. 1971. We Demand. *The Body Politic* 1.

From Landmarks to Spaces, pages 147-62

Angelides, S. 1995. The Economy of (Hetero)sexuality. *Melbourne Historical Journal* 23(44).

Barnes, D. 1937. *Nightwood.* New York: Harcourt, Brace and Co.

Bell, D. 1995. Perverse dynamics, sexual citizenship and the transformation of intimacy. In *Mapping Desire: Geographies of sexualities.* London and New York: Routledge.

Bell, D., and G. Valentine, eds. 1995. *Mapping Desire: Geographies of sexualities.* London and New York: Routledge.

Bi Academic Intervention, ed. 1997. *The Bisexual Imaginary: Desire, representation, identity.* London: Cassell.

Blumstein, P., and P. Schwartz. 1976. Bisexual women. In *The Social Psychology of Sex.* Edited by J. P. Wiseman. New York: Harper and Row.

Bode, J. 1976. *A View from Another Closet: Exploring bisexuality in women.* New York: Hawthorn.

Bowie, M. 1992. Bisexuality. In *Feminism and Psychoanalysis: A critical dictionary.* Edited by E. Wright. Oxford, England: Basil Blackwell.

Bristow, J., and A. Wilson, eds. 1993. *Activating Theory: Lesbian, gay, bisexual politics.* London: Lawrence and Wishart.

Card, C. 1985. Lesbian attitudes and the second sex. *Women's Studies International Forum* 8(3).

Däumer, E. 1992. Queer ethics, or the challenge of bisexuality to lesbian ethics. *Hypatia: A journal of feminist philosophy.* (7)4 (fall).

Faderman, L. 1985. *Surpassing the Love of Men: Romantic friendship and love between women, from the Renaissance to the present.* London: Women's Press.

———. 1991. *Odd Girls and Twilight Lovers: A history of lesbian life in twentieth-century America.* New York: Columbia University Press.

Fast, J., and H. Wells. 1975. *Bisexual Living.* New York: Pocket Books.

Foucault, M. 1971. The discourse on language. In *The Archaeology of Knowledge.* New York: Harper and Row.

Foucault, M. 1978. *The history of sexuality, volume 1: An introduction.* Translated by R. Hurley. London: Penguin Books.

Fraser, M. 1996. Framing contention: Bisexuality displaced. In *RePresenting Bisexualities: Subjects and cultures of fluid desire.* Edited by Donald E. Hall and Maria Pramaggiore. New York: New York University Press.

Freud, S. 1925. Psychogenesis of a case of homosexuality in a woman. In *Collected Papers, Volume II: Clinical Papers, Papers on Technique.* Translated by J. Riviere. London: Hogarth Press.

Freud, S. 1937. The ego and the id. In *The Standard Edition of the Complete Psychological Works of Sigmund Freud.* Translated by J. Strachey. London: The Hogarth Press and the Institute of Psychoanalysis.

Frye, M. 1985. History and responsibility. *Women's Studies International Forum* 8(3).

Garber, M. 1992. *Vested Interests: Cross dressing and cultural anxiety.* New York: Routledge.

———. 1995. *Vice Versa: Bisexuality and the eroticism of everyday life.* New York: Simon and Schuster.

Geller, T., ed. 1990. *Bisexuality: A reader and sourcebook.* Ojai, California: Times Change Press.

George, S. 1993. *Women and Bisexuality.* London: Scarlet Press.

Gregory, D. 1983. The case for a feminist bisexuality. In *Sex and Love: New thoughts on old contradictions*. Edited by S. Cartledge and J. Ryan. London: Women's Press.

Hall, D., and M. Pramaggiore. 1996. *RePresenting Bisexualities: Subjects and cultures of fluid desire*. New York: New York University Press.

Hemmings, C. 1996. From lesbian nation to transgender liberation: A bisexual feminist perspective. *Journal of gay, lesbian,and bisexual identity.* (1)1 (January).

Hutchins, L., and L. Ka'ahumanu, eds. 1991. *Bi Any Other Name: Bisexual people speak out*. Boston: Alyson Publications.

Kermode, F. 1992. Review of *Vice Versa: Bisexuality and the eroticism of everyday life. New York Times Book Review* (July 9).

Kinsey, A. C., W. B. Pomeroy, and C. E. Martin. 1948. *Sexual Behavior in the Human Male*. Philadelphia and London: W.B. Saunders Company.

———. 1953. *Sexual Behavior in the Human Female*. Philadelphia and London: W.B. Saunders Company.

Klein, F. 1978. *The Bisexual Option*. New York: Priam Books.

Klein, F., and T. Wolf, eds. 1985. *Two Lives to Lead: Bisexuality in men and women*. New York: Harrington Park Press.

Masson, ed. and trans. 1985. *Freud S.: The complete letters of Sigmund Freud to Wilhelm Fliess 1887–1904*. Cambridge, Massachusetts: Harvard University Press.

McFarquhar, L. 1994. Review of *Vice Versa: Bisexuality and the eroticism of everyday life. The Nation* (July 24).

Mead, M. 1975. Bisexuality: What's it all about? *Redbook* (January).

Munt, S. 1995. The lesbian *flâneur.* In *Mapping Desire: Geographies of sexualities*. Edited by David Bell and Gill Valentine. London and New York: Routledge.

Off Pink Collective. 1988. *Bisexual Lives*. London: Off Pink Publishing.

Richards, A. ed. 1977. Three essays on the theory of sexuality. In *The Penguin Freud Library Volume 7: On Sexuality.* London: Penguin Books.

Richards, A. ed. 1993. Hysterical phantasies and their relation to bisexuality and A child is being beaten. In *The Penguin Freud Library Volume 10: On Psychopathology.* London: Penguin Books.

Rose, S., and C. Stevens et al, eds. 1994. *Bisexual Horizons*. London: Lawrence and Wishart.

Scott, J. 1992. Experience. In *Feminists theorize the political.* Edited by Judith Butler and Joan Scott. London and New York: Routledge.

Sedgwick, E. 1995. Shame in the cybernetic fold: Reading Silvan Tomkins. *Critical Inquiry* (winter).

Stekel, W. 1934. *Bisexual Love*. New York: Physicians and Surgeons Book Co.

Tucker, N., ed. 1995. *Bisexual Politics*. New York: The Haworth Press.

Upton, D. 1988. White and black landscapes in eighteenth-century Virginia. In *Material Life in America, 1600–1860.* Edited by Blair St. George. Boston: Northeastern University Press.

Weise, E. R. ed. 1992. *Closer to Home: Bisexuality and feminism*. Seattle: Seal Press.

Weisser, S. O., and J. Fleischner, eds. 1994. *Feminist Nightmares: Women at odds*. New York: New York University Press.

White, E. 1995. Review of *Vice Versa: Bisexuality and the eroticism of everyday life. New Yorker* (July 17).

Wolff, C. 1977. *Bisexuality—A Study*. London: Quartet.

Domestic Dykes, pages 163–68

Adler, S., and J. Brenner. 1992. Gender and space: Lesbians and gay men in the city. *International Journal of Urban and Regional Research* 16(1).

Bell, D. 1991. Insignificant others: Lesbian and gay geographies. *Area* 23(4).

Castells, M. 1983. *The City and the Grassroots: A crosscultural theory of urban social movements*. London: Edward Arnold.

Egerton, J. 1990. Out but not down: Lesbians' experience of housing. *Feminist Review* 36.

Kennedy, E. L., and M. D. Davis. 1993. *Boots of Leather, Slippers of Gold: The history of a lesbian community*. New York: Routledge.

Kitzinger, C. 1987. *The Social Construction of Lesbianism*. Newbury Park, California: Sage Publications.

Knopp, L. 1987. Social theory, social movements and public policy: Recent accomplishments of the gay and lesbian movements in Minneapolis, Minnesota. *International Journal of Urban and Regional Research* 11.

———. 1990. Some theoretical implications of gay involvement in an urban land market. *Political Geography Quarterly* 9(4).

———. 1992. Sexuality and the spatial dynamics of capitalism. *Environment and Planning D—Society and Space* 10.

Lauria, M., and L. Knopp. 1985. Toward an analysis of the role of gay communities in the urban renaissance. *Urban Geography* 6(2).

Massey, D. 1993. Questions of locality. *Geography* 78.

Ponse, B. 1978. *Identities in the Lesbian World: The social construction of self.* Westport, Connecticut: Greenwood Press.

Ross, B. 1990. The house that Jill built: Lesbian feminist organising in Toronto, 1976–1980. *Feminist Review* 35.

Stein, A. 1993. *Sisters, Sexperts, Queers: Beyond the lesbian nation.* New York: Plume.

Valentine, G. 1993. Desperately seeking Susan: A geography of lesbian friendships. *Area* 25(2).

Wolf, D. G. 1979. *The Lesbian Community.* Berkeley: University of California Press.

Wolfe, S. J., and J. Penelope. 1993. *Sexual Practice/Textual Theory: Lesbian cultural criticism.* Cambridge, Massachusetts: Blackwell Publishers.

Queer Zones and Enclaves, pages 171–75

Anderson, J. 1996. The shifting stage of politics: New medieval and postmodern territorialities? *Environment and Planning D* 14.

Davis, M. 1992. In LA, burning all illusions—Urban America sees its future. *The Nation* 254(21).

———. 1992. The LA inferno. *Socialist Review* 22(1).

———. 1993. Who killed LA: A political autopsy. *new left review* 197.

———. 1993. Who killed LA: part two: The verdict is given. *new left review* 199.

———. 1994. The suburban nightmare; while older suburbs experience many problems of the inner city, "edge cities" now offer a new escape. *Los Angeles Times* 113 (October 23).

Delany, P. 1994. Vancouver as a postmodern city. In *Vancouver: Representing the postmodern city.* Edited by Paul Delany. Vancouver: Arsenal Pulp Press.

Drucker, P. 1996. In the tropics there is no sin: Sexuality and gay-lesbian movements in the Third World. *new left review* 218.

Groth, P. 1994. San Francisco: Third and Howard—Skid Row and the limits of architecture. In *Streets: Critical perspectives on public space.* Edited by Zeynep Çelik, Diane Favro, and Richard Ingersoll. Berkeley: University of California Press.

Knopp, L. 1990. Exploiting the rent-gap: The theoretical significance of using illegal appraisal schemes to encourage gentrification in New Orleans. *Urban Geography* 11.

———. 1990. Some theoretical implications of gay involvement in an urban land market. *Political Geography Quarterly* 9.

———. 1992. Sexuality and the spatial dynamics of capitalism. *Environment and Planning D—Society and Space* 10.

Lauria, M., and L. Knopp. 1985. Toward an analysis of the role of gay communities in the urban renaissance. *Urban Geography* 6(2).

Patton, C. 1990. *Inventing AIDS.* New York: Routledge.

Smith, N., and C. Katz. 1993. Grounding metaphor: Towards a spatialized politics. In *Place and the Politics of Identity.* Edited by Michael Keith and Steve Pile. New York: Routledge.

Soja, E. W. 1995. Heterotopologies: A remembrance of other spaces in the Citadel-LA. In *Postmodern Cities and Spaces.* Edited by Sophie Watson and Katherine Gibson. Cambridge, Massachusetts: Blackwell Publishers.

Whittle, S. 1994. Consuming differences: The collaboration of the gay body with the cultural state. In *The Margins of the City: Gay men's urban lives.* Edited by Stephen Whittle. Brookfield, Vermont: Ashgate Publishing.

San Francisco, pages 177–96

Bawer, B. 1993. *A Place at the Table: The gay individual in American society*. New York: Poseidon.

Califia, P. 1982. A personal view of the history of the lesbian s/m community and movement in San Francisco. In *Coming to Power: Writings and graphics on lesbian s/m*. Edited by SAMOIS. Boston: Alyson Publications.

———. 1995. Dangerous tongues. In *Forbidden Passages: Writings banned in Canada*. Pittsburgh and San Francisco: Cleis Press.

Delany, S. R. 1975. *Dhalgren*. New York: Bantam Books.

———. 1979. *Tales of Nevèrÿon*. New York: Bantam Books.

———. 1985. *Flight from Nevèrÿon*. New York: Bantam Books.

Duggan, L. 1995. Censorship in the name of feminism. In *Sex Wars: Sexual dissent and political culture*. Edited by Lisa Duggan and Nan D. Hunter. New York: Routledge.

Rubin, G. 1982. The leather menace: Comments on politics and s/m. In *Coming to Power: Writings and graphics on lesbian s/m*. Boston: Alyson Publications.

———. 1984. Thinking Sex: Notes for a radical theory of the politics of sexuality. In *Pleasure and Danger: Exploring female sexuality*. Edited by Carole S. Vance. New York: Routledge.

———. 1991. The Catacombs: A temple of the butthole. In *Leatherfolk: Radical sex, people, politics, and practice*. Edited by Mark Thompson. Boston: Alyson Publications.

Weeks, J. 1977. *Coming Out: Homosexual politics in Britain, from the nineteenth century to the present*. London: Quartet Books.

———. 1981. *Sex, Politics, and Society: The regulation of sexuality since 1800*. London: Longman Group.

———. 1985. *Sexuality and Its Discontents: Meaning, myths, and modern sexualities*. London: Routledge and Kegan Paul.

Gay Male Places of Mexico City, pages 197–212

Bell, D. 1991. Insignificant others: Lesbian and gay geographies. *Area* 23(4).

Carrier, J. 1985. Mexican male bisexuality. *Journal of Homosexuality* 11(1/2).

Cockburn, R. 1988. AIDS spells stop on the Reeperbahn: The geography of prostitution. *Geographical Magazine* LX(4).

Curtis, J., and D. Arreola. 1991. Zonas de tolerancia on the northern Mexican border. *Geographical Review* 81(3).

Ferrari, M., ed. 1993. *Ferrari's Places for Men*. Phoenix: Ferrari Publications.

Jackson, P. 1989. Maps of meaning. In *An Introduction to Cultural Geography*. London: Unwin Hyman.

Knopp, L. 1989. Social consequences of homosexuality. *Geographical, The Royal Geographical Society* 62(5).

Lamundsen, I. 1991. *Homosexuality, Society, and the State*. Mexico: Quinto Sol.

Lerma, J. 1993. La Coyotera: Quieren borrar la mala imagen (La Coyotera: Getting rid of prostitution in Monterrey). *El Norte* 27(8).

Murray, S. 1991. Homosexual occupations in Mesoamerica. *Journal of Homosexuality* 21(4).

Taylor, C. 1985. Mexican male homosexual interaction in public contexts. *Journal of Homosexuality* 11(3/4).

Zendejas, V. 1993. La prostitución masculina en el centro de la Ciudad de México (Hustlers in downtown Mexico City). La Jornada 30(10).

Queer and Gendered Housing, pages 213–32

Adam, B. 1978. *The Survival of Domination*. New York: Elsevier North-Holland, Inc.

Adler, S., and J. Brenner. 1992. Gender and space: Lesbians and gay men in the city. *International Journal of Urban and Regional Research* 16(1).

Altman, D. 1982. *The Homosexualization of America: The Americanization of the homosexual*. New York: St. Martin's Press.

Anlin, S. 1989. *Out but Not Down! The Housing Needs of Lesbians*. London: Homeless Action.

Bawer, B. 1993. *A Place at the Table: The gay individual in American society*. New York: Poseidon.

Beaudry, M. 1988. Joe's. *Vancouver Magazine* (November).

Bouthillette, A. 1994. Gentrification by gay male communities: A case study of Toronto's Cabbagetown. In *The Margins of the City: Gay men's urban lives*. Edited by Stephen Whittle. Aldershot, England: Ashgate Publishing Ltd.

Castells, M. 1983. *The City and the Grassroots: A crosscultural theory of urban social movements*. Berkeley: University of California Press.

Edward, T. 1993. *Erotics and Politics: Gay male sexuality, masculinity, and feminism*. London: Routledge.

Fairclough, T. 1985. The gay community of Vancouver's West End: The geography of a modern urban phenomenon. Paper submitted to the Department of Geography, University of British Columbia, in partial fulfillment of the requirements for a Masters of Arts.

Holcomb, B. 1981. *Revitalizing Cities*. Washington, D. C.: Association of American Geographers.

Humphreys, R. A. L. 1975. *Tearoom Trade: Impersonal sex in public places*. Chicago: Aldine.

Jay, K., ed. 1979. *Lavender Culture*. New York: Jove/HBJ.

Knopp, L. 1995. Sexuality and urban space: A framework for analysis. In *Mapping Desire: Geographies of sexualities*. Edited by David Bell and Gill Valentine. London and New York: Routledge.

Lauria, M., and L. Knopp. 1985. Toward an analysis of the role of gay communities in the urban renaissance. *Urban Geography* 6(2).

Levine, M. 1979. Gay ghetto. *Journal of Homosexuality* 4.

Lockard, D. 1985. The lesbian community: An anthropological approach. *Journal of Homosexuality* 11.

McNee, B. 1984. If you are squeamish . . .. *East Lakes Geographers* 19.

Moore Milroy, B. 1991. Taking stock of planning, space and gender. *Journal of Planning Literature* 6(1).

Murray, S. O. 1979. The institutional elaboration of a quasi-ethnic community. *International Review of Modern Sociology* 9.

Rothenberg, T. 1995. "And she told two friends": Lesbians creating urban social space. In *Mapping Desire: Geographies of sexualities*. Edited by David Bell and Gill Valentine. London and New York: Routledge.

Serafin, B. 1994. Cultural workers and moslem hats: Notes on Commercial Drive. In *Vancouver: Representing the Postmodern City*. Edited by Paul Delany. Vancouver: Arsenal Pulp Press.

Ward, D. 1990. Treatment of lesbians leaves patrons and coffee steaming. *Vancouver Sun* (September 21).

Warren, C. A. 1974. *Identity and Community in the Gay World*. New York: John Wiley and Sons.

White, B. 1980. East side story. *Western Living* (May).

Whittle, S. 1994. Consuming difference: The collaboration of the gay body with the cultural state. In *The Margins of the City: Gay men's urban lives*. Edited by Stephen Whittle. Aldershot, England: Ashgate Publishing Ltd.

Wilson, D. 1990. Vancouver coffee-shop owner embroiled in row over kissing customers. *Globe and Mail* (Toronto) (September 22).

Wolf, D. G. 1979. *The Lesbian Community*. Berkeley: University of California Press.

Wolfe, M. 1992. Invisible women in invisible places: Lesbians, lesbian bars, and the social production of people/environment relationships. *Architecture and Behavior* 8.

The Queer Nation Acts Up, pages 233–74

Altman, D. 1986. *AIDS in the Mind of America: The social, political, and psychological impact of a new epidemic*. New York: Anchor Press.

Baldwin, J. 1962. *The Fire Next Time*. New York: Dial Press.

Banham, R. 1984. *Los Angeles: The architecture of four ecologies*. New York: Penguin Books.

Bly, R. 1991. *Iron John*. Reading, Massachusetts: Addison-Wesley.

Carter, E., and S. Watney. 1989. *Taking Liberties*. London: Serpent's Tail.

Comstock, G. D. 1991. *Violence Against Lesbians and Gay Men*. New York: Columbia University Press.

Crimp, D., ed. 1988. *AIDS: Cultural Analysis, Cultural Activism*. Cambridge, Massachusetts: MIT Press.

Crimp, D., and A. Rolston. 1990. *AIDS demo graphics*. Seattle: Bay Press.

Davis, M. 1990. *City of Quartz: Excavating the future in Los Angeles.* New York: Verso.

Epstein, S. 1991. Democratic science? AIDS activism and the contested construction of knowledge. *Socialist Review* 21(2) (April–June).

Foucault, M. 1975. *The Birth of the Clinic: An archaeology of medical perception.* New York: Vintage.

Gilman, S. 1988. *Disease and Representation.* Ithaca: Cornell University Press.

Grmek, M. 1990. *History of AIDS.* Princeton: Princeton University Press.

Grover, J. Z. 1989. The necessity of metaphor. In *Taking Liberties: AIDS and cultural politics.* Edited by Erica Carter and Simon Watney. London: Serpent's Tail/ICA.

Isherwood, C. 1945. *The Berlin Stories.* New York: New Directions.

———. 1964. *A Single Man.* New York: Farrar, Straus and Giroux.

———. 1976. *Christopher and His Kind.* New York: Farrar, Straus and Giroux.

Kanouse, D., et al. 1991. AIDS-Related Knowledge, Attitudes, Beliefs, and Behaviors in Los Angeles County. Santa Monica: Rand Corporation.

Koonz, C. 1987. *Mothers in the Fatherland. Women, the family, and Nazi politics.* New York: St. Martin's Press.

Lamber, G. 1959. *The Slide Area.* New York: Viking Press.

McBride, D. 1991. *From TB to AIDS: Epidemics among urban blacks since 1900.* Albany: SUNY Press.

McKenzie, N., ed. *The AIDS Reader.* New York: Meridian Press.

McWilliams, C. 1988. *Southern California: An island on the land.* Salt Lake City: Peregrine Smith Books.

Patton, C. 1985. *Sex and Germs: The politics of AIDS.* Boston: South End Press.

———. 1990. *Inventing AIDS.* New York: Routledge.

Showalter, E. 1990. *Sexual Anarchy.* New York: Viking Penguin.

Sontag, S. 1978. *Illness as Metaphor.* New York: Farrar, Straus and Giroux.

———. 1988. *AIDS and Its Metaphors.* New York: Farrar, Straus and Giroux.

Starr, K. 1985. *Inventing the Dream: California through the progressive era.* New York: Oxford University Press.

Timmons, S. 1990. *The Trouble With Harry.* Boston: Alyson Publications.

Wachter, R. M. 1991. *The Fragile Coalition: Scientists, activists, and AIDS.* New York: St. Martin's Press.

Wojnarowicz, D. 1991. Post Cards from America: X-Rays from Hell. In *Close to the Knives: A memoir of disintegration.* New York: Vintage.

Constructing Manchester's "New Urban Village," pages 275–92

Adler, S., and J. Brenner. 1992. Gender and space: Lesbians and gay men in the city. *International Journal of Urban and Regional Research* 16(1).

Castells, M. 1983. *The City and the Grassroots: A crosscultural theory of urban social movements.* Berkeley: University of California Press.

Cooper, D. 1994. *Sexing the City: Lesbian and gay politics within the activist state.* London: Rivers Oram Press.

Corton, S. 1993. Anal Treat: Manchester's Gay Village—Dissection of a "Community." Dissertation for Geography BSc. On file, School of Geography, Manchester University.

de Certeau, M. 1984. *The Practice of Everyday Life.* Translated by Steven F. Rendall. Berkeley: University of California Press.

Evans, D. T. 1993. *Sexual Citizenship.* London: Routledge.

Evans, K., and P. Fraser. 1993. Difference in the city: Locating marginal use of public space. Paper presented to the BSA conference Research Imaginations, Essex, April.

Evans, K., P. Fraser, and I. Taylor. 1993. Going to town: Routine accommodation and routine anxieties in respect of public space and public facilities in two cities in the north of England. Paper presented to Conference on the Public Sphere, Parkers Hotel, Manchester, January.

Gyford, J. 1985. *The Politics of Local Socialism.* London: Allen & Unwin.

Hammill, M. 1994. The city and subculture: A study of Manchester's Gay Village. Unpublished B.A. (Planning) Dissertation. On file, Department of Planning, Manchester University.

Hindle, P. 1994. Gay communities and gay space in the city. In *The Margins of the City: Gay men's urban lives*. Edited by Stephen Whittle. Aldershot, England: Ashgate Publishing Ltd.

Horsfall, A. 1988. Battling for Wolfenden. In *Radical Records: Thirty years of lesbian and gay history*. Edited by Bob Cant and Susan Hemmings. London: Routledge.

Lansley, S., S. Goss, and C. Wolmar. 1989. *Councils in Conflict: The rise and fall of the municipal left*. London: MacMillan.

Lauria, M., and L. Knopp. 1985. Toward an analysis of the role of gay communities in the urban renaissance. *Urban Geography* 6(2).

Lovatt, A., ed. 1994. The 24-Hour City: Selected papers from the First National Conference on the Night-time Economy. Manchester: Manchester Institute for Popular Culture, Manchester Metropolitan University.

Mackintosh, M., and H. Wainwright, eds. 1987. *The Taste of Power: The politics of local economies*. London: Verso.

Manchester City Council. 1991. Strategies for the Gay Village Area. Minutes of meeting, April 15.

Manchester City Council Planning Department. 1991. *City Planning News* N(2).

Manchester 2002. 1994. *Commonwealth Games Bid*. On file, marketing department of Manchester City Council.

O'Connor, J. 1994. Lifestyle and cultural consumption in the city. In *ESRC (UK Economic and Social Research Council) End of Award Report* (R000-23-3075). On file, Manchester Institute for Popular Culture, Manchester Metropolitan University.

O'Connor, J., and D. Wynne. 1993. Margins to the centre: Cultural production in the post-industrial city. Working Paper 7, Manchester Institute for Popular Culture, Manchester Metropolitan University.

Peck, J., and M. Emmerich. 1992. Recession, restructuring, and the greater Manchester labour market: An empirical overview. SPA Working Paper 17, School of Geography, Manchester University, July 17.

———. 1993. Manufacturing Manchester? Industrial and labour market restructuring in greater Manchester. Working Paper 4, Manchester International Centre for Labour Studies.

Thrift, N., and P. Williams, eds. 1987. *Class and Space: The making of urban society*. London: Routledge and Kegan Paul.

Wainwright, H. 1987. *Labour: A tale of two parties*. London: Hogarth.

Weightman, B. A. 1980. Gay bars as private places. *Landscape* 24.

Whittle, S. 1994. Consuming differences: The collaboration of the gay body with the cultural state. In *The Margins of the City: Gay men's urban lives*. Edited by Stephen Whittle. Aldershot, England: Ashgate Publishing Ltd.

Placemaking and the Dialectics of Public and Private, pages 295–99

Boyer, M. C. 1994. *The City of Collective Memory: Its historical imagery and architectural entertainments*. Cambridge, Massachusetts: MIT Press.

Luke, T. W. 1994. Placing power, siting space—The politics of global and local in the new world order. *Environment and Planning D—Society and Space* 12(5).

Murphy, K. 1995. Walking the queer city. *Radical History Review* 62 (spring).

Namaste, K. 1996. Genderbashing: Sexuality, gender, and the regulation of public space. *Environment and Planning D—Society and Space* 14.

Relph, E. 1976. *Place and Placelessness*. London: Pion.

Robbins, M. 1992. *Angles of Incidence*. New York: Princeton University Press.

Wilson, E. 1984. Bodies in public and private. In *Public Bodies—Private States: New views on photography, representation and gender*. Edited by Jane Brettle, and Sally Rice. Manchester, England: Manchester University Press.

Invisible Women in Invisible Places, pages 301–24

Barrett, M. B. 1990. *Invisible Lives: The truth about millions of women-loving women*. New York: Harper and Row.

Bennet, J. M., E. A. Clark, J. F. O'Barr, B. A. Vilen, and S. Westphal-Wihl, eds. 1989. *Sisters and Workers in the Middle Ages*. Chicago: University of Chicago Press.

Bérubé, A. 1979. Lesbians and gay men in early San Francisco. Notes towards a social history of lesbians and gay men in America. New York: Lesbian Herstory Archives Unpublished Papers File.

———. 1991. *Coming Out under Fire: The history of gay men and women in World War II.* New York: Plume, Penguin.

Bowers v. Hardwick. 1986. 478 U.S. 176, 197.

Bradley, E., and M. Wolfe. 1987. Where do the 64-year-old Jewish Latina lesbians live? Diversity of people as an environment issue. *Public environments.* Proceedings of the 18th Conference of the Environmental Design Research Association. Edited by J. Harvey and D. Henning. Washington, D. C.: EDRA.

Brown, J. C. 1986. *Immodest Acts: The life of a lesbian nun.* New York: Oxford University Press.

Bulkin, E. 1980. An old dyke's tale: An interview with Doris Lunder. *Conditions* II(3).

Bullough, V., and B. Bullough. 1977. Lesbianism in the 1920s and 1930s: A newfound study. *Signs* 2(4).

Castells, M. 1983. *The City and the Grassroots: A crosscultural theory of urban social movements.* Berkeley: University of California Press.

Chauncey, G. 1989. From sexual inversion to homosexual: The changing medical concept of female "deviance." In *Passion and Power: Sexuality in History.* Edited by K. Peiss, C. Simmons, and R. A. Padgug. Philadelphia: Temple University Press.

Cott, N. 1977. *The Bonds of Womanhood: "Woman's sphere" in New England, 1780–1835.* New Haven: Yale University Press.

Davidson, J. W., and M. H. Lytle. 1982. 2d ed. *After the Fact: The art of historical detection.* New York: Knopf.

Davis, K. B. 1929. *Factors in the Sex Life of Twenty-Two Hundred Women.* New York: Harper and Row.

Davis, M., and E. L. Kennedy. 1989. Oral history and the study of sexuality in the lesbian community: Buffalo, New York, 1940–1960. In *Hidden from History: Reclaiming the gay and lesbian past.* Edited by M. B. Duberman, M. Vicinus, and G. Chauncey. New York: New American Library.

Dekker, R., and L. van der Pol. 1988. *The Tradition of Female Transvestism in Early Modern Europe.* London: Macmillan.

D'Emilio, J. 1983. *Sexual Politics, Sexual Communities: The making of a homosexual minority in the United States, 1940–1970.* Chicago: Chicago University Press.

D'Emilio, J., and E. Freedman. 1988. *Intimate Matters: A history of sexuality in America.* New York: Harper and Row.

Diamond, I., and L. Quinby. 1988. *Feminism and Foucault: Reflections on resistance.* Boston: Northeastern University Press.

Dreyfuss, H. L., and P. Rabinow. 1983. *Michel Foucault: Beyond structuralism and hermeneutics.* Chicago: University of Chicago Press.

Duggan, L. 1981. The social enforcement of heterosexuality and lesbian resistance in the 1920s. *Class, Race, and Sex: The dynamics of control.* Edited by A. Swerdlow and H. Lessinger. Boston: G. K. Hall.

Editors of the Harvard Law Review. 1990. *Sexual Orientation and the Law.* Cambridge, Massachusetts: Harvard University Press.

Evehard, M. 1986. Lesbian history: A history of change and disparity. In *Historical, Literary, and Erotic Aspects of Lesbianism.* Edited by M. Kehoe. London: Harrington Park Press.

Faderman, L. 1980. *Surpassing the Love of Men: Romantic friendship and love between women, from the Renaissance to the present.* London: Junction Books.

Ferguson, A. 1981. Patriarchy, sexual identity, and the sexual revolution. *Signs* 7 (autumn).

Ferrari, M., ed. 1992. *Places of Interest to Women.* Phoenix: Ferrari Publications.

Garber, E. 1989. A spectacle in color: The lesbian and gay subculture of jazz age Harlem. In *Hidden from History: Reclaiming the gay and lesbian past.* Edited by M. B. Duberman, M. Vicinus, and G. Chauncey. New York: New American Library.

Grahn, J. 1984. *Another Mother Tongue: Gay words, gay worlds.* Boston: Beacon Press.

Gray, J. F. n.d. Memories. *The Other Black Woman* 1(3).

Impact. 1980. The when and now of it; NAB 43 women, girl in bar raid. New York: Lesbian Herstory Archives Lesbian Bar File.

Kennedy, E. L., and M. D. Davis. 1989. The reproduction of butch-femme roles: A social constructionist approach. In *Passion and Power: Sexuality in history.* Edited by K. Peiss, C. Simmons, and R. Padgug. Philadelphia: Temple University Press.

Ladner, J., ed. 1973. *The Death of White Sociology.* New York: Random House.

Lait, J., and L. Mortimer. 1948. *New York Confidential.* New York: Crown Publishers.

Lerner, G. 1979. *The Majority Finds Its Past Placing Women in History*. New York: Oxford University Press.

Letter to Lesbian Herstory Archives. 1984. New York: Lesbian Herstory Archives Lesbian Bar File.

Letter to Lesbian Organizations. 1989. New York: Lesbian Herstory Archives Lesbian Bar File.

Levi, E. 1980. Why do women go to bars? *The Washington Blade* (May 29): 23. New York: Lesbian Herstory Archives Lesbian Bar File.

Manzo, L., and M. Wolfe. 1990. The social production of built forms, environmental settings and people/environment relationships. In *Culture, Space, and History.* Proceedings of the 11th Conference of the International Association for the Study of People and Their Surroundings. Edited by H. Pamir, V. Imamoglu, and N. Teymur. Ankara, Turkey: Middle Eastern Technical University.

Meyerowitz, J. J. 1988. *Women Adrift: Independent wage earners in Chicago, 1880–1930*. Chicago: University of Chicago Press.

Nestle, J. 1987. *A Restricted Country*. Ithaca, New York: Firebrand Press.

New York Times. 1992. Anti-gay crimes are reported on rise in 5 cities (March 19).

Pickett, H. 1984. Women's bar faces eviction in Chelsea. *New York City News* (May 16). New York: Lesbian Herstory Archives Lesbian Bar File.

Piess, K. 1986. *Cheap Amusements: Working women and leisure in turn-of-the-century New York*. Philadelphia: Temple University Press.

Rapp, R., and E. Ross. 1981. The twenties' backlash: Compulsory heterosexuality, the consumer family, and the waning of feminism. In *Class, Race, and Sex: The dynamics of control*. Edited by A. Swerdlow and H. Lessinger. Boston: G. K. Hall.

Rey, M. 1987. Parisian homosexuals create a lifestyle, 1700–1750: The police archives. In *'Tis Nature's Fault: Unauthorized sexuality during the Enlightenment*. Edited by R. Maccubbin, translated by Robert A. Day and Robert Welch. Cambridge, England: Cambridge University Press.

San Francisco Bay Guardian. 1979. Closed doors for the Peg's Place hearing (September 25). New York: Lesbian Herstory Archives Lesbian Bar File.

———. 1979. San Francisco women charge harassment (March 10). New York: Lesbian Herstory Archives Lesbian Bar File.

San Francisco Chronicle. 1958. That was no lady, that was . . . (September 1). New York: Lesbian Herstory Archives Lesbian Bar File.

San Francisco Lesbian & Gay History Project. 1989. She even chewed tobacco. *Hidden from History: Reclaiming the gay and lesbian past*. Edited by M. Duberman, M. Vicinus, and G. Chauncey. New York: New American Library.

Trouble with Bars. 1979. Poem in newspaper, source unknown. New York: Lesbian Herstory Archives Lesbian Bar File.

Trumbach, R. 1987. Sodomitical subcultures, sodomitical roles, and the gender revolution of the eighteenth century: The recent historiography. In *'Tis Nature's Fault: Unauthorized sexuality during the Enlightenment*. Edited by R. Maccubbin. Cambridge, England: Cambridge University Press.

———. 1989. Gender and the homosexual role in modern Western culture. In *Homosexuality, Which Homosexuality?* Edited by D. Altman, C. Vance, M. Vicinus, J. Weeks, et al. London and Uitgeverij, Amsterdam: GMP Publishers.

Truscott, L. 1969. Gay power comes to Sheridan Square. *Village Voice* (3 July).

———. 1969. Queen power: Fags against police in Stonewall bust. *Rat* (July).

Vicinus, M. 1989. They wonder to which sex I belong: The historical roots of modern lesbian identity. *Homosexuality, Which Homosexuality?* Edited by D. Altman, C. Vance, M. Vicinus, J. Weeks, et al. London; Uitgeverij, Amsterdam: GMP Publishers.

Waters, C. 1979. The trouble with women's bars. Newspaper article, source unknown. New York: Lesbian Herstory Archives Lesbian Bar File.

Weeks, J. 1991. *Against Nature: Essays on history, sexuality, and identity*. London: Rivers Oram Press.

Whitebread, H., ed. 1992. *I Know My Own Heart: The diaries of Anne Lister, 1791–1840*. New York: New York University Press.

Zoe, ed. 1991. Gaia's guide. East Haven, Connecticut: Inland Books Co.

Zorbaugh, H. W. 1929. *The gold coast and the slum: A sociological study of Chicago's Near Northside*. Chicago: University of Chicago Press.

Lesbian Spaces in Los Angeles, pages 325–37

Bouthillette, A. 1997. Queer and gendered housing: A tale of two neighbourhoods in Vancouver. In *Queers in Space: Communities, Public Places, Sites of Resistance.* Seattle: Bay Press.

Cassell, J. 1977. *A Group Called Women: Sisterhood and symbolism in the feminist movement.* New York: McKay.

Castells, M. 1983. *The City and the Grassroots: A crosscultural theory of urban social movements.* Berkeley: University of California Press.

Cavin, S. 1990. The invisible army of women: Lesbian social protests, 1969–1988. In *Women and Social Protest.* Edited by G. West and R. Blumberg. New York: Oxford University Press.

Cheney, J. 1985. *Lesbian Land.* Minneapolis: Word Weavers.

Hay, H. 1996. *Radically Gay: Gay liberation in the words of its founder.* Boston: Beacon Press.

Herdt, G., ed. 1992. *Gay Culture in America.* Boston: Beacon Press.

Herrell, R. 1992. The symbolic strategies of Chicago's Gay and Lesbian Pride Day parade. In *Gay Culture in America: Essays from the field.* Edited by Gilbert Herdt. Boston: Beacon Press.

Hoagland, S., and J. Penelope, eds. 1988. *For Lesbians Only.* London: Onlywomen Press.

Kennedy, E. L., and M. D. Davis. 1994. *Boots of Leather, Slippers of Gold: The history of a lesbian community.* New York: Penguin Books.

Lockard, D. 1985. The lesbian community: An anthropological approach. *Journal of Homosexuality* 11(3/4).

Lyman, S., and M. Scott. 1970. In *Social Psychology Through Symbolic Interaction.* Edited by G. Stone and H. Farberman. Waltham, Massachusetts: Xerox College Publishing.

Martin, D. 1970. Good-bye, my alienated brothers. In *Long Road To Freedom: The advocate history of the gay and lesbian movement.* Edited by M. Thompson. New York: St. Martin's Press.

Nestle, J. 1987. *A Restricted Country.* Ithaca, New York: Firebrand Books.

Raphael, S. 1974. Coming out: The emergence of the movement lesbian. Dissertation. Department of Sociology, Case Western Reserve University.

Raven, A. 1977. Through the peephole: Toward a lesbian sensibility in art. *Chrysalis* 14.

Rothenberg, T. 1995. "And she told two friends": Lesbians creating urban social space. In *Mapping Desire: Geographies of sexualities.* Edited by David Bell and Gill Valentine. London and New York: Routledge.

Schon, D. 1971. *Beyond the Stable State.* New York: Norton.

Shugar, D. 1995. *Separatism and Women's Community.* Lincoln: University of Nebraska Press.

Weisen Cook, B. 1979. The historical denial of lesbianism. *Radical History Review* 20.

Zimmerman, B. 1990. *The Safe Sea of Women: Lesbian fiction, 1969–1989.* Boston: Beacon Press.

Leather Nights in the Woods, pages 339–55

Blachford, G. 1981. Male dominance and the gay world. In *The Making of the Modern Homosexual.* Edited by K. Plummer. London: Hutchinson.

Brodsky, J. 1987. A retrospective ethnography of the Mineshaft. *Homosexuality, Which Homosexuality?* International Conference on Gay and Lesbian Studies, December 1987. *Social Sciences*, Vol. 1. Amsterdam: Free University.

Corzine, J., and R. Kirby. 1977. Cruising the truckers: Sexual encounters in a highway rest area. *Urban Life* 6(2).

de Leeuw, A. W. D. 1991. *Het mollebos, een homo-baan.* Notitie Korps Rijkspolitie District Utrecht Groep Driebergen. Driebergen, 2 August. Report by a squad leader of the national Dutch police force.

Delph, E. W. 1978. *The Silent Community: Public homosexual encounters.* Beverly Hills, California: Sage Publications.

Humphreys, R. A. L. 1974. *Tearoom Trade: A study of homosexual encounters in public places.* London: Duckworth.

Kamel, G. W. L. 1983. Leathersex: Meaningful aspects of gay sadomasochism. In *Studies in Sadomasochism.* Edited by T. Weinberg and G. W. L. Kamel. New York: Prometheus.

Lee, J. A. 1983. The social organization of sexual risk. In *Studies in Sadomasochism.* Edited by T. Weinberg and G. W. L. Kamel. New York: Prometheus.

———. 1990. Cruising: Impersonal sex and casual sex. In *Encyclopedia of Homosexuality.* Vol. 1. Edited by W. R. Dynes. New York, London: Garland.

van Lieshout, M. 1989. Nozems, rockers, homo's. Over de stoere bad boy als homoseksuele icoon. *Homologie* 11(6).

Ponte, M. R. 1974. Life in a parking lot: An ethnography of a homosexual drive-in. In *Deviance: Field studies and self-disclosures*. Edited by Jerry Jacobs. Palo Alto, California: National Press Books.

Riemer, J. W. 1977. Varieties of opportunistic research. *Urban Life* 5(4).

Rubin, G. 1991. The Catacombs: A temple of the butthole. In *Leatherfolk: Radical sex, people, politics, and practice.* Edited by Mark Thompson. Boston: Alyson Publications.

Troiden, R. R. 1974. Homosexual encounters in a highway rest stop. In *Sexual Deviance and Sexual Deviants*. Edited by E. Goode and R. R. Troiden. New York: Morrow.

Walsh-Bowers, R. T., and S. J. Parlour. 1992. Researcher-participant relationships in journal reports on gay men and lesbian women. *Journal of Homosexuality* 23(4).

Weinberg, M. S., and C. J. Williams. 1975. Gay baths and the social organization of impersonal sex. *Social Problems* 23(2).

Queer Spaces in New York City, pages 357–70

Boyer, M. C. 1996. *The City of Collective Memory: Its historical imagery and architectural entertainments*. Cambridge, Massachusetts: MIT Press.

Butler, C. 1994. Queer space. *Art+Text* (September).

Chauncey, G. 1994. *Gay New York: Gender, urban culture, and the making of the gay male world, 1890–1940*. New York: BasicBooks.

Duberman, M. 1993. *Stonewall*. New York: Dutton.

Emerson, B. 1995. Uncovering Buttermilk Bottom. *The Atlanta Journal/The Atlanta Constitution* (September 14)

Fox, C. 1995. "City site works" successful in some spots, isn't in others. *The Atlanta Journal/The Atlanta Constitution* (September 19).

Galeano, E. 1982. *Memories of Fire: Genesis*. Translated by Cedric Belfrage. New York: Pantheon.

———. 1984. *Memories of Fire: Faces and masks*. Translated by Cedric Belfrage. New York: Pantheon.

———. 1988. *Memories of Fire: Century of the wind*. Translated by Cedric Belfrage. New York: Pantheon.

Harris, E. 1992. No choice: Elise Harris reviews repro rights representations. *QW* 36 (July 12).

Hayden, D. 1995. *The Power of Place: Urban landscapes as public history*. Cambridge, Massachusetts: MIT Press.

Holloway, L. 1992. Lower Manhattan Journal—Art and history prove a volatile mix. *New York Times* (August 27).

Muschamp, H. 1994. Designing a framework for diversity. *New York Times* (June 19).

OLGAD. 1994. *Guide to Lesbian and Gay New York Historical Landmarks*. New York: OLGAD.

REPOhistory. 1993. *The Lower Manhattan Sign Project*. New York: REPOhistory.

Sullivan. 1994. Design community celebrates gay rights. *Architecture* (August).

Walton, R. 1995. Bottoms up—REPOhistory exhumes Buttermilk Bottom. *Creative Loafing* (September 2).

Making Room, pages 373–80

Betsky, A. 1995. *Building Sex: Men, women, architecture, and the construction of sexuality*. New York: William Morrow.

Colomina, B. 1994. *Privacy and Publicity: Modern architecture as mass media*. Cambridge, Massachusetts: MIT Press.

Deleuze, G., and F. Guattari. 1987. *A Thousand Plateaus: Capitalism and schizophrenia*. Translated by Brian Massumi. Minneapolis: University of Minnesota Press.

Duggan, L. 1995. Queering the state. In *Sex Wars: Sexual dissent and political culture*. New York: Routledge.

Gianni, B., S. Weir, E. Sedgwick, and M. Moon. 1995. Queerying (single family) space. *Sites* 26.

Markus, T. A. 1993. *Buildings and Power: Freedom and control in the origin of modern building types*. New York: Routledge.

Plant, S. 1992. *The Most Radical Gesture: The situationist international in a postmodern age*. London: Routledge.

Sanders, J. 1996. Introduction. In *STUD: Architectures of masculinity*. New York: Princeton University Press.

Scott, D. 1994. Jungle fever—Black gay identity politics, white dick, and the utopian bedroom. *GLQ* 1(3).

Silver, K. E. 1996. Master bedrooms, master narratives: Home, homosexuality, and postwar art. In *Not At Home: The suppression of domesticity in modern art and architecture*. London: Thames and Hudson.

Tschumi, B. 1996. *Architecture and Disjunction*. Cambridge, Massachusetts: MIT Press.

Watson, S., and K. Gibson. 1995. Postmodern politics and planning: A postscript. In *Postmodern Cities and Spaces*. Edited by Sophie Watson and Katherine Gibson. Cambridge, Massachusetts: Blackwell Publishers.

Wigley, M. 1993. *The Architecture of Deconstruction: Derrida's haunt*. Cambridge, Massachusetts: MIT Press.

Having Something to Wear, pages 381–90

Adler, S., and J. Brenner. 1992. Gender and space: Lesbians and gay men in the city. *International Journal of Urban and Regional Research* 16(1).

Berger, J. 1972. *Ways of Seeing*. New York: Penguin Books.

Boyer, M. C. 1993. Straight down Christopher Street: A tale of the oldest street in Greenwich Village. In *Greenwich Village: Culture and counterculture*. Edited by Rich Beard and Leslie Cohen Berlowitz. New Brunswick, New Jersey: Rutgers University Press.

Castells, M. 1983. *The City and the Grassroots: A crosscultural theory of urban social movements*. Berkeley: University of California Press.

Chauncey, G. 1994. *Gay New York: Gender, urban culture, and the making of the gay male world, 1890–1940*. New York: BasicBooks.

D'Emilio, J. 1993. Capitalism and gay identity. In *The Lesbian and Gay Studies Reader*. Edited by Henry Abelove, Michèle Aina Barale, and David M. Halperin. New York: Routledge.

Foucault, M. 1977. *Discipline and Punishment: The birth of the prison*. Translated by Alan Sheridan. New York: Pantheon Books.

Leach, W. 1993. *Land of Desire: Merchants, power, and the rise of a New American culture*. New York: Vintage.

Murphy, K. 1995. Walking the queer city. *Radical History Review* 62 (spring).

White, E. 1933. *The Beautiful Room is Empty*. New York: Quality Paperback Book.

The Meaning at the Wall, pages 391–406

Ackerley, M. H. 1893. *James Everard's Turkish, Roman and Electric Baths*. Marketing Brochure. Private Collection, New York City. Exhibited in *Becoming Visible: The Legacy of Stonewall,* at The New York Public Library, June 18 to September 24, 1994.

Bersani, L. 1988. Is the rectum a grave? In *AIDS: Cultural Analysis, Cultural Activism*. Edited by Douglas Crimp. Cambridge, Massachusetts: MIT Press.

Bolton, R., J. Vincke, and R. Mak. 1994. Gay Baths Revisited. *GLQ* 1(3).

Brook, S. 1985. Get knotted. In *New York Days, New York Nights*. New York: Atheneum.

Brown, M. 1995. Sex, scale, and the new urban politics. In *Mapping Desire: Geographies of sexualities*. Edited by David Bell and Gill Valentine. London and New York: Routledge.

Chauncey, G. 1994. *Gay New York: Gender, urban culture, and the making of the gay male world, 1890-1940*. New York: BasicBooks.

Gay Newspaper (New York City journal). 1969–1974. On file at the National Museum and Archive of Lesbian and Gay History. New York: The Center. Vol. 1–5, a total of 113 issues, from December to June.

Gayellow Pages. 1982. *The Gayellow Pages: The national edition* 12. New York: Renaissance House.

Glassberg, D. 1979. The design of reform: The public bath movement in America. *Journal of American Studies* 20(2) (fall).

Grosz, E. 1992. Bodies-cities. In *Sexuality and Space*. Edited by Beatriz Colomina. New York: Princeton Architectural Press.

Hoffman, M. 1968. *The Gay World: Male homosexuality and the social creation of evil.* New York: BasicBooks.

Holleran, A. 1978. *Dancer from the Dance.* New York: William Morrow.

Katz, J. N. *Gay/Lesbian Almanac.* New York: Harper and Row.

Knopp, L. 1995. Sexuality and urban space. In *Mapping Desire: Geographies of sexualities.* Edited by David Bell and Gill Valentine. London and New York: Routledge.

New York Times. 1994. Bruce Mailman obituary (June 12).

Peters, B. 1994. The sexual revolution Mailman delivered. *OUT* (7/8).

Read, K. E. 1980. *Other Voices.* Novato, California: Chandler and Sharp Publishers Inc.

Ricco, J. P. 1994–1995. Coming together. *a|r|c* 5.

Sadownick, D. 1993. The new sex radicals. *LA Weekly* 15(31) (July 2–8).

Steam. 1994. Listings: Spring '94. *Steam: A quarterly journal for men* 2(1) (spring).

Warner, M. 1995. Why gay men are having unsafe sex again. *The Village Voice* 15(5) (January 31).

Weinberg, J. 1993. *Speaking for Vice.* New Haven: Yale University Press.

Weinberg, M. S., and C. J. Williams. 1979. Gay baths and the social organization of impersonal sex. In *Gay Men: The sociology of male homosexuality.* Edited by Martin P. Levine. New York: Harper and Row Publishers.

Williams, M. T. 1991. *Washing "The Great Unwashed": Public baths in urban America, 1840-1920.* Columbus: Ohio State University Press.

Young, P. D. 1973. So you're planning to spend a night at the tubs. *Rolling Stone* 128 (February 15).

This Is about People Dying, pages 407–37

Clausen, J. 1994. Review of *My American History: Lesbian and gay life during the Reagan/Bush years. The Nation* 259(16) (November 14).

Duggan, L. 1995. Banned in the U.S.A: What the *Hardwick* ruling will mean. In *Sex Wars: Sexual dissent and political culture.* New York: Routledge.

Hunter, N. D. 1995. Life after Hardwick. In *Sex Wars: Sexual dissent and political culture.* New York: Routledge.

Kramer, L. 1978. *Faggots.* New York: Routledge.

Monson, J. 1995. Moving dyke bodies. *Movement Research* 10.

Osborne, T. 1994. Up against the wall. *The Advocate* 652 (April 5).

Patton, C. 1990. *Inventing AIDS.* New York: Routledge.

Schulman, S. 1994. *My American History: Lesbian and gay life during the Reagan/Bush years.* New York: Routledge.

Wolfe, M. 1994. The AIDS Coalition to unleash power, New York (ACT UP NY): A direct action political model of community research for AIDS prevention. In *AIDS Prevention and Services: Community-based research.* Edited by Johannes P. Van Vugt. Westport, Connecticut: Bergin and Garvey.

Do You Love the Dyke in Your Face, pages 439–46

Schorr, C. 1994. Poster girls. *Artforum* (October).

Strategies for (Re)constructing Queer Communities, pages 447–57

Appleyard, D., M. S. Gerson, and M. Lintell. 1981. *Livable Streets, Protected Neighborhoods.* Berkeley: University of California Press.

Arcidi, P. 1994. Defining gay design. *Progressive Architecture* 75(8) (August).

Boyer, M. C. 1988. The return of aesthetics to city planning. *Society* 25(4) (May/June).

———. 1994. *The City of Collective Memory: Its historical imagery and architectural entertainments.* Cambridge, Massachusetts: MIT Press.

Castell, M. 1983. *The City and the Grassroots: A crosscultural theory of urban social movements*. Berkeley: University of California Press.

Dakin, J. 1993. Inhumanities of urban planning. *University of Toronto Quarterly* 62(4).

de Certeau, M. 1984. *The Practice of Everyday Life*. Translated by Steven F. Rendall. Berkeley: University of California Press.

Forester, J. 1993. *Critical Theory, Public Policy, and Planning Practice: Towards a critical pragmatism*. Albany, New York: State University of New York Press.

Immel, M. 1983. Gay urban open space in San Francisco: The landscape of liberation. Thesis for the partial fulfillment of a Master of Landscape Architecture. On file University of California at Berkeley, College of Environmental Design Library. NA25.5.I332.

Jarman, D. 1995, 1996. *Derek Jarman's Garden*. Photographs by Howard Sooley. Woodstock, New York: The Overlook Press.

Marcus, C. C. 1990. Preface. In *People Places: Design guidelines for urban open space*. Edited by Clare Cooper Marcus and Carolyn Francis. New York: Van Nostrand Reinhold.

Marcus, C. C., and C. Francis. 1990. Introduction: Public places and design guidelines. In *People Places: Design guidelines for urban open space*. Edited by Clare Cooper Marcus and Carolyn Francis. New York: Van Nostrand Reinhold.

Moughtin, C. 1992. *Urban Design: Street and square*. Oxford, UK: Butterworth Architecture/Butterworth-Heinemann.

Mumford, L. 1938. *The Culture of Cities*. New York: Harcourt, Brace and Company.

Probyn, E. 1990. Travels in the postmodern: Making sense of the local. In *Feminism/Postmodernism*. Edited by Linda J. Nicholson. New York: Routledge.

Rudofsky, B. 1969. *Streets For People: A primer for Americans*. Garden City, New York: Doubleday.

Sancar, F. H. 1994. Paradigms of postmodernity and implications for planning and design review processes. *Environment and Behavior* 26(3).

Tschumi, B. 1996. *Architecture and Disjunction*. Cambridge, Massachusetts: MIT Press.

Contributors

David Bell teaches Cultural Studies at Staffordshire University. He is coeditor of *Mapping Desire* with Gill Valentine (Routledge 1995) and coauthor of *Consuming Geographies* (Routledge 1997).

Anne-Marie Bouthillette is a recent graduate of the University of British Columbia, where she received an M.A. in Human Geography. Born and raised in Montréal, she has spent most of her adulthood experiencing city life across Canada. She has done extensive research in gay male and lesbian spatialization, and recently contributed to the anthology, *The Margins of the City*. She is currently the full-time executive director of the French-speaking women's network of British Columbia, *Réseau-femmes du Colombie-Britannique*.

Pat Califia is a prolific and promiscuous leatherdyke writer whose fiction, nonfiction, and poetry have appeared in *The Advocate, Co-Evolution Quarterly, Skin Two, The Spectator,* and several other places. Her most recent book is *Public Sex: The Culture of Radical Sex,* a collection of essays about censorship, sex, violence, sexual minority communities, gender, feminism, and the cutting edge of gay politics. She is working on *Sex Changes,* a history of transgenderism, and *The Code,* a novel about the love affair between a queer leatherman and a woman, set in the 1970s.

Michael Carroll is a designer and artist educated in Nova Scotia and based in Montréal. He has worked in Peru, Spain, and England. His work focuses on the body, the landscape, and the built environment with recent works examining erotic desire in architectural design processes. He is currently designing and building a house.

Mark I. Chester is a San Francisco gay radical sex photographer. He's been documenting San Francisco's gay and radical sex underground since 1979 in images that are at once socially, artistically, and politically provocative. His first book of black-and-white fine art sexual photographs, *Diary of a Thought Criminal,* was published in September 1996.

Jim Costanzo is an artist who lives in New York City. He has exhibited in America and Europe. His multimedia installations consist of photography, film, video, and computer graphics.

Jean-Ulrick Désert was born 157 years after the revolutionary liberation of the island nation of Haiti. Educated in the United States, he received his bachelor degree from the Cooper Union School of Architecture and a graduate degree from Columbia University's School of Architecture, Planning, and Preservation. He has exhibited his theoretical works in New York City, and he collaborates regularly with visual artists—including Lyle Ashton Harris, John de Fazio, and Ike Udey—in the United States and abroad. Mr. Désert's studio engagements have spanned involvements with Bernard Tschumi's winning entry for Parc de la Villette, Paris, to the Ralph Appelbaum studio's designs in Soho, New York City, and some of the major museums in the United States, including the Holocaust Memorial in Washington, D.C. Mr. Désert has served as an invited critic at Columbia University's Paris–New York Program, City University of New York (CUNY), and Cooper Union's School of Art, lecturing intermittently while completing a body of work on race, gender, and power.

Ed Eisenberg is a political artist who believes that good art has the power to change the world. He conceived and organized *Groundwork: The Anti-Nukeport Stencil Project* in 1989, which indicated the distances of thousands of New York City street corners from a nearby Navy base. His work contributed to the eventual closure of the facility.

Ty Geltmaker received his B.A. from Trinity College, Hartford, Connecticut, an M.A. from New York University, and his Ph.D. from the University of Southern California. He has taught at Cerritos College, California Institute of the Arts, and the University of Southern California. Before working in academia, he was a journalist in Rome and foreign news editor at United Press International in New York. He has been based in Los Angeles since 1986 and is presently teaching world history at Bronx Community College in New York City.

Blake Goble earned his master's of architecture from Columbia University. He is an artist and registered architect practising in New York City. He has collaborated on architectural projects and art works that have been exhibited in the New York City area.

Del LaGrace Volcano is a *hermaphrodyke* who photographs contemporary forms of sexual expression. She began by photographing leatherdykes in San Francisco during the late 1970s and early 1980s before emigrating to London, where she continues her exploration of the sexual subcultures to which she belongs. Her first book, *Lovebites,* was published in 1991 by Gay Men's Press. She is one of the featured photographers in the 1996 anthology, *Nothing But The Girl: The Blatant Lesbian Image,* published by Cassell.

John Grube was born in Toronto in 1930 and educated at the University of Toronto and the Ontario College of Art, where he taught English and creative writing for over twenty years, until 1992. He has published both popular and scholarly articles on Québecois political culture in *Le Devoir* and authored the books, *Bâtisseur de pays: la pensée de François-Algert Angers* and *Une amitié bien particulière,* a study of Jacques Ferron and the October 1970 Crisis in Québec. He has been active in chronicling the history of the gay men in Toronto, particularly the pre-Stonewall "communities of resistance" that existed in almost all North American cities. He was also a member of the Toronto-based gay art collective JAC.

Morgan Gwenwald is both a movement photographer and a fine arts photographer. Her work has been published in gay, lesbian, and women's publications, including *On Our Backs, The Blade, Curve, Bad Attitude, SEK, Sinister Wisdom,* and *The Village Voice.* Her work has also been included in many books, including *Coming to Power, Dagger, Nothing But The Girl, Butch/Femme,* and *Stolen Glances.* Morgan is a coordinator at the Lesbian Herstory Archives, where she has been a volunteer for many years. She works in the New York Office of the Gay & Lesbian Alliance Against Defamation, where she is director of Special Projects.

Clare Hemmings is a Ph.D. student with the Centre for Women's Studies, University of York, England. Her work focuses on bisexual genealogies of desire. She is joint coordinator of Bi-Academic Intervention, the national network for bisexual research.

Betti-Sue Hertz is a curator and artist who has organized exhibitions for museums, alternative galleries, and unusual public spaces—including a cemetery, an industrial park, and a community garden. She is director of the Longwood Arts Project at the Bronx Council on the Arts and a Ph.D. student in art history at the Graduate Center, CUNY.

Gordon Brent Ingram is from a badly assimilated *franco-colombien* "community" on Vancouver Island. He completed his doctorate in environmental planning at Berkeley in 1989 and has been active in gay/queer and environmental politics for over twenty years. He designs networks of parks, open spaces, and other protected areas, and he has been particularly concerned with social equity and "marginality" in conservation planning and design of public lands. He began his work on gay male use of parks in 1980. He has advised numerous environmental agencies and activist organizations in North America and overseas, and has published in journals ranging from *Environmental Management, Conservation Biology,* and *Landscape and Urban Planning* to contemporary cultural magazines such as *FUSE* and *Border/Lines*. He practices out of San Francisco and Vancouver.

Bill Jacobson is a New York–based photographer who has exhibited in New York, San Francisco, London, Glasgow, Helsinki, and Frankfurt. He completed his photography studies in 1981 and was awarded an M.F.A. from the San Francisco Art Institute. In recent years his solo and group exhibitions have included *Songs of Sentient Beings, Interim Photographs, Spirit & Loss, Large Bodies, Don't Leave Me This Way: Art in the Age of AIDS, The Psycho-Pathology of Everyday Life, Absence, Activism and the Body Politic, Life, Love, Death: Ten Years of Photography About AIDS.*

Elsie Jay is a pseudonym for one of Australia's most influential feminist geographers. She assumes this name when writing about her sexuality in order to protect her children from the many prejudices that still abound around lesbian mothers in Australia and elsewhere. Elsie works in an Australian university where she teaches and researches on the gendering of space. She has a particular interest in the ways in which sexuality is expressed in suburbs and workplaces, as well as the ways in which dominant forms of heterosexuality are enforced in houses, factories, and offices. She has participated in the many theoretical debates that have made up the Women's Liberation Movement of the last twenty years and has a current concern with the concept of "difference" in post-colonial societies like Australia.

Martha Judge is a photo-based installation artist living in Toronto. Her upcoming thesis show deals with issues of power and intimacy.

Isaac Julien is a filmmaker and theoretician best known for the art films *Looking for Langston, Young Soul Rebels,* and *The Attendant.* In addition, his documentary work has examined homophobia in African diaspora communities and the legacies of Frantz Fanon. He has taught at several universities, including the University of California at Santa Cruz and New York University.

Lisa Maya Knauer is an independent media producer, artist, writer, and educator. She was a founder of REPOhistory and was project codirector of the *Lower Manhattan Sign Project.*

Maurice van Lieshout was a lecturer in gay literary studies at the University of Amsterdam. He has published several books and articles on gay history, subcultures, and lesbian and gay youth. Currently he is working as the chief editor of *0|25*, a Dutch monthly about youth and related policy.

Alvaro Lopez-Lopez received a B.A. from the National University of Mexico. He is a postgraduate student at the National University of Mexico, researching the geography of tourism in Mexico. He lives in Mexico City.

Carrie Moyer received a B.F.A. from Pratt Institute, an M.A. from New York Institute of Technology, and attended the Skowhegan School of Art. In 1991 she founded Dyke Action Machine! (DAM!), a lesbian graphics project, with photographer Sue Schaffner. Carrie's other agitprop efforts include campaigns for the Lesbian Avengers, the Irish Lesbian and Gay Organization, the New York City Gay and Lesbian Anti-Violence Project, and Queer Nation, New York. Both her painting and public art projects were included in *In A Different Light,* a survey of late twentieth-century lesbian and gay aesthetic sensibilities mounted by the University Art Museum, University of California, Berkeley, in the spring of 1995. In 1996 her work was included in the "Gender, fucked" exhibition at the Center on Contemporary Art in Seattle.

Joan Nestle is an author, editor, archivist, and teacher. She is cofounder of the Lesbian Herstory Archives, which was housed in her Manhattan apartment for close to twenty years, giving new meaning to the term "public space." The archive now lives in its own building in Park Slope, Brooklyn, New York. Her publications include *A Restricted Country* (Firebrand Books), *The Persistent Desire: Femme-Butch Reader* (Alyson Publications), *Women on Women 1, 2 and 3* (Plume Books), and most recently *Sister and Brother: Lesbians and Gay Men Talk About Their Lives Together* (Harper San Francisco), which she coedited with John Preston. For the last thirty years, she has been a teacher of writing in the SEEK Program at Queens College, CUNY. She is presently working on a collection of international lesbian short fiction and a new collection of her own writings, *A Fragile Union.*

James Polchin has done graduate work at the American University and Drew University, and is currently completing a Ph.D. in American Studies at New York University, where he also teaches writing. His work focuses on the intersections of memory, desire, and social spaces. He is working on a project about queer memory.

Stephen Quilley graduated from Cambridge University in 1989 and earned an M.A. in Soviet studies before going on to doctorate research at Manchester University. His research interests span all areas of urban sociology, linking issues such as globalization and transitions in political economy to broader questions relating to the reconstitution of social and cultural formations in the city.

Robert M. Ransick earned his B.F.A from the School of Visual Arts in New York. He is an artist and photographer and the director of the Photography Department of the New School of Social Research, New York. He teaches photography at The New School and has exhibited in galleries in New York.

REPOhistory, formed in 1989, is based in New York City and produces projects on lost, absent, and neglected histories—often in relation to specific public sites. They use graphic signage, text, historical mapping, and multiple components to address a subject from a variety of perspectives. *The Lower Manhattan Sign Project* consisted of thirty-nine signs placed throughout the Wall Street area. *Choice Histories: Framing Abortion* was presented at Artists Space, New York City, and opened in June 1992. A more recent project, *Entering Buttermilk Bottom,* is on the site of an African-American neighborhood in Atlanta that was destroyed by "urban renewal" in the early 1960s.

Yolanda Retter is an itinerant community worker, a gadfly on the body politic, and a veteran of the lesbian civil wars. In the 1970s she worked with Lesbian Feminists (L.A.), in the 1980s with Lesbians of Color (L.A.), and in the 1990s is a lesbian history and visibility advocate/activist. Of mixed (Peruvian/German) heritage, she was born in Connecticut, grew up in El Salvador (before anyone knew where it was), and has lived in the western part of the United States since 1966. She is ABD in American Studies at the University of New Mexico, has an airplane mechanic's license, works as a reference librarian or a social worker, and sells out-of-print books. She is a member of Metaphysical Activists, a lifelong lesbian, and a modified-by-feminism butch. She assembled the Lesbian History Project Web site on the Internet: *http://wwwlib.usc.edu/~retter/main.html.*

Mark Robbins's installations and constructions explore the architectural frame and the use of design as a medium for social critique. These projects have been exhibited in numerous galleries in the United States and abroad, most recently at the Museum of Modern Art in Saitama, Japan, the Clocktower Gallery of the I.C.A. in New York; and the Wexner Center for the Arts in Columbus, Ohio. Robbins is currently an assistant professor in the School of Architecture at Ohio State University and curator of architecture at the Wexner Center for the Arts. Most recently he was awarded the 1976 Rome Prize of the American Academy in Rome.

Alvaro Sanchez-Crispin received a Ph.D. from the University of London. He is an economic geographer currently based at the Institute of Geography of the National University of Mexico. He has researched several topics in connection with the economic geography of Mexico and has taught in different universities in Mexico, the United States, Finland, Spain, and Argentina. He lives in Mexico City.

Sue Schaffner is a commercial photographer based in New York City. Her work has appeared in *Out, Spin, Guitar World,* and *Request.* As well as being a member of DAM!, Sue also directs and produces feature segments for Dyke TV, the national U.S. news magazine addressing lesbian issues.

Saskia Scheffer is a photographer in New York City. She dedicates much of her time to documenting the lesbian and gay community.

Dana Schuerholz is a white queer activist-artist living in Seattle and currently working in public schools tracking media literacy as well as doing freelance photography and mural painting. She is a member of Impact Visuals, a cooperative of photojournalists distributing quality images of social concern to the alternative and mainstream press. Dana has worked on several media projects with women's groups in El Salvador and Honduras. She is currently involved in public art and activism around queer liberation, homelessness and affordable housing, and environmental issues.

Sarah Schulman is the author of six novels, most recently *Rat Bohemia* (Dutton 1995), and one nonfiction book, *My American History: Lesbian and Gay Life During the Reagan/Bush Years* (Routledge 1994).

Laraine Sommella engaged in movement activities in a variety of groups in the New York, D.C., and Baltimore areas from the late 1960s to the early 1980s. She earned her Ph.D. from the State University of New York at Stony Brook and is now associate professor of English at Quinsigamond Community College in Worcester, Massachusetts.

Ira Tattelman, an architect in Washington, D.C., has become an expert on gay bathhouses. He has presented papers on the topic at the 1996 A.C.S.A. Annual Meeting, Lavender Languages & Linguistics III, Queer Frontiers: The Fifth Annual National Lesbian, Gay, and Bisexual Graduate Student Conference, and at the Architectural Research Centers Consortium Spring '94 Conference. Ira received his masters in architecture from Harvard's Graduate School of Design. His designs have been exhibited in group and solo shows at gallery and exhibit spaces in Washington, D.C., and Boston.

Nick Trubenbach was born in the San Fernando Valley of Los Angeles in 1964 and began his career "swimming with sharks" in the garment, textile, and home furnishings industries. He is a self-taught interior designer now based in San Francisco. Nick is a "queer decorator" who specializes in contemporary reinterpretations of classic designs for residential, hospitality, and commercial environments.

Maxine Wolfe is a lifelong Brooklynite and political organizer. She has been a member of ACT UP New York since 1987 and was a founding member of its Women's Committee and later of Lesbian Avengers. She is also a coordinator of the Lesbian Herstory Archives. She has supported all of this activity and more by working as an academic. She is a professor in the Environmental Psychology Ph.D. program at the Graduate Center, CUNY.

Other Titles By Bay Press

AIDS Demo Graphics
Douglas Crimp with Adam Rolston

The Anti-Aesthetic: Essays on Postmodern Culture
Edited by Hal Foster

But Is It Art? The Spirit of Art as Activism
Edited by Nina Felshin

Clicking In: Hot Links to a Digital Culture
Edited by Lynn Hershman Leeson

The Critical Image: Essays on Contemporary Photography
Edited by Carol Squiers

Culture in Action: A Public Art Program of Sculpture Chicago
Essays by Mary Jane Jacob, Michael Brenson, and Eva M. Olson

The Fact of Blackness: Frantz Fanon and Visual Representation
Edited by Alan Read

How Do I Look? Queer Film and Video
Edited by Bad Object-Choices

Lets Get It On: The Politics of Black Performance
Edited by Catherine Ugwu

Mapping the Terrain: New Genre Public Art
Edited by Suzanne Lacy

Out of Site: A Social Criticism of Architecture
Edited by Diane Ghirardo

Uncontrollable Bodies: Testimonies of Identity and Culture
Edited by Rodney Sappington and Tyler Stallings

Violent Persuasions: The Politics and Imagery of Terrorism
Edited by David J. Brown and Robert Merrill

Discussions in Contemporary Culture is an award-winning series of books copublished by the Dia Center for the Arts, New York, and Bay Press, Seattle. These volumes offer rich and interactive discourses on a broad range of cultural issues in formats that encourage scrutiny of diverse critical approaches and positions.

Discussions in Contemporary Culture
Edited by Hal Foster

Vision and Visuality
Edited by Hal Foster

The Work of Andy Warhol
Edited by Gary Garrels

Remaking History
Edited by Barbara Kruger and Philomena Mariani

Democracy
A Project by Group Material
Edited by Brian Wallis

If You Lived Here: The City in Art, Theory, and Social Activism
A Project by Martha Rosler
Edited by Brian Wallis

Critical Fictions: The Politics of Imaginative Writing
Edited by Philomena Mariani

Black Popular Culture
A Project by Michelle Wallis
Edited by Gina Dent

Culture on the Brink: Ideologies of Technology
Edited by Gretchen Bender and Timothy Druckrey

Visual Display: Culture Beyond Appearances
Edited by Lynne Cooke and Peter Wollen

For information

Bay Press
115 West Denny Way
Seattle, WA 98119-4205
206.284.5913
206.284.1218 (fax)
Bay Press@aol.com
http://www.baypressinc.com/baypress

About The Editors

Anne-Marie Bouthillette is a recent graduate of the University of British Columbia, where she received an M.A. in Human Geography. Born and raised in Montréal, she has spent most of her adulthood experiencing city life across Canada. She has done extensive research in gay male and lesbian spatialization, and recently contributed to the anthology, *The Margins of the City*. She is currently the full-time executive director of the French-speaking women's network of British Columbia, Réseau-femmes du Colombie-Britannique.

Gordon Brent Ingram is from a badly assimilated franco-colombien "community" on Vancouver Island. He completed his doctorate in environmental planning at Berkeley in 1989 and has been active in gay/queer and environmental politics for over twenty years. He designs networks of parks, open spaces, and other protected areas, and he has been particularly concerned with social equality and "marginality" in conservation planning and design of public lands. He began his work on gay male use of parks in 1980. He has advised numerous environmental agencies and activist organizations in North America and overseas, and has published in journals ranging from Environmental Management, Conservation Biology and Landscape and Urban Planning to contemporary cultural magazines such as FUSE and Border/Lines. He sometimes teaches at the University of British Columbia, and he practices out of San Francisco and Vancouver.

Yolanda Retter is an itinerant community worker, a gadfly on the body politic, and a veteran of the lesbian civil wars. In the 1970s she worked with Lesbian Feminists (L.A.), in the 1980s with Lesbians of Color (L.A.), and in the 1990s is a lesbian history and visibility advocate/activist. Of mixed (Peruvian/German) heritage, she was born in Connecticut, grew up in El Salvador (before anyone knew where it was), and has lived in the western part of the United States since 1966. She is ABD in American Studies at the University of New Mexico, has an airplane mechanic's license, works as a reference librarian or a social worker, and sells out-of-print books. She is a member of Metaphysical Activists, a lifelong lesbian, and a modified-by-feminism butch. She assembled the Lesbian History Project web site on the Internet: http://www.lib.usc.edu/~retter/main.html.